Writing the Hit Songs That Defined the Decade

"Songs are like women or cats - fascinating, elusive, seductive, irresistible, infuriating, moody, demanding and contradictory creatures. The writer pursues them like some phantom fantasy - fascinated, intrigued and desperate to find out what they're really like. They should be approached with caution and respect - especially at night."

(Leslie Bricusse 1931-1921)

Michael Francis Taylor

NEW HAVEN PUBLISHING

Published 2025
First Edition
www.newhavenpublishingltd.com
newhavenpublishing@gmail.com

All Rights Reserved

The rights of Michael Francis Taylor as the author of this work, have been asserted in accordance with the Copyrights, Designs and Patents Act 1988.

No part of this book may be re-printed or reproduced or utilized in any form or by any electronic, mechanical or other means, now unknown or hereafter invented, including photocopying, and recording, or in any information storage or retrieval system, without the written permission of the Author and Publisher

Cover Design (C) Pete Cunliffe

Copyright © 2025 Michael Francis Taylor
All rights reserved
ISBN: 978-1-915975-22-5

Foreword

Jimmy Ryan on Songwriting

The year was 1964. Fresh out of high school, we felt like we ruled the world. With summer stretched out before us, we rehearsed daily, gearing up for gigs at the Jersey Shore. To mark our graduation, we ditched our fifties-sounding name, The Vibra-Tones, and rechristened ourselves The Critters. The former was just too Fifties, and current bands were naming themselves after animals, bugs, food, or whatever popped into their heads during last weekend's acid trip. We were also shifting from covers to originals. That was the new trend in music, and like many budding songwriters, our first attempts were pretty lame. But after a short growth spurt, we got the hang of it, and between 1966 and 1967, we cranked out three top forty hits!

For us Critters, and most kids our age, the Sixties were a super-rush. We were coming of age at the same time the music scene was exploding. The world moved out of the doo-wop era into a new musical renaissance with songs that boasted a greater variety of chord changes, more meaningful lyrics, and often recordings by kick-ass bands who wrote their own songs. We sang along with foot stomping, brain pounding, thought-provoking songs from The Beatles, The Stones, The Who, The Animals, The Dave Clark Five, The Kinks, The Beach Boys, The Hollies, The Doors, CCR, CS&N, Cream, Hendrix, and Led Zeppelin, to name a few. These tumultuous years also provided abundant inspiration for protest music. Some songs hit the current chaos head-on, like Barry McGuire's "The Eve of Destruction." Others protested by implication, like Buffalo Springfield's "For What It's Worth," and Jefferson Airplane's "Volunteers." Bob Dylan, with his down-home folksy voice and insightful lyrics, became a musical spokesperson for an entire generation. We had a lot to write about beyond romance - the Vietnam War, the space race, civil rights, nuclear escalation, police brutality and more.

Regarding the craft, writing in the Sixties wasn't much different from writing in the 18th century. It was 100% analog. Our tools of the trade were a pad and pen, a guitar or piano and maybe a dictionary. Some were lucky, rich, or successful enough to have a tape recorder and microphone to record their ideas. Wollensak made a very popular, inexpensive, portable recorder that became an indispensable songwriter's tool. What we did not have was a laptop and a digital audio workstation (DAW) in our bedrooms to puff up a mediocre song with overblown production, disguising its flaws, at next to no cost compared to a commercial recording studio. In the sixties, if the song didn't hold up on your trusty acoustic, it was DOA. Back then, the music world had its gatekeepers. At the top of the list were the A&R execs. These folks and their partners in crime, the publishers, were the sentries who guarded fame like the nuclear codes. They decided which songs landed with signed artists, and whether a band moved on to making records or went back to tending bar, stocking grocery shelves, or driving cabs. If you pitched a song, it might be just you and a guitar—or, if you were lucky enough to own a Wollensak, you handed over a tape. I once brought in a tape of a song I had just written to a NY publisher. He listened for ten seconds, hit the stop button and said, "What else have you got?" Boom. Fail. Hence, I learned it was good practice to write songs that nail it in the first ten seconds, or you may leave the presentation with your tail between your legs.

Today, we still have record companies, A&R execs, and publishers, but even with their massive budgets and influence, success isn't guaranteed. They can spend thousands on advertising and tour support, hoping that streaming platforms like Spotify and Apple Music add their artists' songs to the main playlists. When this doesn't happen, the artists' balance sheets turn red. If your song doesn't make it onto a major streaming playlist, it's almost impossible to be discovered beyond playing bars and small venues. Almost. What gives a new or established songwriter of today an opportunity that didn't exist in the sixties is the ability to self-record, self-mix, self-master, and self-upload to YouTube, TikTok, Instagram, Spotify, Deezer, Amazon, etc. You can have a viral hit and a career without ever going down on your knees for a music business exec. A perfect example is the Filipino singer, Arnel Pineda, who created YouTube tributes to several Journey songs. Journey members saw his videos and were so impressed, they invited him to replace Steve Perry, who had recently left the band. Arnel transitioned from being a YouTube home video creator in the Philippines to Journey's new lead singer!

In the sixties, AM radio stations were the final gatekeepers. If you weren't on the radio, long-term success would be next to impossible. Again, live shows helped, but you'd be unlikely to earn significant money or land substantial bookings unless you were on an AM DJ's playlist. Some acts achieved rotation status organically by releasing an amazing song or even through fan requests. Some didn't and were so determined to tilt the playing field, they slipped cash into the pockets of unscrupulous DJs. That practice, known as payola, took down one of the most popular and innovative DJs in radio history, Alan Freed. His bad judgment got him indicted, fined, and blacklisted from mainstream radio. The scandal ruined his career, but his impact on popularizing rock & roll and R&B on the AM airwaves was undeniable. After his death in 1965 at age 41, the industry made peace with his legacy. He was inducted into the Rock & Roll Hall of Fame in 1981, the Radio Hall of Fame in 1988, and received a star on the Hollywood Walk of Fame in 1991.

Finally, no introduction to an anthology about this era would be complete without a salute to the Brill Building. Here, in this hallowed New York City space, legendary songwriters huddled in their tiny offices, often described as cubbyholes, and cranked out hundreds of hits. Some of them rose to superstardom, like Carole King and her lyricist/husband, Gerry Goffin, Neil Diamond, Neil Sedaka, Paul Simon, Burt Bacharach and Hal David, to mention a few. I remember taking guitar lessons in the Brill Building. In the adjacent office was a somewhat reclusive songwriter named Otis Blackwell. I would often have to endure his relentless piano playing and stereo drifting through the thin walls as I tried to concentrate on my lessons. To me, he was just the annoying musician next door. Many years later, out of curiosity, I looked him up and was astonished to find he wrote some of my favorite songs, "Don't Be Cruel," "All Shook Up," and "Return to Sender" for Elvis, "Great Balls of Fire" and "Breathless" for Jerry Lee Lewis, and "Handy Man" for Jimmy Jones and later, James Taylor. During his fifty-year career, he wrote over a thousand songs and sold over two hundred million records, many of which were composed in his little cubbyhole office at 1619 Broadway, the Brill Building. I've given you a bird's-eye view of what it was like to be a songwriter back in those glorious, sometimes wonderful, sometimes miserable years that brought us a war, a nuclear threat, hope, despair, Woodstock, and a vast trove of songs that still inspire to this day.

Now I'd like to hand things over to my friend, Michael Francis Taylor, who'll take you deeper into this fascinating era - tracing each composer and their songs, from inspiration to chart success, the hits and misses, the quirks, the struggles, and the triumphs behind some of the best songwriting of all time.

Jimmy Ryan
The Superstar Chronicles: Tales of Life Among Rock Royalty, (New Haven 2021)
California Dreaming and Primal Screaming: Gurus and Psychics and Shrinks, Oh My! (New Haven 2021)

Acknowledgments
To Teddie Dahlin, for continuing to have faith in me
To Peter Cunliffe for his amazing cover artwork
To Jimmy Ryan for providing the outstanding foreword
To Angela, for continuing to be my moral compass

Images
Unless stated they are all in the public domain.
Cover images - Goffin & King, Mann & Weil, Jim Morrison, Sam Cooke, Lennon & McCartney, Phil Spector, and Bob Dylan.
Unintentional errors will be corrected in any future edition of this book.

By the same author
Harry Chapin - The Music Behind the Man (New Haven 2019)
Songs From the Vineyard - The Music of Carly Simon (New Haven 2020)
Taylor Swift -The Brightest Star (New Haven 2021)
Taylor Swift - Stolen Lullabies (New Haven 2023)
The Beach Boys Pet Tracks -The Stories behind 100 of their greatest songs (New Haven 2023)

How to use this book

The Writers
Listed alphabetically by surnames.

Chart entries
Only A-side singles that charted in the Sixties are included. Statistics are taken from the US *Billboard Hot 100* and the UK *Official Chart Company*. For historical purposes, the OCC recognises the *New Musical Express* chart until March 1960, followed by *Record Retailer* until February 11th 1969. After that date, the British Market Research Bureau (BMRB) was commissioned by BBC and *Record Retailer* to create the "official" chart based on a comprehensive national sample of sales. US Country, Soul and R&B chart positions are not included.

Number one singles are in **bold** type
Co-writers are in *italics* following the song title

Honours
Rock and Roll Hall of Fame
Established in 1983 by Ahmet Eertegun, with inaugural inductees in 1986. To qualify, artists must have released their first commercial recorded at least 25 years prior to the nomination year and also hinges on influence, significance and overall contribution to the development of rock and roll music.

Songwriters Hall of Fame
Established in 1969. Songwriters qualify if their work demonstrates significant impact on music, and if their first commercial release occurred at least 20 years prior.

Nashville Songwriters Hall of Fame
Established in 1970. Dedicated to honour Nashville's rich songwriting legacy. Qualification is the same as above.

Women Songwriters Hall of Fame
Established in 2021. Dedicated to honour and celebrate the contributions of female songwriters and composers worldwide.

Grammy Lifetime Achievement Award
Established in 1963. Awarded by the Recording Academy to "performers who, during their lifetimes, have made creative contributions of outstanding artistic significance to the field of recording."

Gerry Goffin, Carole King, Barry Mann & Cynthia Weil at the Brill Building c1959
(© *The New York Times*)

The Songwriters

Lou Adler
Born Lester Lou Adler, Chicago 1933.

Raised in Los Angeles, Adler began his musical career on the staff of Doré Records before joining Keen Records and managing artists Johnny Rivers and Jan and Dean. Whilst there, he transitioned to songwriting and using the pseudonym Melvin Schwartz teamed up with co-manager Herb Alpert to produce and write "Baby Talk." Originally given to The Laurels, it failed to chart but went on to give Jan and Dean their second US top ten single in 1959. Greater success for the pair came the following year with "Wonderful World" recorded by Sam Cooke. With its message that neither education nor knowledge can dictate feelings and that only love can make the world a better place, it seemed as if Adler was not taking it seriously, but Cooke revised the lyrics to put more emphasis on schooling. As a pseudonym, Adler used his wife's maiden name Barbara Campbell as writing credit on the label. It was recorded with Keen Records on March 2nd 1959, shortly before Cooke left the label over a royalties dispute. The following year, he moved to RCA, but Keen still held the rights to the song and released it as a single in April 1960.

Craig Werner, a professor of African-American Studies, later claimed that the song had a more politically-charged meaning and that the lines about not knowing much about history or biology were Cooke informing white listeners that these were the things to forget about African-Americans, and that all they needed to remember was love. The song was inducted into the Grammy Hall of Fame in 2014.

Adler's successful publishing house Trousdale included staff writers P F Sloan and Steve Barri to provide material for his roster of artists. In 1964, he founded Dunhill Records with Jay Lasker and Bobby Roberts, and among the successful signings were the Mamas and the Papas, Barry Maguire, and the Grass Roots. In August 1966, Adler teamed up with singer Johnny Rivers to write "Poor Side of Town" for him, thus signalling a turning point Rivers' career, with a move away from rock and roll toward orchestral pop ballads with backing vocalists. Arranged by Marty Paich, it was released on the Imperial label and topped the US charts.

After selling Dunhill to ABC Records in 1967, Adler served as one of the directors of the Monterey Pop Festival and also set up Ode Records, producing former staff writer Carole King's hugely successful album *Tapestry*, which garnered him Grammys for both album and the single "It's Too Late."

Chart entries
Wonderful World *(with Herb Alpert, Sam Cooke)* Sam Cooke (US 1960 # 12; UK # 27); Herman's
    Hermits (UK # 7; US # 4)
Honolulu Lulu *(with Jan Berry, Roger Christian)* Jan & Dean (US 1963 # 11)
Poor Side of Town *(with Johnny Rivers)* Johnny Rivers (US 1966 # 1); Al Wilson (US 1969 # 75)

Paul Anka
Born Paul Albert Anka, Ottawa, Canada 1941.
Songwriters Hall of Fame 1993.

Born to Syrian and Lebanese immigrants, Anka sang in a church choir and briefly studied piano before attending Fisher Park High School in Ottawa. While there, he formed a vocal trio called the Bobbysoxers and performed at local amateur nights, and also honed his writing skills with journalism courses, working for a time at the Ottawa Citizen newspaper. His ambition to become a songwriter grew when he won a trip to New York by winning a Campbell's Soup contest, and in late 1956 convinced his parents to let him travel to Los Angeles, where he called various record companies to get an audition. A meeting with RPM led to the release of his first single, the unsuccessful "Blau-Wile Deveest Fontaine." With $100 given to him by his uncle, Anka went to New York and auditioned for Don Costa's ABC Records. The song he performed was called "Diana," which he later claimed was inspired by having a crush on a girl called Diana Ayoub, whom he had met at church. (In another version, she had been his babysitter). Released in September 1957, it topped the charts on both sides of the Atlantic. This was followed by a string of self-penned hits, including " You Are My Destiny," "Lonely Boy," (a chart-topper), "Put Your Head On My Shoulder," and "It's Time to Cry." 1960's "Puppy Love" was inspired by a crush he had on Disney's mouseketeer Annette Funicello (while also becoming a hit for Donny Osmond in 1972).

Anka also toured the UK and accompanied Buddy Holly on his 1959 Australian tour, for whom he wrote "It Doesn't Matter Anymore," ironically just weeks before he was killed. As a result, he donated all the royalties to his widow.

In the Sixties, he began a career in movies, both as a theme writer and minor actor, most notably in the epic war movie *The Longest Day*. He also purchased the rights and ownership of his ABC-Paramount catalog and re-recorded his earlier hits for his new label RCA. As a songwriter, he continued to have moderate success both for himself and for other artists, but it was hearing a French song while on vacation there that would have a profound impact on his career.

Originally called "Comme d'habitude," it was written by Jacques Revaux, Gilles Thibaut and Claude François and first recorded in 1967. Anka flew out to Paris and negotiated the rights to the song, subject to the three writers retaining their original share of the royalties. Later, at dinner with Frank Sinatra in Florida, Anka suggested he might have a song for him. Back in a New York hotel, he spent the night re-writing the song to suit Sinatra's style, changing its lyrical theme and subtly altering the melodic structure. Although Anka's record company wanted him to record it, Anka insisted it had to be Sinatra. Recorded in just one take in December 1968, "My Way" was released. Although not a big hit in the US, it would win a Grammy and become one of the most-covered songs of all time.

In the Seventies, Anka would return to the top of the US charts with "You're Having My Baby," a duet with Odia Coates. Asked about his songwriting, he once claimed: "Pop music is a creature of the moment; it thrives on the mood of its time. Either you hook into it or you're not going to be part of it."

Chart entries
Puppy Love – Paul Anka (US 1960 # 2; UK # 33)
My Home Town – Paul Anka (US 1960 # 8)
Train of Love – Annette (US 1960 # 36); Alma Cogan (UK 1960 # 27)
I Love You in the Same Old Way – Paul Anka (US 1960 # 40)
Summer's Gone – Paul Anka (US 1960 # 11)
Talk to Me Baby – Annette (US 1960 # 92)
The Story of My Love – Paul Anka (US 1961 # 16)
Tonight My Love, Tonight – Paul Anka (US 1961 # 13)
Dance On Little Girl – Paul Anka (US 1961 # 10)
Broken Heart and a Pillow Filled With Tears – Patti Page (US 1961 # 91)
Love Me Warm and Tender – Paul Anka (US 1961 # 12; UK # 19)
A Steel Guitar and a Glass of Wine – Paul Anka (US 1962 # 13; UK # 41)
Every Night (Without You) Paul Anka (US 1962 # 46)
I'm Coming Home – Paul Anka (US 1962 # 94)
Love (Makes the World Go 'Round) Paul Anka (US 1963 # 26)
Remember Diana – Paul Anka (US 1963 # 39)
Hello Jim – Paul Anka (US 1963 # 97)
Did You Have a Happy Birthday *(with Howard Greenfield)* Paul Anka (US 1963 # 89)
(I'm Watching) Every Little Move You Make – Little Peggy March (US 1964 # 84)
I Love You Baby – Freddie & the Dreamers (UK 1964 # 16)
Diana – Bobby Rydell (US 1965 # 98)
Put Your Head On My Shoulder – The Lettermen (US 1968 # 44)
My Way *(with Claude François, Jacques Revaux)* Frank Sinatra (US 1969 # 27; UK # 5)

Arthur Alexander
Born Sheffield, Alabama 1940. Died 1993.

At the age of 13, Alexander joined a gospel group, which morphed into a cover band a few years later. He began to compose songs, and by overcoming the lack of instrumental skill he sang melodies over and over until he could hear the whole piece in his head. His first published composition was "She Wanna Rock," which was later covered by Canadian rockabilly singer Arnie Derkson. In 1960, with the pseudonym "June" Alexander (short for junior), he was working with Spar Music in Florence, Alabama, and cut his self-penned debut single "Sally Sue Brown" on Jud Records, owned by Jud Phillips (brother of music pioneer Sam). The song was later covered by artists including the Rolling Stones. The following year he scored his first hit, the classic "You Better Move On." It was recorded at the FAME (Florence Alabama Management Enterprises) studio, which later relocated to its more famous location at Muscle Shoals. It was a rare example of Southern whites and blacks working together during the civil rights era and an example of how music could break down barriers.

The next single, "Anna (Go to Him)," scored a top ten on the R&B chart and was later covered by the Beatles, while the following year his "Every Day I Have To Cry" became a minor hit for Steve Alaimo (and recorded by Dusty Springfield a year later). Subsequent recordings were completed in Nashville, which not only undermined the edge of his earlier songs but caused what was a fragile personality to succumb to pressure. Further singles like "Go Home Girl" and a haunting rendition of Buzz Cason's "Soldier of Love" suffered as a result. Out of work for some years, there was renewed interest in his songs in the early Nineties. Performing again with a band, he had just secured a new recording contract in 1993 when he tragically died from a heart attack.

Alexander was one of the first singer-songwriters to embrace what was called "country-soul," and he became one of the cornerstones of the whole "Muscle Shoals Sound." His songs were often mini-tales of morality, delivered in a knowing, sorrowful manner, and the purity and warmth of his voice was rare for the time. Paul McCartney once claimed: "If the Beatles wanted a sound, it was R&B. That's what we used to listen and what we wanted to be like, Black, that was basically it - Arthur Alexander." *AllMusic's* Jason Ankeny summed up the songwriter: "His music is the stuff of genius, a poignant and deeply intimate body of work on par with the best of his contemporaries." He was also the only artist to have his songs covered by the Beatles, the Rolling Stones and Bob Dylan.

Chart entries
You Better Move On (US 1962 # 24)
Anna (Go to Him) (US 1962 # 68)
Every Day I Have to Cry – Steve Alaimo (US 1963 # 46); The Gentrys (US 1966 # 77)

Bill Anderson
Born James William Anderson III, Columbia, South Carolina 1937.
Nashville Songwriters Hall of Fame 1975.
Country Music Hall of Fame 2001.
Songwriters Hall of Fame 2018.

Raised in Decatur, Georgia, he attended Avondale High School, and his interest in music came from his grandparents and listening to country musicians on the radio. At the age of ten, he wrote his first song, "Carry Me Home Texas." Along with school friends, he formed a band which won a school talent contest, and as the Avondale Boys they performed on local radio. Although touted to be a baseball player, he enrolled at the University of Georgia, majoring in journalism. After graduation, he became a radio deejay, even being fired one time for playing country records. Resuming his songwriting, he wrote "City Lights," which would become a major hit for Ray Price. Becoming a regular visitor to Nashville with his compositions, he was signed by Decca's Owen Bradley in 1958, and his first single "That's What It's Like To Be Lonely," became a hit on the country chart the following year.

In 1960, he recorded the self-penned "The Tip of My Fingers" which became his first top ten in the country chart, while 1962's "Mama Sang a Song" gave him his first country chart-topper. The following year, he was inspired to write "Still" after encountering an old girlfriend while promoting a song, and it became his first top ten entry on the Hot 100 and a major country/pop crossover hit. In 1965, he teamed up with label-mate Jan Howard to record "For Loving You," another country number one.

In the Seventies, his longtime producer Owen Bradley was replaced by Buddy Killen, and his musical sound shifted from Nashville ballads toward uptempo countrypolitan songs, receiving negative criticism from many writers.

Chart entries
City Lights – Debbie Reynolds (US 1960 # 55)
It's Not the End of Everything – Tommy Edwards (US 1960 # 78)
I Missed Me – Jim Reeves (US 1960 # 44)
Losing Your Love *(with Buddy Killen)* Jim Reeves (US 1961 # 89)
Mama Sang a Song – Bill Anderson (US 1962 # 89); Stan Kenton & His Orchestra
    (US 1962 # 32); Walter Brennan (US 1962 # 38)
Still – Bill Anderson (US 1963 # 8); Karl Denver (UK 1963 # 13); Ken Dodd (UK
    1963 # 35); The Sunrays (US 1966 # 93)
The Tip of My Fingers – Roy Clark (US 1963 # 45); Eddie Arnold (US 1966 # 43)
My Whole World is Falling Down *(with Jerry Crutchfield)* Brenda Lee (US 1963 # 24)
Still No. 2 *(with Sheb Wooley)* Ben Colder (US 1963 # 98)
8 X 10 *(with Walter Haynes)* Bill Anderson (US 1963 # 53); Ken Dodd as Eight by Ten
    (UK 1964 # 22)
Saginaw, Michigan *(with Don Wayne)* Lefty Frizzell (US 1964 # 85)
Happiness – Ken Dodd (UK 1963 # 31)
Think I'll Go Somewhere and Cry Myself to Sleep – Bill Anderson (US 1966 # 30)
I Love You Drops – Vic Dana (US 1966 # 30)
When Two Worlds Collide *(with Roger Miller)* Jim Reeves (UK 1969 # 17)

Ian Anderson
Born Dunfermline, Scotland 1947.

Moving with his family to Edinburgh at the age of three, he grew up influenced by his father's jazz and big band records and the advent of rock and roll. After relocating again, he attended Blackpool Grammar School, but was asked to leave after refusing corporal punishment. He then studied fine art at Blackpool's College of Art, and in around 1963 formed the soul and blues band the Blades with school friends Jeffrey Hammond and John Evans. With Anderson on vocals, guitar and harmonica, they played their first gig at a church youth club. Drummer Barrie Barloe and guitarist Geoff Stephens were recruited from local band the Atlantics, as well as guitarist Chris Riley.

They changed their name to the John Evan Band (named for their drummer, as his mother paid for the group's van) and then John Evan Smash. Hammond later left the band to attend art school and eventually was replaced by Glen Cornick. Riley also quit to be replaced by Neil Smith.

In November 1967, the band moved to Luton and signed a management deal, replacing Smith with Mick Abrahams of McGregor's Engine. Realising a six-man band was expensive to support, Anderson disbanded, with just him, Abrahams and Cornick staying together and recruiting Abraham's friend Clive Bunker on drums. Changing their name repeatedly to get bookings, it was left to a member of the booking agent's staff, a history buff, to suggest Jethro Tull (the name of an 18th century agriculturist), and as weird as it sounded, the name stuck. With that, they secured a weekly residency at the Marquee Club. Anderson possessed a large overcoat his father had given him, and traded in his guitar for a flute. As his career progressed, he added keyboards, mandolin, sax, whistles and harmonica to his collection of instruments, and adopted the limelight-grabbing oner-legged flute stance and wide-eyed glare that would become his trademarks.

In 1968, their blues-tinged debut album *This Was,* released on the Island label, included the track "Song for Jeffrey," a tribute to former member Hammond, while their first chart success came with their single, "Love Story," released in late 1968. Shortly after, Abrahams left the band to form Blodwyn Pig and was replaced by Martin Barre. The following year, they released the single "Living in the Past", written by Anderson. After being pressed by his booking agency to write a hit single, Anderson composed the song in just one hour, taking inspiration from Dave Brubeck's 1961 jazz instrumental "Take Five," and it scored a top three hit in May 1969. In a later interview, Anderson recalled: "To be honest, I've always loathed and detested that song. In fact, when it was first a hit, I used to hide in a corner and cringe. But the guys in the band now are keen to play it, and you know, I'm beginning to grow accustomed to the damn thing."

Three months later, came the album *Stand Up*, followed by another hit single "Sweet Dream," their first release on the fledgling Chrysalis label. Written by Anderson, it was a mocking critique of grand rock-based concept albums, and, with tongue firmly in cheek, gave fictional schoolboy Gerald Bostock co-writing credit.

In the Seventies, they became only the second rock act after the Beatles to play at New York's Carnegie Hall, and by then their musical style had moved toward progressive rock, with the 1971's *Aqualung* becoming their most successful album. A few years later, they shifted their musical style again to folk-rock.

Chart entries
Love Story – Jethro Tull (UK 1968 # 29)
Living in the Past – Jethro Tull (UK 1969 # 3)
Sweet Dream – Jethro Tull (UK 1969 # 7)

Chris Andrews
Born Christopher Frederick Andrews, Romford, England 1942.

Andrews was still a teenager when he formed and became the lead singer of Chris Ravel and the Ravers. Despite recording several singles, including "I Do" on the Decca label, success eluded them (although it was later claimed that the Rolling Stones' Bill Wyman bought one of their records!). In March 1959, Andrews made his television debut by singing on the British pop show *Oh Boy!*, returning the following month to sing Cliff Richard's latest hit "Move It!" His bluebeat-influenced white-pop songwriting prowess brought him to the attention of manager Eve Taylor, whose roster of artists included top British draws Adam Faith and Sandie Shaw. For Faith he contributed three consecutive hits, "The First Time," "We Are in Love," and "If He Tells You", but it was for Shaw that he achieved the greater success with a string of hits that included the three-week chart topper "Long Live Love."

More hits with Faith would follow, and Andrews would also have some solo chart success beginning with 1965's "Yesterday Man" selling over a million copies and even achieving a four-week chart-topping run in Germany. He went on to write "Our Love Has Gone" for the Fortunes and "I'll Remember Tonight" for the Mamas and the Papas, but these and later releases were not as successful. Only in Europe, particularly Germany, did he remain popular for several years, particularly as he recorded some of the songs in foreign languages.

Chart entries
The First Time – Adam Faith (UK 1963 # 5)
We Are in Love – Adam Faith (UK 1963 # 11)
If He Tells You – Adam Faith (UK 1964 # 25)
I Love Being in Love with You – Adam Faith (UK 1964 # 33)
Girl Don't Come – Sandie Shaw (UK 1964 # 3; US # 42)
It's Alright – Adam Faith (US 1965 # 31)
Stop Feeling Sorry for Yourself – Adam Faith (UK 1965 # 23)
I'll Stop at Nothing – Sandie Shaw (UK 1965 # 4)
Talk About Love – Adam Faith (US 1965 # 97)
Long Live Love – Sandie Shaw (UK 1965 # 1; US # 97)
Someone's Taken Maria Away – Adam Faith (UK 1965 # 34)
Message Understood – Sandie Shaw (UK 1965 # 6)
Yesterday Man – Chris Andrews (UK 1965 # 3; US # 94)
How Can You Tell – Adam Faith (UK 1965 # 21)
To Whom It Concerns – Chris Andrews (UK 1965 # 13)
Tomorrow – Sandie Shaw (UK 1966 # 9)
Something On My Mind – Chris Andrews (UK 1966 # 41)
Nothing Comes Easy – Chris Andrews (UK 1966 # 14)
Whatcha Gonna Do Now – Chris Andrews (UK 1966 # 40)
Stop That Girl – Chris Andrews (UK 1966 # 36)
Run – Chris Andrews (UK 1966 # 32)
Think Sometimes About Me – Sandie Shaw (UK 1966 # 32)
Two Streets -Val Doonican (UK 1967 # 39)
You've Not Changed – Sandie Shaw (UK 1967 # 18)
Today – Sandie Shaw (UK 1968 # 27)
Toy – The Casuals (UK 1968 # 30)
Groovy Baby – Microbe (UK 1969 # 29)
Think It All Over – Sandie Shaw (UK 1969 # 42)

Dave Appell see Kal Mann

Rod Argent
Born Rodney Terence Argent, St Albans, England 1945.

Argent's father was an aeronautical engineer who had fronted two semi-pro dance bands, and Rod's interest in music (particularly keyboards) stemmed from watching him play upright piano in the house. In March 1963, while studying at St. Albans Grammer School and being chorister at the cathedral, he formed a band by recruiting fellow musicians Hugh Grundy (drums) Colin Blunstone (vocals), Paul Atkinson (guitar), and Paul Arnold (bass), although Arnold would later leave to concentrate on exam work and be replaced by Chris White. After rejecting band names such as the Mustangs and the Sundowners, it was Arnold who suggested the Zombies.

In May 1964, the quintet won the newspaper-sponsored Herts Beat competition for the region's new bands with a rendition of Argent's self-penned "She's Not There," with the prize of £250 and a three-year recording deal with Decca Records. With lyrics describing an adolescent breakup, Argent initially sang lead vocals, but with his imaginative keyboard talents becoming increasingly apparent, he saw the advantage of using Bluestone's breathy vocals. With its subtle jazzy arrangement it became their debut single, just missing out on a top ten spot but reaching an impressive number two in the US.

Half a dozen hits followed, including 1968's psychedelic "Time of the Season," taken from the 1968 album *Odessey and Oracle*. Prominent among the unusual and effective components is the bass riff punctuated with a hand clap and the breathy "ahhhh" vocal. Although released twice as a single in the UK, it failed to chart, but surprisingly became a top three hit in the US over a year after its original release.

Changing labels to CBS, the band suffered a decline in demand for live gigs. White and Grundy left the band and Blunstone began a solo career with his version of "She's Not There" under the pseudonym Neil McArthur. By 1969, the remaining Zombies were performing as Argent, with a much heavier sound and a line-up of Argent, White, Bob Henrit (drums) and Russ Ballard (guitar). The hits that followed included "Hold Your Head Up," written by Argent and White.

Chart entries
She's Not There – The Zombies (UK 1963 # 12; US # 2)
Tell Her No – The Zombies (UK 1965 # 42; US # 6)
She's Coming Home – The Zombies (US 1965 # 58)
I Want You Back Again – The Zombies (US 1965 # 95)
She's Not There – Colin Blunstone *(as Neil McArthur)* (UK 1969 # 34)
Time Of the Season – The Zombies (US 1969 # 3)

Jo Armstead
Born Josephine Armstead, Yazoo, Mississippi 1944.

After singing in a church where her mother was a minister, her grandfather introduced her to blues music. As a teenager she began singing in juke joints and at dances, and also performed with Bobby "Blue" Bland's band and Little Melvin & the Downbeats. In 1960, along with Delores Johnson and Eloise Hester, she became a member of the Ikettes as part of Ike & Tina Turner Revue, having been recommended to Ike by her sister, Ike's ex-wife. With the Ikettes, she had a top twenty hit with Ike's "I'm Blue (The Gong Gong Song)." In 1962 she moved to New York and recorded under a pseudonym Deena Johnson to avoid being tracked down by Ike. Armstead then recorded advertising jingles as well as singing backing vocals for artists that included James Brown and B B King.

Following a chance meeting with songwriters Nick Ashford and Valerie Simpson, they teamed up for "Let's Get Stoned," an R&B chart-topper for Ray Charles in 1966. The trio went on to score hits for Maxine Brown, Chuck Jackson and Tina Britt, while Armstead also wrote or co-wrote songs for Garland Green and Sly Johnson. After Ashford and Simpson left Motown in 1967, Armstead moved to Chicago with her husband, record producer Mel Collins, and together formed Giant Productions which released her own single "I Feel an Urge Coming On," later to become a Northern Soul favourite, and "A Stone Good Lover," an R&B hit in 1968.

After the breakup of her marriage, Armstead returned to New York to write for commercials. As advice to budding songwriters, she said: "When the door of opportunity opens, be ready to put your foot in and leave it open for your brother and sister."

Chart entries
Come on Sock It to Me *(with Syl Johnson, Jesse Anderson)* Syl Johnson (US 1967 # 97)
Casanova (Your Playing Days Are Over) *(with Milton Middlebrook)* Ruby Andrews
   (US 1967 # 51)
Jealous Kind of Fella *(with Garland Green, Maurice Dollison, Rudolph Browner)* Garland
   Green (US 1969 # 20)

Jo Armistead with Ashford and Simpson
One Step at A Time - Maxine Brown (US 1965 # 55)
The Hard Way - The Nashville Teens (UK 1966 # 45)

Nick Ashford and Valerie Simpson see also Jo Armstead
Born Nicholas Ashford, Fairfield, South Carolina 1941. Died 2011.
Born Valerie Simpson, New York City 1946.
Songwriters Hall of Fame 2002.
Women Songwriters Hall of Fame 2021 (Ashford).

While a member of a Baptist church, Ashford sang with a group called the Hammond Singers. He later recalled: "Nobody in my family was musical. I had no idea you could be a songwriter and make a living at it. It was all discovery. It was all just thrown at me." He met his future wife Valerie at Harlem's White Rock Baptist Church in 1964 as part of the gospel group the Followers, and following an unsuccessful recording session were introduced to aspiring singer-songwriter Joshie (Jo) Armstead, former member of the Ikettes. Together, they wrote songs for Maxine Brown, the Shirelles, Chuck Jackson and others, including "Let's Go Get Stoned," a chart-topping R&B hit for Ray Charles. In 1966, the couple joined Motown and wrote a string of hits for Marvin Gaye and Diana Ross.

Their second chart hit was the classic "Ain't No Mountain High Enough," the first single for Marvin Gaye and Tammi Terrell. Ashford recalled that the idea for the song came to him upon arriving in New York with no connections, and also spoke about the "bigger than life" persona needed for big stages like Radio City Music Hall. Written before the coupled joined Motown, they were approached by British soul singer Dusty Springfield to record the song but declined in the hope it would give them access to the Detroit label. Simpson recalled, "We played the song for her but wouldn't give it to her, because we wanted to hold that back. We felt like that could be our entry to Motown. Nick called it his 'golden egg.'"

During the recording, Terrell felt nervous and intimidated because she hadn't rehearsed the lyrics, so she recorded her vocals alone, with producers Harvey Fuqua and Johnny Bristol, adding Gaye's vocal at a later date. The soulful "You're All I Need To Get By" was also written as a duet for Gaye and Terrell and recorded at Hitsville. Simpson, who played piano on the recording, recalled it's gospel background: "So much soul comes out of the Baptist Church. It's so embedded in you. You could go out any minute and turn the sweetest ballad into a gospel song if you felt really good about it." At the time, Terrell was recovering from surgery on a malignant brain tumour, and there are moments in the recording when Gaye is heard encouraging Terrell to sing her verses, add-libbing "come on Tammi" a number of times. In real life, Gaye and Terrell were just good friends, with Terrell being romantically involved with the Temptations' David Ruffin at the time.

Ashford also teamed up with Frank Wilson to produce "I'm Gonna Make You Love Me" for Diana Ross and the Supremes & The Temptations, with Ross and Eddie Kendricks on lead vocals (and Otis Williams and Ross doing the spoken interlude). The song was originally a moderate R&B hit for Dee Dee Warwick (sister of Dionne) in 1966, and then recorded by Madeline Bell the following year, reaching number 46 on the R&B chart. The song became the second non-Motown cover song to be a major Motown hit, following on from the Four Tops' "If I Were a Carpenter" in 1967 (written by Tim Hardin).

"The Onion Song" was originally intended for the Supremes but given to Gaye and Terrell to record in January 1969. Featured on their final album *Easy*, the single was recorded first with Gaye's vocals, with a desperately ill Terrell brought two days later to only record a guide vocal. According to Gaye, it is Simpson's voice that appears on the single, later stating that the label were aware of it and kept Tammi's name on the record due to her failing health, but also because of the financial implications of removing her name. Terrell would die six months later, aged just 24. Gaye would later criticise the label for taking advantage of her ill-health.

After getting married in the early Seventies, Ashford and Simpson would enjoy later success as performers, especially with their 1984 hit "Solid."

Chart entries
Let's Go Get Stoned – Ray Charles (US 1966 # 31)
Ain't No Mountain High Enough – Marvin Gaye & Tammi Terrell (US 1967 # 19)
You're Precious Love – Marvin Gaye & Tammi Terrell (US 1967 # 5)
Ain't Nothing Like the Real Thing - Marvin Gaye & Tammi Terrell (US 1968 # 8; UK # 34)
Some Thinks You Never Get Used To – Diana Ross & the Supremes (US 1968 #30; UK #34)
You're All I Need to Get By – Marvin Gaye & Tammi Terrell (US 1968 # 7; UK # 19)
I Am Your Man – Bobby Taylor & the Vancouvers (US 1968 # 85)
Destination: Anywhere – The Marvelettes (US 1968 # 63)
Keep On Lovin' Me Honey - Marvin Gaye & Tammi Terrell (US 1968 # 24)
California Soul – Fifth Dimension (UK 1968 # 25)
Good Lovin' Ain't Easy to Come By – Marvin Gaye & Tammi Terrell (US 1969 # 30; UK # 26)
Didn't You Know (You'd Have to Cry Sometime) – Gladys Knight & The Pips (US 1969 # 63)
The Onion Song – Marvin Gaye & Tammi Terrell (US 1969 # 50; UK # 9)
What You Gave Me - Marvin Gaye & Tammi Terrell (US 1969 # 49)

Ashford and Simpson with Jo Armistead
One Step at A Time - Maxine Brown (US 1965 # 55)
The Hard Way - The Nashville Teens (UK 1966 # 45)

Burt Bacharach and Hal David
Born Burt Freeman Bacharach, Kansas City, Missouri 1928. Died 2023.
Born Harold Lane David, New York City 1921. Died 2012.
Songwriters Hall of Fame 1972.
Nashville Songwriters Hall of Fame 1984 (David).
Grammy Lifetime Achievement Award 2008 (Bacharach).

One of the most successful songwriting partnerships in popular music. Bacharach's father was a noted journalist and his mother a songwriter and amateur painter. As a teenager, he brushed aside classical piano lessons to embrace jazz, especially the styles of Charles Parker and Dizzy Gillespie, that would later influence his writing. He studied music theory and composition at a university in Montreal before serving two years in the army based in post-war Germany. After his discharge in 1952, he was employed as pianist and arranger for a variety of singers such as Vic Damone and Steve Lawrence, and at the age of 28 became music director for Marlene Deitrich on her world tour, soon becoming recognised for his conducting and music arrangements. By 1956, he was working for the worldwide publishing company Famous Music in New York's Brill Building, and it was there that he was paired up with lyricist Hal David. Their first collaboration was "The Blob," written for the Five Blobs and featured in the horror b-movie of the same name. It was when Bacharach was introduced to Mack's lyricist brother Hal that things started to take off.

David was the son of Austrian Jewish immigrants who owned a New York delicatessen, and was the younger brother of lyricist Mack. He attended Thomas Jefferson High School in Brooklyn and studied journalism at New York University. He began his music career by writing lyrics for bandleaders Sammy Kaye and Gut Lombardo, and worked with Morty Nevins of the pop group the Three Suns on four songs for the 1951 movie *Two Gals and a Guy,* as well as the classic Christmas song "I Believe in Santa Claus" by the Stargazers. In 1956 he was working for Famous Music publishers when he met Bacharach. That same year, they wrote several songs, including "I Cry More," which was featured in the movie *Don't Knock the Rock*, "The Morning Mail," and "Peggy's in the Pantry,*"* but their first big success came the following year with "The Story of My Life." Although a country hit for Marty Robbins, it became a UK chart-topper when recorded by Michael Holliday, until replaced by Perry Como's "Magic Moments," also a Bacharach-David composition (the first time any songwriter had back-to-back number ones in that country).

Their first big hit of the Sixties came with "The Man Who Shot Liberty Valance" by Gene Pitney. Although a number three hit, it was apparently never intended to be used in the 1963 Western movie of the same name, as it had already been released before the session (despite it being paid for by the Paramount Studio). The song "Make It Easy On Yourself" was originally recorded by the Isley Brothers as "Are You Lonely By Yourself?" but not released for another 40 years. The song was then picked up Calvin Carter, A&R man for the Veejay label, while on a scouting visit to the Brill Building. Carter played a demo of the song featuring a vocal by the young Dionne Warwick to Vee-Jay singer Jerry Butler, who commented, "Man, it's a great song, and the girl who's singing it, and the arrangement, is a hit." But when Carter explained that Florence Greenberg, head of Scepter Records (who had just signed Warwick) was not interested as it was not in line with his label's signature girl group style, Butler was ecstatic. Wanting the same arrangement featured on the demo, he flew to New York to record the song, with the session overseen by Bacharach. Released in July 1962, it became a top 20 hit. The Walker Brothers' 1965 UK cover was noted for Bacharach's lush Wall of Sound-style production.

At the end of the 1962, Warwick would find her first chart success recording the duo's underrated "Don't Make Me Over." The title was inspired by an outburst made by Warwick after hearing Butler's voice on the radio while out driving: "Needless to say, I was not a happy camper. I let them know that one thing they cannot do is change me. 'Don't make me over'" The song peaked at number 21 on the Hot 100, and signalled the start of what would be an illustrious career.

Gene Pitney's "Twenty Four Hours From Tulsa," with its tale of a travelling man who embarks on a romance in a motel never to return home, became a bigger hit in the UK in 1963. David recalled: "I wrote that to a melody that Burt write and that's what the melody said to me. Music speaks to a lyric writer, or at least it should speak to a lyric writer. And that's what the music said to me. And why it did, I don't know. I don't think I had ever been to Tulsa. I've always kind of liked what I call 'narrative songs' - story songs. And when I hear music, very often I hear a story. The fact that it was Tulsa, as opposed to Dallas, is not terribly meaningful, but the sound of 'Tulsa' rang in my ear." That same year Jack Jones' "Wives and Lovers" came about when the writers were asked to write a song on the theme of marital infidelity to promote the 1963 movie of the same name. Once again, the two writers felt exploited when it was not featured in the actual film.

"Anyone Who Had a Heart", one of their most famous songs, was originally recorded in one take by Dionne Warwick (at the same session as "Walk on By," another Bacharach-David song) and became a top ten hit in the US in January 1964, but only a moderate hit in the UK. Beatles' manager Brian Epstein had heard Warwick's version while in the States and presented to producer George Martin with the suggestion that his protégé Cilla Black record it. Black (aka Priscilla White) had previously worked as a hat-check girl at Liverpool's legendary Cavern Club before gaining a recording contract and who's star potential had yet to be realised. Although Martin preferred Shirley Bassey, Epstein insisted it on Black and had Martin commission Johnny Pearson to arrange the orchestration. With a bassoon replacing the original saxophone solo, and with Black's pensive opening vocal and dramatic, almost shrieking, finale, it shot to the top of the UK charts. Warwick aired her disappointment: "I thought that was quite unfair, in that my recording never received the same kind of airplay because Cilla jumped the gun. So after that, I didn't like her too much."

Two months later, "Walk on By" gave Warwick her second million-selling single and a Grammy nomination. Recorded at the same session as "Anyone Who Had a Heart," her label decided to release it as the b-side to "Any Old Time of the Day," and it was only when top New York deejay Murray the K refused to play the a-side and promoted the b-side instead that the label was compelled to switch the sides. It peaked at number six on the Hot 100. The writers' "Wishin' and Hopin," a track off Warwick's debut album, also became a US top ten hit for Dusty Springfield a short while later.

Springfield's "I Just Don't Know What To Do With Myself" had been written by the duo in 1962 and first recorded by Chuck Jackson, although not released. On an overnight trip to New York, Springfield had met up with Bacharach and was offered the song to record. Although a big hit in the UK in July 1964, its release in the US was held back until October. That same month, the writers had their first UK chart-topper with Sandie Shaw's "(There's) Always Something There To Remind Me." Originally recorded by Dionne Warwick and Lou Johnson, it gave the writers their fourth chart-topping single.

Meanwhile, both writers had collaborated with others on a number of hits. With Bob Hilliard, Bacharach had already scored hits, including the UK number one with Franke Vaughan's "Tower of Strength." David had hits by teaming up with Sherman Edwards for "Johnny Get Angry" by Joanie Summers, and with Paul Hampton for Don Gibson's "Sea of Heartbreak." David once described his career: "One thing a lyricist must learn is not to fall in love with his own lines. Once you learn that, you can walk away from the lyric and look at it with a reasonable degree of objectivity."

In 1965, Bacharach took to the charts himself with "Trains and Boats and Planes," scoring a top five hit in the US, while also covered by Billy J Kramer & the Dakotas in the UK at the same time. "What the World Needs Now is Love" became a hit for fellow songwriter Jackie DeShannon, while Tom Jones had one of his biggest hits with "What's New Pussycat?" The following year, the writers returned to Cilla Black with "Alfie," written to promote the film of the same name starring Michael Caine. David's opening lyric "What's It All About?" was taken from one of Caine's lines in the movie. 1967 saw them score a hit with the instrumental "Casino Royale," the theme to the Bond movie of the same name. Recorded by Herb Alpert & the Tijuana Brass, it was also sung by Mike Redway in the lyric version "Have No Fear Bond Is Here." Later that year came "I Say a Little Prayer," a huge hit for Dionne Warwick (and later for Aretha Franklin). In the lyrics, David intended to convey a woman's concern for her man who's serving in the Vietnam War, but Bacharach disliked Warwick's brisk recording, feeling it had been rushed. Recorded in April 1966 as an album track, the single release was held back seven months until radio stations began playing it. Nevertheless, it was another million-seller for both artists.

The following year, Warwick was given "Do You Know the Way To San Jose," one of her most successful singles. Bacharach composed the music before David had written the lyrics, which were inspired by having been stationed in San Jose while in the navy. Two big hits followed, with Sérgio Mendes' "The Look of Love" and Herb Alpert's romantic solo single, "This Guy's In Love With You," which featured Bacharach's signature horn solo. Warwick also sang a version of the song with the change of gender in the title.

The decade came to an end with two big chart-toppers. First came "I'll Never Fall in Love Again." Originally written in 1968 for the Broadway musical, *Promises, Promises,* based on Billy Wilder's 1960 movie *The Apartment.* It was first recorded by Johnny Mathis and Bacharach himself, but it had the most success in the US when given to Warwick to record. Bobby Gentry's better-known version topped the charts in the UK.

"Raindrops Keep Fallin' on My Head" was written for the 1969 movie *Butch Cassidy and the Sundance Kid.* Director George Roy Hill wanted a romantic song for a particular scene involving a bike ride. After being turned down by singer Ray Stevens (and possibly Bob Dylan too), it was given to B J Thomas who took it to the top of the charts.

Over the years, Bacharach and David wrote over 250 songs together, and to date over a thousand artists have recorded Bacharach compositions, with 52 US top 40 hits and six Grammys along the way. His work with Dionne Warwick became one of the most prolific partnerships in music history. After discovering her working as a session backing singer in 1961, they formed their own production company, enabling them to write and produce songs for her, and secured a recording deal with Scepter Records that would see their songs sell over 12 million copies. Bacharach's style of jazz-influenced chord progressions, odd-changing meters, and syncopated rhythmic patterns has often been referred to as "easy listening" and his selection of instruments commonly referred to as the "Bacharach Sound," much the same as Glenn Miller's music had been tagged two decades before. Looking back on his career, Bacharach wrote: "Music breeds its own inspiration. You can only do it by doing it. You may not feel like it, but you push yourself."

Writer William Farina cited him as "a composer whose venerable name can be linked with just about every other prominent musical artist of his era." Remarkably, neither writer has ever been inducted into the Rock and Roll Hall of Fame.

Chart entries
I Wake Up Crying - Chuck Jackson (US 1961 #59)
The Man Who Shot Liberty Valance – Gene Pitney (US 1962 # 4)
Make It Easy On Yourself – Jerry Butler (US 1962 # 20); The Walker Brothers (UK 1965
   #1; US # 16)
The Love of a Boy – Timi Yuro (US 1962 # 44)
Don't Make Me Over – Dionne Warwick (US 1962 # 21) The Swinging Blue Jeans (UK 1966
   # 31)
This Empty Place – Dionne Warwick (US 1963 # 84)
Blue On Blue – Bobby Vinton (US 1963 # 3)
Be True To Yourself – Bobby Vee (US 1963 # 34)
True Love Never Runs Smooth – Gene Pitney (US 1963 # 21)
Saturday Sunshine – Burt Bacharach (US 1963 #93)
Make The Music Play – Dionne Warwick (US 1963 # 81)
It's Love That Really Counts – The Merseybeats (UK 1963 # 24)
Blue Guitar – Richard Chamberlain (US 1963 # 42)
Reach Out For Me - Lou Johnson (US 1963 # 74) Dionne Warwick (US 1964 # 20; UK # 23)

Twenty Four Hours From Tulsa – Gene Pitney (US 1963 # 17; UK # 5)
Wives and Lovers – Jack Jones (US 1963 #14)
Anyone Who Had A Heart – Dionne Warwick (US 1963 # 8; UK # 42) Cilla Black (UK 1963 # 1)
Who's Been Sleeping In My Bed – Linda Scott (US 1964 # 100)
Walk On By – Dionne Warwick (US 1964 # 6; UK 1964 # 9) Isaac Hayes (US 1969 # 30)
Wishin' And Hopin' – Dusty Springfield (US 1964 # 6) The Merseybeats (UK 1964 # 13)
I Just Don't Know What to Do with Myself – Dusty Springfield (UK 1964 # 3) Tommy Hunt (US 1964 # 100); Dionne Warwick (US 1966 #26)
A House Is Not a Home – Brook Benton (US 1964 # 75) Dionne Warwick (US 1964 # 71)
You'll Never Get To Heaven (If You Break My Heart) – Dionne Warwick (US 1964 # 34; UK # 20)
(There's) Always Something There To Remind Me – Lou Johnson (US 1964 # 49); Sandie Shaw (UK 1964 # 1); Dionne Warwick (US 1968 # 65)
Me Japanese Boy I Love You – Bobby Goldsboro (US 1964 # 74)
Reach Out For Me – Dionne Warwick (US 1964 # 20; UK # 23)
A Message To Martha (Kentucky Bluebird) – Lou Johnson (UK 1964 # 36); Adam Faith 1964 (UK # 12)
Rome Will Never Leave You – Richard Chamberlain (US 1964 #99)
Long After Tonight Is All Over – Jimmy Radcliffe (US 1964 # 40)
Trains And Boats and Planes – Burt Bacharach (US 1965 # 4); Billy J Kramer & the Dakotas (UK 1965 #12; US # 47); Dionne Warwick (US 1966 # 22)
What the World Needs Now Is Love – Jackie De Shannon (US 1965 # 7)
What's New Pussycat? – Tom Jones (UK 1965 # 11; US # 11)
Here I Am – Dionne Warwick (US 1965 # 65)
A Lifetime of Loneliness – Jackie De Shannon (US 1965 # 66)
Looking With My Eyes - Dionne Warwick (US 1965 # 64)
Are You There (With Another Girl) – Dionne Warwick (US 1965 # 39)
Promise Her Anything – Tom Jones (US 1966 # 74)
Alfie – Cilla Black (UK 1966 # 9; US # 95); Cher (US 1966 # 32); Stevie Wonder (US 1968 # 66)
Message To Michael – Dionne Warwick (US 1966 # 8)
  (US 1968 # 66)
My Little Red Book – Love (US 1966 # 52)
Come And Get Me – Jackie DeShannon (US 1966 # 83)
Another Tear Falls - The Walker Brothers (UK 1966 # 12)
Another Night – Dionne Warwick (US 1966 # 49)
The Beginning Of Loneliness – Dionne Warwick (US 1967 # 79)
Only Love Can Break a Heart - Margaret Whiting (US 1967 # 96)
The Windows Of the World – Dionne Warwick (US 1967 # 32)
I Say A Little Prayer – Dionne Warwick (US 1967 # 4)
Do You Know The Way To San Jose? – Dionne Warwick (US 1968 # 10; UK # 8)
The Look Of Love – Sergio Mendez (US 1968 # 4)
This Guy's In Love With You – Herb Alpert (US 1968 # 1; UK # 3); This Girl's In Love With You – Dionne Warwick (US 1969 # 7)
Let Me Be Lonely – Dionne Warwick (US 1968 # 71)
To Wait For Love – Herb Alpert (US 1968 # 51)
Promises, Promises – Dionne Warwick (US 1968 #19)
I Just Don't Know What To Do With Myself – Dusty Springfield (UK 1964 # 3)
The Beginning Of Loneliness – Dionne Warwick (US 1967 # 79)
One Less Bell To Answer – Keely Smith (US 1968 # 2)
Promises, Promises – Dionne Warwick (US 1968 #19)
Any Day Now – Percy Sledge (US 1969 # 86)
The April Fools – Dionne Warwick (US 1969 # 37)
I'll Never Fall In Love Again – Burt Bacharach (US 1969 # 93); Bobby Gentry (US 1969 # 6; UK # 1); Dionne Warwick (US 1969 # 6)

Odds and Ends – Dionne Warwick (US 1969 # 43)
I'm A Better Man (For Having Loved You) – Englebert Humperdinck (US 1969 # 38; UK # 15)
Raindrops Keep Falling On My Head – B J Thomas (US 1969 # 1; UK # 38)

Burt Bacharach
Casino Royale – Herb Alpert & the Tijuana Brass (US 1967 # 27; UK # 27)
We're Only Young Once *(with Robert Colby)* The Avons (UK 1960 # 45)
Baby It's You *(with Mack David & Barney Williams aka Luther Dixon)* The Shirelles (US 1961
 # 8); Dave Berry 1964 (UK # 23); Smith (US 1969 # 5)

Burt Bacharach and Bob Hilliard
Please Stay – The Drifters (US 1961 #14), The Cryan' Shames 1966 (UK # 26)
Tower of Strength – Gene McDaniels (US 1961 #5); Frankie Vaughan 1961 (UK # 1)
You're Following Me – Perry Como (US 1961 # 92)
You Don't Have to Be a Tower of Strength – Gloria Lynne (US 1961 # 100)
Any Day Now (My Wild Beautiful Bird) - Gene McDaniels (US 1962 # 23) Percy Sledge
 (US 1969 # 86)
Don't You Believe it - Andy Williams (US 1962 # 39)
Keep Away from Other Girls– Helen Shapiro (UK 1962 # 40)

Burt Bacharach with others
Baby It's You *(with Mack David, Barney Williams)* Dave Berry (UK 1964 # 24)

Hal David and Sherman Edwards
Outside My Window - The Fleetwoods (US 1960 # 28)
You'll Answer To Me - Patti Page (US 1961 # 46)
Johnny Get Angry - Joanie Sommers (US 1962 # 7); Carol Deeane (UK 1962 # 32)
When the Boys Get Together - Joanie Summers (US 1962 # 94)

Hal David with others
Many a Wonderful Moment *(with Sidny Lippman)* Rosemary Clooney (US 1960 # 84)
Sea of Heartbreak *(with Paul Hampton)* Don Gibson (US 1961 # 21; UK # 14); Joe Brown
 (UK 1966 # 51)
Baby Elephant Walk *(with Henry Mancini)* The Miniature Men (US 1962 # 87)
It Only Took a Minute *(with Mort Garson)* Joe Brown & the Bruvvers (UK 1962 # 6)
Theme From Taras Bulba *(with Franz Waxman)* Jerry Butler (US 1962 # 100)
No Regrets *(with Charles Dumont)* Shirley Bassey (UK 1965 # 39)

Randy Bachman and Burton Cummings
Born Randolph Charles Bachman, Winnipeg, Canada 1943.
Born Burton Lorne Cummings, Winnipeg, Canada 1947.

Bachman studied violin at an early age. Although unable to read music, he would claim he could play anything he heard, but guitar would soon become his favoured instrument. In 1960, he met fellow Canadian musician Chad Allan to form Chad Allan & the Silvertones, with its members from two local teen bands. After changing their name to Chad Allan & the Reflections and listening to imported UK singles, they recorded "Tribute to Buddy Holly," a cover of Mike Berry's hit, after which they signed a deal with Canada's largest label. Their version of Johnny Kidd's "Shakin' All Over" topped the Canadian charts in 1965. With the "British Invasion" in full swing, the song imitated the UK sound so well that the label credited it to "Guess Who?" to make it appear it was actually a UK band moonlighting.

In December 1965 Burton Cummings joined the band. Cummings had played with local R&B band the Deverons before joining Guess Who to share lead vocals with Allan. A few months later Allan quit the band, leaving Cummings as sole singer, and with his departure they officially became the Guess Who.

Cummings and Bachman became the chief songwriters and gave the band four US chart hits in 1969, but it was "American Woman," a band composition with lyrics by Cummings, that saw them become the first Canadian band to top the US charts the following year. Bachman later described it as "an anti-war protest song," Cummings later insisted his lyrics had nothing to do with American pride: "What was on my mind was that girls in the States seemed to get older quicker than our girls and that made them, well, dangerous. When I said 'American woman, stay away from me', I really meant 'Canadian woman, I prefer you'. It was all a happy accident."

Bachman left the band that same year and later formed Bachman Turner Overdrive, while Cummings went on to have a solo career, with his debut album released in 1976.

Chart entries
These Eyes – The Guess Who (US 1969 # 6); Jr Walker & the All-Stars (US 1969 # 16)
Laughing – The Guess Who (US 1969 # 10)
Undun – The Guess Who (US 1969 # 22)
No Time – The Guess Who (US 1969 # 5)

Clint Ballard
Born Clinton Conger Ballard Jr, El Paso, Texas 1931. Died 2008.

Ballard could play the piano at the age of three, and his gift earned him a place studying music at the University of North Texas. After a stint in the army, he became a songwriter and moved to New York. One of his compositions, "Hey, Little Baby," recorded by bandleader Mitch Miller, became the theme of the 1958 World's Fair held in Belgium. While in New York, he "discovered" and managed the Kalin Twins (Harold and Herbert) and wrote their debut single, "Jumpin' Jack." The follow-up single "When," penned by Jack Reardon and Paul Evans, scored a number one in the UK. After leaving the Kalins, Ballard wrote hits for Malcolm Vaughan and Franke Avalon, but it was the next decade that saw their most successful compositions, beginning with 1963s classic "You're No Good." Originally recorded by Dee Dee Clark, it was soon made famous in the US by Betty Everett and in the UK by the Swinging Blue Jeans, although it was left to Linda Ronstadt to record the definitive version and top the US charts in 1974.

This was followed by two chart toppers in 1965. "Game of Love" was recorded by British band Wayne Fontana and the Mindbenders and scored a number one on the US Hot 100, while a little later the Hollies' "I'm Alive" became their first UK chart-topper. Originally offered to Gene Pitney and then Wayne Fontana, who both rejected it, the song was passed on to Manchester band the Toggery Five. Although they recorded it at Abbey Road studios, the Hollies also got to hear of it and quickly recorded it themselves, with a release two weeks ahead of the other band's planned date, resulting in their release being cancelled. Guitarist Alan Doyle later recalled: "After all the work we had laid down on the song, it was a dirty trick to give it to the Hollies. It was a sore point at the time as they got to #1 with the song."

Chart entries
You're No Good – Betty Everett (US 1963 # 51); The Swinging Blue Jeans (UK 1964 #3; US # 97)
The Game of Love – Wayne Fontana & the Mindbenders (UK 1965 # 2; US # 1)
I'm Alive – The Hollies (UK 1965 # 1)
It's Just a Little Bit Too Late *(with Les Ledo)* Wayne Fontana & the Mindbenders (UK 1965 # 20; US # 45)
She Needs Love - Wayne Fontana & the Mindbenders (UK 1965 # 32)
Fiddle Around *(with Larry Kusic)* Jan & Dean (US 1966 # 93)
Speak Her Name – Walter Jackson (US 1967 # 89)

Mark Barkan see also Ben Raleigh
Born Marcus Barkan, New York City 1934. Died 2020.

Barkan honed his songwriting skills in the Brill Building and enjoyed his first major success with "The Writing on the Wall," co-written with Sandy Baron and George Paxton (credited on the record as George Eddy). More hits followed for Connie Francis and Nat King Cole (both with co-writers), but it was his own "Pretty Flamingo" that gave him and the British band Manfred Mann a number one in the UK in 1966. The original demo had been recorded by New York-based singer Jimmy Radcliffe in a Drifters'-style, but Barkan was dissatisfied with the result and had him re-record it with a pared-down arrangement. Another memorable song, co-written with Richie Adams (1938-2017) was "The Tra La La Song (One Banana, Two Banana)," the theme to *The Banana Splits* children's tv show, for which he served as musical director. Barkan and Adams went on to write for the Monkees and the Archies, while Barkan collaborated with songwriters Ben Raleigh, Victor Millrose and Pam Sawyer, as well as being associated with certain cult bands. Records show that the album *Psychedelic Moods* by the Deep, produced by Barkan, was the first album to have the word psychedelic in the title. Barkan and Adams also wrote music for the 1970 sci-fi musical *Toomorrow,* starring Olivia Newton-John.

Chart entries
The Writing on the Wall *(with Sandy Baron, George Eddy (aka George Paxton))* Adam Wade
    (US 1961 # 5); Tommy Steele (UK 1961 # 30)
Mr Happiness *(with Sandy Baron, George Eddy)* Johnny Maestro (US 1961 # 57)
Let True Love Begin *(with Sandy Baron, George Eddy)* Nat King Cole (US 1961 # 73; UK # 29)
I'm Gonna Be Warm This Winter *(with Hank Hunter)* Connie Francis (US 1962 # 18; UK # 48)
If I Didn't Love You *(with Pam Sawyer)* Chuck Jackson (US 1965 # 46)
Pretty Flamingo – Manfred Mann (UK 1966 # 1; US # 29)
I'll Try Anything *(with Victor Millrose)* Dusty Springfield (UK 1967 # 13; US # 40)
I'm Indestructible *(with Victor Millrose)* Jack Jones (US 1967 # 81)
Good Combination – Sonny & Cher (US 1967 # 56)
Help Yourself (To All My Lovin') *(with Scott English, Jerry Ross)* James & Bobby Purify
    (US 1968 # 94)
The Tra La La Song (One Banana, Two Banana) *(with Richie Adams)* The Banana Splits
    (US 1969 # 96)
Swingin' Tight *(with Bob Barish)* Billy Deal & the Rhondels (US 1969 # 85)

Mark Barkan and Ben Raleigh
Hercules - Frankie Vaughan (UK 1962 # 42)
She's a Fool - Leslie Gore (US 1963 # 5)
Do You Really Love Me Too? - Billy Fury (UK 1964 # 13)
That's the Way Boys Are - Lesley Gore (UK 1964 # 12)
I Don't Want To Be a Loser - Leslie Gore (US 1964 # 37)
Bring a Little Sunshine To My Heart - Vic Dana (US 1965 # 66)

Syd Barrett
Born Roger Keith Barrett, Cambridge, England 1946. Died 2006.

Barrett used the nickname Syd from the age of 14 (one account has it derived from Sid "The Beat" Barrett, an earlier Cambridge jazz pianist). He attended Cambridge Art School with his childhood friend Roger Waters and in 1964 enrolled at Camberwell College of Arts in London to study painting. Meanwhile, Waters met Dave Mason and Richard Wright while studying architecture at Regent Stret Polytechnic in London and formed the band Sigma 6 with Clive Metcalf and Wright's future wife Juliette Gale. In 1965, after serving his music apprenticeship with local bands Geoff Mott & the Mottoes and the Hollering Blues, Barrett was invited by Waters to join his band, which at the time was called the Tea Set, although it had also gone by the names the Abdabs and Megadeath. Barrett would eventually come up with the name the Pink Floyd Sound (after two Blues musicians) before Sound was eventually dropped. With the lineup of Barrett (lead vocals, guitar), Waters (bass, vocals), Wright (keyboards) and Mason (drums), their repertoire consisting of a mix of R&B and 12-Bar blues, along with experimental sonic effects, elaborate back-projected film, and extended sets. But it was Barrett's free-form guitar playing and philosophical lyrics (heavily influenced by reading Tolkien and even Grimm fairy tales) that would not only make them popular among London's early psychedelic set but also attracting the attention of the music industry.

When they signed for EMI in late 1966, Barrett had already written songs that would grace their first album. Their first single was "Arnold Layne." With lyrics referring to a cross-dresser stealing women's lingerie from washing lines, was banned by a number of BBC radio stations. Waters explained: "Both my mother and Syd's mother had students as lodgers because there was a girls' college up the road so there were constantly great lines of bras and knickers on our washing lines and Arnold, whoever he was, had bits off our washing lines." The second single, "See Emily Play" also courted controversy. The inspiration behind the track was allegedly about a girl who Barrett had met while he was tripping on LSD and sleeping in the woods, but it later transpired that Emily was in fact the Honorable Emily Young, daughter of Wayland Young, Second Baron Kennet, who had been given the nickname, the "Psychedelic Schoolgirl" (later denied by Young). Barrett commented on his songwriting: "I think it's good if a song has more than one meaning. Maybe that kind of song can reach far more people."

The ground-breaking album *The Piper at the Gates of Dawn* was released in August 1967, but Barrett's reliance upon psychedelic drugs would soon spiral out of control and hasten his downfall. Failing to turn up at concerts, the strain on the other band members became too much to bear. In April 1968 they announced he had left the band. Following a brief and erratic solo career, and two lacklustre albums, he finally retired from the music business and took up painting and gardening in Cambridge.

Chart entries
Arnold Layne – Pink Floyd (UK 1967 # 2)
See Emily Play – Pink Floyd (UK # 6)

Steve Barri see also P F Sloan, James Marcus Smith
Born Steven Barry Lipkin, New York City 1942.

Barri worked as a staff writer with Lou Adler's Dunhill Records, before teaming up with fellow songwriter P F Sloan to produce and co-write a number of hits in the mid-Sixties. They were also largely responsible for the success of the Grass Roots, a band project that the two of them had developed for the label to capitalise on the current folk movement. Having written suitable songs together, they recorded "Where Were You When I Needed You" with Sloan on guitar and lead vocals and several session players, including Wrecking Crew keyboard player Larry Knechtel. Under the name "The Grass Roots," a demo was sent out to radio stations and the writers then looked for a suitable band that could promote the song. They found what they were looking for with the Bedouins, who had just won a competition in the San Francisco area. As the official Grass Roots, the band, with lead singer Willie Fulton, recorded the song themselves, but after two years and half a dozen hit songs, they parted company from Dunhill.

As producer, Barri also scored a chart topper with "Dizzy" for Tommy Roe, while he and his partner co-produced Sloan's global hit song "Eve of Destruction" for Barry Maguire. When Sloan decided to leave Dunhill, Barri continued to produce the Grass Roots as well as co-writing hit songs with James Marcus Smith (aka P J Proby), including "You Baby" for the Turtles and "A Must to Avoid" for Herman's Hermits. When ABC Records acquired Dunhill, Barri was retained as head of A&R, responsible for singing and producing new artists, and he worked on a number of Bobby Bland's critically acclaimed albums.

Chart entries
Bella Linda *(with Lucio Battisti, Barry A Gross)* The Grass Roots (US 1969 # 28)

Steve Barri and P F Sloan
Kick That Little Foot, Sally Ann - Round Robin (US 1964 # 61)
Summer Means Fun - Bruce & Terry (US 1964 # 72)
One Piece Topless Bathing Suite *(with Don Altfeld)* The Rip Chords (US 1964 # 96)
Secret Agent Man - The Ventures (US 1966 # 54); Johnny Rivers (US 1966 # 3)
Where Were You When I Needed You - The Grass Roots (US 1966 # 28)
Only When You're Lonely - The Grass Roots (US 1966 # 96)
Things I Should Have Said - The Grass Roots (US 1967 # 23)
Wake Up, Wake Up - The Grass Roots (US 1967 # 68)

Steve Barri and James Marcus Smith (aka P J Proby)
(Here They Come) From All Over the World - Jan & Dean (US 1965 # 56)
I Found a Girl - Jan & Dean (US 1965 # 31)
A Must To Avoid - Herman's Hermits (UK 1965 # 6; US # 8)
You Baby - The Turtles (US 1966 # 20)
Can I Get To Know You Better - The Turtles (US 1966 # 89)
Another Day, Another Heartache - The Fifth Dimension (US 1967 # 45)

Jeff Barry and Ellie Greenwich see also Phil Spector
Born Joel Adelberg, New York City 1938.
Born Elenor Louise Greenwich, New York City 1940. Died 2009.
Songwriters Hall of Fame 1991.
Rock and Roll Hall of Fame 2010.

Born in Brooklyn to a Jewish family, Barry's parents divorced when he was seven and he moved with his mother and sister to live in Plainfield, New Jersey, only returning to New York seven years later. As a child he only had two interests, cowboys and music. After graduating Erasmus Hall High School he served in the US Army and often sang in military bands before enrolling at the City College of New York to study engineering. In 1958, an introduction via a family friend to music publisher Arnold Shaw led to an audition, where he presented several original songs. Not overly impressed with his voice, Shaw saw potential in his writing, and he was signed to RCA. His first solo release was the self-penned "It's Called Rock and Roll," followed by several others, including "Lonely Lips," written with fellow staff writer Ben Raleigh.

In 1960, Barry's ballad "Teenage Sonata" was an R&B hit for Sam Cooke, while his first pop hit came with "Tell Laura I Love Her," another co-write with Raleigh. The tragic tale of a fatal stock car race was originally intended to be about a rodeo and a guy being killed by a bull, but the label insisted that Barry re-work it as a "teen tragedy" along the lines of the recent hit "Teen Angel." Originally recorded in the US by Ray Peterson, a copy was picked up in the UK by Decca and broadcast on BBC radio. Label executives then panicked, realising it was "too tasteless and vulgar for the English sensibility" and hastily destroying the 25,000 copies already pressed. EMI-Columbia then recruited their new signing Ricky Valence to cover the song, and although BBC banned it, citing a number of recent fatal road accidents, it was too late to see it peak at number one in August 1960.

In October 1962, Barry married Ellie Greenwich, who he had met at a family gathering a couple of years before. Brooklyn-born Greenwich's father was a department store manager, and she was reportedly named after Eleanor Roosevelt. Her interest in music was sparked by listening to records at home, particularly those by Teresa Brewer and Johnny Ray, and she learned to play the accordion at an early age. After the family moved to Levittown, Greenwich and two school friends formed the vocal group the Jivettes, with other members joining later, and they performed at local functions. Around this time she also began writing love songs about a school crush. After graduation, she enrolled at Queens College and taught herself to play piano. Signing with RCA at the age of 17, she recorded her first song, "Silly Isn't It," credited to Ellie Gaye, although it was later changed by the label. After transferring to Hofstra University, she met Barry at a family Thanksgiving party, (her maternal uncle was married to Barry's cousin). Barry was married at the time, but their shared love of music brought them closer together, and they began dating after his marriage was annulled.

Still following separate music careers, Greenwich got her first break at the Brill Building while waiting in a cubicle to see John Gluck, one of the co-writers of "It's My Party." The office happened to be that of established writers Leiber and Stoller, and when they heard someone playing piano from the cubicle, they expected to see fellow writer Carole King. Impressed with what they heard, they eventually signed her to their publishing company Trio Music as a staff writer. At first, Greenwich wrote with other partners, including Raleigh, and also became a much-sought after demo session singer. Her biggest hits at this time were writing with Tony Powers, including the Exciters' "He's Got the Power" and Bob B Soxx's "Why Do Lovers Break Each Other's Hearts?" The latter song was co-written with Phil Spector, who had been introduced to Greenwich by music publisher Aaron Schroeder.

Barry and Greenwich were married in October 1962, and shortly afterward decided to write songs exclusively with each other - a decision that disappointed both Barry's regular wiring partner Artie Resnick, and Greenwich's partner Powers. What followed were some of the finest and most enduring songs of the decade, mainly written with girl groups and teen idols in mind. Signing with Trinity Music, they went on to score hits with "Da Doo Ron Ron," "Then He Kissed Me," "Be My Baby," and "Baby I Love You," just four of the songs co-written with wizz-kid producer Phil Spector.

In early 1963, the duo recorded a demo of "What a Guy," which Barry had written for the Sensations, but the group's label, Jubilee Records, preferred the demo and released it under the name the Raindrops, becoming a top 50 hit. They also released an album at the end of 1963, before their short recording career came to an end two years later. When Red Bird Records was founded by Leiber and Stoller in 1964, the couple were brought in as songwriters and producers, The first release was their "Chapel of Love," co-written with Spector, recorded by the Dixie Cups, and produced along with Leiber and Stoller. They continued to write and produce for Red Bird, including several more singles for the Dixie Cups, the Ad-Libs and the Jelly Beans, as well as co-writing the Shangri-Las' teen-tragedy "The Leader of the Pack" with pop impresario George Shadow Morton. According to Morton, he wrote the song for the girl group the Goodies, but it was needed as a follow-up to Shangri-La's hit "Remember (Walking in the Sand)."

The song was noted for the spoken intro by lead vocalist Mary Weiss, who later recalled: "I don't think I would be able to put feeling into the song unless I had really thought about the lyrics. I put a lot of my own pain into that song. I don't think teenage years are all that rosy for a lot of people - they certainly weren't for me. They are the most confusing time of people's lives and there is a tremendous dark side to the record, which I think teenagers relate to. The studio was a great place to let the pain out." For the sound of the revving engine, Barry later explained that they attached a microphone to a long cable and recorded their engineer's Harley Davidson out in the street, although the noise of the crash was a sound effect.

In 1964, Barry and Greenwich scored a minor US hit with "Do-Wah- Diddy" for the Exciters, but it was soon picked up by the UK's Manfred Mann, and with the re-titled "Do-Wah-Diddy Diddy" became a chart-topper on both sides of the Atlantic. However, this writing love affair did not last, and the couple divorced at the end of 1965. Greenwich recalled: "When things were working, and you're really connecting, what could be better? Here's the person your'e in love with, and you're being creative together, and things are going well - it's the highest high you can imagine. However, when there were disagreements, it was very hard to leave it at the office and go home at night and change hats: 'Hi Honey, what do you want for dinner'"? They continued to write together for a time, including another successful collaboration with Spector. Around this time, Greenwich discovered the young talented writer Neil Diamond, and, along with Barry, formed a company to publish his music. Two of their final hits with Spector were the classic "I Can Hear Music" for the Ronettes and "River Deep Mountain High" for Ike and Tina Turner, but although both became enduring classics, they inexplicably bombed in the US charts.

When NBC began to develop a new sitcom called *The Monkees* in late 1966, the music supervisor Don Kirshner called on Barry to produce songs for the "band" to record and perform on the shows. Barry supplied a few that were written by Neil

Diamond, including "I'm a Believer," which went on to top the charts on both sides of the Atlantic, becoming one of the biggest-selling singles of all time. In 1968, Kirshner quit working with *The Monkees* to become music director for a new Saturday morning cartoon show *The Archies*, and once again called on Barry to provide songs, including the opening theme, "Everything's Archie." During this period, Barry had established his own label, Steed Records, and among his roster of artists was the Canadian singer-songwriter Andy Kim. Between them they wrote and recorded several songs, including "Sugar Sugar" (with lead singer Roy Dante), which became another chart topper on both sides of the Atlantic and also Record of the Year. As advice to budding songwriters, Barry once wrote: "If you finish a song you have to believe it has something or you wouldn't have gone through the time and effort to finish it."

In 1967, Greenwich formed Pineywood Music with Mike Rashkow and released a solo album the following year. During their time together, Barry and Greenwich created music and words that helped define the Brill Building Sound. Reminiscing on her long career, Greenwich wrote: "I still feel it would be nice if that romance can be there, birds could sing if you fell in love, and you could hear violins. I think that would be really terrific - I don't care how old you are, or what generation."

Chart entries
When the Boy's Happy (The Girls Happy Too) – The Four Pennies (US 1963 # 95)
What a Guy – The Raindrops (US 1963 # 41)
Give Us Your Blessing – Ray Peterson (US 1963 # 70); Shangri-Las (US 1965 # 29)
The Kind of Boy You Can't Forget – The Raindrops (US 1963 # 95)
I Have A Boyfriend *(with The Tokens)* – The Chiffons (US 1963 # 36)
That Boy John – The Raindrops (US 1963 # 64)
Do-Wah-Diddy – The Exciters (US 1964 # 78); Manfred Mann (UK 1964 # 1; US #1) *as
    Doo-Wah-Diddy Diddy
I Wanna Love Him So Bad - The Jelly Beans ((US 1964 # 9)
People Say – The Dixie Cups (US 1964 # 12)
Maybe I Know – Leslie Gore (US 1964 # 14)
One More Tear – The Raindrops (US 1964 # 97)
Leader of the Pack *(with George "Shadow" Morton)* The Shangri-Las (US 1964 # 1; UK # 11)
Don't Ever Leave Me – Connie Francis (US 1964 # 42)
You Should Have Seen The Way He Looked At Me – The Dixie Cups (US 1964 # 39)
Little Bell – The Dixie Cups (US 1964 # 51)
Look Of Love – Leslie Gore (US 1964 # 27)
Out In the Streets – The Shangri-Las (US 1964 # 53)
He Ain't No Angel – The Ad Libs (US 1964 # 100)
Give Us Your Blessings – The Shangri-Las (US 1965 # 29)
I'll Take You Where the Music's Playing – The Drifters (US 1965 # 51)
Hanky Pandy – Tommy James & the Shondells (US 1966 # 1; UK # 8)

Barry-Greenwich and Steve Venet
Good Night Baby – The Butterflys (US 1964 # 51)
Baby Be Mine – The Jelly Beans (US 1964 # 51)

Barry-Greenwich and Phil Spector
Da Doo Ron Ron – The Crystals (US 1963 #3; UK # 5)
Not Too Young To Get Married – Bob B Soxx & the Blue Jeans (US 1963 # 63)
Wait 'Til My Bobby Gets Home – Darlene Love (US 1963 # 26)
Then He Kissed Me – The Crystals (US 1963 # 6; UK # 2); The Beach Boys (UK 1967 # 4
   (as Then I Kissed Her)
Be My Baby – The Ronettes (US 1963 # 2; UK # 4)
A Fine, Fine Boy – Darlene Love (US 1963 # 53)
Baby, I Love You – The Ronettes (US 1963 # 24; UK # 11); Andy Kim (US 1969 # 9)
Little Boy – The Crystals (US 1964 # 92)
I Wonder – The Crystals (UK 1964 # 36)
Chapel of Love – The Dixie Cups (US 1964 # 1; UK # 22)
All Grown Up – The Crystals (US 1964 # 98)
River Deep, Mountain High – Ike & Tina Turner (US # 88; UK # 3); Deep Purple (US

1969 # 53)
I Can Hear Music – The Ronettes (US 1966 # 100); The Beach Boys (US 1969 # 24; UK # 10)
I'll Never Need More Than This – Ike & Tina Turner (UK 1969 #64)

Jeff Barry
Teenage Sonata – Sam Cooke (US 1960 # 50)
Tell Me What He Said – Helen Shapiro (UK 1962 # 2)
Bang-Shang-A-Lang – The Archies (US 1968 # 22)
Did You See Her Eyes – The Illusion (US 1968 # 32)

Jeff Barry and Andy Kim
How'd We Ever Get This Way? – Andy Kim (US 1968 # 21)
Shoot Em Up Baby – Andy Kim (US 1968 # 31)
Rainbow Ride - Andy Kim (US 1968 # 49)
Feelin' So Good (S.K.O.O.B.Y - D.O.O) – The Archies (US 1968 # 53)
Sugar Sugar - The Archies (US 1969 #1; UK # 1)
So Good Together - Andy Kim (US 1969 # 36)
Jingle Jangle – The Archies (US 1969 # 10)

Jeff Barry with others
Tell Laura I Love Her *(with Ben Raleigh)* Ricky Valance (UK 1960 # 1; Ray Peterson (US 1963 # 7)
Chip Chip *(with Clifford Crawford & Artie Resnick)* Gene McDaniels (US 1962 # 10)
I Left My Heart in the Balcony *(with Artie Resnick)* Linda Scott (US 1962 # 74)
I Got to Go Back (And Watch That Little Girl Dance) *(with Bert Berns)* The McCoys (US 1967 # 69)
Am I Grooving You *(with Bert Berns)* Freddie Scott (US 1967 # 71)

Ellie Greenwich and Tony Powers
Why Do Lovers Break Each Other's Heart? *(with Phil Spector)* Bob B Soxx & the Blue Jeans (US 1963 # 38)
He's Got the Power - The Exciters (US 1963 # 57)
(Today I Met) The Boy I'm Gonna Marry *(with Phil Spector)* Darlene Love (US 1963 # 39)
One Boy Too Late - Mike Clifford (US 1963 # 96)
I Didn't Mean To Hurt You - The Rockin' Berries (UK 1964 # 43)
All of My Life *(with Helen Miller)* Leslie Gore (US 1965 # 71)

Ellie Greenwich and George Fischoff
Run To My Lovin' Arms - Billy Fury (UK 1965 # 25); Ronnie Welch (US 1965 # 96)
Ain't Gonna Lie - Keith (US 1966 # 39)
98.6 - Keith (US 1966 # 7; UK # 24)
Lazy Day - Spanky & Our Gang (US 1967 # 14)

Ellie Greenwich with others
Remember Then *(with Beverly Ross, Stan Vincent)* The Earls (US 1962 # 24)
Come Dance With Me *(with Matt Maurer)* Jay & the Americans (US 1963 # 76)

John Barry
Born John Prendegast, York 1933. Died 2011.
Songwriters Hall of Fame 1998.

The youngest of four children, Barry's mother was a classical pianist, while his father went from being a projectionist during the silent film era to owning a chain of cinemas in the north of England. As a result, it was inevitable that he would be influenced by both film and music. After attending St Peter's School in York, he did his national service with the army in Cyprus and learned to play trumpet by a correspondence course with jazz musician Bill Russo. On his return home, he worked as an arranger for orchestras led by Ted Heath and Jack Parnell, and in 1957 formed his own band, the John Barry Seven. Among their early recordings was "Hit and Miss," the theme to the BBC show *Juke Box Jury,* as well as a cover of Johnny Smith's "Walk Don't Run."

After appearing as the resident band on BBC's music show *Drumbeat*, he began receiving commissions. In 1959, he was employed by EMI as music arranger for their artists, including Adam Faith. With Les Vandyke, he wrote several songs for Faith, whose movies *Beat Girl* and *Never Let Go* became Barry's first film scores. In 1962, he moved to Ember Records to produce and arrange albums, and all his work came to the notice of United Artists' Noel Rogers, who was making the debut James Bond movie *Dr No.* Unhappy with Monty Norman's "James Bond Theme," he brought in Barry to arrange it, and it would be used in every subsequent Bond movie, although Norman would receive all the royalties.

When the producers hired Lionel Bart to score the title of the second Bond film, *From Russia with Love,* they again decided to use Barry for the rest of the music, thus beginning Barry's 25-year-long collaboration with the Bond franchise (along with lyricist Leslie Bricusse), which also led to chart hits with Shirley Bassey's iconic "Goldfinger" and Tom Jones' "Thunderball." Amongst some of the other non-Bond movie scores he would compose in the Sixties were *Zulu* (1964), *Man in the Middle* (1964), and *King Rat* (1965), although his biggest success came with the Oscar-winning pair *Born Free* (1966) (along with lyricist Don Black) and *The Lion in Winter* (1968). Further success followed with the Grammy-winning *Midnight Cowboy* (1969), despite not given on-screen credit. Looking back on his career, he offered this advice: "If you have a successful run, everything comes to you. Nothing succeeds like success."

Chart entries
Hit and Miss – John Barry Seven (UK 1960 # 10)
Beat For Beatniks – John Barry Seven (UK 1960 # 40)
Never Let Go – John Barry Orchestra (UK 1960 # 49)
Black Stockings – John Barry Seven (UK 1960 # 27)
Cutty Sark – John Barry Seven (UK 1962 # 35)
Goldfinger *(with Leslie Bricusse, Anthony Newley)* Shirley Bassey (UK 1964 # 21; US # 8);
    Billy Strange (US 1965 # 55); Jack LaForge (US 1965 # 96); John Barry Orchestra (US 1965 # 72)
Thunderball *(with Leslie Bricusse)* Tom Jones (US 1965 # 5# UK # 35)
Born Free *(with Don Black)* Roger Williams (US 1966 # 7); The Hesitations (US 1968 # 38)
You Only Live Twice *(with Leslie Bricusse)* Nancy Sinatra (US 1967 # 44; UK # 11)
Midnight Cowboy – Ferrante & Teicher (US 1969 # 10)

Thom Bell and William Hart
Born Thomas Randolph Bell, Kingston, Jamaica 1943. Died 2022.
Hart born Philadelphia Pa. Died 2022.
Songwriters Hall of Fame 2006 (Bell).
Rock and Roll Hall of Fame 2025 (Bell).

Bell and his family moved to Philadelphia when he was just four years old. One of eleven siblings, his mother was a stenographer and pianist and his father, while owning a fish market and restaurant, could also play accordion and Hawaiian guitar. Classically trained as a musician, in his teens Bell sang with friends Kenny Gamble, Leon Huff and Daryl Hall, and got his first break in soul music working as a session player and arranger for Cameo Records in Philadelphia. In 1967, he was introduced to a local group called the Delfonics and produced two of their early singles on the Moon Shot and Cameo labels. The lead vocalist and founding member of the group was William "Poogie" Hart who had previously sung with Little Hart & the Everglows, the Veltones, the Four Guys and the Four Gents, all of which included his brother Wilbert and friends from Overbrook High School.

Around 1964, the two Hart brothers had formed the Orphonics, along with Randy Cain, and were later introduced by Philly Groove Records' Stan Watson to Bell, who at the time was working with Chubby Checker. Hart's "He Don't Really Love Me" was produced and arranged by Bell, and in August 1966 it became their first single on the Moon Shot label (soon to become Cameo-Parkway). With the name of the group changed to the Delfonics, several more singles were released. By the end of 1967, with Cameo about to be defunct, Watson started up his own label called Philly Groove Records, and released "La-La (Means I Love You)" by the Delfonics. Written by Hart and Bell, it featured Hart's incredible falsetto voice, and after first being released on the local market, soon gained national promotion with New York's Amy-Mala-Bell Records, peaking at number four on the Hot 100.

In December 1969, the Delfonics released the Bell-Hart song "Didn't I (Blow Your Mind This Time)," and with it scored another top ten hit, followed by a Grammy award the following year. Bell then joined his old friends Gamble and Huff to work as arranger for a number of acts for their fast-growing company in Philadelphia. In 1971 he became producer for the local group, the Stylistics.

Chart entries
La-La (Means I Love You) – The Delfonics (US 1968 # 4)
I'm Sorry – The Delfonics (US 1968 # 42)
He Don't Really Love Me *(with Stan Watson)* The Delfonics (US 1968 # 92)
Break Your Promise – The Delfonics (US 1968 # 35)
Ready or Not Here I Come (Can't Hide From Love) The Delfonics (US 1968 # 35)
Somebody Loves You – The Delfonics (US 1969 # 72)
Funny Feeling – The Delfonics (US 1969 # 94)
You Got Yours and I'll Get Mine – The Delfonics (US 1969 # 40)
Didn't I (Blow Your Mind This Time) The Delfonics (US 1969 # 10; UK # 22)

Thom Bell and Kenny Gamble
Watch Your Step *(with Luther Dixon)* Brooks O'Dell (US 1963 # 16
Let's Make a Promise *(with Mikki Farrow)* Peaches & Herb (US 1968 # 75)
I Love My Baby - Archie Bell & the Drells (US 1969 # 94)
Moody Woman *(with Jerry Butler)* Jerry Butler (US 1969 # 24)
Girl You're Too Young *(with Archie Bell)* Archie Bell & the Drells (US 1969 # 59)
What's the Use of Breaking Up *(with Jerry Butler)* Jerry Butler (US 1969 # 20)
A Brand New Me *(with Jerry Butler)* Dusty Springfield (US 1969 # 24)

Thom Bell with others
What a Fool I've Been *(with Steve Cropper)* Carla Thomas (US 1963 # 93)

William Bell see also **Booker T Jones and Steve Cropper**
Born William Yarbrough, Memphis, Tennessee 1939.

Singing in church as a child, he was inspired by Sam Cooke's popular gospel group, the Soul Stirrers. He began writing songs at the age of ten, with his first composition called "Alone on a Rainy Night." Four years later, he won a talent contest and became a popular performer in clubs around the Memphis area. Taking his stage name in honour of his grandmother Belle, he was a backing singer for Rufus Thomas, and in 1957 began recording with the teenage vocal group the Del Rios. Noticed by Stax Records, they initially took him on as a songwriter, but he soon became their first male solo artist. While serving in the military, he was able to record a number of singles while on furlough, and after his service was completed in 1967, he released his debut album *The Soul of a Bell,* which included his top twenty hit "Everybody Loves a Winner," one of his first collaborations with Booker T Jones.

Bell was a close friend of Otis Redding and was supposed to have been on the same flight that led to Redding's death in 1967, but as the weather was so bad Bell's show was cancelled. It was this tragedy that led to his long collaboration with Jones, who he had known since high school and church. In honour of Redding, they released "A Tribute to a King." That same year, Bell had an unintended Christmas hit on the R&B chart with "Everyday Will Be Like a Holiday," that still remains one of his most-recorded hits. In 1968, Bell and Jones wrote "Private Number" as a duet for Bell and soul and gospel singer Judy Clay, which went on to score a top ten hit in the UK. The following year, Bell moved to Atlanta and set up the short-lived soul label, Peachtree Records. He also took acting lessons for a stage production of *A Streetcar Named Desire* before signing a two-year deal with Mercury Records. With them, he had his biggest hit with "Trying to Love You," an R&B chart-topper in 1977.

Chart entries
You Don't Miss Your Water - William Bell (US 1962 # 95)
Any Other Way – Chuck Jackson (US 1963 # 81)

William Bell and Booker T Jones
Everybody Loves a Winner - William Bell (US 1967 # 95)
I Got a Sure Thing *(with Ollie Hoskins)* Ollie & the Nightingales (US 1968 # 73)
A Tribute To a King - William Bell (US 1968 # 86; UK #31)
Private Number - Judy Clay & William Bell (US 1968 # 75; UK # 8)
I Forgot To Be Your Lover - William Bell (US 1968 # 45)
All God's Children Got Soul - Dorothy Morrison (US 1969 # 95)

Benny Benjamin see also George David Weiss
Born William Benjamin, Birmingham, Alabama 1925. Died 1969.
Songwriters Hall of Fame 1984
Rock and Roll Hall of Fame 2003.

Benjamin became Motown's first studio drummer in 1958, having honed his skills watching drummers like Buddy Rich and those of the big band jazz groups. He became a much sought after member of the famous Funk Brother session musicians, and his dynamic style led producers such as Berry Gordy insisting on his presence in the studio (as was bassist Jamie Jamerson). As a result, he played on many of Motown's early hits, including "Money (That's What I Want)," "Do You Love Me," "Get Ready," and "My Girl." As an accomplished songwriter, he teamed up in the Fifties with pianist Sol Marcus to write "Lonely Man" for Elvis Presley and "Fabulous Character" for Sarah Vaughan.

In the early Sixties, he co-wrote several hits with George David Weiss, but it was with Sol Marcus (1912-1976) and Horace Ott (b. 1933) that he is best remembered for co-authoring the soul standard "Don't Let Me Be Misunderstood," originally a track on a Nina Simone album, but later a huge hit for the Animals. Ott had started composing the song following a heated argument with Gloria Caldwell, whom he had recently married, and wrote lyrics that expressed how he was well intentioned, but misunderstood. Due to the rules at the time, Ott's credit for the song (he wrote the melody and chorus lyrics) was taken by Caldwell as he was a member of BMI (Broadcasting Music Inc) and not permitted to work with the others as they were members of ASCAP (American Society of Composers, Authors & Publishers).

Notorious for being late for work, Benjamin was known for creating highly fabricated and humorous excuses. When caught sleeping at his drumkit by a producer, he snapped awake and began drumming and calling out "Papa-zita, papa-zita, papa-zita," which earned him the nickname Papa Zita by his fellow Funk Brothers. After a struggle with alcohol and drug addiction, Benjamin found he was being replaced more often by other drummers in the studio.

Chart entries
Wheel of Fortune *(with George David Weiss)* LaVerne Baker (US 1960 # 83)
I'll Never Be Free *(with George David Weiss)* Kay Starr (US 1961 # 94)
Oh! What It Seemed To Be *(with George David Weiss; Frankie Carle)* The Castells (US 1962 # 91)
Don't Let Me Be Misunderstood *(with Gloria Caldwell, Sol Marcus)* The Animals (UK 1965 # 3; US # 15)

Brian Bennett see Hank Marvin

Roy Bennett see Sid Tepper and Roy Bennett

Bert Berns see also Wes Farrell, Jerry Ragovoy
Born Bertrand Russell Berns, New York City 1929 . Died 1967.
Rock and Roll Hall of Fame 2016.
Songwriters Hall of Fame 2025.

Also known as Bert Russell, he began his career in music as a record salesman, copywriter, and session pianist, and later a staff writer in New York's Brill Building. In 1960, he signed a $50 a week contract with Robert Mellin Music, based in Denmark Street (London's Tin Pan Alley). At first he tried his hand as a solo career, using the name Russell Byrd, and recorded the self-penned "You'd Better Come Home," which was a top fifty hit in the US and later recorded by the Isley Brothers. He found greater success with writing "A Little Bit of Soap" for the doo-wop band the Jarmels (also a 1978 UK hit for Showaddywaddy). That year, he formed his first writing partnership with Phil Medley (1916-1997) and their first major success came with "Twist and Shout." Originally recorded by the Top Notes, it was reworked into a rock anthem by the Isley Brothers, whose version gave them their first US top twenty hit in 1962 and induction into the Grammy Hall of Fame in 2010. That same year, Berns' writing scored hits which included "Cry to Me" for Solomon Burke, and the Exciters' "Tell Him," their first top ten success. Now working as an independent producer for different labels, Berns had hits with Gene Pitney (another collaboration with Medley) and Betty Harris.

His association with Solomon Burke brought him to the attention of Jerry Wexler and Ahmet Ertegun, heads of the Atlantic label, and in 1963 he replaced Leiber and Stoller as their staff producer. With Wexler he co-wrote "Everybody Needs Somebody To Love" for Burke, as well as "That's When It Hurts" for Ben E King. As producer, he scored hits for the Drifters with the Young-Resnick's classic "Under the Boardwalk" and the Mann-Weil "Saturday Night at the Movies." In the mid-Sixties, he became the first US producer to work in London, helming a number of records for British artists. In 1964, he wrote "Here Comes the Night," which gave Van Morrison's group Them a number two hit in the UK. Morrison had intended it to be the follow-up to "Baby, Please Don't Go," but Decca had rush-released a version by Lulu three months before (although only reaching the top fifty).

The following year, he formed his own label Bang Records, which specialised in rock acts that included Van Morrison, the McCoys and Neil Diamond. Forming a new writing partnership with Wes Farrell, they gave the McCoys a chart-topper with "Hang on Sloopy," which had already been a hit for the Vibrations in 1964 with the title "My Girl Sloopy." Berns also produced "Brown Eyed Girl" for Morrison. Another venture for him was Shout Records, where the focus was more on soul and R&B. Forging a new writing partnership with Jerry Ragovoy, their most famous song was "Piece Of My Heart," first a hit for Erma Franklin, but made definitive the following year by the Big Brother Holding Company and its relatively unknown lead singer Janis Joplin. It proved to be Berns' last work. A childhood illness that damaged his heart would result in an early death.

Chart entries
You'd Better Come Home – Russell Byrd (US 1961 # 50)
A Little Bit Of Soap – The Jarmels (US 1961 # 12); Garnet Mimms (US 1965 # 95); The
    Exciters (US 1966 # 58)
Cry To Me – Solomon Burke (US 1962 # 44); Betty Harris (US 1963 # 23); The Pretty Things
    (UK 1965 # 28); Freddie Scott (US 1967 # 70)
Tell Him – The Exciters (US 1962 # 4; UK # 46)
Get Him *(with Ray Passman, Jerry Leiber, Mike Stoller)* The Exciters (US 1963 # 76)
His Kiss *(with Mike Stoller)* Betty Harris (US 1964 # 89)
It's All Over *(with Mike Leander)* Ben E King (US 1964 # 72)
Yes I Do – Solomon Burke (US 1964 # 92)
Here Comes the Night – Lulu (UK 1964 # 50); Them (UK 1965 # 2; US # 24)
I Want Candy *(with Bob Feldman, Jerry Goldstein, Richard Gottehrer)* The Strangeloves
    (US 1965 # 11); Brian Poole & the Tremeloes (UK 1965 # 25)
Let the Water Run Down – P J Proby (UK 1965 # 19)
Baby Come On Home – Solomon Burke (US 1966 # 96)
Tell Her – Dean Parrish (US 1966 # 97)
Up In the Streets of Harlem – The Drifters (UK 1966 # 52)
Are You Lonely For Me – Freddie Scott (US 1966 # 39)
I Got To Go Back (And Watch That Little Girl Dance) *(with Jeff Barry)* The McCoys
    (US 1967 # 69)
Am I Grooving You *(with Jeff Barry)* Freddie Scott (US 1967 # 71)

Bert Berns and Phil Medley
Push, Push – Austin Taylor (US 1960 # 90)
Twist and Shout - The Isley Brothers (US 1962 # 17; UK # 42); Brian Poole & the Tremeloes
    (UK 1963 # 4); The Beatles (US 1964 # 2)
If I Didn't Have a Dime (To Play the Jukebox) Gene Pitney (US 1962 # 58)
Killer Joe *(with Bob Elgin)* The Rocky Fellers (US 1963 # 16); The Kingsmen (US 1966 # 77)

Bert Berns and Wes Farrell
My Girl Sloopy - The Vibrations (US 1964 # 26); Little Caesar & the Consuls (US 1965 # 50)
Baby Let Me Take You Home - The Animals (UK 1964 # 21)
Goodbye Baby (Baby Goodbye) Solomon Burke (US 1964 # 33)
Hang On Sloopy - The McCoys (US 1965 # 1; UK # 5); The Ramsey Lewis Trio (US
    1965 # 11)
Everybody Do the Sloopy - Johnny Thunder (US 1965 # 67)

Bert Berns and Jerry Ragovoy
Cry Baby - Garnet Mimms & the Enchanters (US 1963 # 4)
One-Way Love - The Drifters (US 1964 # 56)
It Was Easier To Hurt Her - Wayne Fontana & the Mindbenders (UK 1965 # 36)
I'll Take Good Care Of You - Garnet Mimms (US 1966 # 30)
Heart Be Still - Lorraine Ellison (US 1967 # 89)

Piece Of My Heart - Erma Franklin (US 1967 # 62); Big Brother & the Holding Company
(US 1968 # 12)

Bert Berns and Jerry Wexler
That's When It Hurts - Ben E King (US 1964 # 63)
Everybody Needs Somebody To Love *(with Solomon Burke)* Solomon Burke (US 1964 # 58);
Wilson Pickett (US 1967 # 29)
I Don't Want To Go On Without You - The Moody Blues (UK 1965 # 33)

Jan Berry see also Roger Christian
Born William Jan Berry, Los Angeles 1941. Died 2004.

Jan Berry met fellow student and football player Dean Ormsby Torrence (b. 1940) at Emerson Junior High School in Westwood, Los Angeles. In 1957, they went on to study at the nearby University High School, and while there practiced harmonising with other football players, including future actor James Brolin. Berry and Torrence then formed a doo-wop group the Barons with other students, and at times included Sandy Nelson on drums and future Beach Boy Bruce Johnston on piano. Eventually, various members left, leaving Berry and Torrence to write their own songs.

With Torrence drafted into the US Army, it left Berry to record "Jennie Lee" with Baron member Arnie Ginsburg and fellow student Donald Altfeld (b.1940). As Jan & Arnie, it was released on Joe Lubin's Arwin Records in 1958, and became a surprising number eight hit on the Hot 100. With the moderate success of a second single, they became the featured act on the Summer Dance Party that toured the East Coast and also appeared on the *Dick Clark Show*.

With Torrence completing his six-month military service, he joined Berry to record as Jan & Dean, and with help from producers Lou Adler and Herb Alpert scored a top ten hit with "Baby Talk" on the Dore label. They also became friends of the Beach Boys and shared their love for surfing-related songs, with Berry now co-writing, arranging and producing most of the duo's original material, as well as for other artists such as the Angels, Shelley Fabares and the Rio Chords. Continuing with their studies, Torrence majored in advertising design at USC while Berry entered the California College of Medicine in 1963. Collaborating with Brian Wilson, Berry scored a dozen or more hits, including the chart-topper "Surf City," which was "gifted" to him by Wilson, much to the annoyance of his father Murry Wilson. In 1964, Berry and Torrence were invited to host and perform on the historic televised *T.A.M.I Show,* and also recorded the title song for the movie *Ride the Wild Surf.* After the surfing craze waned, the duo scored hits with "You Really Know How to Hurt a Guy" and "I Found a Girl."

In April 1966, Berry suffered severe head injuries when his Corvette struck a parked truck a short distance from Dead Man's Curve in Beverly Hills. After two months in a coma, he recovered from brain damage and partial paralysis and returned to recording in April 1967. The following year, the duo signed with Warner Bros. and released several singles.

Chart entries
Surf City *(with Brian Wilson)* Jan & Dean (US 1963 #1 ; UK # 26)
Honolulu Lulu *(with Roger Christian, Lou Adler)* Jan & Dean (US 1963 # 11)
I Adore Him *(with Artie Kornfeld)* The Angels (US 1963 # 25)
Drag City *(with Brian Wilson, Roger Christian)* Jan & Dean (US 1963 # 10)
Judy Loves Me *(with Artie Kornfeld, Don Altfeld)* Johnny Crawford (US 1964 # 95)
Dead Man's Curve *(with Roger Christian, Artie Kornfeld, Brian Wilson)* Jan & Dean
(US 1964 # 8)
Three Window Coupe *(with Roger Christian)* The Rip Chords (US 1964 # 28)
Ride the Wild Surf *(with Brian Wilson, Roger Christian)* Jan & Dean (US 1964 # 16)
The Anaheim, Azusa & Cucamonga Sewing Circle, Book Review & Timing Association
(with Don Altfeld, Roger Christian) Jan & Dean (US 1964 # 77)
Sidewalk Surfin' *(with Brian Wilson, Roger Christian)* Jan & Dean (US 1964 # 25)
Bucket T *(with Roger Christian)* Ronny & the Daytonas (US 1964 # 54)
You Really Know How To Hurt a Guy *(with Roger Christian, Jill Gibson)* Jan & Dean
(US 1965 # 27)
Batman *(with Don Altfeld, Fred Weider)* Jan & Dean (US 1966 # 66; UK # 52)

Don Black
Born Donald Blackstone, London 1938.
Songwriters Hall of Fame 2007.

Black is better known as a prolific lyricist for both film and musical theatre, but he has also contributed to Tin Pan Alley, writing a dozen or more hit songs that charted on both sides of the Atlantic. Hackney-born Black worked as a part-time usher at the London Palladium, and as an office boy and trainee journalist for the *New Musical Express,* before going on to work as a song-plugger for a publishing firm in Denmark Street. In 1960, he met "the singer's singer" Matt Monro shortly before recording his breakthrough single, "Portrait of My Love," and becoming his personal manager. It was Monro who encouraged Black to develop his skills as a lyricist, and with vocalist Al Saxon, he wrote "April Fool" for Monro's debut album. Black then collaborated with German compose Udo Jürgens (1934-2014) to write the ballads "Walk Away" and "Without You," both hits for the singer. "Walk Away" was orginally called "Warum nur, warum?" (Tell Her I Send My Love) and performed by Jürgens as the Austrian Eurovision Song Contest entry in 1964 (where Monro sang the UK entry) and later reworked with Monro to give him a top five hit in the UK.

Black also collaborated with French singer-songwriter Charles Aznavour on Monro's hit "For Mama." The following year, Black had his break into film scoring by working with composer Leslie Bricusse on the title theme for the Bond movie *Thunderball.* The song, which had the odd title of "Mr Kiss Kiss, Bang Bang" (after an Italian journalist had described Bond) was soon removed from the title credits for being too short, so composer John Barry was brought in to rewrite it with Black. With the more appropriate title "Thunderball" it became a hit for Tom Jones. Black and Barry achieved greater success later that year with the movie *Born Free*, with Barry's score and Black's evocative lyrics performed by Monro receiving two Academy Awards. Surprisingly, the song never charted.

The following year, Black teamed up with Canadian composer Mark London (b.1940) to write "To Sir, with Love" for the movie of the same name, giving Lulu her first chart-topper in the US. It was initially recorded with the Mindbenders, who were also in the film. More success followed in 1969 when Black joined composer Elmer Bernstein to write the Oscar-nominated title song for the John Wayne movie "True Grit," performed by Glen Campbell.

Since the Sixties, Black has been writing prolifically for stage and screen and sees no signs of stopping. His love for lyrics was infectious: "A song can do more in three minutes than any other art form. From the Heart they come, and to the Heart they stay." In a 2020 interview with Vincent Dowd of the BBC, he recalled: "It's hard to make a living as just a lyric writer and sometimes I think it's not advisable even to try. I've been lucky with the people I knew and worked with…"

Chart entries
Walk Away *(with Udu Jürgens)* Matt Monro (UK 1964 # 4; US # 23)
For Mama *(with Charles Aznavour)* Matt Monro (UK 1964 # 23); Connie Francis (US 1965 # 48)
Without You *(with Udu Jürgens)* Matt Monro (UK 1965 # 37)
My Child *(with Vic Lewis)* Connie Francis (UK 1965 # 26)
Thunderball *(with John Barry)* Tom Jones (UK 1966 # 35; US # 25)
Born Free *(with John Barry)* Roger Williams (US 1966 # 7); The Hesitations (US 1968 # 38)
When the World Is Ready *(with P J Scott)* Vince Hill (UK 1967 # 52)
To Sir, with Love *(with Mark London)* Lulu (US 1967 # 1; UK # 11); Herbie Mann (US 1967 # 93)
Best of Both Worlds *(with Mark London)* Lulu (US 1967 # 32)
Now *(with Henry Meyer, Hans Bradtke)* Val Doonican (UK 1968 # 43)
True Grit *(with Elmer Bernstein)* Glen Campbell (US 1969 # 35)

Charles Blackwell
Born Charles Ramsey, Leytonstone, England 1940. Died 2024.

By the age of 16, Blackwell was taking piano lessons and writing his own songs. Impressed by what material he sent them and the enthusiasm displayed, a music publisher in Denmark Street took him on as a stock clerk. Over the next few months, he learned to write music arrangements and began working as a copyist for another publisher. His big break came in 1957 when he met producer Joe Meek, who at the time was setting up a recording studio and a new label called Triumph Records. Meek recognised Blackwell's talents and soon made him his musical director. Over the next few years, Blackwell was a prolific studio arranger and producer, putting his name to songs like "Johnny Remember Me" (for John Leyton); I'll Never Fall In Love Again" and "What's New Pussycat" (both for Tom Jones); "Please Release Me" (Englebert Humperdinck) and "Hold Me" (P J Proby). He also wrote "Come Outside," a UK chart-topper for Mike Sarne and Wendy Richard. Although born in Middlesbrough, Richard's spoken replies to Sarne's advances were done in a faux-Cockney accent. Employed at the time as a secretary for producer Robert Stigwood, Richard had started making sardonic comments to him from her desk, thus giving him the idea of making the song a duet, despite objections from Blackwell.

Blackwell also arranged "Fireball," the title song to the children's puppet TV series *Fireball XL5*. Written by Barry Gray, it became a minor hit for Don Spencer in 1963. During the mid-Sixties, he produced and arranged for several francophone artists, particularly on hits for Françoise Hardy, as well as doing work with tv producer Jack Good.

Chart entries
Come Outside – Mike Sarne with Wendy Richard (UK 1962 # 1)
Just For Kicks – Mike Sarne (UK 1963 # 22)
Code Of Love – Mike Sarne (UK 1963 # 29)
He's the One – Billie Davis (UK 1963 # 40)

Otis Blackwell and Winfield Scott
Blackwell born New York City 1931. Died 2002.
Scott born Bloomfield, New Jersey 1920. Died 2015.
Nashville Songwriters Hall of Fame 1986 (Blackwell).

Brooklyn-born Blackwell learned to play piano as a child and was influenced by listening to country music and R&B. In 1952, he won a local amateur talent show at Harlem's Apollo Theater, which ultimately led to him being discovered and signed by RCA, and later with Jay-Dee Records. His first single was the self-penned "Daddy Rolling Stone," which became a hit in Jamaica when recorded by Derek Martin, but by 1955 his focus was on writing. His first success came with "Fever," written with his friend Eddie Cooley (1933-2020), who he had met in New York. Cooley asked Blackwell to help him finish a song he had been writing, and when recorded by Little Willie John it became an R&B chart-topper in 1956, and more famously giving Peggy Lee's her signature song two years later.

That same year, Blackwell offered his new song "Don't Be Cruel" to his friend Frankie Valli for his group the Four Lovers to record, but at the last minute asked for it back. Instead, he gave them "You're the Apple of My Eye." Elvis Presley's song publishers Hill & Range had brought him "Don't Be Cruel" to record, with Blackwell offering to give up half the royalties and co-writing credit to the singer to ensure he recorded it. Unfortunately, he had already sold the song for a mere $25. As Presley had made small alterations to the song, as he would do on other occasions, he was given co-writing credit, and it went on to become a worldwide hit and one of his best-known recordings.

Blackwell and Georgia-born Jack Hammer (1925-2016) later wrote "Great Balls of Fire" for Jerry Lee Lewis, and it became a transatlantic chart-topper, selling a million copies in the first ten days of its US release. Later that year, it was reported that while Blackwell was at Shalimar Music, one of the owners, Al Stanton, was shaking a bottle of Pepsi and suggested he write a song for Presley about being "shook up." As a result, "All Shook Up" topped the US charts for nine weeks, and also became his first UK chart-topper.

To help write more songs for Presley, Blackwell brought in New Jersey-born Winfield Scott (1920-2015) who had previously been a member of the vocal group the Cues (as Robie Kirk). Scott had already collaborated with Blackwell on the hit song "Tweedle Dee," so it was logical for Hill & Range to ask them to work together on the Presley movie *Girls! Girls! Girls!*. Without adhering to scripts for the movie, the two writers came up with a random song that was inspired by a demo that had been returned to them with words stamped on it, "Return to sender! No such person! No such zone!" With lyrics describing a failed relationship, it all seemed to work, and it gave Presley another massive hit in October 1962.

Blackwell went on to record for numerous labels before going into semi-retirement.

Chart entries
Return to Sender – Elvis Presley (US 1962 # 2; UK # 1)
One Broken Heart For Sale – Elvis Presley (US 1963 # 11; UK # 12)
(Such an) Easy Question – Elvis Presley (US 1965 # 11)

Otis Blackwell with others
Don't Be Cruel *(with Elvis Presley)* Bill Black's Combo (US 1960 # 11; UK # 32); Barbara
    Lynn (US 1963 # 93)
Nine Times Out of Ten *(with Waldense Hall)* Cliff Richard (UK 1960 # 3)
Fever *(with Eddie Cooley)* Helen Shapiro (UK 1964 # 38)
Handy Man *(with Jimmy Jones, Charles Merenstein)* Del Shannon (US 1964 # 22; UK # 36); The
    McCoys (US 1965 # 7; UK # 44)
Great Balls of Fire *(with Jack Hammer)* Tiny Tim (US 1969 # 85)

Winfield Scott
Many Tears Ago – Connie Francis (US 1960 # 7; UK # 12)

Winfield Scott with others
Long Legged Girl (with the Short Dress On) *(with Leslie McFarland)* Elvis Presley (US
 1967 # 63; UK # 49)

Alan Blaikley see **Ken Howard and Alan Blaikley**

Garry Bonner see **Alan Lee Gordon**

Sonny Bono
Born Salvatore Phillip Bono, Detroit, Michigan 1935. Died 1999 (Skiing accident).

"Sonny" Bono moved with his parents to California, and with a penchant for writing songs from an early age decided his future lay in the music industry. Opting out of education, he took a variety of work while trying to attain his goal. When he became director of A&R with Art Rupe's Speciality Records, he wrote "Things You Do to Me" for Sam Cooke, and using the pseudonym Don Chisty co-wrote with Roddy Jackson "She Said Yeah," a b-side to Larry Williams' 1958 hit "Bad Boy," (later to be covered by the Rolling Stones). He then worked as a promotion man and percussionist for Phil Spector, who inspired him to set up his own label, the ill-fated Rush. With Jack Nitzche, he wrote "Needles and Pins," a minor hit for Jackie DeShannon in 1963, but a UK chart-topper for the Searchers the following year.

    In late 1962, Bono met singer and dancer Cher (born Cheryl Sarkisian 1946) who became his housekeeper. Keen to get a break, Bono introduced her to Phil Spector who then used her as a backing singer on some of his best recordings, including "Be My Baby," and "You've Lost That Lovin' Feelin.'" He also recorded her first single "Ringo, I Love You" under the pseudonym Bonnie Jo Mason. With Cher's deep contralto, some radio presenters thought they were hearing a male voice.

    Bono and Cher married in October 1964, but her fledgling solo career soon gave way to focus on recording as a duo. Over the next six years, they recorded a string of hits together, all penned, produced and arranged by Bono. It began in 1965 with their biggest hit, "I Got You Babe." One story recalls that when she was woken up to sing the lyrics she hated it, feeling it would never be a hit, and then went back to sleep. As it transpired, the oboe-driven song with its simple lyrics was a chart-topper on both sides of the Atlantic, and has since been credited with being one of the finest duets in pop history. Interviewed about his songwriting in Pop Chronicles in 1967, Sono recalled: "What we call a hook hits you … then you're almost not writing, lyrics come to you, sort of a magic takes over, and it's not like work at all." Further success came with "Baby Don't Go" later that year. Although Bono enjoyed some success with a solo career, especially with "Laugh at Me" a top ten hit in 1965, it was Cher who had the biggest success, scoring a number two US hit with "Bang Bang (My Baby Shot Me Down" in 1966. Sonny and Cher's relationship began falling apart by the late Sixties, although "officially" marrying in 1969. They then hosted the hugely successful *Sonny and Cher Comedy Hour* in the Seventies, while Bono produced her massive hit single "Gypsies, Tramps & Thieves" in 1971. Cher, of course, went on to have an incredible solo career over the next three decades.

Chart entries
Needles And Pins *(with Jack Nitzsche)* Jackie DeShannon (US 1963 # 84); The Searchers (UK
 1964 # 1; US # 14)
I Got You Babe – Sonny & Cher (US 1965 # 1; UK # 1); Etta James (US 1968 # 69)
Baby Don't Go – Sonny & Cher (US 1965 # 8; UK # 11)
Laugh At Me – Sonny Bono (US 1965 # 10; UK # 9)
Just You / Sing C'est La Vie *(with Brian Stone, Charles Greene)* Sonny & Cher (US 1965 # 20)
But You're Mine – Sonny & Cher (US 1965 # 15; UK # 17)
Where Did You Go – Cher (US 1965 # 25)
The Revolution Kind – Sonny Bono (US 1965 # 70)
Bang Bang (My Baby Shot Me Down) Cher (US 1966 # 2; UK # 3)
Have I Stayed Too Long – Sonny & Cher (US 1966 # 49; UK # 42)
I Feel Something In the Air – Cher (US 1966 # 43)
Little Man – Sonny & Cher (US 1966 # 21; UK # 4)
Living For You – Sonny & Cher (US 1966 # 87; UK # 44)
The Beat Goes On – Sonny & Cher (US 1967 # 6; UK # 29)
A Beautiful Story – Sonny & Cher (US 1967 # 53)
Plastic Man – Sonny & Cher (US 1967 # 74)
It's the Little Things – Sonny & Cher (US 1967 # 50)
You Better Sit Down Kids – Cher (US 1967 # 9)

Tommy Boyce and Bobby Hart
Born Sidney Thomas Boyce, Charlottesville, Virginia 1939. Died 1994 (suicide).
Born Robert Luke Harshman Hart, Phoenix, Arizona 1939. Died 1994.

With his father a minister, Boyce left high school and later served in the US Army. Upon his discharge, he travelled to Los Angeles to pursue a singing career. After being rejected numerous times he took his father's suggestion and composed a song "Be My Guest" intended for Fats Domino. While waiting for six hours at the hotel where Domino was staying, he finally got the chance to meet him and gave him a demo of the song. Domino gave his word that he would listen to it, and in a matter of weeks went into the studio with producer and arranger Dave Bartholomew, along with co-writer John Marascalco, to finish and record the song. The result was a top ten hit in 1959, Domino's biggest success for several years. Boyce went on to co-write two of Curtis Lee's 1961 hits, "Pretty Little Angel Eyes" and "Under the Moon of Love," (both UK hits for Showaddywaddy in 1976).

Boyce first met Hart in 1959 while playing guitar on Hart's unsuccessful solo single "Girl in the Window" and he seized the opportunity to start a writing partnership. Arizona-born Hart had mirrored Boyce's early life. His father was also a church minister, had joined the army after leaving high school, and was now pursuing his own career in music. Their first success came with "Lazy Elsie Molly," co-written with Elizabeth Harris, and a top 40 hit for Chubby Checker. In late 1965, they were originally cast to be members of the Monkees, but instead secured the music production rights to the forthcoming *Monkees* tv show. They wrote, produced, and even performed the theme song for the pilot (changed, of course, when the show was cast), and also supplied three of their biggest hits. "Last Train to Clarksville" was a reference to a soldier leaving for the Vietnam War. "(I'm Not Your) Stepping Stone" was first recorded in early 1966 by the English band the Liverpool Five, but had remained unreleased before the summer. In the meantime, Paul Revere & the Raiders recorded it as an album track in May. The Monkees' version had Boyce on backing vocal and Hart playing organ.

Screen Gems president and music supervisor Don Kirshner then asked the writers if they had any songs featuring a girl's name. Claiming they had just finished a song, they improvised "Valleri" on the way to his office. As a result they produced the original sessions in August 1966. However, it was found that it could not be used, as union contracts had already been filed with the pair listed as producers, whereas the Monkees' contracts stipulated that all future recordings had them as producers on the label. As a result they re-recorded the song, making it as close to the original as possible.

Conflicts with the show's musical supervisor Don Kirshner and accusations that they were using his studio time for their own projects led to their departure. The two then embarked on a performing career and had success with the 1967 top-ten single, "I Wonder What She's Doing Tonight?" as well as becoming involved in music production with Screen Gems for both film and tv shows.

The following decade saw them reuniting with former Monkees Mickey Dolenz and Davy Jones to form a touring band that performed not only songs written for the show but also new material. In 1994 Boyce, battling illness and depression, took his own life.

Chart entries
Last Train To Clarksville – The Monkees (US 1966 # 1; UK 1967 # 23)
(I'm Not Your) Steppin' Stone – The Monkees (US 1966 # 20)
Out and About – Tommy Boyce & Bobby Hart (US 1967 # 39)
Words – The Monkees (US 1967 # 11)
I Wonder What She's Doing Tonight? - Tommy Boyce & Bobby Hart (US 1967 # 8)
Valleri – The Monkees (US 1968 # 3; UK # 12)
Goodbye Baby (I Don't Want To See You Cry) Tommy Boyce & Bobby Hart (US 1968 # 53)
Alice Long (You're Still My Favorite Girlfriend) Tommy Boyce & Bobby Hart (US 1968 # 27)
Tear Drop City – The Monkees (US 1969 # 56; UK # 44)

Boyce-Hart with others
Lazy Elsie Molly *(with Roberta Harris)* Chubby Checker (US 1964 # 40)
Come A Little Bit Closer *(with Wes Farrell)* Jay and the Americans (US 1964 # 3)

Tommy Boyce
I'll Remember Carol (US 1962 # 80)

Tommy Boyce with others
Sweet Little Cathy *(with Ray Peterson)* Ray Peterson (US 1961 #100)
Pretty Little Angel Eyes *(with Curtis Lee)* Curtis Lee (US 1961 # 7)

Under the Moon of Love *(with Curtis Lee)* Curtis Lee (US 1961 # 46)
Hello Pretty Girl *(with Wes Farrell)* Ronnie Dove (US 1965 # 54)
Peaches 'N' Cream *(with Steve Venet)* The Ikettes (US 1965 # 36)
Action (Where the Action Is) *(with Steve Venet)* Freddy Cannon (US 1965 # 13)

Bobby Hart with others
The Loneliest Night *(with Barry Richards)* Dale and Grace (US 1964 # 65)
Hurt So Bad *(with Teddy Randazzo, Bobby Weinstein)* Little Anthony & the Imperials (US
    1965 # 10); The Lettermen (US 1969 # 12)
Around the Corner *(with Teddy Randazzo, Bobby Weinstein, Wilbur Meshel, Billy Barberis)*
    The Duprees (US 1965 # 91)

Janie Bradford
Born Charleston, Missouri 1939.

Bradford graduated school and attended the Detroit Institute of Technology. In 1958, her neighbour, singer Jackie Wilson, introduced her to Motown founder Berry Gordy Jr, and she was taken on as a secretary. Her penchant for songwriting soon became apparent, and with Gordy she co-wrote two songs that appeared on Wilson's album *Lonely Teardrops.* But it was their collaboration on Barrett Strong's 1960 classic "Money (That's What I Want)" that brought her skills to prominence. Several hits followed, including teaming up with Strong and Norman Whitfield for "Too Busy Thinking About My Baby." Originally recorded by the Temptations as a track on their album *Gettin' Ready*, singer Jimmy Ruffin had also recorded a version with the group providing backing vocals in 1966, but remaining unreleased as a single until 1967. Three years later, Marvin Gaye's version became his second biggest hit of the Sixties. In her career, Bradford also wrote material for Marv Johnson, the Marvelettes, Mary Wells, and Stevie Wonder.

Chart entries
Money (That's What I Want *(with Berry Gordy Jr)* Barrett Strong (US 1960 # 23); Bern Elliott
    & the Fenmen (UK 1963 # 14); The Kingsmen (US 1964 # 16); Jr Walker & the All-Stars
    (US 1966 # 52)
All the Love I Got *(with Berry Gordy Jr & Brian Holland)* Marv Johnson (US 1960 # 63)
Hip City *(with Autry DeWalt Jr)* Jr Walker & the All-Stars (US 1969 # 45)
Too Busy Thinking About My Baby *(with Norman Whitfield & Barrett Strong)* Marvin Gaye
    (US 1969 # 4; UK # 5)

Bob Brass see Irwin Levine

Leslie Bricusse and Anthony Newley
Bricusse born Southfields, London 1931. Died 2021.
Newley born Homerton, London 1931. Died 1999.
Songwriters Hall of Fame 1989.

At the age of two, Bricusse's parents moved to Pinner, Middlesex, and he later attended University College School in Hampstead. After completing two years of national service with the Royal Army Service Corps, he enrolled at Gonville and Caius College in Cambridge, studying modern and medieval languages, and was president of *Footlights* in 1952. He wrote lyrics for its first production, *Lady at the Wheel* and also worked with Beatrice Lillie on her stage show. With his focus shifting to songwriting, he then formed a long-lasting partnership with actor Anthony Newley.
   London-born Newley's parents separated after his birth and he was brought up by his uncle and aunt. By the age of 14, he had left education to work as an office boy for an advertising agency in Fleet Street. Replying to an ad for boy actors, he was offered a job as an office boy at the Italia Conti Stage School. Catching the eye of a producer, he was cast in the children's film series *Dusty Bates*. It was the beginning of a long acting career, which saw him playing the Artful Dodger in David Lean's movie *Oliver Twist* and as a rock singer in *Idol on Parade*, which also launched his career as a singer, with two chart-toppers, "Why" and "Do You Mind."
   Between them, Bricusse and Newley wrote the book, music and lyrics for the 1961 West End musical *Stop the World - I Want To Get Off,* which starred Newley and featured their song, "What Kind of Fool Am I?" chart hits for both Newley and Sammy Davis Jr. In 1964, they wrote lyrics for the title track of the James Bond movie *Goldfinger*, which gave Shirley Bassey

her signature song. One inspiration for the song was "Mack the Knife," which was shown to composer John Barry by director Guy Hamilton who thought it to be a good model for what the movie required. Bricusse and Newley were not shown any film footage or script, but were advised of the fatal gilding suffered by the character Jill Masterson (played by Shirley Eaton). As a result, they utilised "the Midas touch" in the lyric, and the song was completed in a couple of days.

The following year, they composed the musical *The Roar of the Greasepaint - The Smell of the Crowd*, which featured the songs "Who Can I Turn To?" a later hit for Tony Bennett, and "Feel Good," recorded by Nina Simone for her 1965 album I Put a Spell on You. Bricusse also wrote lyrics for Barry's theme tune for the 1965 Bond movie *Thunderball*, giving Tom Jones another transatlantic hit. In 1967, he was asked to write lyrics for the movie *Doctor Dolittle,* starring Rex Harrison and Newley, and among the songs was the popular "I Talk to the Animals," which would win Bricusse an Oscar for Best Original Song. Newley also performed the song "Where Are the Words?" on the soundtrack album. That same year, Bricusse returned to the Bond franchise for a third time, writing lyrics to Barry's theme for *You Only Live Twice*, performed by Nancy Sinatra.

In the early Seventies, Bricusse and Newley wrote the music for the movie Willy Wonka & the Chocolate Factory, starring Gene Wilder, and it included the songs "The Candy Man," (a hit for Sammy Davis Jr), and "Pure Imagination." His advice on songwriting was simple: "Songs are like women or cats - fascinating, elusive, seductive, irresistible, infuriating, moody, demanding and contradictory creatures. The writer pursues them like some phantom fantasy - fascinated, intrigued and desperate to find out what they're really like. They should be approached with caution and respect - especially at night."

Chart entries
My Kind of Girl – Matt Monro (UK 1961 # 5)
D-Darling – Anthony Newley (UK 1962 # 25)
My Kind of Girl – Frank Sinatra with Count Basie (UK 1963 # 35)
If I Ruled the World *(with Cyril Ornadel)* Harry Secombe (UK 1963 # 18); Tony Bennett
    (US 1965 # 34; UK # 40)
Thunderball *(with John Barry)* Tom Jones (US 1965 # 25; UK # 35)
You Only Live Twice *(with John Barry)* Nancy Sinatra (US 1967 # 44; UK # 11)

Leslie Briscusse and Anthony Newley
What Kind of Fool Am I? - Anthony Newley (US 1961 # 85; UK # 36)
Michael Row the Boat *(trad. with Lonnie Donegan)* Lonnie Donegan (UK 1961 # 6)
Gonna Build a Mountain - Matt Monro (UK 1961 # 44)
What Kind of Fool Am I? – Sammy Davis Jr (US 1962 # 17; UK # 26); Robert Goulet
    (US 1962 # 89); Shirley Bassey (UK 1963 # 47)
That Noise – Anthony Newley (UK 1962 # 34)
Who Can I Turn To (When Nobody Needs Me) Tony Bennett (US 1964 # 33); Dionne
    Warwick (US 1965 # 62)
Goldfinger *(with John Barry)* Shirley Bassey (UK 1964 # 21; US # 8)

Eddie Brigati see Felix Cavaliere & Eddie Brigati

Johnny Bristol see Harvey Fuqua

Gary Brooker and Keith Reid
Born Gary Brooker, London 1945. Died 2022.
Born Keith Stuart Brian Reid, Welwyn Garden City, England 1946. Died 2023.

Brooker's father was a professional guitarist but died shortly after the family moved to Southend in 1956. Six years later, having already learned to play piano and other instruments at an early age, Brooker formed the Paramounts with friend and guitarist Robin Trower, and together with other members had a solo hit with a cover of "Poison Ivy" in 1964. After disbanding to focus on songwriting, Brooker was introduced by his old friend and record producer Guy Stevens to lyricist Keith Reid, son of a Holocaust survivor, who had quit school early to pursue a songwriting career. In April 1967, Stevens encouraged them to write together and form a band, suggesting the name Procol Harum, which came from the mis-remembered and misspelled pedigree name of a Siamese cat, and which Stevens felt would fit the ambiguous nature of their music. The eventual line-up became Brooker (piano/lead vocalist), Matthew Fisher (organ); Bobby Harrison (drums); Ray Royer (guitar) and Dave Knights (bass). Lyricist Reid became an "unofficial" member.

The title of their first single allegedly came from Reid hearing at a party that someone looked "a whiter shade of pale." Loosely based on J S Bach's Orchestral Suite No. 3 in D Major and played on Fisher's Hammond organ, it became a worldwide hit, highlighting Brooker's melancholic vocal and Reid's surreal lyrics. In an interview for *Uncut* in 2008 Reid recalled: "I was trying to be evocative. I suppose it seems like a decadent scene I'm describing. But I was too young to have experienced any decadence, then. I might have been smoking when I conceived it, but not when I wrote. It was influenced by books, not drugs." When asked what the lyrics meant, Brooker replied, "They mean I'll never have to work again."

Fisher would later win co-writing credit for the music. In the year that psychedelia became firmly rooted in UK music, it remains its quintessential centrepiece and a fine example of when pop songs become poetry. The follow-up single "Homburg" had the same surreal, dream-like imagery, and a deservedly top five spot on the UK charts.

Chart entries
A Whiter Shade Of Pale *(with Matthew Fisher)* Procol Harum (UK 1967 # 1; US # 5)
Homburg – Procol Harum (UK 1967 # 6; US # 34)
A Salty Dog – Procol Harum (UK 1969 # 44)

Joey Brooks
Born Joseph Kaplan, New York City 1938. Died 2011.

Brooks grew up in Manhattan and later Lawrence, Long Island. After attending the Julliard School of Music (but not graduating) he pursued a music career and adopted the name Joey Brooks. With that name, he recorded several albums for Canadian-American Records before briefly signing with Decca. Although failing to have a successful singing career, he worked in advertising and began writing songs. In the Sixties, he wrote jingles for companies including Pepsi and Maxwell House, winning a number of awards for his work.

In 1965, he wrote the lush ballad "My Ship is Comin' In." With its optimism and promise of good times ahead after a period of struggle, it was first recorded by Jimmy Radcliffe on the Aurora label, and became a top ten UK hit for the Walker Brothers early the following year. Produced by Ivor Raymonde, it followed their huge number one single "Make It Easy on Yourself." The trio of singers, consisting of John Walker (real name John Maus), Scott Walker (Noel Scott Engel) and later Gary Walker (Gary Leeds), had been formed in Los Angeles before moving to the UK in 1965.

With his advertising work making him a rich man, Brooks began composing music for films. In 1977 he wrote, produced, and directed the romantic movie *You Light Up My Life* and his title song, recorded by Debbie Boone, won him a Grammy, an Oscar and a Golden Globe.

Chart entries
Seein' the Right Love Go Wrong *(with Aaron Schroeder)* Jack Jones (US 1965 # 46)
My Ship Is Comin' In – The Walker Brothers (US 1965 # 63; UK # 3)

James Brown
Born James Joseph Brown, Barnwell, South Carolina 1933. Died 2006.
Rock and Roll Hall of Fame 1986.
Grammy Lifetime Achievement Award 1992.
Songwriters Hall of Fame 2002.

The "Godfather of Soul" was born into poverty in a small wooden shack (although he claimed to be born in Macon, Georgia), and his first two names were reversed on the birth certificate. After what was an abusive marriage, his mother moved to New York, and as a young boy Brown began singing at talent shows and later learnt to play piano and other instruments. Inspiration to be a professional musician and entertainer came from watching the legendary blues guitarist Howlin' Wolf and singer Louis Jordan. Convicted of theft at 16, he was sent to a juvenile detention centre in Georgia where he formed a gospel quartet with four cellmates.

Securing an early release on the approbation of local singer Bobby Byrd, he promised the court he would "sing for the Lord." Brown went on to join Byrd's a capella group the Gospel Starlighters. After contacting Little Richard in 1955, they recorded a demo of "Please Please Please," and after sufficient local radio airplay signed a recording deal with King Records' subsidiary label in Cincinnati. Re-recording the song as James Brown and the Famous Flames, it scored their first hit on the R&B chart in March 1956. Further recordings fared poorly, with some of his band walking out on him, but with a new line-up and now officially the Famous Flames, had "Try Me" gain top spot on the R&B chart.

In 1960, the band released "(Do the) Mashed Potato," achieving their first chart entry on the Hot 100, and its success saw the band move to King's parent label. From thereon until the late Seventies, nearly every official single charted, and the 1962 breathtaking album *Live at the Apollo* confirmed Brown's status as the premier dynamic performer. As a writer, the sound of the songs became tighter and leaner, their composition tearing up the accepted rulebook on harmony and structure with its stripped-down interlocking rhythms, all of which were factors in the development of what would become the "funk sound." The unconventional songs that followed displayed the artistic freedom he was now enjoying.

1965's Grammy-winning "Papa's Got a Brand New Bag" was about an old man brave enough to get out on the dance floor of a nightclub, with "brand new bag" meaning a new interest, taste or way of doing things. "I Got You (I Feel Good)" was another Grammy winner, originally released for the 1964 album *Out of Sight*, but later released in an alternate take as a single, becoming his highest charting song on the Hot 100. The following year, "It's a Man's Man's Man's World" was co-written with Betty Jean Newsome, and its title a word play on the 1963 movie *It's a Mad, Mad, Mad, Mad World*. Newsome, his onetime girlfriend, wrote the lyrics from her own view of relationships, claiming years later that Brown did not contribute any lyrics at all, and took him to court when he forgot to pay her royalites.

Over the next two decades Brown's musical style went through changes, but his trademark theatrical performances remained constant. He once said: "When I'm on stage, I'm trying to do one thing: bring people joy. Just like church does. People don't go to church to find trouble, they go there to lose it." Although the years ahead would bring with them much controversy over his personal life, his music legacy remained untarnished, and is still righty regarded as one of the greatest performers in pop history with an undeniable influence on black music.

Chart entries
(Do the) Mashed Potato (US 1960 # 84)
You've Got the Power (*with Johnny Terry*) (US. 1960 # 86)
This Old Heart (US 1960 # 79)
Good, Good Lovin' (*with Albert Schubert*) Chubby Checker (US 1961 # 43)
I Don't Mind (US 1961 # 47)
Baby, You're Right (*with Joe Tex)* (US 1961 # 49)
Lost Someone (*with Bobby Byrd, Lloyd Eugene Stallworth*) (US 1961 # 48;1966 # 94)
Shout And Shimmy (*with Pee Wee Ellis*) (US 1962 # 61)
Mashed Potato U.S.A (US 1962 # 82)
I've Got Money (US 1962 # 93)
I Cried (*with Bobby Byrd*) Tammy Montgomery [aka Tammi Terrell] (US 1963 # 99)
Oh Baby Don't You Weep (Part 1) (US 1964 # 23)
Please, Please, Please (*with Johnny Terry*) (US 1964 # 95)
Try Me – Jimmy Hughes (US 1964 # 65)
Papa's Got A Brand New Bag Pt 1 (US 1965 # 8; UK # 29); Otis Redding (US 1968 # 21; UK # 52)
I Got You (I Feel Good) (US 1965 # 3; UK # 29)
Try Me (US 1965 # 63)
I'll Go Crazy (US 1966 # 73)
Ain't That A Groove Pt. 1(*with Nat Jones)* (US 1966 # 42)
It's A Man's, Man's, Man's World (*with Betty Jean Newsome*) (US 1966 # 8; UK # 13)
Money Won't Change You (Part 1) (*with Nat Jones*) (US 1966 # 53)
Bring It Up (*with Nat Jones*) (US 1967 # 29)
Let Yourself Go (*with Bud Hobgood*) (US 1967 # 46)
Take Me (Just As I Am) – Solomon Burke (US 1967 # 49)
Cold Sweat (Part 1) *(with Alfred Ellis)* (US 1967 # 7)
Get It Together (Part 1) (*with Bud Hobgood & Alfred Ellis*) (US 1967 # 40)
I Can't Stand Myself (When You Touch Me) (US 1967 # 28)
There Was A Time (*with Bud Hopgood*) (US 1967 # 36)
I Got the Feelin' (US 1968 # 6)
America Is My Home, Pt. 1(with *Hayward E Moore*) (US 1968 # 52)
Licking Stick - Licking Stick (Part 1*) (with Bobby Byrd, Alfred Ellis*) (US 1968 # 14)
I Guess I'll Have To Cry, Cry, Cry (US 1968 # 55)
Say It Loud - I'm Black And I'm Proud (*with Alfred Ellis*) (US 1968 # 10)
There Was A Time (*with Buddy Hobgood*) Gene Chandler (US 1968 # 82)
Goodbye My Love (US 1968 # 31)
Tit For Tat (Ain't No Holding Back) (*with Nat Jones*) (US 1968 # 86)
I Don't Want Nobody To Give Me Nothing (Open Up the Door, I'll Get It Myself) (US 1969 # 20)

It's My Thing (*with Marva Whitney*) Marva Whitney (US 1969 # 82)
The Popcorn (US 1969 # 30)
Mother Popcorn (You Gotta Have A Mother For Me) (*with Alfred Ellis*) (US 1969 # 11)
Lowdown Popcorn (US 1969 # 41)
World (Part 1) (US 1969 # 37)
Let A Man Come in And Do the Popcorn (Part 1) (US 1969 # 21)
Ain't It Funky Now (US 1969 # 24)
Let A Man Come in And Do the Popcorn (Part 2) (US 1969 # 40)

Michael Brown
Born Michael David Lookofsky, New York City 1949. Died 2015.

The son of a noted jazz violinist and arranger, his early career in music saw him working with artists such as Reparata & the Delrons and Christopher & the Champs prior to forming the baroque pop band, the Left Banke in 1965. The line-up at the time was Brown (vocals, keyboards) and former sessionists Steve Martin (vocals), Jeff Winfield (guitar), Tom Finn (bass), and George Cameron (drums). Out of a number of demos sent to labels, only "Walk Away Renee," found interest with Smash Records, a subsidiary of Mercury. 16-year-old Brown co-wrote the song with Bob Calilli and Tony Sansone (the latter later claiming to be the lyricist), but Brown stated that this and "Pretty Ballerina" were written about Renée Fladen, a singer who was in a relationship with band member Finn at the time. Fladen was in the control room when Brown tried to record his harpsichord part and later admitted he was so nervous he had to come back later to do it without her there. It earned the band a top five hit in 1966, but the cover by the Four Tops the following year scored a number three on the UK chart, and has been cited as definitive.

Due to internal ructions Brown left the band in 1967, but reunited later in the year for their final chart entry "Desiree." Brown then teamed up with folk singer and songwriter Bert Sommer (1949-1990) to write "And Suddenly," a later hit for the psychedelic band the Cherry People, fronted by Chris and Doug Grimes.

Chart entries
Walk Away Renee (*with Bob Calilli, Tony Sansone*) The Left Banke (US 1966 # 5); Four Tops
    (US 1967 # 14; UK # 3)
Pretty Ballerina – The Left Banke (US 1967 # 15)
Desirée (*with Tom Feher*) – The Left Banke (US 1967 # 98)
And Suddenly (*with Bert Sommer*) – The Cherry People (US 1968 # 45)

Jack Bruce and Pete Brown
Born John (Jack) Symon Asher Bruce, Bishopbriggs, Scotland 1943. Died 2014.
Born Peter Ronald Brown, Ashtead, England 1940. Died 2023.
Rock and Roll Hall of Fame (with Cream) 1993.

Learning to play bass in his teens and performing in jazz combos, Bruce won a scholarship to study cello and composition. In 1962, after a stint playing in another jazz band, he joined the short-lived London band Blues Incorporated, fronted by Alexis Korner, whose members included organist Graham Bond and future Cream drummer Ginger Baker. Bruce then formed the R&B band the Graham Bond Quartet, with Bond, Baker and guitarist John McLaughlin. McLaughlin was later replaced and the band renamed the Graham Bond Organisation, although their output bought little success. Bruce later went on to have a stint with John Mayall's Blues Breakers and Manfred Mann before forming Cream in 1966, along with Baker and Mayall's guitarist Eric Clapton. Meanwhile, Pete Brown had become well known on the Liverpool beat poetry scene and had begun performing with bands at live events. He originally joined Cream as writing partner with Baker, but found after a while he worked better with Bruce.

Between them, they wrote many of the band's hits. Their second single "I Feel Free" had been left off the UK release of their debut album *Fresh Cream* by producer Robert Stigwood, preferring instead to release it as a single. Clapton played a borrowed Les Paul guitar on the recording, as his Beano guitar had been stolen during album rehearsals, and it one of the first times he used what he called the "Woman Tone," by turning the amp all the way up, boosting the treble, cutting the bass, and playing a sustained guitar note.

Brown wrote the opening line to the psychedelic "Sunshine of Your Love" after being up all night and watching the sun rise. With Bruce beginning to play the famous riff on his stand-up bass, Brown looked out the window and sang "It's Getting near dawn now…" Apparently, on first hearing the song, Ahmet Ertegun, head of the band's label, was not that impressed, calling it "psychedelic hogwash." He had been pressing for Clapton to be band leader and did not approve of the bassist being lead singer. Only when Booker T Jones told him of his approval did he relent. With the single "White Room" and its description of hopelessness and depression, the music was written first, and Brown's first attempt at lyrics was about a "doomed hippie girl" with the song titled "Cinderella's Last Goodnight." With Bruce showing disapproval, Brown returned to an eight-page poem written earlier about a new apartment he had moved into that had white wall and bare furnishing. He then whittled it down to a few verses, with Bruce writing music as a tribute to Jimi Hendrix.

When Cream finally broke up, Bruce and Brown continued to write together on solo projects.

Chart entries
Wrapping Paper – Cream (UK 1966 # 34)
I Feel Free – Cream (UK 1966 # 11)
Sunshine Of Your Love (*with Eric Clapton*) Cream (UK 1968 # 25; US # 5)
White Room - Cream (UK 1968 # 28; US # 6)

Eric Burdon see also Alan Price
Born Eric Victor Burdon, Walker, Newcastle-upon-Tyne, England 1941.

Born in an air raid during the war and developing asthma attacks at a young age, Burdon's early education suffered as a result, but while at secondary school a teacher secured him a place at Newcastle College of Art and Industrial Design. In what he later described as a life-changing move, he met other "rebel" teenagers who shared his love of folk and jazz music, including musician John Steel, who played in Burdon's college jazz band the Pagans (with Steel on trumpet). In March 1959, while at a church hop in Byker, Newcastle, Burdon met one of Steel's friends, Durham-born multi-instrumentalist Alan Price, who occasionally sat in with Burdon's band. Price later played for a short time with Bryan "Chas" Chandler in the Kansas City Five (before becoming the Kon-tours), and went on to form the Alan Price Trio with Steel (drums) and Chandler (bass). In 1962, Burdon was invited to join what now had become the Alan Price Rhythm and Blues Combo, with the addition of new guitarist Hilton Valentine from Whiteley Bay's the Wild Cats.

With their gritty, bluesy sound and Burdon's deep powerful vocals, they secured a regular slot at Newcastle's Downbeat Club, where their raucous stage presence may have been one of the reasons for changing their name to the Animals. Attracting much attention in the music world, jazz musician Graham Bond recommended them to his manager Ronan O'Rahilly, and they got a residency at Newcastle's famous Club A-Go Go, even one time backing blues star Sonny Boy Williamson. In 1964, the band moved to London and signed with producer Mickey Most, also securing a record deal with Columbia. Their debut single was the Farrell-Russell song "Baby Let Me Take You Home," but it was the follow-up, "House of the Rising Sun" that made them international stars. Price's arrangement of the traditional US folk-blues song saw it top the charts on both sides of the Atlantic, despite the UK label worrying over its length (4½ minutes) preventing radio play.

Following a successful tour of the US, the single "I'm Crying" saw the first writing collaboration with Burdon and Price. Following a string of cover versions, including John Lee Hooker's "Boom Boom," Nina Simone's "Don't Let Me Be Misunderstood" and Sam Cooke's "Bring It On Home To Me," Price left the band, citing musical disagreements with Burdon and also due to an apparent fear of flying. The following year, a widening division between Burdon and other band members prompted a split, and with a new lineup was reformed as Eric Burdon & the Animals. 1967's semi-autobiographical "When I Was Young" was the first single written by Burdon and four members of the band, which continued with them courting the West Coast sound on their melancholic anti-Vietnam War ballad "San Franciscan Nights," and "Monterey," a song eulogising the famous festival. With Burdon persona seemingly "tamed" and now writing and co-writing more thought-provoking lyrics, he lost some favour with his original fans, and by 1968 they had disbanded.

The following year Burdon re-emerged with the progressive soul band War.

Chart entries
I'm Crying *(with Alan Price)* The Animals (UK 1964 # 8; US # 19)
Inside Looking Out *(with John Lomax, Alan Lomax, Chas Chandler)* The Animals (UK 1966
    # 12; US # 34)

Eric Burdon with Vic Briggs, John Weider, Barry Jenkins, Danny McCulloch
When I Was Young - Eric Burdon & the Animals (UK 1967 # 45; US # 15)
San Franciscan Nights - Eric Burdon & the Animals (UK 1967 # 7; US # 9)
Good Times - Eric Burdon & the Animals (UK 1967 # 20)
Monterey - Eric Burdon & the Animals (US 1967 # 15)
Sky Pilot - Eric Burdin & the Animals (UK 1968 # 40; US # 14)
Anything - Eric Burdon & the Animals (US 1968 # 80)
White Houses - Eric Burdon & the Animals (US 1968 # 11)

Jerry Butler see **Ken Gamble and Leon Huff**

Peter Callander see also Mitch Murray
Born Peter Robin Callander, Lyndhurst, England 1939. Died 2014.

Educated at the City of London School on a scholarship, he followed his father's footsteps and became a chef. He later moved into music publishing, working as a song plugger for Bron Music, where he lobbied bandleaders, record companies and radio producers to feature newly published songs. His first success as a songwriter was 1963's "Walkin' Tall," a top ten hit for Adam Faith, for which Callander chose to be credited as Robin Conrad, as he was also plugging the song. He also became publishing manager for Shapiro Bernstein Music. In the mid-Sixties, he provided English lyrics for several of the grandiose Italian ballads that had become attractive to British singers and arrangers. Among these were "All My Love" for Cliff Richard, "Don't Answer Me" for Cilla Black, "Give Me Time" for Dusty Springfield, "Suddenly You Love Me" for the Tremeloes, and "Monsieur Dupont" for Sandie Shaw.

By now, Callendar was spending most of his time songwriting and he eventually became a full-time lyricist, working alongside Les Reed and Geoff Stephens. Due to having to share royalties with the Italian composers, his most productive and long-lasting partnership was with Mitch Murray, who had already found success writing songs for Gerry & the Pacemakers, but was now finding it difficult to write lyrics. As a result, it became the perfect match. Beginning in 1967, they wrote a string of hits for various artists, beginning with "Even the Bad Times Are Good." Written as a contender for Sandie Shaw to sing at the Eurovision Song Contest in 1967, it ended up losing out to "Puppet on a String," the eventual winner. Picked up by the Tremeloes, it became a top five hit. This was followed by their biggest success, "The Ballad of Bonnie and Clyde." It was suggested to them by singer Georgie Fame, who had watched the controversial gangster movie *Bonnie and Clyde*. It was composed in the style of the period, featuring sound effects of gun battles, car chases and police sirens, and with its piano intro taken from Fats Domono's 1956 "Blue Monday." Fame took the song to the top of the charts in December 1967. Two years later, they wrote "Ragamuffin Man," the last hit for Manfred Mann before the band split up, while Vanity Fare's "Hitchin' a Ride" became a bigger hit when released in the US.

In the Seventies, they produced and wrote for a number of artists, including Paper Lace, Tony Christie and Wayne Newton.

Chart entries
Even the Bad Times Are Good - The Tremeloes (UK 1967 # 4; US # 36)
The Ballad of Bonnie and Clyde – Georgie Fame (UK 1967 # 1; US # 7)
Hush…Not A Word To Mary - John Rowles (UK 1968 # 12)
Ragamuffin Man – Manfred Mann (UK 1969 # 8)
Hitchin' A Ride – Vanity Fare (UK 1969 # 16; US # 5)

Peter Callander with others
A Man Without Love *(with Cyril Ornadel)* Kenneth McKellar (UK 1966 # 30)
I Love Her *(with Ivor Raymonde)* Paul & Barry Ryan (UK 1966 # 17)
Once There Was a Time *(with Tony Del Monaco)* Tom Jones (UK 1966 # 18)
Don't Answer Me *(adapt, with Bruno Zambrini Luis Enriquez)* Cilla Black (UK 1966 # 6)
To Make A Big Man Cry *(with Les Reed)* P J Proby (UK 1966 # 34)
A Fool Am I *(adapt, with Falvio Carraresi, Alberto Testa)* Cilla Black (UK 1966 # 13)
Give Me Time *(adapt, with Pietro Melfa, Atmo)* Dusty Springfield (UK 1967 # 24; US # 76)
All My Love *(adapt, with Frederico Monti Arduini)* Cliff Richard (UK 1967 # 6)
Suddenly You Love Me *(with Daniel Pace, Lorenzo Pilat, Mario Panzeri)* The Tremeloes (UK 1968 # 6; US # 44)
Monsieur Dupont *(with Christian Bruhn)* Sandie Shaw (UK 1969 # 6)

Patrick Campbell-Lyons
Born Lismore, County Waterford, Ireland 1943.

Becoming a part of West London's music scene in the early Sixties, Campbell-Lyons found some initial success as a founding member and vocalist of the Ealing R&B band Second Thoughts, whose original lineup included Andy Newman (aka Thunderclap Newman), Chris Thomas, and co-founder and drummer John "Speedy" Keen. They released the single "Seventh Son" on the Essex label. Splitting up in late 1965, Campbell-Lyons lived in Sweden for a year before returning to London.

In early 1967, he formed the symphonic rock band Nirvana with Greek musician Alex Spyropoulos (b.1941). With a changing lineup of studio musicians, they recorded several acclaimed baroque-style albums. During recordings, they were joined by producer Ray Singer on vocals, with Spyropoulos on keyboards and Campbell-Lyons on guitar.

In October 1967, their debut album *The Story of Simon Simopath* was released on Chris Blackwell's Island label. One of the first narrative concept albums ever released, it included the single "Pentecost Hotel," about a man who finds love in a hotel beneath the ocean run by a goddess called Magdelena. Blackwell launched the album with a "live" show at London's Saville Theatre, sharing the bill with Jackie Edwards, Spooky Tooth and Traffic. Unable to actually perform live as a duo, Campbell-Lyons and Spyropoulos created the Nirvana Ensemble consisting of four musicians, including Singer on guitar (while also appearing on the album cover). Sessionists Sue & Sunny (Sue Glover & Sunny Leslie) provided the vocals.

Following the minor success of the single, the sextet were disbanded and session musicians were used on future recordings. In 1968, they released the sequel album *All of Us*, which included their only chart hit "Rainbow Chaser." Produced by Muff Winwood and released in May 1968, it related the story of Simon, a boy who feels like an outcast both at school and with life in general, and dreams of escaping to a fantastical, surreal place. Although the single was a moderate hit, the wonderful b-side "Tiny Goddess" became a favourite with pirate radio deejays. During a performance of "Rainbow Chaser" on French television, artist Salvador Dali splashed black paint on them.

With Singer leaving the group to produce Peter Sarstedt, a third album *Black Flower* was first rejected by Blackwell but later released on Pye in May 1970, although soon deleted for lack of sales. Further albums continued into the Nineties, and in 1992 the original group filed a lawsuit in California against the more famous Seattle-based band Nirvana. Apparently label owner David Geffen paid the original band $100,000 to continue to use the name.

Chart entries
Rainbow Chaser *(with Alex Spyropoulos)* Nirvana (UK 1968 # 34)

Jim Capaldi see Dave Mason

Leon Carr and Earl Shuman
Carr born Allentown, Pennsylvania 1910. Died 1976.
Born Earl Stanley Shuman, Boston 1923. Died 2019.

Carr was educated at Pennsylvania State University and later studied the Schillinger System of musical composition at New York University. Moving to New York, he worked for a firm marketing jingles and while there also wrote the hit "There's No Tomorrow" by Tony Martin, featured in the 1949 movie *Two Tickets To Broadway*. Earl Shuman grew up in Boston listening to Gershwin, Porter and Berlin. He graduated from Yale University and served in the US Marines in both World War Two and the Korean War. His big break came in 1949 when his mother submitted his "What Happened in April," written with friend Marshall Brown, to a radio station contest Songs for Sale. Rosemary Clooney, described as "a new young singer" performed the song and it won first prize. However, it took four more years for his first big hit, "Seven Lonely Days" by Georgia Gibbs.

On becoming songwriting partners, Carr and Shuman wrote a string of hits for various artists, including "Hotel Happiness," for Brook Benton. One of their best-known songs was "Hey There Lonely Girl," originally a hit for Ruby & the Romantics in 1963 but better known for the high-pitched version by Eddie Holman, a US number two in 1969. Carr also composed the off-Broadway musical *The Secret Life of Walter Mitty* in 1964, which ran for 96 performances in Greenwich Village. Shuman also began an acting career at the age of 77 and later appeared in an episode of *Seinfeld*.

Chart entries
Most People Get Married – Patti Page (US 1962 # 27)
Hotel Happiness – Brook Benton (US 1962 # 3)
Hey There Lonely Boy – Ruby & the Romantics (US 1963 # 27); Eddie Holman (as Lonely Girl)
    (US 1969 # 2)
Our Everlasting Love – Ruby & the Romantics (US 1964 # 64)
Clinging Vine *(with Gary Lane)* Bobby Vinton (US 1964 # 17)
My Shy Violet – The Mills Brothers (US 1968 # 73)

Leon Carr with others
Two Thousand, Two Hundred and Twenty Three Miles *(with Paul Vance)* Patti Page (US
    1960 # 67)
Gina *(with Paul Vance)* Johnny Mathis (US 1962 # 6)
You Don't Need Me for Anything More *(with Richard Ahlert)* Brenda Lee 9US 1969 # 84)

She Lets Her Hair Down (Early in the Morning) *(with Paul Vance)* The Tokens (US 1969 # 61)

Earl Schuman with others
Starry Eyed *(with Mort Garson)* Michael Holliday (UK 1960 # 1)
Theme For a Dream *(with Mort Garson)* Cliff Richard & the Shadows (UK 1961 # 3)
Caterina *(with Bugs Bower)* Perry Como (US 1962 # 23; UK # 37)
Close to Cathy *(with Bob Goodman)* Mike Clifford (US 1962 # 12)

Gregory Carroll
Born John Wayne Carroll, Baltimore, Maryland 1929. Died 2013.

Carroll formed a doo-wop vocal group with school friends (including Johnny Otis) that became the Four Buddies. In 1953, he joined the Orioles for a time before forming a vocal harmony group called the Dappers. In the early Sixties, he created a new quartet that included singer Doris Troy, and co-wrote her "Just One Look," with Troy using the surname Payne on the credit. In October 1962, a quick demo of the song had been recorded for Atlantic and produced by Buddy Lucas, but on hearing it, the label decided not to record it, but instead released it unchanged as a single. It not only became an international hit for her, but also was successfully covered in the UK by the Hollies the following year. He had also co-wrote "What'cha Gonna To Do About It" with Troy.

In the Seventies, Carroll toured with a reformed version of the Orioles until retiring in 1994.

Chart entries
(Ain't That) Just Like Me *(with Billy Guy)* The Hollies (UK 1963 # 25)
Just One Look *(with Doris Payne (aka Troy)* Doris Troy (US 1963 # 10); The Hollies (UK 1964 # 2; US # 98)
What'cha Gonna To Do About It *(with Doris Payne (aka Troy, Rex Garvin)* Doris Troy (UK 1963 # 37)

Wayne Carson
Born Wayne Carson Head, Denver, Colorado 1943. Died 2015.
Nashville Songwriters Hall of Fame 1997.

Carson's parents had sung professionally as "Shorty and Sue." Inspired by country artist Merle Travis, Carson learned to play guitar but quickly took a liking to rock and roll instead. Following a spell fronting bands in Nashville, he worked for a time pitching songs with the help of producer and publisher Si Siman. His song "Somebody Like Me" caught the attention of Siman's producer friend Chet Atkins, who had Carson re-write it for singer Eddy Arnold. It became his first US country chart-topper in 1966. The following year, as Wayne Carson Thompson, he wrote "The Letter," inspired by pages of lyrics sent by his father, who also gave him the line, "Give me a ticket for an aeroplane." It scored a US number one for the Box Tops, receiving two Grammy nominations. It was also the last US chart-topper to be shorter than two minutes in length at 1.58. The self-penned "Keep On" was a later UK hit for Bruce Channel.

In 1972, Carson would go on to have more success with the Grammy award-winning "Always on My Mind," co-written with Johnny Christopher and Mark James, giving Elvis Presley, Willie Nelson, and the Pet Shop Boys huge hits in the Seventies and Eighties.

Chart entries
Somebody Like Me – Eddy Arnold (US 1966 # 53)
Do It Again a Little Bit Slower – Jon & Robin & the In Crowd (US 1967 # 18)
The Letter – The Box Tops (US 1967 # 1; UK # 5); Wayne Fontana & the Mindbenders (UK 1967 # 42); The Arbors (US 1969 # 20)
Drums - Jon & Robin & the In Crowd (US 1967 # 100)
Nine Pound Steel *(with Dan Penn)* Joe Simon (US 1967 # 70)
Neon Rainbow – The Box Tops (US 1967 # 24; UK # 57)
Mr Bus Driver – Bruce Channel (US 1967 # 90)
Dr Jon (The Medicine Man) Jon & Robin & the In Crowd (US 1968 # 87)
Keep On – Bruce Channel (UK 1968 # 12)
I'm Gonna Do All I Can (To Do Right By My Man) – Ike & Tina Turner (US 1969 # 98)
Soul Deep – The Box Tops (US 1969 # 18; UK # 22)

John Carter and Ken Lewis see also Geoff Stephens, Perry Ford
Born John Nicholas Shakespeare, Birmingham, England 1942.
Born Kenneth Alan James Hawker, Birmingham, England 1940.

Carter's family were enthusiastic amateur singers performing folk songs in pubs and at family gatherings. He taught himself to play acoustic guitar and while still at school formed a skiffle group called LVI with his friend Ken Hawker, and together they began writing songs. Looking back, Carter recalled how writing Buddy Holly take-offs inspired them to become professional songwriters. In 1961, deciding to use the pseudonyms of John Shakespeare and Ken Lewis, they went to London and under the guidance of manager Terry Kennedy formed Carter-Lewis and the Southerners to perform and record their songs. For a brief time, they also included guitarist Jimmy Page. Signing with Freddy Webb's Southern Music, they demoed songs for other writers, providing backing vocals on Sandie Shaw's "There's Always Something There To Remind Me,", and the Who's "I Can't Explain." They also performed on BBC's *Easy Beat* and *Saturday Club,* working with jazz singers such as Marion Montgomery and Marion Ryan. Along with Bill Bates, they also wrote "Will I What?" for Mike Sarne as a follow up to his hit "Come Outside."

Eventually, Kennedy convinced them that they needed to create a band to showcase their songs. The vocal harmony group Ivy League was initially formed in August 1964 with recording engineer and budding songwriter Perry Ford (1933-1999). Working with Piccadilly Records, their first single "What More Do You Want" generated little interest, but their second, "Funny How Love Can Be" was a top ten hit. Further hits included "That's Why I'm Crying" and "Tossing and Turning" and one album, 1965's *This is the Ivy League*. Becoming tired of touring, Carter left the group in January 1966 and was replaced by Tony Burrows of the Kestrels, with Lewis leaving too about a year later. They then set up their own production company, Sunny Records.

Carter and Lewis were still much sought after as studio singers, performing on such hits as Jeff Beck's "Hi Ho Silver Lining," Keith West's "Excerpt From a Teenage Opera," and Chris Farlowe's "Out of Time." As a writing team, they also had continued success with Herman Hermit's "Can't You Hear My Heartbeat," a surprising number two hit in the US.

In 1967, they wrote and produced "Let's Go to San Francisco" a psychedelic hit for the Flower Pot Men, with Carter joined in harmonies by Burrows, although a band of session musicians had to be formed for live appearances. The group would re-emerge in the early Seventies as White Plains. Carter also teamed up with Geoff Stephens to write Manfred Mann's "Semi-Detached Suburban Mr James," and two other hits for Herman's Hermits. He also sang lead vocal (through a megaphone) on the Stephens-penned "Winchester Cathedral," a Grammy Award-winning novelty hit for the New Vaudeville Band.

In 1970, the Carter-Stephens song "Knock, Knock Who's There" was favourite to win the Eurovision Song Contest with singer Mary Hopkins, but lost out to Dana's "All Kinds of Everything." Lewis left the music industry in 1971, while Carter with his wife and creative partner Jill Shakespeare wrote the 1974 hit "Beach Baby" by the studio band The First Class, consisting of lead singer Burrows and session singer Chas Mills.

Chart entries
How Can I Tell Her *(with Brian O'Hara)* The Fourmost (UK 1964 # 33)
Is It True? - Brenda Lee (US 1964 # 17; UK # 17)
Can't You Hear My Heartbeat - Herman's Hermits (US 1965 # 2); Goldie & the Gingerbreads
   (UK 1965 # 25)
Sunday For Tea - Peter & Gordon (US 1967 # 31)
Little Bit o' Soul - The Music Explosion (US 1967 # 2)
Let's Go To San Francisco - The Flower Pot Men (UK 1967 # 4)

Carter-Lewis with Perry Ford
Funny How Love Can Be - The Ivy League (UK 1965 # 8)
That's Why I'm Cryin' - The Ivy League (UK 1965 # 22)
Tossing and Turning - The Ivy League (UK 1965 # 3; US # 83)
Willow Tree - The Ivy League (UK 1966 # 50)

John Carter and Geoff Stephens
Semi-Detached Suburban Mr James - Manfred Mann (UK 1966 # 2)
Peek-A-Boo - New Vaudeville Band (UK 1967 # 7; US # 72)
My World Fell Down - Sagittarius (US 1967 # 70)
Sunshine Girl - Herman's Hermits (UK 1968 # 8)
My Sentimental Friend - Herman's Hermits (UK 1969 # 2)

John Carter
Sleepy Joe *(with Russell Alquist)* Herman's Hermits (UK 1968 # 12; US # 61)

Johnny Cash
Born J R Cash, Kingsland, Arkansas 1932. Died 2003.
Nashville Songwriters Hall of Fame 1977.
Country Music Hall of Fame 1980.
Rock and Roll Hall of Fame 1992.

Growing up during the Great Depression, young Cash worked with his family on a cotton plantation in the poverty-stricken town of Dyess, Arkansas, where the personal and economic struggles of the surrounding community forged a lifelong empathy for the poor and working class that inspired many of his most famous songs. Inspired by listening to radio and gospel music, he began playing and writing songs by the age of 12, and over the next few years his high tenor voice gradually changed to a bass-baritone. While at high school, he was also given the chance to sing on local radio. In 1950, he joined the US Air Force and was based in West Germany where he worked as a Morse code operator intercepting Soviet transmissions. While there, he acquired a distinctive scar on the right side of his jaw following surgery to remove a cyst.

Honourably discharged in 1954, he married his first wife and moved to Memphis where he studied to be a radio announcer. While there, he auditioned for Sam Phillips' Sun Records and eventually signed a contract, with his first recordings "Hey Porter" and "Cry! Cry! Cry!" released in 1955. These were followed by the classic songs "Folsom Prison Blues" and "I Walk the Line." The latter had been written backstage at a concert as a pledge of devotion to his new wife and although originally intended as a slow ballad, on Phillips' insistence was recorded as an uptempo version. That same year, he became the first Sun artist to release an album.

Feeling constrained by the label's contract, Cash now signed a more lucrative deal with Columbia, and the single "Don't Take Your Guns to Town," taken from the 1958 album *The Fabulous Johnny Cash,* became one of his biggest hits. With the Sun label continuing to release his backlog of recordings, Cash found himself having singles released concurrently on two different labels. He also revealed that his habit of wearing black clothes on tour was because they were easier to keep looking clean. By this time he had developed a drinking problem and an addiction to amphetamines, both of which led to nervousness and sometimes erratic behaviour. However, despite having being jailed for the night on seven occasions for misdemeanours, he never served a prison sentence.

During the early Sixties, Cash began touring with the Carter Family (mother Maybelle with daughters Anita, June and Helen). In 1963, he released the crossover hit "Ring of Fire." Co-written with June Carter and Merle Kilgore, it described the passions of love. Originally recorded by her sister Anita, June claimed it was inspired after seeing the words "Love is like a burning ring of fire" underlined in an Elizabethan poetry book owned by her uncle. With Cash's signature mariachi-style horn arrangement, it became one of his best-loved singles, topping the Country charts and peaked at 17 on the Hot 100.

Having divorced his first wife after separating in 1962, and with his drug addiction having reached an all-time high, it resulted in concerts being cancelled. However, his chart success continued with the single "Jackson," a duet with June Carter. Written by Billy Ed Wheeler and Jerry Leiber (as Gaby Rodgers), it had first been recorded in 1963 by the Kingston Trio. Although the actual location of Jackson has never been confirmed, it went on to win the artists a well-deserved Grammy and was also a hit for Nancy Sinatra and Lee Hazlewood four months later.

Carter and Cash were married in 1968, and the following two years saw the release of the celebrated "prison" albums, recorded live in front if inmates at Folsom and San Quentin prisons. While the former saw the re-release of "Folsom Prison Blues," the latter had the single "A Boy Named Sue," written by Shel Silverstein, which peaked at number two on the Hot 100. But the clear favourite among the inmates was the song "San Quentin," with Cash proclaiming that the prison should "rot and burn in hell."

In June 1969, Cash starred in his own ABC tv show, with him now having established his public image as the "Man in Black." In the Eighties, he became part of the Highwaymen along with Waylon Jennings, Willie Nelson and Kris Kristofferson.

Chart entries
Straight A's in Love – Johnny Cash & the Tennessee Two (US 1960 # 84)
I Walk the Line – Jaye P Morgan (US 1960 # 66)
Tennessee Flat-Top Box – Johnny Cash (US 1961 # 84)
The Matador *(with June Carter)* Johnny Cash (US 1963 #44)
Understand Your Man – Johnny Cash (US 1964 # 35)
Folsom Prison Blues (live version) *(with Gordon Jenkins)* Johnny Cash (US 1968 # 32; UK # 52)
Get Rhythm – Johnny Cash (US 1969 # 60)
See Ruby Fall *(with Roy Orbison)* Johnny Cash (US 1969 # 75)

Buzz Cason and Mac Gayden
Born James Elmore Cason, Nashville, Tennessee 1939. Died 2024.
Born McGavock Dickinson Gayden, Nashville, Tennessee 1941. Died 2025.
County Music Hall of Fame 2013 (Gayden).

As a teenager, Cason became a founding member of the Casuals, one of Music City's first doo-wop groups, and appeared on bills with Jerry Lee Lewis, Chubby Checker and Brenda Lee, while also singing backing vocals for artists that included Elvis Presley. In 1960, he commenced a solo career under the pseudonym Garry Miles and scored a minor hit with a cover of "Look For a Star" from the movie *Circus of Horrors*. In 1962, he began working as an engineer at Snuff Garrett's Liberty Records in Los Angeles, and while there teamed up with Leon Russell to produce a version of "La Bamba" for the Crickets before going on to tour with the band. That year, his song "Soldier of Love," co-written with Tony Moon, was recorded by Arthur Anderson. He also joined Ronny & the Daytonas and wrote their 1966 hit "Sandy" with John Wilkin. Later that year, he teamed up with Bobby Russell in a music publishing venture and together co-wrote songs for surfing duo Jan and Dean. Under curious pseudonyms, he also worked as a session vocalist for soundalike versions of popular hits, but later began writing under his own name, including his recording of "Adam & Eve" in 1968.

However, Cason had found more success the previous year working with his Nashville friend Mac Gayden. After playing in a number of local bands in the early Sixties, Gayden had joined the pop combo the Escorts led by studio musician Charlie McCoy, and through him had become a Nashville session player (which led to him being involved on Dylan's album *Blonde on Blonde*). According to Gayden, he had first started composing the song "Everlasting Love" on his grandma's piano at the age of five. Many years later, when hearing Robert Knight's voice while performing at a local fraternity, he introduced himself and told him he had a song for him. Gayden then called on his friend Cason to help him complete the song, and together produced the single that became Knight's first hit in September 1967. Three months later, the British band Love Affair, fronted by Steve Ellis, took the song to number one, with the writers also giving them a second chart hit three months later with "Rainbow Valley."

Chart entries
Everlasting Love - Robert Knight (US 1967 # 13; UK # 40); Love Affair (UK 1968 # 1)
Blessed Are the Lonely - Robert Knight (US 1968 # 97)
Rainbow Valley - Love Affair (UK 1968 # 5)

Buzz Cason
Danger *(with Bob Beckham)* Vic Dana (US 1963 # 96)
(They Call Her) La Bamba *(trad. with Jerry Allison)* The Crickets (US 1964 # 21)
Sandy *(with John Wilkin)* Ronnie & the Daytonas (US 1965 # 27)

Buzz Cason and Bobby Russell
Tennessee - Jan & Dean (US 1962 # 69)
Popsicle - Jan & Dean (US 1966 # 21)

Mac Gayden with others
She Shot a Hole In My Soul *(with Chuck Neese)* Clifford Curry (US 1967 # 95)

Felix Cavaliere and Eddie Brigati
Born Felix Cavaliere, Pelham, New York 1942.
Born Edward Brigati, Garfield, New Jersey 1945.
Rock and Roll Hall of Fame 1997 (with the Rascals).
Songwriters Hall of Fame 2009.

Cavaliere studied classical piano from an early age, and later played with local band the Stereos before enrolling at Syracuse University, where he formed his own doo-wop band, the Escorts. Moving on to New York City, he became a backup singer for Sandy Scott and Joey Dee and the Starlighters (whose line-up included percussionist Eddie Brigati, having just replaced his brother David). The Starlighters notched up nine singles between 1961 and 1963, including "Peppermint Twist." When Cavaliere met Starlighters' guitarist Gene Cornish, it gave him the idea of forming his own band, and, convincing both Cornish and Brigati to join, formed the Young Rascals, along with old friend and drummer Dino Danelli. They became the first all-white band signed by Atlantic Records, with Cavaliere and Brigati writing two US chart-toppers with "Groovin'" and "People Got To Be Free."

The inspiration for "Groovin'" came from Cavaliere's then-girlfriend Adrienne Buccheri, and that the song was a reflection of "the bliss I felt relaxing with her on Sunday afternoons, watching the world go by." The song "How Can I Be Sure" (with Cavaliere on lead vocal) also became a UK number one for David Cassidy in 1972. Although Brigati and Cornish quit the band in 1970, Cavaliere continued writing and performing with the band, its name now shortened to the Rascals.

Chart entries
Felix Cavaliere and Eddie Brigati
You Better Run – The Young Rascals (US 1966 # 20)
Come On Up – The Young Rascals (US 1966 # 43)
I've Been Lonely Too Long - The Young Rascals (US 1967 # 16)
Groovin' - The Young Rascals (US # 1; UK # 8)
A Girl Like You – The Young Rascals (US 1967 # 10; UK # 37)
How Can I Be Sure - The Young Rascals (US 1967 # 4)
It's Wonderful - The Young Rascals (US 1967 # 20)
A Beautiful Morning - The Rascals (US 1968 # 3)
People Got To Be Free - The Rascals (US 1968 # 1)
A Ray of Hope – The Rascals (US 1968 # 24)

Felix Cavaliere
Heaven – The Rascals (US 1969 # 39)
See – The Rascals (US 1969 # 27)
Carry Me Back – The Rascals (US 1969 # 26)

Lincoln Chase
Born Lincoln R Chase, New York City 1926. Died 1980.

Chase studied at the American Academy of Music before signing a record deal with Decca in 1951, but he failed to find success as a songwriter with this and several other labels. That changed three years later when his song "Such a Night" became a number two R&B hit for Clyde McPhatter & the Drifters, with later versions recorded by Johnnie Ray (a UK chart-topper) and Elvis Presley. Another success came in 1956 when "Jim Dandy" by LaVern Baker & the Gliders topped the R&B chart. By the end of the decade, Chase was working as manager for soul singer Shirley Ellis, and his song "The Nitty Gritty" gave her a top ten hit in 1964. Perhaps the most famous song for Ellis was the annoyingly catchy "The Clapping Song," originally arranged by Charles Calello.

Chart entries
The Nitty Gritty – Shirley Ellis (US 1963 # 8); Ricardo Ray (US 1968 # 90); Gladys Knight
    & the Pips (US 1969 # 19)
(That's) What the Nitty Gritty Is – Shirley Ellis (US 1964 # 72)
Such a Night – Elvis Presley (US 1964 # 16; UK # 13)
The Name Game *(with Shirley Elliston, aka Shirley Ellis)* Shirey Ellis (US 1964 # 3)
The Clapping Song (Clap Pat Clap Slap) *(arranged; Charles Calello)* Shirley Ellis (US
    1965 # 8; UK # 6)
The Puzzle Song – Shirley Ellis (US 1965 # 78)

Lou Christie and Twyla Herbert
Born Lugee Alfredo Giovanni Sacco, Pittsburgh, Pennsylvania 1943. Died 2025.
Born Twila Moody, Riverside, California 1921. Died 2009.

Attending Moon Area High School in Pittsburgh, Christie studied both music and voice control. He also served as student conductor of the school choir, singing solos at various holiday concerts. Although his teacher wanted him to pursue a career in classical music, he preferred pop, with an ambition to appear on *American Bandstand*. At the age of 15, he met Tyla Herbert at an audition in a hometown church basement. Herbert was a classically-trained musician, twenty years his senior, but who would become his regular writing partner for years to come. California-born Herbert had moved as a child with her family to Pennsylvania. With her flaming red hair, she was described as a "bohemian gypsy, psychic," and predicted a bright future for Christie.

Following graduation, Christie moved to New York where his falsetto voice soon found him work as a sessionist. In 1962, he sent demo tapes to record executive Nick Cenci, who persuaded him to use the stage name Lou Christie. Together, they used the Four Seasons' "Sherry" as a model for a new song, "The Gypsy Cried." Although a slow burner, it eventually charted. Using his real name Sacco for writing credit, the sessions provided the more successful single, "Two Faces Have I." After a spell in the army, his career was resurrected when he signed with MGM. The next single, "Lightnin' Strikes," written with Herbert and produced by Charles Calello, became Christie's first US chart-topper in early 1966.

After being dropped by the label in the late Sixties, he signed with Columbia, who tried unsuccessfully to groom him into being another Frankie Avalon-style artist. His business manager Stan Polley and producer Tony Romeo urged him to sign with Buddah Records, and it led to him recording the Wall of Sound-inspired "I'm Gonna Make You Mine," written by Romeo with backing singers Lesley Gore, Linda Scorr and Valerie Simpson. It became his biggest UK hit when it reached number two in 1969.

In 1971, he released a concept album called *Paint America Love,* now regarded as his finest work. Later describing his songwriting partner, he wrote: "Twyla is a genius. She was going to be a concert pianist but we started writing rock n' roll. The hardest part was that we had too many ideas. If we wanted to write a song, it would never stop."

Chart entries
The Gypsy Cried – Lou Christie (US 1963 # 51)
Two Faces Have I – Lou Christie (US 1963 # 6)
Lightnin' Strikes – Lou Christie (US 1965 #1; UK # 11)
Outside the Gates of Heaven – Lou Christie (US 1966 # 45)
Big Time – Lou Christie (US 1966 # 95)
Rhapsody in the Rain – Lou Christie (US 1966 # 16; UK # 37)
Painter – Lou Christie (US 1966 # 81)
Shake Hands and Wak Away Crying - Lou Christie (US 1967 # 95)
Are You Getting Any Sunshine? – Lou Christie (US 1969 # 73)
She Sold Me Magic – Lou Christie (US 1969 # 40; UK # 25)

Roger Christian see also **Jan Berry, Brian Wilson**
Born Roger Val Christian, Buffalo, New York 1934. Died 1991.

Christian got his break in radio in the mid-Fifties when as a lifeguard he saved a radio executive's wife from drowning in New York. He worked at WSAY in Rochester, New York and later as Mike Melody in Buffalo. In 1959 he moved to California, working for a time as a radio presenter in San Bernadino before moving to Los Angeles in 1965 as one of the original "Boss Jocks" on 93/KHJ. With a keen interest in hot rods, he soon became known as the "Poet of the Strip." When Murry Wilson (father of Beach Boy Brian) got to hear about him, he asked him to collaborate with his son on the Beach Boy tracks "Shut Down," "Little Deuce Coupe" and "Don't Worry Baby." At the same time, Christian began to collaborate on a series of car and surfing-related songs for Jan & Dean (Jan Berry & Dean Torrance) and also teamed up with Gary Usher (1938-1990) on songs that were featured in a string of beach and surfing-related movies.

Chart entries
Shut Down (Part 1) *(with Brian Wilson)* The Beach Boys (US 1963 # 23)
Honolulu Lulu *(with Jan Berry, Lou Adler)* Jan & Dean (US 1963 # 11)
Drag City *(with Jan Berry, Brian Wilson)* Jan & Dean (US 1963 # 10)
Dead Man's Curve *(with Jan Berry, Artie Kornfeld, Brian Wilson)* Jan & Dean (US 1964 # 8)
Three Window Coupe *(with Jan Berry)* The Rip Chords (US 1964 # 28)
The Little Old Lady (From Pasadena) *(with Don Altfeld)* Jan & Dean (US 1964 # 3)
Ride the Wild Surf *(with Jan Berry, Brian Wilson)* Jan & Dean (US 1964 # 16)
The Anaheim, Azusa & Cucamonga Sewing Circle, Book Review & Timing Association
   (with Don Altfeld, Jan Berry) Jan & Dean (US 1964 # 77)
Sidewalk Surfin' *(with Brian Wilson, Jan Berry)* Jan & Dean (US 1964 # 25)
Bucket T *(with Jan Berry)* Ronny & the Daytonas (US 1964 # 54)
You Really Know How To Hurt A Guy *(with Jan Berry, Jill Gibson)* Jan & Dean (US 1965 # 27)

Don Ciccone see **Jimmy Ryan**

Eric Clapton
Born Eric Patrick Clapton, Ripley, England 1945.
Songwriters Hall of Fame 2001.
Rock and Roll Hall of Fame 1992 (The Yardbirds), 1993 (Cream), 2000 (solo).

Now regarded as one of the finest and most influential guitarist in rock history, he learned to play the instrument at the age of 15, heavily influenced by blues music. Having been expelled from Kingston College of Art for showing more interest in music than art, he began busking in London's West End. In 1962, he became a member of the R&B band, the Roosters, and the following year was playing and touring with another R&B band, the Yardbirds, with his reputation as a fine blues guitarist steadily growing. With a habit of remaining on stage to fix a broken string resulting in a slow handclap by the audience, it led to his nickname "Slowhand." When the Yardbirds began veering more toward pop-oriented music, he left the band to join John Mayall's Bluesbreakers. In 1966, he was replaced by Pete Green and then invited by drummer Ginger Baker to join the newly formed Cream.

With the new band, Clapton began a successful career as singer-songwriter, co-writing four of their hits, and leading to their groundbreaking album *Disraeli Gears.* Before the band broke up in 1968, Clapton had written "Badge" with his friend George Harrison, and it became the band's final single. In the original music sheet prepared for the album liner notes, the only discernible word on the page was "bridge" (meaning a bridge section in the song), but due to Harrison's handwriting Clapton misread it as "Badge" and as a result it became the song title.

Clapton also played lead guitar on Harrison's Beatles single "While My Guitar Gently Weeps" as well as Lennon's "Cold Turkey." The following year, he joined the short-lived supergroup Blind Faith along with Ginger Baker, Stevie Winwood and Ric Grech, and wrote the classic "Presence of the Lord," his first solo composition. The next phase of his career saw him making an album with Delaney & Bonnie and Friends and also releasing his first solo album.

Chart entries
Strange Brew (*with Felix Pappalardi, Gail Collins*) Cream (UK 1967 # 17)
Sunshine Of Your Love (*with Jack Bruce, Pete Brown*) Cream (UK 1968 # 25; US # 5)
Anyone For Tennis (*with Martin Sharp*) Cream (UK 1968 # 40; US # 64)
Badge (*with George Harrison*) Cream (UK 1969 # 18; US # 60)
Comin' Home *(with Bonnie Bramlett)* Delaney, Bonnie and Friends (US 1969 # 84; UK # 16)

Dave Clark and Mike Smith
Born David Clark, London, 1939.
Born Michael George Smith, London 1943. Died 2008.
Rock and Roll Hall of Fame 2008 (with the Dave Clark Five).

Clark once claimed to have been a movie stuntman after leaving school aged 15. After teaching himself to play drums, he formed a skiffle band in his late teens as a way of raising funds for his soccer team to play in Holland. In 1958, he and his friend, bass guitarist Chris Walls, placed an ad in *Melody Maker* for musicians to form a band, resulting in a lineup that included Stan Saxon (lead vocals, sax), Rick Huxley (rhythm guitar) and Mick Ryan (lead guitar). Billed as the Dave Clark Five featuring Stan Saxon, they gained experience on the live circuit, and three years later, after going through personnel changes, they signed a long-term contract with the Mecca Ballroom chain. After losing Saxon and Ryan, the band now formed its own identity with new members Lenny Davidson (guitar, backing vocals), Denis Payton (rhythm guitar, sax), and Mike Smith (organ, lead vocals).

Smith had studied classical piano at the age of 13 and had first met Clark when they were both members of a boy's club soccer team. While in his teens, he also developed a strong, throaty vocal, and was working for a finance company when invited to join the band. Their first releases were recorded with engineer Adrian Kerridge at London's Lansdowne Studios, and with Clark as the band's astute manager, he secured the rights not only to produce the songs, but later tap the lucrative US market. In time, Clark would become an entrepreneurial multi-millionaire.

Signing with EMI, over the next few years they spearheaded what was coined by the press as the "Tottenham Sound" as a way to rival Liverpool's Mersey Sound, and developed their trademark pairing of Smith's distinctive vocals with Clark's thumping drumbeat. Having lost out to rivals Brian Poole & the Tremeloes to be the first Brit band to cover the Contours' classic "Do You Love Me," Clark and Smith wrote the band's sixth single "Glad All Over," and in early 1964 it managed to end the Beatles' six-week run at the top of the UK charts with "I Wanna Hold Your Hand." *Billboard* reviewed it as "a rocking, romping group vocal effort much akin to the Liverpool sound and the Beatles' school."

Aiming to take full advantage of this, they released a string of similar-sounding songs, including "Bits and Pieces," which a former lead guitarist claimed to have written earlier without receiving credit. They also became the first British band to follow in the footsteps of the Beatles and appear on the *Ed Sullivan Show* (which they did a record 18 times), while one of the finest songs, the Clark-Davidson "Catch Us If You Can," was featured in the 1965 movie of the same name, seen as their answer to their rival's movie *A Hard Day's Night*. Some of their final singles were actually ballads, including the Reed-Mason "Everybody Knows," surpringly sung by Davidson in 1967.

The band finally broke up in 1970, and in 2008 were inducted into the Rock and Roll Hall of Fame just eleven days after Smith passed away. Being one of the most popular and commercial British bands of the mid-Sixties, it was left to former Rolling Stones manager Andrew Loog Oldham to state in a 2014 interview: "If the Beatles ever looked over their shoulders, it was not the Stones they saw. They saw the Dave Clark 5 or Herman's Hermits."

Chart entries
Glad All Over – The Dave Clark Five (UK 1963 # 1; US # 6)
Bits And Pieces *(credited Ron Ryan)* The Dave Clark Five (UK 1964 # 2; US # 4)
Can't You See She's Mine – The Dave Clark Five (UK 1964 # 10; US # 4)
Thinking Of You, Baby – The Dave Clark Five (UK 1964 # 26)
Come Home – The Dave Clark Five (UK 1965 # 14; US # 16)
Try Too Hard – The Dave Clark Five (US 1966 # 12)
Please Tell Me Why – The Dave Clark Five (US 1966 # 28)
Satisfied With You - The Dave Clark Five (US 1966 # 50)
Live in the Sky – The Dave Clark Five (UK 1968 # 39)

Dave Clark
Because – The Dave Clark Five (US 1964 # 3)
Any Way You Want It – The Dave Clark Five (UK 1964 # 25; US # 14)
Poverty *(with Pearl Woods)* Bobby Bland (US 1966 # 65)
Nineteen Days *(with Dennis Peyton)* The Dave Clark Five (US 1966 # 48)
Why I Sing the Blues *(with B B King)* B B King (US 1969 # 61)

Dave Clark and Lenny Davidson
Everybody Knows (I Still Love You) – The Dave Clark Five (UK 1964 # 37; US # 15)
Catch Us If You Can – The Dave Clark Five (UK 1965 # 5; US # 4)
At the Scene – The Dave Clarke Five (US 1966 # 18)
Look Before You Leap – The Dave Clark Five (UK 1966 # 50)
I've Got To Have A Reason – The Dave Clark Five (US 1967 # 44)
Red and Blue – The Dave Clark Five (US 1967 # 89)

Gene Clark see Roger McGuinn

Rudy Clark
Born Rudolph Clark, New York City 1935. Died 2020.

As mailman and songwriter, Clark discovered and befriended diminutive R&B singer Little Jimmy Ray in a night club, and Gerry Granahan of Caprice Records suggested they could record some of his songs. The first was "If You Gotta Make a Fool of Somebody" which scored a US top thirty hit in 1961,and an even bigger hit in the UK for Freddie & the Dreamers two years later. Clark's "I've Got My Mind Set On You" was also recorded as a b-side to one of Ray's singles (and a US chart-topper for George Harrison in 1987). A songwriting partnership with his friend, singer Bobby Darin, spawned minor hits for King Curtis and Wayne Newton in 1963. While a staff writer for Darin's TM Music, Clark wrote the classic "The Shoop Shoop Song (It's In His Kiss)." First rejected by the Shirelles, it was then recorded by soul and gospel singer Merry Clayton. Although produced by Jack Nitzsche, it never charted. Calvin Carter, who worked as A&R man for Vee-Jay Records, came to New York seeking a follow-up song to Betty Everett's "You're No Good" and suggested Clark's song. Although at first disliking it, she reluctantly agreed to do it, and it became a huge hit for both her and several future artists.

Clark went on to work with songwriter Arthur Resnick and co-wrote "Good Lovin,'" a song first recorded by the Olympics and later revised to become a US chart-topper for the Rascals.

Chart entries
If You Gotta Make a Fool of Somebody – James Ray (US 1961 # 22); Freddie & the Dreamers
   (UK 1963 # 3); Maxine Brown (US 1965 # 63)

Itty Bitty Pieces – James Ray (US 1962 # 41)
Do the Monkey *(with Bobby Darin)* King Curtis (US 1963 # 92)
Shirl Girl *(with Bobby Darin)* Wayne Newton (US 1963 # 58)
The Shoop Shoop Song (It's In His Kiss) Betty Everett (US 1964 # 6; UK 1968 # 34)
Beg Me – Chuck Jackson (US 1964 # 45)
Do It Right – Brook Benton (US 1964 # 67)
Good Lovin' *(with Arthur Resnick)* The Olympics (US 1965 # 81); The Rascals (US 1966 # 1)

Clarke, Hicks and Nash (The Hollies)

Born Harold Allan Clarke, Salford, England 1942.
Born Graham William Nash, Blackpool, England 1942.
Born Anthony Christopher Hicks, Nelson, England 1945.
Rock and Roll Hall of Fame 2010 (with the Hollies).
Songwriters Hall of Fame 2009 (Nash).

During the skiffle craze that swept Britain in the late Fifties, childhood friends Clarke and Nash sang and played guitar together in local clubs under various names such as the Guytones, the Two Teens, and Ricky & Dane Young. They later joined local band the Fourtones before moving on in 1962 to the Deltas, which included bassist Eric Haydock, lead guitarist Vic Steele and drummer Don Rathbone. It was Nash who suggested changing their name to the Hollies (after Buddy Holly), and following a performance at Liverpool's famous Cavern Club, EMI producer Ron Richards auditioned them for the Parlophone label. With Steele not wishing to turn professional, the band's manager invited a local guitar hero Tony Hicks to audition for them. Hicks had become a respected member of the music scene as lead guitarist for Rick Shaw & the Dolphins.

Their first hit singles in 1963 were covers of two Coasters' hits, followed by Maurice Williams' "Stay" (a number 8 hit), Gregory Carroll's and Doris Payne's "Just One Look" (number 2), and Mort Schuman & Clive Westlake's "Here I Go Again" (number 4). In the meantime, drummer Rathbone had decided to leave the band and Hicks brought in ex-Dolphins Bobby Elliott to replace him in August 1963.

Clarke and Nash had already been writing their own material, and their producer Ron Richards allowed them to release "We're Through," although for the time being the writers continued to credit their own material to "L Ransford," the name of Nash's grandfather. Nash later recalled: "Generally, my writing is influenced by living, by absorbing everything that happens to me and my actions." This was followed by two more covers, Gerry Goffin and Russ Titleman's "Yes I Will" (a top ten hit in January 1965) and Clint Ballard's "I'm Alive," which scored their first chart-topper. American Ballard had written it for the band, but they initially passed it over to the Manchester band the Toggery Five before changing their mind.

Their next single "Look Through Any Window," written by Graham Gouldman, became their breakthrough hit in the US, reaching number 32 in January 1966, while their cover of George Harrison's "I f I Needed Someone" was a moderate hit, mainly due to the Beatles releasing it themselves on *Rubber Soul*. Continuing with covers, they next released "I Can't Let Go," written by Chip Taylor and Al Gorgoni, and highlighted by Nash's soaring tenor in the chorus, which had Paul McCartney thinking it was a trumpet. Following its success, bass player Haydock was sacked for missing several gigs and replaced by former Dolphins' member Bernie Calvert, shortly after "Bus Stop," another Gouldman song, became their first US top ten hit.

Finally, Clarke, Nash and Hicks enjoyed their first big success as writers with "Stop Stop Stop." Inspired by a visit to a strip club with a record executive, it was driven by Elliott's cymbal crashes and Hicks' banjo arrangement, which was played through tape deck delay to sound like a balalaika. Their success continued in 1967 with the equally impressive "On a Carousel." Nash later recalled: "We went through a shitload of ideas until inspiration struck. I'm not sure which of the three of us came up with funfairs … [We] realised a love affair was pretty much like going round and round on a carousel. And before we knew it the song just took shape. It was all there, the words, the tune, there was no stopping it." While it was being recorded at Abbey Road Studios, it was filmed by producer George Martin, who was there working on the trumpet parts for "Penny Lane."

Next came their "Carrie Anne," apparently written during a concert they did with Tom Jones, with Clarke supplying the lyrics for the bridge. It also saw one of the first uses on a pop record of a steelpan solo and allegedly was seen as a shy tribute to Marianne Faithful. In anticipation of their next album *Butterfly,* they released the ambitious "King Midas in Reverse." Nash had been influenced by a recent visit to New York and was looking to take the band in a new direction, one that was resisted by the other members. Based on the legend of Midas, the legendary king of Phrygia, who asked the gods to turn everything he touched to gold, and then later regretted and cursed it, Nash recalled that he wrote the lyrics about the time when nothing that he did was successful, and that everything he touched "turned to dust." Another story had Nash overhearing Fairport Convention's Richard Thomson saying he was unlucky with money, sort of like "King Midas in reverse."

Although only just breaking into the top twenty, Nash was proud of the song: "I loved that song. It was very personal and the Hollies really liked it. Normally Hollies singles would go into the top ten, but when 'King Midas' didn't, they started not to trust my desire to keep moving forward and to talk about real stuff rather than 'Moon/June…' songs. ' King Midas' separated us." Its failure to reach higher in the charts and the failure of the subsequent album would later signal Nash's decision to quit the band.

To restore their more popular style, the band returned to the top ten in 1968 with "Jennifer Eccles," named after the wives of Clarke and Nash. When members of the band refused to record Nash's song "Marrakesh Express" as not being commercial enough, they decided to record an album of Dylan songs instead, and with that and clashes with Richards, Nash felt it was time to go. His last recording with them was on Tony Hazzard's "Listen to Me" in August 1968. He moved to Los Angeles with the idea of becoming a songwriter, but later joined ex-Buffalo Springfield guitarist Stephen Stills and ex-Byrds David Crosby to form Crosby, Stills and Nash, with "Marrakesh Express" being their first single.

In January 1969, Terry Sylvester from the Swinging Blue Jeans was brought in to replace Nash and the Hollies continued to have chart success with the Macauley-Stephens "Sorry Suzanne," as well as Bobby Russell and Bob Scott's epic ballad "He Ain't Heavy, He's My Brother."

Chart entries
We're Through - The Hollies (UK 1964 # 7)
Have You Ever Loved Somebody? – Paul & Barry Ryan (UK 1966 # 49); The Searchers (UK 1966 # 48; US # 94)
Stop! Stop! Stop! – The Hollies (UK 1966 # 2; US # 7)
On A Carousel - The Hollies (UK 1967 # 4; US # 11)
Tell Me To My Face – Keith (UK 1967 # 50; US # 37)
Carrie Anne - The Hollies (UK 1967 # 3; US # 9)
Pay You Back With Interest – The Hollies (US 1967 # 28)
King Midas In Reverse - The Hollies (UK 1967 # 18; US # 51)
Dear Eloise – The Hollies (US 1967 # 50)
Jennifer Eccles - The Hollies (UK 1968 # 7; US # 40)
Do the Best You Can – The Hollies (US 1968 # 93)

Graham Nash
Marrakesh Express – Crosby, Stills & Nash (UK 1969 # 17; US # 28)

Graham Nash with others
Annabella *(with Kirk Duncan, Nicky James)* John Walker (UK 1967 # 24; US # 44)

George Clinton
Born George Edward Clinton, Kannapolis, North Carolina 1941.
Rock and Roll Hall of Fame 1997 (with Parliament-Funkadelic).
Grammy Lifetime Achievement Award 2019 (with Parliament-Funkadelic).
Songwriters Hall of Fame 2025.

The first of nine children born in a North Carolina outhouse, Clinton grew up in Plainfield, New Jersey. As a teenager in 1955, he partly-owned a Newark barbershop called Uptown Tonsorial Parlor, which was a hangout for all local singers and musicians. Taking inspiration from Frankie Lyman & the Teenagers, he was having his hair straightened when he came up with the idea of forming his own doo-wop group called the Parliaments with other friends and staff members, including brother and sister Audrey and Eugene Boykins, Glen Carlos, Charles "Butch" Davis, and Herbie Jenkins. While not at work, they played on street corners and at local hops and dances. The following year, Clinton was still at high school and working as foreman of the New Jersey Wham-o Hula Hoop factory, and the Parliaments now consisted of Clinton, Jenkins, Robert Lambert, Danny Mitchell and Grady Thomas. Around this time, they recorded "The Wind" and "A Sunday Kind of Love" on acetate in a Newark record booth. By 1958, the group was in its third incarnation and recorded "Poor Willie" and "Party Boys" for the local Hull label, and the following year the recordings were picked up by ABC-Paramount and released on its subsidiary label APT. The group, now with Johnny Murray on board, recorded two more singles, Lonely Island" and "Cry."

By 1962, Clinton was working in New York as staff writer for Jobete Music, a company affiliated with Motown, and the following year took the group to Detroit to audition for the label, its members now including Clarence "Fuzzy" Hawkins. Although not being signed, they cut a number of demos, and Clinton, commuting to Detroit every week, teamed up with ex-Jobete writer Sidney Barnes and Motown session man Mike Terry to form the Geo-Si-Mik production team, signing with the Golden World and Ric Tic labels. Writing and producing for the team over the next three years, Clinton became disillusioned with the lack of success and returned to Newark to work full-time in his barbershop.

The song "(I Wanna) Testify" was written by Clinton and Daron Taylor and recorded in late 1966 for the Revilot label. When it appeared at number 20 on the Hot 100, Clinton reassembled the group, adding a rhythm section comprising Eddie Hazel (guitar), Lucious Ross (guitar), Billy Nelson (bass) Mickey Atkins (organ) and Ramon Fulwood (drums). Clinton was the only group member to appear on the single, as the others were unable to travel to Detroit. By 1968, he had temporarily lost the rights to the group's name after Motown bought out Golden World. To remain active, he used his rhythm section to assemble a new group, Funkadelic, bringing in Bernie Worrell on keyboards. Signing to Armen Boladian's new Westbound label, they released their debut single "Music For My Mother" and the album *Funkadelic* early in 1970.

The two groups, Funkadelic and the re-named Parliament, would go on to dominate Black music for years to follow with new sounds that embraced both lyricism, new technology and offbeat fashion..

Chart entries
(I Wanna) Testify *(with Deron Taylor)* The Parliaments (US 1967 # 20); Johnny Taylor (as Testify (I Wonna) (US 1969 # 36)
All Your Goodies Are Gone (The Loser's Seat) *(with Billy Nelson, Clarence Haskins)* The Parliaments (US 1967 # 80)
I'll Bet You *(with Patrick Lindsey, Sidney Barnes)* Funkadelic (US 1969 # 63)

Leonard Cohen
Born Leonard Norman Cohen, Westmount, Quebec, Canada 1934. Died 2016.
Rock and Roll Hall of Fame 2008.
Grammy Lifetime Achievement Award 2010.

Born into an Orthodox Jewish family, his father died when he was nine. Cohen attended Westmount High School and studied music and poetry and while there learned to play both acoustic and classical guitar and formed a country-folk group called the Buckskin Boys. After leaving Westmount, he went to live in Montreal where he read his poetry in various clubs. In 1951, he enrolled at McGill University, where he was president of the Debating Union. Three years later he had his first poem published in a magazine. Graduating with a B.A degree, he had his book of poetry *Let Us Compare Mythologies* published in 1956. After a year studying at New York's Columbia University School, he returned to Montreal and had his second poetry book *The Spice-Box of Earth* published, which gained critical recognition.

Moving to live on the Greek island of Hydra in the early Sixties, he continued to write, with the novel *The Favourite Game* published in 1963, and the poetry collection *Flowers For Hitler* the following year. In 1966, he began focusing on songwriting. "Suzanne" was inspired by Cohen's platonic relationship with dancer Suzanne Verdal and the rituals they both enjoyed when they got together, like having a certain kind of tea in her apartment and walking around Old Montreal. The lyrics had first appeared as the poem "Suzanne Takes You Down" in his book *Parasites of Heaven*. The song was first recorded by the Stormy Clovers in 1966 and then by Judy Collins for her album *In My Life*.

Although intending to set out for Nashville to become a country songwriter, Cohen got caught up in New York's folk scene and soon came to the attention of record producer John Hammond who signed him to Columbia Records. Although Hammond was due to produce the album, he fell sick and was replaced by John Simon. "Suzanne" was recorded as a single but failed to chart when released in 1968. In the meantime, Noel Harrison had recorded it and had it peak at 56 on the Hot 100 in November 1967.

The song was included on Cohen's celebrated debut album *Songs of Leonard Cohen,* which also included "So Long, Marianne," inspired by Marianne Jensen who he had met on Hydra in 1960 and brought her and her son back live with him in Montreal. Another song, "Hey, That's No Way To Say Goodbye" was written in a New York hotel and was included on Judy Collins' 1967 album *Wildflowers*.

In 1969, he went to Nashville and recorded the album *Songs From a Room* which included the much-lauded "Bird on a Wire," written and inspired after Jensen handed him a guitar to help him snap out of a depression. The Seventies saw him doing extensive tours, including one in Israel during the war in Sinai, and with changes of style released several more albums. In 1987, Jennifer Warnes released the critically-acclaimed *Famous Blue Raincoat*, an album of Cohen songs, along with the single "First We Take Manhattan."

Cohen always played down his fame: "There are writers who are great visionaries, who can depict huge movements - things like that. They're the great writers. I'm just the other kind."

Chart entries
Suzanne – Noel Harrison (US 1967 # 56)

Roger Cook and Roger Greenaway

Born Roger John Reginald Greenaway, Bristol, England 1938.
Born Roger Frederick Cook, Bristol, England 1940.
Nashville Songwriters Hall of Fame 1997 (Cook).
Songwriters Hall of Fame 2009.

While still a teenage schoolboy, Greenaway joined local vocal group the Kestrels, which also had Roger Maggs and future songwriter Tony Burrows in its line-up. Influenced by US groups such as the Platters and the Penguins, their close harmonies secured them a deal with the Pye label, initially being employed as backing singers for a number of the label's stars. After a spell of military service disrupted their careers, they released a debut single, which almost charted. In 1962, Maggs left the group to pursue a non-music career and was replaced by Cook, who came from the same part of Bristol as Greenaway. The two became close friends, writing songs together as they toured. After working as staff writers for a music publisher, their first success came with "You've Got Your Troubles." Cook recalled it was written while the two of them were in a theatre, with Greenaway asking for help to write the lyrics to a "little tune" he had written. It became a huge hit for the Fortunes in 1965. The following year, they enjoyed their own success as recording artists David and Jonathan, both with a cover of the Beatles' "Michelle" and their own composition "Lovers of the World Unite."

Their 1967 novelty single "I Was Kaiser Bill's Batman" was performed by Whistling Jack Smith, named after the popular baritone singer of the 1920s and 1930s. Originally titled "Too Much Birdseed," it was recorded by studio musicians along with the Mike Sammes Singers, with the whistling supplied by either Noel Walker or the Sammes' John O'Neill, known for his whistling skill. That same year, the ballad "Something's Gotten Hold of My Heart" gave Gene Pitney a top five hit in the UK.

Two years later came "A Way of Life" by the Family Dogg. The group was formed by Albert Hammond and Steve Rowland, with the participation of Mike Hazlewood and Pam "Zooey" Quinn. The single came from their debut album of the same name, which was reported to have among the guest musicians, Elton John and future Led Zeppelin-members Jimmy Page, John Bonham and John Paul Jones.

In the autumn of 1969, Cook joined Blue Mink, a group consisting of singer Madeline Bell, guitarist Alan Parker, bassist Herbie Flowers and drummer Barry Morgan. Their debut single "Melting Pot" scored a top three hit in the UK, but its lyrics have since been criticised for its racist language and phrases.

The following decade saw Cook and Greenaway achieve success with "I'd Like To Teach the World To Sing," a UK chart-topper for the New Seekers (famously rewritten for a Coke Cola ad), as well as hits for artists including Cilla Black and Cliff Richard (both with Jerry Lordan), Andy Williams, and the Hollies.

Chart entries
You've Got Your Troubles – Fortunes (UK 1965 # 2; US # 7)
This Golden Ring – Fortunes (UK 1965 # 15; US # 82)
Green Grass – Gary Lewis & the Playboys (US 1966 # 8)
Lovers Of the World Unite – David & Jonathan (UK 1966 7; US # 53)
I Was Kaiser Bill's Batman – Whistling Jack Smith (UK 1967 # 5; US # 20)
Something's Gotten Hold Of My Heart – Gene Pitney (UK 1967 # 5)
I've Got You On My Mind – Dorain Gray (UK 1968 # 36)
The Way It Used To Be – Engelbert Humperdinck (UK 1969 # 3; US # 42)
A Way Of Life –The Family Dogg (UK 1969 # 6)
Melting Pot – Blue Mink (UK 1969 # 3)

Cook-Greenaway with Jerry Lordan
Good Times (Better Times) – Cliff Richard (UK 1969 # 12)
Conversations – Cilla Black (UK 1969 # 7)

Sam Cooke

Born Samuel Cook, Clarksdale, Mississippi 1931. Died 1964 (murdered).
Rock and Roll Hall of Fame 1986.
Songwriters Hall of Fame 1987.
Grammy Lifetime Achievement Award 1999.

The fifth of eight children whose father was a Baptist minister. Moving with his family to Chicago two years later, Cook performed publicly for the first time singing gospel in his father's church, along with a brother and two sisters known locally as the Singing Children. At the age of 14, Cook became lead singer of the Highway Q.C's and befriended fellow gospel singer Lou Rawls, who sang in a rival group. In 1951, he became lead singer of the innovative gospel group the Soul Stirrers who recorded on the Speciality label. With his unique florid vocal style and star-like charisma, he was credited for bringing gospel music to a younger audience. He left the group in 1957, seeking to branch out into recording pop material. Now adding an "e" to his surname, he signed with Keen Records and his first single, the self-penned "You Send Me," spent three weeks at the top of the US charts. Cooke gave the writing credit to his younger brother, L.C Cook, so his publisher would not profit from the song.

In 1960, he signed with RCA and had success with some of his most famous work, including "Chain Gang" (co-written with elder brother Charles), and inspired while on tour and meeting a real chain gang of convicts on a highway. "Wonderful World" was written with Herb Alpert and Lou Adler, while his own "Cupid" reportedly came about when Cooke's producers had the idea for him to do a song for a girl they had seen on a tv show hosted by Perry Como. His business adviser recalled: "She didn't do anything but just look up at Perry Como in the most wistful-type manner."

1962's "Twistin' the Night Away" was recorded with members of the Wrecking Crew as session musicians and became an R&B chart-topper, while "Bring It On Home to Me" and it's a-side "Having a Party" were written while on tour, with the former song first offered to singer Dee Clark, who turned it down. The song about a guy losing a girl but later missing her badly and willing to do anything to get her back was a bigger hit for the Animals three years later. Cooke's songs were also covered successfully by artists such as Cat Stevens, Johnny Nash, and Otis Redding. He once wrote: "If you observe what's going on and try to figure out how people are thinking and determine the times of your day, I think you can always write something that people will understand."

On December 11th 1964 Cooke was in a Los Angeles motel room having an altercation with a girl he had picked up when he was fatally shot by the manageress. The subsequent posthumous hit single was the poignant "A Change Is Gonna Come," which quickly became an anthem for the Civil Rights Movement. Released as the b-side to "Shake" the previous January, it was inspired by a number of events in his life, especially the time when his entourage were turned away from a whites-only motel in Louisiana and later arrested for disturbing the peace.

Chart entries
Nobody Loves Me Like You – The Flamingos (US 1960 # 30)
Wonderful World *(with Herb Alpert & Lou Adler)* (US 1960 # 12; UK # 27) Herman's Hermits
 (UK 1965 # 7; US # 4)
Chain Gang *(with Charles Cooke Jr)* (US 1960 # 2; UK # 9); Jackie Wilson & Count Basie
 (US 1968 # 84)
Sad Moon – Sam Cooke (US 1960 # 29)
Cupid – Sam Cooke (US 1961 # 17; UK # 7); Johnny Rivers (US 1965 # 76); Johnny Nash
 (UK 1969 # 6; US # 39)
Feel It – Sam Cooke (US 1961 # 56)
It's All Right – Sam Cooke (US 1961 # 93)
Soothe Me – The Sims Twins (US 1961 # 8); Sam & Dave (US 1967 # 56; UK # 35)
Twistin' the Night Away - Sam Cooke (US 1962 # 9; UK # 6)
Meet Me at the Twistin' Place – Johnny Morisette (US 1962 # 63)
Having A Party – Sam Cooke (US 1962 # 17)
Bring It On Home To Me – Sam Cooke (US 1962 # 13); The Animals (UK 1965 # 7;
 US # 32); Eddie Floyd (US 1968 # 17)
Nothing Can Change This Love – Sam Cooke (US 1962 # 12)
I'll Bring It On Home To You – Carla Thomas (US 1962 # 41)
Somebody Have Mercy – Sam Cooke (US 1962 # 70)
Baby, Baby, Baby- Sam Cooke (US 1963 # 66)
Another Saturday Night – Sam Cooke (US 1963 # 10; UK # 23)
When A Boy Falls In Love *(with Clint Lavert)* Mel Carter (US 1963 # 44); Sam Cooke (US
 1965 # 52)
Baby We've Got Love – Johnny Taylor (US 1963 # 98)
Ain't That Good News – Sam Cooke (US 1964 # 11)
Good Times – Sam Cooke (US 1964 # 11)
Cousin of Mine – Sam Cooke (US 1964 # 31; 1965 # 73)
That's Where It's At *(with James W Alexander)* Sam Cooke (US 1964 # 93)
Shake – Sam Cooke (US 1965 # 10); US 1967 # 47; UK # 28)
A Change Is Gonna Come – Sam Cooke (US 1965 # 31)

It's Got the Whole World Shakin' – Sam Cooke (US 1965 # 41)
When a Boy Falls in Love *(with Clint Lavert)* Sam Cooke (US 1965 # 52)
Sugar Dumpling – Sam Cooke (US 1965 # 32)
Feel It – Sam Cooke (US 1966 # 95)
Sweet Soul Music *(with Arthur Conley & Otis Redding)* - Arthur Conley (US 1967 # 2;
   UK # 7)
Soothe Me – Sam & Dave (US 1967 # 56; UK # 35)
You Send Me – Aretha Franklin (US 1968 # 56)
Cupid – Johnny Nash (US 1969 # 39; UK # 6)

Ritchie Cordell and Bo Gentry see also Tommy James
Cordell born Richard Joel Rosenblatt, New York 1943. Died 2004.
Gentry born Robert Allan Ackoff, New York 1942. Died 1983.

After singing and playing guitar in his teens, Brooklyn-born Cordell was introduced to song plugger Sid Prosen in 1961, and via him to singer Paul Simon (at the time using the pseudonym Jerry Landis). Using the name Ritchie Cordell, he released Simon's "Tick Tock" as a single on the Rori label in 1962, and then had his own "Georgiana" produced and arranged by Simon. After having moderate success as writer or performer with the Kama Sutra label, he became a staff writer for Roulette Records in 1966. While there, he struck up a friendship with Tommy James, whose band the Shondells had just scored their first hit with "Hanky Panky." Along with Sal Trimachi and Morris Levy (Roulettes' boss), he wrote their third single "Its Only Love." In the meantime, Cordell had found a new songwriting partner in Bo Gentry.

Gentry had also worked for Kama Sutra, but left after a disagreement with owner Artie Ripp. With Cordell, they wrote the song "I Think We're Alone Now, originally written by Gentry as a mid-tempo ballad for his girlfriend. The two writers recorded a faster version and presented it as a demo to Tommy James, who felt it had hit potential and recorded it with his band. As Gentry was still under contract to Kama Sutra, Roulettes' Morris Levy agreed to a deal naming Cordell as sole writer, but splitting the royalties with Gentry. The song scored a top five hit on the Hot 100 in February 1967 (and a debut chart-topper for Tiffany in 1987). Between them, the two writers scored a number of hits for the Shondells, including "Mirage," "Out of the Blue" and "Get Out Now," but their biggest success came with "Mony Mony." Written with James and Bobby Bloom, it topped the UK charts and reached number three on the Hot 100 in early 1968. Their final hit together was "Indian Giver," written with Bloom, which scored a top five hit for the bubblegum group 1910 Fruitgum Company in January 1969.

In the late Sixties, Cordell left Roulette and joined Super K Productions, set up by Bubblegum-supremo producers Jerry Kazenetz and Jeffry Katz, and wrote several hits for the company, including teaming up with Joey Levine to write "Gimme Gimme Good Lovin'" for Crazy Elephant.

Chart entries
Mirage – Tommy James & the Shondells (US 1967 # 10)
Out of the Blue – Tommy James & the Shondells (US 1967 # 43)
Get Out Now - Tommy James & the Shondells (US 1968 # 48)
Mony Mony *(with Tommy James, Bobby Bloom)* Tommy James & the Shondells (US 1969 # 3;
   UK # 1)
Somebody Cares *(with Harvey Weisenfeld)* Tommy James & the Shondells (US 1968 # 53)
Indian Giver *(with Bobby Bloom)* The 1910 Fruitgum Company (US 1969 # 5)

Ritchie Cordell
I Think We're Alone Now - Tommy James & the Shondells (US 1967 # 4)
I Like the Way - Tommy James & the Shondells (US 1967 # 25)
Getting' Together - Tommy James & the Shondells (US 1967 # 18)

Ritchie Cordell with others
Its Only Love *(with Sal Trimachi)* Tommy James & the Shondells (US 1966 # 31)
Gimme Gimme Good Lovin' *(with Joey Levine)* Crazy Elephant (US 1969 # 12; UK # 12)
Its Only Love *(with Sal Trimachi, Morris Levy)* Tony Blackburn (UK 1969 # 40)
The Train *(with Jeff Katz, Jerry Kasenetz)* The 1910 Fruitgum Company (US 1969 # 57)

Bo Gentry with others
Special Delivery *(with Bobby Bloom)* The 1910 Fruitgum Company (US 1969 # 38)

Make Believe *(with Joey Levine)* Wind (US 1969 # 28)

Henry Cosby
Born Henry R Cosby, Detroit, Michigan 1928. Died 2002.
Songwriters Hall of Fame 2006.

"Hank" Cosby had already served in the Korean War as part of a military band before playing tenor sax in Joe Hunter's jazz band and for various Detroit record labels. In 1959, the band was recruited by Berry Gordy Jr for Motown's ever-growing group of session musicians. Cosby performed on many of the label's early hits before becoming a fine arranger, producer and songwriter, especially working with Little Steve Wonder. Along with Clarence Paul, he wrote "Fingertips," Wonder's first major hit and chart-topper in 1963. Originally a jazz instrumental number, it was recorded for Wonder's first studio album, *The Jazz Soul of Little Stevie*. The single was released on the Tamla label in May 1963, with the b-side a live version entitled "Fingertip Part 2."

Cosby also collaborated with fellow Motown lyricist Sylvia Moy on a number of Wonder's singles, including "Uptight (Everything's Alright), "I Was Made To Love Her" (along with his mother Lula Mae), and "My Cherie Amour." In 1967, the Supremes dropped Florence Ballard and brought in new member Cindy Birdsong, also adding Diana Ross's name to the billing. The changes led to mixed success in the charts, with two of their singles not even reaching the top twenty. This prompted Gordy to hold a special meeting with writers at a Detroit hotel. The group, who dubbed themselves the Clan, decided to break the formula and craft a song about a woman asking her partner not to pressure her into sleeping with him for fear of getting pregnant. "Love Child" (as was Ross in real life), leapt to the top of the charts in September 1968. As a sequel, the Clan also wrote the tragic "I'm Living in Shame" for the Supremes. With inspiration taken from Douglas Sirk's 1959 movie *Imitation of Life,* the lyrics describe how a young girl shuns both her mother and impoverished childhood and passes herself off to her friends as the daughter of a rich parent, only to end with her mother dying without even seeing her daughter become an adult.

Working with Smokey Robinson, Cosby co-wrote "Tears of a Clown," for one of the Miracles' albums in 1967, but when released as a single three years later it topped the charts on both sides of the Atlantic. Cosby left Motown after the label moved to Los Angeles in the early Seventies and continued to write and produce.

Chart entries
Fingertips *(with Clarence Paul)* Little Stevie Wonder (US 1963 # 1)
Work Out Stevie, Work Out *(with Clarence Paul)* Stevie Wonder (US 1963 # 33)
Do the Boomerang *(with Autry DeWalt Jr, Willie Woods)* Jr Walker & the All-Stars (US 1965 # 36)
Uptight (Everything's Alright) *(with Steve Judkins [aka Stevie Wonder], Sylvia Moy)* Stevie Wonder
    (US 1965 # 3; UK # 14); The Jazz Crusaders (US 1966 # 95); Nancy Wilson (US 1966 # 84);
    Ramsey Lewis (US 1966 # 49)
Nothing's Too Good For My Baby *(with Sylvia Moy, William "Mickey" Robinson)* Stevie Wonder
    (US 1966 # 20)
I Was Made To Love Her *(with Stevie Wonder, Sylvia Moy, Lula Mae Hardaway)* Stevie Wonder
    (US 1967 # 2; UK # 5); King Curtis (US 1967 # 76)
Little Ole' Man (Uptight Everything's Alright) *(with Stevie Wonder, Sylvia Moy)* Bill Cosby
    (US 1967 # 4)
I'm Wondering *(with Stevie Wonder, Sylvia Moy)* Stevie Wonder (US 1967 # 12; UK # 23)
Shoo-Be-Doo-Be-Doo-Da-Day *(with Stevie Wonder, Sylvia Moy)* - Stevie Wonder (US 1968 # 9;
    UK # 46)
Love Child *(with Frank Wilson, Pam Sawyer, Deke Richards, R Dean Taylor)* Diana Ross & the
    Supremes (US 1968 # 1; UK # 16)
Home Cookin' *(with Eddie Willis, Melvyn Moy)* Jr Walker & the All-Stars (US 1969 # 42)
I'm Livin' In Shame *(with Pam Sawyer, R Dean Taylor, Frank Wilson, Berry Gordy Jr)* Diana
    Ross & the Supremes (US 1969 # 10; UK # 14)
My Cherie Amour *(with Stevie Wonder & Sylvia Moy)* Stevie Wonder (US 1969 # 4; UK #4)
No Matter What Sign You Are *(with Berry Gordy Jr)* Diana Ross & the Supremes (US 1969 # 31;
    UK # 37)

Phil Coulter see Bill Martin and Phil Coulter

Don Covay

Born Donald James Randolph, Orangeburg, South Carolina 1936. Died 2015.

Covay's family moved to Washington DC in the early Fifties. After being s member of a family gospel quartet, he recorded more secular music with the Rainbows, and in 1957 commenced a solo career with the Little Richard revue, performing as his opening act and also serving as his chauffer. Richard produced an unsuccessful single "Bip Bop Bip" for him, but credited it to "Pretty Boy." After working for a number of labels, Covay eventually signed a deal with Columbia Records who released his first single "Pony Time," with his band the Goodtimers, a song he had co-written with Rainbows' member John Berry. It would become a US number one when recorded by Chubby Checker in 1961. The following year, he was working in New York's Brill Building writing songs for Roosevelt Music, including hits for Solomon King, Gladys Knight & the Pips and Wilson Pickett. Two years later, he wrote and performed "Mercy, Mercy" with Goodtimers' guitarist Ronnie Miller for Atlantic's Rosemart label. With a young Jimi Hendrix playing on the session, it highlighted Covay's bluesy style and scored a top forty hit (and was later covered by the Rolling Stones). While working for Stax Records, he found the relationship with the label's staff difficult, although his songwriting continued.

When asked by Atlantic boss Jerry Wexler to write a song for Otis Redding, he gave a demo of "Chain of Fools," which had been written in his youth. Instead of Redding, Wexler gave the song to Aretha Franklin, which gave her both a massive hit and a Grammy award. In 1968, Covay formed the unsuccessful Soul Clan with Joe Tex, Ben E King, Solomon Burke and Arthur Conley.

Chart entries
I Just Go For You – Jimmy Jones (UK 1960 # 35)
Letter Full of Tears – Glady Knight & the Pips (US 1961 # 19); Billy Fury (UK 1962 # 32)
You Can Run (But You Can't Hide) *(with Paul Griffin)* Jerry Butler (US 1962 # 63)
You Threw A Lucky Punch *(with Smokey Robinson, Ronnie White)* Gene Chandler (US
    1962 # 49)
Crossfire Time *(with Horace Ott)* Dee Clark (US 1963 # 92)
You're Good For Me *(with Horace Ott)* Solomon Burke (US 1963 # 49)
Long Tall Shorty *(with Herb Abramson)* Tommy Tucker (US 1964 # 96)
Mercy, Mercy *(with Ronald Miller)* Don Covay & the Goodtimers (US 1964 # 35)
Take This Hurt Off Me *(with Ronald Miller)* Don Covay (US 1964 # 97)
Tonight's the Night *(with Solomon Burke)* Solomon Burke (US 1965 # 28)
See-Saw *(with Steve Cropper)* (US 1956 # 44); Aretha Franklin (US 1968 # 14)
I Don't Know What You've Got But It's Got Me – Little Richard (US 1965 # 92)
Chain of Fools – Aretha Franklin (US 1967 # 2; UK # 37); Jimmy Smith (US 1968 # 100)
Soul Meeting – The Soul Clan (US 1968 # 91)

Don Covay with John Berry
Pony Time - Chubby Checker (US 1961 # 1; UK # 27)
The Continental Walk - The Midnighters (US 1961 # 33); The Rollers (US 1961 # 80)
I'm Hanging Up My Heart For You - Solomon Burke (US 1962 # 85)
Hey Lover - Debbie Dovale (US 1963 # 81)

Bob Crewe and Bob Gaudio
Born Robert Stanley Crewe, Newark, New Jersey 1930. Died 2014.
Born Robert John Gaudio, New York City 1942.
Rock and Roll Hall of Fame 1990 (Gaudio with The Four Seasons).
Songwriters Hall of Fame 1995.

Lacking formal music training, Crewe had attended New York's Parsons School of Design with an ambition to become an architect, but in 1953, with his affinity for romantic composers of the past and for jazz and swing music, he teamed up with young Texan pianist Frank Slay Jr (1930-2017) to write songs for their small record label XYZ. Their 1957 session with doo-wop band the Rays produced the US hit "Silhouettes," whose story-driven lyrics saw it peak at number three on the US charts (and a UK hit for Herman's Hermits in 1965). The flip side to the Rays' single was "Daddy Cool" (a 1974 hit for British band Darts). Signing with Swan Records, the pair wrote two top ten hits for rising star Freddy Cannon, including "Tallahassee Lassie," and also released two solo albums before Crewe teamed up with Bob Gaudio.

Bronx-born Gaudio studied piano as a youngster and later joined the Royal Teens as their keyboardist, also co-writing with them their popular hit song "Short Shorts." While promoting the single, Crewe and Gaudio met Franke Valli and his band the Four Lovers. When Gaudio agreed with Valli to join with Tommy DeVito and Nick Massi as keyboardist, they became the Four Seasons. In July 1962, Gaudio wrote the gimmick-laden "Sherry." Produced by Crewe, it highlighted Valli's stunning falsetto end of his three-octave tenor range and topped the US charts. They went on to write three more chart-toppers for the band with "Big Girls Don't Cry," "Walk Like a Man," and "Rag Doll," the latter inspired by Gaudio having encountered a girl dressed in rags, wiping the window of his car while stopped at lights.

Two more songs became UK chart-toppers, beginning with the epic ballad "The Sun Ain't Gonna Shine (Anymore)" for the Walker Brothers in 1966. Recorded by the Four Seasons, it was originally released as a solo single for Valli in 1965, but achieved only limited success, not making the Hot 100 at all. This was followed by "Silence Is Golden." Although thrown away as a b-side to "Rag Doll," it was later covered in similar fashion by the Tremeloes the following year and produced by Mike Smith and with guitarist Rick Westwood on lead vocal. Crewe also co-wrote the hit "Lets Hang On!" with Sandy Linzer and Denny Randell, noted for its two-line introduction by Valli and the use of fuzz guitars. In 1965, Crewe also launched his own record label DynoVoice, best known for recording "A Lover's Concerto" a huge hit for the R&B all-girl trio the Toys, with music inspired by the 18th century composition "Minuet in G Major" by Christian Petzold.

Crewe and Gaudio also gave Valli solo hits with "The Proud One" and the much-covered classic "Can't Take My Eyes Of You," which was also a hit the following year for crooner Andy Williams, for whom Crewe also produced the hit single "Music to Watch Girls By." As well as producing and writing album tracks for Lesley Gore, Crewe recorded and co-wrote with Charles Fox the original soundtrack to the 1968 movie *Barbarella,* as well as producing the single "Good Morning Starshine" for Oliver the following year.

Chart entries
Big Girls Don't Cry – The Four Seasons (US 1962 # 1; UK # 13)
Walk Like A Man – The Four Seasons (US 1963 # 1; UK # 12)
Don't Mention My Name – The Shepherd Sisters (US 1963 # 94)
Whatever You Want - Jerry Butler (US 1963 # 68)
Ronnie – The Four Seasons (US 1964 # 6)
Rag Doll – The Four Seasons (US 1964 # 1; UK # 2)
Save It For Me – The Four Seasons (US 1964 # 10)
Bye Bye Baby (Baby Goodbye) – The Four Seasons (US 1965 # 12); The Symbols (UK 1967 # 44)
Toy Soldier – The Four Seasons (US 1965 # 64)
Girl Come Running – The Four Seasons (US 1965 # 30)
The Sun Ain't Gonna Shine (Anymore) – The Walker Brothers (US 1966 # 13; UK # 1)
The Proud One - Frankie Valli (US 1966 # 68)
Silence Is Golden – The Tremeloes (UK 1967 # 1; US # 11)
Can't Take My Eyes Off You - Frankie Valli (US 1967 # 2); The Lettermen (US 1967 # 7); Andy
    Williams (UK1968 # 5); Nancy Wilson (US 1969 # 52)
I Make A Fool of Myself - Franke Valli (US 1967 # 18)
To Give (The Reason I Live) - Frankie Valli (US 1967 # 29)

Bob Crewe and Frank Slay
Mediterranean Moon – The Rays (US 1960 # 95)
Jump Over – Freddy Cannon (US 1960 # 28)
The Urge – Freddy Cannon (US 1960 # 60; UK # 18)
Happy Shades of Blue – Freddy Cannon (US 1960 # 83)
Humdinger – Freddy Cannon (US 1960 # 59)
Pony Express – Danny & the Juniors (US 1961 # 60)
Buzz Buzz A-Diddle-It – Freddy Cannon (US 1961 # 51)
Magic Moon – The Rays (US 1961# 49)
Twistin' All Night Long – Danny & the Juniors (US 1962 # 68)
Teen Queen of the Week – Freddy Cannon (US 1962 # 92)
Silhouettes - Herman's Hermits (UK 1965 # 3; US # 5)

Bob Crewe with others
My Time For Crying (*with Saul Bass*) Maxine Brown (US 1962 # 98)
New Mexican Rose (*with Charles Calello*) The Four Seasons (US 1963 # 36)
Navy Blue (*with Bud Rehak & Eddie Rambeau*) Diane Renay (US 1964 # 6)
Across the Street (*with Charlie Calello & Valmond Harris*) Lenny O'Henry (US 1964 # 98)

Knock! Knock! (Who's There) (*with Larry Santos*) The Orlons (US 1964 # 64)
Society Girl (*with Sandy Linzer, Denny Randell*) The Rag Dolls (US 1964 # 91)
Dusty (*with Sandy Linzer, Denny Randell)* The Rag Dolls (US 1965 # 55)
Let's Hang On! *(with Sandy Linzer, Denny Randell)* The Four Seasons (US 1965 # 3; UK # 4); The Bandwagon (UK 1969 # 36)
Jenny Take A Ride! (*with Enotris Johnson, Richard Penniman*) Mitch Ryder & the Detroit Wheels (US 1965 # 10; UK # 33)
(You're Gonna) Hurt Yourself (*with Charles Calello*) Frankie Valli (US 1966 # 39)
Takin' All I Can Get (*with Gary Knight*) Mitch Ryder & the Detroit Wheels (US 1966 # 100)
Sock It To Me Baby*! (with L Russell Brown)* Mitch Ryder & the Detroit Wheels) (US 1967 # 6)
Summer and Sandy (*with L Russell Brown & Raymond Bloodworth*) Leslie Gore (US 1967 # 65)
More Than the Eye Can See (*with Larry Weiss*) Al Martino (US 1967 # 54)
Birds of Britain (*with Hutch Davie*) The Bob Crewe Generation (US 1967 # 89)
Eternity (*with Charles Fox*) Vikki Carr (US 1969 # 79)

Bob Gaudio
Sherry – The Four Seasons (US 1962 # 1; UK # 8)
Marlena – The Four Seasons (US 1963 # 36)
Dawn (Go Away) *(with Sandy Linzer)* The Four Seasons (US 1964 # 3)
Be My Girl – The Four-Evers (US 1964 # 75)
Big Man In Town – The Four Seasons (US 1964 # 20)
Beggin' (*with Peggy Farina*) The Four Seasons (US 1967 # 16); Timebox (UK 1968 # 38)
Something's On Her Mind (*with Jake Holmes*) The Four Seasons (US 19689 # 98)

Steve Cropper see Booker T Jones

David Crosby see also Roger McGuinn, Stephen Stills.
Born David Van Cortland Crosby, Los Angeles 1941. Died 2023.
Rock and Roll Hall of Fame 1991 (with the Byrds), 1997 (CSN).
Songwriters Hall of Fame 2009.

The son of Oscar-winning cinematographer Floyd Crosby, his older brother Ethan was already a musician and he helped inspire David's early love for jazz music. He attended several schools in California, including Laguna Blanca School in Santa Barbara, and after opting out managed to finish high school via a correspondence course. He began his music career by performing with singer Terry Callier in Chicago and around New York's Greenwich Village, but they were unable to secure a recording contract. After recording his first solo session with the help of producer Jim Dickson, Crosby joined Les Baxter's Balladeers in 1964. At the time, Miriam Makeba was touring with her band, that included Roger McGuinn, and it was his friend Callier who introduced him to McGuinn and Clark who at the time were performing as the Jet Set. Crosby was invited to join the group, which also included drummer Michael Clarke and later bassist Chris Hillman. They would soon become better known as the Byrds.

With the huge success of their cover of Dylan's "Mr Tambourine Man," which featured the wonderful close harmonies of McGuinn, Crosby and Clark, with Crosby chiefly responsible for the soaring harmonies and sometimes unusual phrasing of their songs. Crosby even got to sing lead vocal on the bridge for their second Dylan cover, "All I Really Wanna Do." When Clark left the group in 1966, it gave Crosby the chance to hone his songwriting skills and he collaborated with McGuinn on "I See You," while also penning "What's Happening?" both from their album *Fifth Dimension*. The following album *Younger Than Yesterday* included two Crosby songs, "Everybody's Been Burned" (originally demoed in 1963) and "Mind Gardens."

In early 1967 Crosby wrote "Lady Friend," and oversaw its production, causing issues with the other band members, even more so when Crosby replaced their backing vocals by overdubbing his own. With insufficient airplay and lack of media exposure, the single was a commercial failure.

Tensions between Crosby and the other band members reached breaking point following his diatribes at the Monterey Pop Festival and also when invited by Buffalo Springfield's Stephen Stills to sit in for the departed Neil Young for their set the following evening. There were also rumours that Crosby had been involved with Stills in the writing of Buffalo Springfield's single "Rock & Roll Woman."

In October 1967, McGuinn and Hillman finally asked him to leave the band after he refused to allow them to record a cover of Goffin and King's "Goin' Back" (which they did, anyway). In July 1968 Crosby joined Stills and ex-Hollies Grahan Nash to form Crosby, Stills and Nash. Signing with Atlantic in early 1969, they released their eponymous debut album which included Crosby's beautiful "Guinnevere," a song about three women he had loved (including Joni Mitchell) and "Wooden Ships," the latter co-written with Stills and Jefferson Airplane's Paul Kantner.

Chart entries
Eight Miles High *(with Gene Clark, Jim McGuinn)* The Byrds (US 1966 # 14; UK # 24)
Lady Friend – The Byrds (US 1967 # 82; UK # 55)

Bobby Darin
Born Walden Robert Cassotto, New York 1936. Died 1973.
Songwriters Hall of Fame 1999.

Born to a mother who was only 18, Darin was raised by his maternal grandmother. After graduating from Bronx High School of Science, he enrolled at Hunter College where he soon gravitated to the drama department with ambitions to become an actor and a recording artist. As a young teenager, he could play piano, guitar and drums, and adopted the stage name Bobby Darin for recording. In 1955, he formed a songwriting partnership with Don Kirshner (1934-2011) after running into him at a candy store. Working at New York's Brill Building, they wrote songs and jingles, and the following year Darin's agent secured a recording contract with Decca.

Darin was introduced to singer Connie Francis, and together they wrote several songs, although a romantic relationship was short-lived. Leaving Decca, he then signed with Atco, a subsidiary of Atlantic, and with the help of label head Ahmet Ertegun his career took off. The million-selling single "Splish Splash" was written in an hour with radio deejay Murray Kaufman. The following year, Darin recorded the self-penned ballad "Dream Lover," a UK chart-topper, and then gave "Mack the Knife" his signature jazz-pop interpretation to take it to the top of the charts for nine weeks. "Beyond the Sea" came next, with Darin giving the original French song "La Mer" another jazz version. In December 1960, he married actress Sandra Dee after first meeting her on the set of the movie *Come September*.

In 1962, Darin, while still appearing in movies, turned his hand to writing and performing country music. The hit song "Things" was his last recording for Atco before moving to Capitol and having success with "You're the Reason I'm Living" and "18 Yellow Roses." Returning to Atlantic, he had his final UK hit with a cover of Tim Hardin's "If I Were a Carpenter" in 1966.

Chart entries
I'll Be There – Bobby Darin (US 1960 # 79); Gerry & the Pacemakers (US 1964 # 14; UK 15)
Beachcomber – Bobby Darin (US 1060 # 100)
Somebody to Love – Bobby Darin (US 1960 # 45)
Wait a Minute *(with Don Kirshner)* Bobby Darin (US 1961 # 37)
Theme From Come September – Bobby Darin (UK 1961 # 50); Billy Vaughn (US 1961 # 73)
Multiplication – Bobby Darin (US 1961 # 30; UK # 5)
Things – Bobby Darin (US 1962 # 3; UK # 2)
If a Man Answers – Bobby Darin* (US 1962 # 32; UK # 24) *credited as Walden Cassotto
You're the Reason I'm Living – Bobby Darin (US 1963 # 3)
18 Yellow Roses – Bobby Darin (US 1963 # 10; UK # 37)
Do the Monkey *(with Rudy Clark)* Bobby Darin (US 1963 # 92)
Treat My Baby Good – Bobby Darin (US 1963 # 43)
Shirt Girl *(with Rudy Clark)* Wayne Newton (US 1963 # 58)
Be Mad Little Girl – Bobby Darin (US 1963 # 64)
Jailor, Bring Me Water – Trini Lopez (US 1964 # 94)
Dream Lover – Paris Sisters (US 1964 # 91)
The Things In This House – Bobby Darin (US 1964 # 86)
When I Get Home *(with Russell Alquist)* The Searchers (UK 1965 # 35)
Long Line Rider – Bobby Darin (US 1969 # 79)
Simple Song of Freedom – Tom Hardin (US 1969 # 50)

Ray Davies
Born Raymond Douglas Davies, London 1944.
Rock and Roll Hall of Fame 1990 (with the Kinks).

Songwriters Hall of Fame 2014.

Davies was born one of eight children, including six sisters and a younger brother (future Kinks' guitarist David (born 1947). Weaned on the music of Chuck Berry and Muddy Waters, he was given a guitar by his sister Renee on his 13th birthday, and along with Dave went to the same school as future star Rod Stewart. While there, they formed a band with classmates Pete Quaife (on bass) and John Start (drums) and called themselves the Ray Davis Quartet. Stewart also performed with them one time in 1962 before forming his own band, the Moonrakers. Leaving school at 16 to work in an architect's office, Davies enrolled at Hornsey College of Art to study film, theatre and music (especially blues and jazz). While there, he met Alexis Korner of Blues Incorporated, who through a promoter got Davies to play lead guitar for Dave Hunt's blues combo, while still continuing to play for the quartet, the name of which was soon changed to the Ravens.

Attracting the attention of music publisher Robert Wace and pop impresario Larry Page, the quartet were asked to do a demo tape, with Wace's suggestion that they change their name to the Kinks. In early 1964, after enrolling Mick Avory as drummer, they signed a deal with Pye Records. For their third single, Page suggested that Davies write a song in the style of the Kingsmen's recent hit "Louie Louie." The song "You Really Got Me" was created on the piano in the front room of Davies' home, its jazz-orientated style very different from the finished product. According to Davies, it was inspired while performing during his college days. Seeing an attractive girl on the dance floor, she left before getting the chance to meet her, and how she had "really got me going." Produced by manager Shel Talmy, the single topped the UK charts in August 1964. With Davies' insistent guitar riff and suggestive lyrics he later described as "a love song for street kids," it was a foretaste of what was to follow.

Securing a five-year deal with Reprise, a string of hits followed, including "All Day and All of the Night" with a similar guitar riff, although years later it would spark controversy when the Doors' 1968 "Hello I Love You" showed similarities in the musical structure. The more introspective chart-topper "Tired of Waiting For You" had its music written while travelling on the London underground and the lyrics done at a coffee shop during a break in the recording. Davis recalled: "If after two weeks you still can't write your middle-eight, the best course of action is to see a psychiatrist."

A later hit, "See My Friends," was about the loss of his sister, Renee, who after living for a time in Canada, had returned home. Becoming seriously ill, she later died while dancing in a nightclub. It was just before her death in 1957 that she had bought Ray his first guitar. According to Davies, the inspiration to write it came from being jetlagged on a beach in Bombay and watching two fishermen chanting on their way to work. "Till the End of the Day" was written after being pressured by his managers to write a hit, even going as far as them having songwriting guru Doc Pomus pay him a visit at his home. According to Davies, it was about having the freedom to escape from something.

By this time, Davies' lyrics had also assumed a more sociological character, particularly the psychological effects the British class system was having on ordinary working people. "A Well Respected Man" signalled a move for the band from raucous rock to satirical views on the hypocrisy and superficiality of the British upper middle class, with Davies finding inspiration from old-time music hall and holiday encounters with rich tourists.

With fashion in the UK becoming more daring and outrageous with some trying to avoid looking out of step, Davies came up with the eccentric "Dedicated Follower of Fashion," an almost solo performance and apparently inspired by a fight he had at a party with a fashion designer, with lyrics later typed out in just one sitting. The chart-topping "Sunny Afternoon" referenced the high tax levels set by Harold Wilson's Labour government as seen by an unsympathetic aristocrat lamenting the loss of his enormous unearned fortune (despite the fact that Davies himself was now a wealthy man). Like many of their songs, the anguished "Dead End Street" dealt with misery and poverty, with lyrics about a couple denied passage to Australia during the migration scheme and then being unable to find work.

The melody for 1967's "Waterloo Sunset," arguably their most famous song, had been in Davies' head for several years and initially called "Liverpool Street" until scrapped after the Beatles released "Penny Lane." According to Davies, the choice of location came from boyhood memories of being ill in London's St Thomas' Hospital and being wheeled out on to a balcony that overlooked the Thames and Waterloo railway station. There were also memories of walking by the river with his first wife and sharing their dreams and aspirations. The names of the two characters Terry and Julie were assumed to have been borrowed from the popular British actors Terence Stamp and Julie Christie, who allegedly were romantically linked at the time (although later being refuted by the writer). The song was also noted for the use of a tape-delay echo to get a different guitar sound. The follow-up single "Autumn Almanac" has been described as "a finely observed slice of English custom" and according to the writer was inspired by a local hunch-backed gardener, a drinking friend of his father, who lived close by the family home.

Meanwhile, group co-founder Dave Davies enjoyed the limelight of having two solo singles. The idea for "Death of a Clown," co-written with Ray, came from having to deal with their repetitive touring schedule, and having to perform day after day like circus clowns. With his self-penned follow-up "Susannah's Still Alive," although not as successful, he described a woman consumed by memories of a former lover, and inspired by his first love, Sue Sheenan, who had become pregnant when he was just 16 and then sent away by her parents.

Beginning in 1968, the band cut back on touring to concentrate on studio work, but further singles only had moderate chart success. The album *The Kinks Are the Village Green Preservation Society,* with its vignettes of English village life, was a collection of songs written over the previous two years, but although the lack of a single contributed to moderate sales, it was well-received by critics. As a result, "Days" was rushed out as a single, and seen to be signalling a nostalgic goodbye to his music career. Davies later claimed it was about losing touch with his sister Rosie after she moved to Australia.

In the summer of 1970, the Kinks released their last great single, the controversial "Lola," about a man who falls in love with a transvestite in a club, and inspired after Davies, who wrote the lyrics after his manager had allegedly got drunk at a club and danced with someone whom he took to be a woman.

Chart entries
For the Kinks
You Really Got Me (UK 1964 # 1; US # 7)
All Day And All Of the Night (UK 1964 # 2; US # 7)
Tired Of Waiting For You (UK 1965 # 1; US # 6)
Ev'rybody's Gonna Be Happy (UK 1965 # 17)
Set Me Free (UK 1965 # 9; US # 23)
See My Friends (UK 1965 # 10)
Who'll Be the Next In Line (US 1965 # 34)
A Well Respected Man (US 1965 # 13)
Till the End Of the Day (UK 1965 # 8; US # 50)
Dedicated Follower Of Fashion (UK 1966 # 4; US # 36)
Sunny Afternoon (UK 1966 # 1; US # 14)
Dead End Street (UK 1966 # 5; US # 73)
Waterloo Sunset (UK 1967 # 2)
Mister Pleasant (US 1967 # 80)
Autumn Almanac (UK 1967 # 3)
Wonderboy (UK 1968 # 36)
Days (UK 1968 # 12)
Plastic Man (UK 1969 # 31)
Victoria (UK 1969 # 33)

For other artists
Something Better Beginning – The Honeycombs (UK 1965 # 39)
This Strange Effect – Dave Berry (UK 1965 # 37)
A House In the Country – The Pretty Things (UK 1966 # 50)
Dandy – Herman's Hermits (US 1966 # 5)

Dave Davies
Death Of A Clown *(with Ray Davies)* – Dave Davies (UK 1967 # 3)
Susannah's Still Alive – Dave Davies (UK 1967 # 20)

Billy Davis see Raynard Miner

Mac Davis
Born Morris Mac Davis, Lubbock, Texas 1942. Died 2020.
Nashville Songwriters Hall of Fame 2000.
Songwriters Hall of Fame 2006.

Graduating from high school, Davis moved to live with his mother in Atlanta, who had divorced and remarried. Inspired by the success of Lubbock's most famous son, Buddy Holly, whom he recalled seeing driving through town in a brand new black and pink Pontiac convertible, he also craved a career in music. In Atlanta, he formed a band called the Zots and released two singles for Oscar Kilgo's OEK Records. Following a stint as regional manager for Liberty Records, he began working for Nancy Sinatra's company, Boots Inc., which also served as his publishing company. While playing guitar on some of Sinatra's recordings and guesting on her stage shows, he also began to write songs.

The heartbreaking "In the Ghetto," came from a memory of childhood days, when he couldn't understand why one of his best friends lived in a deprived and crime-ridden part of town. In an interview for the *Tennessean*, he recalled: "I'd always wanted to write a song about it, where a kid is born, he doesn't have a male parent, and falls into the wrong people and dies just as another kid comes along and replaces him. It's just a vicious circle…" Presley was at first hesitant to do it after his manager had warned him that songs with a message could offend some people. Nevertheless, it was recorded during the same session as "Suspicious Minds" and "Don't Cry Daddy" (another Davis song) and it shot to number three on the US charts in 1969.

Davis also co-wrote "Memories," with ex-Wrecking Crew member Billy Strange, which was recorded by a number of artists, including Presley and Nancy Sinatra. For a short period of time he had used the pseudonym Scott Davis to avoid confusion with fellow songwriter Mack David. In 1970, he signed with Columbia and had further success with "Something's Burning" for Kenny Rodgers and his own recording of the Grammy-nominated "Baby Don't Get Hooked On Me," which topped the US chart in 1972.

Chart entries
God Knows I Love You *(with Delaney Bramlett)* – Nancy Sinatra (US 1969 # 97)
In the Ghetto - Elvis Presley (US 1969 # 3; UK # 2)
Friend, Lover, Woman, Wife – O C Smith (US 1969 # 47)
Daddy's Little Man – O C Smith (US 1969 # 34)

Mac Davis and Billy Strange
A Little Less Conversation - Elvis Presley (US 1968 # 95)
Memories - Elvis Presley (US 1969 # 35)
Clean Up Your Own Backyard - Elvis Presley (US 1969 # 35; UK # 21)

Billy Strange
Limbo Rock (*with John Sheldon*) – Chubby Checker (US 1962 # 2; UK # 32)

James Dean see **William Weatherspoon and James Dean**

Desmond Dekker
Born Desmond Adolphus Dacres, St Thomas Township, Jamaica 1941. Died 2006.

Dekker was orphaned at an early age, but his religious upbringing and a love of singing hymns encouraged him to pursue a career in music. After working as a welder in Kingston, he finally secured a record deal, although it was two years before anything was released. Dekker also spotted the music talents of a young fellow welder called Bob Marley and managed to get him noticed by his label boss. Meanwhile, Dekker's own "Honour Your Mother and Father" became the first of a handful of singles to chart in his country under his new stage name." Desmond Dekker, and was picked up by Island Records's Chris Blackwell for a UK release. Following his fourth single "King Of Spa" in 1965, he brought in four brothers to form the Aces. Although his songs celebrated Kingston's "rude boy" lifestyle, they never went to the extremes of other artists who focused on the violence and social problems of ghetto life.

Now looked on as a rude boy icon, his "007 (Shanty Town)" topped the Jamaican chart in 1967 and became an underground club hit for UK mods, as well as scoring a top twenty chart place. The following year he released "Israelites," the first reggae song to top the UK charts, and originally issued in Jamaica as "Poor Me Israelites." Dekker recalled: "I was walking in the park, eating popcorn. I heard a couple arguing about money. She was saying she needs money and he was saying the work he was doing was not giving him enough." More hits followed with the self-penned "It Mek" and 1970's cover of Jimmy Cliff's "You Can Get It If You Really Want," written for the movie *The Harder They Come*.

Chart entries
007 (Shanty Town) – Desmond Dekker & the Aces (UK 1967 # 14)
Israelites - Desmond Dekker & the Aces (UK 1969 # 1; US # 9)
It Mek - Desmond Dekker & the Aces (UK 1969 # 7)

John Densmore see **Jim Morrison**

Jackie DeShannon
Born Sharon Lee Myers, Hazel, Kentucky 1941.
Songwriters Hall of Fame 2010.

DeShannon has been credited for being one of the first female singer-songwriters of the rock & roll era. Growing up on a farm, she was introduced to different music styles, and by the age of six was singing country songs on the local radio before hosting her own radio show five years later. After moving with parents to Illinois, she continued with her radio work, and her vocal talents led to an appearance on Pee Wee King's country and western tv show, billed as Sherry Lee Myers. After leaving school, she was signed by New York's Gone label as a rockabilly singer with the new name of Jackie Dee. After one unsuccessful release, she caught the attention of star Eddie Cochran, who invited her to go with him to Los Angeles and meet up with his songwriting girlfriend Sharon Sheeley (1940-2002). Sheeley had already made a name for herself writing "Poor Little Fool" for Ricky Nelson and co-writing "Something Else" with Cochran, her boyfriend at the time.

In 1960, Jackie signed with Liberty Records under the new name Jackie Dee Shannon (which when mistakenly heard as DeShannon was changed to suit). Writing with Sheeley, they gave Brenda Lee two top ten singles with "Dum Dum" in 1961 and "Heart in Hand" the following year, but her solo recordings of "Faded Love" and the Bono-Nitzsche "Needles and Pins," (for which she would later claim co-writing credit) were only minor hits. Her popularity as a singer faded, perhaps due to her deep vocal and varied choice of music styles, as well as her public profile (she dated Elvis Presley for a time) overshadowing her recording career. However, one of her finest compositions, the poignant "When You Walk In the Room," topped the Canadian charts in 1963. With one of the most recognisable riffs of the Sixties, it was originally written and released as the b-side to "Till You Say You'll Be Mine" on November 23rd 1963, the day after President Kennedy was assassinated, but was later re-released as an a-side, although only scraping into the Hot 100. When later picked up in the UK by the Searchers, it scored a top three hit, as well as climbing to number 35 on the Hot 100. The story of an unrequited love was written when DeShannon was getting ready to go out on a date. In an interview for *Uncut*, she recalled: "It just popped out, along with the word nonchalant. What can I say. I was excited about the date! Those songs are very rare, that come together so quickly. It didn't stand out as special at that point. I was writing a lot, all day, every day."

DeShannon also attracted a growing interest during a stay in the UK, including writing songs with future Led Zeppelin guitarist Jimmy Page, with whom she had a brief relationship. While there, she also provided Marianne Faithful with her biggest hit "Come and Stay With Me," and her work continued to be covered by Helen Shapiro, the Byrds, and the Critters. Meanwhile, "Breakaway," co-written with Sheeley, was recorded by Irma Thomas and used as the b-side to her hit "Wish Someone Would Care,"(and providing Tracy Ullman a hit with her debut single in 1983). Moving to New York in the mid-Sixties, DeShannon achieved a top ten US hit with the Bacharach-David song "What the World Needs Now is Love," and in 1969 recorded "Put a Little Love in Your Heart," her highest-charting US single, which she had co-written with her brother Randy Myers and Jimmy Holiday. On the subject of writing, DeShannon said: "There are many things that influence music and songwriting. It depends upon what things are going on in your life at the time you write the song."

Before marrying singer-songwriter and film composer Randy Edelman in 1976, she recorded "Bette Davis Eyes," originally co-written as a country song with Donna Weiss, but later a huge US chart-topper for Kim Carnes in 1981. Although her recordings failed to reach great heights, she remains one of the Sixties' leading pop composers. Esteemed music writer Dave Marsh saw the irony: "If [she] had grown up a decade later, she'd had been acknowledged as one of the best singer-songwriters. If she'd grown up in New York, rather than Kentucky, she might have been a celebrated Brill Building craftsman like Carole King and Ellie Greenwich; if she'd stuck around Nashville … she'd probably have … a swimming pool shaped like a piano."

Chart entries
Alone With You - Brenda Lee (US 1964 # 48)
When You Walk In the Room (US 1964 # 99); The Searchers (UK 1964 # 3; US # 35)
Come And Stay With Me – Marianne Faithful (UK 1965 # 4)
Put A Little Love In Your Heart (*with Jimmy Holiday & Randy Myers*) (US 1968 # 4); The Dave
   Clark Five (UK 1969 # 31)
Love Will Find A Way (*with Jimmy Holiday & Randy Myers*) (US 1969 # 40)

Jackie DeShannon and Sharon Sheeley
Dum Dum - Brenda Lee (US 1961 # 4; UK # 22)
(He's) The Greatest Imposter – The Fleetwoods (US 1961 # 30)
Tears From An Angel – Troy Shondell (US 1961 # 77)
Heart In Hand - Brenda Lee (US 1962 # 15)
Woe Is Me - Helen Shapiro (UK 1963 # 35)

Sharon Sheeley
Lonely – Eddie Cochran (UK 1960 # 41)

Neil Diamond

Born Neil Leslie Diamond, New York City 1941.
Songwriters Hall of Fame 1984.
Rock and Roll Hall of Fame 2011.

While being a member of a Brooklyn school choral society, Diamond began writing poems for the girls he liked, and judged by their reaction was spurred on to write for other classmates. After graduation, he received a guitar for his 16th birthday, and it was while attending a winter camp and watching celebrated folk singer Pete Seeger perform, he was inspired to writing his own songs. While at New York University on a pre-med major and on a fencing scholarship, he dropped out to spend time going to Tin Pan Alley to get some of his songs heard by local publishers, and eventually signed a 16-week contract with Sunbeam Music to write songs for $50 a week. Afterward, he teamed up with friend Jack Parker as Ned & Jack to form an Everly Brothers'- style duo and cut two unsuccessful songs for Duel Records.

In late 1962, Diamond signed with Columbia and the one-off single "Clown Town," although not a hit, was lauded by *Billboard* and *Cashbox*. Although later dropped by the label, he continued to write for a number of other publishers. In 1965, while performing in a Greenwich Village coffee house, he was noticed by songwriting duo Jeff Barry and Ellie Greenwich, who then added him to their own writing and publishing company. The following year, they arranged an audition with Bert Berns' Bang label, who signed him with Barry and Greenwich as his producers. He scored his first hit with "Solitary Man" (inspired by the Beatles' "Michelle"), while "Cherry, Cherry" had originally been written as "Money, Money," until Barry and Berns convinced him to make it lighter and more teen-friendly. "Kentucky Woman" was written while on the Dick Clark Caravan tour across the country, and although he liked the song, he wanted the label to release the more personal "Shilo" as his next single. Berns felt otherwise and released it against his wishes. It would cause a rift that led to him leaving the label a year later. "Shilo" is now considered one of his best songs up to that time.

The success of "Cherry, Cherry" grabbed the attention of Don Kirshner, who was looking for material for the forthcoming tv show *The Monkees*. Diamond wrote "I'm a Believer," which became a chart-topper on both sides of the Atlantic when recorded by the Monkees. As part of the deal, Diamond was allowed to record it as well, and it appeared on his album *Just For You*. After two singles and two albums, the Monkees frustration grew with Kirshner's ban on them disclosing the fact they never played on the recordings. Kirshner made a deal that in future they would have greater control over their own music and recordings would be split 50-50. It began with Diamond's "A Little Bit Me, a Little Bit You" as the next a-side, with the Monkees playing their own instruments, and with Mike Nesmith's "The Girl I Knew Somewhere" as the b-side (with Mickey Dolenz's lead vocal). Without telling anyone, Kirshner tried to release "A Little Bit You, A Little Bit Me" as a Canadian single with another of his recent productions on the b-side. The group were outraged with the deal being broken, and as result Kirshner was fired by Colgems.

The same year, Diamond had another top ten success with the seductive "Girl, You'll Be a Woman Soon," which solidified his growing connection with his female fan base. He also wrote "The Boat That I Row," a top ten UK hit for Lulu. In 1968, he left Bang and moved to Los Angeles to sign with MCA. The following year brought him two million-selling singles. The anthemic "Sweet Caroline" was written about his second wife, Marcia Murphey, whom he married in 1969. He needed a three-syllable name to fit the melody, so he chose Caroline, after Caroline Kennedy, daughter of the late President. The other song was the gospel-influenced "Holly Holy," which was also a top ten hit.

The Seventies would see Diamond reach superstar status as singer-songwriter, with a string of legendary concerts, movie roles, and singles like "Crackin' Rosie," "I Am…I Said," and "Beautiful Noise."

Chart entries
Sunday And Me – Jay & the Americans (US 1965 # 18)
Solitary Man – Neil Diamond (US 1966 # 55)
Cherry, Cherry – Neil Diamond (US 1966 # 6)
I Got the Feelin' (Oh No No) – Neil Diamond (US 1966 # 16)
I'm a Believer – The Monkees (US 1967 # 1; UK #1)
You Got To Me – Neil Diamond (US 1967 # 18)
A Little Bit Me, A Little Bit You – The Monkees (US 1967 # 2; UK # 3)
Girl, You'll Be A Woman Soon – Neil Diamond (US 1967 # 10)
The Boat That I Row – Lulu (UK 1967 # 6)
My Babe – Ronnie Dove (US 1967 # 50)
I'll Come Running – Cliff Richard (UK 1967 # 26)
Thank the Lord For the Night Time – Neil Diamond (US 1967 # 13)
Kentucky Woman – Neil Diamond (US 1967 # 22); Deep Purple (US 1968 # 38)
Red, Red Wine – Neil Diamond (US 1968 # 62); Jimmy James & the Vagabonds (UK 1968 # 36)

Brooklyn Roads – Neil Diamond (US1968 # 58)
Two-Bit Manchild - Neil Diamond (US 1968 # 66)
Sunday Sun - Neil Diamond (US 1968 # 68)
Brother Love's Travelling Salvation Show – Neil Diamond (US 1969 # 22)
Sweet Caroline (Good Times Never Seemed So Good) Neil Diamond (US 1969 # 4)
Holly Holy – Neil Diamond (US 1969 # 6)

Neil Diamond with others
Ten Lonely Guys (with *Edward Snyder, Cliff Adams, Lockie Edwards, Richard Gottehrer, Jerry Goldstein, Lawrence Weiss, Wes Farrell, Bob Feldman, Stankey Kahan*) – Pat Boone (US 1962 # 45)

Donovan
Born Donovan Phillips Leitch, Glasgow 1946.
Rock and Roll Hall of Fame 2012.
Songwriters Hall of Fame 2014.

Glasgow-born Donovan later moved to Hatfield, England, where his parents' love for folk music encouraged them to buy him a guitar at the age of 14. Dropping out of art school and finding that he did not fit in with the folk establishment, he adopted a beatnik lifestyle, travelling the country busking and playing in folk clubs, waiting tables in cafes, and all the time learning guitar skills. In late 1964, he was discovered by Peter Eden and Geoff Stephens of Pye Records who offered to manage him. Impressive demo recordings led to a three-week mini residency on the tv music show *Ready Steady Go!* and with widespread media comments about his similarity in style and appearance to Bob Dyan, he secured a recording contract. In 1965's fly-on-the-wall documentary *Don't Look Back* by D A Pennebaker, which chronicled Dylan's UK tour, the two singers are seen chatting together in what appears to be friendly rivalry. Meanwhile, Donovan's debut single "Catch the Wind" peaked at number four on the UK charts, seven places above Dylan's "The Times They Are A-Changin.'" Also charting in the US, it was described by *Cashbox* as "a medium-paced, folk-styled low-down bluesy romancer" with a Dylan-like vocal. In a later radio interview, Donovan said he wrote it for the fleeting love affair he had with Linda Lawrence, who shortly after its release became the girlfriend of Rolling Stones' Brian Jones (Donovan would eventually marry her in 1970).

Later that year, Donovan was introduced to producer Mickie Most, and over the next few months their collaboration produced a number of folk-tinged hit singles, including "Colours" and a cover of Buffy Sainte-Marie's "Universal Soldier." The new year, however, brought about a marked change in style, with Donovan becoming one of the first UK artists to embrace the growing "flower power" movement, and with it, writing some of his best work. "Sunshine Superman," although written in 1965, has been cited as being one of the first psychedelic rock songs ever recorded. Playing down the drug implications, Donovan cited that it was written about former girlfriend Linda. In an interview for *Mojo*, he said: "Sunshine is an acid. The Superman is the person capable of entering higher states because it's not easy to go into the fourth dimension and see the matrix of the universe in which everything is connected." The single "Mellow Yellow," which had lyrics with subtle drug references, endeared him to the hippie movement. In another interview, he said it was all about being cool and laid back, with "electrical bananas" not so subtly referring to ladies' sexual toys.

The following year, Donovan joined the Beatles and other artists on a visit to Maharishi Mahesh Yogi in India and later claimed to have interested the Fab Four in transcendental meditation. The single "Jennifer Juniper" was inspired by George Harrison's sister-in-law Jenny Boyd. While there, Donovan wrote the ultra-psychedelic "Hurdy Gurdy Man." Inspired by the sounds he was hearing, he wrote about awakening from a dream to see a hurdy-gurdy man singing songs of love (a hurdy gurdy being a string instrument that produces a sound by a hand-cranked wheel rubbing against strings). According to Donovan, Harrison wrote one of the verses, but was never used in the final recording.

Later hits included the beautiful ballad "Laléna," inspired by actress Lotte Lenya, "Atlantis," with Paul McCartney on backing vocals, and the gutsy "Barabajagal" (credited in the US as "Goo Goo Barabajagal (Love Is Hot)," a collaboration with the Jeff Back Group and a trio of backing vocalists - Madeline Bell, Lesley Duncan and Suzi Quatro. Looking back on his career, he said: "Songwriting is a burst of inspiration and then a long bit of work and a tremendous bit of desperation."

Chart entries
Catch the Wind (UK 1965 # 4; US 1965 # 23)
Colours (UK 1965 # 4; US # 61)
Turquoise (UK 1965 # 30)
Sunshine Superman (UK 1966 # 2; US # 1)
Mellow Yellow (UK 1966 # 8; US # 2)

Epistle To Dippy (US 1967 # 19)
There Is A Mountain (UK 1967 # 8; US # 11)
Wear Your Love Like Heaven (US 1967 # 23)
Jennifer Juniper (UK 1968 # 5; US # 26)
Hurdy Gurdy Man (UK 1968 # 4; US # 5)
Laléna (US 1969 # 33)
To Susan On the West Coast Waiting (US 1969 # 35)
Barabajagal (with the Jeff Beck Group) (US 1969 # 12; US # 36)
Laléna (US 1969 # 33)

Donald "Duck" Dunn see also Booker T Jones
Born Memphis, Tennessee 1941. Died 2012.
Rock and Roll Hall of Fame 1992 (with Booker T & the MGs).

Nicknamed "Duck" by his father for watching Disney cartoons with him, Dunn grew up with his friend and future MG musician Steve Cropper, who both became self-taught guitarists. When Cropper began playing guitar with another friend Charlie Freeman, Dunn switched to bass, and along with drummer Terry Johnson the four Messick High School pals formed the Royal Spades, later adding keyboardist Lee "Smoochy" Smith, and singer Ronnie "Stoots" Angel, as well as a horn section made up of Don Nix (baritone sax), Charles Axton (tenor sax) and Wayne Jackson (trumpet). Axton's mother Estelle and brother Jim Stewart owned Satellite Records, and they signed the band with their new name the Mar-Keys, which eventually would be better known as Booker T & the MGs. In 1965, Dunn would replace Lewis Steinberg as the band's regular bass player.

Over the next four years he collaborated on a string of hits for the MGs, as well as "The Hunter," a minor hit for Ike & Tina Turner in 1969. First recorded by Albert King two years before, the single went on to earn Tina a Grammy nomination. Where the Stax sound became recognised for Al Jackson's drumming and the Memphis Horns, it was Dunn's bass lines on songs like Otis Redding's "Respect," Sam & Dave's "Hold On! I'm Comin'" and Albert King's "Born Under a Bad Sign" that would go on to influence musicians everywhere for decades to come.

Chart entries
Boot-Leg *(with Charles Axton, Isaac Hayes, Al Jackson Jr)* Booker T & the MGs (US 1965 # 58)
Hip Hug-Her *(with Steve Cropper, Al Jackson Jr, Booker T Jones)* Booker T & the MGs (US 1967 # 37; UK # 51)
Slim Jenkins' Place *(with Steve Cropper, Al Jackson Jr, Booker T Jones)* Booker T & the MGs (US 1967 # 70; UK # 58)
The Hunter *(with Steve Cropper, Al Jackson Jr, Booker T Jones, Carl Wells)* Ike & Tina Turner (US 1969 # 93)
Soul Clap 69 *(with Steve Cropper, Al Jackson Jr, Booker T Jones)* Booker T & the MGs (US 1969 # 35)

Bob Dylan
Born Robert Allen Zimmerman, Duluth, Minnesota 1941.
Songwriters Hall of Fame 1982.
Rock and Roll Hall of Fame 1988.
Grammy Lifetime Achievement Award 1991.
Nashville Songwriters Hall of Fame 2002.

Brought up in a close-knit Jewish community in Duluth, the family moved to his mother's hometown of Hibbing, where his father and uncles ran a furniture store. His first exposure to music was listening to the *Grand Ole Opry* radio show, and was captivated by the singing of Hank Williams and Johnnie Ray. While at Hibbing High School, he formed several bands and played covers of songs by Elvis Presley and Little Richard, and at the age of 17 saw Buddy Holly perform at the Duluth armory, just four days before the singer was killed. In 1959, he enrolled at the University of Minnesota and became involved in the local folk music circuit, going by the name of Bob Dylan (after poet Dylan Thomas). After dropping out of college, he went to New York in 1961, where he visited his music idol Woody Guthrie in a psychiatric hospital and began performing at various Greenwich Village clubs, with one gig receiving an enthusiastic review by a *New York Times'* critic. After playing harmonica on an album by folk singer Carolyn Hester, he came to the attention of John Hammond, who signed him to Columbia Records.

The eponymous debut album, released in March 1962, comprised traditional blues, folk and gospel songs, with two Dylan originals, "Song To Woody" (in honour of Guthrie) and "Talkin' New York." Six months later, he signed a management contract with Albert Grossman, and tensions between him and Hammond led to the latter suggesting to Dylan that he work with producer Tom Wilson.

Following a visit to the UK at the end of the year, Dylan worked on his second album, the protest song-laden *The Freewheelin' Bob Dylan,* heavily influenced by the work of Guthrie and Pete Seeger. The opening track "Blowin' in the Wind" had a melody partly taken from the traditional slave song "No More Auction Block" with lyrics calling for an end to injustice and war, and taken into the charts by Peter, Paul & Mary. "Oxford Town" related to the ordeal of James Meredith, the first black student at the University of Mississippi, while "A Hard Rain's a-Gonna Fall," based on the folk ballad "Lord Randall," was seen as a premonition of the Cuban Missile Crisis that came two months later.

Written while in London, the scathing "Masters of War" was directed at the weapons of war industry and based on the English riddle song "Nottamun Town." Balanced against these hard-edged tracks were two love songs. The masterful "Don't Think Twice, It's All Right" was written about his nine-month separation from girlfriend Suze Rotolo, who after holidaying together had contemplated stopping in Italy, while the subject of "Girl From the North Country" had several female contenders in the frame, and leading Dylan to later claim it was written for *all* North Country girls. With these, and the remaining tracks, the album displayed a new direction in songwriting, with its mixture of moral authority, nonconformity, and lyrical stream-of-consciousness attacks. Dylan had become the voice of his generation, although the rough edge of his voice unsettled some listeners. One reviewer wrote that it was the sound made if "sandpaper could sing." Joan Baez recorded several of his early songs and was influential in raising his profile as well as supporting him in the civil rights movement.

The third album, the politicised *The Times They Are a-Changin'* was influenced by more contemporary issues. "Only a Pawn in Their Game" was about the assassination of civil rights activist Medgar Evers in Jackson, Mississippi in June 1963, attributing the blame for the killing and racial violence to rich white politicians. The grimness of "The Ballad of Hollis Brown" related to a South Dakota farmer who, when overwhelmed by the desperation of poverty, kills his starving family before turning the gun on himself, while "North Country Blues" addressed the breakdown of mining and farming communities. "The Lonesome Death of Hattie Carroll," one of his most moving songs, was the true story of the murder of a 51-year-old African-American barmaid at the hands of 24-year-old white socialite William Zanzinger, who was then given an unbelievable six-month sentence. When written, it was arguably the last of his protest songs. But it was the album's anthemic title track that became *the* archetypal protest song. Less than a month after it was recorded, President Kennedy was assassinated.

Disenchanted with the petty politics of the Village scene and frustrated with being tagged the young generation's spokesman, Dylan distanced himself from the expectations of the folk crowd and by immersing himself in reading the poetry of Keats and Arthur Rimbaud, embraced his own poetic consciousness by working on a novel and a play. With its thematic shift, the album *Another Side of Bob Dylan,* with nine of the songs having been written while travelling through Europe, included his disavowal of his past in "My Back Pages," the lyrics of which could be interpreted as his rejection of his earlier political idealism and a desire to follow a new direction. "Chimes of Freedom," inspired by the works of Rimbaud, was written during a road trip across the US with three friends, with lyrics using the dual metaphor of the chimes of a bell representing freedom, and the enlightenment of freedom represented by thunder and lightning. Music critic Paul Williams' called it Dylan's "Sermon on the Mount." The much-covered "All I Really Want to Do" and "It Ain't Me Babe" were said to have been both inspired by his breakup with his girlfriend Rotolo, as was probably the track "To Ramona."

By late 1964, Dylan was feeling constrained and manipulated by the folk and protest movements, and, perhaps inspired by the recent arrival of the Beatles, had transformed from being a folkie songwriter to a folk-rock star, even displaying a new image with jeans and work shirts now replaced with a Carnaby Street-type wardrobe, with obligatory boots, and day-and-night sunglasses. The following year's *Bringing It All Back Home* was another turning point, with the use of electric instruments for the first time (at least on half of the tracks), something that would not only divide the contemporary folk scene but also seen as being instrumental in the birth of folk-rock.

The verbal whirlwind of "Subterranean Homesick Blues" took some of its's inspiration from Chuck Berry's "Too Much Monkey Business" and possibly from reading Jack Kerouac's 1958 novel *The Subterraneans.* The defiant "Maggie's Farm" challenged the capitalist system where employers exploited and devalued their workers, while the surreal imagery of the hard-to-define "Love Minus Zero/No Limit" is generally considered to be about Sara Lownds, the girl he married the year it was recorded and was written in the Chelsea Hotel where she lived. The love song "She Belongs To Me" had some music critics putting Joan Baez in the frame.

According to Dylan, "Mr Tambourine Man" is about an itinerant musician whose music had captivated him, and was actually inspired by folk musician Bruce Langhorne and watching Fellini's 1954 movie *La Strada*. It would also become one of his most celebrated compositions to be covered when the Byrds made it a transatlantic chart-topper in 1965.

That year also saw Dylan undertake an eight-date tour of England and headline the Newport Folk Festival, where he appeared for the first time with an electric guitar and small band. After just three songs, including a blistering "Maggie's Farm," he left the stage after receiving boos from members of the audience, while also triggering a hostile response from the folk music establishment. Unapologetic for his new electric sound, Dylan received praise from many critics for combining his blues-based music with both subtle and surreal poetry to capture the current political and cultural climate.

Highway 61 Revisited has one of his greatest singles, the revolutionary "Like a Rolling Stone." Written on his return from England, its tale of a debutant who falls from grace to become a loner has Dylan's high voltage voice screaming his personal accusations at her, and the title may have been influenced by Hank William's 1949 "Lost Highway" and the line "I'm a rolling stone, all alone and lost." Released as a single ahead of the album (despite its six-minute length), it was well-received by critics and seen to have completed his transformation to a fully-fledged rock star. The magnificent, eleven-minute entropy "Desolation Row," the album's only acoustic track, is both Dylan's most lyrically sophisticated song, but also his most misunderstood, with its huge cast of iconic fictional and real-life characters.

That autumn, Dylan went on tour with musicians that became known as the Band, and for his next album moved what proved to be a problematic production from New York to Nashville, where it was completed with some of its top musicians. The result was the double-album *Blonde on Blonde.* The raucous, party-like opening track "Rainy Day Women #12 and #35" was released as a single, but its chorus about "getting stoned" being interpreted as an invitation to indulge in drugs or alcohol, led to it being banned by some radio stations. The much-praised "Visions of Johanna" about contrasting lovers was written while in New York's Chelsea Hotel with his wife of three months, Sara Lounds, and was another song cited as one of his lyrical masterpieces. "I Want You," with its infectious riff, expression of lust, and a surreal cast of characters, was one of five singles lifted from the album, while the lyrics to another single, "Just Like a Woman" received criticism for being sexist and misogynistic. The whole of side four is taken up by "Sad Eyed Lady of the Lowlands," another paean to Sara.

A tour of Europe in the spring of 1966 led to the infamous cry of "Judas!" from a member of the audience at a Manchester concert, while a motorbike accident that summer put an end to touring for the next eight years. Returning to the studio in late 1967, he recorded the semi-acoustic *John Wesley Harding* with short songs drawn from the Bible and the American West, with the title referring to the Texas outlaw of the same name (although spelt Hardin).The best-known track, "All Along the Watchtower," with its narrative of alienation and apprehension, was another of his songs picked up by Jimi Hendrix as a single (the first being "Like a Rolling Stone"). The following year's *Nashville Skyline* featured a more mellow-voiced Dylan. The sultry "Lay Lady Lay" was originally recorded for the movie *Midnight Cowboy*, but was too late to be included, and instead he dedicated it to Sara, although he would also claim it was originally written as a duet with Barbara Streisand. "Girl From the North Country," a previous album track in 1963, was re-recorded as a duet with Johnny Cash.

The Sixties saw Dylan produce his finest work and become a major figure in popular culture, but with his profound use of lyricism and imagery, he remains one of the greatest songwriters of all time. When asked if he saw himself more as a poet than songwriter, he replied: "It's not me, it's the songs. I'm just the postman. I deliver the songs … I consider myself a poet first and a musician second. I live like a poet and I'll die like a poet."

Chart entries
The Times They Are a-Changin' (UK 1965 # 9)
Subterranean Homesick Blues (US # 39; UK # 9)
Maggie's Farm (UK 1965 # 22)
Like a Rolling Stone (US 1965 # 2; UK # 4)
Positively 4th Street (US 1965 # 7; UK # 8)
Can You Please Crawl Out Your Window? / Highway 61 Revisited (US 1966 # 58; UK # 17)
One Of Us Must Know (Sooner Or Later) / Queen Jane Approximately (US 1966 # 119; UK # 33)
Rainy Day Women #12 & #35 (US 1966 # 2; UK # 7)
I Want You (US 1966 # 20; UK # 16)
Just Like A Woman (US 1966 # 33)
Leopard Skin Pill-Box Hat / Most Likely You'll Go Your Way and I'll Go Mine ((US 1967 # 81)
I Threw It All Away (US 1969 # 85; UK # 30)
Lay Lady Lay (US 1969 # 7; UK # 5)
Tonight I'll Be Staying Here With You (US 1969 # 50)

Cover versions
Blowin' In the Wind – Peter, Paul & Mary (UK 1963 # 2; UK # 13); Stevie Wonder (US 1966 # 9; UK # 36)
The Times They Are a-Changin' - Peter, Paul & Mary (UK 1964 # 44
Don't Think Twice, It's Alright – Peter, Paul & Mary (US 1963 # 9); The Wonder Who? (The Four Seasons) (US 1965 # 12)
It Ain't Me Babe – Johnny Cash (with June Carter) (US 1964 # 58; UK # 28); The Turtles (US 1965 # 8); Davy Jones (UK 1967 # 55)
Mr Tambourine Man - The Byrds (US 1965 # 1; UK #1)

When the Ship Comes In – Peter, Paul & Mary (US 1965 # 91)
All I Really Wanna Do – Cher (US 1965 # 15; UK # 9); The Byrds (US 1965 # 40; UK # 4)
It's All Over Now Baby Blue – Joan Baez (UK 1965 # 22)
If You Gotta Go, Go Now – Manfred Mann (UK 1965 # 2); Fairport Convention (as Si tu dois partir) (UK 1969 # 21)
Farewell Angelina – Joan Baez (UK 1965 # 35)
One Too Many Mornings – The Beau Brummels (US 1966 # 95)
Just Like A Woman – Manfred Mann (UK 1966 # 10); Jonathan King (UK 1966 # 56)
My Back Pages – The Byrds (US 1967 # 30)
Too Much Of Nothing – Peter, Paul & Mary (US 1967 # 35)
The Mighty Quinn (Quinn the Eskimo) - Manfred Mann (UK 1968 # 1; US # 10)
This Wheel's On Fire *(with Rick Danko)* - Judy Driscoll, Brian Auger & the Trinity
   (UK 1968 # 5)
You Ain't Going Nowhere – The Byrds (US 1968 # 74; UK # 45)
All Along the Watchtower – The Jimi Hendrix Experience (UK 1968 # 5; US # 20)
I Shall Be Released – The Tremeloes (UK 1968 # 29); The Box Tops (US 1969 # 67)
Love Is Just a Four Letter Word – Joan Baez (US 1969 # 86)
She Belongs To Me – Ricky Nelson & the Stone Canyon Band (US 1969 # 33)
Ballad Of An Easy Rider – The Byrds (US 1969 # 65)

Jackie Edwards
Born Wilfred Gerald Edwards, Jamaica 1938. Died 1992.

One of fifteen children, Edwards started performing as a singer- songwriter while still in his early teens. In 1959, he was discovered by 22-year-old Chris Blackwell, the British-Jamaican producer who had just formed Island Records, an independent label that would become one of the first to embrace the Jamaican style of music soon to be known a ska. Over the next couple of years, with Blackwell at the helm, Edwards scored four number ones on the Jamaican charts, with self-penned ballads inspired by Nat King Cole and Latin-influenced music. In 1962, he set up his label in London and took Edwards with him, selling records to the Jamaican community from the back of his car. Edwards also recorded duets with Millie Small, but his solo career got underway in 1965 with the album *Come On Home,* which contained four self-penned tracks, including the single "Keep on Running." Although failing to chart, it was picked up by the British blues and R&B band the Spencer Davis Group and became their first chart-topper in January 1966. Their success was repeated several months later when they recorded Edwards' "Somebody Help Me," hitting the top spot for a second time.

Later in the year, Wayne Fontana & the Mindbenders charted with a version of Edwards' "Come on Home," while Stevie Winwood, lead singer of the Spencer Davis Group, teamed up with Edwards to write a new single for the band called "When I Come Home." Edwards continued his solo career into the Eighties, recognised as "the single person most responsible for turning the world on to reggae music."

Chart entries
Keep On Running – The Spencer Davis Group (UK 1966 # 1; US # 76)
Somebody Hep Me – The Spencer Davis Group (UK 1966 # 1; US 1967 # 47)
Come On Home – Wayne Fontana & Mindbenders (UK 1966 # 16)
When I Come Home (*with Stevie Winwood*) The Spencer Davis Group (UK 1966 # 12)

Scott English and Larry Weiss
Born Scott David English, New York City 1937. Died 2018.
Born Laurence D Weiss, Newark, New Jersey 1941.

Signing to the Dot label in 1960, English released his first single "4,000 Miles Away," written by Frank Cariola Three years later, he had a regional hit on the Spokane label with "High On a Hill," co-written by Cariola and Anna Mangravito. It was through arranger Claus Ogerman that English met and befriended singer-songwriter Laurence Weiss. As a teenager, Weiss began writing songs while also working in his family's textile business in Queens, and later became a part-time freelance writer for producer Wes Farrell. One of his first successes came in 1963 with the song "Mr Wishing Well." Co-written with Lockie Edwards Jr, it was recorded by Nat King Cole as a b-side to "That Sunday, That Summer," which peaked at number 12 on the Hot 100. Weiss and Edwards went on to write a number of songs together.

English and Weiss's successful writing partnership began with "Bend Me, Shape Me," first recorded in 1966 as an album track by the Outsiders, but became a bigger hit the following year when the American Breed's version peaked at number five in the US (and a later UK hit for the Amen Corner in 1968). The partnership also gave English guitarist Jeff Beck a rare but memorable UK hit with the anthemic "Hi Ho Silver Lining." In the early stages of its writing, the song had no verses and producer Mickie Most, feeling it had hit potential, persuaded English to write lyrics for verses. Although wanting to record the song himself, Most had British guitarist Jeff Beck in mind instead, so an annoyed English came up with what he thought would be silly, unusable lyrics. However, Most liked what he heard and it gave Beck a surprising and rather catchy hit single in the spring of 1967.

In the Seventies, English recorded "Brandy," co-written with Richard Kerr, and later revised as "Mandy" to give Barry Manilow one of his most famous recordings, despite the singer changing some of its structure. He also co-wrote UK's 1998 Eurovision Song Contest entry by Imaani. Weiss moved to Los Angeles in the Seventies to work for Famous Music and wrote and recorded "Rhinestone Cowboy" for a track on his solo album, but also managed to give Glen Campbell a huge international hit with it in 1975.

Chart entries
In the (Cold Light Of Day) Gene Pitney (UK 1966 # 38)
Help Me Girl - The Outsiders (US 1966 # 37); The Animals (US 1966 # 29; UK # 14)
Hi Ho Silver Lining – Jeff Beck (UK 1967 # 14)
When Love Slips Away (with Vic Millrose) Dee Dee Warwick (US 1967 # 92)
Bend Me, Shape Me – The American Breed (US 1967 # 5; UK # 24); Amen Corner (UK 1968 # 3)

Scott English with others
Now I Know *(with James Last, Stanley Jay Gelber)* Jack Jones (US 1967 # 73)
Help Yourself (To All My Lovin') *(with Jerry Ross, Mark Barkan)* James & Bobby Purify (US 1968 # 94)

Larry Weiss and Lockie Edwards Jr
Getting Ready for the Heartbreak - Chuck Jackson (US 1962 # 88)
Insult to Injury *(with Eddie Snyder)* Timi Yuro (US 1963 # 81)
Leave Me Alone *(with Matt Paul Maurer)* Baby Washington (US 1963 # 62)
The Clock - Baby Washington (US 1964 # 100)

Larry Weiss with others
Does He Really Care For Me *(with Fred Anisfield)* Ruby & the Romantics (US 1965 # 87)
More Than the Eye Can See *(with Bob Crewe)* Al Martino (US 1967 # 54)
Mr Dream Merchant *(with Jonas B Ross)* Jerry Butler (US 1967 # 38)

Georgie Fame
Born Clive Powell, Leigh, England 1943.

Powell had learned to play piano by the age of seven, and after leaving school at 15 spent evenings playing in a band called the Dominoes. In 1959, while on holiday at Butlins camp in Pwllheli, Wales, he was asked to stand-in for the injured pianist of the resident band Rory Blackwell & the Blackjacks. Impressed by his talent, Blackwell urged the 16-year-old to quit his job in a cotton mill and move with the band to London. With their career short-lived, Powell began playing in local pubs and came to the attention of songwriter Lionel Bart who urged him to audition as a pianist for pop impresario Larry Parnes, whose roster of protégés included Tommy Steele, Joe Brown, Marty Wilde and Billy Fury. Like most of his artists, Parnes insisted on a name-change and, despite his objection, he became Georgie Fame. While backing the stars, he was also given the freedom to develop his vocal talents. In 1961, he joined Fury's backing band the Blue Flames, but by the end of the year Fury's manager replaced them with the Tornadoes.

Now billed as Georgie Fame & the Blue Flames, they secured a residency at the Flamingo jazz club, where their mix of jazz, rock and blues spread their reputation, especially with Fame now switching to a Hammond B3 organ, one of the first to be seen in a London band. In 1963, they secured a deal with EMI and cut their first album, recorded at the Flamingo and produced by Ian Samwell. The band would become the only British music act to achieve a trio of chart-toppers with only their top ten chart entries - "Yeh Yeh," a cover of an Afro-Cuban song; his own composition "Getaway" (written as a jingle for a petrol commercial), and the Murray-Callander song "The Ballad of Bonnie and Clyde," which became his biggest success. In 1967, Fame released the ballad "Sitting in the Park," originally written and recorded by US singer and pianist Billy Stewart (1937-1970) who took it to number four on the soul chart in 1965. Fame's version reached number 12 on the UK charts.

Chart entries
Like We Used To Be – Georgie Fame & the Blue Flames (UK 1965 # 33)
Get Away - Georgie Fame & the Blue Flames (UK 1966 #1; US # 70)
Because I Love You – Georgie Fame (UK 1967 # 15)
Try My World *(with Fran Landesman)* Georgie Fame (UK 1967 # 37)

Wes Farrell see also Bert Berns
Born Wesley Donald Farrell, New York City 1939. Died 1996.

Farrell achieved one of his earliest successes with "Boys," co-written with Luther Dixon (1931-2009), which was released in 1960 as the b-side to the Shirelles chart-topping single "Will You Love Me Tomorrow," and also recorded two years later by the Beatles as a track on their debut album *Please Please Me.* In 1964, Farrell collaborated with fellow songwriter Bert Berns on "My Girl Sloopy," inspired by US jazz singer Dorothy Sloop and recorded by the vocal group the Vibrations. While touring in the US with the Strangeloves, who were playing the song as part of their set, the Dave Clark Five announced they would record the song when they returned to the UK, but it never materialised. Instead, 17-year-old Rick Zehringer (aka Rick Derringer) of the US band Rick and the Raiders saw an opportunity and recorded the song themselves as "Hang on Sloopy" with the band's name changed to the McCoys (so as not to be confused with Paul Revere & the Raiders). With the original three verses trimmed down to two for the single, it scored them a US top spot in the summer of 1965. Farrell and Berns also wrote the Animals' hit "Baby Let Me Take You Home," while Farrell collaborated with others on hits, including Jay & the Americans and Ronnie Dove.

In the Seventies, Farrell was hired to produce the music for the tv show *The Partridge Family,* as well as co-writing the theme song "When We're Singin.'"

Chart entries
Wes Farrell and Bert Berns
My Girl Sloopy - The Vibrations (US 1964 # 26); Little Caesar & the Consuls (US 1965 # 50)
Baby Let Me Take You Home - The Animals (UK 1964 # 21)
Goodbye Baby (Baby Goodbye) - Solomon Burke (US 1964 # 33)
Hang on Sloopy - The McCoys (US 1965 # 1; UK # 5); The Ramsey Lewis Trio (US 1965 #11)
Everybody Do the Sloopy - Johnny Thunder (US 1965 # 67)

Wes Farrell with others
Our Favourite Melodies *(with Bob Elgin, Kay Rogers)* Craig Douglas (UK 1962 # 9)
Come a Little Closer *(with Tommy Boyce, Bobby Hart)* Jay & the Americans (US 1964 # 3)
Let's Lock the Door (And Throw Away the Key) *(with Roy Alfred)* Jay & the Americans
   (US 1964 # 11)
Hello Pretty Girl *(with Tommy Boyce)* Ronnie Dove (US 165 # 54)
Think of the Good Times *(with Roy Alfred)* Jay & the Americans (US 1965 # 57)
I'll Make All Your Dreams Come True *(with Bernice Ross)* Ronnie Dove (US 1965 # 21)
Why Can't You Bring Me Home *(with Al Kasha, Joel Hirschhorn)* Jay & the Americans
   (US 1966 # 63)
Happy Summer Days *(with Larry Kusik, Ritchie Adams)* Ronnie Dove (US 1966 # 27)
Look What You've Done *(with Bobby Johnston)* The Pozo-Seco Singers (US 1966 # 32)
Come On Down to My Boat *(with Jerry Goldstein)* Every Mother's Son (US 1967 # 6)
No One Knows *(with Larry Kusik, Ritchie Adams)* Every Mother's Son (US 1968 # 96)

Feldman, Goldstein and Gottehrer
Born Robert C Feldman, New York City 1940. Died 2023.
Born Gerald Goldstein, New York City 1940.
Born Richard Gottehrer, New York City 1940.

Graduating from high school along with Neil Sedaka, Feldman became a member of the All-City Choir along with fellow choristers Neil Diamond and Barbra Streisand. In the late Fifties, he teamed up with friend and neighbour Gerald Goldstein, and in 1957, as budding songwriters, wrote the theme song for Alan Freed's controversial inter-racial music/dance tv show *The Big Beat,* as well as performing as dancers on the show. As Bob and Jerry, they went on to record a number of non-charting singles, including "We Put the Bomp" as an answer to Barry Mann's 1961 hit "Who Put the Bomp," while also being members of other unsuccessful studio-based groups, including Bobbi & the Beaus, the Kittens, and Ezra & the Iveys. In 1962, the two of them met songwriter Richard Gottehrer and formed FGG Productions, for which Feldman was quoted: "I was the dreamer, Jerry was the schemer and Richie was the voice of reason." Their early partnership produced the song "My Boyfriend's Back," originally written as a demo for the Shirelles but recorded by the Angels, who took it to the top of the US charts in 1963.

The following year, in response to the success of the "British Invasion," the writing team formed their own beat group, the Strangeloves, with a fake Australian backstory and band member names Giles, Miles and Niles Strange. Their second single "I Want Candy," written and produced with Bert Berns, was a hit in 1965. That year, the three writers produced the McCoys' US chart-topper "Hang on Sloopy," and the following year wrote another chart hit for them with "Sorrow," which was successfully covered in the UK by the Merseys. In 1966, Feldman and Goldstein set up office in California, with Goldstein becoming producer for the band War's recordings. Gottehrer also went on to produce for artists such as Blondie and the Go-Go's.

Chart entries
I'm Tossin' and Turnin' Again - Bobby Lewis (US 1962 # 98)
What's Gonna Happen When Summer's Gone - Freddy Cannon (US 1962 # 45)
What Time Is It? - The Jive Five (US 1962 # 67)
Ten Lonely Guys *(with Edward Snyder, Cliff Adams, Lockie Edwards, Lawrence Weiss,
   Wes Farrell, Neil Diamond, Stanley Kahan)* Pat Boone (US 1962 # 45)
Let's Stomp - Bobby Comstock (US 1963 # 57)
Patty Baby (*(with Freddy Cannon)* Freddy Cannon (US 1963 # 65)
Bobby Tomorrow - Bobby Vee (UK 1963 # 21)
My Boyfriend's Back - The Angels (US 1963 # 1)
Your Boyfriend's Back *(with Bobby Comstock)* Bobby Comstock & the Counts (US 1963 # 98)
Thank You and Goodnight *(with Mary Sanders)* The Angels (US 1963 # 84)
Wow Wow Wee (He's the Boy For Me) (*with Robert Spencer, Peggy Farina*) The Angels
   (US 1964 # 41)
Giving Up on Love - Jerry Butler (US 1964 # 56)
I'm on Fire - Jerry Lee Lewis (US 1964 # 98)
I Want Candy *(with Bert Berns)* The Strangeloves (US 1965 # 11); Brian Poole & the Tremeloes
   (UK 1965 # 25)
Cara-Lin - The Strangeloves (US 1965 # 39)
Night Time - The Strangeloves (US 1966 # 30)
Sorrow - The Merseys (UK 1966 # 4)
You Make Me Feel (So Good) - The McCoys (US 1966 # 53)

Bob Feldman and Jerry Goldstein
Bubble Gum Music- The Rock and Roll Double Bubble Trading Card Company of
   Philadelphia 1914) (US 1969 # 74)

Jerry Goldstein
It's Nice To Be With You – The Monkees (US 1968 # 51)

Jerry Goldstein and Wes Farrell
Come On Down to My Boat – Every Mother's Son (US 1967 # 6)

Fisher, Matthew see Gary Brooker and Keith Reid

Jack Fishman
Born London 1920. Died 1997.

Born to Jewish refugee parents, his father died when he was young and he left school at 13. His first job was working as a teaboy at a newspaper office, and he soon developed a talent for writing. He worked his way up to become deputy editor of two of Britain's largest national newspapers, before becoming editor of *Empire News*, where he was credited for exposing the spy Kim Philby. As a freelance writer, he wrote best-selling books about Churchill and his wife, but as a songwriter he preferred to use pseudonyms, believing no one would take him seriously as a writer if they knew he wrote pop songs. While recovering from TB after being discharged from the RAF, he began writing lyrics to music he heard on the radio and sent them to publishers in Denmark Street. In 1955, he won an Ivor Novello award for "Everywhere" under the name Larry Kahn. In 1963, he stopped writing music to concentrate on his books, but in 1968 returned to songs with a string of hits, including translating lyrics to some French and Italian songs for artists including Petula Clark, Tom Jones and Herman's Hermits.

One of his most famous translated songs was the Welsh band Amen Corner's "(If Paradise) Is Half As Nice." Written by Lucio Battisi, it was originally recorded in 1968 by Ambra Borelli as "The Paradise of the Life" and the following year by Patty Pravo as "The Paradise." Once translated, Fishman first offered it to the Tremeloes, who turned it down. Amen Corner wanted it as the debut single for their new label Immediate, and after working out the arrangement with producer Shel Talmy, recorded it within two hours. With lead singer Andy Fairweather-Low's distinctive vocal, it topped the charts in February 1969.

Chart entries
Something Missing *(with Gilbert Bécaud, Louis Amade)* Petula Clark (UK 1961 # 44)
My Friend the Sea *(with Ron Goodwin)* Petula Clark (UK 1961 # 7)
If I Only Had Time *(with Michael Fugain, Pierre Delanoë)* John Rowles (UK 1968 # 3);
    Nick DeCaro (US 1968 # 95)
Help Yourself *(with Carlo Donida Labati, Giulio Rapetti)* Tom Jones (UK 1968 # 5; US # 35)
Something's Happening *(with Giancarlo Bigazzi, Riccardo Del Turco)* Herman's Hermits
    (UK 1968 # 6)
(If Paradise) Is Half as Nice (*with Lucio Battisti*) Amen Corner (UK 1969 # 1)

John Fogerty
Born John Cameron Fogerty, Berkeley, California 1945.
Rock and Roll Hall of Fame 1993 (with CCR).
Songwriters Hall of Fame 2005.

Fogerty attended Portola Junior High School in El Cerrito, learned to play guitar, and formed a rock n' roll cover band called the Blue Velvets with friends and fellow students Stu Cook (bassist) and Doug Clifford (drums). A short while later, John's elder brother Tom Fogerty, already a multi-instrumentalist, joined them as rhythm guitarist and co-lead vocalist, re-naming the band Tommy Fogerty & the Blue Velvets. After leaving school, they played in bars and clubs across the Bay area before signing with a local independent label to cut an unsuccessful single "Bonita." In 1964, they signed with the more prestigious Fantasy Records as an instrumental band, although label boss Hy Weiss steered them toward UK-style rock and credited them as the Golliwogs, on what would become a series of unsuccessful singles, although "Fight Fire" and "Walking on the Water," written by John and Tom under the pseudonym Wilde-Green, would become garage band classics.

In 1966, to avoid being drafted to fight in the Vietnam War, John and Clifford enlisted in the US Army Reserves. On discharge two years later, the band's name was changed to Creedence Clearwater Revival (after Creedence Nuball, a friend of Tom's, and the rest from a beer commercial), with John switching to lead vocal. Their first single was "Susie-Q," a cover of the Dale Hawkins' rockabilly hit, and it scored their first chart success in 1968. Their eponymous debut album followed, which included re-workings of some of the Golliwogs' songs, but it would be the single "Proud Mary," released in early 1969, that gave them new-found status. Written by John on the morning of his discharge from the army, his tale of a Mississippi steamboat not only established him as a perceptive songwriter, but also helped develop the band's "swamp-rock" idiom. "Bad Moon Rising," the lead single from their album *Green River,* was inspired by John watching a hurricane scene in the 1941 movie *The Devil and Daniel Webster* and topped the UK charts. He later explained: "It wasn't until the band was learning the song that I realised the dichotomy. Here you've got this song with all these hurricanes and blowing and raging ruin and all that, but it's 'I see the bad moon rising.' It's a happy-sounding tune, right? It didn't bother me at the time."

One of three protest songs on their album *Willy and the Poor Boys*, John's "Fortunate Son" was released during the peak of the Vietnam War, and although not explicit in its criticism of the war itself, it highlighted the unfairness of sons of the wealthy being able to avoid the draft, with the old adage about rich men making war and poor men having to fight them. His social perspective and his increasingly fertile lyricism would continue on future albums. Tom left the band for a solo career in 1971 and CCR finally disbanded in July 1972. Looking back on his career, he said: "I don't know that all the demons have been beaten, but I'm very, very proud of those songs."

Chart entries
Proud Mary – CCR (US 1969 # 2; UK # 8); Solomon Burke (US 1969 # 45); Checkmates Ltd
    (US 1969 # 69)
Bad Moon Rising – CCR (US 1969 # 2; UK # 1)
Lodi – CCR (US 1969 # 52); Al Wilson (US 1969 # 67)
Green River – CCR (US 1969 # 2; UK # 19)

Down On the Corner - CCR (US 1969 # 3; UK # 31)
Fortunate Son – CCR (US 1969 # 14)

Dean Ford and Junior Campbell
Dean born Thomas McAleese, Airdrie, Scotland 1945. Died 2018.
Born William Campbell Jr. Glasgow 1947.

McAleese began his musical career performing with a jazz ensemble at a local parish church dance hall, and at the age of 13 formed his first group the Tonebeats. By the time he completed his education at Clifton High School in Coatbridge, he had become the featured singer for another group. In 1963, he got his first break after performing with the Monarchs at Glasgow's Barrowland Ballroom and was seen by Junior Campbell and Pat Fairley of the Glasgow band the Gaylords (named after the 1930s Chicago street gang) who invited him to join their group. Campbell's paternal grandfather was an Italian immigrant who had changed his name to Campbell once he had settled in Scotland. "Junior" Campbell was educated at Eastbank Academy in Shettleston and had joined the Gaylords in 1961, replacing Pat McGovern as lead guitarist. McAleese replaced Tommy Scott to become their lead singer, guitarist and piano player, and also adopted his stage name (a combination of Dean Martin and Tennessee Ernie Ford).

Under the management of Billy Grainger they became a popular draw in Scotland. Music journalist Gordon Reid managed to get them an audition in Glasgow for EMI's Columbia label and they were signed by Norrie Paramor. One of the four unsuccessful singles they recorded was a cover of Chubby Checker's hit "Twenty Miles." After a tour of Germany in early 1965, they decided to stay in London and change management to Starlite Artistes, owned by Peter Walsh. Building on a healthy club reputation, Walsh suggested they update their image and change their name to the Marmalade. After signing with CBS, a string of covers, as well as the Ford-Campbell song "I See the Rain," failed to chart, and when producer Mike Smith offered them the Cason-Gayden song "Everlasting Love," they turned it down, preferring to record group-based material (Instead, it became a chart-topper for Love Affair). However, giving in to pressure, the agreed to record Artie Schroeck and Jet Loring's "Lovin' Things," which scored a top ten hit in 1968. Their biggest chart success came with a cover of the Beatles' "Obla-Di Obla-Da," which topped the charts in January 1969, followed that summer with a credible version of the Tony Macaulay-penned "Baby Make It Soon."

In November 1969, they signed a deal with Decca which allowed them to write and produce their own songs. With a lineup that now consisted of Ford (lead vocal), Campbell (keyboards), Pat Fairley (acoustic guitar), Graham Knight (bass) and Alan Whitehead (drums), they recorded the dramatic ballad "Reflections of My Life." The bleak outlook on life was penned by Campbell and Ford (credited as McAleese), and with Keith Mansfield's wonderful string arrangement and Campbell's distinctive backwards guitar break, it became their biggest international hit and their only US chart entry.

The early Seventies saw the writing pair having continued success with the singles "Rainbow" and "My Litte One." When Campbell left the group for a solo career in March 1971, ex-Poets Hugh Nicholson was recruited and went on to write further singles "Cousin Norman," "Back on the Road," and "Radancer."

Chart entries
Reflections of My Life – Marmalade (UK # 3; US # 10)

Perry Ford see also John Carter and Ken Lewis
Born Brian Joseph Pugh, Lincoln, England 1933. Died 1999.

After moving to London in 1958 to become a club singer (using the name Lou Bryan), he played with the band Colin Hicks & the Cabin Boys, fronted by the younger brother of Tommy Steele, and later for Vince Taylor & the Playboys. The following year, he secured a record deal with Parlophone, and under the name Perry Ford had a trio of unsuccessful singles produced by George Martin, including Sam Kern and Les Johnson's "Garden of Happiness." As a budding songwriter, he first found success with "Someone Else's Baby," co-written with Les Vandyke (aka John Worsley), and a huge hit for Adam Faith in 1960. "Caroline," which he co-authored with Tony Hiller, was recorded by the Fortunes, and, although not a hit, was better known as the theme song for the famous UK pirate radio station (reportedly named after Caroline Kennedy, daughter of the US president).

After a spell working for the Fortunes' manager Reg Calvert, Ford teamed up with songwriting duo John Carter and Ken Lewis to form the vocal harmony group the Ivy League. After a spell as backing singers for established artists that included Tom Jones and Sandie Shaw, they were signed by the Piccadilly label and released a string of singles, all written by the trio. When Carter left the group in January 1966, followed by Lewis the following year, Ford continued the Ivy League into the Seventies with new members..

Chart entries
Someone Else's Baby *(with Les Vandyke)* Adam Faith (UK 1960 #2)

Perry Ford with John Carter and Ken Lewis
Funny How Love Can Be - The Ivy League (UK 1965 # 8)
That's Why I'm Cryin' - The Ivy League (UK 1965 # 22)
Tossing and Turning - The Ivy League (UK 1965 # 3; US # 83)
Willow Tree - The Ivy League (UK 1966 # 50)

Dallas Frazier
Born Spiro, Oklahoma 1938. Died 2022.
Nashville Songwriters Hall of Fame 1976.

Raised in Bakersfield, California, Frazier began his music career as a teenager playing with country singer Ferlin Husky on the radio and tv show *Hometown Jamboree*. In 1954, he signed with Capitol and released his debut single "Space Command," written by Cousin Herb Henson. Three years later, he wrote the song "Alley Oop," inspired by the tv comic strip of the same name. It was originally a hit for Dante & the Evergreens and later recorded by the short-lived studio band, the Hollywood Argyles, who took it the top of the US charts. Frazier then moved to Nashville, and his songwriting success continued with 1964's "Timber I'm Falling," a hit for Ferlin Husky, and his most famous composition, "There Goes My Everything," initially a crossover hit for country star Jack Greene, and later a huge UK hit for British crooner Engelbert Humperdinck. The song also received a Grammy nomination for Frazier as Best Country Song. Although his career as a solo singer never took off, his songwriting success continued with the memorable "The Son of Hickory Holler's Tramp," the tragic tale of a woman and her 14 children being abandoned by an alcoholic husband and forced into prostitution to support her family. It was first recorded by country singer Johnny Durrell in 1968, but it was Ocie Lee (O C) Smith's definitive version later that year that scored the biggest hit. In 1969, Frazier teamed up with fellow country singer-songwriter Arthur Leo "Doddle" Owens (1930-1999) to write several hits for Charley Pride.

Frazier's songs would go on to receive two more Grammy nominations with Charley Pride's "All I Have to Offer You (Is Me)" in 1970, and the Oak Ridge Boys' "Elvira" in 1981, before leaving the music industry to become a minister.

Chart entries
Alley-Oop - Dante & the Evergreens (US 1960 # 15); The Hollywood Argyles (US 1960 # 1; UK # 24); The Dyna-Sores (US 1960 # 59)
Mohair Sam – Charlie Rich (US 1965 # 21)
Elvira (US 1966 # 72)
There Goes My Everything – Jack Greene (US 1966 # 65); Engelbert Humperdinck (UK 1967 # 2; US # 20)
The Son of Hickory Holler's Tramp - O C Smith (US 1968 # 40; UK # 2)

Dallas Frazier and A L Owens
Johnny One Time - Brenda Lee (US 1969 # 41)
All I Have To Offer You Is Me - Charley Pride (US 1969 # 91)
(I'm So) Afraid Of Losing You Again - Charley Pride (US 1969 # 83)

Harvey Fuqua
Born Louisville, Kentucky 1929. Died 2010.

The nephew of the Inkspots' Charlie Fuqua, he formed his vocal group the Crazy Sounds in Louisville, and later moved with them to Cleveland, Ohio, where they were taken under the wing of deejay Alan Freed. He renamed them the Moonglows after his own nickname "Moondog," and in 1953 had their first releases on his Champagne label. After a short-lived signing with Chicago's Chance label, they signed with Chess Records in 1954, and their single "Sincerely," written by Fuqua and Freed, topped the country charts. In 1957, he broke up the group and recruited new members from the Marques (including Marvin Gaye), and with a new lineup named Harvey & the Moonglows had a hit with "Ten Commandments of Love."

Fuqua left the group in 1958, and the following year, under the name Harvey, appeared in the movie *Go, Johnny, Go!* singing "Don't Be Afraid to Love." Leaving the Moonglows, he joined Anna Records in Detroit, working with Anna Gordy, Billy Davis, Lamont Dozier and Johnny Bristol. After marrying Anna Gordy's sister Gwen, he started his own labels, Tri-Phi and Harvey, but eventually was persuaded to join Motown as producer and A&R man. He was responsible for bringing the Spinners. Johnny Bristol and Tammi Terrell to the label, and suggesting that Terrell should duet with Marvin Gaye.

Over the years, he co-wrote a number of hits with his wife Gwen, Johnny Bristol and Vernon Bullock, ss well as teaming up with singer Jackey Beavers to give Diana Ross & the Supremes a chart-topper with "Someday We'll Be Together." It was originally recorded in 1961 by Bristol and Beavers (as Johnny & Jackey) but failed to chart, but was revived when Motown brought in Bristol to produce a new version for Jr Walker & the All Stars. Although Bristol produced a session with the Funk Brothers house band and backing vocals by sisters Maxine and Julia Waters, Walker never got to record it. With the Supremes about to break up, Motown head Berry Gordy wanted a big hit to launch Diana Ross's solo career and he chose this song, but then as an afterthought decided to have it recorded by the Supremes as a fitting finale to close out their Ross era before launching her solo career. As a result, the single topped the charts, although only Ross's voice appeared on the recording. Looking back on his career, he wrote: "I used to just freak on the Supremes 'cause they were so good. They did everything you told them to do. If you take that out, they take it out."

Around 1971, Fuqua left the label and worked as a producer for RCA.

Chart entries
If I Can't Have You *(with Etta James)* Etta James (US 1960 # 52)
That's What Girls Are Made Of *(with Gwen Gordy Fuqua)* The Spinners (US 1961 # 27)
Love (I'm So Glad) I Found You *(with Gwen Gordy)* The Spinners (US 1961 # 91)
Sincerely *(with Alan Freed)* The Four Seasons (US 1964 # 75)
Cleo's Mood *(with Autry DeWalt, Willie Woods)* Jr Walker & the All Stars (US 1966 # 50)
The Ten Commandments of Love *(with Marshall Paul)* Peaches & Herb (US 1968 # 55); Little
    Anthony & The Imperials (US 1969 # 82)
Sincerely *(with Alan Freed)* Paul Anka (US 1969 # 80)

Harvey Fuqua and Johnny Bristol
I Can't Believe You Love Me -Tammi Terrell (US 1966 # 72)
Come On and See Me - Tammi Terrell (US 1966 # 80)
If I Could Bring My Whole World Around You *(with Vernon Bullock)* Marvin Gaye & Tammi
    Terrell (US 1967 # 10; UK # 41)
My Whole World Ended (the Moment You left Me) *(with Pam Sawyer, Jimmy Roach)* David
    Ruffin (US 1969 # 9; UK # 51)
Twenty Five Miles *(with Edwin Starr)* Edwin Starr (US 1960 # 6; UK # 36)
What Does It Take (To Win Your Love) *(with Vernon Bullock)* Jr Walker & the All Stars (US
    1969 # 4; UK # 13)
Someday We'll Be Together *(with Jackey Beavers)* Diana Ross & the Supremes (US 1969 # 1;
    UK # 13)

Jerry Fuller
Born Jerrell Lee Fuller, Fort Worth, Texas 1938. Died 2024.

Born into a musical family, Fuller began his career by performing around the state with his brother Bill and later signing with the local Lin label. With a talent for songwriting, he decided to move to Los Angeles where he secured a recording contract with Challenge Records, a label which had just had enormous success with the Champs' "Tequila." Fuller toured with the group and also had a minor solo hit with a recording of "Tennessee Waltz," which also led to an appearance on *American Bandstand* in 1959. Two years later, he wrote "Travelin' Man," originally intended for Sam Cooke, but when given to Ricky Nelson it resulted in a US top ten hit. Fuller went on to write eleven of Nelson's recordings. In 1965, after a spell in the army, he moved to New York to manage the label's east coast business, and as producer discovered the garage band the Knickerbockers.

Moving to Columbia Records two years later, he discovered Gary Puckett & the Union Gap in a San Diego bowling alley lounge and signed them to the label. He wrote and produced "Young Girl" for the band, scoring a chart-topper on both sides of the Atlantic in 1968. As a warning to an underage girl of the consequences of men not being able to resist their attraction. Fuller later explained that the inspiration came from the perception that many male stars experienced situations where young girls appeared older. Dealing with the same subject, Fuller also wrote their follow-up single "Lady Willpower", about a man's desire for a younger woman, which almost repeated its chart success.

Fuller went on to produce the hits "The Son of Hickory Holler's Tramp" and "Little Green Apples" by O C Smith, before starting his own Moonchild production company in 1970.

Chart entries
Travelin' Man – Ricky Nelson (US 1961 # 9; UK # 2)
Son-in-Law *(with Dave Burgess)* The Blossoms (US 1961 # 79)
Guilty Of Loving You – Jerry Fuller (US 1961 # 94)
Young World – Ricky Nelson (US 1962 # 5; UK # 19)
It's Up To You – Ricky Nelson (US 1962 # 6; UK # 22)
For Your Sweet Love – The Cascades (US 1963 # 86)
Congratulations – Ricky Nelson (US 1964 # 63)
Please Don't Fight It – Dino, Desi & Billy (US 1965 # 60)
Young Girl - Gary Puckett & the Union Gap (US 1968 # 2; UK # 1)
Lady Willpower – Gary Puckett & the Union Gap (US 1968 # 2; UK # 5)
Over You - Gary Puckett & the Union Gap (US 1968 # 7)

Ken Gamble and Leon Huff
Born Kenneth Gamble, Philadelphia, Pennsylvania 1943.
Born Leon A Huff, Camden, New Jersey 1942.
Songwriters Hall of Fame 1995.
Rock and Roll Hall of Fame 2008.

Gamble spent much of his youth surrounded by and working with music. He cut his first records in penny arcade recording booths and was an assistant on the popular Philly radio station WDAS before running a record store in South Philadelphia. In 1960, he was discovered by producer and music promoter Jerry Ross (1933-2017), and together they wrote the dance song "The 81" for teen girl group Candy and the Kisses (with also featured young keyboard player Leon Huff). Gamble later joined up with Thom Bell (1943-2022) to form the duo Kenny and Tommy, and later the Philly-based harmony group Kenny Gamble & the Romeo's (not to be confused with the Detroit group of the same name). They had a regional hit on the Arctic label with "Ain't It Baby Pt 1." After moving to the Cameo label to become staff writers, Bell and Gamble met musician Leon Huff.

Huff had begun his music career as a session pianist and had worked with Phil Spector before moving to Philadelphia, where he formed the group the Locomotions and did session work for the Cameo and Swan labels. In 1964, he scored his first success as a writer with "Mixed-Up Shook-Up Girl" by Patty & the Emblems. Realising they shared a passion for songwriting, Gamble and Huff secured a deal with CBS and formed Philadelphia International Records, which became the second-largest African-American-owned company after Motown.

The two of them, along with publishing partner and arranger Bell, are credited with laying the groundwork for what became known as the "Philly Sound," with stirring soul music characterised by funk influences and lush horn and string arrangements. "Expressway (To Your Heart)," written for the Soul Survivors, gave the writers their first top ten hit in 1967, while "I'm Gonna Make You Love Me, written with Jerry Ross, become a huge hit for Diana Ross & the Supremes and the Temptations the following year. The song had previously been minor hits for Dee Dee Warwick (sister of Dionne) in 1967 and then Madeline Bell the following year. For the song, Diana Ross and Eddie Kendricks shared lead vocals, with Otis Williams providing the spoken interlude.

In the late Sixties, they teamed up with singer-songwriter Jerry Butler (1935-2025) and composed a string of hits for both him and Betty Everett. The following decade would see them create some of their finest soul music, with songs that included "If You Don't Know Me By Now," "Love Train" and "Me and Mrs Jones." They also received a lifetime achievement Grammy for their work. Huff later recalled: "A great song has to make you feel a certain way. Songs can make you happy and sad, they can help you fall in love. They have to do something. That's when you get a reaction."

Chart entries
(We'll Be) United – The Intruders (US 1966 # 78); The Music Makers (US 1968 # 78)
I Struck It Rich – Len Barry (US 1966 # 98)
I'm Gonna Make You Love Me *(with Jerry Ross)* Dee Dee Warwick (US 1966 # 88); Madeline
    Bell (US 1968 # 26); The Supremes & The Temptations (US 1968 # 2; UK # 3)
Together – The Intruders (US 1967 # 48)
Expressway (To Your Heart) – The Soul Survivors (US 1967 # 4)
Baby I'm Lonely – The Intruders (US 1967 # 70)
A Love That's Real – The Intruders (US 1967 # 82)
Explosion In Your Soul – The Soul Survivors (US 1967 # 33)
United – The Music Makers (US 1967 # 78) Peaches & Herb (US 1968 # 46)
Cowboys To Girls – The Intruders (US 1968 # 6)

Love In Them There Hills (*with Lester Chambers*) The Vibrations (US 1968 # 93)
Love Is Like (A Baseball Game) – The Intruders (US 1968 # 26)
I Can't Stop Dancing – Archie Bell & the Drells (US 1968 # 9)
Do the Choo Choo – Archie Bell & the Drells (US 1968 # 21)
Slow Drag - Archie Bell & the Drells (US 1968 # 54)
(There's Gonna Be a) Showdown - Archie Bell & the Drells (US 1968 # 21)
One Night Affair – The O'Jays (US 1969 # 68)
My Balloon's Going Up - Archie Bell & the Drells (US 1969 # 87)
A World Without Music - Archie Bell & the Drells (US 1969 # 90)

Gamble and Huff with Jerry Butler
Lost – Jerry Butler (US 1967 # 62)
Never Give You Up - Jerry Butler (US 1968 # 20)
Hey, Western Union Man - Jerry Butler (US 1968 # 16)
Only the Strong Survive – Jerry Butler (US 1969 # 4)
It's Been A Long Time – Betty Everett (US 1969 # 96)
Don't Let Love Hang You Up – Jerry Butler (US 1969 # 44)

Kenny Gamble
Finders Keepers, Losers Weepers – Nella Dodds (US 1965 # 96)

Kenny Gamble with Jerry Ross
Everybody Monkey - Freddy Cannon (US 1963 # 52)
Who Do You Love - The Sapphires (US 1964 # 25)
The 81- (US 1964 # 51)
Love Me - Bobby Hebb (US 1966 # 84)

Kenny Gamble with Thom Bell, Jerry Butler and others
Watch Your Step (*with Luther Dixon, Thom Bell*) Brooks O'Dell (US 1963 # 58)
The Boy With the Beatle Hair (*with William Jackson, Joe Renzetti, Jerry Ross*) The Swans (US 1964 # 85)
I Really Love You *(with James Bishop)* Dee Dee Sharp (US 1965 # 78)
Let's Make A Promise (*with Mikki Farrow, Thom Bell*) Peaches & Herb (US 1968 # 75)
Are You Happy (*with Theresa Bell, Jerry Butler*) Jerry Butler (US 1969 # 39)
I Love My Baby *(with Thom Bell)* Archie Bell & the Drells (US 1969 # 94)
Moody Woman *(with Thom Bell, Jerry Butler)* Jerry Butler (US 1969 # 24)
Girl You're Too Young (*with Archie Bell, Thom Bell*) Archie Bell & the Drells (US 1969 # 59)
What's the Use Of Breaking Up (*with Thom Bell & Jerry Butler*) Jerry Butler (US 1969 # 20)
A Brand New Me (*with Thom Bell, Jerry Butler*) Dusty Springfield (US 1969 # 24)

Snuff Garrett
Born Thomas Lesslie Garrett, Dallas, Texas 1938. Died 2015.

After dropping out of school, Garrett worked as a disc jockey in Lubbock where he befriended Buddy Holly and Waylon Jennings, and in 1959, while working for a station in Wichita, he broadcast his own tribute to the singer who had been killed just hours before. That same year, he worked as a recruitment man for Liberty Records, and with a penchant for finding and producing hit songs was soon made head of A&R. Among his roster of artists were Johnny Burnette, Gene McDaniels, Bobby Vee, Del Shannon and Gary Lewis & the Playboys, and he also hired Phil Spector to produce some of the recordings. After leaving Liberty, he worked with Sonny & Cher and founded his own labels, Snuff Garrett Records and its subsidiary Viva, which in the Eighties would be licensed to Warner for $2.5 million. In 1966, he was invited to produce and write songs for the Monkees ahead of their tv show, but following unsuccessful sessions they instead decided to work with songwriters Boyce and Hart.

    Although many of the hit singles he produced came from Brill Building staff writers, he co-wrote some with others, including Gary Lewis and his arranger Leon Russell. He later composed music for movies, including *Every Which Way But Loose* and *The Cannonball Run*.

Chart entries
Cross My Heart (*with Robert Velline, Sonny Curtis*) Bobby Vee (US 1965 # 99)
Everybody Loves a Clown (*with Gary Lewis, Leon Russell*) Gary Lewis & the Playboys
   (US 1965 # 4)
She's Just My Style (*with Al Capps, Gary Lewis, Leon Russell*) Gary Lewis & the Playboys
   (US 1965 # 3)
(You Don't Have To) Paint Me a Picture (*with Leon Russell, Roger Tillison*) Gary Lewis & the
   Playboys (US 1966 # 15)

Mort Garson
Born Morton Sanford Garson, Saint John, New Brunswick, Canada 1924. Died 2008.

Canadian-born Garson later moved to New York to study music before being drafted into the army shortly before the end of the war. On his return, he became a much sought after session musician, composer and arranger. As an accomplished songwriter, he also worked with others on a number of hits, including Michael Holliday's 1960 UK chart-topper "Starry Eyed" and Cliff Richard's "Theme For a Dream" the following year, both co-written with lyricist Earl Shuman (1923-2019). In 1963 he also partnered lyricist Bob Hillaird to give Ruby & the Romantics a US number one with "Our Day Will Come." as well as a string of hits that followed.

In 1967, Garson met Robert Moog at an engineers' convention, and as a result became one of the first composers to work with a Moog synthesiser. In an interview for *Shindig* he explained: "An electronic composer utilises synthesiser as a means of expression…Of course he must remain master of the instrument and not vice versa, but given the unique vehicle, he has the medium in which, almost literally, the sky's the limit for his imagination."

Chart entries
Starry Eyed *(with Earl Shuman)* Michael Holliday (UK 1960 # 1)
Theme For a Dream *(with Earl Schuman)* Cliff Richard & the Shadows (UK 1961 # 3)
It Only Took A Minute *(with Hal David)* Joe Brown & the Bruvvers (UK 1962 # 6)
The World of Lonely People *(with Buddy Kaye)* Anita Bryant (US 1964 # 59)

Mort Garson and Bob Hilliard
Our Day Will Come - Ruby & the Romantics (US 1963 # 1; UK # 38)
My Summer Love - Ruby & the Romantics (US 1963 # 16)
Young Wings Can Fly (Higher Than You Know) Ruby & the Romantics (US 1963 # 47)
Baby Come Home - Ruby & the Romantics (US 1964 # 75)

Bob Gaudio see Bob Crewe

Marvin Gaye
Born Marvin Pentz Gay Jr, Washington DC 1939. Died 1984 (shot by his father).
Rock and Roll Hall of Fame 1987.
Grammy Lifetime Achievement Award 1996.
Songwriters Hall of Fame 2016.

Named after his father, an Apostolic minister, Gaye started singing in church at the age of four and soon learned to play the organ. Encouraged to pursue a musical career, he became a singing star at Cardozo High School, and as a teenager joined several doo-wop groups. In 1956, he dropped out of school to join the US Airforce, but after a while secured an honorable discharge. For a short time, he joined local doo-wop group, the Rainbows, which had been formed by Chester Simmons. That later evolved into the Marquees (the name suggested by Gaye), with Gaye's best friend Reese Palmer joining the group. The new lineup was Simmons (bass), Reese Palmer (first tenor), Gaye (second tenor, baritone) and James Nolan (baritone). When Gaye became soloist, he dropped the "e" from his surname. The quartet performed in the Washington area and soon began working with singer Bo Diddley, who tried unsuccessfully to get his own label Chess to sign them. Instead, he sent them to Okeh Records, a subsidiary of Columbia, where they signed a record deal.

In September 1957 they entered the Brill Building in New York to record five songs, including "Wyatt Earp" and "Hey Little Schoolgirl," backed by Diddley's band. All the records were ignored by the label and were soon dropped. The following year, the Moonglows' co-founder Harvey Fuqua took them under his wing, and under his direction changed their name to

Harvey and the New Moonglows. Relocating to Chicago in 1959, they signed to Chess and recorded the single "Almost Grown."

The following year, Fuqua and Gaye moved to Detroit where Fuqua soon joined forces with Motown's Berry Gordy. In 1961, Gaye married Gordy's sister Anna and signed a solo recording contract with the Tamla label. With initial jazz-balladeer-style recordings proving unsuccessful, he worked as a session vocalist and drummer on recordings by the Miracles and the Marvelettes, also co-writing "Beechwood 4-5789" with George Gordy, a hit for the latter group.

The following year, Gaye joined fellow label artists for the successful Motown Revue tour of the country, which coincided with the release of his first solo hit, the more R&B song "Stubborn Kind of Fellow," produced by William "Mickey" Stevenson. With changes of style in both music and performance, Gaye's career flourished with a string of hits chiefly written by the label's staff writers. In 1963, "Pride and Joy," written with Stevenson and Norman Whitfield, became his first top ten hit on the Hot 100. The song was a tribute to his wife, and had the Vandellas as backing singers. The following year, he co-wrote with Stevenson and Ivy Jo Hunter the classic "Dancing in the Street." Originally offered to Mary Wells, it was turned down, leaving Martha & the Vandellas to record it. Written during the height of the civil rights movement, many African-Americans interpreted it as a call to "demonstrate in the streets," and it went on to peak at number two on the Hot 100. During the recording, co-writer Hunter was unhappy with the drum track, so he went out to his car and came back with a crowbar and with the tape running slammed it against the concrete floor on the downbeat, creating one of most defined drum beats in rock history.

Now portrayed more as a "ladies' man," the label teamed Gaye up with female artists like Mary Wells and Kim Weston, but it was with Tammi Terrell that he found his most enduring partner, their voices blending sensuously. Although the duets took precedence, Gaye had his greatest success as performer in 1968 with the Grammy-nominated "I Heard It Through the Grapevine." Although written by Norman Whitfield and Barrett Strong the previous year for Gladys Knight and the Pips, it was Gaye's dramatically different version that would become the label biggest-selling single of all time.

In 1970, his career was put on hold by the illness and death of soulmate Terrell, but returned to the spotlight the following year with the album *What's Going On,* a creative tour-de-force that blended his sensual vocals with a style of music that infused both classical and jazz influences into his soul roots. On his songwriting, he recalled: "These can't be the only notes in the world, there's got to be other notes some place, in some dimension, between the cracks on the piano keys."

Chart entries
If This World Were Mine – Marvin Gaye & Tammi Terrell (US 1967 # 68)

Marvin Gaye with others
Beechwood 4-5789 (*with George Gordy*) The Marvelettes (US 1962 # 17)
Stubborn Kind Of Fellow (*with George Gordy*) Marvin Gaye (US 1962 # 46)
Hitch Hike (*with Clarence Paul*) Marvin Gaye (US 1963 # 30)
Price And Joy (*with Norman Whitfield, William "Mickey" Stevenson*) Marvin Gaye (US 1963 # 10)
Dancing in the Street (*with William "Mickey" Stevenson, Ivy Jo Hunter*) Martha & the Vandellas (US 1964 # 2; UK # 28); Mamas & the Papas (as Dancing In the Streets) (US 1966 # 73); Ramsey Lewis (US 1967 # 84); Martha & the Vandellas (UK 1968 # 4)
Pretty Little Baby (*with David Hamilton, Clarence Paul*) Marvin Gaye (US 1965 # 25)
Baby I'm For Real *(with Anna Gordy Gaye)* The Originals (US 1969 # 14)

Bobby Gentry
Born Roberta Lee Streeter, Chickasaw County, Mississippi 1942.
Nashville Songwriters Hall of Fame 2020.

Of Portuguese descent, Gentry's parents were divorced soon after her birth. With her mother moving to Palm Springs, she was raised on a poverty-stricken farm by grandparents. When she was seven, they traded in one of their milk cows for a piano so their grandaugher could indulge in her love for music. Six years later, she went to live with her now remarried mother, and for a short while they performed together as Ruby and Bobbie Myers (later taking the stage name Bobby Gentry (from the 1952 movie *Ruby Gentry).*

Moving to Los Angeles after graduation, she performed in clubs before studying at the Conservatory of Music. After being invited to perform two duets with Debbie Reynolds, she signed with Capitol Records with the intention of writing for other artists. She wrote and recorded a demo for "Mississippi Delta" and "Ode to Billy Joe," using her own vocal, as it would be cheaper than hiring someone else. "Ode to Billy Joe" was originally chosen and released as the b-side of the single, but the sides were swapped over by Capitol after hearing a string arrangement by Jimmie Haskell that had been dubbed onto the original demo. The song topped the Hot 100, won two Grammys, and made Gentry an international star. It also created curiosity among listeners as to why Billie Joe committed suicide and what was actually thrown off the Tallahatchie Bridge.

In subsequent interviews, Gentry suggested it could have been a wedding ring but later recalled: "I had my own idea what it was while I was writing it, but it's not that important. Actually it was something symbolic. But I've never told anyone what it was, not even my own dear mother."

In 1968, Gentry's concept album, *The Delta Sweete* drew inspiration from her Mississippi Delta roots, and with most of the instruments played by Gentry, it was later deemed to be one of the masterpieces of the Sixties. Also that year, she was given her own tv variety series on *BBC*. The following year saw a return to the charts, duetting with Glen Campbell on a cover of "All I Have to Do is Dream."

Chart entries
Ode To Billie Joe – Bobby Gentry (US 1967 # 1; UK # 13); Life N Soul (UK 1967 # 62); King
    Curtis (1967 # 28); Ray Bryant (US 1967 # 89)
Okolona River Bottom Band – Bobby Gentry (US 1967 # 54)
Mornin' Glory – Bobby Gentry & Glen Campbell (US 1968 # 74)
Fancy – Bobby Gentry (US 1969 # 31)

Geoff Goddard
Born Reading, England 1937. Died 2000.

Singing in a church choir as a boy, Goddard later studied classical music at London's Royal College of Music. Following national service, his interests steered him more toward popular music with ambitions to become a Liberace-style pianist. Record producer Joe Meek agreed to promote him using the stage name Anton Hollywood, but it came to nothing. Settling on a solo career and using his own name, he recorded several singles with Meek's production, but with his distinctive regional accent they failed to score a hit. However, it was with his songwriting that he found success, providing singer John Leyton with a number of hit singles, including the UK chart-topper "Johnny Remember Me." The tale of a young man haunted by his dead lover came to Goddard while in his sleep. With its eerie, foreboding female wails (by backing vocalist Lissa Gray), it became another of the so-called "death discs" banned by the *BBC* at the time.

The follow-up single, "Wild Wind," also penned by Goddard, followed the same formula. Two years later, Goddard gave singer Heinz Burt his biggest hit with "Just Like Eddie," a tribute to Eddie Cochran, and also co-wrote with Meek two hits for Mike Berry and the Outlaws, who had previously provided backing vocals on "Johnny Remember Me." In 1965, he fell out with Meek over a breach of copyright claim concerning the Honeycombs' hit "Have I the Right?" (written by Howard and Blaikley), which Goddard claimed was borrowed from one of his own earlier songs. Refusing to testify, Goddard lost the case and withdrew from the music industry.

Chart entries
Johnny Remember Me – John Leyton (UK 1961 # 1)
Wild Wind – John Leyton (UK 1961 # 2)
Tribute to Buddy Holly – Mike Berry & the Outlaws (UK 1961 # 24)
Son This Is She – John Leyton (UK 1961 # 15)
Lone Rider – John Leyton (UK 1962 # 40)
Lonely City – John Leyton (UK 1962 # 14)
Just Like Eddie – Heinz (UK 1963 # 5)
Country Boy - Heinz (UK 1963 # 26)
You Were There – Heinz (UK 1964 # 26)
Geoff Goddard and Joe Meek
Don't You Think It's Time – Mike Berry & the Outlaws (UK 1963 # 6)
My Little Baby - Mike Berry & the Outlaws (UK 1963 # 34)

The Gibb Brothers
Born Barry Alan Crompton Gibb, Douglas, Isle of Man 1946.
Born Robin Hugh Gibb, Douglas, Isle of Man 1949. Died 2012.
Born Maurice Ernest Gibb, Douglas Isle of Man 1949. Died 2003.
Songwriters Hall of Fame 1994.
Rock and Roll Hall of Fame 1997 (as the Bee Gees).

Grammy Lifetime Achievement Award 2015.

In 1955, Barry and twin brothers Robin and Maurice (older by one hour) left their home in Douglas, Isle of Man, soon after the birth of their baby brother Andy, to go and live at their father's home town of Chorlton-cum-Hardy in Manchester. With their father being a Mecca-contracted orchestra leader and their mother a singer, music had already played a big part in their lives. With friends Kenny Horricks (on tea-chest bass) and Paul Frost (drums), the three brothers formed the Rattlesnakes, a rock and roll/skiffle band, to play in local cinemas with the Gibb boys singing the hits of the day. By 1957, they had begun to sing more and more in close harmony with aspirations of being a singing trio rather than a band, and with the departure of Frost and Horricks in May 1958, they disbanded to leave the brothers continuing as a trio called Wee Johnny Hayes & the Bluecats. However, three months later the Gibb family (including their older sister and young Andy) emigrated to Australia and settled near Brisbane, Queensland. To raise money, the brothers continued performing as the Rattlesnakes, and it was while at a speedway circus that they were introduced to local radio deejay Bill Gates.

Recognising their potential, Gates dubbed them the B.G's (after his own initials) and played their demo tapes on his show. As interest in the boys grew, Gates secured tv appearances and residences in resort clubs and hotels. Relocating to Sydney in 1962, they were the support act at a Chubby Checker concert, wrote their first composition, "Let Me Love You," and scored their first composing success with "Starlight of Love," a chart-topper for Australian star Col Joye.

In 1963, they signed for Festival Records as the Bee Gees and released their debut single " Three Kisses of Love," while the later single "Wine and Women" gave them their first Australian chart success in 1965. The following year, they signed to Spin Records, and under the guidance of producer Ozzie Byrne, improved their skills as recording artists and vocalists, highlighted by Robin's distinctive vibrato voice. Continuing to write songs with little success, their breakthrough came with Barry's ballad "Spicks and Specks," a top five hit on the Australian chart and later declared the "best single of the year."

Frustrated by their lack of success over the last four years, the Gibbs returned to England with their parents in January 1967, and after a successful audition signed a five-year management contract with Robert Stigwood and Brian Epstein's NEMS Enterprises, as well as a new record deal with Polydor. The following promotion campaign saw them being compared to the Beatles, with Australians Colin Peterson (drums) and Vince Melouney (guitar) now added to the group. Their debut single was Barry and Robin's "New York Mining Disaster 1941," written in a darkened stairway at Polydor during a power cut, and partly inspired by the Aberfan disaster in Wales the previous year.

Their follow-up single, the soulful "To Love Somebody," had originally been a request by Stigwood to write a song for Otis Redding, but it was their next single that would give them the first of what would be five UK chart-toppers. Written by all three brothers in a New York hotel and originally intended for the Seekers, "Massachusetts" was their answer to the magnetic attraction of San Francisco's flower-power culture drawing people away from the east coast but later regretting it. The following year, "I've Gotta Get a Message to You," with lyrics by Robin, described a man awaiting execution for murdering his wife's lover. In an interview, he explained: "What would be going through his mind? Let's not make it doom and gloom, but sort of an appeal to the person he loves. Because right now that's all he cares about." Robin also recalled for *The Mail on Sunday*: "Myself and Barry wrote it. It's a bit like writing a script. Sometimes you can sit three for three hours with your guitar and nothing happens. Then in the last ten minutes something will spark." Barry also commented on songwriting: "When you write a song you have an idea of how it should be sung, but it doesn't work out that way if someone else records it."

The 1968 album *Idea* included "I Started a Joke," about someone who had done or said something terrible resulting in alienation by everyone. Highlighted by Robin's incredible voice, it perfectly suited the lyrics. Robin recalled his part in the writing process: "Melody first, lyrics second ... If the melody doesn't get you off, the chances are it won't get other people off either," while Maurice noted: "I write the music because I can't really write lyrics. But I can write chords like Robin's never heard of. So I provide the music for them to add the lyrics to."

The following year came the ambitious *Odessa,* initially intended to be a concept album about the loss of a fictional ship in 1899. The only single taken from it was "First of May," featuring just Barry on lead vocal, but it also had "Lamplight, a group effort with Robin on lead, as the flip-side. When manager Stigwood made the decision about which song would lead, Robin felt his song had been snubbed (and not for the first time) and temporarily left the group.

His self-penned ballad "Saved By the Bell" (with brother Maurice on piano) gave him a solo number two hit in the UK later in the year. Continuing to record as the Bee Gees, Barry and Maurice failed to retain their success in the charts and in December they too parted ways.

The following year the brothers reunited and went on to have incredible success in the Seventies, beginning with the soundtrack to the disco movie *Saturday Night Fever*.

Chart entries
(The Lights Went Out In) Massachusetts - The Bee Gees (UK 1967 # 1; US # 11)
World - The Bee Gees (UK 1967 # 9)
Words – The Bee Gees (UK 1968 # 8; US # 15)
Jumbo - The Bee Gees (UK 1868 # 25; US # 57)

The Singer Sang His Song - The Bee Gees (UK 1968 # 25)
I've Gotta Get A Message To You – The Bee Gees (UK 1968 # 1; US # 8)
I Started A Joke – Heath Hampstead (UK 1968 # 52; The Bee Gees (US 1968 # 6)
First Of May – The Bee Gees (UK 1969 # 6; US # 37)
The Walls Fell Down – The Marbles (UK 1969 # 28)
Marley Purt Drive – Jose Feliciano (US 1969 # 70)
Tomorrow, Tomorrow – The Bee Gees (UK 1969 # 23; US # 54)
And the Sun Will Shine – Jose Feliciano (UK 1969 # 25)

Barry & Robin Gibb
New York Mining Disaster (1941) – The Bee Gees (UK 1967 # 12; US # 14)
To Love Somebody – The Bee Gees (UK 1967 # 41; US # 17); Nina Simone (UK 1969 # 5)
Holiday - The Bee Gees (US 1967 # 16)

Barry & Maurice Gibb
Only One Woman - The Marbles (UK 1968 # 5)
Don't Forget To Remember – The Bee Gees (UK # 2; US # 73)

Robin Gibb
Saved By the Bell - Robin Gibb (UK 1969 # 2)

Gerry Goffin and Carole King
Born Gerald Goffin, New York City 1939. Died 2014.
Born Carol Joan Klein, New York City 1942.
Songwriters Hall of Fame 1987.
Rock and Roll Hall of Fame 1990.
Grammy Lifetime Achievement Award 2013 (King).

Goffin became a lyricist as a boy, crafting words in his head like a game. After graduating from a Brooklyn high school, he enlisted in the Marine Corps Reserve and later resigned from the US Navy Academy to study chemistry at Queens College. It was there that he met fellow student Carol Klein. Klein had developed a love for music from watching her mother play piano, and from the age of three was taught basic skills, soon displaying she had perfect pitch. In the Fifties, she attended James Madison High School in Brooklyn where she changed her name to Carole King and formed a band called the Co-Sines. While there ,she made demo records with another budding musician called Paul Simon, and her first recording "The Right Girl" was released by ABC Records in 1958.

Both King and Goffin aspired to become professional songwriters, knowing that together they could pool their talents. After King became pregnant, they were married in August 1959. Quitting college, they both took day jobs while spending evenings writing songs together. Goffin added lyrics to the song "Oh Neil," which was King's reply to "Oh Carol," a hit song written by Neil Sedaka, her ex-boyfriend from high school, and Howard Greenfield, who both worked for Don Kirshner's Aldon Publishing Company. Although not successful, attention was brought to the b-side "A Very Special Boy" which was a Goffin-King song, and it helped them both secure writing contracts with Aldon.

Working out of the famous Brill Building, Goffin started by writing with established composers Barry Mann and Jack Keller, including Mann's hit "Who Put the Bomp (In the Bomp, Bomp, Bomp)." Goffin and King's breakthrough hit came with "Will You Still Love Me Tomorrow." Kirshner had assigned them to write a song for the four-girl group the Shirelles as a follow-up to "Tonight's the Night," their biggest success up to that point. King came up with the music, and Goffin, excited about writing for the Shirelles, quickly wrote the lyrics. Keen to get in the door at Columbia, Kirshner offered it to Johnny Mathis, but label boss Mitch Miller declined. Tony Orlando also wanted to record it, but Kirshner explained it was a girl's lyric and that no teenage boy would say those words. (Orlando would end up recording the answer song, "Not Just Tomorrow But Always," using the name Bertell Dache). The Shirelles lead singer Shirley Alston initially disliked the song for being "too Country and Western," but producer Luther Dixon convinced her they could do it in their style and asked the writers if they could add strings and turn it into a more uptempo song. The result was not only a huge transatlantic chart-topper but one of the finest love songs ever written.

Later that year they gave 17-year-old Tony Orlando his debut hit with "Halfway to Paradise," which also became a bigger hit for the UK's Billy Fury. A second US chart-topper came with Bobby Vee's "Take Good Care of My Baby." King had composed the tune on the piano and had almost handed it to fellow songwriter Cynthia Weil until Goffin wrote lyrics for it. Vee was blown away when he heard it, asking Kirshner to come out to Los Angeles to produce it. At the same time, another

Aldon singer Dion DiMucci, was keen to record it, but his first attempt was unsuccessful, and it left the song open for Vee to record it and take it to the top of the charts.

The following year came "The Loco-Motion," written in the hope that it would be recorded by Dee Dee Sharp, who already had a hit with "Mashed Potato Time." Sharp passed on the song, and it was left for 19-year-old Eva Boyd to record a demo. Boyd was King's babysitter, having been introduced to her by local group the Cookies. With a change of name to Little Eva, and with King on backing vocals, it was released on Dimension Records and became the writers' third chart-topper. Later that year, King performed a solo hit with their "It Might as Well Rain Until September," although originally done as a demo for Bobby Vee.

Another of their most celebrated songs was the Drifters' "Up on the Roof." The idea came to King while out driving and thinking of a secret haven where you could escape to and find tranquillity, with an initial title of "My Secret Place." Goffin used scenes of rooftops in the movie *West Side Story* to paint the perfect picture. First recorded as a demo by Little Eva, King preferred to record it herself and it secured her first solo hit. "Go Away Little Girl" by Steve Lawrence was another song intended for Bobby Vee, but when heard by Kirshner, he immediately thought of Lawrence (one half of the Steve and Eydie) and it went on to top the charts.

In 1963 the writers had more success with "One Fine Day." Inspired by the title of the aria "Un bel di vedremo" from Puccini's *Madame Butterfly*, they also intended it for Little Eva. Despite them providing a guide vocal and a distinctive piano riff by King, they were unable to do a viable arrangement and gave it up. Instead, they turned to the Tokens, who had produced the Chiffons' chart-topper "He's So Fine," and saw a potential for another "fine" hit. With King's piano work retained, the demo was radically reworked by the Tokens to give the Chiffons another top five hit. The following year, they gave Cookies' member Earl-Jean a modest hit with "I'm Into Something Good," but once picked up by Herman's Hermits, it topped the UK charts as their debut single. Another song that did better in the UK was "He's In Town," originally a moderate hit for the Tokens, but a top three UK hit for the Rockin' Berries.

In 1966, they wrote their most introspective song, "Goin' Back," with Goffin's emotive lyrics about trying to recapture a youthful innocence. With the definitive version sung by Dusty Springfield, it was also picked up by the Byrds to record in their unique style. The following year came "Pleasant Valley Sunday" by the Monkees, inspired by Pleasant Valley Way in West Orange, New Jersey, where they lived for a time, highlighting Goffin's dissatisfaction with suburban life.

When once asked her views about so-called writer's block, King offered good advice: "Songwriters, both lyricists and melody writers, are often plagued with the thing most often known as writer's block … I have found that the key to not being blocked is to not worry about it. Ever … Trust that it will be there. If it ever was once and you've ever done it once, it will be back. It always comes back and the only thing that is a problem is when you get in your way worrying about it."

"You Make Me Feel Like (A Natural Woman)" with its unmatched vocals by Aretha Franklin, was inspired by producer Jerry Wexler who had been contemplating the concept of a "natural man" when he saw King in the street and shouted to her that he wanted a song about a "natural woman" for Franklin's next album. For the recording, Aretha's sisters Erma and Carolyn sang backing vocals.

Although Goffin fathered a daughter through an affair in 1964, the two writers remained together until finally divorcing in 1969. Two years later, King went on to record *Tapestry*, now cited as one of the greatest albums of all time.

Goffin looked back on his career: "I'm not going to say whether my songs were good or bad. If people like them, that's fine and I'm happy." On hearing of his death in 2014, King paid her own tribute: "His words expressed what so many people were feeling but didn't know how to say … Gerry was a good man and a dynamic force, whose words and creative influence will resonate for generations to come."

Chart entries

Will You Love Me Tomorrow? – The Shirelles (US 1961 # 1; UK # 1); Four Seasons (US 1968 # 24)
How Many Tears – Bobby Vee (US 1961 # 63; UK # 10)
Some Kind Of Wonderful – The Drifters (US 1961 # 32)
Halfway to Paradise – Tony Orlando (US 1961 # 39); Billy Fury (UK 1961 # 3); Bobby Vinton (US 1968 # 23)
How Many Tears – Bobby Vee (US 1961 # 63; UK # 10)
Every Breath I Take – Gene Pitney (US 1961 # 42)
What a Sweet Thing That Was – Shirelles (US 1961 # 54)
Take Good Care Of My Baby – Bobby Vee (US 1961 # 1; UK # 3; US 1968 # 33)
Dear Mr D.J Play It Again *(with Howard Greenfield)* Tina Robin (US 1961 # 95)
Happy Times (Are Here To Stay) *(with Cynthia Weil)* Tony Orlando (US # 82)
Walkin' With My Angel – Bobby Vee (US 1961 # 53)
He Knows I Love Him Too Much - The Paris Sisters (US 1962 # 34)
Her Royal Majesty – James Darren (US 1962 # 6; UK # 36)

I've Got Bonnie – Bobby Rydell (US 1962 # 18)
When My Little Girl Is Smiling – The Drifters (US 1962 # 28; UK # 31); Craig Douglas (UK 1962 # 9); Jimmy Justice (UK 1962 # 9)
Why'd Do Wanna Make Me Cry? – Connie Francis (US 1962 # 52)
Sharing You – Bobby Vee (US 1962 # 15; UK # 10)
Keep Your Love Locked (Deep In Your Heart) Paul Peterson (1962 # 58)
Don't Ever Change – The Crickets (UK 1961 # 5)
The Loco-Motion – Litte Eva (US 1962 # 1; UK # 2); The Vernon Girls (UK 1962 # 47)
Point Of No Return – Gene McDaniels (US 1962 # 21)
It Might As Well Rain Until September – Carole King (US 1962 # 22; UK # 3)
Keep Your Hands Off My Baby – Little Eva (US 1962 # 12; UK # 30)
Up On the Roof – The Drifters (US 1962 # 5); Kenny Lynch (UK # 10); Julie Grant (UK 1963 # 33); The Cryan' Shames (US 1968 # 85)
Chains – The Cookies (US 1962 # 17; UK # 50)
Go Away Little Girl – Steve Lawrence (US 1962 # 1); Mark Wynter (US 1962 # 6), The Happenings (US 1966 # 12)
Let's Turkey Trot – Little Eva (UK 1963 # 13)
Don't Say Nothin' Bad (About My Baby) The Cookies (US 1963 # 7)
This Litte Girl – Dion (US 1963 # 21)
He's A Bad Boy – Carole King (US 1963 # 94)
Poor Little Rich Girl – Steve Lawrence (US 1963 # 27)
Old Smokey Locomotion – Litte Eva (US 1963 # 48)
One Fine Day – The Chiffons (US 1963 # 5; UK # 29)
Will Power – The Cookes (US 1963 # 72)
I Want To Stay Here – Steve & Eydie (US 1963 # 28; UK # 3); Miki & Griff (UK 1963 # 23)
Hey Girl – Freddie Scott (US 1963 # 10)
I Can't Stay Mad At You – Skeeter Davis (US 1963 # 7)
Everybody Go Home – Eydie Gormé (US 1963 # 80)
Walking Proud – Steve Lawrence (US 1963 # 26)
I Can't Stop Talking About You – Steve & Eydie (US 1963 # 35)
Where Does Love Go – Freddie Scott (US 1964 # 82)
I Can't Hear You – Betty Everett (US 1964 # 66)
I'm Into Something Good – Earl-Jean (US 1964 # 38); Herman's Hermits (UK 1964 # 1; US # 13)
He's In Town – The Tokens (US 1964 # 43); The Rockin' Berries (UK 1964 # 3)
Oh No Not My Baby – Maxine Browne (US 1964 # 24); Manfred Mann (UK 1965 # 11)
Show Me Girl – Herman's Hermits (UK 1964 # 19)
I Just Can't Say Goodbye – Bobby Rydell (US 1964 # 94)
At the Club – The Drifters (US 1965 # 43; UK # 35)
It's Gonna Be Alright – Maxine Browne (US 1965 # 56)
I Need You – Chuck Jackson (US 1965 # 75)
You're My Girl – Rockin' Berries (UK 1965 # 40)
Some Of Your Lovin' – Dusty Springfield (UK 1965 # 8)
Don't Forget About Me – Barbara Lewis (US 1965 # 91); Dusty Springfield (1965 # 64)
Don't Bring Me Down – The Animals (US 1966 # 12; UK # 6)
So Much Love – Ben E King (US 1966 # 96); Steve Alaimo (US 1966 # 92)
Goin' Back – Dusty Springfield (UK 1966 # 10) The Byrds (US 1968 # 89)
On This Side Of Goodbye – The Righteous Brothers (US 1966 # 47)
Pleasant Valley Sunday – The Monkees (US 1967 # 3; UK # 11)
(You Make Me Feel Like (A Natural Woman) Aretha Franklin (US 1967 # 8)
So Much Love – Tony Blackburn (UK 1968 # 31)
I Can't Make It Alone – P J Proby (UK 1966 # 37); Bill Medley (US 1968 # 95); Lou Rawls (US 1969 # 63)
Yours Until Tomorrow – Gene Pitney (UK 1968 # 34)
Don't Forget About Me – Dusty Springfield (US 1969 # 64)

Porpoise Song – The Monkees (US 1968 # 62)
I Can't Make It Alone – Lou Rawls (US1969 # 63)
Goffin & King with Phil Spector
Just Once In My Life – Righteous Brothers (US 1965 # 9)
Is This What I Get For Loving You? - The Ronettes (US 1965 # 75)
Hung On You – The Righteous Brothers (US 1965 # 47)

Goffin & King with Howard Greenfield
(Dear Mr D.J) Play It Again – Tina Robin (US 1961 # 95)

Gerry Goffin and Jack Keller
That Lovin' Touch – Mark Dinning (US 1960 # 84)
Run To Him – Bobby Vee (US 1961 #2; UK # 3)
A Forever Kind Of Love – Bobby Vee (UK 1962 # 13)
How Can I Meet Her?– Everly Brothers (US 1962 # 75; UK # 12)
It Started All Over Again – Brenda Lee (US 1962 # 29; UK # 15)
Don't Ask Me To Be Friends – The Everly Brothers (US 1962 # 48)
No One Can Make My Sunshine Smile – The Everly Brothers (UK 1962 # 11)
Don't Try To Fight It, Baby - Eydie Gormé (US 1963 # 53)
Girls Grow Up Faster Than Boys – The Cookies (US 1963 # 33)

Gerry Goffin and Russ Titelman
Yes I Will – The Hollies (UK 1965 # 9)

Gerry Goffin and Barry Mann
Who Put the Bomp (In the Bomp, Bomp, Bomp) – Barry Mann (US 1961 # 7); The Viscounts
    (UK 1961 # 21)
I Could Have Loved You So Well – Ray Peterson (US 1961 # 57)

Carole King
Are You Growing Tired Of My Love – Status Quo (UK 1969 # 46)

Carole King and Howard Greenfield
Crying In the Rain – The Everly Brothers (US 1962 #6; UK # 6)

Wally Gold see **Aaron Schroeder and Wally Gold**

Bobby Goldsboro
Born Richard Charles Goldsboro, Marianna, Florida 1941.

Moving to Alabama while still very young, Goldsboro later learned to play guitar, although he had ambitions to be a baseball player. While at high school, he joined the band Spider & the Webbs and continued playing with them while at college. Their manager took the chance to have the boys play for Roy Orbison, who was without a backing band for a show. It went so well that they were asked to become his permanent band for the next two and a half years, touring the US and Europe. When not on tour, the band continued playing local concerts with songs written by Goldsboro, and their performances came to the attention of producer Jack Gold, who offered Goldsboro a solo recording contract with United Artists. His first hit "See the Funny Little Clown" sold a million copies and over the next few years, although only finding moderate success as a singer, gave the UK's Dave Berry a top five hit with "Little Things." Two of his rare soul singles, "It's Too late" and "Too Many People" became huge hits on the UK's Northern Soul scene.

In 1968, Goldsboro's version of Bobby Russell's "Honey" topped the US charts for five weeks. The following year, his composition "With Pen in Hand," sung by Vikki Carr, won a Grammy nomination for Best Female Vocal Performance .

Chart entries
Baby's Gone *(with Roy Orbison)* Gene Thomas (US 1963 # 84)
See the Funny Little Clown (US 1964 # 9)

Whenever He Holds You (US 1964 # 39)
Little Things – Dave Berry (UK 1965 # 5)
Voodoo Woman (US 1965 # 27)
If You Wait For Love (US 1965 # 75)
If You've Got a Heart (US 1965 # 60)
Broomstick Cowboy (US 1965 # 53)
It's Too Late (US 1966 # 23)
Whenever She Holds You – Patty Duke (US 1966 # 64)
I Know You Better Than That (US 1966 # 56)
It Hurts Me (US 1966 # 70)
Blue Autumn (US 1966 # 35)
Autumn of My Life (US 1968 # 19; UK # 58)
With Pen In Hand – Billy Vera & the Beaters (US 1968 # 43); Vicki Carr (US 1969 # 35; UK # 39)
I'm A Drifter (US 1969 # 46)
Muddy Mississippi Line (US 1969 # 53)

Jerry Goldstein see Feldman, Goldstein and Gottehrer

Phillip Goodhand-Tait
Born Kingston upon Hull, England 1945.

Phil Tait, as he was known at school, began his music career after the family moved to Guildford in 1957. He formed a band called Phill Tone & the Vibrants, which four years later became Phill and the Stormsville Shakers. They released their first singles in 1966, including "I'm Gonna Put Some Hurt On You." With another name-change to Circus the following year, they released further singles, also without chart success. By 1969, Tait decided to pursue a solo career and went on to write and record songs, many covered by different artists, especially Love Affair, for whom he wrote or co-wrote three of their hits.

In 1971, he wrote the soundtrack for the movie *Universal Soldier,* and five years later played on Chris de Burgh's album *Spanish Train and Other Stories*.

Chart entries
A Day Without Love – Love Affair (UK 1968 # 6)
One Road – Love Affair (UK 1969 # 16)
Bringing On Back the Good Times *(with John Cokell)* Love Affair (UK 1969 # 9)

Alan Gordon and Garry Bonner
Born Alan Lee Gordon, Natick, Massachusetts 1944. Died 2008.
Born Garry Owen Bonner, Lighthouse Point, Florida 1943.

In 1965, Gordon formed the band the Magicians, which had evolved from Tex & the Chex. The line-up included Gordon (drums, songwriter), Everett Jacobs (bass) Mike Appell (guitar) and Rod Bristow (lead vocals). Gordon wrote the single "An Invitation To Cry," with non-member Jimmy Woods, but prior to recording the song, Jacobs was replaced by Garry Bonner. By 1965 Gordon and Bonner were emerging as a songwriting duo and began working with publishers Charles Koppelman and Don Rubin to write for other artists. Gordon had already written some of the lyric for "Happy Together" a couple of years before, and the chorus had come to him after a visit to his father. Unable to get Jacobs to help him finish the song, he now turned to Bonner for help. The completed song was offered to the Happenings, the Vogues and the Tokens, but was rejected by all three. Although hungry for a hit song, the Turtles were not happy with the quality of the demo they received, but after several months of rehearing decided to record it. It became a huge hit, knocking the Beatles' "Penny Lane" off the top of the Hot 100 at the beginning of 1967. The songwriting duo also penned the Turtles' "She's Rather Be With Me," which peaked at number three on the charts several months later.

Chart entries
Happy Together – The Turtles (US 1967 # 1; UK # 12)
Melancholy Music Man – The Righteous Brothers (US 1967 # 43)
Girls In Love – Gary Lewis & the Playboys (US 1967 # 39)
She'd Rather Be With Me – The Turtles (US # 3; UK # 4)

Me About You – The Mojo Men (US 1967 # 83); The Lovin' Spoonful (US 1969 # 91)
Two In the Afternoon – Dino, Desi & Billy (US 1967 # 99)
You Know What I Mean – The Turtles (US 1967 # 12)
Jill – Gary Lewis & the Playboys (US 1967 # 52)
The Cat In the Window (The Bird In the Sky) – Petula Clark (UK 1967 # 66; US #26)
She's My Girl – The Turtles (US 1967 # 14)
Me About You – The Lovin' Spoonful (US 1969 # 91)

Berry Gordy Jr
Born Berry Gordy III, Detroit, Michigan 1929.
Rock and Roll Hall of Fame 1988.
Songwriters Hall of Fame 2017.

Gordy was born the seventh of eight children to Berry Gordy II. Dropping out of high school in 11th grade, he became a professional boxer until drafted into the army in 1950 to serve in the Korean War. On his return to Detroit three years later, he married and ran a record store for a while. After being introduced through a friend to singer Jackie Wilson in 1957, he arranged for him to record "Reet Petite," a song Berry had written with his sister Gwen and writer-producer Billy Davis. Although a minor hit in the US, Berry went on to co-write other songs for Wilson, including "Lonely Teardrops." With the money made from his songwriting, Berry began building a roster of artists that included the Miracles, whose lead singer Smokey Robinson encouraged him to set up his own R&B company, Tamla Records. Its first recording was "Come To Me" by Marv Johnson. Berry's third release, "Bad Girl" by the Miracles, was the first on the Motown label. In August that year, Gordy and former Motown secretary Janie Bradford co-wrote what would become the much-covered classic "Money (That's What I Want)" for Barrett Strong to give Anna Records its first hit single. The label had been formed in 1959 by Berry's sisters Anna and Gwendolyn along with songwriter Roquel Billy Davis, and it had a better distribution system in place which helped promote the single.

In April 1960, Gordy merged the Tamla and Motown labels into a new company, Motown Record Corporation, and later that year teamed up with Robinson to write "Shop Around," giving the label its first million-selling hit single and the first Motown song to be released in the UK. Robinson had written the lyrics in about twenty minutes, recalling his mother telling him when he was ten to date lots of girls in pursuit of the perfect one. Originally having Barrett Strong in mind to record it, Gordy insisted he record it himself with his wife Claudette singing lead. After its release, Gordy woke Robinson up in the middle of the night to say he had thought up a different arrangement for the song and called the Miracles into the studio to record it. Everyone made it to the studio except the piano player, and Gordy sat in to play instead. The 3am re-recording had a faster tempo with Robinson now on lead vocal.

Gordy continued to produce hits for the label and co-write with Robinson for the Miracles, including "You Really Got a Hold On Me," but he also had solo songwriting credit for a number of hits, including "Do You Love Me?" for the Contours (later a UK number one for Brian Poole & the Tremeloes). Although written for the Temptations, they failed to arrive for the recording session. At the same time but in a different studio, the Contours arrived to record "It Must Be Love," but Gordy asked them to cut "Do You Love Me?" instead. It would be another two years before the Temptations had their hit, "The Way You Do the Things You Do."

Over the next decade, Gordy was responsible for signing a roster of artists that included the Four Tops, Gladys Knight & the Pips, and Stevie Wonder. In 1969, he brought together a trio of songwriters - Freddie Perren, Alphonso Mizell and Deke Richards - to form The Corporation and write songs for the Jackson Five, fronted by 11-year-old Michael Jackson.

Gordy had an innate gift for identifying artists' talents, and by controlling their recordings and choreographing their image, managed to create for Motown a whole new genre of music.

Chart entries
(You've Got To) Move Two Mountains – Marv Johnson (US 1960 # 20)
Merry-Go-Round – Marv Johnson (US 1961 # 61)
Let Me Go the Right Way – The Supremes (US 1962 # 90)
Shake Sherry – The Contours (US 1962 # 43)
Do You Love Me? – The Contours (US 1962 # 3); Brian Poole & Tremeloes (UK 1963 # 1); Dave
    Clark Five (UK 1963 # 30)
Don't Let Her Be Your Baby – The Contours (US 1963 # 64)
My Daddy Knows Best – The Marvelettes (US 1963 # 67)
Try It Baby – Marvin Gaye (US 1964 # 15)

Berry Gordy with Smokey Robinson
Shop Around - The Miracles (US 1960 # 2)
Don't Let Him Shop Around (*with Loucye Gordy Wakefield*) Debbie Dean (US 1961 # 92)
Ain't It Baby – The Miracles (US 1961 # 49)
Broken Hearted – The Miracles (US 1961 # 97)
Way Over There – The Miracles (US 1962 # 94)
You've Really Got A Hold On Me - The Miracles (US 1962 # 8)
Two Wrongs Don't Make a Right – Mary Wells (US 1963 # 100)
A Love She Can Count On – The Miracles (US 1963 # 31)
I'll Try Something New – The Miracles (US 1962 # 39); Diana Ross & the Supremes & the Temptations (US 1969 # 25)

Berry Gordy with others
Money (That's What I Want (*with Janie Bradford*) Barrett Strong (US 1960 # 23); Bern Elliott & the Fenmen (UK 1963 # 14); The Kingsmen (US 1964 # 16); Jr Walker & the All-Stars (US 1966 # 52)
You Got What It Takes (*with Tyran Carlo, Gwen Fuqua, Marv Johnson*) Marv Johnson (UK 1960 # 25)
I Love the Way You Love (*with "Mikaljon"* [*Mike Ossman, Al Abrams & John O'Den*] Marv Johnson (US 1960 # 9; UK # 35)
All I Could Do Was Cry (*with Billy Davis & Gwen Gordy*) Etta James (US 1960 # 33)
I Don't Want To Take A Chance (*with William "Mickey" Stevenson*) Mary Wells (US 1961 # 33)
All I Could Do Was Cry (*with Gwen Gordy & Tyran Carlo*) Etta James (US 1960 # 33)
Ain't Gonna Be That Way (*with Marv Johnson*) Marv Johnson (US 1960 # 74)
All the Love I Got (*with Brian Holland & Janie Bradford*) Marv Johnson (US 1960 # 63)
Happy Days (*with Tom McKnight*) Marv Johnson (US 1960 # 58)
I Don't Want To Take A Chance (*with William "Mickey Stevenson"*) Mary Wells (US 1961 # 33)
You Made Me So Very Happy (*with Brenda Holloway, Patrice Holloway & Frank Wilson*) Brenda Holloway (US 1967 # 39); Blood Sweat and Tears (UK 1969 UK # 35; US # 2)
I'm Living In Shame (*with Pam Sawyer, R Dean Taylor, Frank Wilson, Henry Cosby*) Diana Ross & the Supremes (US 1969 # 10; UK # 14)
No Matter What Sign You Are (*with Henry Cosby*) Diana Ross & the Supremes (US 1969 # 31; UK # 37)
I Want You Back (*with The Corporation (Gordy), Freddie Perren, Deke Richards, Fonz Mizell*) The Jackson 5 (US 1969 # 1; UK # 2)

Al Gorgini see Chip Taylor

Richard Gottehrer see Feldman, Goldstein and Gottehrer

Graham Gouldman
Born Graham Keith Gouldman, Salford, England 1946.
Songwriters Hall of Fame 2014.

Although not academically gifted as a child, Gouldman praised his parents for encouraging him to seek a career in music, and later recalled for *The Guardian*: "They recognised that songwriting is a gift and I was lucky enough to have it." With his father being an amateur poet and playwright, he was able to seek advice with his burgeoning songwriting craft. In his late teens, Gouldman played guitar and sang in various Manchester bands, including the High Spots and the Planets, but it was with the Whirlwinds that they managed to get a recording contract with HMV in 1964. The debut single "Look at Me," was a Buddy Holly cover (the b-side of which was written by future friend and 10cc-member Lol Crème). The Whirlwinds broke up later that year and Gouldman formed a new band the Mockingbirds, which included another future 10cc-member Kevin Godley on drums. Signing with Columbia, they released several songs, including the Gouldman-penned "You Stole My Heart" and "That's How (It's Gonna Stay)," but turned down "For Your Love," a song he had written at the age of 18 while working by day in a gents' outfitters and performing at night. Eventually, it would be recorded by the Yardbirds and top the UK charts in 1965.

Switching to the Immediate label, further releases followed, including Gouldman's "You Stole My Love." After signing a management agreement with impresario Harvey Lisberg, Gouldman wrote a string of hit singles for artists that included Herman's Hermits and the Hollies. In 1967, he began writing songs for Kennedy Street Enterprises and the following year released three solo singles. Two years later, he joined the Mindbenders as their temporary bass player, and became friends with Eric Stewart (another future 10cc member). A low point in his career came when he was approached by Jerry Kasenetz and Jeffry Katz of the US Super K Productions to come to New York and write throwaway, two-minute "bubblegum pop" songs. He accepted the advance payment, wrote the songs, and even sang lead vocal on one of them by the Ohio Express. At the end of the year, he convinced the studio that he could write songs for them back in England with Lol Crème and ex-Mindbenders friend Stewart.

In 1972, the three of them were signed by entrepreneur/producer Jonathan King and given the name 10cc, becoming one of the great British bands of the Seventies.

Chart entries
For Your Love – The Yardbirds (UK 1965 # 1; UK # 6)
Heart Full Of Soul – The Yardbirds (UK 1965 # 2; US # 9)
Look Through Any Window (*with Charles Silverman*) The Hollies (UK 1965 # 4)
Evil Hearted You – The Yardbirds (UK 1965 # 3)
Listen People – Hermans Hermits (US 1966 # 3)
Bus Stop – The Hollies (UK 1966 # 5; US # 5)
No Milk Today – Hermans Hermits (UK 1966 # 5; US # 7)
Behind the Door – Cher (US 1966 # 97)
East West – Hermans Hermits (UK 1966 # 37; US # 27)
Pamela, Pamela – Wayne Fontana & the Mindbenders (UK 1966 # 11; US # 76)
Tallyman – Jeff Beck (UK 1967 # 30)
Sausalito (Is the Place To Go) Ohio Express (US 1969 # 86)

Peter Green
Born Peter Allen Greenbaum, London 1946. Died 2020.

Green was a self-taught guitarist and was playing professionally by the age of 15. While working for several shipping companies, he joined Bobby Denis & the Dominoes as bass guitarist, playing a mixture of covers. Inspired by the Shadows' Hank Marvin, he later played with other bands, including the Muskrats and the Tridents. In October 1965, he was asked to stand in for John Mayall's Bluesbreakers' guitarist Eric Clapton on several gigs. He then joined Peter Barden's band Peter B's Looners, whose lineup included future Fleetwood Mac drummer Mick Fleetwood. The following year, Green and other members quit to form the soul band Shotgun Express, whose lineup included vocalist Rod Stewart, and later was invited to join the Bluesbreakers after Clapton's departure. Among the lineup was future Fleetwood Mac bassist John McVie. Green wrote a number of songs for the band, including the trademark "The Supernatural," and was soon referred to by fellow guitarists as the "Green God."

In 1967, with the band seen to be veering away from playing blues, Green formed his own band with Fleetwood, McVie, and slide guitarist Jeremy Spencer (from the blues trio Levi Set). The new band was called Peter Green's Fleetwood Mac featuring Jeremy Spencer, and later that year were signed to Mike Vernon's Blue Horizon label. Green's songwriting became more prominent with blues-styled originals like "Black Magic Woman" (covered by Santana in 1970), but it was his instrumental "Albatross" that gave them their biggest chart success. Inspired by reading the poem *The Rime of the Ancient Mariner* and his liking for Hawaiian guitar playing found on Santo & Johnny's 1959 instrumental "Sleep Walk," it also featured new member Danny Kirwan (ex-Boilerhouse) on guitar. In 1969, the band signed to the short-lived Immediate label and released "Man of the World," a beautiful cry from the heart written by Green, who at the time was frequently taking LSD and on a mental decline. He later recalled for *NME,* "It was how I felt at the time. It's me at my saddest." The last single with Green was "Oh Well," released in two parts, with radio stations playing the a-side "Part 1," while the b-side "Part 2" was an orchestral piece that sounded completely different.

Green would leave the band in 1970, giving all his money away to charity, while Fleetwood Mac continued with McVie's wife Christine (ex-Chicken Shack), and with the later addition of American duo Lindsey Buckingham and Stevie Nicks became global superstars.

Chart entries
Black Magic Woman – Fleetwood Mac (UK 1968 # 37)

Albatross – Fleetwood Mac (UK 1968 # 1)
Man of the World – Fleetwood Mac (UK 1969 # 2)
Oh Well – Fleetwood Mac (UK 1969 # 2; US # 55)

Roger Greenaway see Roger Cook and Roger Greenaway

Howard Greenfield see also Neil Sedaka
Born New York City 1936. Died 1986.
Songwriters Hall of Fame 1991.

Neil Sedaka was 13 years old and living with his family in a Brooklyn apartment when he was heard playing by a neighbour who introduced him to her 16-year-old son Howard Greenfield. Greenfield, an aspiring poet and lyricist, had attended the same high school as Sedaka and the two of them soon formed a writing partnership. In 1956, they wrote their first recorded song for the vocal group the Tokens, of which Sedaka was briefly a member. Inspired by show tunes, they wrote non-hit singles for other vocal groups the Cardinals and the Clovers, and to supplement their modest income, Greenfield took a job as a messenger for National Cash Register. In 1958, they were signed as songwriters to Don Kirshner and Al Nevin's Aldon Music, whose New York offices soon relocated to the Brill Building. Their first major success came later that year with "Stupid Cupid," originally intended for the Shepherd Sisters, but successfully recorded by Connie Francis.

With Sedaka signing to RCA as a solo artist, the two of them continued to write songs for him to record, including "Oh! Carol," and "Happy Birthday Sweet Sixteen," but it was "Breaking Up Is Hard to Do" that gave him his first chart-topper. Greenfield had written the lyrics at Sedaka's urging, and the song was then presented to Barry Mann for appraisal. Mann was not that impressed, so Sedaka added the more catchy "dooby-doo" intro.

In 1960, with Sedaka's touring commitments taking up more time, Kirshner suggested to Greenfield that he should collaborate with other staff writers, and as a result partnered Jack Keller for the next six years. Together they wrote hits for a number of artists, including "My Heart Has a Mind of Its Own," a chart-topper for Connie Francis, and Jimmy Clanton's "Venus in Blue Jeans."

At the same time, Greenfield worked with another writer Helen Miller on a number of hits, with "Foolish Little Girl" giving the Shirelles a top ten single. The Everly Brothers' hit "Crying in the Rain" came about when two of the Aldon songwriting partnerships chose to swap partners for the day, with Gerry Goffin (of Goffin-King) joining Jack Keller, leaving Carole King with Greenfield. The song would prove to be their only collaboration. With Kirshner having been eager to produce a hit for the Everlys, it was recorded shortly before the brothers were inducted in to the Marine Corps in November 1961and released while they were serving.

Greenfield moved to California in 1966 but continued to write with Keller and Sedaka whenever possible, although increasing arguments would see the partnership with Sedaka end in 1973.

Chart entries
Howard Greenfield and Neil Sedaka
Oh Carol - Neil Sedaka (US 1959 # 9; UK # 3)
Calendar Girl - Neil Sedaka (US 1960 # 4; UK # 8)
Another Sleepless Night – Jimmy Clanton (US 1960 # 22)
Run Samson Run – Neil Sedaka (US 1960 # 28)
You Mean Everything To Me – Neil Sedaka (US 1960 # 17)
Stairway To Heaven - Neil Sedaka (US 1960 # 9; UK # 8)
What Am I Gonna Do – Jimmy Clanton (US 1961 # 50); Emile Ford & the Checkmates
    (UK 1961 # 33)
Little Devil - Neil Sedaka (US 1961 # 11; UK # 9)
Happy Birthday, Sweet Sixteen - Neil Sedaka (US 1961 # 6; UK # 3)
Breaking Up Is Hard To Do - Neil Sedaka (US 1962 # 1; UK # 7); The Happenings (US 1968
    # 67)
Next Door To An Angel - Neil Sedaka (US 1962 # 10; UK # 29)
Where The Boys Are - Connie Francis (US 1961 # 4; UK # 5)
King Of Clowns – Neil Sedaka (US 1962 # 45)
Alice In Wonderland – Neil Sedaka (US 1963 # 17)
Let's Go Steady Again – Neil Sedaka (US 1963 # 26; UK # 42)
Bad Girl – Neil Sedaka (US 1963 # 33)

Sunny – Neil Sedaka (US 1964 # 86)
We Had a Good Thing Goin' – The Cyrkle (US 1967 # 72)

Howard Greenfield and Jack Keller
Everybody's Somebody's Fool - Connie Francis (US 1960 # 1; UK #5)
My Heart Has A Mind Of Its Own - Connie Francis (US 1960 # 1; UK # 3)
Loving Touch – Mark Dinning (US 1960 # 84)
I Wish I'd Never Been Born – Patti Page (US 1960 # 52)
Don't Read the Letter – Patti Page (US 1960 # 65)
Poor Little Puppet – Cathy Carroll (US 1962 # 91)
Breakin' in a Brand New Heart – Connie Francis (US 1961 # 7; UK # 12)
Venus In Blue Jeans – Jimmy Clanton (US 1962 # 7) Mark Wynter (UK 1962 # 4)
You Used To Be – Brenda Lee (US 1963 # 32)

Howard Greenfield and Helen Miller
Rumors – Johnny Crawford (US 1962 # 12)
Foolish Little Girl – The Shirelles (US 1963 # 4; UK # 38)
Charms – Bobby Vee (US 1963 # 13)
It Hurts to Be in Love – Gene Pitney (US 1964 # 7; UK # 36)
I'll Make Him Love You – Barbara Lewis (US 1967 # 72)

Howard Greenfield and Kenny Karen
Darkest Street in Town – Jimmy Clanton (US 1963 # 77)
Town Crier – Craig Douglas (UK 1963 # 36)

Howard Greenfield and Carole King
Crying In the Rain – The Everly Brothers (US 1961 # 6; UK # 6)
(Dear Mr D.J) Play It Again *(with Gerry Goffin)* Tina Robin (US 1961 # 95)

Howard Greenfield and Barry Mann
The Way Of a Clown – Teddy Randazzo (US 1960 # 44)
Girls Girls Girls – Steve Lawrence (UK 1960 # 49)
Counting Teardrops – Emile Ford & the Checkmates (UK 1960 # 4)
Warpaint – Brook Brothers (UK 1961 # 5)

Howard Greenfield with others
Hail to the Conquering Hero *(with Gloria Shayne)* James Darren (US 1962 # 97)
Did You Have a Happy Birthday *(with Paul Anka)* Paul Anka (US 1963 # 89)
My Special Dream *(with Freddie Douglass, Sol Kaplan)* Shirley Bassey (UK 1964 # 32)

Ellie Greenwich see **Jeff Barry and Ellie Greenwich**

Marvin Hamlisch
Born Mavin Frederick Hamlisch, New York City 1944. Died 2012.
Songwriters Hall of Fame 1986.

Although better known for his film work, Hamlisch was also a songwriter. As a child prodigy he could mimic piano music heard on the radio by the age of five, and two years later was accepted into what became the Julliard School Pre-College Division. After gaining a Bachelor of Arts degree from Queens College, he worked as a rehearsal pianist for the movie *Funny Girl,* and later scored the 1968 movie *The Swimmer*. As songwriter he had his first success partnering Howard Liebling (1928-2006) on "Sunshine and Lollipops" and "California Nights," both hits for Leslie Gore.

In the Seventies he composed the scores for the Broadway musical *A Chorus Line,* winning both a Tony Award and a Pulitzer Prize.

Chart entries
Wake Up – The Chamber Brothers (US 1969 # 92)

Marvin Hamlisch and Howard Liebling
Sunshine, Lollipops And Rainbows – Leslie Gore (US 1965 # 13)
California Nights – Leslie Gore (US 1967 # 16)

Albert Hammond and Mike Hazlewood
Born Albert Louis Hammond, London 1944.
Born Michael Edward Hazlewood, Crawley, England 1941. Died 2001.
Songwriters Hall of Fame 2008 (Hammond).

Hammond was born in London shortly after his parents were evacuated from Gibraltar during the war, and in 1960 began a music career with the Gibraltarian band the Diamond Boys. Although unsuccessful, they performed throughout Spain and played a large part in introducing pop music to the country. Mike Hazlewood began his career as a deejay on Radio Luxembourg in the early Sixties, and in 1966, along with Hammond, founded the group Family Dogg. Together, they wrote hit songs for Leapy Lee and Irish singer Joe Dolan, and as Family Dogg scored a hit in 1969 with the Cook-Greenaway song "Way of Life." Among the musicians on the recording were Elton John and future Led Zeppelin-members Jimmy Page, John Bonham, and John Paul Jones.

In the Seventies, Hammond and Hazlewood would go on to write "The Air That I Breathe" for the Hollies and "It Never Rains in Southern California" and "Free Electric Band" for Hammond to record.

Chart entries
Litte Arrows - Leapy Lee (UK 1968 # 2; US # 16)
Make Me an Island – Joe Dolan (UK 1969 # 3)
Teresa – Joe Dolan (UK 1969 # 20)

Tim Hardin
Born James Timothy Hardin, Eugene, Oregon 1941. Died 1980 (accidental heroin overdose)

Hardin was born to parents with musical backgrounds, his mother a violinist and father a concertmaster. Learning to play guitar at college, he later dropped out to join the Marines and served in Southeast Asia. Following his discharge in 1961, he moved to New York to attend the American Academy of Dramatic Arts, but again dropped out to pursue a music career. With a repertoire of folk songs under his belt, he performed around Greenwich Village, befriending fellow artists like John Sebastian and Cass Elliot. Moving on, he joined the folk scene in Boston where he was discovered by young producer Eric Jacobsen, who secured him a recording contract with Columbia. Unsuccessful demos led to the contract being terminated, and in 1965 Hardin moved to Los Angeles for a while before returning to New York. While there he signed with Verve Folkways, and in 1966 recorded his first album, the deeply poignant *Tim Hardin 1*, which included the single "How Can We Hang on to a Dream," a minor hit in the UK (and later a regular part of the Nice's live gigs) as well as the magnificent and much-covered "Reason to Believe." A *Los Angeles Times* reviewer described Hardin having "a voice which quavers between the tugs of the blues and the render side of joy. He can sing nasty, but his forte is gentle songs whose case allows him to slip and slide through a rainbow of emotions."

His second album *Tim Hardin 2* contained his most famous song "If I Were a Carpenter." Dealing with male romantic insecurity, it was rumoured to have been inspired by his love for actress Susan Morss, as well as the less romantic suggestion that it came from the construction of his recording studio. It also became an international hit in the hands of Bobby Darin and the Four Tops, although Hardin was deeply disappointed with those releases and reportedly broke down on hearing them. In 1969, he signed with Columbia again, recording three more albums, and also performed at the Woodstock festival. But he also spent the year travelling between the US and the UK trying unsuccessfully to cure his heroin addiction. Following his untimely death in 1980, one reviewer wrote: "Few people who have ever heard the poignant, often lonely, tone of [his] body of work would dispute the suggestion that he was one of the most affecting singer-songwriters of the modern pop era."

Chart entries
How Can We Hang On to a Dream – Tim Hardin (UK 1966 # 50)
If I Were A Carpenter – Bobby Darin (US 1966 # 8; UK # 9) Four Tops (US 1968 # 20; UK # 7)
The Lady Came From Baltimore – Bobby Darin (US 1967 # 62)

George Harrison see also **John Lennon and Paul McCartney**
Born Liverpool, England 1943. Died 2001.
Rock and Roll Hall of Fame 1998 (with the Beatles), 2004 (solo).

Harrison enrolled at the Liverpool Institute High School for Boys, and developed an early love of music from listening to artists like Cab Calloway, Hoagy Carmichael and Slim Whitman. In 1956, he was out riding a bike when he heard Elvis's "Heartbreak Hotel" playing from a nearby house, and it sparked an interest in rock and roll and especially the sound of guitars. After being bought one by his mother, he was taught to play by a friend of his father, and with the skiffle craze sweeping the country, he formed his own skiffle group the Rebels with his brother and a friend.

He first met fellow-Institute scholar Paul McCartney while on a bus, and they began a lasting friendship over their love of music. McCartney and his friend John Lennon had formed their own skiffle group the Quarrymen, and in March 1958, urged by McCartney, Harrison auditioned and was finally accepted as their lead guitarist. Two years later, with their new name the Beatles, promoter Allan Williams organised a club residency for them in Hamburg, which ended with Harrison being deported for being too young to work in nightclubs. With Brian Epstein becoming their manager in December 1961, he smartened their image and secured a record deal with EMI.

The rest is history with Beatlemania soon sweeping the world with a succession of singles and albums topping the charts, with Harrison's serious and focused stage persona earning him the moniker "the quiet Beatle." Lennon gave him lead vocal on "Do They Want To Know a Secret?" recalling: "It only had three notes and he wasn't the best singer in the world," although that view would soon change. Harrison's first writing credit came with "Don't Bother Me" on their second album *With the Beatles*, the name apparently inspired by his answer when asked to write a song. It would be his last writing credit until the album *Help!* two years later. Harrison's love for soul and folk music would eventually lead the band in that direction, as well as Indian classical music. After struggling for months to complete a song, he wrote two tracks for the *Help!* album. "I Need You" and "I Like You Too Much," both inspired by his love for girlfriend-model Pattie Boyd during a period of separation.

That love for her continued on *Rubber Soul* with "If I Needed Someone," its music inspired by the Byrds. The following album *Revolver* had Harrison's "Taxman" as the opening track. With it being the first Beatles' song to make a political statement (about policies of the current Labour government) it elevated Harrison's status as a writer. Other tracks on the album used traditional Indian instruments such as sitar, tambura and tabla, all played by Harrison.

His one song on the *Sgt Pepper* album was the Indian-inspired spiritual "Within You Without You," for which no other Beatle played a part, but had Harrison bring in musicians from the London Asian Music Circle. In response to criticism, Harrison said: "We're not trying to outwit the public. The whole idea is to try a little bit to lead people into different tastes." "The Inner Light," the b-side to "Lady Madonna," became the first Harrison song to appear on a Beatles single and again had local musicians playing traditional Indian instruments. The wonderful "My Guitar Gently Weeps on the *"White"* album, written while on a visit to his parents' home, had Harrison bring in Eric Clapton to play lead guitar. In 1969, the two friends co-wrote the single "Badge" for Cream.

Two of Harrison's classic compositions were highlights of the penultimate album *Abbey Road*. "Here Comes the Sun," was written in Clapton's garden while avoiding a group meeting with the Apple Corporation, but it was the ballad "Something" that would become his signature song. As another love song dedicated to wife Pattie, the lyric was inspired by label-mate James Taylor's album track "Something in the Way She Moves." The beautiful song would lead Frank Sinatra to call it "the greatest love song ever written." It became the first Beatles' chart-topper that was not written by Lennon and McCartney.

Before the Beatles finally split up, Harrison recorded two albums, with *Wonderwall Music* consisting mainly of a blend of Indian and Western instrumentation. In 1970, Harrison recorded a triple album *All Things Must Pass*, now considered to be his best work, and one that included the chart-topping gospel-like "My Sweet Lord," his first single as a solo artist.

On his songwriting, Harrison once revealed: "If I write a tune and people think it's nice, then that's fine by me, but I hate having to compete and promote the thing. I really don't like promotion."

Chart entries
If I Needed Someone – The Hollies (UK 1965 # 20)
Badge (*with Eric Clapton*) Cream (UK 1969 # 18; US # 60)
Something – The Beatles (UK 1969 #4; US # 1)

William Hart see Thom Bell and William Hart

Tony Hatch and Jackie Trent
Born Anthony Peter Hatch, Pinner, England 1939.
Born Yvonne Ann Burgess, Newcastle-under-Lyme, England 1940. Died 2015.
Songwriters Hall of Fame 2013 (Hatch).

With encouragement from his mother, a pianist herself, Hatch had musical ability at a young age and was just ten-years-old when he was enrolled at the London Choir School. Rather than continuing studies at the Royal College of Music, he opted to drop out of school in 1955 to work as a tea boy for Robert Mellin Music in London's Tin Pan Alley. With an aptitude for songwriting, he began composing songs under the pseudonym Mark Anthony and later joined Top Rank Records, working for their A&R man Dick Rowe. After doing national service he became a producer for artists such as Adam Faith and Bert Weedon, as well as beginning a solo recording career, but still using his pseudonym.

His first hit as composer came with Garry Mills' chart hit "Look For a Star" in 1960. When Top Rank was sold to EMI, Hatch switched to Pye Records and wrote songs for American artists, including the top ten hit "Forget Him" for teen idol Bobby Rydell. Under the name Fred Nightingale, he also wrote "Sugar and Spice," a UK number two hit for the Searchers in 1963. The following year, he began using his own name and wrote a string of hits for Petula Clark, with her most famous "Downtown" being inspired by a trip to New York. Clark had already carved a successful career in French, Italian and German-speaking territories and Hatch suggested she should be recording again in English. He had an unfinished song he played for her on a piano, and she said if he could write a suitable lyric she would record it. The song peaked at number two in the UK charts, but a while later Joe Smith of Warner Brothers, who was in England looking for material, heard the song and offered her a record deal. The song topped the US charts, making Clark the first UK female artist to have a US number one during the rock era.

That year, Hatch also wrote "I Love the Little Things" for Matt Monro, which came second in the Eurovision Song Contest in Copenhagen (won by Italy with "Non ho l'età," by Gigliora Cinquetti). "I Couldn't Live Without Your Love," another hit for Clark, was inspired by his ongoing affair with Jackie Trent (he was still married to his first wife). Trent had won a poetry competition at the age of nine and two year later won a talent show, after which she began using the stage name Jackie Trent. She recorded her first singles for Oriole Records in 1962 before moving to Pye. It was there she met Hatch who produced her records. When Hatch was asked to provide a song for the tv series *It's Dark Outside*, he co-wrote "Where Are You Now (My Love)?" with Trent and when recorded gave her a UK number one in 1965.

The following year, he scored another US number one with Petula Clark's "My Love." On a flight from New York to Los Angeles in November 1965, Hatch had been putting the finishing touches to a song he called "The Life and Soul of the Party," which he planned to record in Los Angeles. During a conversation with an American passenger, he was advised that the song's title would be meaningless to the American public. Hatch then adapted the lyrics and changed the title to "My Love," and completing the music soon after arriving in New York. Around the same time, Trent wrote "What Would I Be" for the popular Irish singer Val Doonican, while Hatch began to write for tv, including the themes to *Crossroads, Man Alive, The Doctors* and *The Champions*.

Married in 1967, they went on to write more hits for Clark. "Don't Sleep in the Subway" was a combination of three different songs which Hatch had written but not completed. He later described the meaning behind the lyrics: "It's two adult people and they've had a row. As the man often does, he said 'Oh I'm going. I'm leaving.' You walk out the door and you're not sure what you're doing or why you're doing it." "The Other Man's Grass Is Always Greener" was written after Clark's previous single "The Cat in the Window (The Bird in the Sky)" had flopped and there was need for an advanced single for her next album. Hatch recalled that the song contained "a lot of deep thought [and] a lot of philosophy … [Clark] enjoyed singing those kind of songs." Unfortunately, it still only found moderate chart success.

The following year they gave Scott Walker a huge hit with the ballad "Joanna," for which the singer declined co-writing credit for some of the lyrics. Hatch had written the song for the 1968 movie of the same name at the request of the director Michael Sarne, but the film company insisted it had to be performed by Rod McKuen, to whom they had already paid an advance in an earlier deal. Instead, they released the single around the same time the movie went out. Former Walker Brothers' singer Gary Leeds, who also played on the recording, recalled that Scott hated singing the song, feeling that his manager was trying to make him into "another Andy Williams or Frank Sinatra."

In the Seventies, the couple switched to musical theatre, with Hatch continuing to score tv themes that included *Emmerdale Farm, Hadleigh* and *Sportsnight*. The couple divorced in 2002. Hatch described his career: "I just love the music business. I love being part of it. I love the challenge. I love working with musicians and I love working in the recording studio."

Chart entries
Where Are You Now (My Love)? – Jackie Trent (UK 1965 # 1)
When Summertime Is Over – Jackie Trent (UK 1965 # 39)
Love Is Me Love Is You – Connie Francis (US 1966 # 66)
I Couldn't Live Without Your Love – Petula Clark (UK 1966 # 6; US # 9)
Who Am I – Petula Clark (US 1966 # 21)
Colour My World – Petula Clark (US 1966 # 16)
Don't Sleep In the Subway – Petula Clark (UK 1967 # 12; US # 5)
If You Ever Leave Me – Jack Jones (US 1968 # 92)
You've Got To Be Loved – The Montanas (US 1968 # 58)
Joanna – Scott Walker (UK 1968 # 7)

Look At Mine – Petula Clark (US 1969 # 89)
The Other Man's Grass Is Always Greener – Petula Clark (UK 1967 # 20; US # 31)
Where Will You Be – Sue Nicholls (UK 1968 # 17)
Don't Give Up – Petula Clark (US 1968 # 37)
American Boys – Petula Clark (US 1968 # 59)
I'll Be There – Jackie Trent (UK 1969 # 38)
Look At Mine – Petula Clark (US 1969 # 89)

Tony Hatch
Look For A Star – Deane Hawley (US 1960 # 29); Billy Vaughn (US 1960 # 19)
    *as Mark Anthony); Garry Mills (UK 1960 # 7; US 26) (*as Mark Anthony)
Top Teen Baby *(as Mark Anthony, with Bunny Lewis)* Garry Mills (UK 1960 # 24)
Transistor Radio *(as Mark Anthony, with Benny Hill)* Benny Hill (UK 1961 # 24)
Count On Me – Julie Grant (UK 1963 # 24)
Harvest Of Love *(as Mark Anthony, with Benny Hill)* Benny Hill (UK 1963 # 20)
Forget Him *(as Mark Anthony)* Bobby Rydell (US 1963 # 4)
Sugar And Spice *(as Fred Nightingale)* The Searchers (UK 1963 # 2; US # 44); The Cryin'
    Shames (US 1966 # 49)
Downtown – Petula Clark (UK 1964 # 2; US # 1) Mrs Miller (UK 1966 # 56; US # 82)
I Know A Place – Petula Clark (UK 1965 # 17; US # 3)
Crazy Downtown *(with Allan Sherman)* Allan Sherman (US 1965 # 40)
You'd Better Come Home – Petula Clark (UK 1965 # 44; US # 22)
Roundabout – Connie Francis (US 1965 # 80)
'Round Every Corner – Petula Clark (UK 1965 # 43; US # 21)
You're the One *(with Petula Clark)* The Vogues (US 1965 # 4) Petula Clark (UK 1965 # 23)
Call Me – Chris Montez (US 1965 # 22)
My Love – Petula Clark (UK 1966 # 4; US # 1)
A Sign Of the Times – Petula Clark (UK 1966 # 49; US # 11)
To Show I Love You – Peter & Gordon (US 1966 # 98)
The Other Man's Grass Is Always Greener (with Yvonne J Harvey) Petula Clark (UK
    1967 # 20; US # 31)
I Love the Little Things – Matt Monro (UK 1964 *Eurovision entry

Jackie Trent
What Would I Be – Val Doonican (UK 1966 # 2)

Ken Hawker see John Carter and Ken Lewis

Mike Hawker and John Schroeder
Born Michael Edwin Hawker, Bath, England 1936. Died 2014.
Born John Francis Schroeder, London 1935. Died 2017.

With his father in the Royal Air Force, Hawker spent part of his childhood in Singapore before returning to Barnsley to live with relatives. After leaving university, he followed his father's footsteps and joined the RAF. He began writing concert reviews of US jazz musicians for music magazines before getting a job in publicity at EMI in the late Fifties. Later, he did promotion work for pop impresario Larry Parnes and began writing songs. He then linked up with composer John Schroeder, who at the time was working as an A&R assistant to Norrie Paramor at Columbia. Together, they wrote several songs for Paramor's young protégée Helen Shapiro, including "Don't Treat Me Like a Child," and two back-to back UK chart toppers with "Walkin' Back to Happiness" and "You Don't Know." Hawker would go on to receive an Ivor Novello Award for "Happiness." Schroeder later became A&R chief for the independent Oriole label and secured an early licensing deal with Motown. He then moved to Pye and formed Sounds Orchestral with Johnny Pearson, scoring an international hit with "Cast Your Fate to the Wind." He was also largely responsible for launching the career of Status Quo in the late Sixties, and producing their first hit "Pictures of Matchstick Men" in 1968.
   In the meantime, Hawker had joined up with composer Ivor Raymonde (1926-1990) to write several hits for Dusty Springfield, including "I Only Want to Be With You." According to Hawker's then-wife Jean Ryder, it was written shortly

after their marriage in December 1961 and was inspired by his romantic feelings for his new bride. Ryder, who had been a member of the vocal group the Vernon Girls and would later join the Breakaways, later claimed the intention had been to record the song herself.

In the Seventies, Hawker continued to write for artists and discovered singer songwriter Labi Siffre. Schroeder formed Alaska Records before moving to Canada.

Chart entries
Don't Treat Me Like a Child – Helen Shapiro (UK 1961 # 3)
You Don't Know – Helen Shapiro (UK 1961 # 1)
Walkin' Back To Happiness – Helen Shapiro (UK 1961 # 1; US # 100)
Little Miss Lonely - Helen Shapiro (UK 1962 # 8)
Look Who It Is - Helen Shapiro (UK 1963 # 47)

Mike Hawker and Ivor Raymonde
I Only Want To Be With You - Dusty Springfield (UK 1963 # 4; US # 12)
Stay Awhile - Dusty Springfield (UK 1964 # 13; US # 38)
My World of Blue - Karl Denver (UK 1964 # 29)
You're Hurtin' Kind of Love - Dusty Springfield (UK 1965 # 37)

Isaac Hayes & David Porter
Born Isaac Lee Hayes, Covington, Tennessee 1942. Died 2008.
Porter born Memphis, Tennessee 1941.
Rock and Roll Hall of Fame 2002 (Hayes)
Songwriters Hall of Fame 2005.
Grammy Lifetime Achievement Award 2020 (Hayes).

With his mother dying young and father abandoning the family, Hayes was raised by his maternal grandparents and spent his early years working on farms. By the age of five, he was singing in his local church and became a self-taught musician, playing piano, organ, saxophone and flute, and all the time developing a love of performing. After graduating from high school, he was offered several music scholarships, but turned them all down to provide for his family. With a day job at a Memphis meat-packing plant, he spent evenings playing in juke joints and nightclubs. In the late Fifties, he was invited to perform as a singer at Memphis's Curry Club by bandleader Ben Branch, whose house band the Largos providing backing. In the early Sixties, Hayes was working as a session man at Stax Records where he teamed up with songwriter David Porter.

Porter was one of 12 children, and like Hayes, sang in church and school, where one of his closest friends was classmate Maurice White (later the founder of Earth, Wind and Fire). Performing at various venues and in local competitions, Porter later attended LeMoyne College, and while still a student and working at a grocery store met producer Chips Moman, whose Satellite Records (soon to become Stax) was across the street. Offered the job as their first staff songwriter, Porter was able to arrange for friends to make recordings (including William Bell and Booker T Jones). As A&R man for the re-branded Stax label, he signed artists that included Homer Banks, the Emotions and the Soul Children, before inviting Hayes to be his writing partner.

Over the next few years, they wrote a string of hits for the label's roster of artists, especially Sam & Dave (Sam Moore & Dave Prater) and Carla Thomas (daughter of Rufus), later to be dubbed the Queen of Memphis Soul. As producers, they were also credited with the development of the Stax sound and style, which was provided by Booker T Jones' house band the MGs (Memphis Group).Their first success as writers came with Sam & Dave's "Hold On! I'm Comin,'" released in March 1966. The title actually came from Porter's reply to Hayes when told to hurry up out of a restroom. With its "suggestive nature," however, some radio stations lodged complaints, and on most copies of the single it has "Hold On! I'm A-Comin'" Around the same time, they gave Carla Thomas hits with "Let Me Be Good To You," written along with staff writer (Lewis) Carl Wells, and the top 20 "B-A-B-Y."

In 1967, Hayes and Porter wrote and produced "Soul Man" by Sam & Dave." After watching a tv newscast of the aftermath of a Detroit riot, Hayes noticed that black residents had marked buildings that had not been destroyed (chiefly black-owned premises) with the word "soul," and he later explained that it was about "one's struggle to rise above his present conditions … like boasting, 'I'm a soul man.' It's a pride thing." The following year's "Soul Sister, Brown Sugar" was deemed to mean admiration for a person who is "as sweet, like brown sugar."

As a recording artist, Hayes released his largely improvised debut album *Presenting Isaac Hayes* in 1969. After losing their biggest artist Otis Redding in 1967, and then losing their back catalog to Atlantic the following year, Stax went through a major upheaval, and its vice-president Al Bell called for 27 new albums to be released by mid-1969. Hayes' second album *Hot Buttered Soul* became the most successful of these releases. One of the tracks was a cover of Bacharach & David's "Walk on By," which Hayes transformed into a 12-minute funk vamp, as was "I Just Don't Know What To Do With Myself" and "The Look of Love" on the following album. Hayes once explained: "You know, you can't put bread in a cold oven. You know, you've got to take your time. You've got to heat it up. So that's what I like to do with my music. I like to build it, and build it into a maddening, exciting crescendo."

In 1971, Hayes composed music for the soundtrack to the movie *Shaft,* and with its half-spoken vocal, became a worldwide hit single, winning an Oscar for Best Original Song. Hayes had only agreed to do it on condition he got the starring role in the movie, but with no acting experience he lost out to Richard Roundtree. Porter also recorded solo albums for Stax in the early Seventies, and released recordings for other labels with the pseudonyms Little David and Kenny Cain.

Chart entries
You Don't Know Like I Know – Sam & Dave (US 1966 # 90)
Hold On! I'm Comin' – Sam & Dave (US 1966 # 21); Chuck Jackson & Maxine Brown (US 1967 # 91)
Let Me Be Good To You *(with Carl Wells)* Carla Thomas (US 1966 # 62)
Your Good Thing (Is About to End) Mable John (US 1966 # 95); Lou Rawls (US 1969 # 18)
B-A-B-Y – Carla Thomas (US 1966 # 14)
Said I Wasn't Gonna Tell Nobody – Sam & Dave (US 1966 # 64)
You Got Me Hummin' – Sam & Dave (US 1966 # 77)
Something Good (Is Gonna Happen to You) Carla Thomas (US 1967 # 74)
When Something is Wrong with My Baby – Sam & Dave (US 1967 # 42)
When Tomorrow Comes -Carla Thomas (US 1967 # 99)
I Take What I Want *(with Mabone "Teenie" Hodges)* James & Bobby Purify (US 1967 # 41)
How Can You Mistreat the One You Love – Jean & the Darlings (US 1967 # 96)
Soul Man – Sam & Dave (US 1967 # 2; UK 24); Ramsey Lewis (US 1967 # 49)
I Thank You – Sam & Dave (US 1968 # 9; UK # 4)
60 Minutes of Your Love – Homer Banks (UK 1968 # 55)
Everybody Got To Believe in Somebody – Sam & Dave (US 1968 # 73)
Soul Sister, Brown Sugar – Sam & Dave (US 1968 # 41; UK # 15)
Born Again – Sam & Dave (US 1969 # 92)
The Sweeter He Is Pt 1 – The Soul Children (US 1969 # 52)

Isaac Hayes with others
Boot-leg *(with Charle Axton, Donald "Duck" Dunn, Al Jackson Jr)* Booker T & the MGs (US 1965 # 58)
Candy *(with Steve Cropper)* The Astors (US 1965 # 63)

Justin Hayward
Born David Justin Hayward, Swindon, England 1946.
Rock and Roll Hall of Fame 2018 (with The Moody Blues).

The son of two teachers, he later played in several bands while still at school and bought his first guitar at the age of 15 (one that he played throughout most of his career). Performing in venues with several local bands, their repertoire consisted mainly of Buddy Holly songs, and even opened for the Hollies and Brian Poole & the Tremeloes. At the age of 18, he signed an eight-year publishing contract with Lonnie Donegan's Tyler Music, without realising that all songs written prior to 1974 would be owned by them. In 1965, he answered an ad in *New Musical Express* for a guitarist for Marty Wilde, and after auditioning joined the singer and his wife as the trio The Wilde Three.

The following year, he answered another ad, this time one placed by Eric Burdon in *Melody Maker.* Burdon then passed on the letter and the demo to his friend Mike Pinder of the Moody Blues. In a matter of days, Pinder invited Hayward to join the band, replacing the departed Denny Laine. Around the same time, bass player John Lodge (b.1943) replaced Clint Warwick, who had also left the band. The two songwriters Hayward and Lodge would be instrumental in transforming the band into one of the UK's most celebrated progressive bands. While touring in Belgium, Hayward wrote "Nights in White Satin," inspired by a girlfriend who gave him a gift of satin sheets. In 2008, he explained to the *Daily Express*: "I wrote our most famous song when I was 19. It was a series of random thoughts and was quite autobiographical. It was a very emotional time and I was at the end of one big love affair and the start of another. A lot of that came out in the song."

Released as a single in 1967, it went on to sell two million copies. Its parent album *Days of Future Passed* was based around three different times of day, and the longer version of the song had the London Festival Orchestra providing the lush accompaniment for the introduction, the final chorus, and the "final lament" section, all arranged by Peter Knight. Hayward also wrote the single "Never Comes the Day" from the album *On the Threshold of a Dream* and just managed to make the US Hot 100 in 1969. In a later interview he said: "I can be stupid in my lyrics or say whatever I want without having to worry about anybody else's feeling or anybody being embarrassed by it or anything like that."

Hayward would perform with the Moody Blues for decades to come. In 1974, he teamed up with Lodge to record the album *Blue Jays,* which spawned the single "Blue Guitar," and in 1978 became part of Jeff Lynne's concept album *The War of the Worlds,* which yielded the self-penned single "Forever Autumn."

Chart entries
Nights in White Satin – The Moody Blues (UK 1967 # 19)
Tuesday Afternoon (Forever Afternoon) – The Moody Blues (US 1967 # 24)
Voices in the Sky – The Moody Blues (UK 1968 # 27)
Never Comes the Day – The Moody Blues (US 1969 # 91)

Tony Hazzard
Born Anthony Hazzard, Liverpool, England 1943.

Learning to play ukelele and guitar at an early age, Hazzard attended Durham University before being encouraged by BBC television producer Tony Garnett to move to London. There, he signed a recording contract with music publisher Gerry Bron's Orchestral Service. Over the next decade, he wrote songs for a number of artists, including Simon Dupree & the Big Sound, The Family Dogg, the Hollies, and the Swinging Blue Jeans.

Chart entries
You Won't Be Leaving – Herman's Hermits (UK 1966 # 20)
Ha! Ha! Said the Clown – Manfred Mann (UK 1967 # 4); The Yardbirds (UK 1967 # 45)
Me, the Peaceful Heart – Lulu (UK 1968 # 9; US # 63)
Listen to Me – The Hollies (UK 1968 # 11)
Fox on the Run – Manfred Mann (UK 1968 # 5; US # 97)
Maria Elena – Gene Pitney (UK 1969 # 25)
Hello World – The Tremeloes (UK 1969 # 14)

Lee Hazlewood
Born Barton Lee Hazlewood, Mannford, Oklahoma 1929. Died 2007.
Songwriters Hallof Fame 2011.

The son of a half-Creek mother, Hazlewood spent his youth listening to pop and bluegrass music in Texas. He studied for a medical degree in Dallas and then joined the army to serve in the Korean War. On his return, he worked as a deejay in Phoenix and formed his own record label Viv. As songwriter and producer, he scored his first hit in 1955 with "The Fool" by Sanford Clark, and then struck up a partnership with guitarist Duane Eddy, producing and co-writing hits for him like "Rebel Rouser," "Shazam!" and "Dance With the Guitar Man." His collaboration with Nancy Sinatra began when her father asked him to help guide her career. Inspired by a line spoken by Sinatra in the 1963 movie *4 for Texas,* Hazlewood wrote and produced "These Boots Are Made For Walkin'" for Nancy (despite wanting to record it himself) and it topped the US charts in 1965. He also wrote her hit "Sugar Town," albeit an allusion to sugar cubes laced with LSD, and duetted with her on "Some Velvet Morning," a hit in the fall of 1967.

Chart entries
A Stranger In Your Town *(with Marty Cooper)* The Shacklefords (US 1963 # 70)
Surfin Hootenanny – Al Casey Combo (US 1963 # 48)
Baja – The Astronauts (US 1963 # 94)
Houston – Dean Martin (US 1965 # 21)
Not the Lovin' Kind – Dino, Desi & Billy (US 1965 # 25)
So Long, Babe – Nancy Sinatra (US 1965 # 86)
These Boots Are Made For Walkin' – Nancy Sinatra (US 1965 # 1; UK # 1)
How Does That Grab You, Darlin'? – Nancy Sinatra (US 1966 # 7; UK # 19)
Friday's Child – Nancy Sinatra (US 1966 # 36; UK # 55)
In Our Time – Nancy Sinatra (1966 # 46)
Sugar Town – Nancy Sinatra (US 1966 # 5; UK # 8)

Summer Wine – Nancy Sinatra & Lee Hazlewood (US 1967 # 49)
Love Eyes – Nancy Sinatra (US 1967 # 15)
Lightning's Girl - Nancy Sinatra (US 1967 # 24; UK # 54)
Lady Bird – Lee Hazlewood & Nancy Sinatra (US 1967 # 20; UK # 47)
This Town – Frank Sinatra (US 1967 # 53)
Tony Rome - Nancy Sinatra (US 1967 # 83)
Some Velvet Morning –Lee Hazlewood & Nancy Sinatra (US 1968 # 26)
In Some Time – Ronnie Dove (US 1968 # 99)
100 Years - Nancy Sinatra (US 1968 # 69)
Happy - Nancy Sinatra (US 1968 # 74)

Lee Hazlewood and Duane Eddy
Shazam! – Duane Eddy (US 1960 # 45; UK # 4)
Kommotion – Duane Eddy (US 1960 # 78; UK # 13)
Dance With the Guitar Man – Duane Eddy (US 1962 # 12; UK # 4)
Boss Guitar – Duane Eddy (US 1963 # 28; UK # 27)
Lonely Boy, Lonely Guitar- Duane Eddy (US 1963 # 82)
Your Baby's Gone Surfin' – Duane Eddy (US 1963 # 93; UK # 49)

Mike Hazlewood see Albert Hammond and Mike Hazlewood

Jimi Hendrix
Born Johnny Allen Hendrix, Seattle, Washington 1942. Died 1970 (overdose).
Rock and Roll Hall of Fame 1992.
Grammy Lifetime Achievement Award 1992.

Of African-American and alleged Cherokee descent, Hendrix learned to play guitar at the age of 15 and in 1961 enlisted in the US Army, although discharged the following year. Moving to Clarksville, Tennessee, he formed a band, the King Kasuals, where he learned to play the guitar with his teeth in low-paying venues. Moving on to Nashville, he began playing on the Chitlin' Circuit, a group of Midwest venues that provided accepted black performers. He also performed as a backing musician for various artists, including Wilson Pickett and Sam Cooke. In 1964, he decided to go solo, and after winning an amateur concert was asked by Ronald Isley to become part of the backing band for the Isley Brothers.

Moving on, Hendrix joined Little Richard's touring band, the Upsetters, and later Curtis Knight & the Squires. After a couple of recording contracts proved short-lived, he moved to Greenwich Village in 1966 and formed his own band, Jimmy James and the Blue Flames. During one of the gigs he met Linda Keith, girlfriend of Stones' guitarist Keith Richards, who was impressed by his playing. She referred him to Chas Chandler, who at the time was leaving the Animals to go into management. When he saw Hendrix in a nightclub playing Billy Roberts' "Hey Joe," he invited him to come to London, where he signed a management and production contract with himself and ex-Animals manager Michael Jeffrey. Chandler and Hendrix then sought musicians for a band and chose bass guitarist Noel Redding (ex-Neil Landon & the Burnettes) and drummer Mitch Mitchell (ex-Georgie Fame & the Blue Flames). It was Chandler who persuaded Hendrix to change the spelling of his first name to Jimi.

In October 1966, Chandler brought Hendrix to the London Polytechnic where Cream were scheduled to perform. Asking Cream's Eric Clapton if he could do a few numbers, Hendrix played Howlin' Wolf's "Killing Floor." Clapton recalled later: "He walked off, and my life was never the same again." Later that month, Hendrix was signed to Track Records, and for their first single recorded Roberts' "Hey Joe," as the Jimi Hendrix Experience. With the need for a flip-side, Hendrix suggested another cover song, but Chandler persuaded him to come up with an original number so he could receive publishing royalties. After a jam at a London club, he wrote "Stone Free." Recorded in just an hour, it was his first composition for the band.

Further success came the following year with two more top ten hits. "Purple Haze," was a song Hendrix finished writing in the dressing room at East London's Upper Cut Club, run by former boxer Billy Walker. In the studio, Hendrix and Chandler came up with some unusual tricks to get the unique sound. The distant-sounding background track was created by putting headphones around a microphone to get the echo effect. Later asked about its inspiration, he replied, "I dream a lot and I put my dreams down as songs."

According to Hendrix, the lyrics for "The Wind Cries Mary" came after an argument with then-girlfriend Kathy Etchingham over her cooking lumpy mashed potatoes. After some plate throwing, she stormed out to stay with a friend for the rest of the day. When she returned, he had written the song, using her middle name Mary. The lyrics for "The Burning of the Midnight Lamp" were written on a flight from New York to Los Angeles, expressing the confusion he was feeling at the time.

In June 1967, Hendrix appeared at the Monterey Festival and rock music would never be the same again. Setting his guitar on fire remains one of rock's most iconic moments. In 1968, his version of Dylan's "All Along the Watchtower" gave him his biggest-selling UK single and his only US top 40 hit. Redding left the band the following year, a few months before Hendrix stole the Woodstock Festival with his legendary performance of "The Star Spangled Banner."

After forming and touring with the short-lived trio, Band of Gypsys, Hendrix invested in the new Electric Ladyland Studios in Greenwich Village. On September 8th 1970 he was found unconscious by his girlfriend in her London apartment. Taken to hospital, he was pronounced dead. The post mortem revealed he had died of asphyxia while intoxicated with barbiturates (which according to his girlfriend were nine sleeping tablets).

Hendrix once said of his songwriting: "Imagination is the key to my lyrics. The rest is painted with a little science fiction."

Chart entries
Purple Haze (UK 1967 # 3; US # 65) Dion (US 1969 # 63)
The Wind Cries Mary (UK 1967 # 6)
Burning Of the Midnight Lamp (UK 1967 # 8)
Foxy Lady (US 1967 # 67)
Up From the Skies (US 1968 # 82)
Fire – Five By Five (US 1968 #52)
Crosstown Traffic (UK 1968 # 37; US # 58)

Twyla Herbert see Lou Christie

Tony Hicks see Clarke, Hicks and Nash

Bob Hilliard see also Mort Garson
Born Hilliard Goldsmith, New York City 1918. Died 1971.
Songwriters Hall of Fame 1983.

With an early talent for writing lyrics, Hilliard left high school and worked for a music publisher in the Brill Building. One of his earliest successes was "The Coffee Song (They've Got An Awful Lot of Coffee in Brazil)" co-written with Dick Miles and recorded by Frank Sinatra in 1946. Over the next decade, he wrote scores for several Broadway shows and also supplied the lyrics for the 1951 movie *Alice in Wonderland*. In 1963, he teamed up with composer Mort Garson to write "Our Day Will Come," a US chart-topper for Ruby & the Romantics, and also partnered Burt Bacharach to write lyrics for a number of artists, with their "Tower of Strength," a top ten hit for Gene McDaniels and UK number one for Frankie Vaughan.

Chart entries
In My Little Corner of the World *(with Lee Pockriss)* Anita Bryant (US 1960 # 20; UK # 48)
A Kookie Little Paradise *(with Lee Pockriss)* The Tree Singers (US 1960 # 73); Jo Ann Campbell
    (US 1960 # 61); Frankie Vaughan (US 1960 # 31)
The Coffee Song *(with Dick Miles)* Frank Sinatra (UK 1961 # 39)
Dear Hearts and Gentle People *(with Sammy Fain)* The Springfields (US 1962 # 95)
Angry at the Big Oak Tree *(with Paul Hampton)* Frank Ifield (UK 1964 # 25)
Careless Hands *(with Carl Sigman)* Des O'Connor (UK 1967 # 6)

Bob Hilliard and Mort Garson
Our Day Will Come - Ruby & the Romantics (US 1963 # 1; UK # 38)
My Summer Love - Ruby & the Romantics (US 1963 # 16)
Young Wings Can Fly (Higher Than You Know) Ruby & the Romantics (US 1963 # 47)
Baby Come Home - Ruby & the Romantics (US 1964 # 75)

Bob Hilliard and Burt Bacharach
Please Stay – The Drifters (US 1961 #14), The Cryin' Shames 1966 (UK # 26)
Tower of Strength – Gene McDaniels (US 1961 #5; Frankie Vaughan 1961 (UK # 1)
You're Following Me – Perry Como (US 1961 # 92**)**
You Don't Have To Be A Tower Of Strength – Gloria Lynne (US 1961 # 100)
Any Day Now (My Wild Beautiful Bird) - Gene McDaniels (US 1962 # 23); Percy Sledge
    (US 1969 # 86)

Don't You Believe It - Andy Williams (US 1962 # 39)
Keep Away From Other Girls– Helen Shapiro (UK 1962 # 40)

Jimmy Holiday
Born Sallis, Mississippi 1934. Died 1987.

Raised in Iowa, Holiday had early aspirations of becoming a professional boxer, but at the age of 13 hung up the gloves and sought a new direction, devoting himself to music. He first learned to play alto sax and performed in jazz combos before concentrating on writing and performing R&B songs. He joined the Futuretones, and in 1958 released an unsuccessful single "Voice of the Drums" on the Los Angeles-based Four Star label. Taking a while to get over its failure, Holiday signed for Everest Records in 1963 and released "How Can I Forget?" which became a top ten hit on the R&B chart. Written by Ed Townsend, it proved to be the label's most successful single of the year, even doing better than a cover by Ben E King. Further singles followed with little chart success, and Holiday switched to various labels before signing with Minit Records in 1966.

His first single for the label was the self-penned "Baby I Love You," which peaked into the R&B charts, but further releases failed to repeat its success. However, his soulful debut album *Turning Point* was well received, as were the singles "Everybody Needs Help," "Spread Your Love," and "I'm Gonna Use What I Got." In 1969, he spent time writing with Jackie DeShannon and her brother Randy Myers, with the much-covered "Put A Little Love in Your Heart" becoming her highest-ever chart hit at number four. "Love Will Find A Way," a second single by the trio, also became a moderate hit.

Chart entries
Baby I Love You *(with Ronnie Shannon)* Jimmy Holiday (US 1966 # 98); Aretha Franklin (US
    1967 # 4; UK # 39)
I Chose To Sing the Blues *(with Ray Charles)* Ray Charles (US 1966 # 32)
Make A Little Love *(with Mike Akapoff)* Lowell Fulsom (US 1967 # 97)
That's A Lie *(with Ray Charles)* Ray Charles (US 1968 # 64)
Let Me Love You – Ray Charles (US 1969 # 94)
Put a Little Love in Your Heart *(with Jackie DeShannon, Randy Myers)* Jackie DeShannon
    (US 1969 # 4); Dave Clark Five (UK 1969 # 31)
Love Will Find a Way *(with Jackie DeShannon, Randy Myers)* Jackie DeShannon (US
    1969 # 40)

Holland-Dozier-Holland see also Norman Whitfield
Born Brian Holland, Detroit, Michigan 1941.
Born Herbert Lamont Dozier, Detroit, Michigan 1941. Died 2022.
Born Edward James Holland Jr, Detroit, Michigan 1939.
Songwriters Hall of Fame 1988.
Rock and Roll Hall of Fame 1990.

Although interested in becoming an accountant and claiming to have no musical ambition as a teenager, Eddie Holland Jr accompanied a friend to an audition and was unexpectedly asked to sing. It ended with him being referred to songwriter and aspiring music executive Berry Gordy Jr. Since his vocals sounded similar to those of rising star Jackie Wilson, he was taken on to sing demos that Gordy had written for Wilson to record, including "To Be Loved," "Lonely Teardrops," and "I'll Be Satisfied." In 1958, Gordy secured a deal with the Chicago-based Mercury label and produced Holland's first single, "Little Miss Ruby," written by Neal Matthews and featured in the movie *Country Music Holiday*. The following year, a third single, "Merry-G-Round," written by Berry, was recorded at Hitsville on the Tamla label, but leased to United Artists. These and three further singles failed to chart.

Toward the end of 1961, Gordy's United Artists agreement with Holland expired and he returned to in-house releases at Motown. Holland recorded "Jamie," a song written by William Stevenson and Barrett Strong, and one that Strong had intended to record himself before suddenly leaving the label. It became Holland's first and biggest hit, reaching six on the R&B chart and thirty on the pop chart. With stage fright later becoming a problem, he began working behind the scenes as lyricist and in vocal production.

Older brother Brian had also started in the music business with an erratic career as a solo singer, releasing a single in 1958 under the name of "Briant Holland." He then partnered longtime friend and future songwriting partner Freddie Gorman in the group the Fidalatones. Proving to be short-lived, he then joined the Satintones, the first group to record on the label, and whose lineup included Robert Bateman. Brian also belonged to the vocal quartet the Rayber Voices, who were backing singers on several early Motown releases.

In 1961, he formed the writing partnership "Brianbert" with Bateman, and along with others co-wrote "Please Mr Postman," a chart topper on both side of the Atlantic for the Marvelettes (although the writing credits have long been disputed). The title of the song may have been inspired by Bateman being a former Detroit postman. In 1963, Brian partnered Lamont Dozier under the name Holland-Dozier and released one single in 1963 before remaining inactive for a number of years.

Dozier was the oldest of five children and was educated at Edgar Allan Poe elementary school, where his love of words and poetry began. While at Hutchins Junior High, he met Aretha Franklin, daughter of the local Baptist preacher, and later, while at Northwestern High School, began picking out songs on a piano, which nurtured an interest for a music career. While still at school, he and some friends formed the doo-wop group the Romeos, and "Fine Fine Boy" became a regional hit. When Atlantic got to hear it, they gave it a national release. A chance to record further singles with them was scuppered after Dozier insisted they would sign only if they could record an entire album straight away, which was refused.

In 1962, Dozier's wife Anne Brown introduced him to the Hollands. She was working for Motown as an office girl, typing and packing records. Meanwhile, after mopping floors at another label while trying to get his singing and writing career off the ground, Dozier accepted an offer of $25 a week from Gordy, the money to be advanced against future royalties. From that day, he began to strike up a working partnership with the Holland brothers as both songwriters and producers. With shared backgrounds in the church and a mutual love for classical music, they would become as tough as their boss in getting the best out of the artists.

According to Dozier, he would collaborate with Eddie on the lyrics and with Brian on the melodies, then he and Brian would take it to the studio and produce the record, with Eddie also helping by teaching the artists the tune once the lyrics were finished, often recording two or three songs in a day. Dozier commented on his songwriting: "I don't think about commercial concerns when I first come up with something. When I sit down at the piano, I try to come up with something that moves me."

Their first success came with a trio of hits for Martha & the Vandellas, soon followed by "Can I Get a Witness" by Marvin Gaye, with backing vocals by the Supremes. With Gaye, they would write songs in keys that were higher than he was comfortable with, which allowed him to develop his own style. Their first big chart success came in 1964 with the Supremes' chart-topper "Where Did Our Love Go." Inspired by one of Dozier's romantic breakups, it was originally offered to the Marvelettes, but rejected. As their lead singer Gladys Horton sang in a lower key than Diana Ross, it forced her, too, it would have meant her singing in a style she wasn't comfortable with.

After seeing the Four Tops perform in a Detroit nightclub, Brian invited them to the Motown studio and spent the night recording "Baby I Need Your Lovin,'" which became their first chart hit. Like many of the trio's songs, they would be written as ballads, but once in the studio would pick up the tempo to give them more commercial appeal (dance music being in vogue among youngsters at the time).

Inspired by Dozier's first love affair, the Supremes "Baby Love" made them the label's first act with two chart-topping singles, and within months it became three with their "Come See About Me." Altogether, the Supremes would score a total of ten chart-topping singles for the label during the Sixties. The Four Tops' number one "I Can't Help Myself (Sugar Pie, Honey Bunch)" was inspired by Dozier recalling as a child the nicknames his grandfather gave to his wife, while "This Old Heart of Mine" by the Isley Brothers was typical of Dozier's writing, using an upbeat tune for a sad story, in this case a man devastated by the loss of his girl. "(I'm a) Roadrunner" by Jr Walker & the All Stars, featured the sax playing of Walker and Mike Terry, with its title inspired by the popular tv cartoon series.

One of their finest moments came in 1966 with the Four Tops epic "Reach Out I'll Be There," which was the result of the writers in agreement that what women wanted the most was for their man to always be there for them.
For the recording, they told lead singer Levie Stubbs to sing like Bob Dyan did on "Like a Rolling Stone," hence the urgency in his voice. Recorded in just two takes, it became the label's second chart-topper in the UK. "You Keep Me Hanging On" by the Supremes was another inspired by Dozier's past relationships, and he also created the news flash-style stuttering guitar line (played by studio band member Robert White). The spoken line "there ain't nothing I can do about it," sounding very much like an ad-lib, was in fact intentional. The dramatic "Bernadette" by the Four Tops was another tour-de-force vocal by Stubbs, the name being chosen from Dozier's unrequited love for an Italian girl when he was 12.

"The Happening" by the Supremes was written for the 1967 movie of the same name. Co-authored with the director Frank DeVol, it was recorded at Columbia Studios in Los Angeles with a whole new group of musicians. The single was the last to be credited to the Supremes, with all future releases listed as Diana Ross & the Supremes, and was also the last to feature Florence Ballard, who would soon be replaced by Cindy Birdsong. The first hit for the new lineup was "Reflections," about a woman who looks back in anguish at a lost love. The music also saw a departure from the old formula, with electric piano, tambourine, and oscillator-generated sound effects added during the recording.

Eddie Holland would also write songs with other collaborators, including Norman Whitfield and R Dean Taylor, while Brian worked with Motown staff writers, including William "Mickey" Stevenson, Janie Bradford and Robert Bateman.

In 1967, Dozier and the Hollands were in dispute with Gordy over royalties and profit-sharing leading them to stage a work slowdown, and early the next year they left Motown to set up their own labels, Invictus and Hot Wax, which had moderate success. Dozier also had a solo recording career at the time. When Gordy sued them for breach of contract, they countersued and it led to one of the most drawn out legal battles in music history. As they were legally contracted to Gordy's publishing arm Jobete, it was ruled that they could not use their names on songs they wrote, and as a result recordings from 1969-1972 were credited to the collective pseudonym "Edythe Wayne" (named after a friend and an associate).

In 1973, Dozier left and was replaced by Harold Beatty as producer and arranger. During their five years at Motown, Lamont and Brian wrote and produced every song they recorded, with Eddie also writing lyrics and arranging the vocals. The trio's list of artists is like a who's who in soul and R&B music, with over a dozen chart-topping singles to their names.

Eddie Holland looked back on their careers: "We were very, very fortunate to have a place where we could record that many pieces of product, and experiment that much, with somebody paying for it. That was like going to school, and somebody paying for your classes."

Chart entries
Locking Up My Heart – The Marvelettes (US 1963 # 44)
Come and Get These Memories – Martha & the Vandellas (US 1963 # 29)
(Love Is Like A) Heat Wave - Martha & the Vandellas (US 1963 # 4)
Mickey's Monkey – The Miracles (US 1963 # 8)
Can I Get A Witness – Marvin Gaye (US 1963 # 22)
I Gotta Dance To Keep From Crying – The Miracles (US 1963 # 35)
Quicksand - Martha & the Vandellas (US 1963 # 8)
When the Lovelight Starts Shining Through His Eyes – The Supremes (US 1963 # 23)
Leaving Here - Eddie Holland Jr (US 1964 # 76)
Live Wire - Martha & the Vandellas (US 1964 # 42)
Run, Run, Run – Supremes (US 1964 # 93)
You Are a Wonderful One – Marvin Gaye (US 1964 # 15)
In My Lonely Room - Martha & the Vandellas (US 1964 # 44)
Just Ain't Enough Love – Eddie Holland (US 1964 # 54)
Where Did Our Love Go – The Supremes (US 1964 # 1; UK # 3)
Baby I Need Your Lovin' – Four Tops (US 1964 #11); The Fourmost (UK 1964 # 24)
Candy To Me – Eddie Holland (US 1964 # 58)
Baby Don't You Do It – Marvin Gaye (US 1964 # 27)
Baby Love – The Supremes (US 1964 # 1; UK # 1)
Come See About Me – The Supremes (US 1964 # 1; UK # 27); Nella Dodds (1964 US # 74);
    Jr Walker & the All-Stars (US 1967 # 24; UK # 51)
How Sweet It Is (To Be Loved By You) – Marvin Gaye (US 1964 # 6; UK # 49); Jr Walker
    & the All-Stars (US 1966 # 18; UK # 22)
Without the One You Love (Life's Not Worth While) – Four Tops (US 1964 # 43)
Stop! In the Name of Love – The Supremes (US 1965 # 1; UK # 7)
Nowhere To Run – Martha & the Vandellas (US 1965 # 8; UK # 26; UK 1969 # 42)
Back In My Arms Again – The Supremes (US 1965 # 1; UK # 40)
I Can't Help Myself (Sugar Pie, Honey Bunch) Four Tops (US 1965 # 1; UK # 23)
It's the Same Old Song – Four Tops (US 1965 # 5; UK # 34)
Nothing But Heartaches – The Supremes (US 1965 # 11)
1-2-3 *(with John Medora, David White, Len Borisoff (Barry)* Len Barry (US 1965 # 2; UK # 3);
    Ramsey Lewis (as "One, Two, Three") (US 1967 # 67
Take Me In Your Arms (Rock Me A Little While) Kim Weston (US 1965 # 50; Jr Walker
    & the All-Stars (US 1967 # 24; UK # 51); The Isley Brothers (UK # 52)
I Hear A Symphony – The Supremes (US 1965 # 1; UK # 39)
Something About You – Four Tops (US 1965 # 19)
Love (Makes Me Do Foolish Things) – Martha & the Vandellas (US 1965 # 70)
My World Is Empty Without You – The Supremes (US 1966 # 5); Jose Feliciano (US 1969 # 87)
Put Yourself In My Place – The Elgins (US 1966 # 92); Isley Brothers (UK 1969 # 13)
Shake Me, Wake Me (When It's Over) – Four Tops (US 1966 # 18)
This Old Heart Of Mine (Is Weak For You) (*with Sylvia Moy*) Isley Brothers (US 1966 # 12;
    UK # 47); Isley Brothers (UK 1968 # 3); Tammi Terrell (US 1969 # 67)
Helpless – Kim Weston (US 1966 # 56)
(I'm a) Roadrunner – Junior Walker & the All-Stars (US 1966 # 20; UK # 12)
Love Is Like An Itching In My Heart – The Supremes (US 1966 # 9)

I Guess I'll Always Love You – Isley Brothers (US 1966 # 61; UK 1966 # 45; UK 1969 # 11)
How Sweet It Is (To Be Loved By You) Jr Walker & the All-Stars (US 1966 # 18; UK # 22)
You Can't Hurry Love – The Supremes (US 1966 #1; UK # 3)
Little Darling (I Need You) – Marvin Gaye (US 1966 # 47; UK # 50)
Reach Out, I'll Be There – Four Tops (US 1966 # 1; UK # 1); Merrilee Rush (US 1968 # 79)
Heaven Must Have Sent You – The Elgins (US 1966 # 50)
A Love Like Yours (Don't Come Knocking Every Day) – Ike & Tina Turner (UK 1966 # 16)
I'm Ready For Love - Martha & the Vandellas (US 1966 # 9; UK # 22)
You Keep Me Hanging On – The Supremes (US 1966 # 1; UK # 8); Vanilla Fudge (US 1967 # 67; UK # 18); Wilson Pickett (US 1969 # 92)
(Come 'Roud Here) I'm the One You Need – Miracles (US 1966 # 17; UK # 37)
Standing In the Shadows of Love – Four Tops (US 1866 # 6; UK # 2)
Love Is Here And Now You're Gone – The Supremes (US 1967 # 1; UK # 17)
Jimmy Mack - Martha & the Vandellas (US 1967 # 10; UK # 21)
Bernadette - Four Tops (US 1967 # 4; UK # 8)
The Happening *(with Frank De Vol)* The Supremes (US 1967 # 1; UK # 6); Herb Alpert (US 1967 # 32)
7 Rooms Of Gloom – Four Tops (US 1967 # 14; UK # 12)
Your Unchanging Love – Marvin Gaye (US 1967 # 33)
I'll Turn To Stone – Four Tops (US 1967 # 76)
Reflections – Diana Ross & the Supremes (US 1967 # 2; UK # 5)
You Keep Running Away – Four Tops (US # 19; UK # 26)
In And Out Of Love – Diana Ross & the Supremes (US 1967 # 9; UK # 13)
Forever Came Today – Diana Ross & the Supremes (US 1968 # 28; UK # 28)
Take Me In Your Arms (Rock Me A Little While) – Isley Brothers (UK 1968 # 52)
Reach Out – Merrilee Rush (US 1968 # 79)

Holland-Dozier-Holland with Ron Dunbar (aka Edyth Dunbar)
While You're Out Looking For Sugar? – The Honey Cone (US 1968 # 62)
Mind Body and Soul – The Flaming Ember (US 1968 # 26)
Crumbs Off the Table – The Glass House (US 1969 # 59)
Girl It Ain't Easy – The Honey Cone (US 1969 # 68)
Too Many Cooks (Spoil the Soup) *(with Angelo Bond)* 100 Proof (Aged in Soul) (US 1969 # 94)

Brian Holland & Lamont Dozier
Forever - The Marvelettes (US 1963 # 78)
Strange, I Know *(with Freddie Gorman)* The Marvelettes (US 1962 # 49)

Brian Holland, Lamont Dozier & R Dean Taylor
I'm In A Different World – Four Tops (US 1968 # 51; UK # 27)

Brian Holland and others
All the Love I Got *(with Berry Gordy Jr, Janie Bradford)* Marv Johnson (US 1960 # 63)
Please Mr Postman *(with Georgia Dobbins, William Garrett, Freddie Gorman)* The Marvelettes (US 1961 # 1# UK # 1)
Greetings (This Is Uncle Sam) *(with Robert Bateman, Ronald Dunbar, Stuart Avig, Marty Coleman, Art Glasser, Jerry Light)* The Valadiers (US 1961 # 89); The Monitors (US 1966 # 100)
Twistin' Postman *(with Robert Bateman, William "Mickey" Stevenson)* The Marvelettes (US 1962 # 34)
Playboy *(with Robert Bateman; Gladys Horton, Mickey Stevenson)* The Marvelettes (US 1962 # 7)

Eddie Holland Jr and Norman Whitfield
Price And Joy *(with Marvin Gaye & William "Mickey" Stevenson)* Marvin Gaye (US

1963 # 10)
Girl (Why You Wanna Make Me Blue) - The Temptations (US 1964 # 26)
Needle In A Haystack *(with William "Mickey" Stevenson)* - The Marvelettes (US 1964 # 45)
Too Many Fish In the Sea - The Marvelettes (US 1964 # 25)
He Was Really Saying Something *(with William "Mickey" Stevenson)* The Velvelettes
    (US 1964 # 45)
Ain't Too Proud To Beg - The Temptations (US 1966 # 13; UK # 21)
Beauty Is Only Skin Deep - The Temptations (US 1966 # 3; UK # 18)
I Know I'm Losing You *(with Cornelius Grant)* The Temptations (US 1966 # 8; UK #19)
Too Many Fish In the Sea / Three Litte Fishes *(with Saxie Dowell)* Mitch Ryder & the
    Detroit Wheels (US 1967 # 24)
Everybody Needs Love - Gladys Knight & the Pips (US 1967 # 39)
You're My Everything *(with Cornelius Grant & Roger Penzabene)* The Temptations
    (US 1967 # 6; UK # 26)
(Loneliness Made Me Realize) It's You That I Need - The Temptations (US 1967 # 14)
It Should Have Been Me *(with William "Mickey" Stevenson)* Gladys Knight & the Pips (US
    1968 # 40)

Eddie Holland Jr with others
Gotta See Jane *(with R Dean Taylor Ronald Miller)* R Dean Taylor (UK 1968 # 17)

Jim Holvay
Born James Steven Holvay, Chicago 1945.

Young Holvay's interest in music was elevated when his brother brought home Bill Haley's "Rock Around the Clock." Saving money to buy a guitar and a chord book, he developed his playing and writing skills and formed a school band, the Rockin' Rebels. Later, while still at high school, he played guitar with Jimmy & the Jesters. On a trip with his father to Chicago's Record Row, a meeting with Curtis Mayfield and Leonard Chess had a big influence on his career. With a new guitar in hand, he recorded a couple of songs with the Maybees for a local label, and after graduation in 1963 joined the Chicagoans with his longtime collaborator Gary Beisbier. They became the house band on the live tv show *Danceville USA* and began touring across the country. Returning to college, he wrote and produced songs for various local artists and was invited to become the permanent guitarist on Dick Clark's *Caravan of Stars* road show. While on tour, Holvay and Brian Hyland wrote songs together, including the Phillips' release, "Stay Away From Her." In 1966, Holvay returned to Chicago to concentrate on songwriting, and along with Mike Sistak from the Clark tour formed The MOB, a rock & soul horn band, with Holvay and ex-Maybees member Beisbier co-writing many of their hit songs. Later that year, Holvay was approached by the manager of the Chicago-based group The Buckinghams and asked if he had any songs for them. Holvay went on to pen four top ten hits for the group, including the million-selling chart-topper "Kind of a Drag." With lead singer Dennis Tufano, they had three more chart hits, all occurring in 1967, with *Billboard* magazine declaring them "the "most-listened-to band of the year."

Chart entries
Kind of a Drag – The Buckinghams (US 1966 # 1)
Don't You Care *(with Gary Beisbier, James William Guercio)* The Buckinghams (US 1967 # 6)
Hey Baby (They're Playing Our Song *(with Gary Beisbier)* The Buckinghams (US 1967 # 12)
Susan *(with Gary Beisbier, James William Guercio)* The Buckinghams (US 1967 # 11)

Harlan Howard
Born Harlan Perry Howard, Detroit, Michigan 1927. Died 2002.
Nashville Songwriters Hall of Fame 1973.
Songwriters Hall of Fame 1997.
Country Music Hall of Fame 1997.

Growing up on a farm, Howard listened to country artists on the *Grand Ole Opry* radio show, immersing himself in true-life sad songs. Although an avid reader, he only completed nine years of formal education, and with an "ear for a telling phrase" had started writing songs at the age of 12. After serving in the war as a US Army paratrooper, he travelled to Los Angeles to work and find a record company for his music. His first success came in late 1958 with "Pick Me Up on Your Way Down," a number two country hit for Charlie Walker, that also became the artist's best-selling record. The following year, he wrote "Heartaches By the Number" for Ray Price to have a top ten country hit, although a few months later becoming a chart-topping single on the Hot 100 for Guy Mitchell. Spurred on by these early successes, Howard moved to Nashville in 1960 with a large portfolio of songs and signed with Acuff-Rose Music. The following year, fifteen of these songs became hits on the country charts. These included Patsy Cline's "I Fall To Pieces," written with Hank Cochran.

Chart entries
Everglades – The Kingston Trio (US 1960 # 60)
I Fall To Pieces *(with Hank Cochran)* Patsy Cline (US 1961 # 12)
Pick Me Up on Your Way Down – Pat Zill (US 1961 # 91)
When I Get Through With You (You'll Love Me Too) Patsy Cline (US 1962 # 53)
Call Me Mr Inbetween – Burl Ives (US 1962 # 19)
Mary Ann Regrets - Burl Ives (US 1962 # 39)
Busted – Ray Charles (US 1963 # 4; UK # 21)
I Won't Forget You – Jim Reeves (US 1964 # 93 # UK # 3)
I Got a Tiger by the Tail *(with Buck Owens)* Buck Owens (US 1965 # 25)
Too Many Rivers – Brenda Lee (US 1965 # 13; UK # 22)
Heartaches by the Number – Johnny Tillotson (US 1965 # 35)
Sally Was a Good Old Girl – Trini Lopez (US 1968 # 99)
He Called Me Baby – Ella Washington (US 1969 # 77)
The Chokin' Kind – Joe Simon (US 1969 # 13)
Baby, Don't Be Looking in My Mind – Joe Simon (US 1969 # 72)

Ken Howard and Alan Blaikley
Born Kenneth Charles Howard, Worthing, England 1939. Died 2024.
Born Alan Tudor Blaikley, London 1940. Died 2022.

Born early during the war, Howard was evacuated with his brother to Cleveland, Ohio, and on returning to London enrolled at University College School in 1947 where he became friends with fellow student Alan Blaikley. Educated at University College School and later at Wadham College in Oxford, Blaikley read English and Classical Moderations (Latin and Greek) and became a reviews editor of the university newspaper *Cherwell*. In 1956, Howard continued his education at a Swiss college for a year, before returning to London to work for Granada TV. The following year, he studied Social Anthropology at Edinburgh University, and in 1959 won a weekly spot on Scottish tv singing with fellow student Eva Hermann as Eva & Ken and recorded for the Fontana label. Graduating with an MA, he found work with BBC's drama department in London and with friends Blaikley and Paul Overy ran and edited the magazine *Axle Quarterly* which published early works by among others, Melvyn Bragg, Ray Gosling and Simon Raven.

Their songwriting career began in the mid-Sixties, with Howard writing lyrics to Blaikley's compositions. Over the years, they wrote many hits for bands and solo artists, scoring two number ones along the way, beginning in 1964 with "Have I the Right?" for London group the Honeycombs, with its female drummer and former hairdresser Honey Lantree. It was also their suggestion to change the name of the band Dave Dee & the Bostons to the more catchy Dave Dee, Dozy, Beaky, Mick & Titch, and went on to write all their hits, including the chart-topping "Legend of Xanadu." They also wrote several hits for the Herd, fronted by 16-year-old Peter Frampton, while Blaikley partnered Len "Chips" Hawkes of the Tremeloes to write several of their hits in the late Sixties.

Howard and Blaikley became the first British composers to write for Elvis Presley, including the 1970 hit "I've Lost You," and continued to write theme music for tv dramas and West End musicals As a film maker, Howard also made several tv documentaries.

Chart entries
Have I the Right? – The Honeycombs (UK 1964 # 1)
Is It Because – The Honeycombs (UK 1964 # 34)
You Make It Move – Dave Dee Dozy Beaky Mick and Tich (UK 1965 # 26)
Hold Tight! - Dave Dee Dozy Beaky Mick and Tich (UK 1966 # 4)
Hideaway - Dave Dee Dozy Beaky Mick and Tich (UK 1966 # 10)
Bend It! - Dave Dee Dozy Beaky Mick and Tich (UK 1966 # 2)
Save Me - Dave Dee Dozy Beaky Mick and Tich (UK 1966 # 3)
Touch Me, Touch Me - Dave Dee Dozy Beaky Mick and Tich (UK 1967 # 13)
Okay! - Dave Dee Dozy Beaky Mick and Tich (UK 1967 # 4)

From the Underworld – The Herd (UK 1967 # 3; US # 52)
Zabadak! - Dave Dee Dozy Beaky Mick and Tich (UK 1963 # 3; US # 52)
Paradise Lost – The Herd (UK 1967 # 15)
The Legend Of Xanadu - Dave Dee Dozy Beaky Mick and Tich (UK 1967 # 1)
I Don't Want Our Loving To Die – The Herd (UK 1968 # 5)
Last Night In Soho - Dave Dee Dozy Beaky Mick and Tich (UK 1968 # 8)
The Wreck Of the Antoinette - Dave Dee Dozy Beaky Mick and Tich (UK 1968 # 14)
Wait For Me Mary-Anne – Marmalade (UK 1968 # 23)
Don Juan - Dave Dee Dozy Beaky Mick and Tich (UK 1969 # 23)
Snake in the Grass - Dave Dee Dozy Beaky Mick and Tich (UK 1969 # 23)

Howard-Blaikley with others
Boy (*with Geoff Stephens*) Lulu (UK 1968 # 15)
Bluer Than Blue (with *Barry Mason*) Rolf Harris (UK 1969 # 30)

Alan Blaikley
That's the Way - The Honeycombs (UK 1964 # 12)

Alan Blaikley and Len (Chip) Hawkes
Helule Helule (*with David Kabaka*) The Tremeloes (UK 1968 # 14)
My Little Lady (*with Daniele Pace, Mario Panzeri, Lorenzo Pilat*) The Tremeloes (UK 1968 # 6)
I Will See You There – Linda Kendrick (UK 1969 # 41)
(Call Me) Number One - The Tremeloes (UK 1969 # 2)

Leon Huff see **Ken Gamble and Leon Huff**

Ivy Jo Hunter
Born George Ivy Hunter, Detroit, Michigan 1940. Died 2022.

Urged on by his mother, Hunter attended Cass Tech High School to study commercial art, although many others his age wanted to become professional musicians. Undeterred, he still managed to sing in local amateur vocal groups and later play trumpet and baritone sax in the Detroit All City Orchestra. Following a spell in the US Army, he returned home to take a job with an electrical company while performing at clubs in the evening. He became friends with Motown saxophonist Hank Cosby, and through him met A&R man William "Mickey" Stevenson who signed him as an artist, songwriter, producer and manager. Using his professional name Ivy Jo Hunter, it would later lead record buyers to assume he was a woman. Working as keyboard player on various recording sessions, he soon developed a songwriting partnership with Stevenson, and success followed with Martha & the Vandellas' "Dancing in the Street," (co-written with Marvin Gaye), followed by the dance-craze song "Can You Jerk Like Me" by the Contours, and the Four Tops' ballad "Ask the Lonely."

Although mainly limited to writing for the label's second-tier acts, Hunter also contributed to some of Motown's best-loved songs, and in 1969 co-wrote with Beatrice Verdi "Behind a Painted Smile," which highlighted the brothers' unhinged vocal style. Ironically, it became a UK top ten hit after the Isleys had quit Motown to form their own label, T Neck Records.

Hunter was also a talented vocalist and recorded much material during the Sixties, but the label's failure to promote him as a solo act proved a disappointment to him. The barely noticed release of his 1970 single "I Remember When" was followed by a planned album which was later shelved.

Chart entries
Loving You Is Sweeter Than Ever (*with Stevie Wonder*) Four Tops (US 1966 # 12)
Got To Have You Back (*with Leon Ware, Stephen Bowden*) Isley Brothers (US 1967 # 93)
You (*with Jeffrey Bowen, Jack Coga*) Marvin Gaye (US 1968 # 34; UK # 52)
Yesterday's Dreams (*with Vernon Bullock, Jack Coga, Pam Sawyer*) Four Tops (US 1968 # 49; UK # 23)
Behind A Painted Smile (*with Beatrice Verdi*) Isley Brothers (UK 1969 # 5

Ivy Jo Hunter and William "Mickey" Stevenson
Dancing In the Street (*with Marvin Gaye*) Martha & the Vandellas (US 1964 # 2; UK # 28); Mamas & the Papas (as Dancing In the Streets) (US 1966 # 73); Ramsey Lewis (US 1967 # 84); Martha & the Vandellas (UK 1969 # 4)
Wild One - Martha & the Vandellas (US 1964 # 34)
Ask the Lonely - Four Tops (US 1965 # 24)
I'll Keep Holding On – The Marvelettes (US 1965 # 34)
I'll Always Love You - The Spinners (US 1965 # 35)
You've Been In Love Too Long (*with Clarence Paul*) Martha & the Vandellas (US 1965 # 36)
My Baby Loves Me (*with Sylvia Moy*) Martha & the Vandellas (US 1966 # 22)

John Hurley and Ronnie Wilkins
Born John David Hurley, Pittsburgh 1941. Died 1986.
Born Ronald Stephen Wilkins, Lumberton, North Carolina 1941.

After performing as a child with his uncle in Pittsburgh barrooms, Hurley went on to co-host a local radio show and sang with the Pittsburgh Opera Society. Once he discovered rock and roll, he relocated to Nashville, and in 1962 joined Tree music publishers as a songwriter, as well as serving for a time in the US Army. While at Tree, he formed a writing partnership with Ronnie Wilkins.

Wilkins had begun writing songs and performing while at high school, and in his teens appeared on WAGR radio where he got word from a Charlotte talent agent that Tree were looking for new songwriters. After an audition in Nashville, he was taken on, and he had his first solo success with Joe Dowell's "Poor Little Cupid" in 1963. With Hurley, they focused on writing for soul artists, including Joe Tex. In 1965 they had their first chart hit was the Gentry's "Spread It on Thick", written along with Bill Cates, and later had more success with "Love of the Common People." First recorded by the Four Preps and released by Capitol, it became a country hit for Waylon Jennings in 1967 (and many years later by UK's Paul Young), but it only broke into the Hot 100 when recorded by the Winstons in 1969.

While working at Muscle Shoals, they were asked by Jerry Wexler to write a song for Aretha Franklin, and, remembering her father was a preacher, they came up with "Son of a Preacher Man." Instead of Franklin recording it, Wexler gave it to Dusty Springfield as an album track for *Dusty in Memphis.* When released as a single in 1968 it became a top ten hit on both sides of the Atlantic.

In 1970, both writers moved to California to work on Hurley's first solo album for RCA.

Chart entries
Spread It on Thick – The Gentrys (US 1966 # 50)
The Land of Milk and Honey – The Vogues (US 1966 # 29)
Son of a Preacher Man – Dusty Springfield (US 1968 # 10; UK # 9)
Love of the Common People – The Winstons (US 1969 # 54)

Alan Jackson Jr see also Booker T Jones
Born Albert J Jackson Jr, Memphis, Tennessee 1935. Died 1975 (murdered).
Rock and Roll Hall of Fame (with Booker T & the MGs).
Nashville Songwriters Hall of Fame 2011.
Songwriters Hall of Fame 2012.

Born the son of big band leader Al Jackson, he began playing drums on stage with his father's band in 1940 at the age of five. Some ten years later, he played in producer and trumpeter Willie Mitchell's band while also drumming with Ben Branch's popular Memphis band. Stax label musicians Steve Cropper and Donald "Duck" Dunn first heard him play at the Flamingo Room and at the all-white Manhattan Club in Memphis, along with Booker T Jones. It was Jones who suggested that Jackson be signed to Stax as a session musician, although Jackson felt he could get a regular salary playing live. With that, the label boss offered him a weekly salary, the first Stax musician to be given one.

Stax's house band were called the Mar-Keys, although the live lineup was not always the same as the band heard on the recordings. Subject to changes from session to session, it included over the next several years: Steve Cropper (guitar); Donald "Duck" Dunn or Lewis Steinerg (bass); Smoochy Smith, Marvell Thomas, but mainly Booker T Jones and Isaac Hayes (keyboards); Howard Grimes, Terry Johnson and Al Jackson (drums), and Wayne Jackson, Floyd Newman, Don Nix, Gilbert Caple, Vinny Trauth, Packy Axton and Andrew Love (horns).

In the summer of 1962, Jackson made his debut for the label when playing with Jones, Cropper and Steinberg on a Billy Lee Riley recording. During downtime, the four of them began playing around with a bluesy organ riff and were heard by label president Jim Stewart who decided to let them record this and a second track. The result was the instrumental "Green Onions," credited to all four musicians and released as Booker T and the MGs. It scored a number three hit that August. It was the first of a number of chart hits under the new name, all featuring Jackson's instantly recognisable backbeat.

Jackson went on to produce songs for blues guitarist Albert King, co-writing with him his 1968 hit "Cold Feet." In the Seventies, he co-wrote and played on several of Al Green's hits, including "Let's Stay Together," before being tragically murdered at his home by an intruder in 1975.

Chart entries
Al Jackson Jr with Jones, Cropper and Lewis Steinberg
Green Onions - Booker T & the MGs (US 1962 # 3)
Mo' Onions - Booker T & the MGs (US 1964 # 97)
Chinese Checkers - Booker T & the MGs (US 1963 # 90)
Soul Dressing - Booker T & the MGs (US 1964 # 95)
Soul Limbo - Booker T & the MGs (US 1968 # 17; UK # 30)
Hang 'Em High - Booker T & the MGs (US 1968 # 9)

Al Jackson Jr with Jones & Steve Cropper
Hole In the Wall *(with Nathaniel Nathan)* The Packers 9US 1965 # 43)
My Sweet Potato - Booker T & the MGs (US 1966 # 85)
Hip Hug-Her *(with Donald "Duck" Dunn)* Booker T & the MGs (US
    1967 # 37; UK # 51)
The Hunter *(with Carl Wells, Donald Dunn)* Ike & Tina Turner (US 1969 # 93)
Soul Clap 69 *(with Donald Dunn)* Booker T & the MGs (US 1969 # 35)

Al Jackson with others
Boot-Leg *(with Charles Axton, Donald Dunn, Isaac Hayes)* Booker T & the MGs (US
    1965 # 58)
Cold Feet *(with Albert King)* Albert King (US 1968 # 67)

William Jackson see also Jimmy Wisner
Born William Edward Jackson III, Philadelphia. Died 2016.

In 1963, Jackson joined the Cameo Parkway label as a staff writer and producer, and along with arranger Roy Straigis produced recordings by the Tymes, scoring a hit with "So Much In Love," co-written with and Straigis and Tymes' lead singer George Williams. Jackson continued working with the band and produced many of their recordings for Columbia and RCA. He also partnered songwriter Jimmy Wisner (1931-2018) on a number of hits, including "Don't Throw Your Love Away," originally a b-side for the Orioles in 1963 but a UK number one when recorded by the Searchers the following year.

Chart entries
So Much in Love *(with John Joseph - aka Roy Straigis, George Williams)* The Tymes
    (US 1963 # 5; UK # 49)
Groovy Baby *(with Roy Straigis)* Billy Abbott & the Jewels (US 1963 # 55)
Let's Make Love Tonight *(with Roy Straigis, George Williams)* Bobby Rydell (US 1963 # 98)
The Boy With the Beatle Hair *(with Joe Renzetti, Jerry Ross)* The Swans (US 1964 # 85)
Don't Be Afraid (Do as I Say) – Frankie Karl & the Dreams (US 1968 # 93)

William Jackson and Jimmy Wisner
Willyam, Willyam - Dee Dee Sharp (US 1964 # 97)
Don't Throw Your Love Away - The Searchers (UK 1964 # 1; US # 16)
The Magic of Our Summer Love - The Tymes (US 1964 # 99)
Here She Comes *(with Roy Straigis)* The Tymes (US 1964 # 92)
What in the World's Come Over You - The Rockin' Berries (UK 1965 # 23)

Mick Jagger and Keith Richards

Born Michael Philip Jagger, Dartford, England 1943.
Born Keith Richards, Dartford, England 1943.
Rock and Roll Hall of Fame 1989 (with The Rolling Stones).
Grammy Lifetime Achievement Award 1986 (with the Rolling Stones).
Songwriters Hall of Fame 1993.

Although encouraged by his father to follow in his footsteps as a physical education teacher, Jagger once said: "I always sang as a child. I was one of those kids who just liked to sing." He loved listening to singers on radio, tv and in the movies, and in September 1950 he befriended his neighbour Keith Richards while both at Wentworth Primary School in Dartford. Richards' parents both served as town mayors, and as a boy he was given a guitar by his grandfather, although his father disparaged any musical notions he might have. Richards loved to listen to Louis Armstrong, Billie Holiday and Duke Ellington. Jagger and Richards lost contact in 1954 when the Jagger family moved away. At the age of 12, Jagger went to Dartford Grammer School and formed a garage band with friend and guitarist Dick Taylor, playing songs by artists like Chuck Berry and Muddy Waters. Jagger then met up with Richards again at Dartford railway station where conversations revealed a shared love for R&B music.

In late 1961, they formed a quintet called the Blues Boys, which included Taylor. After leaving school, Jagger continued to study finance at London School of Economics, while Richards moved into a flat with guitarist friend Brian Jones. The trio later began playing at the Ealing Jazz Club with Alexis Korner's band Blues Incorporated, with Jagger becoming lead singer until replaced with Long John Baldry. In July 1962, Jagger, Richards, Jones and Taylor, along with pianist Ian Stewart and drummer Tony Chapman, made their debut at the Marquee Jazz Club as the Rolling Stones, the name taken from a Muddy Waters song, and three months later made their first recordings at Curly Clayton Studios, although proving unsuccessful.

By the end of the year, Jagger had quit university and bassist Bill Wyman and ex-Blues Incorporated drummer Charlie Watts had replaced Taylor and Chapman. Fixing a management deal with 19-year-old ex-Beatles PR-man Andrew Loog Oldham and his associate Eric Easton, the band signed with Decca and recorded Chuck Berry's "Come On" as their first single at Olympic Studios in London on May 10th 1963. Although not charting, it was followed by a string of other covers, two of which topped the UK charts. They included Lennon & McCartney's "I Wanna Be Your Man" (UK # 12); the Buddy Holly-Norman Petty "Not Fade Away" (UK # 3; US # 98); the Womacks' "It's All Over Now" (UK # 1; US # 26), and Willie Dixon's "Little Red Rooster (UK # 1).

Although their writing partnership took time to develop, one of their earliest successes was "As Tears Go By," written for 17-year-old Marianne Faithful, a singer Oldham was promoting at the time. According to one account, he had locked the two writers in a kitchen, forcing them to come up with something, and telling them: "I want a song with brick walls all around it, high windows and no sex." With Jagger writing the lyrics and Richards the melody, it was recorded with musicians that included future Led Zeppelin Jimmy Page on 12-string acoustic guitar. Released in June 1964, it reached number nine on the charts.

In December 1964, they scored their first chart success as writers with the ballad "Heart of Stone," first issued in the US where it peaked at 19 on the charts. In the song, the narrator describes his life as a womaniser and how one girl in particular won't end up breaking his heart. Their first chart-topping success as writers came with "The Last Time." Richards recalled later: "We didn't find it difficult to write pop songs, but it was *very* difficult, and I think Mick will agree, to write one for the Stones. It seemed to us it took months and months and in the end we came up with The Last Time, which was basically re-adapting a traditional gospel song that had been sung by the Staple Sisters, but luckily the song itself goes back into the mists of time." It was recorded in Los Angeles on a one day stopover on their way to Australia, with Phil Spector assisting production. The flip-side to the single was "Play With Fire." Originally called "A Mess of Fire," Jagger described it as a "don't mess with me" song, by telling a well-dressed woman he's not intimidated by her wealth. Apparently, only Jagger and Richards were on the recording, as the rest of the band were sleeping after a long session. Spector filled in on bass, while his assistant Jack Nitzsche played harpsichord. The following day, the band headed off to Australia.

This was followed by what is considered to be one of their finest singles, "(I Can't Get No) Satisfaction." According to Richards, the famous guitar riff and the title of the song came to him in his sleep while staying at the Fort Harrison Hotel in Clearwater, Florida. He recorded it on a portable tape deck then went back to sleep. When he brought it into the studio later that week, the tape allegedly included the sound of snoring. Apart from the title, Jagger wrote the rest of the lyrics. Dealing with what he saw as the real and fake side of America, he described a man looking for authenticity but being unable to find it through "the haze of commercialism." The song topped the charts on both sides of the Atlantic. Initially banned by BBC radio for lyrics being considered too sexually suggestive, a later performance on the US *Ed Sullivan Show* in February 1966, had the line "trying to make some girl" bleeped out by the show's censors.

"Get Off of My Cloud" was their response to the media's clamour to give them another "Satisfaction," with Jagger writing the lyrics and Richards the melody. Jagger later recalled the meaning behind the song: "It's a stop-bugging-me, post-teenage-alienation song. The grown-up world was a very ordered society in the 60's and I was coming out of it. America was even more ordered than anywhere else. I found it was a very restrictive society in thought and behaviour and dress." It's alleged drug references led some radio stations to ban it.

Jagger also came up with the lyrics to "19th Nervous Breakdown" after five weeks touring the US, and making the comment, "Dunno about you blokes, but I feel about ready for my nineteenth nervous breakdown." Around this time, Jagger had been in a relationship with English model Christine Shrimpton for several years which would shortly end amid allegations of philandering and an alleged affair with Marianne Faithful.

With the incredible "Paint It Black," the duo were emulating the Beatles' more sophisticated music, and it highlighted Jones' use of a sitar, which augmented the complexity and texture of their sound. Richards recalled how on a three-day trip to Fiji, they had come across sitars made out of materials like dried watermelons or pumpkins and bringing two back with them, with Richards and Jones trying them out in the studio to get the right sound on the record.

"Mother's Little Helper" was a satirical view of a middle-aged woman with children being dependent upon pills, and was inspired by their recording engineer asking his wife to bring him some depressants to the studio. The b-side to the single was the ballad "Lady Jane," written in early 1966 after Jagger had read *Lady Chatterley's Lover*, which uses the term Lady Jane to mean female genitalia, and not inspired, as believed at the time, to be about Jane Ormsby-Gore, daughter of the former British ambassador to the US. Also that year, they wrote "Out of Time" for their album *Aftermath*, a song which ex-Thunderbirds singer Chris Farlowe recorded with Jagger as producer and took to the top of the UK charts.

1967's beautiful "Ruby Tuesday" was chiefly a Richards' song, with music contribution from Brian Jones. It was inspired by Linda Keith, who was Richards' girlfriend at the time, and who had left him deeply hurt when she went off to New York in a confused, drug-related state of mind, becoming involved with Jimi Hendrix and others. In the song, he describes her as an uncontainable spirit, changing her mood with every new day, a "Ruby Tuesday" who cannot be held on to. Also on the double a-sided single was "Let's Spend the Night Together," a title so suggestive that before being performed live on *the Ed Sullivan Show*, the censors insisted the lyric had to be changed to "Let's Spend Some *Time* Together."

Two songs that defined the summer of love for the band were "We Love You," written as a message of gratitude to their fans for giving their support during the drug tests of Jagger and Richards. It also featured guest backing vocals by Lennon and McCartney, as did the other single "Dandelion." With lyrical references to British nursery rhymes, it was first demoed in November 1966 and originally titled "Sometimes Happy, Sometimes Blue," with different lyrics and sung by Richards.

The title of 1968's chart-topper "Jumpin' Jack Flash" came about while they were at Richards' country house and heard the clumping footsteps of Jack, his gardener. Richards told Jagger it was "jumpin' Jack." "Sympathy for the Devil" from their album *Beggar's Banquet,* was mainly a Jagger song, with a working title of "The Devil is My Name," having earlier been called "Fallen Angels." In the song, the narrator is the devil, boasting of his role in each of several historical atrocities, and repeatedly demanding the listener's courtesy toward him and asking them to "guess my name." Jagger later stated he drew influence from French poet Charles Baudelaire and Mikhail Bulgakov's novel *The Master and Margarita*, which had recently been translated to English and given to him by Marianne Fairthful. Jagger later stated: "I see songwriting as having to do with experience, and the more you're experienced the better it is. But it has to be tempered, and you just must let your imagination run."

"Honky Tonk Women," their last chart entry and final chart-topper of the Sixties, was inspired by them staying on a ranch in a rural part of Brazil and watching the local inhabitants. This, and two more of their songs, "Satisfaction" and "Paint it Black, would later be inducted into the Grammy Hall of Fame.

In 1981, *Rolling Stone* wrote that the band "are the great rock & roll rhythm section of our time ... special primarily because they understand that a great rock & roll band never takes too much for granted." But maybe Keith Richards summed it up the only way he could: "Everyone talks about rock these days; the problem is they forget about the roll."

Chart entries
For the Rolling Stones
Tell Me (You're Coming Back) (US 1964 #24)
Heart Of Stone (US 1964 # 19)
The Last Time (UK 1965 # 1; US # 9; The Who (UK 1967 # 44)
(I Can't Get No) Satisfaction (UK 1965 # 1; US #1); Otis Redding (as Satisfaction) (UK
    1966 # 33; US # 31); Aretha Franklin (as "Satisfaction") (UK 1967 # 37)
Get Off of My Cloud (UK 1965 # 1; US # 1)
19th Nervous Breakdown (UK 1966 # 1; US # 2)
Paint It Black (UK 1966 # 1; US # 1)
Mother's Little Helper (US # 8)
Have You Seen Your Mother Baby, Standing In the Shadow (UK 1966 # 5; US # 9)
Let's Spend the Night Together (UK 1967 # 3; US # 55)
Ruby Tuesday (UK 1967 # 3; US # 1)
Dandelion (UK 1967 # 8; US # 14)

We Love You (UK 1967 # 8; US # 50)
She's A Rainbow (US 1967 # 35)
Jumpin' Jack Flash (UK 1968 # 1; US # 3)
Street Fighting Man (US 1968 # 48)
Sympathy For the Devil (UK 1969 # 9)
Honky Tonk Women (UK 1969 # 1; US # 1)

For other artists
That Girl Belongs To Yesterday – Gene Pitney (UK 1964 # 7; US # 49)
As Tears Go By (*with Andrew Loog Oldham*) Marianne Faithful (UK 1964 # 9; US # 22);
    The Rolling Stones (US # 6)
So Much In Love – The Mighty Avengers (UK 1964 # 46)
Think – Chris Farlowe (UK 1966 # 37)
Blue Turns To Grey – Chris Farlowe (UK 1966 # 15)
Take It Or Leave It – The Searchers (UK # 31)
Lady Jane – David Garrick (UK 1966 # 28)
Sittin' On a Fence – Twice as Much (UK 1966 # 25)
Ride On Baby – Chris Farlowe (UK 1966 # 31)
Out Of Time – Chris Farlowe (UK 1966 # 1; US # 122)

Bill Wyman
In Another Land (US 1967 # 87)

Mark James
Born Francis Rodney Zambon, Houston Texas 1940. Died 2024.
Songwriters Hall of Fame 2014.

James not only played violin and accordion at school, but also conducted their orchestra. Later switching to guitar as his favoured instrument, he became friends with B J Thomas. After being advised to change his name if he wanted to be star, he chose Mark James and began performing in local clubs. Initially intending to write songs for himself to record, he cut his first single and formed the Mark James Trio, co-writing songs with Bobby Winder. After being drafted into the army and serving in Vietnam, he moved to Memphis in 1968, working as a staff writer for producer Chips Moman's publishing company. He wrote several songs that became hits for his friend Thomas, including 1968's "Hooked on a Feeling," which was inspired by his high school girlfriend Karen Taylor. It also was the inspiration for his song "Suspicious Minds" which he recorded himself on the Scepter label. In 1969, when Presley was looking for a song to relaunch his career, Moman played him the song and it became a chart-topper with an almost identical arrangement to James' version.

In the Seventies, Presley recorded more of James' songs, including "Moody Blue" and "Always on My Mind" (the latter co-written with Johnny Christopher and Wayne Carson). Although issued as a b-aside by Presley, it was later a huge hit for both Willie Nelson and the Pet Shop Boys.

Chart entries
The Eyes of a New York Woman – B J Thomas (US 1968 # 28)
Hooked on a Feeling – B J Thomas (US 1968 # 5)
It's Only Love *(with Steve Tyrell)* B J Thomas (US 1969 # 45)
Pass the Apple, Eve *(with Johnny Christopher)* B J Thomas (US 1969 # 97)
Suspicious Minds – Elvis Presley (US 1969 # 1; UK # 2)
Turn on a Dream – The Box Tops (US 1969 # 58).

Tommy James
Born Thomas Gregory Jackson, Dayton, Ohio 1947.

In 1959, at the age of 12, schoolboy James moved with his family to Niles, Michigan, and formed his first band the Echoes, which by the following year had become Tom & the Tornadoes with Larry Coverdale (guitar), Craig Villeneuve (keyboards), Larry White (bass) and Jim Payne (drums). While James was working for local label Spin-It Records in 1962, they cut a single called "Long Pony Tail." In 1964, James re-named the group the Shondells, in honour of singer Troy Shondell and in February recorded the Barry-Greenwich song "Hank Panky" on the small local label Snap Records, owned by local deejay Jack Douglas. Without national promotion, it failed to chart. When the members graduated from high school the following year, the band was broken up.

Although now considering a non-music career, James decided to form a new band called the Koachmen, along with Coverdale and members of another local group the Spinners. Although going on tour, bookings soon began to dry up, leaving James to consider his next move.

The following year, Pittsburgh dance promoter Bob Mack got hold of a copy of "Hank Panky" and had it played regularly on radio stations and at dance parties, leading to a soar in demand. Unable to track down members of the original band, James made promotional appearances by himself until finally recruiting a quintet of musicians from Greensburg, where they had performed as the Raconteurs, and formed the new Shondells, with Mike Vale (bass), Ron Rosman (organ), Joe Kessler (guitar), George Magura (sax, piano) and Vincent Pietropaoli (drums).

Signing a record contract with New York's Roulette Records, the label chose to re-release "Hank Panky," and saw it climb to the top of the US charts in 1966. The following year, Kessler and Pietropaoli left the group after a payment disputes and were replaced by Eddie Gray and Peter Lucia. Magura also departed.

Their third single for the label was "I Think We're Alone Now" written by Ritchie Cordell and his songwriting partner Bo Gentry (although uncredited due to a contract issue). Cordell and Gentry would go on to write or co-write more singles for the band. In 1968, the party rock single "Mony Mony" became the band's first and only chart-topper in the UK. Written by James, Cordell and Bobby Bloom, it was inspired by James' view from his apartment of the illuminated sign M.O.N.Y atop the Mutual of New York building. After the single's success, James decided to change the band's direction, becoming more of an album-orientated band with the blessing of his label.

It was drummer Lucia who claimed to have come up with the name of "Crimson and Clover" for the album and new single after watching a high school football game between his hometown team (wearing crimson kit) and their opponents (in green or "clover"). The single, a shortened version of the five-minute album track, launched the new self-helmed Shondells with its hints of psychedelia, highlighted by the guitar's tremolo effect set to vibrate in sync with the song's rhythm. With its ethereal, layered harmony, it became their first US chart-topper in February 1969 and described by James as "our second renaissance." An invitation to play at Woodstock that year was declined, and the band folded in 1970.

Chart entries
Mony Mony (*with Bo Gentry, Richie Cordell, Bobby Bloom*) Tommy James & the Shondells
   (US 1968 # 3; UK # 1)
Crimson and Clover (*with Peter Lucia Jr*) Tommy James & the Shondells (US 1968 # 1)
Sweet Cherry Wine (*with Richie Grasso*) Tommy James & the Shondells (US 1969 # 7)
Crystal Blue Persuasion (*with Eddy Gray, Mike Vale*) Tommy James & the Shondells (US
   1969 # 2)
Sugar on Sunday (*with Mike Vale*) The Clique (US 1969 # 22)
Ball Of Fire (*with Paul Naumann, Bruce Sudano, Mie Vale, Woody Wilson*) Tommy James
   & the Shondells (US 1969 # 19)
She (*with Mike Vale, Robert King*) Tommy James & the Shondells (US 1969 # 23)

Antonio Carlos Jobim
Born Antônio Carlos Brasileiro de Almeida, Rio De Janeiro, Brazil 1927. Died 1994.
Songwriters Hall of Fame 1991.
Grammy Lifetime Achievement Award 2012.

Born to a prominent family, he studied medicine in Europe where his uncle added Jobim to his last name, as homage to the family's Portuguese home they came from. While an infant, his parents separated and his mother moved the family to Ipanema. When his mother re-married, it was his stepfather who encouraged him to pursue a music career and taught him to play piano (which at first he hated). In the 1940s, he began playing in nightclubs and bars in Rio De Janeiro, and in the early Fifties worked as an arranger for the Continental Studio. In April 1953, he had his first composition "Incerteza" recorded by Brazilian singer Mauricy Moura, with lyrics by Newton Mendonça (1921-1960). Jobim then went on to co-write music for a play with poet and diplomat Vinicius de Moraes (1913-1980), who would go on to pen lyrics for many of Jobim's most popular songs.

In 1958, Brazilian singer and guitarist João Gilberto recorded his first album which had two of Jobim's most famous song, "Desafinado" and "Chega de Saudade." Merging samba and cool jazz with sophisticated harmonies, they introduced the Bossa Nova movement in the country. In the early Sixties, he collaborated with US jazz saxophonist Stan Getz (1927-1991) and husband and wife João and Astrud Gilberto to record two albums that created a bossa nova craze in the US and subsequently around the world. Getz teamed up with Charlie Byrd, who had just returned from a US State Department tour of Brazil, and recorded the album *Jazz Samba* which featured a cover of Jobim's "Desafinado." The English lyrics by Jon

Henricks and "Jesse Cavanaugh," (a pseudonym used by the music publisher Richmond Organization) responded to critics who claimed that the bossa nova genre was created for singers who couldn't sing.

The album *Getz/Gilberto* became one of the best-selling jazz albums of all time, winning the Grammy for Album of the Year, and turned Astrud Giberto into an international sensation with "Garota de Ipanema" (The Girl From Ipanema), for which Jobim composed the melody on a piano at his new house in Ipanema, while Moraes wrote the lyrics, as he had done six years earlier with "Chega de Saudade."

In 1967, Jobim worked with Frank Sinatra on his album *Francis Albert Sinatra & Antônio Carlos Jobim,* which received a Grammy nomination.

Chart entries
Desafinado (with *Newton Mendonça, Jon Hendricks & Jessie Cavanaugh)* Stan Getz & Charlie Byrd (US 1962 # 15; UK # 11); Ella Fitzgerald (UK 1962 # 38); Pat Thomas (US 1962 # 78)
Meditation (Meditacao) *(with Newton Mendonça)* Charlie Byrd (US 1963 # 66; Pat Boone *(with Norman Gimbel)* ((US 1963 # 91); Claudine Longet (US 1966 # 98)
The Girl From Ipanema *(with Vinicius de Moraes, Norman Gimbel)* Stan Getz & João Gilberto (US 1964 # 5; UK # 29)
Quiet Night of Quiet Stars (Corcovado*)(with Gene Lees)* Andy Williams (US 1965 # 92)

Booker T Jones and Steve Cropper see also **William Bell, Al Jackson Jr, Donald "Duck" Dunn, Lewis Steinberg**

Born Booker Taliaferro Jones Jr, Memphis, Tennessee 1944.
Born Steven Lee Cropper, Dora, Missouri 1941.
Rock and Roll Hall of Fame 1992 (as Booker T Jones and the MGs).
Nashville Songwriters Hall of Fame 2010 (Cropper).
Songwriters Hall of Fame 2005 (Cropper).
Grammy Lifetime Achievement Award 2007 (as Booker T Jones and the MGs).

Named in honour of the educator Booker T Washington, Jones was a child prodigy and the son of a science teacher, playing multiple instruments at school as well as organ in church. While at school, he collaborated with future stars, including singer William Bell and Maurice White (of Earth, Wind & Fire). His entry into a music profession came at the age of 16 when he played sax on Carla & Rufus Thomas's hit single "Cause I Love You." He was then hired by bandleader Willie Mitchell to play sax and later bass. It was here that he met producer and drummer Al Jackson, who brought him to Stax Records to join the label's house band. In the summer of 1962, he met 14-year-old record clerk Steve Cropper.

As a boy, Cropper had moved with his family to Memphis. With his exposure to black church music, he soon acquired a guitar and with fellow guitarist Charlie Freeman formed the Royal Spades while still in high school. With a lineup that included producer Chips Moman, Wayne Jackson and Jerry Lee Smith, they soon changed their name to the Mar-Keys. Signed to the Satellite label (a forerunner of Stax), they recorded a hit single "Last Night." With a floating membership that included at times Isaac Hayes, Al Jackson Jr and Lewis Steinberg, they became the racially-integrated house band for Jim Stewart's new Stax label. On meeting Cropper, Jones eventually joined the group as a keyboard player.

After session work, the group recorded impromptu tracks, with the bluesly instrumental "Behave Yourself" leading Stewart to release it on his subsidiary label Volt Records under the moniker Booker T and the MGs (standing for the Memphis Group). With local deejays preferring to play the b-side instrumental "Green Onions," Stax reissued it. Co-written by Jones, Cropper, bass guitarist Steinberg and drummer Al Jackson Jr,. the name and his iconic Fender Telecaster riff were inspired by seeing a cat called Green Onions walk a certain way. The song topped the US R&B charts and peaked at three on the Hot 100. The group's intuitive playing became the foundation on which the label's studio sound was built, and the quartet played on many of the labels great singles.

"Knock on Wood" became Eddie Floyd's biggest hit in 1966. It was allegedly co-written with Jones, Cropper and Jim Stewart in the Lorraine Hotel where Martin Luther King Jr would be assassinated two years later. Working into the night, they came up with the famous line, "It's like thunder, lightning, the way you love me is frightening," after Floyd told Cropper a story about how he and his brother would ride out a storm in Alabama. "In the Midnight Hour" by Wilson Pickett had also been written in the same hotel, with the title coming from Cropper after hearing Pickett singing a gospel track with a line "See my Jesus in the midnight hour" sung over and over again, and then turning it into a song about waiting for his girl.

Otis Redding died in a plane crash on December 10th 1967, a month before "(Sittin' On) The Dock Of the Bay" was released and three days after he recorded it. Redding had been playing at the Fillmore in San Francisco and Bill Graham, who ran the hotel, gave him the choice of staying in the hotel or at a boathouse across the bay in Sausalito. He chose the boathouse, as he liked being outdoors. According to Cropper, that's where he got the idea of the ships coming in and "watching them roll out again." With that, Cropper took what he had away with him and finished the song. The famous whistling at the end wasn't planned, but when Cropper and Stax engineer Ronnie Capone heard it, they realised it had to stay. Beach sound effects were dubbed in after the recording. The plan had also been to use backing singers on the record, possibly the Staple Sisters, but when Redding died there was no time left as there was a rush to get it out.

Continiung his classical music studies, Jones eventually earned a BA. As well as session work, the MGs recorded their own material and had further top ten hits with the instrumentals "Time is Tight," and "Soul Limbo," the latter soon becoming the theme for BBC's test cricket coverage.

In 1970, Jones was made Vice President at Stax, but becoming frustrated with the punishing session schedule and the label continuing to treat the MGs as employees instead of musicians, he decided to go and live and work in Los Angeles, where he signed with A&M as songwriter and soul vocalist. Cropper also quit Stax later that year and started TMI, his own label and recording studio in Memphis. Between them and with other writers, Jones and Cropper were responsible for giving artists some of the most famous R&B hits of the Sixties.

Chart entries
Pop-Eye Stroll – The Mar-Keys (US 1962 # 94)
Knucklehead - The Bar-Kays (US 1967 # 76)

Booker T Jones
Jelly Bread (US 1962 # 82)
Let Me Come On Home *(with Al Jackson Jr & Otis Redding)* Otis Redding (UK 1967 # 48)
Time Is Tight - Booker T & the MGs (US 1969 # 6; UK # 4)

Jones-Cropper with Al Jackson Jr & Lewis Steinberg
Green Onions - Booker T & the MGs (US 1962 # 3)
Mo' Onions - Booker T & the MGs (US 1964 # 97)
Chinese Checkers - Booker T & the MGs (US 1963 # 90)
Soul Dressing - Booker T & the MGs (US 1964 # 95)
Soul Limbo - Booker T & the MGs (US 1968 # 17; UK # 30)
Hang 'Em High - Booker T & the MGs (US 1968 # 9)

Jones-Cropper with Rufus Thomas
Can Your Monkey Do the Dog - Rufus Thomas (US 1964 # 48)
Somebody Stole My Dog - Rufus Thomas (US 1964 # 86)

Jones-Cropper with Eddie Floyd
634-5789 (Soulsville U.S.A) - Wilson Pickett (US 1966 # 13)
Ninety-Nine and a Half (Won't Do) *(with Wilson Pickett)* Wilson Pickett (US 1966 # 53)
Knock On Wood *(with Jim Stewart)* Wilson Pickett (US 1966 # 28; UK # 19); Otis Redding &
    Carla Thomas (US 1967 # 30; UK # 35)
Raise Your Hand *(with Alvertis Isbell)* Eddie Floyd (US 1967 # 79; UK # 42)
Slim Jenkin's Place - Booker T & the MGs (US 1967 # 70; UK # 58)
Things Get Better *(with Wayne Jackson)* Eddie Floyd (UK 1967 # 31)
Love Is a Doggone Good Thing - Eddie Floyd (US 1967 # 97)
On a Saturday Night - Eddie Floyd (US 1967 # 92)
You Don't Know What You Mean To Me - Sam & Dave (US 1968 # 48; UK # 50)

Jones-Cropper with Wilson Pickett
In the Midnight Hour - Wilson Pickett (US 1965 # 21); The Mirettes (US 1868 # 45)
Don't Fight It - Wilson Pickett (US 1965 # 53; UK # 29)
Ninety-Nine and a Half (Won't Do) *(with Eddie Floyd)* Wilson Pickett (US 1966 # 53)

Jones-Cropper with Otis Redding
Mr Pitiful - Otis Redding (US 1964 # 41)
Just One More Day *(with McElvoy Robinson)* Otis Redding (US 1965 # 85)
Fa-Fa-Fa-Fa-Fa (Sad Song) - Otis Redding (US 1966 # 29; UK # 23)
(Sittin' On) The Dock Of the Bay - Otis Redding (US 1968 # 1; UK # 3); King Curtis (US

1968 # 84); Sérgio Mendes (US 1969 # 66); The Dells (US 1969 # 42)
The Happy Song (Dum-Dum) - Otis Redding (US 1968 # 25; UK # 24)

Jones-Cropper with Al Jackson Jr
Hole In the Wall (*with Nathaniel Nathan*) The Packers 9US 1965 # 43)
My Sweet Potato - Booker T & the MGs (US 1966 # 85)
Hip Hug-Her (*with Donald "Duck" Dunn*) Booker T & the MGs (US
    1967 # 37; UK # 51)
The Hunter *(with Carl Wells, Donald Dunn)* Ike & Tina Turner (US 1969 # 93)
Soul Clap 69 *(with Donald Dunn)* Booker T & the MGs (US 1969 # 35)

Jones-Cropper with others
What A Fool I Am *(with Thom Bell)* Carla Thomas (US 1963 # 93)
I've Got No Time To Lose *(with William Parker)* Carla Thomas (US 1964 # 67)
Woman's Love *(with Carla Thomas)* Carla Thomas (US 1964 # 71)
Candy *(with Isaac Hayes)* The Astors (US 1965 # 63)
See Saw *(with Don Convay)* Don Convay & the Goodtimers (US 1965 # 44); Aretha Franklin
    (US 1968 # 14)

Booker T Jones and William Bell
Everybody Loves A Winner - William Bell (US 1967 # 95)
I Got a Sure Thing *(with Ollie Hoskins)* Ollie & the Nightingales (US 1968 # 73)
A Tribute to a King - William Bell (US 1968 # 86; UK # 31)
Private Number - Judy Clay & William Bell (US 1968 # 75; UK # 8)
I Forgot To Be Your Lover - William Bell (US 1968 # 45)
All God's Children Got Soul - Dorothy Morrison (US 1969 # 95)

Booker T Jones and Eddie Floyd
Big Bird - Eddie Floyd (UK 1968 # 53)
I've Never Found a Girl (To Love Me Like You Do) *(with Eddie Floyd, Alvertis Bell)* Eddie
    Floyd (US 1968 # 40)
Why Is the Wine Sweeter (On the Others Side *(with Eddie Floyd)* Eddie Floyd (US 1969 # 98)

Paul Kantner see also Grace Slick
Born Paul Lorin Kantner, San Francisco 1941. Died 2016.
Rock and Roll Hall of Fame 1996 (with Jefferson Airplane).

At the age of eight, Kantner lost his mother and was sent by his father, a travelling salesman, to a Catholic military boarding school. Finding an interest in both music and science fiction, he later rebelled against authority and, like his hero Pete Seeger, chose to become a protest singer. While at the University of Santa Clara, he met future Jefferson Airplane member Joran Kaukonen, but continuing his education at San Jose College he dropped out to share a house in Los Angeles with folk singers David Freiberg and David Crosby. For a time, Kantner and Freiberg tried unsuccessfully to form a folk duo, and in the summer of 1965 he met singer Marty Balin while performing in a folk club. Balin had spent some time in Los Angeles with the folk quartet the Town Criers, and was now looking to recruit musicians for a new house band. Along with three investors, he had bought a former pizza parlour on Fillmore Street in San Francisco to convert into a nightclub the Matrix. With Kantner joining the band as vocalist and rhythm guitarist, he recommended his old friend and blues player Kaukonen for lead guitarist.

It was Kaukonen who suggested the band's name Jefferson Airplane, the nickname given to him by an old friend. Completing the line-up were bass player Bob Harvey, drummer Jerry Peloquin, and singer Signe Anderson. Over the next few months, internal disagreements saw Harvey and Peloquin replaced by Skip Spence and Jack Casady. With promoter Billy Graham, the band soon became popular playing gigs and benefits and were regular performers at the Fillmore Auditorium and Carousel Ballroom. In December 1965, they appointed Matthew Katz as manager and signed a recording contract with RCA with a then unheard-of advance of $25,000.

After the release of their debut single, they played at the Fillmore West along with other top bands from the Bay Area, including the Great Society with its charismatic lead singer Grace Slick. Their debut album *Jefferson Airplane Takes Off* consisted of traditional folk music with elements of jazz, and had Balin writing or co-writing all of the tracks. By May, Spencer Dryden had replaced Spence on drums, and following the band's appearance at the Monterey Jazz Festival (the first rock band to do so), Anderson also quit for personal reasons, leaving Slick to be invited to join as lead singer. She brought with her two songs, "Somebody To Love," written by her brother-in-law Darby, and her own composition, "White Rabbit," both of which had been performed but not released by her former band. They both featured on the band's second album, the psychedelic *"Surrealistic Pillow."*

After a much-lauded and reputation-enhanced appearance at the legendary Monterey Pop Festival, they released the somewhat erratic album *After Bathing at Baxters* early in 1968, with Kantner's songwriting now becoming the dominant force in the band. His penchant for coupling sci-fi or fantasy themes with whimsical lyrics was clearly evident in the opening track "The Ballad of You and Me and Pooneil," which was also released as a single. Inspired by the work of Winnie the Pooh creator A A Milne, some of Kantner's lyrics were taken almost word-for-word from two of Milne's poems. (the "neil" of the title referenced Fred Neil, a pioneer of folk-rock, who Kantner admired.

The album *Crown of Creation* included the Kantner-Balin tracks "In Time" and the dark sequel "The House at Pooneil's Corner," as well as the title track, written by Kantner. With lyrics borrowed (with permission) from John Wyndham's 1955 sci-fi novel *The Chrysalids,* it took the shape of a counterculture anthem. By the end of the decade, band members had begun other projects, with Kantner and Slick (now in a relationship) later forming the hugely successful Jefferson Starship with some ex-Airplane members.

Chart entries
The Ballad of You and Me and Pooneil – Jefferson Airplane (US 1967 # 42)
Watch Her Ride – Jefferson Airplane (US 1967 # 61)
Crown of Creation – Jefferson Airplane (US 1968 # 64)
Volunteers *(with Marty Balin)* Jefferson Airplane (US 1969 # 65)

Buddy Kaye
Born Jules Leonard Kaye, New York City 1918. Died 2002.
Songwriters Hall of Fame 1991.

By the age of eight, Kaye had created a business for himself by answering the corner pharmacy pay phone and then running to the recipient's apartment to notify them there was a call waiting. During the prohibition years he earned a little more money doing nighttime booze deliveries for his mother, who had been abandoned by her husband. With the little money he earned, it paid for a 25-cent music lesson on saxophone and clarinet. In 1935, he graduated from high school and enrolled at Brooklyn College, where his enjoyment of reading classical literature inspired him to write poetry. Coupling this with his love for music, he became a promising lyricist. As a professional sax player, he joined local bands before forming a quintet that played in nightclubs and on cruise ships. But yearning to write songs, he spent the next decade visiting New York's Brill Building to find a composer to collaborate with.

One of his earliest successes was "Speedy Gonzales," co-written with David Hess and Ethel Lee, and a transatlantic hit for Pat Boone. He also had several hits with composer Ted Mossman, with the chart-topping "Till the End of Time, recorded in 1945 by Perry Como, and also an adaptation of Rachmaninoff's Piano Concerto in C Minor which became "Full Moon and Empty Arms," a later hit for Frank Sinatra. In the early Sixties, Kaye travelled abroad to write English translations of songs for artists like Charles Aznavour and Antonio Carlos Jobim. In 1964, he established Budd Music in London and with composer Phil Stringer wrote chart hits for a number of artists, with "The Next Time," from the movie *Summer Holiday,* becoming a UK number one for its star Cliff Richard. He later moved with his family to California to do film and tv work, including composing the theme to tv's *I Dream of Jeannie* with Hugo Montenegro, and songs for five Elvis Presley movies.

In 1974, he would receive a Grammy for Best Children's Recording by producing the album *The Little Prince narrated by Richard Burton,* with music scored by Mort Garson.

Chart entries
Banjo Boy *(with Charlie Niessen)* Jan & Kjeld (US 1960 # 58; UK 36); Art Mooney (US
    1960 # 100); Dorothy Collins (US 1960 # 79)
Happy Go Lucky Me *(with Paul Evans, Al Byron)* George Formby (UK 1960 # 40)
The Next Kiss (Is the Last Goodbye) *(with David Hess & Ethel Lee)* Conway Twitty (US
    1961 # 72)
Speedy Gonzales *(with David Hess & Ethel Lee)* Pat Boone (US 1962 # 6; UK # 2)
Boys Cry *(with Tommy Scott)* Eden Kane (UK 1964 # 8)
The World of Lonely People *(with Mort Garson)* Anita Bryant (US 1964 # 59)
Till the End of Time *(with Ted Mossman)* The Ray Charles Singers (US 1964 # 83)
In the Middle of Nowhere *(with Bea Verdi)* Dusty Springfield (UK 1965 # 8)

Little By Little *(with Bea Verdi, Eddie Gin)* Dusty Springfield (UK 1966 # 17)
Goodbye Bluebird *(with Bob Halley)* Wayne Fontana & the Mindbenders (UK 1966 # 49)

Buddy Kaye and Phil Springer
Time - Craig Douglas (UK 1961 # 9)
Welcome Home, Baby - The Brook Brothers (UK 1962 # 33)
The Next Time - Cliff Richard & the Shadows (UK 1962 # 1)
Sweet William - Millie (UK 1964 # 30; US # 40)
All Cried Out - Dusty Springfield (US 1964 # 41)
Last Night - The Merseybeats (UK 1964 # 40)
This Is My Prayer *(with Mario Panzen, Nicola Salerno)* The Ray Charles Singers (US 1965 # 72)

Jack Keller
Born Jack Walter Keller, New York City 1936. Died 2005.

Brooklyn-born Keller was the son of dance band musician Mal Keller. Learning to play piano and accordion, he later worked in a camera repair store following his father's death. While still a teenager, he played in local dance bands and began writing songs with his friend Paul Kaufman. After regular visits to the Brill Building, he met up with lyricist Lee Cathy and together wrote "Just Between You and Me," a hit for the Chordettes in 1957. Further collaborations followed, including songs with Noel Sherman and Hank Hunter. In 1959, he became one of the first songwriters to work for Don Kirshner and Al Nevins' publishing company Aldon Music, and was instrumental in developing a staff of young writers that included Neil Sedaka, Howard Greenfield, Carole King and Gerry Goffin. Over the next few years, Kaye wrote dozens of songs, alternating with lyricists Goffin and Greenfield, the latter pairing producing two chart-toppers for Connie Francis in 1960.

With Columbia Pictures (Screen Gems) buying Aldon in 1963, Keller and Greenfield began writing theme songs to tv series, including the successful *Bewitched* and *Gidget*. With them both moving to Los Angeles in 1966, Keller continued with tv theme work as well as having songs recorded by leading artists, and that same year was asked to co-produce the Monkees' debut album. For the band's second album *More of the Monkees*, Keller collaborated with Diane Hildebrand to write the track "Your Auntie Grizelda," and with Billy Carr and Ben Raleigh for "Hold On Girl."

In 1970, Keller and Hildebrand wrote "Easy Come, Easy Go," a top ten hit for Bobby Sherman, before moving to Nashville in the Eighties to write for country artists.

Chart entries
The World In My Arms *(with Noel Sherman)* Nat King Cole (UK 1961 # 36)
Just For Old Time's Sake *(with Hank Hunter)* The Maguire Sisters (US 1961 # 20)
Please Don't Ask About Barbara *(with Bill Buchanan)* Bobby Vee (US 1962 # 15; UK # 29)
Gotta Have Your Love *(with Tony Powers)* The Sapphires (US 1965 # 77)
Seattle *(with Hugo Montenegro, Ernie Sheldon)* Perry Como (US 1969 # 38)

Jack Keller and Gerry Goffin
That Lovin' Touch – Mark Dinning (US 1960 # 84)
Run To Him – Bobby Vee (US 1961 #2; UK # 3)
A Forever Kind Of Love – Bobby Vee (UK 1962 # 13)
How Can I Meet Her?– Everly Brothers (US 1962 # 75; UK # 12)
It Started All Over Again – Brenda Lee (US 1962 # 29; UK # 15)
Don't Ask Me To Be Friends – The Everly Brothers (US 1962 # 48)
No One Can Make My Sunshine Smile – The Everly Brothers (UK 1962 # 11)
Don't Try To Fight It, Baby - Eydie Gormé (US 1963 # 53)
Girls Grow Up Faster Than Boys – The Cookies (US 1963 # 33)

Jack Keller and Howard Greenfield
Everybody's Somebody's Fool - Connie Francis (US 1960 # 1; UK #5)
My Heart Has a Mind of Its Own - Connie Francis (US 1960 # 1; UK # 3)
Loving Touch – Mark Dinning (US 1960 # 84)
I Wish I'd Never Been Born – Patti Page (US 1960 # 52)

Don't Read the Letter – Patti Page (US 1960 # 65)
Poor Little Puppet – Cathy Carroll (US 1962 # 91)
Breakin' in a Brand New Heart – Connie Francis (US 1961 # 7; UK # 12)
Venus In Blue Jeans – Jimmy Clanton (US 1962 # 7) Mark Wynter (UK 1962 # 4)
You Used To Be – Brenda Lee (US 1963 # 32)

Al Kent
Born Albert Prentis Hamilton, Detroit 1937. Died 2021.

His first forays into music were with the doo-wop group the Nite-Caps, and he also had a spell working in Chicago with several other labels. Returning to Detroit, he signed with Ric Tic Records, who at the time were competing with the fledgling Motown to become Detroit's premier soul label. Among his achievements was Edwin Starr's "SOS (Stop Her on Sight)," written with Richard Morris, although he is probably best remembered for his own Northern Soul classics "You Got To Pay the Price" and "The Way You've Been Acting Lately." When Ric Tic was bought out by Motown, Kent joined with Berry Gordy Jr and worked with Edwin Starr , J J Barnes and the Fantastic Four. After Motown, he joined Armen Boladien at Westbound, working again with the Fantastic Four.

Chart entries
Hungry For Love *(with Bob Hamilton, Joanne Jackson)* Sam Remo Golden Strings (US 1965 # 27)
Stop Her on Sight (SOS) *(with Richard Morris, Edwin Starr)* Edwin Starr (US 1966 # 48; UK # 35)
Real Humdinger *(with Bob Hamilton, Richard Morris)* J J Barnes (US 1966 # 80)
Headline News *(with Richard Morris, Edwin Starr)* Edwin Starr (US 1966 # 84; UK # 39); The Bown Set (UK # 51)
The Whole World is a Stage *(with Ronnie Savoy, Eddie Wingate)* The Fantastic Four (US 1967 # 63)
You Gave Me Something (and Everything is All Right) *(with Norma Toney, Ronnie Savoy, William Garrett)* The Fantastic Four (US 1967 # 55); Gloria Taylor (US 1969 # 49)
You Got To Pay the Price *(with Hermon Weems)* Al Kent (US 1967 # 49)
Show Time *(with Hermon Weems)* The Detroit Emeralds (US 1968 # 89)

Carole King see Gerry Goffin and Carole King

Terry Kirkman
Born Terry Robert Kirkman, Salina, Kansas 1939. Died 2023.

Kirkman's parents both had musical backgrounds, with father a singer and saxophonist and mother a church organist. Raised in California, he learned to play brass instruments as a child and while later attending Chaffey College as a music major, met fellow student Frank Zappa. For two years they performed together in local coffee bars, and following graduation Kirkman worked as a salesman. While working in Hawaii he befriended US Navy man Jules Alexander and agreed to get together again after his discharge. In 1963, they both moved to Los Angeles where they worked behind the scenes as arrangers and directors for other artists. He then joined Doug Dillard to form the Inner Tubes, a folk group which for a while had members drifting in and out, including David Crosby and Cass Elliot. The group would later evolve into the much larger act, the Men, which for a time became the house band at the Troubadour. In 1965, Kirkman and five of its members decided to go it alone and formed a new band, the Association, the name suggested by Kirkman's then-fiancée. The original lineup had Kirkman (vocals, various instruments); Alexander (vocals, lead guitar); Brian Cole (vocals); Russ Giguere (vocals, percussion, guitar); Ted Bluechel Jr (drums, guitar, bass, vocals), and finally Bob Page (guitar, banjo, vocals), who was soon replaced by Jim Yester.

Eventually, they signed with Valiant Records and released a cover of Dylan's "One Too Many Mornings," but the breakthrough came with Tandyn Almer's "Along Comes Mary." Sung by Yester, it became a top ten hit in 1966, but also courted controversy when both Almer and Leonard Bernstein admitted Mary was a reference to marijuana. Kirkman contributed vocals to a number of their hits, as well as writing the slow-tempo "Cherish" in half an hour, giving the band a US chart-topper later in the year. Kirkman and Larry Ramos shared lead vocals on the beautiful ballad "Never My Love," written by the Adrissi brothers (Don and Rich), which had Kirkman's epic Vietnam War song "Requiem For the Masses" on the flip side. Kirkman left the band twice in 1972 and 1984.

Chart entries
Cherish – The Association (US 1966 # 1)
Everything That Touches You – The Association (US 1968 # 10)
Six Man Band – The Association (US 1968 # 47)

Larry Kolber see Barry Mann and Cynthia Weil

Al Kooper see also Irwin Levine
Born Alan Peter Kuperschmid, New York City 1944.
Rock and Roll Hall of Fame 2023.

At the age of 14, Kooper played guitar with the Royal Teens but did not appear on their 1958 recording of the novelty song "Short Shorts." Two years later, he collaborated with songwriters Irwin Levine (1938-1997) and Bob Brass to write and record demo songs for the publisher Sea-Lark Music. In 1965, they wrote "This Diamond Ring," a number one hit for Gary Lewis & the Playboys, and "I Must Be Seeing Things," a hit for Gene Pitney. Moving to New York at the age of 21, Kooper was invited by producer Mike Bloomfield to watch sessions for Dylan's "Like a Rolling Stone," and ended up playing the organ riffs on the famous recording. In 1965, while Kooper continued to play with Dylan in concert and in the studio, he joined the Blues Project as keyboardist, alongside Danny Kalb, Andy Kulberg, Tommy Flanders and Steve Katz. Shortly before he was due to appear with them at the Monterey Pop Festival, he left to form the group Blood, Sweat and Tears with Katz, Bobby Colomby, Jim Fielder and a trio of horn players. Citing creative differences, Kooper left the following year and was hired as a producer at Columbia Records, working with Bloomfield and Stephen Stills. After moving to Atlanta in 1972, he discovered the band Lynyrd Skynyrd.

Chart entries
This Diamond Ring *(with Bob Brass, Irwin Levine)* Gary Lewis & the Playboys (US 1965 # 1)
I Must Be Seeing Things *(with Bob Brass, Irwin Levine)* Gene Pitney (US 1965 # 31; UK # 6)
The Water Is Over My Head *(with Irwin Levine)* The Rockin' Berries (UK 1966 # 43)
No Time Like the Right Time – The Blues Project (US 1967 # 96)
I Can't Quit Her *(with Irwin Levine)* The Arbors (US 1969 # 67)

Bobby Krieger see Jim Morrison

Ronnie Lane see Steve Marriott and Ronnie Lane

Mike Leander
Born Michael George Farr, Walthamstow, England 1941. Died 1996.

After Leander won a scholarship at Bancroft's School in Woodford Green, he began his music career as an arranger for Decca Records in 1963. At a serendipitous meeting at London's Marquee Club, he saw young guitar player and art college student Jimmy Page and invited him to come and do session work for the label. Later that year, Leander signed a three-year deal with them as musical director. Among his early signings were the Rolling Stones and Joe Cocker. With his name now becoming known in the music industry, it reached Jerry Wexler in the US, who together with the Ertegun brothers, invited Leander to New York to work as arranger on some of their projects.

For the Drifters' classic "Under the Boardwalk," Leander added a wonderful string orchestration to Bert Berns' Spanish-tinted arrangement, and also co-wrote with him "It's All Over," a minor hit for Ben E King. Returning to London, he worked on recordings by Marianne Faithful and teamed up with Chas Mills to co-write a number of hits for Peter & Gordon and Paul & Barry Ryan. In 1967, he wrote "I've Been a Bad, Bad Boy" with Canadian composer Mark London (b.1940) to give ex-Manfred Mann's Paul Jones a solo top five hit, while also providing the lush string arrangement on David McWilliams' "Days of Pearly Spencer." When producer George Martin was unavailable, he was asked by Paul McCartney to provide the string arrangement on Sgt Pepper's beautiful ballad "She's Leaving Home."

Leander left Decca to work for MCA's UK branch, where he discovered Paul Gadd (aka Paul Raven) and set him on the road to success in the Seventies as Gary Glitter.

Chart entries
It's All Over *(with Bert Russell)* Ben E King (US 1964 # 72)
Choc Ice – The Long & the Short (UK 1964 # 40)
I've Been A Bad, Bad Boy *(with Mark London)* Paul Jones (UK 1967 # 5)
Early In the Morning *(with Ed Seago)* Vanity Fare (UK 1969 # 8; US # 12)

Mike Leander and Charles (Chas) Mills
Lady Godiva - Peter & Gordon (UK 1966 # 16; US # 6)
High Time - Paul Jones (UK 1966 # 4)
Missy Missy - Paul & Barry Ryan (UK 1966 # 43)
The Knight In Rusty Armour - Peter & Gordon (US 1966 # 15)
The Jokers - Peter & Gordon (US 1967 # 97)

Jerry Leiber and Mike Stoller
Born Jerome Leiber, Baltimore, Maryland 1933. Died 2011.
Born Michael Stoller, Belle Harbor, NY 1933.
Songwriters Hall of Fame 1985.
Rock and Roll Hall of Fame 1987.

Leiber was born to Jewish parents whose origins were in Russia and Poland. and encountered antisemitism while growing up in a Polish Catholic district of Baltimore. Losing his father at the age of five, he was 12 years old when his mother moved with the family to Los Angeles. As a student at Fairfax High School, he had a penchant for writing lyrics, and the following year was introduced by a classmate to Mike Stoller, whose own family had moved from New York. Stoller had been given piano lessons by James P Johnson and had hung out in the jazz bars of 52nd Street. In a more recent interview, Stoller recalled the first meeting: "He got my number from a drummer. The phone call was from Jerry Leiber, a guy who wanted to write songs. I wasn't interested at first, he finally wangled an invitation to come over to my house, because I wasn't eager, but then after I saw what he was writing when he came over and showed me, I saw they were in the form of twelve-bar blues. And so I started to play some blues on the piano, he started to sing, and we shook hands and said, "We'll be partners." And we were for 61 years."

Despite their different characters (Stoller being reserved, Leiber extroverted), they bonded immediately, and having immersed themselves in New York's thriving R&B scene were able to have a handle on black vernacular.
In 1950, Jimmy Witherspoon became the first artist to perform one of their songs, "Real Ugly Woman" (credited to Stoller-Leiber), while their first hit composition was "Hard Times" by Charles Brown, an R&B hit in 1952. That same year, bandleader Johnny Otis invited the two 19-year-olds to his house to meet blues singer Willie Mae "Big Mama" Thornton. After hearing her sing, they "forged a tune to suit her personality - brusque and badass." According to Leiber, "Hound Dog" "just came leaping out," and it went on to give the singer a number one hit on the R&B charts in 1953. Although the writers detested Presley's later version as being "too white," once it sold a million copies they were inundated with requests to write more for him, and they went on to give the singer hits in the late Fifties with "Love You," "Jailhouse Rock," "Don't," and "King Creole." Around 1954, they founded Spark Records in Los Angeles with artists including the Robins, for whom they wrote the hit "Riot in Cell Block #9," one of the first R&B hits to use sound effects. Wanting to focus more on writing, the duo later sold the label to Atlantic, and in 1957 moved to New York after accepting A&R roles with the new label. They also persuaded two members of the Robins to go with them and form a new group, the Coasters. Among the hits they wrote for them were "Searchin,'" "Charlie Brown," and the number one, "Yakety Yak." In 1959, with Atlantic's Ertegun and Wexler too busy to produce, Leiber and Stoller were hired to write and produce for the Drifters. They also brought in songs by other writers for the group to record, including Pomus & Shuman's "Save the Last Dance For Me." The duo also co-wrote their "Dance With Me" using the pseudonym Elmo Glick.

In December 1960, Leiber teamed up with the young Phil Spector, who had been taken on after a request by music publisher Lester Sill. Together they wrote "Spanish Harlem" for Ben E King, his first chart success away from the Drifters. King had started writing an updated version of the 1905 gospel song written by Charles Tindley and based on Psalm 46, although the most popular adaptation was by the Staple Sisters in 1955. It was this version that King first got to hear. Although intended for the Drifters, they decided not to do it. When first presented to the label bosses, it had Leiber singing and Spector on guitar, with its memorable riff apparently conceived by Spector's then-girlfriend Beverly Ross. After a recording session, King had some studio time left over, and Leiber, one of the session's producers, asked him if he had any mores songs. King then sang an a cappella version of the beginnings of the melody. When Stoller walked in the office, King and Leiber were working on the lyrics, and he went to the upright piano and began working on the harmonies and developed the bass pattern. With lyrics completed, the session musicians were called back in to do the recording. The resulting song not only became a top ten hit for King in 1961, but has since been cited as one of the greatest songs of all time.

In 1963, Leiber and Stoller launched another label called Red Bird with record promoter George Goldner, with 90% of its charted recordings coming from female artists, including the Shangri-Las and the Dixie Cups, with a number of songs written by Brill Building writers. During the time Phil Spector worked with the duo, he was learning their production techniques and playing guitar on sessions, including his solo on the Drifter's "On Broadway," the 1963 hit that had Leiber & Stoller sharing writing credits with Barry Mann & Cynthia Weil. After selling Red Bird to Goldner in 1966, they continued as independent producers and wrote a string of hits for various artists including the Monkees' "D W Washburn," Ray Stevens' "Along Came Jones," and Peggy Lee's "Is That All There Is?" which earned her a Grammy for Best Female Vocal. Their last major production was Stealers Wheel's "Stuck in the Middle With You" in 1972, and a few years later produced an album for Procul Harum before going on to work for A&M Records.

Leiber famously wrote: "Red-hot songs were born on the black streets of Baltimore, where I delivered five-gallon cans of kerosene and ten-pound bags of coal," while Stoller offered simple advice for any budding songwriter: "Just keep writing and explore every opportunity that comes your way."

Chart entries
Lorelei – Lonnie Donegan (UK 1960 # 10)
Shopping For Clothes (*with Kent Harris*) The Coasters (US 1960 # 83)
You're the Boss – Jimmy Ricks & LaVern Baker (US 1960 # 81)
Saved – LaVern Baker (US 1961 # 81)
Little Egypt (Ying-Yang) – The Coasters (US 1961 # 37)
Stand By Me (*Elmo Click [Leiber & Stoller], Ben E King*) Ben E King (US 1961 # 4;
 UK # 27); Kenny Lynch (UK1964 # 39); Earl Grant (US 1965 # 75); Spyder Turner (US
 1966 # 12)
I'll Be There (*with Ben E King & Ollie Jones*) Damita Jo (US 1961 # 12)
You're So Square (Baby I Don't Care) Buddy Holly (UK 1961 # 12)
My Claire De Lune – Steve Lawrence (US 1961 # 68)
Girls! Girls! Girls! – The Coasters (US 1961 # 96); The Fourmost (UK 1965 # 33)
Searchin' – Jack Eubanks (US 1961 # 83)
She's Not You (*with Doc Pomus*) Elvis Presley (US 1962 # 5; UK # 1)
I Keep Forgettin' – Chuck Jackson (US 1962 # 55)
What To Do With Laurie (*with Billy Ed Wheeler*) Mike Clifford (US 1962 # 68)
I'm A Woman – Peggy Lee (US 1963 # 54)
Ruby Baby – Dion (US 1963 # 2)
Reverend Mr Black (*with Billy Ed Wheeler)* The Kingston Trio (US 1963 # 8)
Some Other Guy (with Richard Barrett) The Big Three (UK 1963 # 37)
Lucky Lips – Cliff Richard & the Shadows (UK 1963 # 4; US # 62)
Get Him (*with Bert Russell & Ray Passman*) The Exciters (US 1963 # 76)
I (Who Have Nothing) (*with Mogol & Carla Donita*) Ben E King (US 1963 # 29); Shirley
 Bassey (UK 1963 # 6); Terry Knight & the Pack (US 1966 # 46)
Searchin' – The Hollies (UK 1963 # 12); Ace Cannon (US 1964 # 84)
Bossa Nova Baby – Elvis Presley (US 1963 # 8; UK # 13)
Drip Drop – Dion Di Muci (US 1963 # 6)
Kansas City – Trini Lopez (US 1963 # 23; UK # 35); James Brown (US 1967 # 55)
Poison Ivy – The Paramounts (UK 1964 # 35)
Love Potion No. 9 – The Searchers (US 1964 # 3)
D W Washburn – The Monkees (US 1968 # 18; UK # 17)
Do Your Own Thing – Brook Benton (US 1968 # 99)
Along Came Jones – Ray Stevens (US 1969 # 27)
Is That All There Is? – Peggy Lee (US 1969 # 11)

Leiber & Stoller with Barry Mann & Cynthia Weil
On Broadway (*with Barry Mann & Cynthia Weil*) The Drifters (US 1963 # 9)
Only In America (*with Barry Mann & Cynthia Weil)* Jay and the Americans (US
 1966 # 25)

Jerry Leiber and others
Spanish Harlem *(with Phil Spector)* Ben E King (US 1960 #10); Jimmy Justice (UK
1962 # 20);
Sounds Incorporated (UK 1964 # 35); King Curtis (US 1965 # 89)
Past, Present and Future *(with Artie Butler, George "Shadow" Morton)* The Shangri-Las
(US 1966 # 59)

Paul Leka and Shelley Pinz
Leka born Bridgeport, Connecticut 1943. Died 2011.
Pinz born Rochelle Pinz, New York 1944. Died 2004.

After taking piano lessons as a boy, Leka was writing songs at the age of 16 and trying to sell them to New York publishers. Later becoming a multi-instrumentalist, he played piano with the doo-wop group the Chateaus and recorded singles for the Coral label in the early Sixties. Preferring to produce and arrange music, he left the group to become a full-time songwriter for Circle Five Productions in the Brill Building. In early 1966, fellow staff writer and former college student Rochelle "Shelley" Pinz was standing in front of the Brill Building watching a man with a tambourine begging for money, and it inspired her to write a poem "Green Tambourine." Based on the poem, Leka and Pinz wrote a song with the same name, reluctantly recorded by the short-lived Ohio band the Lemon Pipers. With their debut single having just failed, it became a worldwide hit, and the duo went on to write two more hits for them the following year. Leka also produced the Peppermint Rainbow, another sunshine pop group.

While working for Mercury in 1969, Leka urged the label to record studio musician Gary DeCarlo (aka Garrett Scott), a former member of the Chateaus. Although subsequent releases failed to chart, the label asked Leka and DeCarlo to cut a b-side along with Dale Frahuer, also an ex-member of the Chateaus. The trio chose to record "Na Na Hey Hey Kiss Him Goodbye," a previously unrecorded song from their Chateaus days. When label head Bob Reno decided to release it as an a-side, Leka thought it was "an embarrassing record … an insult," so to avoid clashing with a planned solo career for lead singer DeCarlo, it was released on its Fontana subsidiary under the name Steam, a name conceived by Leka. It became a platinum-selling chart-topper later in the year. During this period, Leka also worked with the Left Banke as producer and arranger.

In the Seventies, Leka owned a recording studio in Bridgeport, Connecticut, and continued to work with artists that included Reo Speedwagon and singer-songwriter Harry Chapin, for whom he produced three albums.

Chart entries
Green Tambourine – The Lemon Pipers (US 1967 # 1; UK # 7)
Rice Is Nice – The Lemon Pipers (US 1968 # 46; UK # 41)
Jelly Jungle (of Orange Marmalade) The Lemon Pipers (US 1968 # 51)

Paul Leka with others
Na Na Hey Hey Kiss Him Goodbye *(with Gary DeCarlo, Dale Frashuer)* Steam (US 1969 # 1;
UK # 9)

John Lennon and Paul McCartney see also George Harrison
Born John Winston Lennon, Liverpool 1940. Died 1980 (murdered).
Born James Paul McCartney, Liverpool 1942.
Songwriters Hall of Fame 1987 (with the Beatles).
Grammy Lifetime Achievement Award 1990 (McCartney) 2014 (with the Beatles).
Grammy Lifetime Achievement Award 1991 (Lennon) 2014 (with the Beatles).
Songwriters Hall of Fame 1994 (Lennon).
Rock and Roll Hall of Fame 1994 (Lennon).
Rock and Roll Hall of Fame 1999 (McCartney).

Born at Liverpool's Maternity Hospital, John was the only child of Alfred and Julia Lennon. His father was a merchant seaman, absent at the time of his birth, and they gave him his middle name in respect for the current prime minister. After being away from home for six months, his father offered to look after the family, but with Julia now pregnant with another man's child, she rejected the idea and gave custody of John to her sister Mimi, who looked after him through to his adolescence. John and his mother kept in touch with regular visits, and it was her that taught him to play banjo and listen to pop tunes on the radio. John attended Dovedale Primary School and Quarry Bank High School, and at the latter, despite getting involved in fights and having a disruptive influence in class, was usually a good-natured, likeable student.

In 1956, his mother bought her 15-year-old son an inexpensive guitar and he formed a skiffle group called the Quarrymen with his close friend Eric Griffiths, with John's mother showing them how to tune guitars and to play simple chords. Pete Shotton joined the group as washboard player, while school friend Bill Smith played a tea-chest bass. Smith was eventually replaced by Len Garry, and when drummer Colin Hanton and banjo player Rod Davis came on board, the group had its stable lineup. With rehearsals taking place in various houses, former tea-chest player Nigel Walley became their manager and secured several gigs during 1957, including one at Liverpool's Cavern Club. On July 6th 1957, they played at a church fête in Woolton in a procession on the back of a moving flatbed lorry. After moving to a permanent stage behind the church, they were playing "Come Go With Me" when 15-year-old Paul McCartney arrived.

Born at Walton Hospital, Paul's parents had moved to Speke after the war, with father Jim returning to his job as a salesman for a cotton merchants and mother Mary a visiting midwife. After attending Joseph Williams Junior School, he went on to the grammar school, Liverpool Institute. In 1954, he met and befriended George Harrison.

On being introduced to John at the church fête, the two of them chatted in the scout hut, talking about music and guitars. Paul had recently written his first song, "I Lost My Little Girl" on his Framus Zenith acoustic guitar, shortly after his mother had died. John was impressed by his ability to tune a guitar and his knowledge of rock lyrics, and later suggested to group member Shotton that they should ask him to join them. When word got back to Paul, who was about to go on holiday with his family, he accepted the invitation. While he was away, Shotton and Davis left the group, feeling that moving away from skiffle would make their instruments redundant. On his return, Paul made his debut with the group at New Clubmoor Hall in Norris Green on October 18th 1957. However, his poor performance on lead guitar signalled the need for an additional guitarist, and he recommended his friend Harrison, who later auditioned for the group and, despite initial reservations from John, was accepted. Griffiths and Garry would subsequently leave the group. Around this time, John wrote his first song, "Hello Little Girl," a later chart hit for the Fourmost.

Lennon and McCartney soon became perfect songwriting partners, beginning by scribbling down songs in a school notebook. They also made a "gentleman's agreement" that all songs written by either one would be jointly credited to them equally as a partnership, thus ensuring they shared equal songwriting royalties.

By January 1959, Griffiths and Garry had left the group and John returned to his studies. The three guitarists, Lennon, McCartney and Harrison, now billed themselves as Johnny & the Moondogs (and at times the Rainbows), playing rock and roll with whatever drummer was available (including Paul's brother Mike). In August, they secured a four-month regular Saturday-night spot at the Casbah Coffee Club in Liverpool, run by Mona Best. In January the following year, John's art school friend Stuart Sutcliffe (1940-1962) joined the group as bass guitarist, and it was he that suggested they change their name to the *Beatals* as a tribute to Buddy Holly & the Crickets. By early July, the name had changed to the Silver Beetles, and after a tour of Scotland backing singer Johnny Gentle, they finally became the Beatles. In mid-August 1960, their unofficial manager Allan Williams arranged a 48-night residency in a Hamburg club, and after an audition for a drummer, recruited Pete Best, son of Casbah Club's Mona. While in Germany, Harrison would be deported when found to be underage.

In February 1961, the Beatles played their first lunch-time session at Liverpool's Cavern Club, and two months later returned to Hamburg for another 92-night club residency. While there, German producer Bert Kaempfert signed both the Beatles and Norwich-born singer Tony Sheridan to his company. With the Beatles backing Sheridan (as the Beat Brothers) they recorded *My Bonnie*, an album of mainly covers, and released the title track as a single. Charting in both the UK and US, it was the Beatles' first commercial recording. In July, bass guitarist Sutcliffe announced he was leaving the group to study art, giving instructions to left-handed McCartney, who now switched to bass, not to change the strings on his guitar.

During a performance at the Cavern Club in November 1961 they group encountered Brian Epstein, a music columnist and owner of local record store NEMS, and the following January appointed him as their manager. That month, they failed an audition for Decca in London (which was won by Brian Poole & the Tremeloes). Meanwhile, Epstein negotiated an early release from their Hamburg contract, and began to direct their image away from leather jackets to matching suits and respectful bows, whist also getting them onto mainstream radio. In April 1962, shortly before the group returned to Hamburg for a residency at the Star Club, they heard that Sutcliffe had died from a brain haemorrhage. The following month, Epstein met EMI producer George Martin and had the group sign a provisional contract to record demos.

On June 6th they had their debut session at EMI's Abbey Road Studios to record a test for the Parlophone label and record three Lennon-McCartney songs, "P.S I Love You," "Ask Me Why" and "Love Me Do." Two months later, having being long dissatisfied with his drumming, Best was fired and replaced by Ringo Starr (b. Richard Starkey 1940) of Rory Storm & the Hurricanes, although a later recording for the songs had sessionist Andy White on drums, and Starr relegated to tambourine. Although coming close to having the group record Mitch Murray's "How Do You Do It?" for their first single, he relented after pressure from EMI's publishing arm who preferred an original song. "Love Me Do" became their first single release. McCartney wrote the verse and chorus with Lennon contributing the bridge. Although only reaching number 17 on the UK charts, it would become a chart-topper in the US in 1964.

In March 1963, they released their debut album *Please Please Me*. The title track became their first UK number one. Written by John, it was an attempt to write a Roy Orbison-style composition, and the title came from having been intrigued by lyrics to a Bing Crosby song that went, "Please lend a little ear to my pleas."

While on tour with Helen Shapiro and heading to Shrewsbury on a coach (or maybe car), they began writing their next single, "From Me To You," and were inspired by reading the letters section of the *New Musical Express,* which was headed "From You to Us." It went on to top the charts for seven weeks beginning in May 1963. Their third chart-topper, "She Loves You," was conceived on a tour bus after a concert in Newcastle, continued that night at a hotel, and completed at Paul's family home. According to Paul, the original idea came from Bobby Rydell's "Forget Him" with its call-and-response pattern. "I Want to Hold Your Hand" was written while Paul was lodging at his girlfriend Jane Asher's parents' home in London, composing the song with John at a piano in the basement. "All My Loving," taken from the second album *With the Beatles* and a later US hit, was another written on a tour bus, and the first song for which Paul wrote the words first (a rare occurrence). Paul once revealed with tongue firmly in cheek: "There are two things John and I always do when we're going to sit down and write a song. First of all we sit down. Then we think about writing a song."

On February 9th 1964, the Beatles made their legendary appearance on the *Ed Sullivan Show* following major pre-publicity engineered by Epstein. Watched by 73 million viewers, it changed pop music forever.

For their debut film *A Hard Day's Night*, directed by Richard Lester in July 1964, the title track and single originated from a comment made by Ringo, who, waking up after working, was thinking it had been hard day's work, until realising it was in fact night. The first single taken from the album of the same name was "Can't Buy Me Love." Paul wrote this after having an upright piano moved into his room in a luxury Paris hotel, and later claimed the idea behind it was that despite having lots of material possessions, it doesn't buy you what you really want. Both singles became transatlantic hits. John wrote the guitar riff for "I Feel Fine" while the group were recording "Eight Days a Week." Lennon and Harrison claimed it was influenced by a riff in Bobby Parker's 1961 "Watch your Step," a song they had covered in the early days. The single was also famous for the feedback note created when Paul was plucking the A-string on his bass, and John's guitar, which was leaning against the bass amp, picked up the feedback. Doing it again to show Martin, he agreed to edit the sound on the front. According to Paul, the title of the US single "Eight Days a Week" came from a chauffeur's comment made while driving him to John's house.

In July 1965, the release of their second movie *Help!* (inspired by the Marx Brothers' *Duck Soup*) was preceded by two of the group's (and Lennon's) greatest singles. The title track had John's lyrics expressing the stress felt with their rapid rise to fame and a cry for help, and he also saw it as a turning point in his songwriting style. No longer "writing to order," he could at last express personal feelings in a song. The wonderful "Ticket to Ride," mainly attributed to John, had conflicting stories about the title's origin, with Paul saying it referred to a railway ticket to Ryde on the Ise of Wight.

"Yesterday," released as a single in the US, was written by Paul after the entire melody came to him in a dream while staying at the home of then-girlfriend Jane Asher, and then hurriedly played it on a piano. Worrying it was someone else's work, he left it for a month and went round people in the music business to find anyone who had heard it. Becoming satisfied, he wrote the lyrics to what has become one of the most covered songs in pop history. For "We Can Work It Out," another song probably referring to Asher, Paul wrote music and lyrics to the chorus, while John's intimations of mortality contributed the bridge. "Daytripper" was written during the early sessions for the *Rubber Soul* album. Like "I Feel Fine," John based his guitar riff on Parker's "Watch Your Step," while Paul contributed to some of the lyrics, admitting that the "trip" was a drug reference and that day-trippers were those only partly-committed to the experience, while also following John's style of writing about women who claimed to be more than what they delivered. Paul's lyrics to "Paperback Writer" were inspired by an aunt who once asked him if he could write something other than about love, and later when seeing Ringo reading a book. Writing the framework for the song while driving from London to John's house in Surrey, he used the story of an aspiring author's letter sent to a publisher as a response to the pressure the group were getting from EMI for another single. According to John, the album track "In My Life" came about after journalist Kenneth Allsop remarked he should write songs about his childhood. It resulted in one his finest songs. Although the autobiographical lyrics were John's, he and Paul would disagree over who wrote the melody.

While *Rubber Soul* had marked a distinct creative departure from the previous albums' pure-pop and the beginning of greater songwriting and instrument experimentation, the next album *Revolver* saw their most overt use of studio technology yet and the start of their psychedelic period. "Yellow Submarine" was a children's song written especially for Ringo to sing, and according to John the melody came from combining two different songs they had been working on separately. Paul came up with the melody for "Eleanor Rigby" on a piano, with the original protagonist being named Miss Daisy Hawkins and the name McKenzie taken from a telephone book. He also revealed that Eleanor had probably come from actress Eleanor Bron, who had starred in the movie *Help!* while another time saying it was inspired by an lonely old lady he knew from his youth and did her shopping. He also said that Rigby was the name of a Bristol store Rigby & Evans he had noticed while visiting his girlfriend. Paul wrote the melody and first verse, while Harrison came up with "Ah, look at all the lonely people," and Starr contributed "writing the words of a sermon that no one will hear" and "Father McKenzie, darning his socks." John would later claim he wrote 70% of the lyrics, and it became the only song for which they disagreed over ownership. Other tracks included John's drug-influenced "I'm Only Sleeping" and the Timothy O'Leary-inspired mantric "Tomorrow Never Knows" with its reverse guitar and looped tape effects, and Paul's beautiful ballads "For No One" and "Here, There and Everywhere." The Beatles played their last concert at San Francisco's Candlestick Park on August 29th 1966.

Ahead of their much-vaunted album *Sgt Pepper's Lonely Hearts Club Band,* the group released another double A-side, with "Strawberry Fields Forever" / "Penny Lane." John wrote the former and based it on his childhood memories of playing in the garden of Strawberry Field, a Salvation Army's children's home in Liverpool. With a total of 45 hours recording, it fused two different versions of the same song, using reverse-recorded instrumentation, and a brass and cello arrangement by Martin. John started writing the song while on the set of Richard Lester's movie *How I Won the War* in Almeria, and probably took inspiration from a novel he was reading, Nikos Kazantzakis's autobiographical *Report to Greco* which described a writer searching for spiritual meaning. With this and his experiences with LSD, it caused him to question his own identity. Working without his bandmates no doubt left him feeling vulnerable. He called it one of the most honest songs he had written, describing it as "psychoanalysis set to music." Paul wrote the nostalgic "Penny Lane" in response to John's song. With some lyrical help from John, they painted a bustling landscape describing real-life Liverpool locations and characters recalled from their schooldays.

When released, *Sgt Pepper* became a cultural icon, lauded by critics for its innovations in songwriting and production, and for bridging the cultural divide between popular music and high art. John's "Lucy in the Sky with Diamonds" was quickly identified with the initials LSD being a drug reference, although he insisted it was derived from a drawing by his four-year-old son Julian. Paul's "She's Leaving Home" was inspired by a front page story in the *Daily Mail* about 17-year-old Melanie Coe who had left her parents with her croupier boyfriend, who had previously worked in the motor trade. John adapted the lyrics for "Being For the Benefit of Mr Kite!" from an 1843 poster for Pablo Fanque's circus he had bought at an antique shop in Kent. Paul's "When I'm Sixty Four" evoked memories of George Formby and seaside postcards, while John's epic "A Day in the Life" was inspired by random articles in the *Daily Mail* about potholes in Blackburn and the death in a car crash of the Guinness heir and socialite Tara Browne. The "dream sequence" bridge was part-written and sung by Paul.

In November, they released the EP *Magical Mystery Tour,* a project that Paul had initiated after work on *Sgt Pepper* was completed the previous April. His idea was to create a psychedelic-themed film similar to Ken Kesey's *Merry Prankster's* in the US. Unscripted, it would take the form of various characters taking a coach ride and have an unspecified series of magical adventures. However, the idea lay dormant for several months while the group began work on John's "All You Need Is Love" and it's *Our World* satellite broadcast in June and focusing on launching their company Apple. After the death of Brian Epstein in late August, work commenced on writing new material for the project.

Continuing the psychedelic sound of *Sgt Pepper,* the double album saw the group members exerting more control over production and indulging in sound experimentation, with lyrics embracing pure randomness and simplicity. The lyrics for John's ultra-surreal "I Am the Walrus" came from three song ideas he had been developing, and unable to finish them had combined them into one. The name Walrus referenced the famous Lewis Carroll's poem, while the lines "yellow matter custard" and "dead dog's eye" were taken from an old playground nursery rhyme. There's even a nod to "Lucy in the Sky with Diamonds." The song was released as the flip-side to Paul's "Hello, Goodbye," but the line "let your knickers down" quickly got it banned by BBC radio. Paul's song, however, took it to number one, with lyrics that came from an exercise in word association with Epstein's assistant Alistair Taylor.

The following year came Paul's "Lady Madonna," describing the plight of a working mother through each day of the week, and according to Paul was inspired after seeing a photo in *National Geographic* of a breastfeeding woman entitled "Mountain Madonna." Their first release on the Apple label came with Paul's "Hey Jude," which evolved from "Hey Jules," a song he had written to comfort John's son Julian after he had left his wife for Yoko Ono. This was followed by Paul's "Get Back," which evolved from being a satirical comment on anti-immigrant sentiment to being about returning to one's roots. In a later interview, John felt Paul was referring to Yoko Ono when he sang "get back to where you belong." The flip-side "Don't Let Me Down" was John's anguished love song to Yoko. "The Ballad of John and Yoko" chronicled the events surrounding their wedding in March 1969 and was written while in honeymoon in Paris.

Lennon once revealed the emotional pressure of creating a song: "Songwriting is about getting the demon out of me. It's like being possessed. You try to go to sleep, but the song won't let you. So you have to get up and make it into something, and then you're allowed to sleep."

John's relationship with avant-garde artist and performer Yoko Ono had begun in 1966, and three years later the song "Give Peace a Chance," was released as a single. Recorded on honeymoon in a Montreal hotel room with a group of friends, including Patrick O'Leary and Petula Clark, the anti-war song was credited to Plastic Ono Band. A second single, John's anti-drug "Cold Turkey," became the first song he wrote with solo credit, and was banned by US radio due to its graphic description of heroin withdrawal.

John's "Come Together," the opening track to the album *Abbey Road,* came about after psychologist Timothy Leary, running for state governor of California, asked him to write a campaign song based on his slogan "Come Together - Join the Party!" As a double A-side single, it was paired with George Harrison's beautiful and much-covered "Something," his paean for his wife Patti Boyd, with its first line borrowed from James Taylor's 1968 album track "Something in the Way She Moves."

The Beatles' final studio album before breaking up was 1970's *Let It Be.* The recording of Paul's title track had begun in January 1969, and was inspired by a dream about his late mother Mary, who died from cancer when he was 14, and her words to him, "It will be all right, just let it be." Another song dating back to 1968 was Paul's "The Long and Winding Road," written at his Scottish farm and inspired by growing tensions within the group. John's meditative and spiritual "Across the

Universe" had an even longer history, with its first recording dating back to the "Lady Madonna" sessions of February 1968, where both songs were written as possible singles before they embarked on the trip to India. It was originally released in December 1969 as part of the various-artists' charity album *No One's Gonna Change Our World*.

These two young musicians from an English seaport changed the course of rock and roll and transformed youth culture, serving as the benchmark for the aspiration and dreams of a worldwide generation that came of age in the Sixties.

Chart entries
*Main writer in italics

Love Me Do (UK 1962 # 17; US 1964 # 1)
Please Please Me *(John)* (UK 1963 # 1; US # 3)
From Me To You (UK 1963 # 1; US #116)
She Loves You (UK 1963 # 1; US # 1)
I Want To Hold Your Hand (UK 1963 # 1; US # 1)
Sie Liebt Dich (She Loves You) German version (US 1964 # 97)
All My Loving *(Paul)* (US 1964 # 45)
Can't Buy Me Love *(Paul)* (UK 1964 # 1; US # 1)
Do You Want To Know A Secret? *(John)* (US 1964 # 2)
A Hard Day's Night *(John)* (UK 1964 # 1; US # 1)
I'll Cry Instead *(John)* (US 1964 # 25)
And I Love Her *(Paul)* (US 1964 # 12)
I Feel Fine *(John)* (UK 1963 # 1; US # 1)
Eight Days A Week *(Paul)* (US 1965 # 1)
Ticket To Ride *(John)* (UK 1965; US # 1)
Help! *(John)* (UK 1965 # 1; US # 1)
Yesterday *(Paul)* (US 1965 # 1)
We Can Work It Out *(Paul)* / **Daytripper** *(John)* (UK 1965 # 1; US # 1)
Nowhere Man *(John)* (US 1966 # 3)
Paperback Writer *(Paul)* (US 1966 # 1; US # 1)
Yellow Submarine / **Eleanor Rigby** *(Paul)* (UK 1966 # 1; US # 2)
    Magical Mystery Tour (UK EP 1967 # 2; UK LP # 1)
    Magical Mystery Tour *(Paul)*
    Fool On The Hill *(Paul)*
    I Am the Walrus *(John)*
    Blue Jay Way (George)
    Your Mother Should Know *(Paul)*
    Baby, You're A Rich Man *(John)*
Penny Lane *(Paul)* / **Strawberry Fields Forever** *(John)* (UK 1967 # 2; US # 1)
All You Need Is Love *(John)* (UK 1967 # 1; US # 1)
Hello Goodbye *(Paul)* (UK 1967 # 1; US # 1)
Lady Madonna *(Paul)* (UK 1968 # 1; US # 4)
Hey Jude *(Paul)* (UK 1968 # 1; US # 1)
Get Back *(Paul)* (UK 1969 # 1; US # 1)
Don't Let Me Down *(John)* (with Billy Preston) (US 1969 # 35)
The Ballad of John and Yoko *(John)* (UK 1969 # 1; US # 8)
Something *(George)* / **Come Together** *(John)* (UK 1969 #4; US # 1)

Lennon-McCartney covers that charted
Do You Want To Know A Secret – Billy J Kramer with the Dakotas (UK 1963 # 2)
From Me To You – Del Shannon (US 1963 # 77)
Bad To Me *(possibly John)* Billy J Kramer with the Dakotas (UK 1963 # 1; US # 9
Hello Litte Girl *(John)* The Fourmost (UK 1963 # 9)
Love of the Loved *(Paul)* Cilla Black (UK 1963 #35)
I'll Keep You Satisfied *(Paul)* Billy J Kramer with the Dakotas (UK 1963 #4; US # 30)
I Wanna Be Your Man *(Paul)* Rolling Stones (UK 1963 #12)

I'm In Love *(possibly John)* The Fourmost (UK 1963 # 17)
All My Loving - Dowlands (UK 1964 # 33); The Holyridge Strings (US 1964 # 93)
A World Without Love *(Paul)* Peter & Gordon (UK 1964 # 1; US #1); Bobby Rydell (US 1964 # 80)
Nobody I Know *(Paul)* Peter & Gordon (UK 1964 #10; US # 12)
Like Dreamers Do *(Paul)* The Applejacks (UK # 20)
I Want To Hold Your Hand – Boston Pops Orchestra (US 1964 # 55)
From a Window *(Paul)* Billy J Kramer & the Dakotas (UK 1964 # 10; US # 23); Chad & Jeremy (US 1965 # 97)
Ringo's Theme (This Boy) *(John)* George Martin & His Orchestra (US 1964 # 53)
I Should Have Known Better *(John)* The Naturals (UK 1964 # 24
It's For You *(Paul)* Cilla Black (UK 1964 # 7; US # 79)
I Don't Want To See You Again *(Paul)* Peter & Gordon (US 1964 #16)
And I Love Her (as And I Love Him) Esther Phillips (US 1965 # 54)
You've Got To Hide Your Love Away *(John)* The Silkie (UK 1965 # 28; US # 10)
That Means A Lot *(Paul)* P J Proby (UK 1965 # 30)
Yesterday –Matt Monro (UK 1965 # 8); Marianne Faithful (UK 1965 # 36); Ray Charles (UK 1967 # 44; # 25)
A Hard Day's Night – Peter Sellers (UK 1965 # 14); The Ramsey Lewis Trio (US 1966 # 29)
Girl *(John)* St Louis Union (UK 1966 # 11); The Truth (UK 1966 # 27)
Michelle *(Paul)* Billy Vaughn (US 1966 # 18); The Overlanders (UK 1966 # 1); Bud Shank (US 1966 # 65); David and Jonathan (UK 1966 # 11; US # 18))
Woman *(Paul)* Peter & Gordon 1966 (UK # 28; US # 14)
Drive My Car *(Paul)* Bob Kuban & the In-Men (US 1966 # 93)
Got To Get You Into My Life *(Paul)* Cliff Bennett & the Rebel Rousers (UK 1966 # 6); Billy Vaughn (US 1966 # 77); Bud Shank (US 1966 # 65)
Daytripper – The Vontastics (US 1966 # 100); Ramsey Lewis (UK 1966 # 74); Otis Redding (UK 1967 # 43)
Eleanor Rigby– Vanilla Fudge (UK 1967 # 53); Ray Charles (US 1968 # 35; UK # 36); Aretha Franklin (US 1969 # 17)
With a Little Help From My Friends – Young Idea (UK 1967 # 19); Joe Brown (UK 1967 # 32) Joe Cocker (UK 1968 # 1; US # 68)
When I'm Sixty Four *(Paul)* Kenny Ball & His Jazzmen (UK 1967 # 43)
Good Day Sunshine *(Paul)* Claudine Longet (US 1967 # 100)
Step Inside Love *(Paul)* Cilla Black (UK 1968 # 8)
The Fool On the Hill *(Paul)* Sérgio Mendes (US 1968 # 6)
Lady Madonna – Fats Domino (US 1968 # 100)
Ob-La-Di Ob-La-Da *(Paul)* Marmalade (UK 1968 # 1); The Bedrocks (UK 1968 # 20); Athur Conley (US 1969 # 51)
Hey Jude – Wilson Pickett (US 1968 # 23; UK # 16)
Back In the USSR *(Paul)* Cliff Bennett & His Band (UK 1969 # 54); Chubby Checker (US 1969 # 82)
Goodbye *(Paul)* Mary Hopkin (UK 1969 # 2; US # 13)
Birthday *(Paul)* Underground Sunshine (US 1969 # 26)
Golden Slumbers / Carry That Weight *(Paul)* Trash (UK 1969 # 35)
She Came In Through the Bathroom Window *(Paul)* Joe Cocker (US 1969 # 30)
Ticket To Ride – The Carpenters (US 1969 # 54)
Julia *(John)* Ramsey Lewis (US 1969 # 76)

George Harrison
Something – The Beatles (UK 1969 #4; US # 1)
If I Needed Someone – The Hollies (UK 1965 # 20)
Badge *(with Eric Clapton)* Cream (UK 1969 # 18; US # 60)

John Lennon & Plastic Ono Band
Give Peace A Chance (UK 1969 # 2; US # 14)
Cold Turkey (UK 1969 # 14; US # 30)

Irwin Levine
Born Irwin Jesse Levine, Newark, New Jersey 1938. Died 1997.

The son of prizefighter Benny Levine, his first success in the music business came in 1961 by co-writing two singles with Bob Brass. "You're Gonna Need Magic," a minor hit for Roy Hamilton, which was soon followed by "A Thing of the Past," the b-side to the Shirelles' "What a Sweet Thing That Was." Three years later, the duo joined Al Kooper to write and record demo songs for the publisher Sea-Lark music, and with the song "This Diamond Ring" by Gary Lewis & the Playboys, scored their first chart-topper. Although originally recorded as a demo by Jimmy Radcliffe, it made its first chart appearance when recorded by Sammy Ambrose in January 1965. Lewis' version had been produced by Snuff Garrett with members of the Wrecking Crew, although Lewis later denied claims that the Playboys did not actually play on the record and that the session musicians were only there to do overdubs. Kooper was unhappy with their version and would have preferred the Drifters to record it in the style of Radcliffe's original demo.
    Levine and Brass went on to write "I Must Be Seeing Things" for Gene Pitney, and "Little Lonely One" for Tom Jones, while Levine teamed up with other writers, including Phil Spector and Toni Wine, to have moderate hits for a number of artists.
    In 1970, Levine and Wine wrote "Candida," an international hit for Tony Orlando, who for the recording created the group Dawn with top session singers Telma Hopkins and Joyce Vincent. Toward the end of the year, Orlando would have even greater success with "Knock Three Times," penned by Levine and L Russell Brown, which became a chart-topper on both sides of the Atlantic. The following year that success was repeated with "Tie a Yellow Ribbon Round the Ole Oak Tree."

Chart entries
You're Gonna Need Magic *(with Bob Brass)* Roy Hamilton (US 1961# 80)
A Thing of the Past *(with Bob Brass)* The Shirelles (US 1961 # 41)
This Diamond Ring *(with Bob Brass, Al Kooper)* Gary Lewis & the Playboys (US 1965 # 1)
I Must Be Seeing Things *(with Bob Brass, Al Kooper)* Gene Pitney (US 1965 # 31; UK # 6)
Little Lonely One *(with Bob Brass)* Tom Jones (US 1965 # 42)
The Water Is Over My Head *(with Al Kooper)* The Rockin' Berries (UK 1966 # 43)
Let's Call It A Day Girl *(with Neil Sheppard)* Razor's Edge (US 1966 # 77); Bobby Vee
   (US 1969 # 92)
Black Pearl *(with Phil Spector, Toni Wine)* Sonny Charles & the Checkmates (US 1969 # 13)
I Can't Quit Her *(with Al Kooper)* The Arbors (US 1969 # 67)
You're Husband - My Wife *(with Toni Wine)* The Brooklyn Bridge (US 1969 # 46)

Howard Liebling see Marvin Hamlisch

Gordon Lightfoot
Born Gordon Meredith Lightfoot Jr, Orillia, Ontario, Canada 1938. Died 2023.
Songwriters Hall of Fame 2012.

Schooled by his mother to become a successful child performer, Lightfoot sang an Irish-American lullaby while in fourth grade and had it broadcast over the school's p.a system during a parents' day. Having a clear soprano voice, it was left to his choirmaster to give him the confidence to perform and sing with emotion, and as a result was invited to make appearances on local radio and at music festivals. At the age of 12, after winning a number of competitions, he learned to play folk guitar, piano and drums.
    In 1958, he moved to Los Angeles and enrolled at Westlake College of Music to study jazz orchestration and composition. To pay his way, he sang on demo records and wrote and produced jingles. Returning to Toronto two years later, he became well-known as a folk singer in the city's coffee houses and performed with a number of folk groups, including Singin' Swingin' Eight, who appeared on the tv series *Country Hoedown*. In 1961, he signed with RCA in Nashville and recorded two solo singles that became moderate hits in Canada. He also dueted with Terry Whelan as the Two-Tones/Two-Timers and released a live album in the Chateau label in 1962.
    Lightfoot then spent a year in the UK as host of BBC's *Country and Western Show,* and on his return to Canada in 1964 appeared at the Mariposa Folk Festival. With a growing reputation as a songwriter, the Canadian folk duo Ian and Sylvia recorded his songs "Early Mornin' Rain" and "For Loving Me," both of which were later recorded by Peter, Paul and Mary

and a number of other artists. The following year he signed a management contract with Albert Grossman and a recording contract with United Artists. His much-covered single "I'm Not Sayin'" peaked at number 12 on the Canadian charts. An appearance at the Newport Folk Festival, followed by the release of his debut album *Lightfoot!* bolstered his reputation as a singer-songwriter.

Over the next three years, Lightfoot recorded four more albums with a number of singles charting in Canada, the most successful being his cover of Dylan's "Just Like Tom Thumb's Blues," peaking at number three. The single "Black Day in July" from his 1968 album *Did She Mention My Name?* was about the Detroit riots of the previous year, and when Martin Luther King was assassinated weeks later, many US radio stations pulled it for "fanning the flames," despite the fact that the lyrics were a plea for racial harmony.

Feeling he lacked the support of his label, he moved to Warner Brothers and in early 1971 had his biggest success with the ballad "If You Could Read My Mind," with lyrics reflecting on his recent divorce and comparing it to a ghost movie. It was written one summer while staying in a vacant Toronto house.

Further albums included the singles "Sundown" (1974), the epic true-life tragedy "The Wreck of the Edmund Fitzgerald" (1976), and "Daylight Katy" (1978).

Chart entries
For Lovin' You – Peter, Paul & Mary (US 1965 # 30)
Early Mornin' Rain – Peter, Paul & Mary (US 1965 # 91)
I Can't Make It Anymore – Spyder Turner (US 1967 # 95)

Sandy Linzer and Denny Randell
Born Sanford Roy Linzer, New York City 1941
Born Dennis Joel Rafklin, New York City 1941.
Songwriters Hall of Fame 2012.

At an early age, Randell had already learned to play a variety of instruments, and spent his high school years in Silver Spring, Maryland. Choosing to use whatever spare time he had honing his skills in the school music room, he spent his evenings writing songs and playing in a band that was managed by a popular local deejay, who also played Randell's tapes on his radio show. In the early Sixties, he was given the opportunity to record one of the songs he had written, arranged and produced. Not only did it have regional success, but it also caught the attention of New York's famous music publisher Shapiro Bernstein, who employed him as a staff writer. Before long, he was working on producing and arranging songs for a number of artists on their roster, including siblings Jean and Don Thomas. Through this role, he came to the attention of Bob Gaudio of the Four Seasons, who invited him to work with the group. Following a meeting with their producer/songwriter Bob Crewe, Randall was introduced to 20-year-old lyricist Sandy Linzer and the trio set about writing, arranging and producing songs for the Four Seasons, beginning with the Crewe-Linzer penned "Dawn (Go Away)," a US top three in 1964, while Randell arranged and produced a number of tracks on their debut album *Rag Doll*.

The following year, Randall and Linzer produced the hit "A Lover's Concerto" for the all-girl trio the Toys, with the melody adapted from Bach's classical Minuet in G major. This was soon followed by him teaming up with Crewe to write "Let's Hang On," another top three hit for the Four Seasons.

Success for the group continued in 1966 with hits that included Randall & Linzer's "Working My Way Back To You" and "Opus 17 (Don't You Worry 'Bout Me)," the latter so-called for being the group's 17th single and notable for the near-absence of lead singer Frankie Valli's trademark falsetto. By year's end, they had earned sufficient prestige to set up their own label, Oliver. In 1968, Randell went to Los Angeles to work with Don Kirshner at Screen Gems and also as producer/A&R man for Epic/CBS Records. Continuing to write with Linzer, they provided songs for *The Monkees* tv show as well as hits for Jay & the Americans and Al Hirt. One of their last hits of the decade was 1968's "Breakin' Down the Walls of Heartache," a UK number four for Johnny Johnson's Bandwagon.

Chart entries
Society Girl *(with Bob Crewe)* The Rag Dolls (US 1964 # 91)
Dusty *(with Bob Crewe)* The Rag Dolls (US 1965 # 55)
Let's Hang In *(with Bob Crewe)* The Four Seasons (US 1964 #3; UK # 4); Jonny Johnson & the
    Bandwagon (UK 1969 # 36)
A Lover's Concerto *(adapt. Johann Sebastian Bach)* The Toys (US 1965 # 2; UK # 5); Sarah
    Vaughan (US 1966 # 63)
Attack – The Toys (US 1965 # 18; UK # 36)
Working My Way Back To You – The Four Seasons (US 1966 # 9; UK # 50)
May My Heart Be Cast Into Stone – The Toys (US 1966 # 85)
Opus 17 (Don't You Worry 'Bout Me – The Four Seasons (US 1966 # 13; UK # 20)

Baby Toys *(with Tony Decilis, Richard Layton)* The Toys (US 1966 # 76)
Can't Get Enough of You Baby – Question Mark & the Mysterions (US 1967 # 56)
Penny Arcade – The Cyrkle (US 1967 # 95)
Keep the Ball Rollin' – Jay & the Techniques (US 1967 # 14); Al Hirt (US 1968 # 100)
Baby Make Your Own Sweet Music – Jay & the Techniques (US 1968 # 64)
Breakin' Down the Walls of Heartache – Johnny Johnson & the Bandwagon (UK 1968 # 4)

Sandy Linzer and others
Dawn (Go Away) *(with Bob Gaudio)* The Four Seasons (US 1964 # 3)
Electric Stories *(with Mike Petrillo)* The Four Seasons (US 1968 # 61)

Mark London
Born Montreal, Canada 1940.

Working first as a comedian in London, he scored his first success as a composer working with lyricist Don Black on the title track of the 1967 movie *To Sir, with Love,* starring Sidney Poitier and Lulu (London would later marry Lulu's longtime manager Marion Massey). When released in the US, it shot to number one and became the best-selling single of the year. Also that year, he partnered Mike Leander on the soundtrack to the movie *Privilege,* which starred ex-Manfred Mann singer Paul Jones and Jean Shrimpton. As well as having a part in the movie, London co-wrote "I've Been a Bad, Bad Boy," one of the singles taken from it. Performed by Jones, it became a top UK five hit in January 1967.

London continued working with Lulu on her next single "Best of Both Worlds," with lyrics again penned by Black, and later went on to compose the soundtrack for a series of children's animated films.

Chart entries
I've Been a Bad, Bad Boy *(with Mike Leander)* Paul Jones (UK 1967 # 5)
To Sir, with Love *(with Don Black)* Lulu (US 1967 # 1; UK # 5); Herbie Mann (US 1967 # 93)
Best of Both Worlds *(with Don Black)* Lulu (US 1967 # 32)

Jerry Lordan
Born Jeremiah Patrick Lordan, London 1937. Died 1995.

Paddington-born Lordan was a self-taught pianist and guitarist. After attending Finchley Catholic School, he did national service as a radar operator in the RAF before working in advertising and also performing as a comedian and singer in local clubs and pubs. In 1958, with a talent for songwriting, his advertising work also allowed him to make demos, and one song, "A House, A Car and a Wedding Ring," came to the attention of a Decca record producer who had it recorded by ex-boxer Mike Preston. Although not successful, it was later covered by US rockabilly artist Dale Hawkins. Lordan had his first UK chart success with "I've Waited So Long," a top ten hit in 1959 for a young Anthony Newley. Signing with Parlophone in 1960, he went on to have a trio of chart hits as a solo artist, including the George Martin-produced "Who Could Be Bluer?"

One of his biggest successes as writer was the instrumental "Apache." Inspired in the late Fifties by watching the 1954 Western movie of the same name, he later recalled that he "wanted something noble and dramatic, reflecting the courage and savagery of the Indian Apache warrior Massai," played in the movie by Burt Lancaster. Unimpressed with the original recorded version by guitarist Bert Weedon, Lordan played it on ukelele to Shadows' bass player Jet Harris while on tour with Cliff Richard. The group quickly recorded it in July 1960 and took it to the top the UK charts. With Weedon's version finally seeing a release shortly after, despite having merit, it only scraped into the top 30. To compensate, the Shadows' Hank Marvin and Bruce Welch wrote "Mr Guitar" for Weedon to record. The following year, Lordan wrote "A Girl Like You," a UK top three for Cliff Richard, and also "I'm a Moody Guy" for Shane Fenton (aka Alvin Stardust).

Following the success of "Apache," Lordan decided to concentrate on songwriting, and in 1962 gave the Shadows a second chart-topper with "Wonderful Land." Recalling the difficulties in the writing, he said, "I got the first phrase and it took me six months to get to the middle. I knew it had to have a second part and I couldn't think of anything." It remained top of the charts for eight weeks, sharing that record with Presley and the Archies for the whole decade. More success came for the Shadows over the next couple of years with Lordan's instrumental "Atlantis" and "Mary Anne" (a rare vocal), while also giving ex-Shadows' guitarist Jet Harris and drummer Tony Meehan back-to-back instrumental hits with "Diamonds" (a chart-topper) and "Scarlett O'Hara," named after a fictional character in the novel *Gone With the Wind* (but not actually featuring Harris on the recording!). In 1966, he co-wrote "A Place in the Sun" with his wife Petrina, his final hit for the Shadows.

Although collaborations with fellow songsmiths Roger Cook and Roger Greenaway brought success for a time, by the end of the decade the hits stopped coming and an attempt at acting also proved fruitless.

Chart singles
I'll Stay Single *(with Thomas Mould)* Jerry Lordan (UK 1960 # 26)
Who Could Be Bluer? – Jerry Lordan (UK 1960 # 16)
Sing Like An Angel – Jerry Lordan (UK 1960 # 36)
Apache – The Shadows (UK 1960 # 1); Bert Weedon (UK 1960 # 24); Jørgen Ingmann (US
 1961 # 2); Sonny James (US 1961 # 87)
A Girl Like You – Cliff Richard & the Shadows (UK 1961 # 3)
I'm A Moody Guy – Shane Fenton & the Fentones (UK 1961 # 22)
Walk Away - Shane Fenton & the Fentones (UK 1962 # 38)
Wonderful Land – The Shadows (UK 1962 # 1)
I'm Just A Baby – Louise Cordet (UK 1962 # 13)
Diamonds – Jet Harris & Tony Meehan (UK 1963 # 1)
Scarlett O'Hara – Jet Harris & Tony Meehan (UK 1963 # 2); Lawrence Welk & His Orchestra
 (US 1963 # 89)
Atlantis – The Shadows (UK 1963 # 2)
Song of Mexico – Tony Meehan (UK 1964 # 39)
Apache '65 – The Arrows (US 1965 # 64)
Mary Anne – The Shadows (UK 1965 # 17)
A Place In the Sun *(with Petrina Lordan)* The Shadows (1966 # 24)
Conversations (*with Roger Cook & Roger Greenway*) Cilla Black (UK 1969 # 7)
Good Times (Better Times) (*with Roger Cook & Roger Greenway*) Cliff Richard & the
 Shadows (UK 1969 # 12)

John D Loudermilk
Born John Dee Loudermilk Jr, Durham, North Carolina 1934. Died 2016.
Nashville Songwriters Hall of Fame 1976.

Raised in the old tobacco warehouse city of Durham to parents who were members of the Salvation Army, young Loudermilk was influenced by church music and choirs, and had two cousins who performed as the Louvin Brothers, appearing regularly on the *Grand Ole Opry*. Learning to play guitar, Loudermilk graduated from the private Campbell College, and while still in his teens gained work as a graphic artist for a local tv station. A poem that he had set to music called "A Rose and a Baby Ruth" (the name referring to a chocolate bar) was picked up by the station owner who allowed him to play it on air. Country star George Hamilton IV heard it, and when recorded by himself in 1956, it became a top ten hit.

The following year, using the pseudonym Johnny Dee, he wrote and recorded the top 40 hit "Sittin' in the Balcony" on the Columbia label, which at the same time also charted with a version by Eddie Cochran. He also wrote and recorded the original version of "Tobacco Road," which was inspired from a road in town where hogsheads of tobacco were rolled down to the riverside to be loaded onto barges. Although failing to chart, it would be made famous by the Nashville Teens a few years later. In 1959, Loudermilk teamed up with songsmith Marijohn Wilkin to write "Waterloo," a country chart-topper for Stonewall Jackson. Two years later, he signed with RCA and had a string of minor hits as a solo singer. Although largely unsuccessful, he found greater success writing for other artists. "Sad Movies (Make Me Cry)" was a top five hit for Sue Thompson, while "Norman" also repeated that success for her three months later.

The Everly Brothers' sombre "Ebony Eyes," while scoring a UK chart-topper, was initially banned from BBC radio due to its death-related theme, while lyrics to "This Little Bird," sung by 17-year-old Marianne Faithfull, may have foreshadowed her later struggle with alcohol. Another song, the Casinos' "Then You Can Tell Me Goodbye," had originally been recorded six years before by Don Cherry, but now peaked at number ten on the Hot 100.

Perhaps Loudermilk's most famous song was 1969's "Indian Reservation" (or to give it its full title, "The Lament of the Cherokee Reservation Indian") by ex-Sorrows' member Don Farndon, a top five hit in the singer's home country. Known to be a self-professed prankster, Loudermilk had written and recorded the song in 1959, claiming he had been asked by Cherokees to write a song about their plight after being "kidnapped" when his car got stuck in mountain snow. (The plight referred to was the 1838 tragedy of Cherokee Indians being displaced from their homes in Georgia to a reservation in Oklahoma). In 1959, Marvin Rainwater, who claimed to be part-Cherokee himself, had recorded the song as "Pale Faced Indian," but the song went on to top the US charts in 1971 with a version by Paul Revere & the Raiders.

Chart entries
Angela Jones – Johnny Ferguson (US 1960 # 27); Michael Cox (UK 1960 # 7)
Ebony Eyes - The Everly Brothers (US 1961 # 8; UK 1961 # 1)

Stayin' In – Bobby Vee (US 1961 # 33; UK # 4)
Top Forty, News, Weather and Sports – Mark Dinning (US 1961 # 81)
The Great Snowman – Bob Luman (UK 1961 # 49)
Sad Movies (Make Me Cry) – Sue Thompson (US 1961 # 5); The Lennon Sisters (US 1961 # 56); Carol Deene (UK 1961 # 44)
(He's My) Dreamboat – Connie Francis (US 1961 # 14)
The Language of Love - John D Loudermilk (US 1961 # 32; UK # 13)
Norman – Sue Thompson (US 1961 # 3); Carol Deene (UK 1961 # 24)
Thou Shall Not Steal - John D Loudermilk (US 1962 # 73); Dick & Dee Dee (US 1964 # 13)
Callin' Dr Casey – John D Loudermilk (US 1962 # 83)
Torture – Kris Jensen (US 1962 # 20)
James (Hold the Ladder Steady) Sue Thompson (US 1962 # 17)
Road Hog – John D Loudermilk (US 1962 # 65)
Abilene (*with Bob Gibson, Lester Brown*) George Hamilton IV (US 1963 # 15)
Talk Back Trembling Lips – Johnny Tillotson (US 1963 # 7)
Tobacco Road – The Nashville Teens (US 1964 # 14; UK # 6)
Everything's Alright – Johnny Cash (US 1964 # 16)
Google Eye – The Nashville Teens (UK 1964 # 10)
Paper Tiger – Sue Thompson (US 1965 # 23)
This Little Bird – Marianne Faithful (UK 1965 # 6; US # 32); Nashville Teens (UK 1965 # 38)
Then You Can Tell Me Goodbye – The Casinos (US 1967 # 6; UK # 28); Eddy Arnold (US 1968 # 84)
What A Woman In Love Won't Do – Sandy Posey (US 1967 # 31; UK # 48)
I Wanna Live – Glen Campbell (US 1968 # 36)
It's My Time – The Everly Brothers (UK 1968 # 39)
Indian Reservation - Don Farndon (US 1968 # 20; UK 1970 # 3)

Mike Love see Brian Wilson and Mike Love

Bernie Lowe see Kal Mann and Dave Appell

Kenny Lynch
Born Kenneth Lynch, London 1938. Died 2019.

Of Jamaican/ Barbadian heritage, Lynch grew up in Stepney, the youngest of 13 children. His sister Gladys was a respected jazz singer using the pseudonym Maxine Daniels. At the age of 12 he made his first stage appearance singing with his sister. After leaving school at 15, he did a variety of jobs and the following year played with a string of bands that included those of Ed Nichols and Bob Miller. In 1957, he began his national service with the Royal Army Service Corps, for which he became the regiment's featherweight boxing champion. Three years later, he released a cover of Harold Dorman's "Mountain of Love" on the RCA label and took it to number 33 on the UK charts.

More cover versions followed, including two top ten hits with "Up on the Roof" and "You Can Never Stop Me Loving You." In 1962, Bert Weedon's single "Twist Me Pretty Baby" included the credit "Shouts by Kenny Lynch," while the following year Lynch's single "Misery" became the first Beatles cover to be released. The group then went on to emulate Lynch's more pop-oriented arrangement for the track on their debut album, and later showed their respect for him by including him on the album cover for *Sgt Pepper*. In 1964, Lynch had his first chart success as a writer with "What Am I to You?" co-authored with Mort Shuman and Clive Westlake, and over the next couple of years continued working with Schuman on hits for Cilla Black and the Small Faces. With an infectious personality and also being an accomplished actor, Lynch was a popular tv celebrity, appearing in many programmes over the years.

Chart entries
What Am I To You? *(with Clive Westlake, Mort Schuman)* Kenny Lynch (UK 1964 # 37)
It's Gotta Last Forever *(with Clive Westlake, Bill Giant)* Billy J Kramer & the Dakotas (US 1965 # 67)
I'll Stay By You *(with Hal Shaper)* Kenny Lynch (UK 1965 # 29)

Follow Me *(with Mort Schuman)* The Drifters (US 1965 # 91)
Love Is Just A Broken Heart *(with Michelle Vendome, Mort Schuman)* Cilla Black (UK 1966 # 5)
Sha-La-La-La-Lee *(with Mort Schuman)* Small Faces (UK 1966 # 3)
What Good Am I? *(with Mort Schuman)* Cilla Black (UK 1967 # 24)

Tony Macaulay and John MacLeod see also Geoff Stephens
Born Anthony Gordon Instone, Fulham, England 1944.
Born John MacLeod, Canada c1926.
Songwriters Hall of Fame 2025 (Macaulay)

While a 19-year-old student at Brighton's College of Advanced Technology, Macaulay also played in bands and was passionate about getting into the music industry as a songwriter. In the early Sixties, he took the job as a song plugger for Essex Publishing, persuading radio stations to play the label's new releases. Gaining experience in the industry, he later worked for Pye Records, and it was there that he teamed up with the experienced Canadian songwriter John MacLeod, who had moved to the UK in the Forties, eventually coming to live in Macaulay's hometown of Brighton. In 1947, he and his brother joined the vocal quartet Maple Leaf Four, releasing a couple of albums and making a number of tv appearances. By the early Sixties, he was also working on advertising jingles.

In 1966, Macaulay had his first chart success as songwriter with "Don't Let a Little Pride Stand in the Way" by Billy Fury, co-authored with actor Don Michael Paul, but it was with MacLeod that they had back-to-back chart-toppers. The Foundations' "Baby, Now That I've Found You" and Long John Baldry's "Let the Heartaches Begin," was the first time in UK chart history that a writer had one of his songs displaced at number one by another of his songs. When told of the fact, Macaulay recalled: "Everyone said how incredible that was. I said, no, its bloody awful planning!" More writing success for the Foundations and Baldry followed, as well as a hit for the girl trio the Paper Dolls with the catchy "Something Here In My Heart." Macaulay also teamed up with Manfred Mann's Mike D'Abo for the Foundations' "Build Me Up Buttercup," as well as having solo credit for Marmalade's "Baby Make It Soon" in 1969.

His final collaboration of the Sixties was with ex-schoolteacher Geoff Stephens, scoring hits for the Hollies and Scott Walker and a top five US hit with the Flying Machine's "Smile a Little Smile For Me." In the meantime, MacLeod penned "Baby Take Me In Your Arms" for British singer Jefferson (aka Geoff Turton), which became a surprise top 30 hit in the US.

Chart entries
Baby, Now That I've Found You – The Foundations (UK 1967 # 1; US # 11)
Let the Heartaches Begin – Long John Baldry (UK 1967 # 1; US # 8)
Back On My Feet Again – The Foundations (UK 1968 # 18; US # 59)
Hold Back the Daybreak – Long John Baldry (UK 1968 # 54)
Something Here In My Heart (Keeps A-Tellin' Me No) The Paper Dolls (UK 1968 # 11)
Any Old Time (You're Lonely And Sad) - The Foundations (UK 1968 # 48)
Mexico – Long John Baldry (UK 1968 # 15)
It's Too Late Now – Long John Baldry (UK 1969 # 21)
In the Bad, Bad Old Days (Before You Loved Me) The Foundations (UK 1969 # 8)
My Little Chickadee – The Foundations (US 1969 # 76)

Tony Macaulay
Build Me Up Buttercup (*with Mike d'Abo*) The Foundations (UK 1968 # 2; US # 3)
Baby Make It Soon - Marmalade (UK 1969 # 9)

Tony Macaulay and Geoff Stephens
Sorry Suzanne – The Hollies (UK 1969 # 3; US # 56)
Lights of Cincinnati – Scott Walker (UK 1969 # 13)
Smile A Little Smile For Me – The Flying Machine (US 1969 # 5)

Tony Macaulay with others
Don't Let A Little Pride Stand In the Way *(with Don Michael Paul)* Billy Fury (UK 1966 # 51)

John MacLeod
Baby Take Me In Your Arms *(with Anthony Gordon Instone)* Jefferson (US 1969 # 23)

Henry Mancini see also Johnny Mercer
Born Enrico Nicola Mancini, Cleveland, Ohio 1924. Died 1994.
Grammy Lifetime Achievement Award 1995.

Raised in Pennsylvania, he was the son of Italian immigrants. With his father an amateur musician, by the age of eight he had learnt to play the piccolo. He was inspired to write music composition after watching Cecil B DeMille's 1935 movie *The Crusades*. Four years later, he studied piano and orchestral arrangement with Pittsburgh's conductor Max Adkins and began writing arrangements for bandleader Benny Goodman. After graduation in 1942 he attended the Julliard School of Music in New York and in 1943 joined the US Army Air Force and was recommended by Glen Miller to an airforce band, before going overseas to serve with US engineers in France. On his return home, he became pianist and arranger for the newly-formed Glen Miller Orchestra and in 1952 joined Universal-International's music department. Over the next half dozen years he scored music for over 100 movies, including many sci-fi and "creature features," as well as receiving an Oscar nomination for *The Glen Miller Story*. He also had his first success as a pop songwriter with "I Won't Let You Out of My Heart" by Guy Lombardo & His Royal Canadians.

In 1958, he began working as an independent composer/arranger and struck up a long-lasting partnership with writer/producer Blake Edwards, beginning with scoring the theme to the tv series *Peter Gunn*. This was followed by working on movies including *Breakfast at Tiffany's* (with the wonderful "Moon River"), *Days of Wine and Roses*, *The Pink Panther* (and its sequels), *The Great Race* and *Victor Victoria*. With director Stanley Donen he worked on *Charade*, *Arabesque* and *Two for the Road;* with Howard Hawks on *Hatari!*(including "Baby Elephant Walk"); with Vittorio de Sica on *Sunflower*, and with Arthur Hiller on *Silver Streak*.

Nominated for 72 Grammys, he went on to win 20 (including "Moon River" and "Days of Wine and Roses,") while also receiving 19 Academy Award nominations and winning four.

Among his tv work were the movies *The Thorn Birds* and *The Moneychangers* and the series *Peter Gunn*, *Newhart*, *Hotel*, and *Remington Steele*.

Chart entries
Mr Lucky – Henry Mancini (US 1960 # 21)
Theme From the Great Imposter – Henry Mancini (US 1961 # 90)
Moon River *(with Johnny Mercer)* Jerry Butler (US 1961 # 11); Henry Mancini (US 1961 # 11;
  UK # 44; US 1962 # 32); Danny Williams (UK 1961 # 1)
Baby Elephant Walk *(with Hal David)* The Miniature Men (US 1962 # 87); Lawrence Welk
  & His Orchestra (US 1962 # 48)
Theme From Hatari! – Henry Mancini (US 1962 # 95)
Days of Wine and Roses *(with Johnny Mercer)* Henry Mancini (US 1963 # 33); Andy Williams
  (US 1963 # 26)
(I Love You) Don't You Forget It *(with Al Stillman)* Perry Como (US 1963 # 39)
Banzai Pipeline – Henry Mancini (US 1963 # 93)
Charade *(with Johnny Mercer)* Henry Mancini (US 1963 # 36); Andy Williams (US 1964 # 100);
  Swing and Sway with Sammy Kaye (US 1964 # 36)
The Pink Panther Theme – Henry Mancini (US 1963 # 31)
A Shot in the Dark – Henry Mancini (US 1964 # 97)
How Soon? *(with Al Stillman)* Henry Mancini (UK # 10)
Dear Heart *(with Ray Evans, Jay Livingston)* Jack Jones (US 1964 # 30); Andy Williams (US
  1964 # 24); Heney Mancini (US 1964 # 77)
In the Arms of Love *(with Ray Evans, Jay Livingston)* Andy Williams (US 1966 # 49; UK # 33)

Barry Mann and Cynthia Weil
Born Barry Imberman, New York City 1939.
Born Cynthia Weil, New York City 1940. Died 2023.
Songwriters Hall of Fame 1987.
Rock and Roll Hall of Fame 2010.
Women Songwriters Hall of Fame 2023 (Weil).

Born two days before fellow songwriter Gerry Goffin, Mann took occasional piano lessons as a child. Although having an ambition to become an architect, he had begun to write songs by the age of 14. As well as becoming president of his senior class, he was leader of the Junior and Senior Sings as well as being a member of the cheering squad, the Go-Getters. He graduated from James Madison High School in 1956 (the same school future songsmiths Jack Keller and Carole King attended), and it was Keller who offered to try and sell Mann's songs in New York. The following year, he quit studying architecture at Pratt Institute to begin a career as a professional songwriter. While booking into a Brill Building studio to record some of his songs, he met Lou Stallman who invited him to join Round Music, a publishing company he had set up with Joe Shapiro. Using the name Mann, he spent the following months writing songs with Shapiro and Sid Jacobson, although his first chart success was co-writing with Mike Anthony "She Say (Oom Dooby Doom)" for the Diamonds, a top 20 hit in 1959.

In 1960, he was hired as a staff writer at Don Kirshner's Aldon Records at $150 a week, and was teamed up with a number of other writers, including Hank Hunter (1929-2017) for Steve Lawrence's "Footsteps," and Howard Greenfield for Emile Ford & the Checkmates' "Counting Teardrops." With Larry Kobler (aka Kolberg 1931-2015) he wrote "I Love How You Love Me" for the girl trio, the Paris Sisters (Albeth, Sherrell and Priscilla). The song was originally intended for Tony Orlando to be recorded in a similar upbeat style to his "Halfway to Paradise." It took Kobler just seven minutes to write the lyrics on a napkin in a café, just across the street from Aldon Music. He then went back to the office to find someone to record it, and ran into Mann who was with Phil Spector. Spector then asked him if he could have the song for one of his girl groups, and, with Aldon boss Don Kirshner persuading him that it would have more potential if recorded by a female act, Kolber reluctantly gave him the song.

Mann also recorded a solo album which yielded the novelty hit "Who Put the Bomp (in the Bomp, Bomp, Bomp," co-written with Gerry Goffin, which was self-mocking look at the gibberish lyrics being used by songwriters for the then-popular doo-wop craze. Mann and Goffin had written it during a playful experiment to see how many songs they could write in half an hour. This one took just five minutes!

Mann was known to have few roots in rock and roll, disliked songs by Chuck Berry and Little Richard, and preferred the vocal rhythm and blues of contemporary pop records.

While at Aldon, Mann met 21-year-old Cynthia Weil. Raised in Manhattan, her father owned a couple of furniture stores but died when she was seven. She took ballet and piano lessons at the private Walkden School and was inspired by a maternal aunt who was a chorus dancer. After a year at the University of Michigan, she transferred to Sarah Lawrence College in New York where she attained a major in theatre. During this time, she had performed in nightclubs as a dancer and singer, and it was an agent who urged her to become a lyricist.

Just weeks after meeting Mann at Aldon, the couple were married and almost immediately began writing songs together. With her love for show tunes, they made a perfect match. Among their early chart hits were "Bless You" for Tony Orlando (for which they received a first royalty check for $3,000), "If a Woman Answers (Hang Up the Phone)" for Leroy Van Dyke, and "My Dad" by Paul Peterson.

One of the most famous of the early songs was "On Broadway." They had written it in its original form in 1962, and with an upbeat lyric was recorded by the Crystals for their album *Twist Uptown*. When Leiber and Stoller let it be known that the Drifters had booked studio time for the following day and were short of a song, Mann and Weil sent him their song. Feeling there was something missing, the four of them held an overnight meeting, giving it a more rock-oriented groove and more bluesy feel, together with some lyrical changes by Leiber. Recorded by the Drifters, it scored a US top ten hit in 1963.

The following year saw some of their greatest work. "I'm Gonna Be Strong" was originally recorded by Frankie Laine, but it was Gene Pitney's stronger version that became a transatlantic hit and his greatest success. "Saturday Night at the Movies" was another hit for the Drifters, with Johnny Moore now replacing Rudy Lewis on lead vocal. The wonderful "Walking in the Rain" by the Ronettes was co-written with Phil Spector, and recorded with lead singer Ronnie Spector in the summer of 1964. According to Ronnie, the three writers were still adjusting the lyrics right up to the minute she recorded it and recalled how Spector placed headphones on her and told her to listen closely. "Then all of a sudden I hear a low rumble, like there was thunder coming from every corner of the room." The sound effects were used throughout the song, which was recorded in just one take, and audio engineer Larry Levine received a Grammy nomination for his work.

Their next collaboration with Spector came with the incredible "You've Lost That Lovin' Feelin'" by the Righteous Brothers, destined to become the most played song on radio and tv of the 20th Century and one of the greatest pop songs of all time. It was written after a request from Spector for a hit song for a new act he had just signed to his Philles label. Mann and Weil then listened to some of the artists' previous singles on the Moonglow label, including "Little Latin Lupe Lu" and "My Babe" to get a feel for their sound and then made the decision to write a ballad about a desperate attempt to rekindle lost love. Using the Four Tops' "Baby, I Need Your Loving," which was rising in the charts, as their inspiration, they chose the title as a temporary measure until they had something better, but Spector liked it as it was and so it remained. Completing the lyrics at Spector's house, Mann wrote the melody and came up with the opening line which was influenced by a lyric from another of his songs, "I Love How You Love Me." The two of them quickly wrote the first two verses, but having difficulty with the bridge, asked Spector for help, who then experimented on the piano with a "Hang on Sloopy"-type riff. Spector also tacked on the words "gone, gone, gone, whoa, whoa, whoa" to the end of the chorus, something that Weil disliked, claiming later he only "inspired" words, not actually wrote any.

When they presented it to the artists, Bill Medley felt the song (which the writers had sung in a higher key) did not suit his low baritone voice, so they lowered the key from F to C♯ for the recording, and, according to Medley, changed the whole vibe of the song. With Bobby Hatfield unhappy about him not been given equal prominence in the song, he went to Spector asking what he was supposed to do during Medley's solo, and the reply was, "You can go directly to the bank!" Two years later, Mann and Weil wrote "(You're My) Soul and Inspiration" for the Righteous Brothers, giving them their second US chart-topper and with Hatfield's voice now given more prominence.

Some of the other songs the couple intended to be more socially conscious included "We Gotta Get Out of This Place" by the Animals, and "Uptown" by the Vogues. However, they were unhappy when their song "Only in America," co-written with Leiber & Stoller and originally conceived as a protest song against racial prejudice when recorded by the Drifters, was re-worked by their co-writers with less controversial lyrics and recorded by Jay & the Americans.

In the late Sixties, the couple, now rich and famous, left Aldon and moved to Los Angeles, writing mainly for Broadway shows and country artists. In 1987 their song "Somewhere Out There" from the animation movie *An American Tail* won two Grammys. Weil once offered advice to budding songwriters: "You just have to believe in yourself when you've got something, and just keep pounding on the door, because if you pound long enough, someone is going to open it."

Chart entries
Bless You – Tony Orlando (US 1961 # 15; UK # 5)
A Girl Has To Know – The G-Clefs (US 1962 # 81)
If A Woman Answers (Hang Up the Phone) Leroy Van Dyke (US 1962 # 35)
Uptown – the Crystals (US 1962 # 13)
Conscience – James Darren (US 1962 # 11; UK # 30)
Where Have You Been All My Life – Arthur Alexander (US 1962 # 58)
Jonny Loves Me – Shelley Fabares (US 1962 # 21)
Mary's Little Lamb – James Darren (US 1962 # 39)
My Dad – Paul Peterson (US 1962 # 6)
He's Sure the Boy I Love – The Crystals (1962 # 11)
Proud – Johnny Crawford (US 1963 # 29)
Blame It On the Bosa Nova – Eydie Gormé (US 1963 # 7; UK # 32)
Don't Be Afraid, Little Darlin' – Steve Lawrence (US 1963 # 26)
Amy – Paul Peterson (US 1963 # 65)
Heart – Kenny Chandler (US 1963 # 64); Wayne Newton & the Newton Boys (US 1963 # 82),
    Rita Pavone (UK 1966 # 27)
Don't Make My Baby Blue – Frankie Laine (US 1963 # 51); The Shadows (UK 1965 # 10)
I'm Gonna Be Strong – Gene Pitney (US 1964 # 9; UK # 2)
Only in America – Jay and the Americans (US 1963 # 25)
Cindy's Gonna Cry – Johnny Crawford (US 1963 # 72)
I'll Take You Home – The Drifters (US 1963 # 25; UK # 37); Cliff Bennett & the Rebel
    Rousers (UK 1965 # 42)
The Girl Sang the Blues – The Everly Brothers (UK 1963 # 25)
I Want You To Meet My Baby – Eydie Gormé (US 1963 # 17)
Saturday Night At the Movies – The Drifters (US 1964 # 18; UK # 35)
Talk To Me Baby – Barry Mann (US 1964 # 94)
Born To Be Together – The Ronettes (US 1965 # 52)
Come On Over To My Place – The Drifters (US 1965 # 60; UK # 40)
Love Her – Walker Brothers (UK 1965 # 20)
Looking Through the Eyes of Love – Gene Pitney (US 1965 # 28; UK # 3)
It's Gonna Be Fine – Glenn Yarborough (US 1965 # 54)
We Gotta Get Out Of This Place – The Animals (US 1965 # 13; UK # 2)
Don't Make My Baby Blue – The Shadows (UK 1965 # 10)
Home of the Brave – Bonnie & the Treasures (US 1965 # 77; Jody Miller (1965 # 25)
Magic Town – The Vogues (US 1966 # 21)
(You're My) Soul and Inspiration – The Righteous Brothers (US 1966 # 1; UK # 15)
Kicks – Paul Revere & the Raiders (US 1966 # 4)
Hungry - Paul Revere & the Raiders (US 1966 # 6)
It's A Happening World – The Tokens (US 1967 # 69)
It's Not Easy – The Will-O-Bees (US 1968 # 95)
Brown Eyed Woman – Bill Medley (US 1968 # 43)
Shape Of Things To Come – Max Frost & the Troopers (US 1968 # 22)

Peace Brother Peace – Bill Medley (US 1968 # 48)
It's Getting Better – Mama Cass (US 1969 # 30; UK # 8)
Make Your Own Kind of Music – Mama Cass (US 1969 # 36)

Mann-Weil with Phil Spector
Walking in the Rain – The Ronettes (US 1964 # 23; UK # 3); The Walker Brothers (UK 1967 # 26); Jay & the Americans (US 1969 # 19)
You've Lost That Lovin' Feelin' – Righteous Brothers (US 1964 # 1; UK # 1); Cilla Black (UK 1965 # 2); Dionne Warwick (US 1969 # 16); Righteous Brothers (UK 1969 # 10)
Born To Be Together – The Ronettes (US 1965 # 52)

Mann-Weil with Leiber & Stoller
On Broadway – The Drifters (US 1963 # 9; UK # 7)
Only in America – Jay & the Americans (US 1963 # 25)

Barry Mann
Come Back Silly Girl – The Lettermen (US 1962 # 17)

Barry Mann with Larry Kolber
Sweet Little You *(with Larry Kolber)* Neil Sedaka (US 1961 # 59)
I Love How You Love Me *(with Larry Kolber)* The Paris Sisters (US 1961 # 5); Jimmy Crawford (UK 1961 # 18); Maureen Evans (UK 1964 # 34); Paul & Barry Ryan (UK 1966 # 21); Bobby Vinton (US 1968 # 9)
Let Me Be the One *(with Larry Kolber)* The Paris Sisters (US 1962 # 87); Peaches & Herb (US 1969 # 74)
Patches *(with Larry Kolber)* Dickey Lee (US 1962 # 6)

Barry Mann with Howard Greenfield
The Way of a Clown - Teddy Randazzo (US 1960 # 44)
Girls Girls Girls - Steve Lawrence (UK 1960 # 49)
Counting Teardrops - Emil Ford & the Checkmates (UK 1960 # 4)
Warpaint - The Brook Brothers (UK 1961 # 5)

Barry Mann with Gerry Goffin
Who Put the Bomp (In the Bomp, Bomp, Bomp) Barry Mann (US 1961 # 7); The Viscounts (UK 1961 # 21 as Who Put the Bomp)

I'd Never Find Another You - Billy Fury (UK 1961 # 5)
I Could Have Loved You So Well - Ray Peterson (US 1961 # 57)

Barry Mann with others
Footsteps *(with Hank Hunter)* Steve Lawrence (US 1960 # 7; UK # 4); Ronnie Carroll (UK 1960 # 36)
I'll Never Dance Again *(with Mike Anthony)* Bobby Rydell (US 1962 # 14)
The Grass is Greener *(with Mike Anthony)* Brenda Lee (US 1963 # 17)

Kal Mann and Dave Appell
Born Kalman Cohen, Philadelphia Pa 1917. Died 2001.
Born Dave Appell, Philadelphia Pa 1922. Died 2014.

Mann (no relation to Barry Mann) began his career in the Forties as a comedy writer for Red Buttons, Danny Thomas and Jack Leonard, but it was his friend and songwriter Bernie Lowe (1917-1993) that convinced him that if he could write comic parodies, he could also write song lyrics for the music industry. Lowe had started Teen Records in 1955 while working with Freddie Bell & the Bellboys. He asked Bell to re-write the lyrics to Leiber & Stoller's "Hound Dog" to appeal to a broader radio audience, and the version he came up with was the one Presley later recorded. Lowe would also use the pseudonym Harold Land so he could be affiliated to both BMI and ASCAP. In 1956, Mann and Lowe wrote "(Let Me Be Your) Teddy Bear," a chart-topper for Presley the following year, and together formed the Philadelphia-based Cameo Records (later to become Cameo-Parkway).   When they brought in Dave Appell, the three of them worked together as a production team on many of the label's early releases. Appell had begun his music career during the war as arranger for several of the US Navy's big bands, and then did the same for post-war dance orchestras, including those of Benny Carter and Earl Hines. He also spent time recording for Decca as the Dave Appell Four, the name of which was soon changed to the Applejacks, and in 1955 joined ASCAP as a publisher, collaborating with Max Freedman.

For a time, the Applejacks became the studio band for Ernie Kovacs' tv and radio shows in Philadelphia, and later played in Las Vegas before Appell went on to work for Cameo as a session guitarist, arranger and producer. The Applejacks played on Charlie Grace's hits, including the 1957 million-seller "Butterfly." In 1958, Mann signed unknown singer Ernest Evans (aka Chubby Checker) and wrote the song "The Class" for him as the label's first release. Their subsequent success with Checker's recordings made Cameo-Parkway one of the biggest independent labels in the country.

Capitalising on current dance crazes, Appell took just 45 minutes to write "Bristol Stomp" for the Philly band the Dovells, which had been inspired by watching teenagers slamming their heels on a Pennsylvania dance floor. "Wah-Watusi" and "South Street" for the Orlons also went national through *American Bandstand*. Some of the songs attributed to Mann and Appell were often the work of deceased songwriters whose songs were now out of copyright. The Orlons' "South Street" was actually Stephen Foster's "Camptown Races" with nonsense lyrics, while they were sued over "Mashed Potato Time" being too similar to Motown's "Please Mr Postman."

That summer, Appell wrote the instrumental dance song "The Mexican Hat Rock" for the Applejacks, becoming a top twenty hit after exposure on tv. In 1960, Mann and Appell, along with Lowe, scored their first chart hit with Bobby Rydell's "Wild One," and the following year, in response to the need for a follow-up to Checker's Hank Ballard-penned hit "The Twist," they wrote the Grammy award-winning top ten hit "Let's Twist Again." Some songs written by Mann, such as "Limbo Rock," used the pseudonym Jon Sheldon to enable him to be affiliated (like Lowe) with both BMI and ASCAP. Appell left Cameo in 1964 and in the Seventies enjoyed success producing for Tony Orlando and Dawn.

Chart entries
Time Machine *(with Howard Greenfield)* Dante & the Evergreens (US 1960 # 73)
Twistin' U.S.A - Danny & the Juniors (US 1960 # 27); Chubby Checker (US 1961 # 68)
Let's Twist Again - Chubby Checker (US 1961 # 8; UK # 22)
You Can't Sit Down *(with Dee Clark, Cornell Muldrow)* Philip Upchurch Combo (US 1961
    # 29)
The Fish *(with Luther Dixon)* Bobby Rydell (US 1961 # 25)
Bristol Stomp - The Dovells (US 1961 # 2)
Do the New Continental - The Dovells (US 1962 # 37)
The Wah-Watusi - The Orlons (US 1962 # 2)
Gravy (For My Mash Potatoes) - Dee Dee Sharp (US 1962 # 9)
Dancin' Party - Chubby Checker (US 1962 # 12# UK # 19)
Hully Gully Baby - The Dovells (US 1962 # 25)
Don't Hang Up - The Orlons (US 1962 # 4# UK # 39)
The Cha-Cha-Cha - Bobby Rydell (US 1962 # 10)
 Butterfly Baby - Bobby Rydell (US 1963 # 23)
Let's Limbo Some More - Chubby Checker (US 1963 # 20)
South Street - The Orlons (US 1963 # 3)
Do the Bird - Dee Dee Sharp (US 1963 # 10); The Vernon Girls (UK 1963 # 44)
Mother, Please! - Jo Ann Campbell (US 1963 # 88)
Wildwood Days - Bobby Rydell (US 1963 # 17)
Rock Me in the Cradle of Love - Dee Dee Sharp (US 1963 # 43)
Surf Party - Chubby Checker (US 1963 # 55)
Betty in Bermudas *(with Rose Marie)* The Dovells (US 1963 # 50)
Crossfire! - The Orlons (US 1963 # 19)
Wild! - Dee Dee Sharp (US 1963 # 33)
Loddy Lo - Chubby Checker (US 1963 # 12)
Stop Monkeyin' Aroun' - The Dovells (US 1963 # 94)
Bon-Doo-Wah - The Orlons (US 1963 # 55)
Where Did I Go Wrong - Dee Dee Sharp (US 1964 # 82)

Hey, Bobba Needle - Chubby Checker (US 1964 # 23)
Rules Of Love - The Orlons (US 1964 # 66)
She Wants T'swim - Chubby Checker (US 1964 # 50)

Mann-Appell with Bernie Lowe
Wild One - Bobby Rydell (US 1960 # 2; UK # 7)
Ding-a-Ling - Bobby Rydell (US 1960 # 18)
Good Time Baby - Bobby Rydell (US 1961 # 11; UK # 42)
The Door To Paradise - Bobby Rydell (US 1961 # 85)

Kal Mann with others
Birdland (*with Huey Smith*) Chubby Checker (US 1963 # 12)
You Can't Sit Down *(with Dee Clark, Cornell Muldrow)* Philip Church Combo (UK 1966 # 39)

Nancie Mantz see Annette Tucker

Ray Manzarek see Jim Morrison

Steve Marriott and Ronnie Lane
Born Stephen Peter Marriott, Plashet, England 1947. Died 1991 (house fire).
Born Ronald Frederick Lane, Plaistow, England 1946. Died 1997.

Marriott was born to East End working-class parents, and as a premature baby weighing just 1.9kg was hospitalised for a month after developing jaundice. His father, an accomplished pianist, worked as a printer and later had a jellied eels stall, while his mother worked in a sugar factory. Lane, along with his mother and brother, would be diagnosed with multiple sclerosis at different points in their lives.

With their son showing an early interest in singing and performing, his parents bought him a harmonica and ukulele which he taught himself to play. To earn extra money, he later busked at local bus stops and went on to win local talent concerts while on holiday. At the age of 12, Marriott formed a band with school friends called The Wheels (later the Mississippi Five). Mimicking his idol Buddy Holly, they played in local coffee bars and at a local cinema. Despite being accused of pranks and being disruptive at school, he developed a taste for acting, and in 1960 successfully auditioned for the role of the Artful Dodger in Lionel Bart's musical *Oliver!*.

Encouraged by his parents to pursue an acting career, he enrolled at London's Italia Conti Academy of Theatre Arts and went on to appear in film and tv, usually typecast as an energetic Cockney kid. His most notable role was alongside Peter Sellers in the movie *Heaven's Above*. Eventually he would lose interest in acting and resume his music ambition. In 1963, he wrote "Imaginary Love," and after taking it to a number of record labels was signed as a solo artist by Decca, and his first (unsuccessful) single was "Give Her My Regards," written by fellow Londoner Kenny Lynch. Later that year, he formed the Frantiks and recorded a cover version of "Move It," although it was never released. With a name-change to Marriott & the Moments, they supported a number of artists and played at some of London's top venues. Marriott was later dropped from the band after members claimed he was too young to be lead singer. In July 1964, he first saw future Small Faces' partners Ronnie Lane and Kenny Jones performing with their bands.

Leaving school at 16, he met drummer Jones at a local pub and formed the Outcasts, switching from lead guitar to bass. Marriot again met Lane while working in a music shop, and becoming friends through their shared love for music set out to form a new band. According to David Bowie, a friend of Marriott's, they had planned to form an R&B duo called David and Goliath, but nothing came of it. Marriott then recruited old friend Jimmy Winston to play organ (later replaced by Ian McLagan), while a college friend called Annabel suggested the name Small Faces.

Signing a management deal with impresario Don Arden and a recording deal with Decca. they released a string of high-octane singles, beginning with "Whatcha Gonna Do About It," with lyrical help from Brian Potter and Ian Samwell. "Sha-La-La-La-Lee," written by Mort Schuman and Kenny Lynch, was a bigger hit, although Marriott felt it did not represent their sound. The next single was "Hey Girl," the first hit to be written by Marriott and Lane, but it was their follow-up "All or Nothing" that raised the bar. Claimed to be inspired either by Marriott's breakup with his ex-fiancée Sue Oliver or by his first wife who once dated Rod Stewart, it became their first chart-topper in 1966.

Following a dispute over unpaid royalties, relations with Arden broke down the following year. With Arden selling them to Andrew Loog Oldham, they were signed with his Immediate label which allowed them to spend more time in the studio and less time playing live. With the new label, they quickly embraced psychedelic pop with three more outstanding singles, both written by the duo. "Here Comes the Nice," with sound effects and lyrics alluding to drug use and drug dealing, signalled a starting point for the band as studio musicians. This was followed by "Itchycoo Park," arguably their finest single. With Lane both conceiving the idea and being its main writer, its inspiration was said to have been a park in a London suburb near to where the writers grew up, with the "Itchycoo" referring to the stinging nettles that grew there, although the lyric about getting "high" led to a short ban by the BBC. "Tin Soldier" had originally been written for singer P P Arnold, but Marriott felt the band should release it themselves (using her great voice as backing singer). When the BBC misheard the last line of the song as "sleep with you," they insisted it had to be changed before allowed airplay, but with Marriott explaining it was about "getting into someone's mind - not their body" and that the lyric was actually "sit with you," they backtracked.

"Lazy Sunday" saw Marriott singing large parts in a greatly exaggerated, music hall-type Cockney accent and was inspired by having arguments with his neighbours, while "The Universal," their final authorised single, was from a party tape recorded by Marriott in his garden, with other instruments added in the studio. With its complex wordplay, various background noises (including a dog), and Marriott's unusual offhand vocal, it proved less successful than some of their previous singles.

Marriott once observed: "People who got on their feet and freaked about were called idiot dancers, and nobody wants to be called an idiot dancer. But the whole idea of rock and roll is to get people off their arses - that's what it's all about."

With the success of their concept album *Ogden's Nut Gone Flake*, with its innovative round cover and Stanley Unwin's comical commentary, Marriott felt the band needed to evolve and wanted to bring in ex-Herd singer Peter Frampton. When the other members refused, Marriott spent more time with Frampton and eventually quit the band by storming off stage at a New Year's gig in December 1968. Shortly after, he joined the newly formed band Humble Pie with Frampton and released a debut album and the Marriott-penned single, "Natural Born Bugie."

With the Small Faces disbanding in 1969, Lane formed the Faces with McLagan, Jones and Rod Stewart. With the breakup of his marriage and growing drug dependence, Marriott became difficult to work with, and Humble Pie disbanded in 1975. A reunion of the Small Faces ended with Lane suffering with MS before quitting the band, and after the commercial failure of two albums, the band called it a day.

In 1991, Marriott died in a house fire just days after beginning work on an album with Frampton. Lane passed away six year later after battling his illness for 20 years.

Chart entries
Whatcha Gonna Do About It? (*with Ian Samwell*) The Small Faces (UK 1965 # 14)
Hey Girl – The Small Faces (UK 1966 # 10)
All Or Nothing – The Small Faces (UK 1966 # 1)
My Mind's Eye – The Small Faces (UK 1966 # 4)
My Way Of Giving In – Chris Farlowe (UK 1967 # 48)
I Can't Make It – The Small Faces (UK 1967 # 26)
Here Comes the Nice – The Small Faces (UK 1967 # 12)
Itchycoo Park – The Small Faces (UK 1967 # 3; US # 16)
Tin Soldier – The Small Faces (UK 1967 # 9)
(If You Think You're) Groovy – P.P Arnold (UK 1968 # 41)
Lazy Sunday - The Small Faces - (UK 1968 # 2)
The Universal - The Small Faces - (UK 1968 # 16)
Afterglow of Your Love – The Small Faces (UK 1969 # 36)

Steve Marriott
Natural Born Bugie – Humble Pie (UK 1969 # 4)

Gerry Marsden
Born Gerald Marsden, Liverpool 1942. Died 2021.

Born during the war in the Toxteth area of Liverpool, his interest in music began at an early age, when he recalled singing "Ragtime Cowboy Joe" to onlookers from on top of an air raid shelter. He first attended Our Lady of Mount Carmel school and while at the Florence Institute youth club learned to box and play guitar. At the age of 14, he was working as a delivery boy for British Rail and joined the skiffle group Red Mountain Boys, along with his older brother Freddie (drums), Les Chadwick (bass) and Arthur McMahon (piano). They later renamed themselves the Mars Bars, hoping to get sponsorship from the confectionary company. Instead, Mars demanded they change their name. In 1959, they called themselves the Pacemakers, and by December they all had to give up their jobs when contracted to undergo a four-month stint in Hamburg along with the Beatles.

In 1961 McMahon was replaced by Les Maguire and the group shared the same bill with the Beatles on many occasions, at one venue even joining together as the Beatmakers. The following year, they signed a management deal with Brian Epstein and were later spotted playing by George Martin, who signed them to Columbia, then part of EMI. Martin had just recorded the Mitch Murray song "How Do You Do It?" with the Beatles, but with them not wanting to release it, it was given to the Pacemakers as their first single in March 1963. It topped the charts for three weeks. With Martin continuing to be at the helm, this was followed by "I Like It," another Murray song, and a cover of Richard Rodgers' "You'll Never Walk Alone" (from the musical *Carousel*), both of which became chart-toppers. They would become the only UK act to score three number ones with their first three releases.

Marsden's penchant for songwriting was evident with the next single, "I'm the One," although it failed to continue their chart-topping streak. The next single to chart was the beautiful ballad "Don't Let the Sun Catch You Crying," co-written by the Marsdens, Chadwick and Maguire. Originally given to Louise Cordet, a singer who regularly toured with the band, they released their own version around the same time and it became a top ten hit on both sides of the Atlantic.

Marsden's sentimental opus "Ferry Cross the Mersey," a homage to his hometown river and the ferry that links Liverpool to Birkenhead, continued the band's successful chart run, but also signalled its demise. In October 1966, they disbanded, with Marsden moving on to feature in West End musicals and tv shows.

Chart entries
I'm the One – Gerry & the Pacemakers (UK 1964 # 2; US # 82)
Don't Let the Sun Catch You Crying *(with John Chadwick, Leo Maguire, Fred Marsden)* Gerry
    & the Pacemakers (UK 1964 # 6; US # 4)
It's Gonna Be Alright – Gerry & the Pacemakers (UK 1964 # 24; US # 23)
Ferry Cross the Mersey – Gerry & the Pacemakers (UK 1964 # 8; US # 6)
Give All Your Love To Me – Gerry & the Pacemakers (US 1965 # 8)
La La La – Gerry & the Pacemakers (US 1966 # 90)

Bill Martin and Phil Coulter
Born William Wylie MacPherson, Glasgow 1938, Died 2020.
Born Philip Coulter, Derry, NI 1942.

Martin was educated at Govan High School and began writing songs at the age of ten. With the intention of working in the shipyards, he completed his apprenticeship as a marine engineer. While at college, he heard Bobby Darin's "Dream Lover" and it inspired him to follow a career in music. As well as enrolling at the Royal Academy of Music in London, he was also a promising footballer and had trials for the Scottish club Partick Thistle. Moving with his new wife to Johannesburg in 1960, he played for their local team before returning to the UK to focus on songwriting. Using the "less Scottish" name Bill Martin, he worked for a time in London's Denmark Street and his "Kiss Me Now," recorded by Tommy Quickly & the Remo Four, was released on the Piccadilly label in November 1963, the same day JFK was assassinated.

The following year, he teamed up with Tommy Scott, and as Scott & Martin wrote what became non-charting songs for the Bachelors, Van Morrison, the Dubliners and Twinkle. Better success came in 1965 when he first met the successful Irish songwriter Phil Coulter. The son of a fiddle-playing policeman and a piano-playing mother, Coulter was encouraged to embrace music and later enrolled at Queen's University, Belfast, studying French and classical music. While there, he formed his first band and wrote a few songs that became local hits.

Moving to London in 1964, he worked as an arranger and songwriter in Denmark Street, working with artists that included Van Morrison and Tom Jones, and arranging the hit song "Terry" for Twinkle. The meeting with Martin led to a ten-year successful writing partnership, with Coulter's melodies and Martin's lyrics producing a string of hits for established artists, including two Eurovision Song entries. After joining KPM Music, they managed to get a number of their songs recorded as album tracks for artists that included Dave Dee, Dozy, Beaky, Mick & Tich, Ken Dodd, and Los Bravos, but finally achieved a top 50 chart hit in 1966 with "Hi! Hi! Hazel" by Geno Washington & the Ram Jam Band.

For the UK's 1967 Eurovision entry, Sandie Shaw had to be talked into performing the Martin-Coulter song "Puppet on a String" by her mentor Adam Faith, later recalling, "I hated it from the very first 'oompah' to the final 'bang' on the big bass drum." Despite her reaction, it became the UK's first winner at the final held in Vienna, as well as Shaw's third UK chart-topper. The following year, the writing team were asked to repeat their success with a song for the 1968 contest held in London to be performed by Cliff Richard. Coulter wrote a song called "I Think I Love You," but having doubts about the lyrics, asked Martin for help, and it was re-written as "Congratulations." Although favourite to win on the night, it just lost out to Spain's entry, although giving Richard another UK number one. Their final chart success of the Sixties was "Surround Yourself With Sorrow," a huge hit for Cilla Black and produced by George Martin.

Martin and Coulter would go on to write several hits for the glam-rock band Bay City Rollers, and in 1975 won an Ivor Novello Award for Songwriter of the Year. They also tried two more unsuccessful attempts at the Eurovision Song Contest with Luxembourg's 1975 entry "Toi, performed by Coulter's future wife Geraldine, and in 1978 with the UK entry "Shine On" sung by Christian.

Coulter later confessed: "Most composers and arrangers these days use computer programs and keyboards, but I'm one of those dinosaurs that still writes it down on score paper and still dreams it up in his ears first."

Chart entries
Hi! Hi! Hazel – Geno Washington & the Ram Jam Band (UK 1966 # 45), Gary & the Hornets (US 1966 # 96) The Troggs (UK 1967 # 42)
Puppet On A String –Sandie Shaw (UK 1967 # 1)
Tonight In Tokyo – Sandie Shaw (UK 1967 # 21)
Congratulations – Cliff Richard (UK 1968 # 1; US # 99)
Surround Yourself With Sorrow – Cilla Black (UK 1969 # 3)

Hank Marvin see also Bruce Welch
Born Brian Robson Rankin, Newcastle England 1941.

The son of an army officer, he played both piano and banjo at a young age, but after seeing and hearing Buddy Holly decided to learn guitar, and at the same time wear Holly-style dark-rimmed glasses. After attending Rutherford Grammar School, he secured his parents' permission and moved to London with school friend Bruce Welch to pursue a music career. He used the stage name of Hank Marvin (Hank being his childhood nickname, and his surname after US country singer Marvin Rainwater). The two of them met Cliff Richard's manager Johnny Foster in a Soho coffee bar. Foster was on the lookout for a guitarist to play with Richard's new backing group the Drifters on his upcoming tour. Although also considering Tony Sheridan, who at the time had a residency at the coffee bar, Marvin was offered the post but only agreeing if Welch could join him. After rehearsing at Richard's family home, the Drifters were set to go.

With the lineup of Marvin (lead guitar), Welch (rhythm guitar), Jet Harris (bass) and Terry Smart (drums) they recorded the Lionel Bart song "Living Doll," a top 20 hit for Richard in 1959. With the threat of legal action by the management of US group the Drifters, they changed their name to the Shadows and recorded as such for Richard's chart-topping single "Travellin' Light," written by Sid Tepper and Roy C Bennett.

In 1960, the Shadows had their first solo hit with Jerry Lordan's "Apache." With Tony Meehan now replacing Smart on drums, it became their first UK number one. The following year, Marvin, Welch and Harris penned the hit "F.B.I," but due to complicated publishing contracts it was credited to their manager Peter Gormley. In 1963, the Marvin-Welch song "Foot Tapper" became the group's final chart-topper, while Marvin and Shadow's new drummer Brian Bennett penned "Summer Holiday" for Richard's movie of the same name. Later in the year Marvin, Welch and Richard wrote "On the Beach" for the movie *Wonderful Land*. With the Shadows continuing to collaborate on Richard's singles (including new member John Rostill) Marvin had the chance to write alone Richard's 1967's ballad "The Day I Met Marie" and on 1969's duet "Throw Down a Line," the latter while the Shadows had temporarily split up and originally recorded by the Jeff Beck Group.

In 1970, Marvin and Welch teamed up with ex-Strangers guitarist John Farrar to form the vocal trio Marvin, Welch & Farrar, later scoring a hit with "Lady of the Morning," with critics comparing them favourably with Crosby, Stills, Nash and Young. Five years later, the re-formed Shadows performed the Paul Curtis song "Let Me Be the One" as the UK's entry in the Eurovision Song Contest (coming second).

Chart entries
F.B.1. (*with Jet Harris & Tony Meehan*) The Shadows (UK 1961 # 6)
Gee Whizz, It's You (*with Ian Ralph Samwell*) Cliff Richard & the Shadows (UK 1961 # 4)
Mr Guitar *(with Bruce Welch)* (UK 1961 # 47)
Foot Tapper *(with Bruce Welch)* The Shadows (UK 1963 # 1)
Shindig (*with Bruce Welch*) The Shadows (UK 1963 # 6)
Geronimo – The Shadows (UK 1963 # 11)
The Rise And Fall Of Flingel Blunt (*with Brian Bennett & John Rostill*) The Shadows (UK 1964 # 5)
On the Beach (*with Cliff Richard & Bruce Welch*) Cliff Richard & the Shadows (UK 1964 # 7)
Rhythm And Greens (*with Brian Bennett & John Rostill*) The Shadows (UK 1964 # 22)
Genie With the Light Brown Lamp ((*with Bruce Welch, Brian Bennett & John Rostill*) The Shadows (UK 1964 # 17)
I Could Easily Fall In Love With You *(with Bruce Welch, Brian Bennett & John Rostill)* Cliff Richard & the Shadows (UK 1964 # 9)
I Met A Girl – The Shadows (UK 1966 # 22)

Time Drags By *((with Bruce Welch, Brian Bennett & John Rostill)* Cliff Richard & the
    Shadows (UK 1966 # 10)
The Dream I Dream – The Shadows (UK 1966 # 42)
In the Country *(with Bruce Welch, Brian Bennett & John Rostill)* Cliff Richard & the
    Shadows (UK 1966 # 6)
The Day I Met Marie – Cliff Richard (UK 1967 # 10)
London's Not Too Far (UK 1968 # 52)
Don't Forget To Catch Me (*with Bruce Welch & Brian Bennett*) Cliff Richard & the
    Shadows (UK 1968 # 21)
Goodnight Dick (US 1969 # 52)
Throw Down A Line - Cliff Richard & Hank Marvin (UK 1969 # 7)

Barry Mason and Les Reed see also Geoff Stephens
Born John Barry Mason, Wigan, England 1935. Died 2021.
Born Leslie David Reed, Woking, England 1935. Died 2019.

Growing up in the village of Coppull near Chorley, Lancashire, Mason's father was a journalist for the *Wigan Observer* and his mother a motor-racer. After his father died when Mason was nine, his mother married a US G.I. and he was sent to a boarding school in Wales. By the time he had completed national service with the Royal Marines, his mother and stepfather had emigrated to Columbus, Ohio, and he went out to live with them. Although their marriage failed and his mother returned to the UK, Mason stayed to complete his education at Ohio University. After hitchhiking to California to follow his dream of becoming an actor or singer, he too returned home. Disillusioned with acting after being understudy to Albert Finney in John Osborne's play *Luther,* he switched his focus to a music career and became manager for his friend and neighbour Tommy Bruce. With financial help from Mason, Tommy Bruce & the Bruisers recorded "Ain't Misbehavin'" and scored a top three hit in 1960, while also writing "You're My Little Girl" as a b-side to another of his recordings. In 1964, he co-wrote "Don't Turn Around" with Birmingham songwriter Peter Lee Sterling to give the Merseybeats a follow-up chart hit to "I Think Of You," also written by Sterling.

Around this time, Mason met Les Reed. An accomplished multi-instrumentalist by the age of 14, Reed had studied at the London College of Music and had later joined the Willis Reed Group for four years. After doing national service, where he was a member of the East Kent Military band, he played jazz piano in London clubs until being invited to join the John Barry Seven as pianist. In 1962, he decided to pursue a career as a songwriter and worked for publisher Mills Music. While there, he struck up a writing partnership with Geoff Stephens, scoring a hit with "Tell Me When" for the Applejacks in 1964.

Meanwhile, Mason and Reed had also been writing together, and in 1965 their "Here It Comes Again," was a top ten hit for the Fortunes. While Mason produced and co-wrote "She Just Satisfies," the first solo single for future Led Zeppelin member Jimmy Page, Reed joined Tom Jones' manager Gordon Mills to write "It's Not Unusual" for the then-relatively unknown Welsh singer. With Reed's arrangement, it launched the Welsh singer to super-stardom. In an interview for the *Mail on Sunday,* Jones recalled: "I did the demo on this song when it was being offered to Sandie Shaw. I was just starting out and, God bless her, she said: 'Whoever's singing this, it's his' "

In 1967, Mason and Reed gave Herman's Hermits a surprising top five US hit with "There's a Kind of Hush," followed by Engelbert Humperdinck's "The Last Waltz," which famously kept the Beatles' "Penny Lane/Strawberry Fields Forever" from the top spot. Later that year, their ballad "Everybody Knows" by the Dave Clark Five featured Lenny Davidson on a rare lead vocal. The following year, they wrote what is perhaps their most famous song with Tom Jones' "Delilah." With its crime of passion storyline, Mason's lyrics had similarities to the plot of Bizet's *Carmen,* and with its big-band sound and Jones' breathtaking performance, it won the Ivor Novello Award for Song of the Year. In later years, a court case had Mason's ex-wife Sylvan Whittingham claiming credit for half of the lyrics, as well as several other songs, and the two-year legal battle was settled out of court in 1986.

The final years of the decade saw Mason and Reed continuing their success with Des O'Conner's chart-topping "I Pretend," and three top ten ballads by Englebert Humperdinck. In 1970, Mason had his final UK chart-topper with "Love Grows (Where My Rosemary Goes)" for Edison Lighthouse, and in the following years Reed wrote music for stage musicals productions.

Chart entries
Here It Comes Again - Fortunes (UK 1965 # 4; US # 27)
Have Pity On the Boy – Paul & Barry Ryan (UK 1966 # 18)
The Last Waltz – Engelbert Humperdinck (UK 1967 # 1; US # 25)
Everybody Knows – Dave Clark Five (UK 1967 # 2; US # 43)

I'm Coming Home – Tom Jones (UK 1967 #2; US # 57)
Kiss Me Goodbye – Petula Clark (UK 1968 # 50; US # 15)
Delilah *(with Sylvan Whittingham)* Tom Jones (UK 1968 # 2; US # 15)
It's Your Day Today – P J Proby (UK 1968 # 32)
When We Were Young - Solomon King (UK 1968 # 21)
I Pretend - Des O'Connor (UK 1968 # 1)
Les Bicyclettes de Belsize - Engelbert Humperdinck (UK 1968 # 5; US # 31)
An Olympic Record *(with Steve Marriott, Ronnie Lane)* The Barron Knights (UK 1968 # 35)
Winter World Of Love - Engelbert Humperdinck (UK 1969 # 7#; US # 16)
Love Is All – Malcolm Roberts (UK 1969 # 12)

Barry Mason with others
Don't Turn Around *(with Peter Lee Sterling)* The Merseybeats (UK 1964 # 13)
Super Girl *(with Graham Bradly)* Graham Bonney (UK 1966 # 19)
A Man Without Love (*with Roberto Livraghi, Daniele Pace, Mario Panzeri*) Engelbert Humperdinck (UK 1968 # 2; US # 19)
1-2-3 O'Leary *(with Michael Carr)* Des O'Conner (UK 1968 # 4)
Bluer Than Blue *(with Alan Blaikely & Kenneth Howard)* Rolf Harris (UK 1969 # 30)
Love Me Tonight *(with Lorenzo Pilat, Mario Panzeri)* Tom Jones (UK 1969 # 9; US # 13)

Les Reed and Geoff Stephens
Tell Me When - Applejacks (UK 1964 # 5)
There's A Kind Of Hush – Hermans Hermits (UK 1967 # 7; US # 4)
Claire – Paul & Barry Ryan (UK 1967 # 47)
Tears Won't Wash Away These Heartaches – Ken Dodd (UK 1969 # 22)

Les Reed with others
Everybody Knows *(with Jimmy Duncan)* Steve Lawrence (US 1964 # 72)
It's Not Unusual *(with Gordon Mills)* Tom Jones (UK 1965 # 1; US # 10)
Leave A Little Love *(with Robin Conrad)* Lulu (UK 1965 # 8)
Don't Bring Me Heartaches *(with Robin Conrad)* Paul & Barry Ryan (UK 1965 # 13)
To Make a Big Man Cry *(with Peter Callander)* P J Proby (UK 1966 # 34); Roy Head (US 1966 # 95)
La Dernière Valse *(with Hubert Ithier)* Mireille Mathieu (UK 1967 # 26)
No One Can Break A Heart Like You *(with Jackie Raye)* Dave Clark Five (UK 1968 # 28)
Please Don't Go *(with Jackie Raye)* Donald Peers (UK 1968 # 3)

Dave Mason see also Stevie Winwood
Born David Thomas Mason, Worcester, England 1946.
Rock and Roll Hall of Fame 2004 (with Traffic).

By the age of 16 Mason had already formed the band the Jaguars as vocalist and lead guitarist. The other teenage members were Michael Mann (rhythm guitar), Dennis Morgan (bass) and Roger Moss (drums). With a repertoire of mainly instrumentals, they were heavily influenced by the Shadows, and in 1963 financed their own limited edition single "Opus To Spring," penned by Mason, on Worcester's Impression Records. The following year, Mason joined another Worcester band called the Hellions, which at the time featured Jim Capaldi (vocals, drums), Gordon Jackson (guitar) and later Dave Meredith (bass). Turning professional, the band secured an engagement at the Star Club in Hamburg backing singer Tanya Day. Sharing the same hotel, they met members of fellow Midlanders, the Spencer Davis Group, and befriended their young vocalist Stevie Winwood.

On their return to England, the experience the Hellions had gained made them a much-sought after band, securing them a residency at London's Whisky-A-Go-Go Club. While there, they met visiting US record producer Kim Fowley and songwriter Jackie DeShannon, who offered to give them a song to record and help them to get a recording contract with Piccadilly Records. The song "Daydreaming of You" failed to chart, as did two further singles the following year, but the Mason-Capaldi song "Shades of Blue," their first collaboration, was recorded by Birmingham label-mates the Rockin' Berries.

By 1966, with no chart success and business expenses mounting, Mason quit to play with other local bands while Capaldi formed a new band, Deep Feeling. Over the next few months, Mason and Capaldi often played gigs at Birmingham's new hip club the Elbow Room with both Winwood (who had recently left the Spencer Davis Group) and ex-Locomotive musician Chris Wood. By April 1967, they had decided to form the band Traffic. Signing to Island Records, they retreated to an isolated cottage to rehearse for their debut album. The first single was Capaldi and Winwood's "Paper Sun," and with Mason's sitar lines and Winwood's distinctive lead vocal, it scored a top five hit. Later in the year came Mason's psychedelic "Hole In My Shoe." With Mason on lead vocal, it was said to have been inspired by a dream he had while in a "haunted" cottage, but the other members disliked the song as not representing their style. It also featured a spoken-word midsection by label boss Chris Blackwell's six-year-old stepdaughter Francine Heimann's dream of flying on the back of a giant albatross. The next single "Here We Go Round the Mulberry Bush," written by all four members, was featured in the romantic movie of the same name.

With Mason citing differences of musical opinion with Winwood, he quit the band after the release of their first album, and although returning for a while, eventually left for good. Winwood went on to join Eric Clapton's "supergroup" Blind Faith, while Capaldi and Wood teamed up with Mick Weaver to form the short-lived Wooden Frog. Going to the US, Mason worked with Delaney and Bonnie for a time before embarking on a solo career, while also collaborating with Cass Elliott, George Harrison, the Stones, McCartney and many others.

Chart entries
Hole In My Shoe – Traffic (UK 1967 # 2)
Here We Go Round the Mulberry Bush *(with Jim Capaldi, Stevie Winwood, Chris Wood)* Traffic (UK 1967 # 8)
Feeling Alright - Joe Cocker (US 1969 # 69); Mongo Santamaria (US 1969 # 96)

Curtis Mayfield

Born Curtis Lee Mayfield, Chicago 1942. Died 1999.
Grammy Lifetime Achievement Award 1995.
Rock and Roll Hall of Fame 1991 (with the Impressions), 1999 (solo).
Songwriters Hall of Fame 2002.

One of five children, Curtis's father left the family when he was 12. He later attended Wells Community Academy High School before dropping out in his second year. Presented with a guitar at the age of ten, his mother also taught him to play piano two years later. He later sang with a gospel group at his aunt's church and, inspired by Muddy Waters and Spanish guitarist Andres Segovia, taught himself to play the instrument. At 14, he formed the singing group the Alphatones, and in 1956 joined the Roosters, formed by his school friend Jerry Butler, brothers Richard and Arthur Brooks, and later Sam Gooden. Mayfield wrote and composed songs for the group, and two years later they were re-named the Impressions. Butler departed after their first two hit singles, "For Your Precious Love" and "Come Back My Love," and Mayfield followed, co-writing and performing on Butler's 1960 hit "He Will Break Your Heart."

After Mayfield returned to the Impressions, they signed with ABC-Paramount Records, working with the label's A&R man Johnny Pate. With Butler being replaced by former Roosters member Fred Cash, Mayfield became lead singer and songwriter. Their first hit "Gypsy Woman" peaked at number 20 on the charts. During this time, Mayfield also wrote for other artists, including Jan Bradley's "Mama Didn't Lie" and Major Lance's "Monkey Time," "Hey Little Girl," and "Um, Um, Um, Um, Um," the latter scoring number one on the R&B charts and becoming a later UK hit for Wayne Fontana. In 1963, the Impressions' "It's All Right" became the first of six chart-toppers on the R&B charts, including "Keep On Pushing" and "Amen," the latter an updated old gospel song, co-written by Mayfield, and featured in the Sidney Poitier 1964 movie *Lillies of the Field*.

1965's "People Get Ready," one of their most famous songs, had a significant impact on the civil rights movement, while 1967's "We're a Winner" became an anthem of the black power movement. Mayfield later owned the Mayfield and Windy C labels and was also a partner in the Curtom and Thomas labels. He also wrote for the female vocal group the Fascinations, and in 1967 gave them their most famous hit with "Girls Are Out To Get You." Three years later, he left the Impressions to begin a solo career as writer and producer for other artists, as well as recording songs with socially conscious themes. His 1970 solo album Curtis included the soul classic "Move On Up," although it failed to chart in the US.

Mayfield looked back on his career: "My art and my creativities were totally something that was of my own heart and mind. I could never let anybody dictate to me what I should write and how I would write it."

Chart entries
Gypsy Woman – The Impressions (US 1961 # 20)
Grow Closer Together – The Impressions (US 1962 # 99)
Little Young Lover - The Impressions (US 1962 # 96)

Mama Didn't Lie – Jan Bradley (US 1963 # 14)
I'm the One Who Loves You - The Impressions (US 1963 # 73)
Sad, Sad Girl and Boy - The Impressions (US 1963 # 84)
The Monkey Time – Major Lance (US 1963 # 8)
Man's Temptation – Gene Chandler (US 1963 # 71)
It's Alright – The Impressions (US 1963 # 4)
It's All Right – Impressions (US 1963 # 4)
Hey Little Girl – Major Lance (US 1963 # 13)
Need To Belong – Jerry Butler (US 1963 # 31)
Um, Um, Um, Um, Um, Um – Major Lance (US 1963 # 5; UK # 40); Wayne Fontana & the Mindbenders (UK 1964 # 4)
Taking About My Baby – The Impressions (US 1964 # 12)
I'm So Proud – The Impressions (US 1964 # 14)
It Ain't No Use – Major Lance (US 1964 # 68)
Keep On Pushing – The Impressions (US 1964 # 10)
Just Be True – Gene Chandler (US 1964 # 19)
Rhythm – Major Lance (US 1964 # 24)
You Must Believe Me – The Impressions (US 1964 # 15)
It's All Over – Walter Jackson (US 1964 # 67)
Amen (*trad. With Jester Hairston, Johnny Pate*) The Impressions (US 1964 # 7)
What Now – Gene Chandler (US 1964 # 40)
Sometimes I Wonder – Major Lance (US 1964 # 64)
People Get Ready – The Impressions (US 1965 # 14)
Come See – Major Lance (US 1965 # 40)
You Can't Hurt Me No More – Gene Chandler (US 1965 # 92)
Woman's Got Soul – The Impressions (US 1965 # 29)
Nothing Can Stop Me – Gene Chandler (US 1965 # 18; UK # 41)
Meeting Over Yonder – The Impressions (US 1965 # 48)
I Can't Work No Longer – Billy & the Chanters (US 1965 # 60)
I Need You – The Impressions (US 1965 # 64)
(Gonna Be) Good Times – Gene Chandler (US 1965 # 92)
Just One Kiss From You – The Impressions (US 1965 # 76)
You've Been Cheatin' – The Impressions (US 1965 # 33)
Rainbow '65 Pt 1 – Gene Chandler (US 1965 # 81)
Since I Lost the One I Love – The Impressions (US 1966 # 90)
(I'm Just a) Fool For You – Gene Chandler (US 1966 # 88)
Too Slow – The Impressions (US 1966 # 91)
Can't Satisfy – The Impressions (US 1966 # 65)
Danger! She's a Stranger (*with Clarence N Burke, Greg K Fowler*) – The Five Stairsteps (US 1967 # 89)
Girls Are Out To Get You – The Fascinations (US 1967 # 92)
You Always Hurt Me - The Impressions (US 1967 # 96)
I Can't Stay Away From You - The Impressions (US 1967 # 80)
We're a Winner - The Impressions (US 1967 # 14)
We're Rolling On - The Impressions (US 1968 # 59)
I Loved and I Lost - The Impressions (US 1868 # 61)
Don't Change Your Love – The Five Stairsteps & Cubie (US 1968 # 59)
Fool For You - The Impressions (US 1968 # 22)
Don't Cry My Love - The Impressions (US 1968 # 71)
This Is My Country - The Impressions (US 1968 # 25)
Stay Close To Me – The Five Stairsteps & Cubie (US 1968 # 91)
Can't Satisfy – The Impressions (UK 1969 # 53)
Seven Years – The Impressions (US 1969 # 84)
Choice of Colours – The Impressions (US 1969 # 21)
Say You Love Me – The Impressions (US 1969 # 58)

We Must Be In Love – The Five Stairsteps & Cubie (US 1969 # 88)

Curtis Mayfield with Jerry Butler & Calvin Carter
He Will Break Your Heart (*with Jerry Butler, Calvin Carter*) – Jerry Butler (US 1960 # 7); The
    Righteous Brothers (US 1966 # 91)
Find Another Girl (*with Jerry Butler*) Jerry Butler (US 1961 # 27)
I'm Telling You (*with Jerry Butler*) Jerry Butler (US 1961 # 25)

Paul McCartney see John Lennon and Paul McCartney

Van McCoy
Born Van Allen Clinton McCoy, Washington DC 1940. Died 1979.

As a youngster, McCoy learned to play piano and sang with the Metropolitan Baptist Church choir, and by the age of 12 was writing his own songs. While attending Theodore High School in the mid-Fifties, he formed a doo-wop quartet the Starlighters with older brother Norman and two friends and released the novelty dance single "The Birdland." Receiving some success, it led to a tour alongside sax player Vi Burnside, followed by a recording contract with Hollywood Records in 1959, McCoy wrote both tracks on their debut single "You're the One to Blame/ I Cried." When they disbanded, McCoy sang for a while with the Baltimore-based doo-wop group the Marylanders. He then went on to study philosophy at Howard University before quitting after two years to move to Philadelphia where he set up his own recording company, Rockin' Records.

One of the first releases was in 1961 with the self-penned "Mr D.J," and although just missing out on the Hot 100, it came to the attention of Scepter Records' Florence Greenberg, who then hired him as a staff writer and A&R man. His first writing success for them was with the Shirelles' "Stop the Music," arranged by McCoy and co-authored with Willie Dixon.

In 1964, McCoy worked for Jerry Teifer at April-Blackwood Music, connected with Columbia Records, while at the same time his song "Giving Up" by Gladys Knight & the Pips was breaking into the top 40. During this time, he wrote a number of classic hit songs, including "When You're Young and in Love" for Ruby & the Romantics, featuring lead singer Ruby Nash, and later giving the Marvelettes their only UK chart hit. It was also the last Marvelettes' single to feature their former lead singer Gladys Horton, although only appearing on backing vocals (the lead now sung by Wanda Rogers). Other popular songs included "Getting Mighty Crowded" by Betty Everett, and "Baby I'm Yours" by Babara Lewis.

In 1967, McCoy formed the short-lived Vando Records with Philadelphia dee-jay Douglas "Jocko" Henderson, as well as going on to own the Share record label and co-own Larry Maxwell's Maxx label. The following year, he teamed up with Alicia Evelyn to write "I Get the Sweetest Feeling" for Jackie Wilson (also a UK top ten in 1972), and was reported to have formed VMP (Van McCoy Productions).

In the Seventies, McCoy would go on to arrange several hits for the Stylistics, and in 1975 score a huge hit with the Grammy award-winning instrumental "The Hustle."

Chart entries
Ready For Love (*with Michael Burton & Jeff Lane*) Jimmy Jones (UK 1960 # 46)
Stop the Music (*with Willie Denson*) The Shirelles (US 1962 # 36)
Giving Up – Gladys Knight & the Pips (US 1964 # 38).
Lovers Always Forgive – Gladys Knight & the Pips (US 1964 # 89)
When You're Young And In Love – Ruby & the Romantics (US 1964 # 48); The Marvelettes
    (US 1967 # 23; UK # 13)
Times Have Changed – Irma Thomas (US 1964 # 98)
Maybe Tonight – The Shirelles (US 1964 # 88)
Getting Mighty Crowded – Betty Everett (US 1964 # 65; UK # 29)
He's My Guy – Irma Thomas (US 1964 # 63)
Suddenly I'm All Alone – Walter Jackson (US 1965 # 96)
Keep On Trying – Bobby Vee (US 1965 # 85)
Before and After – Chad and Jeremy (US 1965 # 17)
Baby I'm Yours – Barbara Lewis (US 1965 # 11) Peter and Gordon (UK 1965 # 19)
You've Come Back – P J Proby (UK 1966 # 25)
I've Lost You – Jackie Wilson (US 1967 # 82)
The Sweetest Thing This Side Of Heaven – Chris Bartley (US 1967 # 32)
I Get The Sweetest Feeling (*with Alicia Evelyn*) Jackie Wilson (US 1968 # 34)

Roger McGuinn see also David Crosby, Stephen Stills
Born James Joseph McGuinn III, Chicago 1942.
Rock and Roll Hall of Fame 1991 (with The Byrds).

McGuinn's love for music began as a 14-year-old listening to Presley's "Heartbreak Hotel" on the radio, which led to him asking his parents to buy him a guitar (they had written a best-selling book called *Parents Can't Win*). Among his other early influences were Johnny Cash, Gene Vincent, Carl Perkins and the Everly Brothers. In 1957, he enrolled at Chicago's Old Town School of Folk Music and learned to play both 12-string guitar and five-string banjo. On graduating, he began playing on the local folk circuit and at coffee houses before being hired as a sideman by a number of folk music artists, including Judy Collins and the Chad Mitchell Trio. A break came when singer Bobby Darin, looking to add a folk element into his music, hired him as backup guitarist and harmony singer. When Darin started T.M Music Publishing in New York's Brill Building, McGuinn was employed as a songwriter for $35 a week. Just 18 months later, Darin retired from singing due to illness.

By 1963, McGuinn was working as a studio musician, and among the artists he worked with were Simon & Garfunkel and Judy Collins. It was when he saw the Beatles' George Harrison playing a 12-string Rickenbacker guitar in the movie *A Hard Day's Night*, that persuaded him to buy the instrument that would later become his trademark. The following year, he was given an opportunity by Doug Weston to perform at his Troubadour night club in Los Angeles. Opening for country artists Hoyt Axton and Roger Miller, McGuinn played traditional folk songs but with a rock-edge, and it soon caught the attention of folkie and fellow-Beatles fan Gene Clark.

The third of 13 children, Clark (1944-1991) was born in Tipton, Missouri. With the family later moving to Kansas City, his father taught him to play guitar and harmonica, and by the age of eleven he was writing songs.
Developing a rich, tenor voice, he later formed a local rock & roll combo called Joe Meyers & the Sharks. With a growing love for folk music, he graduated Bonner Springs High School and formed the folk group, the Rum Runners. Clark was later invited to join the folk band the Surf Riders, who were based at the Castaway Lounge in the city, and in 1963 he was discovered and hired by the folk ensemble The New Christy Minstrels. With them, he recorded two albums before departing the following year, once he had become aware of the Beatles. Moving to Los Angeles, he met McGuinn, a fellow Beatles convert.

The two of them began performing together at the Folk Den, and it was while there that they met David Crosby (1941-2023), of Les Baxter's Balladeers, who persuaded them to let him sing harmony with them. The three of them then formed the Jet Set, and Crosby introduced them to Jim Dickson, who had access to World Pacific Studios where they could hone their craft and develop their distinctive folk rock sound. With Michael Clarke recruited as drummer, Dickson, now their manager, arranged a one-off deal with Elektra's Jac Holtzman and recorded the single "Please Let Me Love You" using two Wrecking Crew session musicians (Ray Pohlman on piano and Earl Palmer on drums), with their one-off British-sounding name, The Beefeaters.

In August 1964, they acquired a copy of Dylan's then-unreleased "Mr Tambourine Man," and, after rehearsing it with a new rock arrangement, won Dylan's approval after he was invited to the studio. In the meantime, Dickson had recruited ex-Green Grass Group mandolin player Chris Hillman to join the band. In November 1964, having now acquired new instruments, including McGuinn's Rickenbacker 12-string guitar, they signed a contract with Columbia on the recommendation of Miles Davis, and shortly after, at the suggestion of Dickson, changed their name to the Byrds, replacing the "I" with a "Y" to mimic the Beatles' similar spelling.

In January 1965, they recorded "Mr Tambourine Man," which apparently only had McGuinn playing, as producer Terry Melcher brought in Wrecking Crew musicians. It became a global million-seller and would define much of their music with its rich harmony arrangement (McGuinn and Clark in unison, with Crosby providing high harmony) and, of course, McGuinn's signature "jingle jangle" 12-string. With this one song they established their position as the frontrunners of folk-rock. In June 1965, the US music press first coined the term "folk rock" to describe the Byrds' sound.

The next single, "All I Really Wanna Do" was another Dylan cover, chosen by the label to ensure another hit (despite the band's disapproval). With Cher's version released the same time and reaching the US top ten, the Byrds single stalled at number 40. For the third single, the Byrds dismissed the idea of doing another Dylan cover, and instead chose "Turn! Turn! Turn!," adapted by Pete Seeger with lyrics taken from the Book of Ecclesiastes. Produced by Dickson, the song had originally been recorded in 1962 as an album track for the folk group, the Limeliters. McGuinn presented it to the band after arranging a version on Judy Collins' album *Judy Collins 3*. It gave the Byrds their second chart-topper with its lyrical message resonating with the current anti-war feelings.

1966's "Eight Miles High" was written by McGuinn, Clark and Crosby following a flight to London (although Clark claimed the lyrics were mainly his, with some cooperation from Crosby). With McGuinn taking music inspiration from sitar player Ravi Shankar and sax player John Coltrane, the song was influential in the development of psychedelic rock music and cited as its first example. Although subject to a US radio ban due to alleged drug references, the group insisted it was about the experience of being at 40,000 feet in an aircraft. When asked in 2016 about the song, McGuinn stated: "Well, it was done on an airplane ride to England and back. I'm not denying that the Byrds did drugs at that point - we smoked marijuana - but it wasn't really about that."

"So You Want To Be a Rock 'n' Roll Star," written by McGuinn and Hillman, was said to have been inspired by the overnight success of the Monkees, although McGuinn later stated it was more about the whole music business. It was also the first chart song to have the term "rock star" mentioned in the lyrics.

Around this time, with his decision to follow a Subud religious cult, McGuinn wished to be known henceforth as Roger McGuinn. In 1968, after a year of internal disputes and members taking extended solos, McGuinn helped to create the groundbreaking album *Sweetheart of the Rodeo,* consisting mainly of covers, but laying the foundations for the early-Seventies country-rock genre. McGuinn also performed a solo cover of Bob Dylan's "It's Alright, Ma (I'm Only Bleeding)" for the soundtrack of the 1969 movie *Easy Rider,* as well as co-writing with him the single "Ballad of Easy Rider."

After the breakup of the Byrds, McGuinn went on to record several solo albums in the Seventies and worked and toured with Dylan on his *Rolling Thunder Revue*. Looking back, McGuinn recalled: "I've always considered myself a folk singer, even though we strapped on Rickenbacker guitars and played pretty loud."

Chart entries
It Won't Be Wrong (*with Harvey Gerst*) The Byrds (US 1966 # 63)
Eight Miles High (*with Gene Clark & David Crosby*) The Byrds (US 1966 # 14; UK # 24)
5D (Fifth Dimension) The Byrds (US 1966 # 44)
Mr Spaceman – The Byrds (US 1966 # 36)
So You Wanna Be A Rock 'n' Roll Star *(with Chris Hillman)* The Byrds (US 1967 # 29)
You Showed Me *(with Gene Clark)* The Turtles (US 1969 # 6)
Ballad of Easy Rider *(with Bob Dylan)* The Byrds (US 1969 # 65)

David Crosby
Lady Friend – The Byrds (US 1967 # 82; UK # 55)
Rock 'N Roll Woman (*with Stephen Stills*) Buffalo Springfield (US 1967 # 44)

Gene Clark
Set You Free This Time – The Byrds (US 1966 # 79)

John Medora and David White
Born John L Madora, Philadelphia Pa 1936.
Born David Ernest White Tricker, Philadelphia Pa 1939. Died 2019.

Before going to school, White had toured the country with his parents in their acrobatic act called Barry and Brenda & Company. He also learned to play a variety of instruments as a child, and was writing songs by the age of 14. In the mid-Fifties, he joined local vocal group the Juvenaires under the name Dave White Tricker. The group had been formed in 1955 at John Bertram High School in Philadelphia, with Danny Rapp (lead vocalist), Frank Maffei (second tenor), Bobby Maffei (first tenor) and Joe Terry (baritone). They sang at school parties and local events and were eventually noticed by local record producer John Madora, who introduced them to local dee-jays Larry Brown and Artie Singer, owners of the label Singular Records. One of six children, Medora (sometimes spelt Madora) had taken vocal lessons before beginning a music career. Signing to the Prep label, his first recording was in 1957 with Singer's "Be My Girl."

Later in the year, with the new name Johnny Medora & the Juvenaires, they recorded "Do the Bop," a song written by Medora and White and inspired by a popular dance featured on dee-jay Dick Clark's tv show *American Bandstand.* Singer was impressed by the song and took it to Clark who suggested they change the song's name to "At the Hop" and the group's name to the more contemporary Danny & the Juniors. With Singer given co-writing credit, the song was re-recorded with lyric alterations and Rapp singing lead vocal. A subsequent appearance on *Bandstand* with what was originally a local hit, saw it leap to the top of the charts in 1958.

Two years later, Medora and White formed their own production company and secured an independent deal with the Mercury label. In 1961, the two of them wrote the Twist-inspired "The Fly," a top ten hit for Chubby Checker, and two years later continued their success with Leslie Gore's "You Don't Own Me." With lyrics that inspired a second wave of the feminist movement, it was described by the *New York Times* as "indelibly defiant." Gore later recalled, "My take on the song was: I'm 17, what a wonderful thing, to stand up on a stage and shake your finger at people and sing you don't own me."

Moving on to work for Decca, they collaborated with Holland-Dozier-Holland and blue-eyed soul singer Len Barry to write "1-2-3" for Barry to score a number two hit. Despite its chart success, Motown sued the writers, claiming it was a re-working of the Supremes' song "Ask Any Girl", the b-side to "Baby Love." Following their denial and two years of litigation, they finally agreed to give the writers Holland-Dozier-Holland co-writing credit as well as 15% of the writing and publishing royalties.

Medora and White teamed up with Ray Gillmore to form the pop trio the Spokesmen and had a hit with "The Dawn of Creation," which was a reply to Barry Maguire's depressing hit "Eve of Destruction."

Medora would go on to discover both Leon Huff and Kenny Gamble and spend time in Las Vegas working with singer Wayne Newton. In the mid-Seventies, he moved to Los Angeles to write and produce songs for movies and tv. Meanwhile, White continued to write and produce, becoming a member of the group Crystal Mansion and penning their 1968 hit "The Thought of Loving You."

Chart entries
The Fly - Chubby Checker (US 1961 # 7)
Doin' the Continental Walk - Danny & the Juniors (US 1962 # 93)
Dancin' the Strand - Maureen Gray (US 1962 # 91)
Pop Pop Pop-Pie - The Sherrys (US 1962 # 35)
Slop Time - The Sherrys (US 1963 # 97)
Oh-La-La-La-Limbo- Danny & the Juniors (US 1963 # 99)
Birthday Party – The Pixies Three (US 1963 # 40)
The Boy Next Door – The Secrets (US 1963 # 18)
Cold, Cold Winter – The Pixies Three (US 1963 # 79)
You Don't Own Me – Leslie Gore (US 1963 # 2)
Lip Sync *(with Leonard Borisoff - aka Len Barry)* Len Barry (US 1965 # 84)
1,2,3 *(with Len Barry, Holland-Dozier-Holland)* Len Barry (US 1965 # 2; UK # 3); Ramsey Lewis (US 1967 # 67)
Like a Baby *(with Len Borisoff - aka Len Barry)* Len Barry (US 1966 # 27; UK # 10)
Hey You Little Boo-Ga-Loo *(with Len Barry, Leon Huff)* Len Barry (US 1966 # 76)

John Medora
It's That Time of Year *(with Barry White, Leon Huff)* Len Barry (US 1966 # 91)

David White
The Thought of Loving You – Crystal Mansion (US 1968 # 84)

Joe Meek
Born Robert George Meek, Newent, England 1929. Died 1967 (suicide).

As a youngster, Meek had an interest in electronics and was believed to have made the region's first working television. During national service, he indulged in his hobby for space-age music as a radio technician in the RAF and later worked for the Midlands Electric Board, where he used their resources to develop his interest in music production. His next job was as an audio engineer for a radio production company, making a name for himself with his work on Ivy Benson's album *Music For Lonely Lovers.* Soon he would become the UK's premier independent record producer, renowned for his innovative studio techniques.

In 1954, he joined the top recording studio IBC as an engineer and worked on various hit records, including "Green Door" by Frankie Vaughan, Lonnie Donegan's "Cumberland Gap," and Johnny Duncan's "Last Train to San Fernando." Using the pseudonym Robert Duke, he also wrote hit songs, including 1958s "Put a Ring on My Finger," a hit for Les Paul & Mary Ford. After setting up Lansdowne Studios with Denis Preston, he worked on recordings by various jazz artists before leaving to begin an independent career.

In 1960, he founded Triumph Records with William Barrington-Coupe and nearly scored a chart-topper with Meek's production of Michael Cox's single "Angela Jones." Despite its success, Meek felt that he needed the distribution network of the major labels to increase sales. Leaving Triumph, he set up his own company, RGM Sound, and with financial backing from a toy importer used a recording studio in his London flat to release tapes to major labels. One of his first hits was the atmospheric, echo-laden "Johnny Remember Me," written by Geoff Goddard and recorded by John Leyton. It topped the charts in 1961, helped by Charles Blackwell's arrangement and the eerie female wails provided by Lissa Gray. Leyton's follow-up single "Wild Wind" repeated the same formula. Meek would recall later: "I wish I could have taken a class on becoming a Rock Star. It might have prepared me for this."

In 1962, the increasingly-inventive Meek reached his peak with writing and producing the instrumental "Telstar" for the Tornadoes. Inspired by the communications satellite which had been launched in July, the transatlantic chart-topper made Meek a production superstar way ahead of his rivals. This was followed by more production successes with Heinz's "Just Like Eddie" and the Honeycombs' "Have I the Right?" However, by the mid-Sixties his commercial standing and credibility was waning and his work began to be branded novel rather than innovative, and his production techniques predicable.

The departure of songwriter Goddard and a string of failing singles led to mental instability and a violent nature. In February 1967, affected by bipolar disorder and schizophrenia, he shot and killed his landlady who had argued about the studio noise, before turning the gun on himself.

Chart entries
Can't You Hear the Beat of a Broken Heart *(as Robert Duke)* Les Paul & Mary Ford
   (UK1962 # 39)
Walk With Me My Angel *(as Robert Duke)* Don Charles (UK 1962 # 39)
Telstar – The Tornadoes (UK 1962 # 1; US # 1)
Globetrotter – The Tornadoes (UK 1963 # 5)
Robot – The Tornadoes (UK 1963 # 17)
The Ice Cream Man – The Tornadoes (UK 1963 # 18)
Diggin' My Potatoes - Heinz (UK 1965 # 49)

Joe Meek and Geoff Goddard
Don't You Think It's Time – Mike Berry & the Outlaws (UK 1963 # 6)
My Little Baby - Mike Berry & the Outlaws (UK 1963 # 34)

Johnny Mercer see also **Henry Mancini**
Born John Herndon Mercer, Savannah, Georgia 1909. Died 1976.

The son of a prominent attorney and great-grandson of a Confederate general, Mercer was sweeping the floors of an ice cream parlour at the age of ten, and his first exposure to music was hearing his mother sing old Scottish romantic ballads and being taken to see minstrel and vaudeville shows. Having already sung in a choir and memorised words to songs, he became more interested in finding out who wrote them.

At the age of 19, he moved to New York's Greenwich Village and worked for a brokerage house, while spending evenings acting, singing, and writing lyrics. In 1930, he penned "Out of Breath (and Scared to Death of You)," composed by his friend Everett Miller and later appearing in a musical revue *The Garrick Gaieties.* Steadily learning the trade from other songwriters, his early songs proved unsuccessful, but he had his first break meeting Hoagy Carmichael. Impressed with his writing, Carmichael had Mercer labouring for a year to write lyrics for his song "Lazy Bones."

Becoming a member of ASCAP (American Society of Composers, Authors and Publishers), Mercer became a well-respected member of the Tin Pan Alley fraternity. In 1935, he was offered a job by RKO to write for low-budget musicals, and his first big song was "I'm an Old Cowhand from the Rio Grande," sung by Bing Crosby in the 1936 movie *Rhythm on the Range.* Moving on to work for Warner Brothers. he partnered composer Richard Whiting on "Hooray for Hollywood" for the movie *Hollywood Hotel.* After Whiting's death, he teamed up with Harry Warren and received his first Oscar nomination for "Jeepers Creepers," sung by Louis Armstrong in 1938's *Going Places*. This was soon followed by the popular "You Must Have Been a Beautiful Baby," sung by Dick Powell in *Hard to Get.* Among the songs Mercer wrote over the next few years were "Fools Rush In," (with Rube Bloom), "One For My Baby (and One More For the Road)" and "That Old Black Magic" (with Harold Arlen).

In 1942, Mercer founded Capitol Records with producer Buddy DeSylva and record store owner Glen Wallichs, and signed a number of famous artists, including Nat King Cole. He also enjoyed a chart hit with "Zip-a-Dee-Doo-Dah" as Johnny Mercer and the Pied Pipers (although not writing the song). By the mid-Forties, Mercer had become one of Hollywood's top lyricists and was able to style his songs on the changing language and cultural fashions, preferring to have the music first for him to add lyrics, and even writing English lyrics to foreign songs, as was the case with "Autumn Leaves." The Fifties saw him writing lyrics for the MGM musical *Seven Brides for Seven Brothers,* and along with composer Henry Mancini, winning Oscars for "Moon River," from *Breakfast at Tiffany's*, and the title song from *Days of Wine and Roses.*

In 1969, along with publishers Abe Olman and Howie Richmond, he founded the Academy of Popular Music's Songwriters Hall of Fame, and after his death it established the annual Johnny Mercer Award as its highest honour, given to songwriters with a history of outstanding creative works.

Chart entries
Skylark *(with Hoagy Carmichael)* Michael Holliday (UK 1960 # 39)
Fools Rush In (Where Angels Fear to Tread) *(with Rube Bloom)* Brook Benton (US
   1960 # 24; UK # 50); Etta James (US 1962 # 87); Ricky Nelson (US 1963 # 12; UK # 12)
Come Rain or Come Shine *(with Harold Arlen)* Ray Charles (US 1960 # 83)
The Bilbao Song *(with Bertolt Brecht, Kurt Weill)* Andy Williams (US 1961 # 37)
That Old Black Magic *with Harold Arlen)* Bobby Rydell (US 1961 # 21)

You Must Have Been a Beautiful Baby *(with Harry Warren)* Bobby Darin (US 1961 # 5; UK # 10); Dave Clark Five (UK 1967 # 35)
Moon River *(with Henry Mancini)* Jerry Butler (US 1961 # 11); Henry Mancini (US 1961 # 11; UK # 44; US 1962 # 32); Danny Williams (UK # 1)
Dream – Dinah Washington (US 1962 # 92)
I Remember You *(with Victor Schertzinger)* Frank Ifield (US # 5; UK # 1)
I Wanna Be Around *(with Sadie Vimmerstedt)* Tony Bennett (US 1963 # 14)
Days of Wine and Roses *(with Henry Mancini)* Henry Mancini (US 1963 # 33); Andy Williams (US 1963 # 26)
Charade *(with Henry Mancini)* Henry Mancini (US 1963 # 36); Andy Williams (US 1964 # 100)
Love With the Proper Stranger *(with Elmer Bernstein)* Jack Jones (US 1964 # 62)
Summer Wind *(with Henry Mayer)* Wayne Newton (US 1965 # 78); Frank Sinatra (US 1966 # 25; UK # 36)
Autumn Leaves -1965 *(with Joseph Kosmer, Jacques Prévert)* Roger Williams (US 1965 # 92)

Helen Miller see Howard Greenfield

Roger Miller
Born Roger Dean Miller Snr, Fort Worth, Texas 1936. Died 1992.
Nashville Songwriters Hall of Fame 1973.
Country Music Hall of Fame 1995.

Miller's mother died when he was a year old, and with his father unable to support the family during the Depression his three sons were sent to live with her brothers on a farm outside Erick, Oklahoma. Educated in a one-room schoolhouse, he often daydreamed and wrote songs. As a later member of the FFA student organisation at high school, he was taught to play guitar by his cousin's husband Sheb Wooley. With his growing desire to become a singer-songwriter, he ran away from home to perform in Texas and Oklahoma, and after stealing a guitar turned himself in to the police next day. To avoid jail, he joined the army and served in Korea, and on his return went to Nashville where he got a job in a hotel as a "singing" bellhop. Comedian and country singer Minne Pearl hired him to play fiddle in her band, and through her he met musician George Jones, who got him an audition for Starday Records.

Getting married and becoming a father put his career on hold, and he worked as a firefighter in Amarillo while still performing at night. After meeting singer Ray Price, he became a member of his band, the Cherokee Boys. Returning to Nashville, his song "Invitation to the Blues" was recorded by both Price and Rex Allen, and after signing with Tree Publishing, his song "Bill Bayou" became his first country chart-topper when recorded by Jim Reeves. Described as "the most talented, and least disciplined, person you could imagine," Miller became one of the main songwriters of the Fifties. In 1960, he scored his first solo hit with "You Don't Want My Love," which was also covered by Andy Williams. Two years later, he wrote "The Swiss Maid." First recorded by Miller as "Fair Swiss Maiden," which just missed out on becoming a UK chart-topper for yodelling singer Del Shannon.

On the subject of songwriting, Miller once declared: "The human mind is a wonderful thing. It starts working before you've even born and doesn't stop again until you sit down and write a song." In 1964, he had two solo recordings on the Smash label that were both top ten hits on the Hot 100, but it was the following year that would see his writing status elevated, particularly in the UK. His signature song "King of the Road," with its tale of a travelling hobo, was inspired by seeing a sign on the side of a barn that read, "trailers for sent or rent," thus giving him the opening line to the song. It went on to top the UK charts and win him five Grammys. This was shortly followed by "England Swings," with Miller's lyrics relating to traditional mid-Sixties notions of the country. In 1969, the song "When Two Worlds Collide," recorded by Miller eight years before and co-written with Bill Anderson, became a posthumous top 20 hit for the late Jim Reeves.

Later in life, Miller appeared in and wrote songs for the 1985 Broadway musical *Big River*. With a unique style that defied classification, Miller once explained that in trying to do what other artists were doing, he became frustrated when the end result came out different, realising "I'm the only one that knows what I'm thinking."

Chart entries
You Don't Want My Love – Andy Williams (US 1960 # 64)
The Swiss Maid – Del Shannon (US 1962 # 64; UK # 2)
Dang Me – Roger Miller (US 1964 # 7)
Chug-a-Lug – Roger Miller (US 1964 # 9)
Do-Wacka-Do- Roger Miller (US 1964 # 31)

King of the Road – Roger Miller (US 1965 #4; UK # 1)
Queen of the House *(with Mary Taylor)* Jody Miller (US 1965 # 12)
Engine, Engine # 9 – Roger Miller (US 1965 # 7; UK # 33)
One Dyin' and A-Buryin' – Roger Miller (US 1965 # 34)
Kansas City Star - Roger Miller (US 1965 # 31# UK # 48)
England Swings- Roger Miller (US 1965 # 8; UK # 13)
Husbands and Wives - Roger Miller (US 1966 # 26)
The Last Word in Lonesome Is Me – Eddy Arnold (US 1966 # 40)
You Can't Roller Skate in a Buffalo Herd - Roger Miller (US 1966 # 40)
My Uncle Used To Love Me But She Died - Roger Miller (US 1966 # 58)
When Two Worlds Collide *(with Bill Anderson)* Jim Reeves (UK 1969 # 70)

Ron Miller
Born Ronald Norman Gould, Chicago 1932. Died 2007.

With his father dying when he was still young, Gould adopted his stepfather's surname. Around the age of nine, he was constantly listening to the radio and began writing patriotic songs in his head about America winning the war, and at the age of 18 he joined the US Marines. On discharge in 1953, he held a variety of jobs, including selling washing machines, and also had a failed attempt at becoming a prop-baseball player. After joining a theatre group for a while, he decided acting wasn't for him, and instead started writing songs again. Around the age of 30, Miller got the chance to play piano in the lounge of a Chicago hotel, and it was while there that he was noticed by Motown's Berry Gordy Jr and William "Mickey" Stevenson, who invited him to come to Detroit and write songs for their artists. Three months later, he was introduced to 12-year-old Stevie Wonder and the two became friends and later songwriting partners.

Shortly after JFK was killed, Miller and Wonder were sitting on a lawn outside Motown when Wonder started to cry, saying, "You know I'm glad I'm blind… because I see everything the way I want to see it." With that, Miller penned the lyrics to "A Place in the Sun" with a melody composed by staff writer Bryan Wells. It became the first of several hits for the two songwriters. On the night that Miller's daughter was born in 1965, he penned the lyrics to "For Once In My Life" to music written by Orlando Murden. Although written as a slow ballad and passed around various artists as try-outs, it was first recorded by Jean DuShon. However, it was Wonder's more upbeat version in 1968 that became the Grammy-winning hit and one of the most covered songs in pop history. "Yester-Me, Yester-You, Yesterday," written with Murden, was originally recorded in 1966 by blue-eyed Motown artist Chris Clark, but it was Wonder again who had a memorable a top ten hit with it.

In the Seventies, Miller would go on to write Wonder's hit "Heaven Help Us All," showcasing an earthier, gospel sound, and also co-write Diana Ross's beautiful ballad "Touch Me in the Morning" (with Michel Masser) and Charlene's "I've Never Been To Me" (with Kenneth Hirsch).

Miller later reflected on his career: "I thought that writing songs was the easy way to paradise! I thought I was pretty good at it and maybe I was, but I surely wasn't as good as I thought I was."

Chart entries
A Place in the Sun *(with Bryan Wells)* Stevie Wonder (US 1966 # 9; UK # 20); David Isaacs (UK 1969 # 51)
Travelling Man *(with Bryan Wells)* Stevie Wonder (US 1967 # 32)
For Once in My Life *(with Orlando Murden)* Tony Bennett (US 1967 # 91); Jackie Wilson (US 1968 # 70); Stevie Wonder (US 1968 # 2; UK # 3); Dorothy Squires (UK 1969 # 24)
Gotta See Jane *(with Eddie Holland Jr; R Dean Taylor)* R Dean Taylor (UK 1968 # 17)
Yester-Me, Yester-You, Yesterday *(with Bryan Wells)* Stevie Wonder (US 1969 # 7; UK # 2)

Charles Mills see Mike Leander

Gordon Mills
Born Gordon William Mills, Madras, British India 1935. Died 1986.

Mills's parents had met and married in India while his father was serving in the British Army. Returning to England shortly after, they lived in Trealaw, South Wales. His mother taught him to play harmonica, and by the age of 15, he had joined his first group, playing in local clubs and pubs. Two years later, he was called up to do national service in Germany and Malaya. On his return, he came second in a contest held by the harmonica-makers Hohner, before going on to win for the UK when it was staged in Europe. He was later invited to join the Morton Fraser Harmonica Gang, and later, with two of its members, formed the vocal trio the Viscounts, who had a minor hit in 1961 with the Mann-Goffin song "Who Put the Bomp (In The Bomp, Bomp, Bomp)."

Mills had begun writing songs after an inherent shyness made him more comfortable composing than performing. His first recorded song was "I'll Never Get Over You," a top ten UK hit for Johnny Kidd & the Pirates in 1963. This was followed by more hits for Kidd, as well as for the Applejacks and Cliff Richard. But it was while watching a performance by the Welsh beat group Tommy Scott & the Senators in 1964 that he first came across their frontman Thomas Woodward. The group had recorded several solo tracks with producer Joe Meek with little success, and while performing in a club later in the year had been spotted by Decca producer Peter Sullivan, who introduced them to manager Phil Solomon.

Although their partnership was short-lived, Woodward's career took off when Mills saw him perform in a Cwmtillery club and offered to be his manager. Inviting him to come to London, he gave him the stage name of Tom Jones (after the 1963 movie) and secured a recording contract with Decca. The second attempt at a chart single was "It's Not Unusual." Written with Les Reed (1935-2019), it had first been offered to Sandie Shaw who instead recommended that it suited Jones better. As a result, it shot to the top of the charts and made Jones an international star, with Mills redesigning the singer's image into that of a slick crooner. Apart from writing a minor hit for Freddie & the Dreamers, Mills made no further impact as a songwriter, although that same year he did the same for struggling singer Gerry Dorsey by giving him the stage name of Englebert Humperdinck and turning him into another superstar crooner.

In the Seventies, Mills founded his own record label MAM whose artists included Lynsey De Paul, but only the continuing success of new-found Irish singer-songwriter Gilbert O'Sullivan kept the business booming. Their relationship would sour when the singer discovered that his contract greatly favoured the label owner. The drawn-out lawsuit that followed ended with O'Sullivan being awarded £7 million in damages. One of O'Sullivan's biggest hits had been 1972's "Clair," named after Mills' three-year-old daughter, and featuring the girl's laughter.

Chart entries
I'll Never Get Over You – Johnny Kidd & the Pirates (UK 1963 # 4)
I'm the Lonely One – Cliff Richard & the Shadows (UK 1964 # 8; US # 92)
Three Little Words – Applejacks (UK 1964 # 23)
It's Not Unusual *(with Les Reed)* Tom Jones (UK 1965 # 1; US # 10)
A Little You – Freddie & the Dreamers (UK 1965 # 26; US # 48)
Once Upon A Time – Tom Jones (UK 1965 # 32)
Not Responsible – Tom Jones (UK 1966 # 18; US # 58)

Reynard Miner
Born Chicago 1946. Died 2024.

Miner began his career as a writer and producer for Chess Records in Chicago. His first success as producer came with two chart hits for guitarist and blues singer Little Milton, both of which he co-authored with in-house writers Billy Davis, Carl William Smith and Gene Barge. In 1964, he teamed up with Smith to write "Rescue Me" a number one R&B hit for soul singer Fontella Bass, who was claimed by some sources to also be a co-writer. Recorded in only three takes, Bass's powerful vocal performance was later described by top rock journalist Dave Marsh as "the best non-Aretha Franklin ever." Miner played piano on the recording and a young Minne Ripperton sang backing vocals.

More success with David and Smith followed over the next two years, but it was 1967's "(Your Love Keeps Lifting Me) Higher and Higher" that became his biggest achievement. Written with Smith and Kansas-born Gary Jackson (1945-2014), it was recorded by Jackie Wilson. Originally sung as a soul ballad, it was producer Carl Davis who suggested it sounded totally wrong, saying, "You have to jump and go with the percussion … if he didn't want to sing it that way, I would put my voice on the record and sell millions," The advice was taken and it became a multi-million dollar hit.

When Davis left Chess in 1968, Miner moved to Motown and wrote or co-write songs for artists including Martha & the Vandellas, Jimmy Ruffin, and the Marvelettes, and then went on to work with William Weatherspoon for the Holland-Dozier-Holland Invictus/Hot Wax labels.

Chart entries
We're Gonna Make It *(with Billy Davis, Carl William Smith, Gene Barge)* Little Milton
　(US 1965 # 25)
Who's Cheating Who? *(with Billy Davis, Carl William Smith, Gene Barge)* Little Milton (US 1965 # 43)
Rescue Me *(with Carl William Smith)* Fontella Bass (US 1965 # 4; UK # 11)

Recovery *(with Billy Davis, Carl William Smith)* Fontella Bass (US 1965 # 37# UK # 32)
In the Basement Pt. 1 *(with Billy Davis, Carl Smith)* Etta James & Sugar Pie DeSanto
  (US 1966 # 97)
(Your Love Keeps Lifting Me) Higher and Higher *(with Carl Smith & Gary Jackson)* Jackie
  Wilson (US 1967 # 6; UK 1969 # 11)
There Is *(with Bobby Miller)* The Dells (US 1968 # 20)

Joni Mitchell
Born Robert Joan Mitchell, Fort MacLeod, Alberta, Canada 1943.
Rock and Roll Hall of Fame 1997.
Songwriters Hall of Fame 1997.
Grammy Lifetime Achievement Award 2002.

During the war, young Mitchell moved with her mother (a teacher) and father (an air force officer) to various bases around the country before settling in Saskatchewan at war's end. At the age of nine, she contracted polio and despite struggling with her education she embraced painting and poetry and began studying classical piano. She later taught herself to play guitar, although polio had weakened her left hand. At the age of 18, Mitchell began singing and playing with friends covers of hits by Edith Piaf and Miles Davis, and also performed in clubs where she had her first experience of jazz music. With the intention of becoming a folk singer, she sang at hootenannies and on local tv and radio, before heading off to Toronto. Despite playing non-union gigs in meeting halls and church basements, she still resorted to busking and shop work to pay her union fees. In 1964, she had an unexpected pregnancy with an ex-boyfriend, and following the birth of a daughter placed her for adoption (all of which would remain a secret until 1993). Mitchell continued playing in folk clubs, but now with more of her own material.

In 1965, she moved to Detroit with her friend and fellow singer Chuck Mitchell and performed together in coffee houses. By the end of the year they had married, with Joni taking his surname, and she appeared several times on Oscar Brand's tv show *Let's Sing Out*. After her divorce two years later, she moved to New York to pursue a solo career, and performed in clubs and coffee houses along the East Coast with her innovative guitar playing and unique vocal. She struck up a friendship with David Crosby while playing in a Florida nightclub, and followed him to Los Angeles where she came under the management of Elliot Roberts, who had a connection with producer David Geffen. After signing to the Reprise label, Crosby convinced them to let Mitchell record a solo acoustic album. Produced by Crosby, it was finally released as *Song to a Seagull*, the cover of which featured a Mitchell painting. Some of her earlier songs like "Both Sides Now" and "Chelsea Morning" had already been recorded by artists such as Judy Collins by the time Mitchell starting on her second album *Clouds*, and she now included her own versions. "Chelsea Morning," with its strong imagery, had been inspired by the distinct décor of her apartment while staying in the Big Apple, while "Both Sides Now," originally a minor hit for Harper's Bizarre, was inspired by a passage in Saul Bellow's 1959 novel *Henderson the Rain King* where the writer looks out of a plane window to observe the clouds. Mitchell later confessed: "The writing has been an exercise - trying to work my way towards clarity. Get out the pen and face the beast yourself…"

The Seventies saw Mitchell rise to become one of the most influential singer-songwriters of her generation. Her 1970 album *Ladies of the Canyon* was written while living in Laurel Canyon with Graham Nash, and later seen as a transition between her earlier folk songs and the more sophisticated work that followed. However, the 1971 album *Blue* would go on to be cited as one of the greatest of all time.

Chart entries
Both Sides Now – Judy Collins (US 1968 # 8; UK # 14); Dion (US 1969 # 91)
Chelsea Morning – Judy Collins (US 1969 # 78)

Chips Moman
Born Lincoln Wayne Moman, La Grange, Georgia 1937. Died 2016.
Nashville Songwriters Hall of Fame 2022.

After moving to Memphis in his teens, Moman played in Warren Smith's road band before moving on to Los Angeles around 1957 with Johnny Burnette's band. He also toured with Gene Vincent and for a time was a guitar session player at Gold Star Studios. Returning to Memphis, he assisted the setting up of Satellite Records (later Stax) by helping find a disused movie theatre that became their headquarters. As their recording engineer and producer, his first single was 1960's "Gee Whiz (Look at His Eyes)" by Carla Thomas. In 1964 he left Stax following a monetary dispute with the label owner, and set up his own Memphis studio, American Sound, with musicians Reggie Young and Bobby Womack (guitars), Tommy Cogbill and Mike

Leech (bass), Bobby Woods and Bobby Emmons (piano) and Gene Chrisman (drums). Amongst their recordings were songs by the Box Tops, Merrilee Rush, Bobby Womack, Joe Tex, Wilson Pickett, Herbie Mann, Sandy Posey and Petula Clark. Moman also established a songwriting partnership with fellow Memphis producer Dan Penn, and among their successes were Aretha Franklin's R&B hit "Do Right Woman, Do Right Man," and James Carr's "The Dark End of the Street."

Moman also produced Elvis Presley's 1969 album *From Elvis in Memphis*, arguably one of the artist's best, and the recording sessions included the hit songs "In the Ghetto," "Suspicious Minds," and "Kentucky Rain," although the latter two did not appear on the album.

Chart entries
Last Night *(with Charles Axton, Jerry Lee Smith, Floyd Newman, Gil Capie)* The Mar-Keys
   (US 1961 # 3)
This Time – Troy Shondell (US 1961 # 6; UK # 22)
The Dark End of the Street *(with Dan Penn)* James Carr (US 1967 # 77)

Bob Montgomery
Born Robert Montgomery, Lampasas, Texas 1937. Died 2014.

Montgomery met his best friend and future songwriting partner Buddy Holly at Hutchinson High School in Lubbock, Texas, in 1949. While there, they performed bluegrass songs as Buddy and Bob and soon appeared on local radio shows, with Montgomery on lead vocal and Holly harmonising. In October 1955, along with bass player Larry Welborn, they supported Bill Haley and the Comets at Fair Park Auditorium, and while there Marty Robbins' manager Eddie Crandall showed interest in working with Holly as a solo performer and asked for demos of his music to be sent to Decca Records. Montgomery went on to co-write a number of Holly's hits, including "Heartbeat," "Wishing," and "Love's Made a Fool of You." He also wrote the pop standard "Misty Blue" with Brenda Lee in mind, but after she turned it down it was first recorded by Wilma Burgess and later Eddie Arnold.

In 1968, Montgomery worked as producer on Bobby Goldsboro's chart-topper "Honey," and in the Seventies continued that relationship by producing "Summer (The First Time)."

Chart entries
Heartbeat *(with Norman Petty)* The England Sisters (UK 1960 # 33); Buddy Holly (UK 1960 # 30)
Two of a Kind *(with Earl Sinks)* Sue Thompson (US 1962 # 42)
Wishing *(with Buddy Holly)* Buddy Holly (UK 1963 # 10)
Somebody Else's Girl – Billy Fury (UK 1963 # 18)
Love's Made a Fool of You *(with Buddy Holly)* Buddy Holly (UK 1964 # 39); The Bobby Fuller
   Four (US 1966 # 26);
Wind Me Up (Let Me Go) *(with John Talley)* Cliff Richard & the Shadows (UK 1965 # 2)
Misty Blue – Eddie Arnold (US 1967 # 57)

Jim Morrison
Born James Douglas Morrison, Melbourne, Florida 1943. Died 1971.
Rock and Roll Hall of Fame 1993 (with The Doors).
Grammy Lifetime Achievement Award 2007 (with the Doors).

The son of a future US Navy Rear Admiral, Morrison was raised in a military family and spent his early childhood in San Diego before later moving around the country to live wherever his father was based. He finally graduated from George Washington High School in Alexandria with an IQ of 149, and in the early Sixties attended Florida State University. He was an avid reader, drawing inspiration from the work of several philosophers and poets that included French symbolist Arthur Rimbaud. While at UCLA, Morrison enrolled in Jack Hirschman's class on French artist Antonin Artaud and his surrealistic theatre brand had an enormous impact on Morrison's later work. Graduating with a bachelor's degree, he enjoyed the Bohemian lifestyle of Venice Beach, "living on beans and LSD," and writing lyrics to his early songs.

Along with fellow UCLA student Ray Manzarek (1939-2013), Morrison began forming Rick & the Ravens. They were soon joined by guitarist Robby Krieger (b.1946) and drummer John Densmore (b.1944) and changed their name to the Doors, after the title of Aldous Huxley's book *The Doors of Perception,* which referred to such doors being unlocked through the use of psychedelic drugs. In June 1966, they opened for Van Morrison's band Them at the Whisky-A-Go Go, and on the final night jammed together on "Gloria." Morrison was heavily influenced by the Irish singer's stage craft, especially his subdued menace and recklessness.

Later in the year, the Doors released their first single, "Break On Through (To the Other Side)," with writing credited to all four band members. With Morrison the main lyricist, Krieger would contribute certain lines, while other band members offered rhythm and chords to Morrison's vocal melodies. After signing with Elektra, the single "Light My Fire" spent three weeks topping the Hot 100. Originally composed by Krieger, it was inspired by the Rolling Stones' "Play With Fire" as well as the melody of the song "Hey Joe." The team effort saw Densmore suggesting a more Latin rhythm and the single snare-drum opening, Manzarek adding the Bach-style organ riff, and Morrison writing the second verse and part of the chorus. While appearing on the *Ed Sullivan Show* to perform it live, the show's censors insisted the lyric "girl we couldn't get much higher" had to be changed to "get much better," but, with his customary defiance, Morrison deliberately sang the original lyric, leading to the band being barred from any further appearances. Their celebrated second album *Strange Days* saw Morrison's rebellious image now firmly installed in him, and the Doors soon became one of the most popular rock bands in the US with their distinctive blend of blues and psychedelic rock.

Continuing bad behaviour led to arrests on a number of occasions, even becoming the first rock star to be arrested while on stage. "People Are Strange" was apparently written while Morrison was feeling depressed, and while going for a walk with Densmore in Laurel Canyon the words came to him "in a flash" and were hastily scribbled down on paper. "Hello, I Love You" was one of six songs recorded by Rick & the Ravens in 1965, with lyrics inspired by Morrison after seeing a young black woman at Venice Beach. In 1968 it became their second US chart-topper, while also leading to accusations of plagiarism when it was alleged the musical structure was similar to that of Ray Davies' "All Day and All of the Night." It was apparently settled out of court.

After an extended break, their final album, the intimate *L.A Woman,* was released in 1970. Together with the atmospheric single "Riders On the Storm," it was cited as one of their finest achievements. Morrison retreated to live in Paris, hoping to follow a literary career and quitting music altogether. On July 3rd 1971 he was found dead in his apartment, officially recorded as from a heart attack, but those years of pleasure-seeking excess had tragically taken its toll. He once claimed: "I'll always be a word man, better than a bird man."

Chart entries
Light My Fire - The Doors (US 1967 # 1; UK # 49); Jose Feliciano (US 1968 # 3; UK # 6); The Doors (US 1968 # 87)
People Are Strange - The Doors (US 1967 #12)
Love Me Two Times - The Doors (US 1967 # 25)
The Unknown Soldier - The Doors (1968 # 39)
Hello, I Love You - The Doors (US 1968 # 1; UK # 15)

Van Morrison
Born George Ivan Morrison, Belfast NI 1945.
Rock and Roll Hall of Fame 1993.
Songwriters Hall of Fame 2003

With his father a shipyard electrician and mother a former singer and dancer, their only child was called Van from an early age. His entry into music began by listening to his father's immense record collection, which had been acquired during a spell in Detroit. By listening to artists such as Ray Charles, Lead Belly, Muddy Waters and Solomon Burke, he both emulated them and was inspired by them. His father bought him a guitar when he was eleven and he learned to play it from a chord book. In 1957, aged just 12, he formed the skiffle group the Sputniks and performed at local cinemas, with Morrison singing lead and writing and arranging most of their material. After forming a second short-lived group, he persuaded his father to buy him a tenor saxophone after hearing Jimmy Giuffre play. Taking lessons in both sax playing and reading music, he was able to join other local bands, one of which became the Monarchs, fronted by his friend Georgie Sproule.

Leaving school in 1960 with no qualifications, he took a job as a window cleaner while playing in the evenings with the Monarchs. The following year, he toured Europe with the band (now called Georgie & the Monarchs), playing sax, guitar and harmonica, and while in Germany they recorded the single, "Boozoo Hully Gully/Twingy Baby." On their return to Belfast in 1963, the band split up and Morrison and Sproule played in the Manhattan Showband, along with guitarist Herbie Armstrong. Later, Morrison and Armstrong joined Brian Rossi and the Golden Eagles (later becoming the Wheels) with Morrison their blues singer. In 1964, he left the group and replied to an ad for musicians to perform at Belfast's Maritime Hotel. For that, he created a new band from members of the Gamblers and shared vocals with Billy Harrison. As a new name for the band, piano player Eric Weixon suggested Them, after the 1954 horror film of the same name.

As well as playing covers, the band also performed some of Morrison's early material, and the debut of "Gloria" actually took place on stage. Dick Rowe of Decca Records got to hear of their performances and signed them to a standard two-year contract. "Gloria" was one of seven songs recorded in London. Although having no explicit lyrics, the song was alleged to be about a girl looking for a sexual encounter. It became b-side to the single "Baby Please Don't Go," which was derived from

John Lee Hooker's 1949 version as "Don't Go Baby." The following single "Here Comes the Night," written and produced by Bert Berns, became their most successful hit in 1965. Among the session musicians was guitarist Jimmy Page.

With their singles becoming more successful in the US, the band undertook a two-month tour of the country, and were supported by the Doors at the Whisky A Go Go club in Los Angeles. Following revenue issues with their manager and with their visas expiring, they returned to Belfast to do a couple of concerts before breaking up and leaving Morrison to concentrate on a solo career.

In 1967, Morrison was offered a contract by Berns, who owned the Bang label, and hastily flew to New York to sign the contract. Eight songs were recorded, with "Brown Eyed Girl" becoming the lead single and a top ten US hit. Originally called "Brown Skinned Girl" about an interracial relationship, Morrison changed it at the recording to make it more palatable for radio, although the lyric "making love in the green grass" still had some stations removing the song from their playlists. Hoping to capitalise on its success, Berns quickly put the songs on an album, *Blowin' Your Mind!* without Morrison's knowledge or input, and on its release it flopped. Apparently, Morrison had not fully studied the contract which gave Berns full control.

To escape the contract, Morrison next recorded a batch of non-sensical "novelty" songs. Following Berns death shortly afterward, Warner Records bought Morrison's contract and gave him three sessions to record what would be his debut album *Astral Weeks*. With its deeply intellectual lyrics, it became a cult classic in the US, despite at the time being largely ignored in the UK.

In the fall of 1969, Morrison moved to upstate New York and wrote more formally-composed material for his next album *Moondance*. Both a critical and commercial success, it became his first million seller. His 1989 romantic single "Have I Told You Lately" became a Grammy winner and cited as one of the finest love songs of the century.

Looking back on the pitfalls of a music career, Morrison said: "That's the way things go. You win some, you lose some. You're not going to be, as someone put it, divinely inspired all the time. But you might have to just get on with it."

Chart entries
Brown Eyed Girl – Van Morrison (US 1967 # 10)
Gloria – Them (US 1966 # 60); Shadows of Knight (US 1966 # 10)
One More Time – Them (UK 1965 # 48)
Mystic Eyes – Them (US 1965 # 33)

George "Shadow" Morton
Born George Francis Morton, Richmond, Virginia 1941. Died 2013.

After being raised in Brooklyn, young Morton got himself into so much trouble that his parents moved to Hicksville, Long Island. While there he would meet his high school sweetheart (and future wife) Lois Berman. In 1957, he and four friends formed the doo-wop vocal group the Markeys and played for school audiences. One of its members was accordion-player Ellie Gaye (later Greenwich) who offered the other members encouragement. They recorded "Hot Rod," written by Morton and Joe Monaco, which was released as a single on RCA. Following graduation, Morton did jobs while hitchhiking across the country, and when picked up by a friend after being stranded in a snowstorm, was told that Ellie Gaye was now writing hit songs as Ellie Greenwich in New York's Brill Building.

Fixing an invitation to her office, he also met her husband Jeff Barry, who asked him to come back the following week with a song he had written. With that, Morton found some musicians and went looking for singers. He heard that the Markeys' Tony Michaels had been writing songs for four girls from Queens called the Shangri-Las, and Morton arranged studio time to hear them. On the day, he realised he still had no song to offer, so he sat in his car until he came up with an idea. Back in the studio, he went to 14-year-old pianist Billy Joel and dictated the opening piano line. Returning to Barry the next day, he gave him the tape. Although initially taking a dislike to Morton's bravado, Barry took the tape to Jerry Leiber who, on hearing it, realised what he had written and produced was nothing less than a teenage soap opera. With that, Leiber signed Morton and the Shangri-Las to his Red Bird label. However, another version of the story had Morton presenting the demo to other Red Bird staff-writers who then took it to a studio with the four girls and session musicians to record. The song was the classic "Remember (Walking in the Sand)." Peaking at number five on the Hot 100, it was said to have been inspired while Morton was parked next to a beach, with the song's demo having surf and seagull sound effects.

With the Shangri-Las needing another hit, Morton produced the Barry-Greenwich teenage-tragedy song "Leader of the Pack," which, while becoming a US chart-topper, was refused airplay on UK radio stations due its death theme. As staff producer for Red Bird, Morton was given the nickname "Shadow" by record company executive George Goldner, as his whereabouts were sometimes in question. In the two years he worked there, Morton continued to produce and write teen melodramas, incorporating sound effects and Spector-style inventive percussion. He later wrote: "I've never written a song. I write productions. I'm a storyteller. I do soap operas. I'm more director than a producer."

In 1967, following the collapse of the label, Morton found 15-year-old folk singer Janis Fink playing in Greenwich Village. With a change of name she became Janis Ian and he produced her debut single "Society's Child." That same year, he discovered Mark Stein & the Pigeons, who later became Vanilla Fudge, and went on to produce their first three albums.

Chart entries
Remember (Walking in the Sand) The Shangri-Las (US 1964 # 5; UK # 14)
Leader of the Pack *(with Jeff Barry, Ellie Greenwich)* The Shangri-Las (US 1964 # 1;
    UK # 11)
Leader of the Laundromat *(with Jeff Barry, Ellie Greenwich, Paul Vance, Lee Pockriss)* The
    Detergents (US 1964 # 19)
Give Him a Great Big Kiss – The Shangri-Las (US 1964 # 18)
I Can Never Go Home Anymore – The Shangri-Las (US 1965 # 6)
Past, Present and Future *(with Jerry Leiber, Artie Butler)* The Shangri-Las (US 1966 # 59)

Sylvia Moy
Born Sylvia Rose Moy, Detroit, Michigan 1938. Died 2017.
Songwriters Hall of Fame 2006.
Women Songwriters Hall of Fame 2025.

One of nine children, Moy and her young siblings embraced music by playing on pots and pans, and at Northern High School she studied classical and jazz music. In 1963, she was noticed singing in a club by Motown's Marvin Gaye and William "Mickey" Stevenson and was given a recording and songwriting contract, with the emphasis on writing due to the label's lack of material for their artists to record. Moy would soon become mainly associated with Stevie Wonder, and it was at her urging to Gordy that the label retained the singer after his voice changed through puberty. Luckily, producer Clarence Paul had now found it much easier to work with Wonder's more-mature tenor voice.

Becoming the first woman to write for the label, Moy's first success came with Wonder's "Uptight (Everything's Alright)," co-written with Wonder (as Stevie Judkins) and Henry "Hank" Cosby. They based the song upon an instrumental riff that Wonder had developed after listening to the Stones' "(I Can't Get No) Satisfaction" while he was touring with the band. With Moy completing the lyrics, there was no braille copy for the singer to read, so during the recording she sang ahead of him and he just had to repeat the lines as he heard them. It peaked at number three on the Hot 100 in 1965. The following year, she co-wrote "This Old Heart of Mine (Is Weak For You)" with Holland-Dozier-Holland. Originally intended for the Supremes, it was instead given to the Isley Brothers. According to Dozier, it had been inspired by a girl he just couldn't give up, recalling, "I made excuses for her and all the wrong she had done to me. She was a necessary evil that I just couldn't overcome."

1967's Marvin Gaye - Kim Weston duet "It Takes Two" was written by Moy and Weston's then-husband William "Mickey" Stevenson. In a later interview for *Mojo*, Weston recalled working with Gaye in the studio: "I saw a new side to him. I'd travelled and shared bills with him so we knew how each other worked. In the studio he was really encouraging. He added little ad libs, intonations here and there and suggested things for the arrangements. I saw the genius shine out of him but also the frustration. You could hear it in his voice. He wanted more control."

That same year Moy joined Wonder, his mother Lula Mae Hardaway and Hank Cosby to pen the soulful "I Was Made To Love Her," a song that Wonder later cited as his favourite, and being inspired by Angie, his first love, and how he would call her up and talk until they both fell asleep while still on the phone.

In 1969 came the beautiful love song "My Cherie Amour," (My Dearest Love), the origin of which dated back to 1966 with "Oh, My Marcia," a song Wonder had written for a girlfriend while at blind school. When Gordy first heard it, he asked Moy and Cosby to develop it, and it was Moy who came up with the intriguing French/English title. Wonder's vocals were added in 1968, but the song was then shelved, only appearing as the b-side to his single "I Don't Know Why." However, with the b-side getting sufficient airplay, Motown released it in 1969 as an a-side single.

Moy would go on to co-write more hits for Wonder, including 1970's "Never Had a Dream Come True," before moving into film and tv work.

Chart entries
Uptight (Everything's Alright) *(with Stevie Judkins -aka Stevie Wonder; Henry Cosby)* Stevie
    Wonder (US 1965 # 3; UK # 14); The Jazz Crusaders (US 1966 # 95); Nancy Wilson (US
    1966 # 84); Ramsey Lewis (US 1966 # 49)
My Baby Loves Me *(with William "Mickey" Stevenson, Ivy Jo Hunter)* Martha & the Vandellas
    (US 1966 # 22)
This Old Heart of Mine (Is Weak For You) *(with Brian Holland, Lamont Dozier, Eddie
    Holland Jr)* Isley Brothers (US 1966 # 12; UK # 47; UK 1968 # 3); Tammi Terrell

(US 1969 # 67)

Nothing's Too Good For My Baby *(with Henry Cosby, William "Mickey" Robinson)* Stevie Wonder (US 1966 # 20)

What Am I Going To Do Without Your Love *(with William "Mickey" Stevenson)* Martha & the Vandellas (US 1966 # 71)

It Takes Two *(with William "Mickey" Stevenson)* Marvin Gaye & Kim Weston (US 1967 # 14; UK # 4)

I Was Made To Love Her *(with Stevie Wonder, Lula Mae Hardaway, Henry Cosby)* Stevie Wonder (US 1967 # 2; UK # 5); King Curtis (US 1967 # 76)

Love Bug Leave My Heart Alone *(with Richard Morris)* Martha & the Vandellas (US 1967 # 25)

Little Ole' Man (Uptight Everything's Alright) *(with Stevie Wonder, Henry Cosby)* Bill Cosby (US 1967 # 4)

I'm Wondering *(with Stevie Wonder, Henry Cosby)* Stevie Wonder (US 1967 # 12; UK # 23)

Honey Chile *(with Richard Morris)* Martha Reeves & the Vandellas (US 1967 # 11)

Shoo-Be-Doo-Be-Doo-Da-Day *(with Stevie Wonder, Henry Cosby)* Stevie Wonder (US 1968 # 9; UK # 46)

I Promise To Wait My Love *(with George Gordy, Billie-Jean Brown, Margaret Johnson Gordy, Allen Story)* Martha Reeves & the Vandellas (US 1968 # 62; UK # 55)

(We've Got) Honey Love *(with Richard Morris)* Martha Reeves & the Vandellas (US 1969 # 56)

My Cherie Amour *(with Stevie Wonder & Hank Cosby)* Stevie Wonder (US 1969 # 4; UK #4)

Mitch Murray see also Peter Callander
Born Lionel Michael Stitcher, Hove, England 1940.

In his teens, Murray loved listening to his father's record collection and songs of the Thirties, and when he became a songwriter his melodic structure would bear similarities to those recordings. Growing up in London's Golders Green, however, he had no dreams of a musical career. Working for his father's handbag business, he travelled all over the country, and by the age of 17 had begun writing songs just for fun. He taught himself to play guitar using his father's 1930's sheet music, and almost by accident began writing tunes to fit the chord sequences. One of his first songs to be recorded was in 1962 with Terry Scott's childrens' favourite "My Brother."

After changing his legal name by deed poll, he wrote "How Do You Do It?" and offered it to Adam Faith and Brian Poole, who both showed no interest. However, EMI producer George Martin liked the song and felt it good enough to become the debut single for the Beatles. At first, the group felt it didn't fit their sound and were hesitant to record it, but after some structural and slight lyrical changes (which Murray disliked), it was recorded in September 1962. With the label's publisher Ardmore & Beechwood being more interested in publishing Lennon-McCartney material, Martin settled instead on their "Love Me Do," which was recorded at the same session. The Beatles' version of Murray's song would remain unreleased until 1995. Meanwhile, Martin still had faith in Murray's song, and while working with the Beatles in January 1963, he had fellow producer Ron Richards record it with the label's other Liverpool group, Gerry & the Pacemakers. As their debut single, it topped the UK charts for three weeks.

Encouraged by its success, Murray offered EMI another similar song, "I Like It," and that, too, scored a chart-topper for the Pacemakers a few months later. Also that year, Murray teamed up with Freddie Garrity to write two enjoyable top ten hits for his group the Dreamers, with "I'm Telling You Now" (a US number one) and "You Were Made For Me." In 1964, Murray's book *How To Write a Hit Song* would go on to inspire many budding songwriters, including 12-year-old schoolboy Gordon Sumner (aka Sting). Murray pointed out: "A freelance songwriter is only as good as the song itself. It's not like being in a band where you have fans waiting for your next song even before it is written."

The following year, Murray forged a writing partnership with lyricist and former chef Peter Callander (b.1939), and one of their first collaborations was Murray's novelty single "Down Came the Rain." Using the moniker "Mister Murray," it was non-charting single on the Fontana label in 1965. While a number of their songs were adapted from European hits, their first success was "Even the Bad Times Are Good," a contender for Sandie Shaw to perform at 1967's Eurovision Song Contest, before losing out to the eventual winning song "Puppet On a String." However, the song was soon picked up by the Tremeloes, who scored a top five hit on the UK charts. The writing team's greatest success came toward the end of 1967 with "The Ballad of Bonnie and Clyde." R&B singer Georgie Fame had already been inspired after watching the gangster movie and approached the writers to compose a song for him to record. The result was a 1930's music-style recreation of their story, with jazz trumpets, trombones and piano embellished with the sound of guns, sirens and car chases. Although lyrically it had its historical inaccuracies, it nevertheless topped the UK charts.

In 1968, Murray became the youngest ever director of the copyright collective PRS for Music and later founded the Society of Distinguished Songwriters. The following year, Murray and Callander wrote "Ragamuffin Man" for Manfred Mann, a tale about the son of a wealthy family casting away the life he had known, and then being asked if he had regrets. That same year they gave Vanity Fare the song "Hitchin' a Ride" about a young man with no money trying to hitchhike home to see his girl. Noted for the two recorders heard in the intro, it was a surprising top ten hit in the US.

With Callander, he formed their own label Bus Stop in 1972 and wrote and produced singles for Paper Lace and Tony Christie, while Murray went on to be more involved in comedy, doing voice characterisations for film and tv and becoming a professional speechwriter.

Chart entries
How Do You Do It? – Gerry & the Pacemakers (UK 1963 # 1; US 1964 # 9)
I Like It – Gerry & the Pacemakers (US 1963 # 1; US # 1964 # 17)
By the Way – The Big Three (UK 1963 # 22)
I'm Telling You Now (*with Freddie Garrity*) Freddie & Dreamers (UK 1963 # 2; US 1965 # 1)
You Were Made For Me (*with Freddie Garrity)* Freddie & the Dreamers (UK 1963 # 3; US
    1965 # 21)
I Knew It All the Time – Dave Clark Five (US 1964 # 53)

Mitch Murray and Pete Callander
Even the Bad Times Are Good - The Tremeloes (UK 1967 # 5; US # 36)
The Ballad of Bonnie and Clyde – Georgie Fame (UK 1967 # 1; US # 7)
Hush…Not A Word To Mary - John Rowles (UK 1968 # 12)
Ragamuffin Man – Manfred Mann (UK 1969 # 8)
Hitchin' A Ride – Vanity Fare (UK 1969 # 16; US # 5)

Graham Nash see Clarke, Hicks and Nash

Willie Nelson
Born Abbott, Texas 1933
Nashville Songwriters Hall of Fame 1973.
Country Music Hall of Fame 1993.
Grammy Lifetime Achievement Award 2000
Songwriters Hall of Fame 2001.

With his mother leaving home soon after he was born and his father later moving away and re-marrying, Nelson and his sister were raised by their grandparents. At the age of six, his grandfather bought him a guitar and he sang gospel in a local church. Three years later, he was playing in a local band called Bohemian Polka. While at Abbott High School, he earned cash by singing in taverns, dance halls and honky tonks, and later joined the Texans, a band formed by his sister's husband, and played on KHBR radio in Hillsboro. After leaving school in 1950, he joined the US Air Force for a while before being medically discharged. On his return, he married and studied agriculture at Baylor University, before dropping out to pursue a music career. After playing with country singer Johnny Bush's band, he moved with his new family to Pleasanton, Texas, and became a deejay at KBOP. While there in 1955, he made a demo of the song "The Storm Has Just Begun." After working with other radio stations and playing nightclubs, he moved to San Diego and later Portland, Oregon, where he was hired as a radio announcer by KVAN in Vancouver, Washington. Regarding the music, he simply said: "Three chords and the truth - that's what a country song is."

In 1956, Nelson made his first record, the unsuccessful "No Place For Me," and for the next four years he moved around the country taking various work, writing songs, and eventually settled in Nashville in 1960. While there, he met songwriter Hank Cochran who worked for Pamper Music, part-owned by Ray Price, who took him on as a staff writer. Faron Young recorded Nelson's "Hello Walls," a portrayal of a man's lonely conversation with his walls after being jilted by his lover, and it peaked at number 12 on the Hot 100. After Price recorded Nelson's "Night Life," he asked him to become bass player for his touring band, the Cherokee Cowboys. When Nelson and Cochran met Patsy Cline's husband, Charlie Dick, they played a demo of the song "Crazy." Cline eventually decided to record it and it became not only her biggest hit but also her signature song.

In 1961, Nelson signed with Liberty Records and recorded two successful singles, one being a duet with his future wife Shirley Collie, followed by his debut album. Three years later, he signed with Fred Foster's Monument Records and wrote "Pretty Paper," a hit for Roy Orbison, before moving to RCA. That same year, he joined the *Grand Ole Opry* radio show and befriended Waylon Jennings, and a few years later formed his own backing band, the Record Men, which included Johnny Bush.

In 1982, Nelson had a new lease of life when his version of "Always on My Mind" topped the country charts.

Chart entries
Hello Walls – Faron Young (US 1961 # 12)
Crazy – Patsy Cline (US 1961 # 9)
Funny How Time Slips Away – Jimmy Elledge (US 1961 # 22); Johnny Tillotson (US 1963 # 50)
Night Life – Rusty Draper (US 1963 # 50)
Pretty Paper – Roy Orbison (US 1963 # 15; UK # 6)
Funny (How Time Slips Away) – Joe Hinton (US 1964 # 13)

Anthony Newley see Leslie Bricusse and Anthony Newley

Randy Newman
Born Randall Stuart Newman, Los Angeles 1943.
Songwriters Hall of Fame 2002.
Rock and Roll Hall of Fame 2013.

After spending his childhood summers in New Orleans, Newman's parents returned to Los Angeles where three of his uncles were Hollywood film-score composers - Alfred, Lionel and Emil Newman. After graduating from University High School, he studied music at the University of California and finally completed his degree at UCLA. Citing Ray Charles as a big influence, he was already a professional songwriter by the age of 17. After the song "Golden Gridiron Boy" his first as a performer, failed to chart, he decided to focus on writing and arranging. In 1962, one of his first writing credits was "They Tell Me It's Summer" for the vocal group the Fleetwoods, and it led to commissions for other artists including Pat Boone, Gene Pitney and Jackie DeShannon.

His first chart success came two years later, co-writing "Anyone Who Knows What Love Is" for soul singer Irma Thomas. Further UK chart success came with songs by Cilla Black and Gene Pitney, all of which broke into the top twenty, but his most memorable hit of the Sixties was 1967's unconventional and ragtime-influenced "Simon Smith and the Amazing Dancing Bear." Written three years before for Frank Sinatra but never recorded, it told the tale of a young man who entertained rich diners with his dancing bear. It was next offered to Harper's Bizarre, who recorded it as an album track in 1967. That same year, it was recorded by ex-Animals member Alan Price, and coupled with Newman's "Tickle Me," peaked at number four on the UK charts. Price, a great admirer of Newman's writing, included seven of his songs on his album *A Price on His Head*. It's success also earned Newman a recording contract with Warner Records. Harper's Bizarre would record six of his songs during their short career. "I Think It's Going To Rain Today," from Newman's crucially acclaimed eponymous debut album, became an early standard and much-covered song.

In the mid-Sixties, Newman's childhood friend Lenny Waronker had him work for the independent label Autumn Records. Along with Leon Russell and Van Dyke Parks, they played on sessions for artists like the Beau Brummels and the Mojo Men. When Waronker became A&R manager for Warner in late 1966, the trio of Newman, Russell and Parks became instrumental in its success as a rock music label. In 1969, Newman worked with Gordon Lightfoot and Peggy Lee, and the following year Harry Nilsson recorded the album *Nilsson Sings Newman*, consisting entirely of his songs.

Looking back, Newman recalled: "I started recording because I was always complaining about the records that I was getting of my songs. At least if I did them and messed them up, I wouldn't have anyone else to blame."

Chart entries
Anyone Who Knows What Love Is (*with Judith Arbuckle, Jeannie Seely, Pat Sheeran*) Irma
    Thomas (US 1964 # 52)
I Don't Want To Hear It Anymore – Jerry Butler (US 1964 # 95)
I've Been Wrong Before – Cilla Black (UK 1965 # 17)
Nobody Needs Your Love – Gene Pitney (UK 1966 # 2)
Just One Smile – Gene Pitney (UK 1966 # 8; US # 64)
Simon Smith and His Amazing Dancing Bear – Alan Price Set (UK 1967 # 4)
So Long, Dad – Manfred Mann (UK 1968 # 52)
Love Story – Alan Price Set (UK 1968 # 56)

Harry Nilsson
Born Harry Edward Nilsson III, New York City 1941. Died 1994.

Born in Brooklyn, Nilsson's father abandoned the family when he was three (as later referenced in his autobiographical album track "1941"). Although completing his education through ninth grade, he was still in his teens when he escaped poverty by moving to Los Angeles. Finding work for a time at the Paramount Theatre, he settled into a bank job as a computer programmer while spending evenings pursuing a singer-songwriting career. While working at the theatre, he had formed a close-harmony vocal duo with a friend Jerry Smith and also learned to play guitar. In 1962, with his natural talent and singing lessons that his uncle had given him, Nilsson began singing demos for songwriter Scott Turner and was paid $5 for each track recorded.

The following year, he co-wrote a song for Little Richard with Turner's friend John Marascalco, who also paid for some of Nilsson's independent singles. The song "Donna, I Understand" caught the attention of Mercury Records, who offered him a contract using the name Johnny Niles. 1964 saw Nilsson writing several songs with Phil Spector and beginning a working relationship with songwriter and publisher Perry Botkin Jr, who managed to find a market for Nilsson's material. Through Botkin, he also befriended his music copyist (and later composer and arranger) George Tipton, who invested his life savings to finance the recording of four Nilsson songs. When Nilsson later signed with RCA, Tipton would arrange most of his recordings. Meanwhile, his contract was handled by Tower Records, and later that year they released the first singles credited to his real name as well as his non-charting debut album *Spotlight on Nilsson*.

Joining RCA at the end of 1967, they released the critically acclaimed album *Pandemonium Shadow Show,* which included the much-covered ballad "Without Her," about the sadness of dreaming of someone you love being there, but then having to live another day alone. That September, he also wrote the infectious "Cuddly Toy," which was recorded by the Monkees and performed in one of their tv shows. With all this success, Nilsson finally quit his bank job. The year also saw him achieve his first chart success as a performer with the Lennon-McCartney song, "You Can't Do That." Taken from the *Shadow Show* album, it became a top ten hit in Canada. In 1968, the album *Aerial Ballet,* named after the highwire circus act of his parents, included the single "One," a later top ten hit for Three Dog Night, as well as his version of folk singer Fred Neil's "Everybody's Talkin.'" Written in 1967 for Neil's self-titled album, it was released as a single by Nilsson the following year, but then pulled and not re-released until the movie *Midnight Cowboy* came out.

Film director John Schlesinger was working on the movie when Derek Taylor recommended Nilsson to write the soundtrack. The new song "(I Guess) the Lord Must Be in New York City" was first offered, but Schlesinger preferred Nilsson's version of "Everybody's Talkin,'" and agreeing to use it as the movie's theme song, it was re-recorded with a slightly different arrangement to suit the movie's requirements. The single peaked at number six on the Hot 100 and won Nilsson a Grammy. In the meantime, "(I Guess) the Lord Must Be in New York City" became a moderate hit for Wayne Newton and was also used for a Sophia Loren movie, while his own version later peaked at number 34 in the charts.

The Seventies would see him secure his biggest success with his cover of Badfinger's power ballad "Without You."

Chart entries
Ten Little Indians (US 1967 # 96)
1941 – Tom Northcott (US 1968 # 88); Billy J Kramer (UK 1968 # 57)
The Story Of Rock and Roll – The Turtles (US 1968 # 48)
Together – Sandie Shaw (UK 1968 # 54)
One – Three Dog Night (US 1969 # 5)
Without Her – Herb Alpert & the Tijuana Brass (US 1969 # 63; UK # 36)
(I Guess) The Lord Must Be in New York City – Wayne Newton (US 1969 # 34); Nilsson
   (US 1969 # 34)

Jack Nitzsche
Born Bernard Alfred Nitzsche, Chicago 1937. Died 2000.

The son of German immigrants, he was later raised on a farm in Michigan before moving to Los Angeles in 1955. With ambitions to become a jazz saxophonist, he was taken on as a music copyist by Sonny Bono, the head of A&R at Speciality Records. While working there in 1960 he co-wrote the novelty hit "Bongo, Bongo, Bongo" for percussionist Preston Epps. Three years later, he teamed up with Bono to write "Needles and Pins," a minor hit for Jackie DeShannon but a UK chart-topper for the Searchers in 1964. His own recording of "The Lonely Surfer," written with Martin Cooper, was also a top 40 hit.

During the Sixties, he became Phil Spector's right-hand man, conducting, arranging and orchestrating the famous Wall of Sound on almost all of his hit records. He also arranged the beautiful title song of Doris Day's 1963 movie *Move Over, Darling*. Written by Terry Melcher (Day's son), Hal Kanter and Joe Lubin, and produced by Melcher, the single peaked at number eight on the UK chart the following year. While becoming the music organiser for the *TAMI Show* tv special, Nitzsche met the Rolling Stones and was subsequently invited to play keyboards on a number of their hits.

The final years of the Sixties saw him co-write "I Could Be So Good to You," a moderate hit for the Portland-based garage rock band Don and the Goodtimes, and also working with Neil Young on his eponymous debut album.

Chart entries
Bongo, Bongo, Bongo *(with Arthur Egnoian)* Preston Epps (US 1960 # 78)
Needles and Pins *(with Sonny Bono)* Jackie DeShannon (US 1963 # 84); The Searchers
(UK 1964 # 1; US # 13)
The Lonely Surfer *(with Martin Cooper)* Jack Nitzsche (US 1963 # 39)
I Could Be So Good To You *(with Greg Dempsey)* Don & the Goodtimes (US 1967 # 56)

Laura Nyro
Born Laura Nigro, New York City 1947. Died 1997.
Songwriters Hall of Fame 2010.
Rock and Roll Hall of Fame 2012.

Born in the Bronx, Nyro's father was a jazz musician and her mother a bookkeeper, and it was music that helped her cope with a difficult childhood. A self-taught pianist at an early age, she read poetry and was inspired by female artists like Nina Simone and Billie Holiday, as well as classical composers. At the age of eight, she composed her first songs and attended the New York Society for Ethical Culture and later Manhattan's High School of Music & Art. Along with friends, she sang on street corners and in subway stations, and her mother's work brought her into contact with record executives Artie Mogull and Paul Barry who offered her a recording and management contract.

Her debut album *More Than a New Discovery* included her songs "Wedding Bell Blues" (a 1969 hit for the Fifth Dimension) and "Stoney End" (a 1970 hit for Barbra Streisand). Her own versions were released in 1966, but only "Wedding Bell Blues" became a minor hit. After a poorly received appearance at the Monterey Pop Festival, David Geffen became her manager, and together they founded the publishing company Tuna Fish Music, with proceeds of future compositions being divided equally. Geffen then secured her a contract with Clive Davis at Columbia, a move that gave her more artistic freedom. 1968's album *Eli and the Thirteenth Confession* received high critical praise for its sophistication and depth. The single "Eli's Coming" had been written in high school to prove to her teacher that rock and roll "wasn't junk." It was also a top ten hit when recorded by Three Dog Night. Another track "Stoned Soul Picnic" was a top three hit for the Fifth Dimension.

In 1969, Geffen and Nyro sold Tuna Fish to CBS for $4.5 million, making them both millionaires, and the following year she had her only Hot 100 entry with a cover of Goffin-King's "Up on the Roof." But their friendship soon came to an abrupt end. While preparing to launch a new recording label called Asylum, Geffen announced that Nyro would be its first artist, but just before the signing he learned she had re-signed with Columbia without telling him, leaving Geffen, in his own words, feeling betrayed.

Chart entries
Stone Soul Picnic – The 5th Dimension (US 1968 # 3)
Sweet Blindness – The 5th Dimension (US 1968 # 13)
Wedding Bell Blues – The 5th Dimension (US 1969 # 1; UK # 16)
And When I Die – Blood, Sweat & Tears (US 1969 # 2)
Eli's Coming – Three Dog Night (US 1969 # 10)

Spooner Oldham see Dan Penn and Spooner Oldham

Dan Penn and Spooner Oldham
Born Wallace Daniel Pennington, Vernon, Alabama 1941.
Born Dewey Lindon Oldham Jr, Center Star, Alabama 1943.
Nashville Songwriters Hall of Fame 2020 (Penn).

Penn spent most of his late teenage years in the Muscle Shoals area and was a regular at Rick Hall's FAME (Florence Alabama Music Enterprises) studios, where he performed, produced and wrote songs. While there in 1960, he cut his first record "Crazy Over You" as well as writing his first hit with Conway Twitty's "Is a Bluebird Blue?" Penn then began a writing partnership with fellow FAME session musician Spooner Oldham.

Oldham had been blinded in his right eye as a child. Reaching for a frying pan, he was hit by a spoon he knocked off a shelf, leaving schoolmates to give him the lifelong nickname. He began his music career by playing piano in a jazz band at

Lauderdale County High School and then attending the University of North Alabama, but that was cut short when he decided to join FAME as a session pianist. His first collaboration with Penn was "I'm Your Puppet," a top ten US hit in 1966 for singing cousins James & Bobby Purify, and its success convinced the writers they were following a lucrative career. More hits followed over the next two years, with songs recorded by the Box Tops, Percy Sledge and Sandy Posey, as well as scoring a top ten UK hit with Plastic Penny's "Everything I Am."

In early 1966, Penn moved to Memphis to work at Chip Moman's American Sound Studio, with Oldham joining him the following year. With Moman, Penn wrote some of his best songs. "The Dark End of the Street" was written while taking a break from playing cards (and cheating) with dee-jay Don Schroeder. In a hotel room, it took them just 30 minutes to write what they called the "best cheatin' song ever." Although a minor hit when recorded by R&B singer James Carr, it would in time be much covered by a number of top artists. While at a recording session, the pair were introduced by Jerry Wexler to Aretha Franklin and later wrote for her "Do Right Woman, Do Right Man," which became the b-side to her hit single "I Have Never Loved a Man (The Way I Love You)." That same year, Penn also produced the Box Tops' hit "The Letter." Oldham, as part of the famous Muscle Shoals Rhythm Section, continued to play organ on a number of R&B hits including Sledge's "When A Man Loves a Woman" and Wilson Pickett's "Mustang Sally." He later moved to Los Angeles, and as a much sought-after backing musician performed on recordings by artists that included Bob Dylan, Linda Ronstadt and Bob Seger.

Penn later revealed: "I'm always amazed when I hear who has recorded one of my songs. Amazed and happy when I receive my royalties."

Chart entries
I'm Your Puppet – James & Bobby Purify (US 1966 # 6)
It Tears Me Up - Percy Sledge (US 1966 # 20)
Wish You Didn't Have To Go - James & Bobby Purify (US 1967 # 38)
Out Of the Left Field - Percy Sledge (US 1967 # 59)
Are You Never Coming Home - Sandy Posey (US 1967 # 59)
Everything I Am - Plastic Penny (UK 1968 # 6)
Cry Like a Baby - The Box Tops (US 1968 # 2; UK # 15)
Sweet Inspiration - The Sweet Inspirations (US 1968 # 18)
I Met Her In Church - The Box Tops (US 1968 # 37)

Dan Penn
Is a Blue Bird Blue? – Conway Twitty (US 1960 # 35; UK # 43)
Come On *(with Tommy Roe)* Tommy Roe (US 1964 # 36)
My Dreams *(with David Briggs)* Brenda Lee (US 1964 # 85)
The Dark End of the Street *(with Chips Moman)* James Carr (US 1967 # 77)
Nine Pound Steel *(with Wayne Carson Thompson)* Joe Simon (US 1967 # 70)
Up Tight, Good Man *(with Lindon Oldham)* Laura Lee (US 1967 # 93)

John Phillips
Born John Edmund Andrew Phillips, Parris Island, South Carolina 1935. Died 2001.
Rock and Roll Hall of Fame 1998 (with the Mamas & the Papas).

The son of retired US Marine Corps officer Claude Phillips, he grew up in Alexandria, Virginia, and later enrolled at the Catholic Linton Hall Military School in Bristow, where, according to Phillips, he was subjected to traumatic beatings by the nuns. In 1946, he continued his education at George Washington High School, and with his height (1.95m) he excelled in basketball. Graduating in 1953, he gained entry to the US Naval Academy, but resigned during his first year. Three years later, he quit studying art at Hampden-Sydney College and went to New York in search of a record contract and the Greenwich Village folk scene. With Scott McKenzie (1939-2012), Bill Clearly and Michael Rand, Phillips formed the doo-wop quartet the Abstracts, which later became the Smoothies. In 1960, they cut two singles for Decca, "Softly" and "Lonely Boy and Pretty Girl," both produced by Milt Gabler.

By 1961, Phillips and McKenzie had joined singer and banjo player Dick Weissman to form the trio, the Journeymen and secured a residency at a Village nightclub. Their manager, Frank Werber, who also had the Kingston Trio on his books, got them a record contract with Capitol Records for which they recorded their eponymous debut album, with two of the songs written by Phillips. Two more albums followed, and the Phillips-Weissman single "River Come Down" was well received and it highlighted Phillips' skills as the main singer, writer and arranger. With McKenzie beginning to having mental health issues, relationships within the group became strained, and the label began showing signs of losing interest.

In 1963, Phillips married Long Beach model Michelle Gilliam (b.1944), who he met while in San Francisco, and the group soon began to fall apart, partly due to the "British invasion" making their style of music appear out of fashion. The following year, along with his new wife and banjo-player Marshall Brickman, he formed the New Journeymen, and when Brickman departed soon after, Phillips brought in Canadian singer Denny Doherty (1940-2007), formerly of the short-lived group the Mugwumps, whose lineup included future Lovin' Spoonful members John Sebastian and Zal Yanonsky, and also Ellen Cohen (aka Cass Eliot) (1941-1974). When the New Journeymen broke up in early 1965, a new group called the Magic Cyrcle was formed, with Doherty suggesting that his out-of-work friend Eliot should become a member.

Later that year, with the new name the Mamas & the Papas, singer Barry Maguire introduced them to Lou Adler, head of Dunhill Records, for whom they signed a record deal. "California Dreamin'" was a song that Phillips and his wife had written in 1963 while still members of the New Journeymen and living in New York. During one cold winter, they were reminiscing about California's sunshine, with lyrics inspired by Michelle's loneliness. The song was first recorded by Maguire on his album *This Precious Time,* with the Mamas and Papas singing backing vocals, but producer Adler was so impressed with their singing he decided to re-record it with Doherty's lead vocal. Other changes included an improvised alto flute played by Bud Shank replacing the original harmonica solo, and the addition of a new guitar intro by 20-year-old P F Sloan. (Maguire's original vocal can be briefly heard at the beginning by listening to the left channel).

The resulting single was released in December 1965, ahead of their debut album *If You Can Believe Your Eyes and Ears.* With tracks that embraced soul, pop/rock and folk/rock, it was a showcase for Phillips' ability to write optimistic, feel-good songs in what had quickly become a counterculture climate. The wonderful "Monday, Monday," written by Phillips in just twenty minutes, relates to someone disliking the day because it was the day his lover left him. Doherty had put pressure on Phillips to come up with more new material and he came back the following morning with one that he felt had "universal appeal." The group felt otherwise, especially Doherty who would again be singing lead vocal, stating: "Nothing about it stood out to me; it was a dumb f**kin' song about a day of the week." Despite the criticism, it not only became a US chart-topper but won the group a Grammy award.

The following year, their second, eponymous album brought with it some controversy when Phillips discovered that Michelle had been having affairs with both Doherty and the Byrds' Gene Clark. He fired her and brought in Adler's girlfriend Jill Gibson. Although the album cover featured the group with Michelle, it was re-shot with Gibson. (Elliot also had long-standing unrequited love for Doherty). After a brief expulsion, Michelle returned to the group just before the album's release, and the original cover was reinstated. The album contained another big single "I Saw Her Again," written by Phillips and Doherty. Although inspired by the affairs, it is best remembered for Doherty's false start at the beginning of the third chorus, intentionally left in by Adler following a mistake during the mixing by engineer Bones Howe.

In February 1967, the group released their third album, *Deliver,* and again included two memorable hits. Their cover of the Pauling-Bass song "Dedicated To the One I Love," a former hit for the Shirelles, was beautifully delivered by Michelle, her first lead vocal (on the first verse), and when performed live on the *Ed Sullivan Show* was just enchanting to watch. For the auto-biographical "Creeque Alley," John and Michelle namechecked a number of artists and locations that had figured in their history, with recurring emphasis on Mama Cass remaining "fat." Phillips stated that the song had been written to explain to producer Adler a "who's who" in their history, while the song title referred to a club in the Virgin Islands where the New Journeymen had vacationed.

Later in the year, Phillips and Adler masterminded the Monterey Pop Festival with the group performing as one of the headline acts. With local authorities in Monterey getting concerned about the influx of hippies ahead of the festival, Phillips tried to smooth things over by writing "San Francisco (Be Sure To Wear Flowers In Your Hair)" in just twenty minutes and giving it to his friend Scott McKenzie to record. Regarded as a hippie anthem, it brought thousands of them to San Francisco during the summer of 1967.

Eliot left the group later that year before returning to record their fourth album *The Papas and the Mamas.* Released in 1968, it was recorded at the Phillips' home and was reviewed as being more downbeat. The highlights were Elliot's cover version of the 1930 song "Dream a Little Dream Of Me," with music by Fabian Andre and lyrics by Gus Kahn. Inspired by hearing of the death of one of the songs original composers, it included Phillips' spoken intro, "And now, to sing this lovely ballad, here is Mama Cass."

The single "Safe In My Garden," with its layered vocal lines, was a showcase for their exquisite harmonies and a soothing tonic for a year that saw myriad protests and civil unrest. "Twelve Thirty (Young Girls Are Coming to the Canyon)" was their last great single. It was written by Phillips in 1965, shortly after moving to California, and inspired by the L.A neighbourhood of Laurel Canyon, a haven for the folk-rock community of artists, where, allegedly, young girl "groupies" would go to party all night. The 12.30 of the title referred to a broken church clock in the "dirty" city of New York with the hands stopped at that time.

Shortly after the release of the album, the band was officially dissolved, as was Michelle's marriage to Phillips. A later attempt at a group reunion resulted in the album *People Like Us* in 1971, but then they split for good. Eliot went on to have a short but successful solo career until her premature death in 1974, while Phillips beat his drug addiction and released a solo album in 1970. Michelle became an actress, while Doherty continued to record, as well as getting a refusal from Eliot to marry!

Chart entries
California Dreamin' *(with Michelle Phillips)* The Mamas & the Papas (US 1965 # 4; UK # 23);
    Bobby Womack (US 1968 # 43)
Monday, Monday – The Mamas & the Papas (US 1966 # 1; UK # 3)
I Saw Her Again *(with Denny Doherty)* The Mamas & the Papas (US 1966 # 5; UK # 11)
Look Through My Window – The Mamas & the Papas (US 1966 # 24)
Go Where You Wanna Go – The Fifth Dimension (US 1967 # 16)
Creeque Alley *(with Michelle Phillips)* The Mamas & the Papas (US 1967 # 5; UK # 9)
San Francisco (Be Sure To Wear Some Flowers In Your Hair) – Scott Mckenzie (US
    1967 # 4; UK # 1)
Twelve Thirty (Young Girls Are Coming To the Canyon) The Mamas & the Papas (US
    1967 # 20)
Like an Old Time Movie – Scott McKenzie (US 1967 # 24)
Dancing Bear – The Mamas & the Papas (US 1967 # 51)
Safe In My Garden – The Mamas & the Papas (US 1968 # 53)
For the Love Of Ivy – The Mamas & the Papas (US 1968 # 81)

Wilson Pickett
Born Prattville, Alabama 1941. Died 2006.
Rock and Roll Hall of Fame 1991.

One of eleven children, young Pickett sang in Baptist church choirs before going to live with his father in Detroit in 1955. With his passionate style of singing inspired by listening to his hero Little Richard, he joined the gospel group the Violinaires and toured the country with one group before fronting a new gospel-harmony group called Pickett for the next four years. In 1959, he recorded the song "Let Me Be Your Boy" with the all-girl group the Primettes as his backing singers. It later became the b-side of his self-penned single "My Heart Belongs To You." The following year, he was heard singing and playing his guitar on the front porch of his home by Willie Schofield, a member of the R&B vocal group the Falcons. Invited to join the group (which included Eddie Floyd), he replaced Joe Stubbs as their lead singer.

His biggest success with the Falcons was "I Found a Love," co-written with Schofield and Rob West, with Pickett on lead vocals. Although a minor hit, it spearheaded his path to a solo career. A demo he had cut for "If You Need Me" written with Robert Bateman and Sonny Sanders, was given to Atlantic producer Jerry Wexler, who then had his star artist Solomon King record it and turn it into a huge soul standard. As a result, Pickett's own version released on the Double L label only had moderate chart success. However, the self-penned "It's Too Late" and subsequent album of the same name not only helped to showcased his raw soulful voice, but also persuaded Wexler to sign him to his label.

The first single "I'm Gonna Cry," co-written with Don Covay and produced by Pickett, failed to chart, as did "Come Home Baby", a duet with Tammy Lynn. But the third single proved to be the breakthrough. Recorded at the famous Stax studio in Memphis, "In the Midnight Hour" was co-written with session guitarist Steve Cropper, who also handled production with Jim Stewart. It was Cropper who based his groove on the current dance step known as the Jerk. Despite its powerful rhythm track, it only peaked at number 21 on the Hot 100, it's sales probably dented by the song's title having a suggestion of after-hours sex and thereby restricting radio play.

Further sessions at Stax led to the singles "Don't Fight It" (another co-write with Cropper), and "Ninety-Nine and a Half (Won't Do)" (with Cropper and Eddie Floyd). In late 1965, Stax owner Jim Stewart decided to ban all outside productions, so Wexler took Pickett to FAME studios in Muscle Shoals, Alabama, where he had his greatest success. In 1966, his cover of Chris Kenner's 1963's "Land of 1000 Dances" which namechecked a number of the popular dance crazes, reached number six on the Hot 100, while the incredible "Mustang Sally, a cover of the Bonny "Mack" Rice song from the previous year, repeated its success and became arguably his greatest recording. Pickett also had a third top R&B single and million-seller with Dyke Chritian's "Funky Broadway."

Toward the end of 1967, Pickett switched recording to Memphis's American Studios. Working with new producers Tommy Cogbill and Tom Dowd, one of the songs recorded was "I'm a Midnight Mover" co-written with Bobby Womack. A year later, he went back to FAME to record a cover of the Beatles' "Hey Jude" and a remake of Hendrix's hit "Hey Joe," and in 1970, after recording sessions at Criteria in Miami, teamed up with Philly writers Gamble and Huff, who gave him a top 20 hit with their "Engine No. 9."

Pickett looked back on his career: "If I wasn't in show business I don't know what I would have been - a wanderer or something, you know? But God blessed me with the talent and the chance. I knocked on enough doors, and this is what I can give myself credit for."

Chart entries
I Found A Love (*with Willie Scofield & Robert West*) The Falcons and Band (US 1962 # 75);
    Wilson Pickett (as I Found A Love Pt 1) (US 1967 # 32)
If You Need Me (*with Robert Bateman & Sonny Sanders*) Wilson Pickett (US 1963 # 64)
    Solomon Burke (US 1963 # 37)
It's Too Late – Wilson Pickett (US 1963 # 49)
In the Midnight Hour (*with Steve Cropper*) Wilson Pickett (US 1965 # 21; UK # 12); The Mirettes
    (US 1968 # 45)
Don't Fight It (*with Steve Cropper*) Wilson Pickett (US 1965 # 53; UK # 29)
Ninety-Nine and a Half (Won't Do) (*with Steve Cropper & Eddie Floyd*) Wilson Pickett (US 1966
    # 53)
Soul Dance Number Three (*with Jerry Wexler*) Wilson Pickett (US 1967 # 55)
I'm A Midnight Mover (*with Bobby Womack*) Wilson Pickett (US 1968 # 24; UK # 38)

Lee Pockriss and Paul Vance
Born Lee Julian Pockriss, New York City 1924. Died 2011.
Born Joseph Paul Florio, New York City 1929. Died 2022.

Brooklyn-born Pockriss graduated from Erasmus College and went on to Brooklyn College before his education was cut short with the outbreak of war. He then served as a cryptographer for the US Air Force. After the war, he continued studying English and music at Brooklyn College and then studied musicology at New York University. In 1950, he won a competition for a new song from the American Federation of Music Clubs and for a time composed for television, primarily for NBC's *U.S Steel Hour*. With the continuing ambition of becoming a professional songwriter, he began associating with writers and publishers at New York's Brill Building. It was there that he met fellow Brooklyn writer Paul Vance, who had begun writing lyrics in his early teens before serving in the US Army at Fort Leavenworth in Kansas. After the war, he ran an auto salvage business, but, like Pockriss, yearned to be a songwriter.

    The two of them soon formed a writing partnership and their first success came with the infectious "Catch a Falling Star," a transatlantic chart-topper for Perry Como when released in 1957 as a double-header with "Magic Moments." Keen-eared musicologists recognised the melody having similarities to a theme in Brahm's *Academic Festival Overture*. The single paved the way for their future success as professional writers, with Pockriss describing their ideal working relationship: "He [Vance] understands the public, I understand the profession."

    In 1959, as Lee and Paul, they wrote and released the novelty song "The Chick" on the Columbia label, while that same year singer-songwriter Paul Evans began recording demoes for Pockriss. One of the songs, "My Heart Is An Open Book" was co-written with Hal David and a hit for rockabilly singer Carl Dobkins Jr. Another was "Seven Little Girls (Sitting in the Back Seat)," a collaboration with Bob Hilliard. Originally intended for tv host Merv Griffin to record, they instead preferred Evans' version for the single, and in doing so scored another transatlantic hit when two months later the vocal trio the Avons took it to number three on the UK charts.

    In the summer of 1960, Pockriss and Vance wrote what would become their greatest success. Inspired by a comment made by Vance's young daughter while wearing a swimsuit on a beach, the novelty of "Itsy Bitsy Teenie Weenie Yellow Polkadot Bikini" seemed a surefire hit once Pockriss had added the catchy melody, but it took six months of being turned down before they found a suitable artist to record it in 16-year-old Brian Hyland. His version gave the writers their second US chart-topper.

    Later that year, Pockriss adapted a 1958 German tune by composer Heino Gaze, originally titled "Tivoli Melody," but with a later name-change to "Calcutta," the harpsichord-driven instrumental was recorded on Artie Ripp's Dot label by veteran Lawrence Welk & His Orchestra. Featuring handclaps and "la la la" backing vocals, it was a departure for Welk, but nevertheless gave him a million-selling number chart-topper. In the fall of 1961, Pockriss was commissioned to write a new song for 18-year-old actress Shelley Fabares to perform as Mary Stone in the sitcom, *The Donna Reed Show*. With fellow writer Lyn Duddy, they came up with "Johnny Angel" as a sequel to the show's "Johnny Loves Me," written by Barry Mann & Cynthia Weil, and it once again climbed to the top of the charts. Several years later, Pockriss teamed up with Hal Hackaday (1922-2015) to write "Kites," the final release for country-folk group the Rooftop Singers in 1967. Later in the year, it gave the UK band Simon Dupree & the Big Sound a top ten hit, noted for its distinctive Japanese-inspired version.

    Before the decade came to an end, Pockriss and Vance had a final flourish creating the group the Cuff Links, comprising hired studio musicians and lead singer Roy Dante, who had previously sang with the Detergents on their 1964 novelty hit, "Leader of the Laundromat." With Dante suppling all the harmony vocals, the singles "Tracy" and "When Julie Comes Around" both scored top ten hits in the UK. Pockriss went on to write for both stage and screen and also provide songs for tv's *Sesame Street*, while Vance continued to produce various artists.

Chart entries
Starbright - Johnny Mathis (US 1960 # 25; UK # 47)
Itsy Bitsy Teeny Weeny Yellow Polkadot Bikini – Brian Hyland (US 1960 # 1; UK # 8)
No - Dodie Stevens (US 1960 # 73)
Four Little Heels (The Clickety Clack Song) Brian Hyland (US 1960 # 73; UK # 29); The Avons (UK 1960 # 45)
Wait For Me - The Playmates (US 1960 # 37)
Calcutta (*with Heino Gaze, Hans Bradtke)* Lawrence Welk Orchestra US 1960 # 1); The Four Preps (US 1961 # 96)
Little Miss Stuck Up - The Playmates (US 1961 # 70)
Leader Of the Laundromat (*with Shadow Morton, Jeff Barry, Elle Greenwich*) The Detergents (US 1964 # 19)
Double-O-Seven - The Detergents (US 1965 # 89)
In My Room (*with Joaquin Prieto)* Verdelle Smith (US 1966 # 62)
Tar And Cement (*with Adriano Celentano*) Verdelle Smith (US 1966 # 38)
Dommage, Dommage (Too Bad, Too Bad) - Jerry Vale (US 1966 # 93); Paul Vance (US 1966 # 97)
I Don't Need Anything - Sandie Shaw (UK 1967 # 50)
Walk Tall – 2 of Clubs (UK 1967 # 92)
Tracy - Cuff Links (UK # 4; US # 9)
When Julie Comes Around - Cuff Links (UK 1969 # 10; US # 41)

Lee Pockriss and others
In My Little Corner Of the World *(with Anita Bryant)* Anita Bryant (US 1960 # 10)
A Kookie Little Paradise *(with Bob Hilliard)* The Tree Swingers (US 1960 # 73); Jo Ann Campbell (US 1960 # 31); Frankie Vaughan (UK 1960 # 31)
Johnny Angel (*with Lyn Duddy*) Shelley Fabares (UK 1962 # 1; UK # 41); Patti Lynn (UK 1962 # 37)
The Cheerleader (*with Fred Tobias*) Paul Peterson (US 1963 # 78)
Kites (*with Hal Hackady*) Simon Dupree & the Big Sound (UK 1967 # 8)

Paul Vance with others
Two Thousand, Two Hundred, and Twenty Three Miles *(with Leon Carr)* Patti Page (US 1960 # 67)
Keep Your Hands In Your Pockets *(with Jack Segal)* The Playmates (US 1962 # 88)
Gina *(with Leon Carr)* Johnny Mathis (US 1962 # 6)
What Will Mary Say *(with Eddie Synder)* Johnny Mathis (US 1963 # 9; UK # 49)
Bye Bye Barbara *(with Jack Segal)* Johnny Mathis (US 1964 # 53)
Can I Trust You *(with Eddie Snyder, Emidio Remigi, Al Testa)* The Bachelors (US 1966 # 49; UK # 26)
She Lets Her Hair Down (Early in the Morning) *(with Leon Carr)* The Tokens (US 1969 # 61)

Doc Pomus and Mort Schuman
Pomus born Jerome Solon Felder, New York City 1925. Died 1991.
Schuman born Mortimer Schuman, New York City 1938. Died 1991.
Rock and Roll Hall of Fame 1992.
Songwriters Hall of Fame 1992.

Brooklyn-born Pomus contracted polio as a young boy and spent a year in an iron lung. Although homeschooled for much of his early education, he had a high IQ and a passion for writing his own lyrics to current songs recorded by blues artists, especially those of Big Joe Turner. In 1943, after attending Bushwick High School, he went on to study music and play piano and saxophone at Brooklyn College. While still in his teens, he used the stage name Doc Pomus (partly a nod to blues singer Doctor Calyton) and began performing well-received blues standards in jazz clubs, debuting at Greenwich Village's George's Tavern in front of a largely black audience.

For the next ten years or so, he performed in New York with a band that included King Curtis and Mickey Baker, with a reported fifty recordings to his name with labels such as Chess, Atlantic and Coral. In 1957, when the company that had the rights to his songs learned more about his background and began to take less interest in promoting his career as a singer, Pomus switched to concentrating on his songwriting. His 1956 song "Lonely Avenue" had become a top ten hit for Ray Charles, but had made him little money. After getting married, he sent a demo of the song "Young Blood" to his role models Leiber and Stoller who then rewrote it for the Coasters. With him getting co-credit as lyricist, he received his first royalty check of $2,500 once it became a hit. Now even more convinced about his future, Pomus met 16-year-old composer Mort Shuman, who was dating his younger cousin. Shuman was also born in Brooklyn and had been educated at Abraham Lincoln High School, and as a lover of R&B had studied music at the New York Conservatory.

On meeting Shuman, producer Otis Blackwell introduced them to Hill & Range Music in the Brill Building. With Shuman being more acquainted with current artists, Pomus asked him to compose melodies to his lyrics, although they would also have a hand in both. Pomus was foremost a writer of streetwise blues lyrics, describing the realities of being a teenager rather than painting an idealised portrait. Shuman's strength was with his effortless melodies. Their first success came with Joe Turner's "Love Roller Coaster," an R&B hit in 1957. Two years later, their song "A Teenager In Love" was commissioned by Laurie Records. First intended for the white doo-wop group the Mystics, it was instead given by the label to Dion & the Belmonts to record and went on to score a top five hit in 1959. With the UK's Marty Wilde also having a hit with the song, Pomus and Shuman, as a way of compensation, wrote the lullaby-style song "Hushabye" for the Mystics to record and have their own hit (and a later album track for the Beach Boys).

Further top ten hits were recorded by Fabian and Jimmy Clanton, including "A Mess of Blues," the flip-side to Presley's "It's Now or Never" in 1960. That same year, the writing duo had perhaps their finest moment with "Save the Last Dance For Me." In 1957, Pomus had been inspired to write the lyrics at his wedding to Willi Burke, a Broadway singer-actress. Although not being able to dance with her due to the effects of polio, he insisted she danced with everyone else, which reluctantly she did. As he watched her, he scribbled on a napkin, "Don't forget who's taking you home, and in who's arms you're gonna be," a heartfelt lyric to what would become their most famous song. With Shuman's melody based on a popular Cuban style, it was recorded by the Drifters and produced by Leiber & Stoller. Although intended to be the flip-side of "Nobody But Me," it was deejay Dick Clark who persuaded the label that it was the stronger song. Released several months after lead singer Ben E King left the group, it topped the US charts for three weeks in August 1960.

In 1961, they wrote a trio of songs for Elvis Presley (the first of 25 songs they would pen for the artist). "Surrender" was adapted from the 1901 Neapolitan song "Torna a Surriento (Come Back to Sorrento)" and became both a transatlantic chart-topper and one of the artist's best-selling singles. This was followed by "(Marie's the Name Of) His Latest Flame" and "Little Sister," a double A-side number one in the UK later in the year. These were soon followed by the Drifter's UK number one "Sweets For My Sweet," their first single with new lead singer Charlie Thomas (and a later number one hit for the Searchers). In 1962, Pomus collaborated with Leiber & Stoller on Presley's "She's Not You," another UK chart-topper, while the two of them wrote the beautiful ballad "Can't Get Used To Losing You," a top ten hit for crooner Andy Williams when released the following year.

In 1964, their success continued with "Suspicion." Originally cut as a demo for Presley in 1962, it became a huge hit for Terry Stafford, which led to the re-release of Presley's version (although the flip-side "Kiss Me Quick" became the bigger hit). That same year, their legendary "Viva Las Vegas," was recorded by Presley for the movie of the same name, despite only reaching number 29 on the US charts. Later that year, they moved to England and teamed up with others to write dozens of songs, although it was Shuman who had the greater success, collaborating with US composer J Leslie McFarland to score a UK number one with "Little Children" by Billy J Kramer & the Dakotas. Kramer (real name William Ashton) had been a British Rail fitter until Beatles' manager Brian Epstein signed him in 1963.

In 1965, Pomus had a bad fall that confined him to a wheelchair for the rest of his life. The partnership ended when he left the music business for ten years to become a professional gambler, only returning in the late Seventies to write with B B King and Dr John. Looking back on his career, he revealed: "I didn't want to be the crippled songwriter or the crippled singer. I wanted to be the singer or the songwriter who was crippled. I wanted to be larger than life and a man amongst men."

After writing more hits with others, Shuman moved to Paris to begin a recording career, and in 1968 translated Jacques Brel's lyrics and starred in the stage production of *Jacques Brel Is Alive and Well and Living in Paris*. Many years later, he moved back to London to write for musical productions.

Chart entries
Too Good – Little Tony & His Brothers (UK 1960 # 19)
This Magic Moment – The Drifters (US 1960 # 16); Jay and the Americans (US 1968 # 6)
Lonely Winds – The Drifters (US 1960 # 54)
A Mess Of Blues – Elvis Presley (UK 1960 # 2)
Save the Last Dance For Me – The Drifters (US 1960 # 1; UK # 2)
Wait – Jimmy Clanton (US 1960 # 91)
I'll Save the Last Dance For You – Damita Jo (US 1960 # 22)

I Count the Tears – The Drifters (US 1960 # 17; UK # 28)
Your Other Love – The Flamingos (US 1960 # 54)
No One – Connie Francis (US 1961 # 34); Ray Charles (US 1963 # 21; UK # 35); Brenda Lee (US 1965 # 98)
Havin' Fun – Dion (US 1961 # 42)
A Texan and a Girl From Mexico – Anita Bryant (US 1961 # 85)
Surrender *(adapted)* Elvis Presley (US 1961 # 1; UK # 1)
Little Sister – Elvis Presley (UK 1961 # 1)
(Marie's the Name) His Latest Flame – Elvis Presley (US 1961 # 4; UK # 1)
Sweets For My Sweet – The Drifters (US 1961 # 16); The Searchers (UK 1963 # 1)
Room Full of Tears – The Drifters (US 1961 # 72)
Ecstasy – Ben E King (US 1962 # 56)
Seven Day Weekend – Gary U.S Bond (US 1962 # 27)
Spanish Lace – Gene McDaniels (US 1962 # 31)
Can't Get Used To Losing You – Andy Williams (US 1963 # 2; UK # 2)
It's Been Nice (Goodnight) – Everly Brothers (UK 1963 # 26)
It's A Lonely Town (Lonely Without You) – Gene McDaniels (US 1963 # 64)
Viva Las Vegas - Elvis Presley (US 1964 # 29; UK # 17)
Suspicion – Terry Stafford (US 1964 # 64; UK # 31)
Wrong For Each Other – Andy Williams (US 1964 # 34)
Petticoat White (Summer Sky Blue) – Bobby Vinton (US 1966 # 81)
World Of Broken Hearts – Amen Corner (UK 1967 # 24)
This Magic Moment – Jay & the Americans (US 1968 # 6)
Hushabye – Jay & the Americans (US 1969 # 62)

Doc Pomus and others
First Taste Of Love *(with Phil Spector)* Ben E King (UK 1960 # 27)
She's Not You *(with Jerry Leiber & Mike Stoller)* Elvis Presley (US 1962 # 5; UK # 1)
Don't Try To Change Me *(with Peter Anders & Vini Poncia)* The Crickets (UK 1963 # 37)
Hopeless *(with Alan Jeffreys)* Andy Williams (US 1963 # 13)
Let's Do the Freddie *(with Dave Appell)* Chubby Checker (US 1965 # 40)
I Feel That I've Known You Forever *(with Alan Jeffreys)* Elvis Presley (US 1965 # 70)

Mort Schuman and others
Young Boy Blues *(with Phil Spector)* Ben E King (US 1961 # 66)
Kiss Me Quick *(with Jerome Felder)* Elvis Presley (US 1963 # 34; UK # 14)
Little Children *(with J Leslie McFarland)* Billy J Kramer & the Dakotas (UK 1964 # 1; US # 7)
Here I Go Again *(with Clive Westlake)* The Hollies (UK 1964 # 4)
What Am I To You *(with Clive Westlake & Kenny Lynch)* Kenny Lynch (UK 1964 # 37)
Follow Me *(with Kenny Lynch)* The Drifters (US 1965 # 91)
The River *(with Renato Angiolini)* Ken Dodd (UK 1965 # 3)
Love Is Just a Broken Heart *(with Kenny Lynch & Michelle Vendome)* Cilla Black (UK # 5)
Sha La La La Lee *(with Kenny Lynch)* Small Faces (UK 1966 # 3)
Look At Granny, Run, Run *(with Jerry Ragovoy)* Howard Tate (US 1966 # 19)
Time, Time *(with Armand Canfora, Joss Baselli & Michel Jourdan)* Ed Ames (US 1967 # 61)
What Good Am I? *(with Kenny Lynch)* Cilla Black (UK 1967 # 24)
Daylight Saving Time *(with Jerry Ross)* Keith (US 1967 # 79)
What's It Gonna Be? *(with Jerry Ragovoy)* Dusty Springfield (US 1967 # 49; UK # 52)
Jackie *(with Jacques Brel & Gérard Jouannest)* Scott Walker (UK # 22)
Stop *(with Jerry Ragovoy)* Howard Tate (US 1968 # 76)

Tony Powers see also **Beverly Ross**, **Jeff Barry and Ellie Greenwich**
Born Howard Stanley Puris, New York City 1938.

In the late Fifties, Bronx-born Powers began writing songs for Leiber & Stoller's publishing company Trio Music in New York's Brill Building. One of his first compositions was "Remember Then" which became a hit for the white doo-wop group Larry Chance & the Earls in 1962 (although some versions have Beverly Ross (1934-2022) as co-author). A short while later, he began working alongside Ellie Greenwich, writing "He's Got the Power" by the Exciters, and "This Is It" by Jay & the Americans. With Phil Spector coming on board, they also co-wrote "(Today I Met) The Boy I'm Gonna Marry" by Darlene Love, followed by "Why Do Lovers Break Each Other's Heart?" by Bob B Soxx & the Blue Jeans as a tribute to Frankie Lyman & the Teenagers.

By the mid-Sixties, Powers had signed for Don Kirshner's Screen Gems publishing company, a subsidiary of Colpix Records, and as lyricist teamed up with George Fischoff (1938-2018) to pen "Lazy Day" by Spanky & Our Gang" and "98.6" for Keith (aka James Keefer). The latter title referred to the normal body temperature, symbolising how a woman's love can make you feel healthy and normal again.

By the Seventies, Powers began writing more about social and political issues and released a solo album in 1971.

Chart entries
Remember Then *(with Stan Vincent, Beverly Ross)* The Earls (US 1962 # 24)
Come Dance With Me *(with Matt Maurer)* Jay & the Americans (US 1963 # 76)
All of My Life *(with Helen Miller)* Lesley Gore (US 1965 # 71)
Gotta Have Your Love *(with Jack Keller)* The Sapphires (US 1965 # 77)

Tony Powers and Ellie Greenwich
Why Do Lovers Break Each Other's Heart? *(with Phil Spector)* Bob B Soxx & the Blue Jeans (US 1963 # 38)
He's Got the Power - The Exciters (1963 # 57)
(Today I Met) The Boy I'm Gonna Marry *(with Phil Spector)* Darlene Love (US 1963 # 39)
One Boy Too Late - Mike Clifford (US 1963 # 96)
I Didn't Mean to Hurt You - The Rockin' Berries (UK 1964 # 43)

Tony Powers and George Fishchoff
Run to My Loving Arms - Billy Fury (UK 1965 # 25); Lenny Welch (US 1965 # 96)
Ain't Gonna Lie - Keith (US 1966 # 39)
98.6 - Keith (US 1966 # 7; UK # 24)
Lazy Day - Spanky & Our Gang (US 1967 # 14)

Reg Presley
Born Reginald Maurice Ball, Andover, England 1941. Died 2013.

Leaving school at 15, Ball became an apprentice bricklayer and played bass for a local skiffle group in the evenings. His break came in the early Sixties when a fellow worker Howard Mansfield suggested they form a band called the Troglodytes, with Mansfield as lead singer, along with Dave Wright (guitar), fellow brickie Ronnie Bond (drums) and Ball (bass). When Mansfield and Wright left the group, there was a need to find replacements, and with another local group Ten Foot Five having a similar personnel upheaval, their respective managers suggested the two amalgamate, with survivors Chris Britton (guitar) and Peter Staples (bass) joining the group. Despite initial reluctance, Ball was chosen to be leads singer (he would not be using the stage name Presley until 1966).

In 1965, after rehearsing above the Copper Kettle café in Andover, they won a Battle of the Bands talent contest in Oxford. When the Kinks' manager Larry Page saw the Troglodytes singing a raw rendition of "You Really Got Me," he invited them to send him a demo. Page signed them to his label, Page One Records, and had them record Ball's self-penned "Lost Girl" in London to be released through CBS. At the same time, Page approached *New Musical Express* writer Keith Altham to help find a suitable stage name for Ball and suggested Presley. The name of the group was also abbreviated to the Troggs.

With Page striking a new deal between Page One and the Fontana label, he came across a demo of US writer Chip Taylor's "Wild Thing," which had been an unsuccessful single by the Wild Ones, and gave it to the Troggs to record. Despite misgivings over the corny lyrics, the innuendo-laden arrangement and Presley's mock-seductive vocals saw it peak at number two in the UK charts and going even one better in the US. A dispute over rights in the US saw it released on both Fontana and Atco labels, with Atco coupling it with the band's follow-up single.

With its success, Presley finally quit his bricklaying job, and went on to write most of their remaining chart hits, beginning with "With a Girl Like You," their first and only UK number one, and the lustful "I Can't Control Myself," with its blatantly suggestive lyrics seeing it banned from being played or performed on radio in both the UK and US. The gentle ballad "Any Way That You Want Me," another Chip Taylor song, was far removed from the band's previous garage-rock singles. However, 1967's "Give It To Me" would see a return to their old formula. Presley later revealed: "I don't know anything about music. In my line you don't have to … Truth is like the sun. You can shut it out for a time, but it ain't going away."

Later that year, they released the infectious "Night of the Long Grass," a deliberate change of sound with hints of psychedelia, and it served as a prelude to perhaps their finest song, the ballad "Love Is All Around." Written in just ten minutes by Presley, it was inspired by watching a Sunday afternoon tv program that had the Salvation Army band the Joystrings perform an evangelical song called "Love That's All Around." It became their final top twenty single in the UK (and later a 15-week chart-topper for Wet Wet Wet in 1994). Presley finally announced his retirement following a series of strokes in 2012.

Chart entries
With A Girl Like You – The Troggs (UK 1966 # 1; US # 29)
I Can't Control Myself – The Troggs (UK 1966 # 2; US # 43)
Give It To Me – The Troggs (UK 1967 # 12)
Night Of the Long Grass – The Troggs (1967 # 19)
Love Is All Around – The Troggs (1967 # 4; US # 7)
Little Girl – The Troggs (UK 1968 # 37)

Alan Price see also **Eric Burdon**
Born Fatfield, Durham, England 1942.

Educated at Jarrow Grammar School, Price, became a self-taught musician, starting his music career as part of the Newcastle-based group Kansas City Five, whose initial members were Eric Burdon (b.1941) and drummer John Steel (b.1941), before Geoff Hedley and George Stoves completed the lineup. After disbanding, Price joined the Kon-Tours with bass guitarist Bryan "Chas" Chandler (b.1938), and when Steel joined they became the Alan Price Rhythm & Blues Combo. In 1962, Price invited Burdon to join, with new guitarist Hilton Valentine (b.1943) from Whitley Bay's Wild Cats soon completing the lineup. The band soon adopted the name the Animals because of their raucous live performances, and Price would remain a key part of the group as their organist, recording and touring with them for the next three years. In that time, he was given co-writing credit with Burdon for "I'm Crying", a top ten single in 1964. Burdon's deep gravelly vocal and Price's pulsating organ (a Vox Continental) were key ingredients to the success of songs like "The House of the Rising Sun" and "Don't Let Me Be Misunderstood."

In May 1965, shortly after their cover of "Bring It On Home To Me," Price announced he was leaving the band due to musical disagreements (possibly a feud with Burdon over unpaid royalties for "The House of the Rising Sun"), as well as a growing fear of flying ahead of a planned Swedish tour. His place was taken by Dave Rowberry from the Mike Cotton Sound. He then formed the Alan Price Set with Clive Burrows (baritone sax), Steve Gregory (tenor sax), John Walters (trumpet), Peter Kirtley (guitar), Rod "Boots" Slade (bass) and Little Roy Mills (drums). Quickly securing a contract with Decca, they released their debut single, a cover of Bacharach's "Any Day Now (My Wild Beautiful Bird)." The next single was also a cover. Screamin' Jay Hawkins' "I Put a Spell On You" which had also been a single for Nina Simone, and it may have been her version which inspired Price to record it. According to him, it was "the cheapest record to produce" at a cost of £16. Around this time, Price also made an appearance in D A Pennebaker's *Don't Look Back* documentary film covering Dylan's UK tour.

The much-covered 1952 song "Hi-Lili, Hi-Lo," was followed by Randy Newman's "Simon Smith and the Amazing Dancing Bear," the profits of which also funded the recording of "The House That Jack Built," Price's first self-composed single which he also produced. With the melody coming first, Price struggled with lyrics that described the hobbies of people living under one roof, referring to them as simple "nonsense poetry." The following year the band covered Sonny Rollins' "Don't Stop the Carnival," which peaked at 13 on the charts.

Price went on to be a tv host and later teamed up with his friend Georgie Fame for an album and the 1971 single "Rosetta," written by Mike Snow. Looking back, he simply declared: "Success has a thousand fathers, and failure is an orphan."

Chart hits
I'm Crying (*with Eric Burdon*) The Animals (UK 1964 # 8# US # 19)
The House That Jack Built - Alan Price Set (UK 1967 # 4)
Shame – Alan Price (UK 1967 # 14)

Jerry Ragavoy see also Bert Berns
Born Jordan Ragovoy, Philadelphia Pa 1930. Died 2011.

Ragavoy learned to play piano as a child, and inspired by European classical music wrote his first song at the age of eight, describing it as "a direct steal from the Nutcracker Suite." On leaving school, he also became interested in African-American music while working in a record store, and earned extra money by giving piano lessons. When a group of black teenagers called the Castelles played a demo to the store owner Herb Slotkin, he and Ragavoy decided to form Grand Records to release their songs. With Ragavoy as producer and pianist, the single "My Girl Awaits Me," written by Frank Vance, became an R&B hit. Without much further success, Ragavoy moved to Chancellor Records in Philadelphia and co-wrote "About This Thing Called Love," a b-side to a single by Fabian. Also at the label were the local R&B/doo-wop group the Majors, for which Ragavoy wrote their novelty single, "A Wonderful Dream." Using the pseudonym Norman Margolies, he persuaded the group's lead vocalist to sing falsetto.

Disappointed with the commercialism of the label, Ragavoy moved to New York where he met Bert Berns (aka Bert Russell), a rep for a music publisher whose job was pitching songs to record companies. Berns needed a new song for the black vocal group Garnet Mimms & the Enchanters, and Ragavoy suggested "Cry Baby," an unfinished song he had been working on for months. Completing it with Berns while at his house, it was later recorded by the group with Ragavoy now using the pseudonym Norman Meade, and, with Dionne Warwick on backing vocals, it became a million-seller. Working mainly with Berns, they had a string of hits over the next few years, including "Time Is On My Side" by Irma Thomas (a later hit for the Rolling Stones); "Piece of My Heart" by Erma Franklin (a later hit for Janis Joplin), and the almost-operatic "Stay With Me" by Lorraine Ellison, co-written with George David Weiss (and later recorded as "Stay With Me Baby" by the Walker Brothers).

Away from soul music, Ragavoy also co-wrote two hits with exiled South African Miriam Makeba, and later bought the New York studio, the Hit Factory, where a number of albums were made, including Stevie Wonder's *Songs In the Key Of Life*, before it was sold in 1975.

Chart entries
A Little Bit Now *(with Ed Marshall)* The Majors (US 1962 # 63); The Dave Clark Five
 (US 1967 # 67)
Let's Kiss and Make Up *(with Marjorie McCoy)* Bobby Vinton (US 1962 # 38)
I Can't Wait Until I See My Baby *(with Chip Taylor)* Justine Washington (US 1964 # 93)
A Quiet Place *(with Samuel Bell)* Garnet Mimms & the Enchanters (US 1964 # 78)
I Wanna Thank You *(with Samuel Bell)* The Enchanters (US 1964 # 91)
Time Is On My Side – The Rolling Stones (US 1964 # 6)
Ain't Nobody Home – Howard Tate (US 1966 # 63)
Pata Pata (*with Miriam Makeba)* Miriam Makeba (US 1967 # 12)
Malayisha (*with Miriam Makeba)* Miriam Makeba (US 1968 # 85)

Jerry Ragovoy and Bert Berns
Cry Baby - Garnet Mimms & the Enchanters (US 1963 # 4)
One-Way Love - The Drifters (US 1964 # 56)
It Was Easier To Hurt Her - Wayne Fontana & the Mindbenders (UK 1965 # 36)
I'll Take Good Care Of You - Garnet Mimms (US 1966 # 30)
Heart Be Still - Lorraine Ellison (US 1967 # 89)
Piece Of My Heart - Emma Franklin (US 1967 # 62); Big Brother & the Holding Company
 (US 1968 # 12)

Jerry Ragovoy and Mort Schuman
Look At Granny, Run, Run - Howard Tate (US 1966 # 19)
What's It Gonna Be? - Dusty Springfield (US 1967 # 49; UK # 52)
Stop - Howard Tate (US 1968 # 76)

Jerry Ragovoy and George David Weiss
Stay With Me - Lorraine Ellison (US 1966 # 64); The Walker Brothers (as Stay With Me Baby)
 (UK 1967 # 26)

Ben Raleigh
Born New York 1913. Died 1997 (kitchen fire).

Raleigh began his music career by teaming up with Bernie Wayne (1919-1993) to write a number of hits in the early Sixties. Wayne was best known for the much-covered "Blue Velvet," which he co-wrote with Lee Morris in 1951. In the meantime, Raleigh and Wayne found early chart success with "You Walk By," a 1941 hit for Eddy Duchin and his Orchestra, and "Laughing on the Outside (Crying on the Inside)" originally a hit for Teddy Walters in 1946. In 1955, he partnered New York-born Sherman Edwards (1919-1981) to write "Wonderful! Wonderful!" an early hit for crooner Johnny Mathis, and a later hit for the Tymes. More success followed with Don Wolf, but it was his pairing with Jeff Barry that gave him his biggest success. Recorded by Ricky Valance in 1960, Barry's lyrics to "Tell Laura I Love Her" originally concerned a rodeo, not a car race, as the writer loved cowboy culture. With the label preferring the song to resemble "Teen Angel," the chart-topping tale of teenage car tragedy, Barry re-wrote the lyrics accordingly. Raleigh also wrote songs with Mark Barkan (1934-2020), including several for Leslie Gore, including the 1963 hit "She's a Fool," produced by Quincy Jones.

Later moving into tv work, he co-wrote with Earl Hagen the theme to the 1967 ABC sitcom *Rango,* and, more famously, the theme song to 1969's *Scooby Doo, Where Are You!* with David Mook (and sung by Larry Marks).

Chart entries
Exclusively Yours *(with Don Wolf)* Carl Dobkins Jr (US 1960 # 62); Mark Wynter (UK 1961 # 32)
Tell Laura I Love Her *(with Jeff Barry)* Ricky Valance (UK 1960 # 1)
Queen For Tonight *(with Artie Wayne)* Helen Shapiro (UK 1963 # 33)
That's How Heartaches Are Made *(with Bob Halley)* Baby Washington (US 1963 # 40); The Marvelettes (US 1969 # 97)
Wonderful! Wonderful! *(with Sherman Edwards)* The Tymes (US 1963 # 7)
Your Other Love *(with Klaus Ogermann)* Connie Francis (US 1963 # 28)
Midnight Mary *(with Artie Wayne)* Joey Powers (US 1963 # 10)
Blue Winter *(with John Gluck)* Connie Francis (US 1964 # 24)
Love Is All We Need *(with Don Wolf)* Vic Dana (US 1964 # 53); Mel Carter (US 1966 # 50)
Love Is a Hurtin' Thing *(with Dave Linden)* Lou Rawls (US 1966 # 13)
You Can Bring Me All Your Heartaches *(with H B Barnum)* Lou Rawls (US 1966 # 55)
Dead End Street *(with Lou Rawls, David Axelrod)* Lou Rawls (US 1967 # 29)

Ben Raleigh and Mark Barkan
Hercules - Frankie Vaughan (UK 1962 # 42)
She's a Fool - Leslie Gore (US 1963 # 5)
That's the Way Boys Are - Leslie Gore (US 1964 # 12)
Do You Really Love Me Too - Billy Fury (UK 1964 # 13)
I Don't Wanna Be a Loser - Leslie Gore (US 1964 # 37)
Bring a Little Sunshine To My Heart - Vic Dana (US 1965 # 66

Otis Redding
Born Otis Ray Redding Jr, Dawson, Georgia 1941. Died 1967 (plane crash).
Rock and Roll Hall of Fame 1989.
Songwriters Hall of Fame 1994.
Grammy Lifetime Achievement Award 1999.

Redding was one of six children born to a sharecropping family, whose father was a part-time preacher in local Baptist churches. When he was three, they moved to Macon where he later sang in a Baptist church choir and went on to learn to play piano, guitar and drums, as well as having singing lessons. While attending Ballard-Hudson High School, he was a regular member of the school band. This also led to appearances on the local radio station WIBB, with singing inspired by his heroes Sam Cooke and Little Richard. When his father became too ill to support the family, Redding quit school in tenth grade to take various jobs, occasionally earning money singing and playing in local clubs. In 1958, he took part on deejay Hamp Swain's *Teenage Party* talent show which was broadcast on radio on Saturday mornings. His imitation of Little Richard proved a success, and he went on to win for 15 consecutive weeks.

During a performance with a backing band at the Douglass Theatre in Macon, he was spotted by local guitarist Johnny Jenkins, who after being unimpressed by his band, asked Redding to back him instead. As a result, he replaced Willie Jones as frontman of Jenkins' group Pat T Cake & the Mighty Panthers.

After a short stay with the Upsetters, Little Richard's former backing band, Redding moved to Los Angeles in mid-1960 and recorded several singles for Fine Art Records, including "She's All Right," co-written with James McEachin. After touring the southern states, Jenkins left the band to become frontman of the Pinetoppers, while Redding met Bobby Smith and signed with his label Confederate Records. With them, he recorded the single "Shout Bamalama" as Otis and the Shooters.

With Jenkins looking for another label, Atlantic showed an interest and Redding drove Jenkins and his band to the Stax studio in Memphis. Although the session with Jenkins was unproductive (despite being backed by house band Booker T and the MGs), spare studio time allowed Redding to perform two songs, one of which, the self-penned ballad "These Arms of Mine," had Jenkins on guitar and Steve Cropper on piano. It impressed studio manager Jim Stewart enough to see its potential and have Redding release the song as a single on their new Volt label. It peaked at number 20 on the R&B chart in early 1963. Further sessions produced the singles "That's What My Heart Needs" and "Pain In My Heart," the latter an adapted cover of Irma Thomas's current R&B hit "Ruler of My Heart," which led to copyright issues with its writer Naomi Neville.

On the strength of these hits, Redding secured a residency at Harlem's Apollo Theatre for $400 a week, backed by King Curtis's house band. In May 1964, his debut album *Pain In My Heart* was released, as well as the extracted single, the slow-tempo and much-covered "Security." Later that year, Redding teamed up with guitarist Cropper to write the single "Mr Pitiful," in response to the nickname Memphis deejay Moonah Williams had given Redding for sounding pitiful while singing ballads. When Cropper heard of this, it was his suggestion to write the song, which was done in about ten minutes. "I've Been Loving You Too Long (To Stop Now)," written with ex-Impressions singer Jerry Butler in a Buffalo, New York hotel room, became Redding's breakthrough single on the Hot 100, peaking at 21 in June 1965.

Later that year, Earl "Speedo" Sims of the Singing Demons brought the ballad "Respect" to Redding's attention. Uncertain of who did the original lyrics, Redding rewrote them and sped up the tempo for Sims and his band to record it. With sessions at Muscle Shoals failing to produce a good version, Redding then had Sims permission to record it himself with producer Cropper. Although becoming a top five R&B success, two years later it would give Aretha Franklin a million-selling chart topper. With the success of the album *Otis Blue/Otis Redding Sings Soul,* Redding was able to buy a ranch in Georgia. After an acclaimed performance at the Whisky-G-Go in Los Angeles (one of the first soul artists to do so), he returned to Stax and recorded a cover of the standard ballad "Try a Little Tenderness," originally written in 1932. His soulful opening and frenetic conclusion made his version definitive.

In August 1966, Redding launched his own label, Jotis Records, and among its acts was Arthur Conley, for whom Redding wrote and produced "Sweet Soul Music," a reworking of Sam Cooke's "Yeh Man." In June 1967, he duetted with Stax's Carla Thomas (daughter of Rufus) on an adaption of Lowell Fulson's song "Tramp" while also becoming the closing act at the Monterey Pop Festival. After an extensive tour of the UK, he returned to the studio in December to record "(Sittin' on) The Dock of the Bay." He had begun writing the lyrics in August while on a rented houseboat in Sausalito and then completed it with Cropper in Memphis, where sound effects were added, along with Redding's whistling (either intentionally or because he forgot Cropper's "fadeout rap.")

Four days after the recording, Redding took a flight to Madison, Wisconsin, with his rock band, the Bar-Keys but the plane went down in icy waters in a lake near Madison, killing all but one member of the band. Stax Records, at the time on the verge of bankruptcy, were devastated with the loss, and also discovered that the Atco division of Atlantic still owned the rights to their best-selling artist's back catalog.

Redding once offered advice for writers: "You've got to concentrate on the business of entertaining and writing songs. Always think different from the next person. Don't ever do a song as you heard somebody else do it."

Chart entries
These Arms of Mine – Otis Redding (US 1963 # 85)
Come to Me *(with Phil Walden)* Otis Redding (US 1964 # 69)
Security – Otis Redding (US 1964 # 97); Etta James (US 1968 # 35; UK # 53)
Chained and Bound – Otis Redding (US 1964 # 70)
I've Been Loving You Too Long (to Stop Now) *(with Jerry Butler)* Otis Redding (US
    1965 # 21); Ike & Tina Turner (US 1969 # 68)
Respect – Otis Redding (US 1965 # 35); The Rationals (US 1966 # 92); Aretha Franklin (US
    1967 # 1; UK # 10)
I Can't Turn You Loose – Otis Redding (UK 1965 # 29); Chamber Brothers (US 1968 # 37)
My Lover's Prayer – Otis Redding (US 1966 # 61; UK # 37)
Fa-Fa-Fa-Fa-Fa (Sad Song) *(with Steve Cropper)* Otis Redding (US 1966 # 29; UK # 23)
Sweet Soul Music *(with Arthur Conley, Sam Cooke)* Arthur Conley (US 1967 # 2; UK # 7)
Let Me Come On Home *(with Al Jackson Jr, Booker T Jones)* Otis Redding (UK 1967 # 48)
Shout Bamalama – Mickey Murray (US 1967 # 54)

(Sittin' on) The Dock of the Bay *(with Steve Cropper)* Otis Redding (US 1968 # 1; UK # 3);
King Curtis (US 1968 # 84); Sérgio Mendes (US 1969 # 66); The Dells (US 1969 # 42)
The Happy Song (Dum Dum) *(with Steve Cropper)* Otis Redding (US 1968 # 25; UK # 24)
Amen – Otis Redding (US 1968 # 36)
I've Got Dreams To Remember *(with Zelma Redding)* Otis Redding (US 1968 # 41)
Hard to Handle *(with Allen Jones, Alvertis Isbell)* Patti Drew (US 1968 # 93)
Love Man – Otis Redding (US 1969 # 72; UK # 43)

Les Reed see Barry Mason and Les Reed

Keith Reid see Gary Brooker and Keith Reid

Artie Resnick and Kenny Young
Born Arthur Resnick, New York 1937.
Young born Shalom Giskan, Jerusalem 1941. Died 2020.
Songwriters Hall of Fame 2012.

After attending Valley Forge Military Academy, Resnick became a songwriter, working out of the Brill Building in New York. His first success came with co-writing "Chip Chip" with Jeff Barry and Clifford Crofford, and giving Gene McDaniels a top ten hit in 1962. Two years later, he met Shalom Giskan. Born in Jerusalem, he had moved with his parents to the US as a child and was raised in Manhattan. He later attended the City University of New York where he studied psychology and sociology. By the age of 22, he had changed his name to Kenny Young and was working as a songwriter for Bobby Darin's TM Music at the Brill Building.

His first chart success as writer was "Please Don't Kiss Me Again" for the New York-based trio the Charmettes, which became an R&B hit in 1963. The following year, Resnick and Young scored their first hit with the Drifters' "Under the Boardwalk." With an opening line that references the group's prior hit "Up on the Roof," it was recorded the day after the groups' lead singer Rudy Lewis died from a suspected drug overdose. Instead of rescheduling the session, the song was recorded by their other lead vocalist Johnny Moore. Despite the change, it became a top five hit and a much-covered classic. More hits followed, including "One Kiss For Old Times' Sake" and "A Little Bit of Heaven" for pop and country singer Ronnie Dove, while Young also self-penned "When Liking Turns to Loving" for him.

The following year, Resnick wrote "Good Lovin'" with Rudy Clark (1935-2020), a minor hit for the Olympics, but later giving the Rascals' a UK chart-topper. Meanwhile, Young's success continued with hits for Herman's Hermits and the Seekers, and with Ben Yardley he wrote the memorable "Captain of Your Ship" for girl group Reparata & the Delrons. Young also had a career as a singer, and released several singles both as solo artist and with groups including the Squirrels.

In the late Sixties, Young wrote top ten singles for Irish singer Clodagh Rodgers, including her first and biggest hit, "Come Back and Shake Me." He had first seen her perform with the group Honeybus on the UK tv show *Colour Me Pop,* and after meeting her and husband/manager Johnny Morris, agreed to write and produce for her.

In 1966, Resnick formed the group The Third Rail with his wife Kris and singer/producer Joey Levine, and wrote and recorded "Run, Run, Run," a modest hit for them in 1967. Resnick and Levine then set up a writing partnership as part of Super K Productions, the company behind what was termed "bubblegum" pop, and achieved success with hits for the Ohio Express and the Kasenetz-Katz Singing Orchestral Circus. Young, meanwhile, went on to have a solo career as a singer-songwriter and released two albums, later forming, producing and singing with two UK bands, Fox and Yellow Dog.

Chart entries
Under the Boardwalk - The Drifters (US 1964 # 4; UK # 45)
I've Got Sand in My Shoes - The Drifters (US 1964 # 33)
One Kiss For Old Time's Sake - Ronnie Dove (US 1965 #14)
The Record (Baby I Love You) Ben E King (US 1965 # 84)
A Little Bit of Heaven - Ronnie Dove (US 1965 # 16)

Artie Resnick
Chip Chip *(with Jeff Barry, Clifford Crawford)* Gene McDaniels (US 1962 # 10)
I Left My Heart in the Balcony *(with Jeff Barry)* Linda Scott (US 1962 # 74)
Never Love a Robin *(with Mickey Gentile)* Bobby Vee (US 1963 # 99)
Good Lovin' *(with Rudy Clark)* The Olympics (US 1965 # 81); The Rascals (US 1966 # 1)

Artie Resnick and Joey Levine
That's the Tune - The Vogues (US 1966 # 99)
Run, Run, Run *(with Kris Resnick)* The Third Rail (US 1967 # 53)
Yummy, Yummy, Yummy - Ohio Express (US 1968 # 4; UK # 5)
Down at Lulu's - Ohio Express (US 1968 # 33)
Quick Joey Small (Run, Joey, Run) The Kazenetz-Katz Singing Orchestral Circus (US 1968
    #25; UK # 19)
Chewy Chewy - Ohio Express (US 1968 # 15)
Sweeter Than Sugar - Ohio Express (US 1969 # 96)
Mercy - Ohio Express (US 1969 # 30)

Kenny Young
Please Don't Kiss Me Again – The Charmettes (US 1963 # 100)
Just a Little Bit Better – Herman's Hermits (UK 1965 # 15; US # 7)
When Liking Turns to Loving – Ronnie Dove (US 1966 # 18)
Don't Go Out in the Rain (You're Gonna Melt) Herman's Hermits (US 1967 # 18)
When Will the Good Apples Fall – The Seekers (UK 1967 # 11)
Captain of Your Ship *(with Ben Yardley)* Reparata & the Delrons (UK 1968 # 13)
Come Back and Shake Me – Clodagh Rodgers (UK 1969 # 3)
Goodnight Midnight – Clodagh Rodgers (UK 1969 # 4)
Biljo – Clodagh Rodgers (UK 1969 # 22)
Highway Song – Nancy Sinatra (UK 1969 # 21)
Arizona – Mark Lindsay (US 1969 # 10)

Deke Richards
Born Dennis Lussier, Los Angeles 1944. Died 2013.

The son of a Hollywood screenwriter, Richards was 18 when he appeared in the horror comedy movie *Eegah: The Name Written in Blood.* By the mid-Sixties, he had adopted his stage name and was fronting the band Deke & the Deacons. In 1966, after meeting Berry Gordy Jr while the Supremes were performing at the Hollywood Palace, he signed for Motown's fledgling operation in Los Angeles as producer and songwriter. He also met up with Debbie Dean (1928-2001), who his band had once backed. She had been the first white artist to sign for Motown in 1960, but had since lost touch with them. Richards managed to get her reconnected with the label and the two of them became songwriting partners. One of their songs was "I Can't Dance To That Music You're Playing," a hit for Martha Reeves & the Vandellas in 1968. The following year, Richards became part of the Corporation, with Berry Gordy, Freddie Perren, and Alphonzo Mizell, a group put together to write hit songs for the label's new artists, the Jackson 5.

In 1971, Richards and fellow writer Sherlie Matthews formed the vocal sextet Celebration and released an album on Motown's West Coast label Mowest, as an attempt to replicate the success of the Fifth Dimension. Richards also wrote the hits "I'm Still Waiting" and "Doobedood'Ndoobe, Doobedood'Ndoobe" for Diana Ross.

Chart entries
Bless You *(with Berry Gordy, Freddie Perren, Fonz Mizell)* Tony Orlando (US 1961 # 15;
    UK # 5)
I Can't Dance To That Music You're Playing *(with Debbie Dean)* Marhta Reeves & the Vandellas
    (US 1968 # 42)
Love Child *(with Henry Cosby, Frank Wilson, Pam Sawyer, R Dean Taylor)* Diana Ross & the
    Supremes (US 1968 # 1; UK # 15)
I Want You Back *(with Berry Gordy, Freddie Perren, Fonz Mizell)* Jackson 5 (US 1969 # 1;
    UK # 2)

Keith Richards see Mick Jagger and Keith Richards

Robbie Robertson
Born Jamie Royal Robertson, Toronto Canada 1943. Died 2023.
Rock and Roll Hall of Fame (with The Band).
Grammy Lifetime Achievement Award 2008 (with the Band).

Robertson's mother was Cayuga and Mohawk, raised on a reserve near Toronto, before marrying in 1942. As a boy, he was taught guitar by a cousin on the reserve and listened to Rock and R&B on the radio. At 16, after having summer jobs in a travelling circus, he joined the band Little Caesar & the Consuls and for a year performed at local dances. In 1957, he formed Robbie & the Rhythm Chords along with a friend, but soon changed the name to Robbie & the Robots. When they added a pianist, they became the Suede. After opening for Arkansas-based Ronnie Hawkins & the Hawks, Robertson heard Hawkins say they wanted new songs to record, and then spent the night writing two and handing them to Hawkins the next day. Impressed with the songs, he recorded both for their new album and invited Robertson to the Brill Building to help choose more songs.

When the Hawks' bass player left the band, Robertson was invited to replace him, but soon switched to playing lead guitar and learning new techniques from temporary band member Roy Buchanan. He also became friends with the band's drummer Levon Helm, as well as Rick Danko, Richard Manuel and Garth Hudson, who joined in 1961. The lineup would later become the Band. When the Hawks left Hawkins to go on their own in early 1964, they became the Levon Helm Sextet and later Levon and the Hawks. The following year, they recorded their own singles, including Robertson's "The Stones I Throw," and also worked on an album by blues artist John P Hammond.

In August 1965, Robertson and the band began working with Bob Dylan after being recommended to Albert Grossman by his secretary Mary Martin. They joined him for his world tour and were present when an angry folk-lover in the audience shouted out "Judas!" In 1966, Dylan sustained injuries in a motorcycle crash and quit touring for a time. The following year, he invited the band to Woodstock, New York, to work on new music, with some of the members renting a nearby house dubbed Big Pink. Recordings by Dylan and the band were carried out in the basement all through the summer, with Robertson and the musicians developing a sound of their own. Capitol then brought them to New York to begin recording songs with producer John Simon, and then on to Los Angeles to complete the album, *Music From Big Pink,* released in August 1968.

Robertson wrote four of the tracks, including "The Weight," "To Kingdom Come," (with Robertson on lead vocal), "Caledonia Mission," and "Chest Fever." "The Weight" was inspired by watching films made by director Luis Buñuel, which reflected the recurring theme about the impossibility of sainthood, while Nazareth is a reference to the Pennsylvania town, which was also the place where his guitar had been made.

The following year, the Band rented a Hollywood Hills home from Sammy Davis Jr to record their eponymous album, loosely based on themes of old Americana. Robertson's single "Rag Mama Rag," with Helm singing what were mainly nonsensical lyrics, would achieved the band's highest chart placing in the UK, although not released there until early 1970. For many, the highlight of the album was Robertson's Civil War-themed "The Night They Drove Old Dixie Down," a first-person narrative about a white Southerner's life in the dying days of the war, although in more recent times questions were raised about the lyrics endorsing slavery and "Lost Cause" ideology. Despite its popularity, it was seldom sung live, one of the reasons being that Helm was in dispute with Robertson over songwriting credit. Whatever its merits, it was confined to the b-side of the single "Up on Cripple Creek," a Roberton song that dealt with long-distance truck driving.

In 1971, Joan Baez would record a slightly more sanitised version of "The Night They Drove Old Dixie Down" and take it to number three on the US charts.

Chart entries
The Weight – The Band (US 1968 # 63); Jackie De Shannon (US 1968 # 55), Aretha Franklin
   (US 1969 # 19); Diana Ross & Supremes & Temptations (US 1969 # 49)
Up On Cripple Creek - The Band (US 1969 # 25)

Smokey Robinson
Born William Robinson Jr, Detroit, Michigan 1940.
Rock and Roll Hall of Fame 1987.
Songwriters Hall of Fame 1990.
Grammy Lifetime Achievement Award 1999.

Born into a poor family, his parents divorced when he was three, and when his mother died he went to live with his older sister. It was his favourite uncle and godfather who gave him the cowboy nickname "Smokey Joe" for his love of Westerns. Attending Northern High School, he was both an excellent scholar and promising athlete, but his main interest was music. With a young Aretha Franklin living several houses away, he often heard her playing piano, and was also influenced by listening to Detroit-native Barrett Strong on the radio, as well as groups like Billy Ward & his Dominoes and Nolan Strong & the Diablos. In 1955 he formed a doo-wop vocal group called the Five Chimes with school friends Warren "Pete" Moore and Ronald White. Two years later, they expanded to become the Matadors, with cousins Bobby & Emerson Rogers. Guitarist Marv Tarplin was added to the group several years later.

Once established on the Detroit club scene, they changed their name to the Miracles, and with Emerson joining the army, he was replaced by his sister Claudette (who would go on to marry Robinson). In 1957, they failed an audition for Jackie

Wilson's manager at Brunswick Records, but then met Berry Gordy Jr, who had just written "Reet Petite" for Wilson, a singer who was still working at the Ford factory and trying to get a full-time career in music. Impressed with Robinson's vocals and the extent of his songwriting, many of which were done at high school, Gordy helped secure them a deal with End Records. Their first single, "Got A Job," written by Gordy and Tyran Carlo, was released in 1958 as an answer song to the Silhouettes' "Get a Job." Robinson, who was attending college at the time, dropped out to pursue his new career. Now becoming closely involved with the group, Gordy released the Berry-Robinson single "Bad Girl" to the Chess label and it became their first US chart hit. In 1960, with the help of a loan and royalties from Wilson and Marv Johnson, Gordy formed his own company, Motown Records, with the Miracles becoming the first to sign with their subsidiary label Tamla.

For their debut single "Shop Around," Gordy and Robinson described a mother giving her grown-up son advice on how to find a woman worthy of being his wife. Once re-recorded as a more pop version, it became Motown's first million-seller, just missing out on the chart's top spot. It was the beginning of one of the most successful careers for the label, with Robinson responsible for 26 top forty hits as chief songwriter, producer and lead singer. As producer, he was also tasked with overseeing the development of the label's female artists Mary Wells and the Supremes, although he was unable to mold the latter into hit-making artists. That was not the case with the Miracles.

The self-penned beat-ballad "You've Really Got a Hold on Me," was written in a hotel room while on business in New York, taking inspiration from hearing Sam Cooke's "Bring It On Home To Me." Originally released as a b-side to "Happy Landing," it reached the top ten in its own right. Robinson had a gift for being able to turn out high-quality songs to order, and adept at writing for other Motown artists, with Bob Dylan later referring to him as "America's greatest living poet." In early 1964, Robinson and band member Bobby Rogers penned "The Way You Do the Things You Do" for the Temptations, their first charting single, and the same year he wrote and produced "My Guy" for his protégé Mary Wells, a chart-topping hit for Motown's first female star. The song was about a woman rejecting a sexual advance while affirming her fidelity to her boyfriend, and during the recording Wells jokingly sang over the song's outro with a Mae West-style huskiness, but the producers loved it, saying, "Keep it going, keep it going."

The following year, "My Girl", written by Robinson and Ronald White, gave the Temptations their first number one hit and the first with David Ruffin on lead vocal. Inspired by Robinson's love for his wife and Miracles' member Claudette, the song was written in the Apollo Theater when the Temptations were performing as part of a package tour with the Miracles. While working on the song at a piano, he was joined by his band mate Ronald White and together they completed the song. Rather than have the Miracles record it, Robinson had Temptations' David Ruffin in mind, someone who he had described as the group's "sleeping giant." (Eddie Kendricks and Paul Williams had previously sung lead on their records). On their return to Detroit, Robinson and White produced the single, allowing them to create their own background vocals, including their "hey hey hey," while White's opening bass line became one of the most recognisable guitar riffs in pop history.

July 1965 brought with it one of the band's finest recordings. The multi-award winning "The Tracks of My Tears" was written by Robinson with band members Warren Moore and Marv Tarplin. Robinson was looking in the mirror one day and thinking to himself, "What if a person would cry so much that you could see tracks of their tears in their face?" It took him six months to write the lyrics to Tarplin's melody, a riff developed after listening to Harry Belefonte's calypso-tinged "The Banana Boat Song(Day-O)." When it was first recorded, Robinson left out the last chorus and instead faded it out on the "I need you, I need you" line, but at a meeting with label executives he was convinced to end it on the chorus. Despite being a top 20 hit in the US, it would do much better when re-released in 1969, and is now cited as one of the greatest singles of all time.

Also in 1965, Robinson and band members wrote "Ain't That Peculiar" for Marvin Gaye, while also collaborating on "Going To A Go-Go," a hit for the Miracles as their debut UK chart entry. The next year, the Temptations scored another top 30 hit with Robinson's "Get Ready." Written as an answer to the latest dance craze called "the Duck," the uptempo song featured Eddie Kendrick's distinct falsetto.

In April 1967, the lyrically-impressive single "The Love I Saw In You Was Just a Mirage" became the first to be credited to Smokey Robinson & the Miracles, confirming the artist's status. That same year, "I Second That Emotion," written with staff writer Al Cleveland, was inspired when the two of them were shopping in Detroit and Robinson bought pearls for his wife. When the salesperson said "I sure hopes she likes them," he replied, "I second that emotion."

The arrival of Holland-Dozier-Holland, as well as the writing team of Norman Whitfield and Barrett Strong, would impact on Robinson as top writer and producer, as did the growing trend of artists like Stevie Wonder and Marvin Gaye composing their own material. Robinson stayed on with the label as vice president for a while, and the song "Tears of a Clown," written with Hank Cosby and Stevie Wonder as an album track back in 1967, was resurrected in 1970, becoming their first US and UK chart-topper. Wonder had first come up with the instrumental track but could not find lyrics to suit, and it was Robinson who suggested that the distinctive organ motif sounded like a circus and provided lyrics that reflected that vision.

Robinson commenced a successful solo career in 1973, culminating with the single "Being There" topping the Uk charts in 1981. He finally left Motown in 1999.

Chart entries
Who's Loving You – The Miracles (US 1960 # 66); Brenda & the Tabulations (US 1967 # 66)

What's So Good About Goodbye – The Miracles (US 1962 # 35)
Your Heart Belongs To Me – The Supremes (US 1962 # 95)
The One Who Really Loves You – Mary Wells (US 1962 # 8)
Two Lovers - Mary Wells (US 1962 # 7)
You've Really Got A Hold On Me - The Miracles (US 1962 # 8)
A Breathtaking Guy – The Supremes (US 1963 # 75)
Laughing Boy – Mary Wells (US 1963 # 15)
What's So Easy For Two Is So Hard For One – Mary Wells (US 1963 # 29)
As Long As I Know He's Mine – The Marvelettes (US 1963 # 47)
He's A Good Guy (Yes He Is) - The Marvelettes (US 1964 # 55)
(You Can't Let the Boy Overpower) The Man In You – The Miracles (US 1964 # 59); Chuck Jackson (US 1968 # 94)
My Guy – Mary Wells (US 1964 # 1; UK # 5)
I'll Be In Trouble – The Temptations (US 1964 # 33)
You're My Remedy – The Marvelettes (US 1964 # 48)
When I'm Gone – Brenda Holloway (US 1965 # 25)
Operator – Brenda Holloway (US 1965 # 78)
Don't Mess With Bill – The Marvelettes (US 1966 # 7)
Get Ready - The Temptations (US 1966 # 29; UK 1969 # 10)
You're the One – The Marvelettes - (US 1966 # 48)
The Hunter Gets Captured By the Game – The Marvelettes (US 1967 # 13)
More Love - The Miracles (US 1967 # 23)
My Baby Must Be A Magician – The Marvelettes (US 1967 # 17)
If You Can Wait – The Miracles (US 1968 # 11; UK # 50)
(You Can't Let the Boy Overpower) The Man In You – Chuck Jackson (US 1968 # 94)
Here I Am Baby - The Marvelettes (US 1968 # 44)
I'm Gonna Hold On As Long As I Can – The Marvelettes (US 1969 # 76)
I'll Try Something New – Diana Ross & the Supremes & the Temptations (US 1969 # 25)
The Composer – Diana Ross & the Supremes (US 1969 # 27)

Smokey Robinson and Berry Gordy Jr
Shop Around - The Miracles (US 1960 # 2)
Ain't It Baby – The Miracles (US 1961 # 49)
Don't Let Him Shop Around (*with Loucye Gordy Wakefield*) Debbie Dean (US 1961 # 92)
Broken Hearted – The Miracles (US 1961 # 97)
Way Over There – The Miracles (US 1962 # 94)
Too Wrongs Don't Make A Right – Mary Wells (US 1963 # 100)
A Love She Can Count On – The Miracles (US 1963 # 31)
I'll Try Something New – The Miracles (US 1962 # 39); Diana Ross & the Supremes & The Temptations (US 1969 # 25)

Smokey Robinson and Ronald White
Everybody's Got To Pay Some Dues - The Miracles (US 1961 # 52)
You Beat Me To the Punch - Mary Wells (US 1962 # 9)
You Threw A Lucky Punch *(with Don Covay)* Gene Chandler (US 1962 # 49
Come On Do the Jerk *(with Bobby Rogers)* The Miracles (US 1964 # 50)
My Girl - The Temptations (US 1965 # 1; UK # 43); Otis Redding (UK 1965 # 11); Bobby Vee (US 1968 # 35)
My Girl Has Gone *(with Pete Moore, Ronald White, Marv Tarplin)* The Miracles (US 1965 # 14)
My Baby *(with Pete Moore & Ronald White)* The Temptations (US 1965 # 13)
Don't Look Back *(with Ronald White)* The Temptations US 1965 # 83)

Smokey Robinson and Al Cleveland
I Second That Emotion - The Miracles (US 1967 # 4; UK # 27; Diana Ross & the

Supremes & the Temptations (UK 1969 # 18)
Girls, Girls, Girls – Chuck Jackson (UK 1968 # 59)
Yester Love - The Miracles (US 1968 # 31)
Special Occasion - The Miracles (US 1968 # 26)
Malinda (*with Terry Johnson*) Bobby Taylor & the Vancouvers (US 1968 # 48)
Baby, Baby Don't Cry (*with Terry Johnson*) The Miracles (US 1969 # 8)
Doggone Right (*with Terry Johnson*) The Miracles (US 1969 # 32)
Here I Go Again (*with Pete Moore, Terry Johnson*) The Miracles (US 1969 # 37)
Point It Out - The Miracles (US 1969 # 37)

Smokey Robinson and others
The Way You Do The Things You Do (*with Bobby Rogers*) The Temptations (US 1964 # 11)
I Like It Like That *(with Marv Tarplin)* The Miracles (US 1964 # 27)
That's What Love Is Made Of (*with Bobby Rogers & Warren Moore*) The Miracles (US 1964 # 35)
I'll Be Doggone (*with Pete Moore & Marv Tarplin*) Marvin Gaye (US 1965 # 8)
Ooh Baby Baby *(with Pete Moore)* The Miracles (US 1965 # 16); The Five Stairsteps (US 1967 # 63)
It's Growing (*with Pete Moore*) The Temptations (US 1965 # 18)
The Tracks Of My Tears (*with Pete Moore & Marv Tarplin*) The Miracles (US 1965 # 16); Johnny Rivers (US 1967 # 10)
Since I Lost My Baby (*with Pete Moore*) The Temptations (US 1965 # 17)
First I Look At the Purse *(with Bobby Rogers)* The Contours (US 1965 # 57)
Ain't That Peculiar (*with Pete Moore, Marv Tarplin, Bobby Rogers*) Marvin Gaye (US 1965 # 8)
Going To A Go-Go (*with Pete Moore, Bobby Rogers, Marv Tarplin*) The Miracles (US 1965 # 11)
One More Heartache (*with Pete Moore, Bobby Rogers, Marv Tarplin*) Marvin Gaye (US 1966 # 29)
Take This Heart Of Mine (*with Pete Moore, Marv Tarplin*) Marvin Gaye (US 1966 # 16; UK # 56)
The Love I Saw In You Was Just A Mirage *(with Marv Tarplin)* The Miracles (US 1967 # 20

Tommy Roe
Born Thomas David Roe, Atlanta Georgia 1942.

In 1958, while still attending Brown High School, Roe formed a rock and roll combo called Tommy Roe & the Satins and played at school hops and fraternity parties held at Georgia University. With their performances heavily influenced by Buddy Holly & the Crickets, Roe was offered a solo contract by local label Judd Records, run by Judd Phillips, brother of Sun Records' Sam Phillips. The band recorded "Sheila," a song Roe had written at the age of 14 about a girl called Freda he had a crush on at school. With Phillips unhappy with the name, he sent Roe home to think of a different title, and when his aunt Sheila came to visit that weekend, as Roe later recalled, "the rest is history!" Unfortunately, the label only gave it local promotion without going national. After graduation, Roe worked as a technician at the General Electric Company and spent evenings and weekends performing live gigs, some of them on radio with Atlanta deejay Paul Drew. When Drew recommended them to producer Felton Jarvis at ABC/Paramount Records, Jarvis recognised their potential, especially Roe's songwriting, and signed them to the label.

In 1962, "Sheila" was re-recorded in a similar vein to Holly's "Peggy Sue" with a drum-laden intro and Roe's Holly-like vocal. Roe recalled being a little apprehensive with the recording: "I wasn't really crazy about the whole idea because I was a big fan of Buddy Holly's and I felt like we were sponging off of him and his whole sound." Originally released as a b-side, sufficient airplay saw it enter the charts, and given a $5,000 advance Roe was able to quit his job and go on a promotional tour. Three months later, the song hit the number one spot for three weeks and became a million-seller. Following a revival of Robin Luke's "Susie Darlin,'" Roe embarked on a UK tour, headlining with Chris Montez, and with its success the label released a cover of Merle Kilgore's "The Folk Singer," later becoming a UK top ten hit. A few months later, Roe's self-penned, gospel-styled rocker "Everybody" would repeat its success.

Capitalising on his recent UK fame, Roe would soon move to England to live there for several years. In 1964, he was invited by producer George Martin to support the Beatles at their first US concert in Washington, and, to avoid being drafted volunteered to join the US Army Reserves. On his return two years later, his bubblegum-style "Sweet Pea" saw a return to the charts, as did several more singles over the coming months. By 1969, he had gained a new producer in Steve Barri, and in an attempt to resurrect his Holly-style sound, the two of them came up with the song "Dizzy." Written by Roe while touring with his hometown friend Freddy Weller (now a member of Paul Revere & the Raiders), it was recorded in pure sophisticated bubblegum-fashion, with Hal Blaine's sledgehammer drums and Jimmie Haskell's offbeat violin. The result was a month-long run at the top of the US charts, with sales eventually topping two million copies, and even deposing the Beatles' "Get Back" to head the UK charts. The top ten "Jam Up Jelly Tight," another collab with Weller, would become his fifth and final million-seller at the end of 1969.

Chart entries
Sheila – Tommy Roe (US 1962 # 1# UK # 3)
Everybody – Tommy Roe (US 1963 # 3; UK # 9)
Come On *(with Dan Penn)* Tommy Roe (US 1964 # 36)
Sweet Pea – Tommy Roe (US 1966 # 8); Manfred Mann (UK 1967 # 36)
Hooray For Hazel – Tommy Roe (US 1966 # 6)
It's Now Winter's Day – Tommy Roe (US 1966 # 23)
Sing Along With Me – Tommy Roe (US 1967 # 91)
Little Miss Sunshine – Tommy Roe (US 1967 # 99)
Dizzy *(with Freddy Weller)* Tommy Roe (US 1969 # 1; UK # 1)
Heather Honey – Tommy Roe (US 1969 # 29)
Jack and Jill *(with Freddy Weller)* Tommy Roe (US 1969 # 53)
Jam Up and Jelly Tight *(with Freddy Weller)* Tommy Roe (US 1969 # 8)

Beverly Ross
Born New York City 1934. Died 2022.

Raised in the Bronx, her family later moved to Lakewood, New Jersey, to become chicken farmers. As a young girl, she learned to play piano and write poetry and lyrics, and while still at school had one of her songs performed on television by Peggy Lee. In 1952, she moved to New York to canvass her songs to publishers at the Brill Building and was taken on as a staff writer. Teaming up with Julius Dixson (1913-2004), they wrote "Dim, Dim the Lights (I Want Some Atmosphere)," a later crossover hit for Bill Haley & the Comets in 1954 (and also becoming the first rock and roll song recorded by a white singer to reach the R&B chart).

Four years later, they wrote and performed "Lollipop" as Ronald and Ruby (aka back Ronald Gumps and white "Ruby" Ross). According to Dixson, the title came about after being late for a session because his daughter had gotten a lollipop stuck in her hair. Originally recorded as a demo to promote the song, RCA decided to release it and it peaked at number 20 on the charts. Once it was discovered that the artists were an inter-racial duo, tv appearances that had already been booked were cancelled and as a result they made no public appearances. The song was later covered by the Chordettes in the US and the Mudlarks in the UK.

In the late Fifties, Ross began working with Jeff Barry and was recruited by publishers Hill & Range. She wrote "Dixieland Rock" with Aaron Schroeder, using the pseudonym Rachel Frank, and with Sam Bobrick wrote "Girl of My Best Friend," originally recorded by Charlie Blackwell in 1959 (and later hits for Ral Donner and Elvis Presley). Around this time, she also made solo recordings for Columbia and met Phil Spector, who she collaborated with for some six months. In that time, she alleged that he "stole" a riff that she had composed and used it for his later hit "Spanish Harlem," written with Jerry Leiber. For that, she never forgave him.

In the Sixties, her hits included Roy Orbison's "Candy Man" (with Fred Neil), the Earls' "Remember Then" (with Tony Powers and Stan Vincent), and Leslie Gore's sequel hit "Judy's Turn to Cry" (with Edna Lewis).

Chart entries
Girl of My Best Friend *(with Sam Bobrick)* Ral Donner (US 1961 # 19)
Candy Man *(with Fred Neil)* Roy Orbison (US 1961 # 25; UK # 20); Brian Poole & the
　　Tremeloes (UK 1964 # 6)
Remember Then *(with Tony Powers, Stan Vincent)* The Earls (US 1962 # 24)
Judy's Turn to Cry *(with Edna Lewis)* Lesley Gore (US 1963 # 5)
Teenage Cleopatra – Tracey Dey (US 1963 # 75)

Jerry Ross see also **Gamble and Huff**

John Rostill see **Hank Marvin**

Bobby Russell
Born Robert L Russell, Nashville 1940. Died 1992.
Songwriters Hall of Fame 1970.
Nashville Songwriters Hall of Fame 1994.

As a budding songwriter raised in what was on the verge of becoming America's Music City, Russell's first success came collaborating with Buzz Cason (1939-2024), a fellow writer working for the Nashville-based Rising Sons music publishing firm. Their song "Tennessee," became a minor hit on the Liberty label for Jan & Dean in 1962. Two years later, they wrote "Ruby Red, Baby Blue" for the vocal group the Fleetwoods, although the single failed to break into the Hot 100. Another two years passed before Russell's self-penned "Sure Gonna Miss Her" was released. Recorded on the Liberty label with session leader Leon Russell, it became a top ten hit for Gary Lewis & the Playboys in March 1966. A few months later, Russell & Cason gave Jan & Dean greater success with "Popsicle." Written in 1962, it had first been recorded by the Indiana garage band, the Todds for their album *Drag City*. Jan & Dean then recorded it as the lead single of a greatest hits album which followed Jan Berry's near-fatal crash near Dead Man's Curve. Around the same time, Russell wrote "The Joker Went Wild," a top 20 hit for Brian Hyland, but it would be almost another two years before he came back with his most famous songs.

According to Cason, Russell recorded both "Little Green Apples " and "Honey" in 1968 as "an experiment in composing" and anticipating a potential market for true-to-life songs. First recorded by Roger Miller, "Little Green Apples" gave him his final country hit and moderate success on the Hot 100, but it was O C Smith's later version that really took off, peaking at number two and going on to win the writer two Grammy Awards.

Hot on its tail came "Honey," which had been inspired after Russell noticed how much a tree had grown since planting it in his front yard. It was first recorded by the Kingston Trio's Bob Shane and produced by Russell, but before its release it came to the attention of Bobby Goldsboro's producer Bob Montgomery. Goldsboro felt the song had been over-produced and felt he could do a simpler rendition. Russell agreed, with the caveat that it did not compete in the charts with Shane's record. As a result, the release of Goldsboro's version was delayed for a month. Recorded in one take, it spent five weeks at number one, and was the fastest-selling single for United Artists at the time. Ironically, Shane's version failed to chart.

In 1969, Russell was introduced by lyricist Johnny Mercer to writer/composer Bobby Scott (1937-1990), best-remembered for co-writing the Grammy Award-winning song "A Taste of Honey" in 1960. The two of them collaborated on the epic ballad "He Ain't Heavy, He's My Brother." The title was taken from James Wells' 1884 book telling the story of a little girl carrying a big baby boy, and when asked if she was tired, replied, "No, he's not heavy; he's my brother." The title was also used as the motto of Boys Town, a community in Omaha, Nebraska. Formed in 1917, Catholic priest Father Edward Flanagan later commissioned a statue that bore the inscription.

Originally recorded by Kelly Gordon as a track on his album *Defunked*, the writers sent a demo to Tony Hicks of the Hollies when they were looking for a new song to record. In an interview for the *Guardian*, Hicks recalled: "[The demo] sounded like a 45rpm record played at 33rpm, the singer was slurring, like he was drunk. But it had something about it. There were frowns when I took it to the band but we speeded it up and added an orchestra. The only thing left recognisable were the lyrics." Recorded in June 1969, it had session player Elton John on piano, and it went on to peak at number three on the UK charts as well as being a top ten hit in the US.

In 1972, Russell wrote "The Night the Lights Went Out in Georgia," a critique of Southern country justice, and although first offered to Cher, it was eventually sung by his then-wife, singer and comedian Vicki Lawrence, and topped the US charts early the following year.

Chart entries
Sure Gonna Miss Her – Gary Lewis & the Playboys (US 1966 # 9)
The Joker Went Wild – Brian Hyland (US 1966 # 20)
Little Green Apples – Roger Miller (US 1968 # 39; UK # 19); Patti Page (US 1968 # 96);
    O C Smith (US 1968 # 2)
Honey - Bobby Goldsboro (US 1968 # 1; UK # 2); O C Smith (US 1969 # 44)
Sudden Stop – Percy Sledge (US 1968 # 63)
1432 Franklin Pike Circle Hero – Bobby Russell (US 1968 # 36)
Vance – Roger Miller (US 1968 # 80)

Bobby Russell and Buzz Cason
Tennessee - Jan & Dean (US 1962 # 69)

Popsicle - Jan & Dean (US 1966 # 21)

Bobby Russell and Bobby Scott
He Ain't Heavy, He's My Brother - The Hollies (UK 1969 # 3; US # 7)

Jimmy Ryan
Born Plainfield, New Jersey 1946.

At the age of ten, Ryan had already decided he wanted a career in music and convinced his parents to buy him a guitar. While at junior high school he formed his first band, the Fliptones, before moving on to his next school where he formed the Vibra-Tones. In 1964, after firing their rhythm guitarist, band member Bob Podstawski recommended replacing him with future Four Seasons' singer/guitarist Don Ciccone (1946-2016). Impressed with his playing and his talent for songwriting, he was invited to join, and the band soon had a new name, the Critters. That same year, producer Jimmy Radcliffe signed them to Musicor Records, and released their first single, the Ciccone-penned "Georgiana."

The following year, they were signed to the Kama Sutra label, who in turn made a deal with Kapp Records. Kapp then released the Critter's cover version of Jackie DeShannon's "Children and Flowers," which made it into the Hot 100 (with the b-side "He'll Make You Cry" written by Ryan). Their debut album of the same name also included a cover of John Sebastian's "Younger Girl," which had been selected for a single by their producer Artie Ripp. With Ciccone, Ryan and Podstawski all enrolling at Villanova University, the record was held back and not completed until late 1965. On release it ended up doing better in the UK, where it peaked at number 38 in May 1966. However, their biggest success came a few months later with Ciccone's "Mr Dieingly Sad." In an interview for *Goldmine*, Ciccone recalled he was inspired not by a love gone bad but by the sadness of knowing that due to the draft he would have to leave his wife Kathy. He joined the US Air Force and served four years as a hydraulics mechanic in Vietnam. It became their biggest hit, reaching number 17 on the Hot 100. charts.

In July 1967, the Critters had their final chart hit with Ryan's "Don't Let the Rain Fall Down On Me," inspired after getting drenched in a downpour after class. With its complex arrangement, they hired several elite studio musicians for a backing track to compliment Ryan's 12-string guitar, but with studio time running out, he only had the chance to lay down a quick one-take reference vocal. To everyone's surprise, Kama Sutra released it in its unfinished state, likely because the band had terminated their contract due to bogus accounting. Nevertheless, it still secured a chart position, peaking at number 39. By this time, with Ciccone in the Air Force and two other members also enlisted in the military to avoid the draft, the others were left to recruit new members and keep the band going for a few more years (and two more albums) before finally calling it a day. In 1973, three years after his completion of duty, Ciccone joined Frankie Valli and the Four Seasons as guitarist, and three years later sang the memorable falsetto sections on their transatlantic chart-toppers "December, 1963 (Oh, What a Night) and "Who Loves You."

Ryan became a much sought-after session player, recording and touring with Carly Simon from 1970 to 1991 and noted for his guitar solos on "You're So Vain," and "Let the River Run," the theme song for the movie Working Girl," which earned a Grammy, A Golden Globe, and an Oscar.

Chart entries
Don't Let the Rain Fall Down On Me – The Critters (US 1967 # 39)

Buffy Sainte-Marie
Born Beverley Jean Santamaria, Stoneham, Massachusetts 1941.

Teaching herself to play piano and guitar as a child, she attended Wakefield High School before going on to the University of Massachusetts in Amherst, where she earned a degree in teaching and Asian philosophy. At the time, some of the songs she had already written included the Indian lament "Now That the Buffalo's Gone." Touring alone in her early twenties, she played at concert halls, festivals and for First Nation communities across the country, as well as the coffee houses of Greenwich Village's folk scene. While there, Joni Mitchell introduced her to Eliot Roberts, who became her manager.

In 1963, after recovering from an addiction to codeine brought on by a throat infection, she wrote the much-covered song "Cod'ine." That same year, images of wounded soldiers returning from Vietnam (a war for which the government were still in denial) inspired her to write "Universal Soldier." Originally recorded by the Highwaymen, it later appeared as a track on her debut album *It's My Way!* in April 1964, and went on to be successfully covered by both Donovan and Glen Campbell in 1965.

That same year, the ballad "Until It's Time For You To Go" was released as a track on her album *Many a Mile.* It became a top 20 hit for the UK group the Four Pennies, and was later covered by a number of artists, including Elvis Presley and Barbra Streisand. A few of the songs she recorded focused on the mistreatment of Native Americans and as a result courted controversy, none less so than the 1970 single "Soldier Blue," the theme to the movie of the same name about the 1864 Sand Creek massacre of a Cheyenne and Arapaho village by Colorado State Militia.

In 1983, she co-wrote with Jack Nitzsche and lyricist Will Jennings the Oscar-winning song "Up Where We Belong" for the movie *An Officer and a Gentleman*, and became a US chart-topper when recorded by Joe Cocker and Jennifer Warnes.

Chart entries
The Universal Soldier – Glen Campbell (US 1965 # 45); Donovan (US 1965 # 53)
Until It's Time For You To Go – The Four Pennies (UK 1965 # 19)

Ian Samwell
Born Ian Ralph Samwell, London 1937. Died 2003.

Samwell grew up in Harrow and learned to play guitar before joining the RAF. Once back in civvy street, he showed an interest in becoming a pop star. Looking to join a band, he first came across Harry Webb, a credit control clerk who was singing with his group the Drifters at the 2i's Coffee Bar in Soho. Invited to join them, Webb's manager Johnny Foster suggested Webb use the stage name Cliff Richards, but at Samwell's suggestion also dropped the "s" from his surname. Samwell became second guitarist alongside founding members Norman Mitham, Ken Pavey, and Terry Smart. In 1958, they auditioned for producer Norrie Paramor. A week before, Samwell had written his very first song while travelling by bus to Richard's house for a rehearsal. Playing his guitar, he stumbled on a riff that would become the song's intro, with lyrics scribbled down on a packet of guitar strings. Arriving at the rehearsal, he re-wrote the lyrics and played it to the band, with Foster suggesting the title "Move It." With additional musicians, it was recorded (with Samwell on bass) as the b-side to their debut single, a cover of Bobby Helms' "Schoolboy Crush," but when later switched to the a-side, it shot to number two on the charts. It is now considered as the first rock and roll song to originate from the UK.

Although squeezed out of the band when Hank Marvin and Jet Harris joined, Samwell was offered a songwriting contract with the label and later wrote Richard's second single "High Class Baby," which Samwell revealed was about having his advances spurned by the actress daughter of singer Sarah Cracknell.

More of his songs became hits for Richard, including "Never Mind" and "Dynamite," but it was 1960's ballad "Fall in Love With You" that again became one spot away from being a chart-topper. The previous year, Samwell had written "Say You Love Me Too," which was recorded by the Isley Brothers, thus becoming the first song by a British writer to be recorded by a US R&B artist. In 1965, the Small Faces' manager Don Arden asked him and Brian Potter (b.1939) to provide lyrics to a Solomon King-inspired melody that Steve Marriott and Ronnie Lane had for their debut single, "Whatcha Gonna Do About It." The result was a top twenty chart hit.

For a time, Samwell became resident deejay at London's Lyceum Ballroom before becoming staff producer at Warner Records' London office. In that capacity, he discovered the band America and produced their first album, even wisely suggesting the name of their "Desert Song" be changed to "A Horse With No Name."

Chart entries
Fall in Love With You – Cliff Richard & the Shadows (UK 1960 # 2)
Gee Whiz, It's You *(with Hank Marvin)* Cliff Richard & the Shadows (UK 1961 # 4)
You Can Never Stop Loving Me *(with Jean Slater)* Kenny Lynch (UK 1963 # 10); Johnny
    Tillotson (US 1963 # 18)
 Whatcha Gonna Do About It? *(with Steve Marriott, Ronnie Lane)* The Small Faces (UK 1965
    # 14)

Pam Sawyer
Born Pamela Joan Sawyer, Romford, London 1938.
Women Songwriter Hall of Fame 2023.

Eager to become a songwriter, Sawyer got in touch with impresario Lew Grade who was impressed enough to introduce her to visiting US composer and pianist Bob Mersey. The two of them later married and went to live in New York in 1961. Following a separation, Sawyer went on to work as a lyricist with other songwriters, including Mark Barkan and Helen Miller, before teaming up with US singer-songwriter Lori Burton (1940-2021). Together they wrote hits for several artists including 1965's "Try to Understand" by Lulu, and Patti LaBelle & the Bluebelles' "All or Nothing." She also recorded with Burton as Whyte Boots, although the label promoted them as a "trio" of female singers. In 1967, Sawyer and Burton signed for Motown after auditioning for Holland, Dozier and Holland. Sawyer worked with Ivy Jo Hunter and others on the Four Tops hit "Yesterday's Dreams," before becoming part of a writing collective known as the Clan, which included Motown's Henry

"Hank" Cosby, Frank Wilson, Deke Richards and R Dean Taylor. Their greatest success was the Supremes' "Love Child," a US chart-topper in 1968.

In the Seventies, her continuing ability to craft emotionally resonant lyrics led to more chart success, co-writing "Last Time I Saw Him" with Michael Masser, and "Love Hangover" with Marilyn McLoed, both hits for Diana Ross. Finally leaving Motown in the Eighties, she founded Pam Sawyer and Barley Lane Music.

Chart hits
You're My Baby (And Don't You Forget It) *(with Helen Miller, Steve Venet)* The
    Vacels (US 1965 # 63)
If I Didn't Love You *(with Mark Barkan)* Chuck Jackson (US 1965 # 46)
Yesterday's Dreams *(with Vernon Bullock, Jack Goga, Ivy Jo Hunter)* Four Tops (US
    1968 # 49; UK # 23)
Love Child *(with Henry Cosby, Frank Wilson, Deke Richards, R Dean Taylor)*
    Diana Ross & the Supremes (US 1968 # 1; UK # 2)
I'm Living In Shame (*(with Henry Cosby, Frank Wilson, Berry Gordy, R Dean Taylor)*
    Diana Ross & the Supremes (US 1969 # 10; UK # 8)
My Whole World Ended (the Moment You Left Me) *(with Harvey Fuqua, Johnny
    Bristol, Jimmy Roach)* David Ruffin (US 1969 # 9; UK # 51)

Pam Sawyer and Lori Burton
Try to Understand - Lulu (UK 1965 # 25)
All Or Nothing - Patti LaBelle & the Bluebelles (US 1965 # 68)
I Ain't Gonna Eat My Heart Out Anymore - The Young Rascals (US 1965 # 52)
Baby Let's Wait - The Royal Guardsmen (US 1968 # 35)

Aaron Schroeder and Wally Gold
Born Aaron Harold Schroeder, New York City 1926. Died 2009.
Born (Jack) Wally Gold, New York City 1928. Died 1998.
Songwriters Hall of Fame 1991 (Gold).

Brooklyn-born Schroeder graduated from the High School of Music & Art in New York and in 1948 became a member of ASCAP (American Society of Composers, Authors & Publishers). Having his first break with writing one of Rosemary Clooney's first recordings, he scored his first chart hit in 1956 co-writing Guy Mitchell's "Crazy With Love" with Josephine Peoples. One of the most prolific songwriters in the business, he would go on to compose over 500 recorded songs, including co-writing 17 chart hits for Elvis Presley, five of which topped the charts. His most successful partnership came with fellow Brooklyner Wally Gold (1928-1998).

Gold later moved with his family to New Jersey and during the war played saxophone in the US Navy band. On his return, he studied at Boston University and also formed the vocal group Jack Gold & the Four Esquires with Bill Courtney as lead singer, and Gold, Robert Golden and Frank Mahoney as backing vocalists. They recorded two singles on the Paris label, "Love Me Forever" and "Hideaway," both top thirty hits in 1957-58. After appearing on the *Ed Sullivan Show*, they disbanded in the early Sixties.

In 1959, the writing team of Schroeder and Gold had their first chart hit with Nat King Cole's "Sweet Bird of Youth," and continued their success with songs for Pat Boone, Carl Dobkins and Gene Vincent. The following year, they joined Don Costa to write the instrumental "Because They're Young" for guitarist Duane Eddy, quickly followed by having their first chart-topper with Presley's "It's Now or Never," adapted from Eduardo di Capua's Neapolitan song "O Sole mio." When Presley had heard a 1949 version by Tony Martin called "There's No Tomorrow," it inspired him to record it and his music publisher then found Schroeder and Gold to write the English lyrics, which were completed in just half an hour. In 1962, their "Good Luck Charm" gave Presley his second hat-trick of chart-toppers in the UK.

In the early Sixties, Schroeder set up his own Musicor Records label with United Artists as distributor, and as its manager launched the career of Gene Pitney. Working out of New York's Brill Building, Schroeder and Pitney co-wrote "Rubber Ball," a hit for Bobby Vee, with Pitney using the pseudonym Anne Orlowski (his mother's name). Schroeder was also largely responsible for developing the blend of Pitney's voice with the songs of Bacharach & David that generated some of the artist's best-known work.

Gold would go on to be credited with writing or co-writing over 80 songs, his most famous being Leslie Gore's "It's My Party." Co-authored with Herb Wiener and John Gluck Jr,, it gave the singer her first chart-topper in 1963. A few years later, he became a house producer for Columbia Records, working with artists that included Barbra Streisand and Tony Bennett, and in the Seventies was Vice-President of Don Kirshner's music organisation.

Chart entries
Wild Cat - Gene Vincent (UK 1960 # 21)
Time And the River - Nat King Cole (US 1960 # 30; UK # 23)
Lucky Devil - Frank Ifield (UK 1960 # 22)
Hither, Thither and Yon - Brook Benton (US 1960 # 58)
Because They're Young (*with Don Costa*) Duane Eddy (US 1960 # 4; UK # 20); James Darren (UK 1960 # 29
It's Now Or Never (*with Eduardo di Capua*) Elvis Presley (US 1960 # 1; UK # 1)
Utopia (*with Martin Kalmanoff*) Frank Gari (US 1960 # 27)
Good Luck Charm - Elvis Presley (US 1962 # 1; UK # 1)
Half Heaven - Half Heartache (*with George Goehring*) Gene Pitney (US 1963 # 12)
Yesterday's Hero (*with Carl Spencer, Alfred Cleveland*) Gene Pitney (US 1964 # 64)

Aaron Schroeder and others
Stuck On You (*with J Leslie McFarland*) Elvis Presley (US 1960 # 1; UK # 3)
Rubber Ball (*with Anne Orlowski, aka Gene Pitney*) Bobby Vee (US 1960 # 6; UK # 4); The Avons (UK 1961 # 30); Marty Wilde (UK 1961 # 9)
I'm Gonna Knock On Your Door (*with Sid Wayne*) Eddie Hodges (US 1961 # 12)
Bandit of My Dreams (*with Anne Orlowski, aka Gene Pitney*) Eddie Hodges (US 1962 # 65)
Today's Teardrops *(with Gene Pitney)* Ricky Nelson (US 1963 # 54)
Seeing the Right Love Go Wrong (*with Joey Brooks*) Jack Jones (US 1965 # 46)

Wally Gold
Exodus – The Tornadoes (UK 1964 # 41)
Look Homeward Angel – The Monarchs (US 1964 # 47)

Wally Gold with others
She Can't Find Her Keys *(with Roy Alfred)* Paul Peterson (US 1962 # 19)
It's My Party *(with Herb Wiener, John Gluck Jr)* Leslie Gore (US 1963 # 1; UK # 9)
Questions and Answers *(with Phillip Springer)* The In Crowd (US 1966 # 92)

John Schroeder see Mike Hawker and John Schroeder

Mort Schuman see Doc Pomus and Mort Schuman

Winfield Scott see Otis Blackwell

John Sebastian
Born John Benson Sebastian, New York City 1944.
Rock and Roll Hall of Fame 2000 (with The Lovin' Spoonful).
Songwriters Hall of Fame 2008.

With his father a noted classical harmonica player and mother a radio script writer, Sebastian grew up in Greenwich Village, surrounded by musical artists. After graduating from Blair Academy, a private boarding school, he attended New York University but dropped out after a year to pursue a career in music. Much influenced by blues musicians Lightnin' Hopkins and Sonny Terry, he managed to meet them through his father's connections and soon became part of the folk/blues scene which was developing in the Village. In the early Sixties, having learnt to play a variety of instruments including blues harmonica, guitar, piano and auto-harp, Sebastian began working as a studio musician and played on progressive folk albums by local artists Fred Neil and Tom Rush.

In February 1964, Sebastian was invited to Cass Elliot's apartment to watch the Beatles television debut on the *Ed Sullivan Show*. Also there was guitarist Zal Yanovsky, a member of the Canadian folk group the Halifax Three, who like the others was active on the local folk music scene. All three would be greatly influenced by the Beatles' performance, and after being encouraged by Elliot to play guitars together late into the night, Sebastian and Yanovsky realised they had a musical affinity for one another. When Yanovsky's band folded a few months later, he and founder member Denny Doherty joined Elliot,

James Hendricks and Tim Rose to form the electric folk group the Mugwumps. Although short-lived and unsuccessful, Sebastian played with them for a time. Once disbanded, Doherty and Elliot went away to join the Mamas and the Papas.

In January 1965, along with producer Erik Jacobsen, Sebastian and Yanovsky formed a new outfit called the Lovin' Spoonful, named after a phrase from Mississippi John Hurt's *Coffee Blues*, along with fellow members Steve Boone (bass, vocals) and Joe Butler (drums, vocals). Working on Sebastian's innovative compositions, they were given a residency at Greenwich's Night Owl club while Jacobsen secured them a deal with the recently-formed Kama Sutra label. In the meantime, Bob Dylan, who had seen Sebastian perform, invited him to play bass for his *Bringing It All Back Home* sessions and to join his new all-electric band on tour. Not only did Sebastian's parts probably not appear on the album, but he also declined touring to concentrate on his new band. Their first single was Sebastian's celebratory "Do You Believe in Magic?" inspired by a teenage girl seen in the audience at the Night Owl. Standing in contrast to the older beatnik crowd, it seemed to symbolise that the audience was changing along with the music they were now playing. Written and arranged the following night, it became their first chart hit, peaking at number nine on the Hot 100 in October. The following album, named after the single, displayed their light, lyrical synthesis they dubbed "good-time music."

Seeking to avoid being typecast by their music, Sebastian suggested at the time that it showcased how the group was not defined by any particular sound. Their second album *Daydream* was released early the following year, and its lead single bearing the same name just lost out on being a chart-topper. Sebastian had written the song to lift his spirits after a grueling tour and had initially been inspired by the music of the Supremes, with whom they had toured, along with his earlier involvement in jug band music. This was soon followed by the next single, "Did You Ever Have To Make Up Your Mind," another number two in the charts and written in the back of a taxi en route to the studio.

The summer of 1966 brought their biggest hit, "Summer in the City" a rare song that laments the heat of the daytime instead of romanticising summer's warmth. Sebastian recalled a song that his 14-year-old brother Mark had composed and taped called "It's a Different World." With it's bossa nova-like sound and rudimentary, yet soulful, lyrics, Sebastian reworked the melody and replaced the laconic verses with upbeat ones. But the song is best remembered for its iconic opening. For music aficionados, and I quote, "it opens with two descending notes (a flattened or minor sixth) followed by a perfect fifth degree of a minor scale) played three times by lead guitar, bass and electric piano. On the fourth beat of each bar, a snare and bass drum smash." The song enjoyed a three-week run at the top of the charts. A third album followed, but after Yanovsky was caught in a marijuana bust in San Francisco, it led to a backlash by fans and increased tension within the band over diverging musical interests.

The beginning of 1967 saw the release of the single "Nashville Cats," Sebastian's ode to the Nashville A-Team, the name given to a loose group of session musicians based in Music City, and inspired when they saw an unknown guitarist playing in a hotel bar. It became the band's first conscious effort to record a country hit. In June, Yanovsky quit the band after media indignation over allegedly incriminating others over his drug bust. Replaced by Jerry Yester, the band's musical style was now perceived to be veering away from their previous eclectic blend to becoming increasingly more pop-oriented.

In October 1968, Sebastian left the band to begin a solo career, and as a Broadway musical composer found success with *Jimmy Shine*, which had Dustin Hoffman in the lead role. In 1969 he appeared at Woodstock, and recalled, "I did not show up there with a road manager and a couple of guitars. I showed up with a change of clothes and a toothbrush." After performing original songs there and at the Big Sur Folk Festival, he went on to release several solo albums in the Seventies and worked as a session player for another of artists.

Chart entries
Do You Believe In Magic? – The Lovin' Spoonful (US 1965 # 9)
You Didn't Have To Be So Nice (*with Steve Boone)* The Lovin' Spoonful (US 1965 # 10)
Good Time Music – Beau Brummels (US 1965 # 97)
Daydream – The Lovin' Spoonful (US 1966 # 2; UK # 2)
Did You Ever Have To Make Up Your Mind? – The Lovin' Spoonful (US 1966 # 2)
Younger Girl – The Hondells (US 1966 # 52); The Critters (US 1966 # 42)
Summer In the City (*with Mark Sebastian, Steve Boone*) The Lovin' Spoonful (US # 1;
 UK # 7)
Rain On the Roof – The Lovin' Spoonful (US 1966 # 10; UK # 47)
Nashville Cats – The Lovin' Spoonful (US 1966 # 8; UK # 23)
Lovin' You – Bobby Darin (US 1967 # 32)
Darling Be Home Soon – The Lovin' Spoonful (US 1967 # 15; UK # 45); Bobby Darin
 (US 1967 # 93)
Six O'Clock – The Lovin' Spoonful (US 1967# 18)
She Is Still A Mystery – The Lovin' Spoonful (US 1967 # 27)
Money – The Lovin' Spoonful (US 1968 # 48)
She's A Lady - John Sebastian US 1969 # 84)

Neil Sedaka see also Howard Greenfield
Born New York City 1939.
Songwriters Hall of Fame 1983.

Brooklyn-born Sedaka was the son of a taxi driver, whose paternal grandparents had emigrated from Turkey in 1910. Even in a second-grade choral class, Sedaka demonstrated musical aptitude and was urged by a teacher to take piano lessons. In 1947, he auditioned successfully for a piano scholarship at the Julliard School of Music's Preparatory Division for Children which he attended each Saturday. Although his mother wanted him to become a classical pianist, Sedaka's interest lay with popular music, although he often played classical throughout his life. Graduating from Abraham Lincoln High School, he and several classmates formed a group called the Linc-Tones and recorded some minor regional hits. They changed their name to the Tokens shortly before Sedaka left to start a solo career and went on to have four top-forty hits on their own. When Sedaka was 13, a neighbour had heard him playing, and introduced him to her son Howard Greenfield, who was an aspiring poet and lyricist.

In 1958, Sedaka joined Aldon Music, Don Kirshner's Brill Building school of songwriters, where he teamed up with Greenfield as a staff writer. One of their first collaborations was "The Diary," inspired by Connie Francis, one of their most important clients, who they asked (but refused) to have access to her diary to find lyrical material. Although intended for Little Anthony & the Imperials, their recording of it failed to impress. With Sedaka signing to RCA Records, he felt he should record the song himself as his debut single, and it went on to become a top twenty hit.

Keen to give Francis what would be a third hit single, Kirshner got the writing pair to visit her home to pitch songs. When Greenfield suggested to Sedaka to play "Stupid Cupid" to her, he felt that the "classy lady" would be insulted by the lyrics. Not so, on hearing it Francis jumped up and down and said, "That's It! You guys got my next record!" The single would top the UK charts for six weeks.

The following year, their novelty song "I Go Ape" scored a moderate solo hit for Sedaka, who at the time was also doing session work for other artists, including playing piano on Bobby Darin's "Dream Lover." However, with RCA losing money on Sedaka's last releases, they were ready to drop him from the label when they were urged to give him one last chance. Sedaka and Greenfield responded by studying the lyrics, song structure, chord progressions and harmonies before composing their next songs, and it resulted in some of the biggest-selling singles of the time. "Oh! Carol" referenced Carol Klein, Sedaka's ex-girlfriend from high school, and now a fellow Brill Building songwriter married to Gerry Goffin. It became a top ten hit toward the end of 1959. In playful response, she recorded "Oh Neil" using her stage name Carole King. Four months later, came "Stairway to Heaven," which repeated the chart placing, followed by "Calendar Girl," a top four single at the beginning of 1961. Over the next couple of years, Sedaka and Greenfield wrote hit after hit for the singer, including "Little Devil," "Happy Birthday Sweet Sixteen," "Breaking Up Is Hard To Do," and "Next Door To An Angel." They also wrote for other artists, including Jimmy Clanton's "Venus in Blue Jeans."

With the British Invasion taking the country by storm, Sedaka was soon left without a recording career. After working with Roger Atkins on the Fifth Dimension's "Workin' On a Groovy Thing," he mutually agreed with Greenfield to end their long collaboration with the appropriately-titled "Our Last Song Together," a hit for Sedaka in 1973. However, Sedaka would enjoy several years of success teaming up with Phil Cody to write "Solitaire," a hit for Andy Williams, and giving his own solo career a boost with hits like "Laughter in the Rain" (a US number one) and "The Immigrant." Another of the songs written with Greenfield was "Love Will Keep Us Together," originally as an album track on one of Sedaka's solo albums in 1973, but becoming a worldwide hit two years later when released by pop duo Captain and Tennille.

Chart entries
Neil Sedaka and Howard Greenfield
Calendar Girl - Neil Sedaka (US 1960 # 4; UK # 8)
Another Sleepless Night – Jimmy Clanton (US 1960 # 22)
Run Samson Run – Neil Sedaka (US 1960 # 28)
You Mean Everything To Me – Neil Sedaka (US 1960 # 17)
Stairway To Heaven - Neil Sedaka (US 1960 # 9; UK # 8)
What Am I Gonna Do – Jimmy Clanton (US 1961 # 50); Emile Ford & the Checkmates
    (UK 1961 # 33)
Little Devil - Neil Sedaka (US 1961 # 11; UK # 9)
Breaking Up is Hard To Do – The Happenings (US 1968 # 67)

Neil Sedaka and Roger Atkins
Workin' on a Groovy Thing *(with Roger Atkins)* Patti Drew (US 1968 # 62); Fifth Dimension
    (US 1969 # 20)

Pete Seeger

Born New York City 1919. Died 2014.
Songwriters Hall of Fame 1972.
Grammy Lifetime Achievement Award 1993.
Rock and Roll Hall of Fame 1996.

Born into a musically gifted family, it was perhaps the introspective poems of his uncle Alan Seeger that most inspired him to become a songwriter. Graduating from Harvard University in 1938, he hitchhiked and rode trains across the country picking up country ballads, hymns and work songs, while becoming an expert five-string banjo player. In 1940, he formed the quartet the Almanac Singers, which also included Woody Guthrie, and played at farm meetings, union halls or wherever populist political sentiments were readily welcomed. After the war, he formed the Weavers, along with Lee Hays, Fred Hellerman and Ronnie Gilbert, and recorded a number of records. Once they had achieved national fame, it stirred up controversy concerning Seeger's previous activities in left-wing and labour politics and were subsequently blacklisted by the music industry. They disbanded in 1952 but reunited three years later with renewed interest in their music.

Finally leaving the group in 1958, Seeger continued working, usually with his family. Brother Mike was a member of the New Lost City Ramblers, while sister Peggy had teamed up with British folk singer Ewan McColl to spearhead the UK's folk music revival in the early Sixties. Still blacklisted as a solo performer, Seeger was convicted of contempt of Congress in 1961, although overturned the following year. He became a regular fixture at folk festivals and was credited for the growing popularity of the hootenanny, as well as turning the old song "We Shall Overcome" into an anthem for the civil rights movement. As a mentor for young artists like Joan Baez and Bob Dylan, he wrote or co-wrote "Where Have All the Flowers Gone," "If I Had a Hammer," and "Kisses Sweeter Than Wine."

In 1959, he wrote "Turn! Turn! Turn! (To Everything There Is a Season)," the lyrics of which - except for the title and the final two lines - consist of the eight verses of the third chapter of the biblical Book of Ecclesiastes. It was originally released in 1962 as "To Everything There Is a Season" an album track by the folk group the Limeliters, but in 1965 it became a worldwide hit when adapted by the Byrds.

On the subject of songwriting, Seeger once offered this advice: "If you've got a lot of people writing songs, you're more liable to get some good songs. Anybody can write a third rate song, but, if there's one where people say, 'Hey, give me the words to that, I've really got to learn it, 'then it's a good song."

Chart entries
Where Have All the Flowers Gone? *(with Joe Hickerson)* The Kingston Trio (US 1962 # 21);
   Johnny Rivers (US 1965 # 26)
If I Had a Hammer *(with Lee Hays)* Peter, Paul & Mary (US 1962 # 10); Trini Lopez (US
   1963 # 3; UK # 4)
On Top of Spaghetti *(trad, with Tom Glazer)* Tom Glazer (US 1963 # 14)
Gotta Travel On *(with Paul Clayton, Lee Hays, Fred Hellerman, Ronnie Gilbert, Larry
   Ehrlich, Dave Lazer)* Tim Yuro (US 1963 # 64)
We Shall Overcome *(with Guy Carawan, Lee Hamilton, Zilphia Horton)* Joan Baez (US
   1963 # 50; UK # 26)
Turn! Turn! Turn! *(adapt. Book of Ecclesiastes)* The Byrds (US 1965 # 1; UK # 26); Judy
   Collins (US 1969 # 69)
Guantanamera *(with Joseíto Fernández, Héctor Angulo, José Martí)* The Sandpipers (US
   1966 # 9; UK # 7)

Del Shannon

Born Charles Weedon Westover, Grand Rapids, Michigan 1934. Died 1990 (suicide).
Rock and Roll Hall of Fame 1999.

Learning to play ukelele and guitar as a youngster, Westover was inspired by country & western singers Hank Williams and Hank Snow. Drafted into the US Army in 1952, he was stationed in Germany where he formed a band called the Cool Flames. On his return, he worked as a carpet salesman and truck driver, and in evenings found part-time club work as a guitarist for singer Doug DeMott's group, the Moonlight Ramblers. When DeMott was fired, he took over as lead singer with a new name Charlie Johnson, and the band now called the Big Little Show Band. In July 1960, demos were sent off by a local deejay, and along with keyboard player Max Crook signed a recording and writing deal for Bigtop Records, with the suggestion that he change his name to Del Shannon.

First sessions in New York proved unsuccessful, but they were persuaded to re-write and record one of their earlier songs called "Little Runaway." In January 1961, Shannon recorded the re-named "Runaway" with its distinctive Musitron sound, and it topped the charts a month later. A second single, "Hats Off to Larry, penned by Shannon and recorded the same day, gave him a top five hit, but further hits only achieved moderate chart success. In 1962, he co-wrote several songs with Maron McKenzie, with "Little Town Flirt" being the most successful. By August 1963, Shannon's relationship with Bigtop had soured and he decided to form his own label, Berlee Records, named after his parents. He returned to the charts with "Handy Man," written by Jimmy Jones and Otis Blackwell, but achieved bigger success in 1964 with the self-penned top ten hit "Keep Searchin' (We'll Follow the Sun)." Two years later, he signed with Liberty Records.

By the Seventies, Shannon's career had slowed down dramatically, partly due to his alcoholism. By 1990, he was on anti-depressants and struggling to finish a new album, and on February 8th he tragically took his own life.

Chart entries
Runaway *(as Charles Westover, Max Crook)* Del Shannon (US 1961 # 1; UK # 1); Lawrence
   Welk & His Orchestra (US 1962 # 56)
Hats Off to Larry – Del Shannon (US 1961 # 5; UK # 6)
So Long, Baby – Del Shannon US 1961 # 28; UK # 10)
Hey! Little Girl – Del Shannon (US 1961 # 38; UK # 2)
Cry Myself to Sleep – Del Shannon (US 1962 # 99; UK # 29)
Sue's Gotta Be Mine – Del Shannon (US 1963 # 71; UK # 21)
Keep Searchin'(We'll Follow the Sun) – Del Shannon (US 1964 # 9; UK # 3)
I Go To Pieces *(as Charles Westover)* Peter & Gordon (US 1965 # 9)
Stranger in Town – Del Shannon (US 1965 # 30; UK # 40)
Break Up *(as Charles Westover)* Del Shannon (US 1965 # 95)

Del Shannon and Maron McKenzie
Little Town Flirt – Del Shannon (US 1962 # 12; UK # 4)
Two Kind of Teardrops – Del Shannon (US 1963 # 50; UK # 5)
Two Silhouettes – Del Shannon (UK 1963 # 23)
Mary Jane – Del Shannon (UK 1964 # 35)

Martha Sharp
Born Martha Marion Sharp, Charlotte, North Carolina 1937. Died 2024.

Following her education at Thomas Jefferson High School in Richmond, Virginia, and Mary Baldwin University in Staunton, Sharp travelled to Nashville and signed with Painted Desert Music as a staff writer. Her first success came with writing "The Special Years," a hit for Irish crooner Val Doonican in 1965. The following year, Sandy Posey's manager Chips Moman liked Sharp's song "Born a Woman" and the following year brought the Memphis singer to Muscle Shoals to record the single, which went on to peak at number 12 in the charts. This was followed by Sharp being signed by Bob Beckham to Combine Records in Nashville, where Beckham published the songwriter's next song "Single Girl" for Posey to score another top twelve hit. In appreciation, Sharp wrote the liner notes for Posey's third album. The next artist to dip into Sharp's catalog at Painted Desert was Bobby Vee & the Strangers, who in 1967 recorded "Come Back When You Grow Up" and gave Sharp her biggest songwriting hit. Her songs were recorded by many other artists, including Tom Jones, Cilla Black and Waylon Jennings.

Chart entries
The Special Years – Val Doonican (UK 1965 # 7)
Born a Woman – Sandy Posey (US 1966 # 12; UK # 24)
Single Girl – Sandy Posey (US 1966 # 12; UK # 15)
Come Back When You Grow Up – Bobby Vee & the Strangers US 1967 # 3)
Maybe Just Today – Bobby Vee & the Strangers (US 1968 # 46)

Gloria Shayne
Born Gloria Adele Shain, Brookline, Massachusetts 1923. Died 2008.

As a child, Shayne grew up next door to Joseph and Rose Kennedy, including their son John F Kennedy. Her career in music began as being part of the family vocal trio, the Shain Sisters, with siblings Esther and Thelma. Changing her surname for professional reasons, she graduated Boston University School of Music and moved to New York during the 1940s. Working as a pianist, she arranged music for famous composers Irving Berlin and Stephen Sondheim. and in 1951 met her first husband Noël Regney (1922-2002) while playing in a hotel.

With Shayne usually the lyricist, they wrote some well-known songs, including "Rain, Rain, Go Away," "Sweet Little Darlin'" and "Another Go Around." Away from her husband, she also wrote "Goodbye Cruel World," a top three hit for James Darren in 1961. At the height of the Cuban missile crisis in 1962, the pair of them wrote the Christmas carol "Do You Hear What I Hear" as a plea for peace. Released shortly after Thanksgiving, it was first recorded by the Harry Simeone Chorale and sold a quarter of a million copies. Bing Crosby also recorded it in 1963 and made it a worldwide hit. In this instance, it was Regney who wrote the lyrics and Shayne the music. Shayne later recalled: "Noel wrote this beautiful song and I wrote the music. We couldn't sing it, though; it broke us up. We cried. Our little song broke us up."

The following year, she teamed up with Jerry Keller to write "Almost There" for Andy Williams. After her divorce, she married her second husband William Baker in 1973.

Chart entries
Goodbye Cruel World – James Darren (US 1961 # 3; UK # 28)
Rain, Rain, Go Away *(with Noël Regney)* Bobby Vinton (US 1962 # 12)
Hail to the Conquering Hero *(with Howard Greenfield)* James Darren (US 1962 # 97)
Almost There *(with Jerry Keller)* Andy Williams (US 1964 # 67; UK # 2)
The Men in My Little Girl's Life *(with Mary Candy, Eddie Deane)* Mike Douglas (US
   1965 # 6)

Carl Sigman
Born New York City 1909. Died 2000.
Songwriters Hall of Fame 1972.

Brooklyn-born Sigman studied law at New York University, and, although loathing the profession, practiced it for a year. Encouraged by his friend Johnny Mercer to become a songwriter, he was always trying to "make conversational lyrics" from phrases people used on the phone or at the dining table. While still an attorney, he also worked as a typist and a piano teacher while trying to find the time to visit the Brill Building where the songwriters "hung out." In 1940, he co-wrote "Pennsylvania 6-5000" with Jerry Gray, a hugely popular hit for the Glenn Miller Orchestra, and one of a number of compositions written for some of the popular band leaders of the day. During the war, he served in Europe with an army glider crew and won a bronze star, while also composing "The All-American Soldier," the official war song for the 82nd Airborne Division. In the post-war years, Sigman had success writing for musicals, one of the most famous being the much-covered "Civilisation (Bongo, Bongo, Bongo)" from the Broadway show *Angel In the Wings*.

Although primarily a lyricist, Sigman also wrote his own music and adapted a number of foreign songs, although not attempting to translate the words. In 1951, he wrote lyrics to music that future US Vice President Charles Dawes had composed in 1912, and the song "It's All in the Game" became a later chart-topper for Tommy Edwards (and also finding later success for both Cliff Richard and the Four Tops). Other songs that became hits during this period included Jane Morgan's "The Day That the Rains Came Down," Ray Peterson's "Answer Me," the Platters' "Ebb Tide," and Tony Bennett's "Till."

In 1964, UK record producer George Martin became aware of an Italian ballad called "Il mio mondo" ("My World"), it's haunting melody written the previous year by Umberto Bindi and Gino Paoli and recorded by Bindi. Although not a hit, Martin commissioned Sigman to write original English lyrics for singer Cilla Black to record as "You're My World." With Johnny Pearson conducting the orchestra and the Breakaways on backing vocals, it topped the UK charts for four weeks in May and became her only US chart hit.

In the Seventies, Sigman collaborated with French composer Francis Lai to write the Oscar-winning song "(Where Do I Begin?) Love Story" for singer Andy Williams, and also teamed up with James Last to write "Fool" for Elvis Presley.

Chart entries
Answer Me *(with Gerhard Winkler, Fred Rauch)* Ray Peterson (UK 1960 # 47)
Ebb Tide *(with Robert Maxwell)* The Platters (US 1960 # 56); Lenny Welch (US 1964 # 25);

The Righteous Brothers (US 1965 # 5; UK # 48)
Buona Sera *(with Peter DeRose)* Mr Acker Bilk & the Paramount Jazz Band (UK 1960 # 7)
'Till *(with Charles Danvers)* Tony Bennett (UK 1961 # 35); The Angels (US 1961 # 14); The Vogues (US 1968 # 27)
That's the Way With Love *(with Piero Soffici, Gualtiero Malgoni)* Piero Soffici (US 1961 # 59)
What Now My Love *(with Gilbert Bécaud, Pierre Delanoë)* Shirley Bassey (UK 1962 # 5); Sonny & Cher (US 1966 # 14; UK # 13); Mitch Ryder & the Detroit Wheels (US 1967 # 30)
Losing You *(with Jean Renard)* Brenda Lee (US 1963 # 6; UK # 10)
It's All in the Game *(with Charles Dawes)* Cliff Richard & the Shadows (UK 1963 # 2; US # 25)
Shangri-La *(with Matty Malneck, Robert Maxwell)* Robert Maxwell & His Orchestra (US 1964 # 15); Vic Dana (US 1964 # 27); The Lettermen (US 1969 # 64)
You're My World *(with Umberto Bindi, Gino Paoli)* Cilla Black (UK 1964 # 1; US # 26)
Just Yesterday *(with Klaus Ogermann)* Jack Jones (US 1965 # 73)
A Day in the Life of a Fool *(with Luiz Bonfá, Antonio Mariz)* Jack Jones (US 1966 # 62)
The World We Knew (Over and Over) *(with Bert Kaempfert, Herbert Rehbein)* Frank Sinatra (US 1967 # 30; UK # 33)
Careless Hands *(with Bob Hilliard)* Des O'Connor (UK 1967 # 6)
Lonely Is My Name (*(with Bert Kaempfert, Herbert Rehbein)* Sammy Davis Jr (US 1968 # 93)
(You Are) My Way of Life (*(with Bert Kaempfert, Herbert Rehbein)* Frank Sinatra (US 1968 # 63; UK # 53)

Paul Simon

Born Paul Frederic Simon, Newark, New Jersey 1941.
Songwriters Hall of Fame 1982.
Rock and Roll Hall of Fame 1990 (as Simon & Garfunkel), 2001 (solo).
Grammy Lifetime Achievement Award 2003 (as Simon & Garfunkel).

Simon's parents were both teachers, with his father also being a musician and dance bandleader performing as Lee Sims. In 1945, the family moved to Kew Garden Hills in Queens, and Simon attended Public School 164. His future singing partner Art Garfunkel (b.1941) lived just three block away, and over the years they both went to the same schools, Parsons Junior High and Forest Hills High. Simon first noticed Garfunkel when he saw him sing a rendition of Nat King Cole's "Too Young" at a fourth-grade talent show, but they only became friends in 1953 when they both took part in a sixth-grade graduation production of *Alice in Wonderland*. Sharing a love for music, they quickly developed their ability to harmonise. Along with friends, they formed a streetcorner quintet called the Peptones, but soon realised they could perform better as a duo and occasionally sang at school dances.

Around the age of 13, Simon wrote his first song "The Girl For Me" for them to perform, and his father wrote the words and chords on paper for the boys to use. He then sent it to the Library of Congress to register a copyright, with Simon under the name Jerry Landis and Garfunkel being Tom Graph.

In 1955, inspired by their idols the Everly Brothers, Simon was trying to remember the lyrics to their "Hey Doll Baby," but instead came up with a different song altogether called "Hey Little Schoolgirl." For a fee of $25, they recorded it at Sanders Recording Studio in Manhattan. While there, the two 15-year-olds were noticed by music promoter Sid Prosen who, after speaking to their parents, signed them to his independent label Big Records as Tom and Jerry. Released in 1957, with their "Dancin' Wild" on the flip-side, it sold over 100,000 copies and peaked at 49 on the charts, no doubt helped by Prosen bribing deejay Alan Freed with $200 to play the single on his nightly radio show!

Still using the name Jerry Landis, Simon wrote and recorded over three dozen songs during this period, sometimes solo and occasionally as Tom and Jerry, and all released on various minor labels under different pseudonyms. The novelty song "The Lone Teen Ranger" was his only chart entry. In 1961, he moved to Madison Records and recorded as Tico & the Triumphs, and when the label and Simon's contract were bought by Amy Records the following year, the single "Motorcycle" scraped into the charts. Some of the recordings from this period were credited to Simon/Landis (the Simon being his brother Eddie.) While at Amy, Simon worked as writer and producer for several artists on the label while also performing at Greenwich Village clubs at night.

After graduating high school, Simon attended Queens College, majoring in English before graduating in 1963, while at the same time Garfunkel was studying mathematics at Manhattan's Columbia University. Simon then went on to Brooklyn

Law School, but dropped out after one semester to travel to England to play on the folk circuit (with Garfunkel joining him in the summer). While there, Simon recorded the solo single "He Was My Brother" for the independent Oriole label, with lyrics describing a friend killed during the civil rights disturbances. (In the US it was credited to Kane). During this time, Simon made money cutting demos for music publishers, having been introduced to contacts by fellow demo-maker Carole Klein (later Carole King).

In September 1963, while performing at Gerde's Folk City club in Greenwich, they caught the attention of Tom Wilson, a producer for Columbia Records, and they convinced him to let them have a studio audition. Performing Simon's new song, "The Sounds of Silence" (as it was originally titled), Columbia executive Clive Davis signed them to a record deal, but as Simon & Garfunkel instead of Tom & Jerry (which, according to Simon, was the first time in pop music that artists' surnames had been used without their first names).

Their debut album *Wednesday Morning, 3 A.M* was released in 1964, with five of the 12 tracks written by Simon. The standout one, of course, was "The Sounds of Silence." Written in a darkened bathroom when he was 21, Simon recalled how he was able to sit by himself, play and dream. Two years later, he reflected that the song was about the inability of people to communicate with each other, especially emotionally, and therefore unable to love each other. Although the album was a commercial failure, "The Sounds of Silence" began to get increasing airplay, and with folk rock now beginning to make waves on the radio, Wilson took the initiative to record a new version, albeit without the singer's knowledge. In June 1965, during sessions for Bob Dylan's "Like a Rolling Stone," Wilson retained some of the musicians and had engineer Roy Halee employ a heavy echo to the recording, which was now re-named "The Sound of Silence." Months later, while on tour in Denmark, Simon got to hear it for the first time and was "horrified." Nevertheless, it topped the Hot 100.

While abroad, Simon's contract with Columbia allowed him to record with their British label CBS. At a cost of £60, he recorded solo acoustic versions of songs at a London studio that would later reappear on his debut solo album *The Paul Simon Songbook,* which was initially only made available in the UK. The opening track, "I Am a Rock," dealt with isolation and emotional detachment, while the beautiful "Kathy's Song" was dedicated to Simon's girlfriend Kathy Chitty during his sojourn in England.

In September 1965, Simon was apparently waiting on the platform of Widnes railway station in Cheshire after appearing at the Howff folk club. Missing his girlfriend Kathy, he began writing "Homeward Bound" on a scrap of paper. The song would first appear on the UK release of the album *Sounds of Silence* (but held back in the US for the following album). Some of the other tracks from *Songbook* would also be re-recorded by Wilson for the album. However, among the other songs was the standout "Richard Cory," based on Edwin Arlington Robinson's 1897 poem of the same name which they had both read and studied while students at Forest Hills. It explores the themes that status and wealth do not ensure happiness, as demonstrated by the rich and admired Cory, who kills himself and shocks the people who had envied him.

Simon later offered advice to would-be songwriters: "It's very helpful to start with something that's true. If you start with something's that false, you're always covering your tracks. Something simple and true, that has a lot of possibilities, is a nice way to begin."

With the success of the single "The Sound of Silence", the duo regrouped after a time apart and spent three months in the studio recording the new album, *Parsley, Sage, Rosemary and Thyme*. Many of the acoustic numbers were written while in England, as well as the re-recorded versions from his solo album. "Scarborough Fair/Canticle" was inspired by the traditional 18th century English ballad about the number of impossible tasks given to a former lover who lives in the North Yorkshire town. The melody used by the duo had originally been sung to folk singer Ewan McColl by a retired lead miner in 1947. The song was recorded in counterpoint with "Canticle," a re-working of Simon's lyrics to his anti-war song "The Side of a Hill," while the arrangement was by Martin Carthy, although not credited. "The 59th Street Bridge Song (Feelin' Groovy)" was inspired by Simon taking a daytime walk across New York's Queensboro Bridge and later became a hit for Harpers Bizarre. "The Dangling Conversation," with Simon's most ambitious lyrics to date, failed to make a big impression on the charts, leaving him bitterly disappointed with what he considered the album's best track. Garfunkel also had one of his finest moments in "For Emily, Now That I've Found Her," with his ethereal vocal describing the moment of finding solace in a lover, albeit an imaginary one. The album closes with "7 O'Clock News/Silent Night," which juxtaposed the traditional carol with a simulated news bulletin voiced by radio deejay Charlie O'Connell, and describing actual events from the summer of 1966, and referencing among others Richard Nixon, Lenny Bruce, and Martin Luther King.

Their fourth studio album *Bookends* was loosely biographical, explored life's journey from child to old age and contained many of Simon's major themes. Beginning lyrically with "Save the Life of My Child" about a mother-child relationship, the cycle of life ends with "At the Zoo" in which he anthropomorphised animals in various amusing ways. Inbetween, there were three of Simon's most popular songs. "America," one of his strongest writing efforts, came from a 1964 road trip with his girlfriend Chitty, who he had brought back with him from England, while "A Hazy Shade of Winter" dates back to his time in England when he was unsure of his achievements. Around the time of the recording, film director Mike Nichols was working on *The Graduate* and was interested in two of Simon's songs. Granted permission by Clive Davis, Nicholls met up with Simon who agreed to write at least one new song for the movie. Although two of the songs offered were not to Nichols' liking, a third one, an early version of "Mrs Robinson," was readily accepted. The song was originally titled "Mrs Roosevelt" until they all agreed to change it for the movie. The Grammy Award-winning single shot to number one in April 1968 and became one of their biggest international hits.

Following the release of *Bookends*, Garfunkel took an acting role in the movie *Catch-22* while Simon began working on songs for their next album *Bridge Over Troubled Water*, writing all the tracks except a cover of "Bye Bye Love." In March 1969 one of those songs, "The Boxer" was released as a stand-alone single. Having taken some 100 hours to produce at various locations, the largely autobiographical song was partially inspired by the Bible and composed at a time when Simon felt that his work was being unfairly criticized. Produced by Roy Halee, the song was recorded in a number of locations, including Columbia University's St Paul's Chapel, and mixed in synchrony on two 8-track tape recorders. For the "lie-la-lie" refrain, Halee and Wrecking Crew drummer Hal Blaine found a spot for the drums in front of an elevator in the Columbia offices, with Blaine pounding the snare drum "like a cannon shot" at the end of the "lie-la-lie" vocals that were being played on his headphones.

Released in January 1970, the title track for *Bridge Over Troubled Water* had been written early in 1969 and had come to Simon very quickly. It was inspired by gospel singer Claude Jeter's line "I'll be your bridge over deep water if you trust in my name" in the song "Mary Don't You Weep," recorded by his group the Swan Silvertones in 1959. For the melody, Simon referenced Bach's "O Sacred Head Now Wounded" for inspiration. Although Garfunkel felt Simon should do the lead vocal, it ended up with him and producer Halee asking Simon to add a third verse with a "bigger ending" with both sharing lead. The lyrics of the added verse were inspired by Simon's then-wife Peggy Harper after noticing her first grey hairs (hence the line, "Sail on, silver girl") The single topped the US charts for six weeks, and ended up selling over six million copies.

The album also had other fine moments. The angelic "The Only Living Boy In New York," was written while Garfunkel was filming in Mexico and Simon left alone and isolated back in the city. The heaven-sent "aaahs" at the end of the song were produced by the two of them screaming 13 times in an echo chamber and then having it multi-tracked eight times. In the song, Simon refers to Tom, which alludes to their early days when Garfunkel was the "Tom" of Tom and Jerry. "El Cóndor Pasa (If I Could)," was a Peruvian song, originally composed as an instrumental by Daniel Robles in 1913, and had Simon writing the English lyrics, although later losing a lawsuit over copyright. "So Long, Frank Lloyd Wright" was both Simon's tribute to the famous architect but also a look back on their earlier career, with Garfunkel's ambition to be an architect and a prediction that they will eventually split up. During the recording, Halee can even be heard shouting the portentous message, "So long already, Artie."

The two artists indeed became irascible due to the long recording sessions and their partnership came to an abrupt end just a month after the album was released. Simon continued recording as a solo artist with several ground-breaking albums, while Garfunkel also had success with albums of covers. They eventually reunited in 1975 for the Simon-penned single "My Little Town," which appeared on both their solo albums, and a string of well-received concerts followed over the coming years.

Chart entries
Motorcycle – Tico & the Triumphs (US 1962 # 99)
The Lone Teen Ranger – Paul Simon *(as Jerry Landis)* US 1963 # 97)
The Sound Of Silence - Simon & Garfunkel (US 1965 # 1); The Bachelors (UK 1966 # 3)
Homeward Bound - Simon & Garfunkel (US 1966 # 5; UK # 9); The Quiet Five (UK 1966
  # 44)
Someday, One Day – The Seekers (UK 1966 # 11)
I Am A Rock - Simon & Garfunkel (US 1966 # 3; UK # 17)
Red Rubber Ball *(with Bruce Woodley)* The Cyrkle (US 1966 # 2)
The Dangling Conversation - Simon & Garfunkel (US 1966 # 25; UK # 51)
A Hazy Shade of Winter - Simon & Garfunkel (US 1966 # 13)
The 59th Street Bridge Song (Feelin' Groovy) – Harpers Bizaare (US 1967 # 13; UK # 34)
At the Zoo - Simon & Garfunkel (US 1967 # 16)
Fakin' It -Simon & Garfunkel (US 1967 # 23)
Scarborough Fair/Canticle *(trad, with Art Garfunkel)* Simon & Garfunkel (US 1968 # 11)
Mrs Robinson - Simon & Garfunkel (US 1968 # 1; UK # 4); Booker T & the MGs (US
  1969 # 37)
The Boxer – Simon & Garfunkel (US 1969 # 7; UK # 6)

Grace Slick see also **Paul Kantner**
Born Grace Barnett Wing, Highland Park, Illinois 1939.
Rock and Roll Hall of Fame 1996 (with Jefferson Airplane).

As a child, her parents moved several times before settling at Palo Alto in the San Francisco area of California in the early Fifties. After graduating from a private all-girl school, she completed her education at Finch College in New York and the University of Miami. Learning to play guitar and compose music, she took a job as a model in a department store and later married musician and cinematographer Jerry Slick. Although initially uncertain about pursuing a career in music, that all changed in August 1965. After reading an article in the *San Francisco Chronicle* about a newly-formed rock band called Jefferson Airplane, she went to see them perform at Frisco's Matrix nightclub and it inspired her to form her own rock band, the Great Society, with her becoming its visual and musical focal point. The other members were her husband (drums), brother-in-law Darby Slick (lead guitar), David Miner (rhythm guitar), and Bard DuPont (bass), who would soon be replaced by Peter van Gelder (flute, bass, sax). They made their debut at the Coffee Gallery in October, and then recorded several tracks at Golden State Recorders under the supervision of Sly Stone.

In February 1967, the band released their only single, Darby Slick's "Somebody to Love," on the Northbeach label. Written after realising his girlfriend had left him, it featured Grace on guitar, piano and recorder, and despite her impressive lead vocal, made little impact outside the Bay area. Once they began to open for more successful local bands, including Jefferson Airplane, the Great Society were offered a recording contract with Columbia Records, but before anything was signed Grace was asked by Airplane's Jack Cassidy to join the band, replacing their lead singer Signe Toly Anderson who left to raise a child. Slick also stated that she decided to join them as they were a more professional band. Without her, the Great Society dissolved that fall, and so did Grace and Jerry's marriage in 1971.

On October 16th 1966, Slick made her debut performance with Airplane and almost immediately it became their commercial breakthrough. With her good looks and stage presence, and, of course, her powerful contralto voice, it was well-suited for the band's heavier psychedelic music. The first album she recorded with them was 1967's *Surrealistic Pillow,* which not only saw the band turn from folk-rock to a more psychedelic direction, but is now considered one of the most quintessential albums of the era with its musical portrait of the free-thinking Summer of Love. When Slick joined the band, she brought along Darby's "Somebody to Love" and her own "White Rabbit." With lyrics written around late December 1965, "White Rabbit" was based on Lewis Carroll's 1865 children's book *Alice's Adventures in Wonderland* and its sequel *Through the Looking Glass.* Slick saw a surfeit of drug references in the books, including mushrooms, a smoking caterpillar, and substances that changed appearance and perception.

She combined the would-be harmless tales with an LSD trip. although she saw it as a wake-up call to parents who read such novels to their children, claiming that unlike most fairytales there was no Prince Charming to save them, just a girl on her own in a strange place following her curiosity - the White Rabbit. She also took the line "feed your head" to mean read some books and pay attention. For the music, Slick spent hours listening to Miles Davis's album *Sketches of Spain,* especially the opening track "Concierto de Aranjuez." The song's dark Spanish march-style track was also influenced by Ravel's *Boléro*. Slick composed the music on a second-hand upright piano that had keys missing and felt it was perfectly in tune with what was going in the Bay area at the time (also admitting it was written after an acid trip.) The Great Society's version had a lengthy instrumental passage and was performed in a raga style that typified their musical approach. Rock critic Michael Gallucci called it "one of the druggiest cuts ever recorded." Both "Somebody to Love" and "White Rabbit" became top ten singles.

Slick also wrote "Lather," the opening track on Airplane's third album *Crown of Creation* in 1968, which was inspired by the band's drummer Spencer Dryden, who, almost thirty years her senior, was her boyfriend at the time. The following year, Slick began a long-term relationship with band member Paul Kantner and they had a child together. In 1974, after two members left the band, Slick and Kantner formed Jefferson Starship.

Asked about her writing, she once replied: "So I get finished writing a song and what I hear is the vocal and the instrument I'm playing, and everything else is a delightful surprise. 'Cause I don't picture anything else."

Chart entries
White Rabbit – Jefferson Airplane (US 1967 # 8)
Greasy Heart – Jefferson Airplane (US 1968 # 98)

P F Sloan see also Steve Barri
Born Philip Gary Schlein, New York City 1945. Died 2015.

Born to an American father and Romanian mother, his family moved to West Hollywood in 1957, where his father, a pharmacist, changed the family name to Sloan to be able to sell liquor in the store. Learning to play guitar at the age of 13, he met Elvis Presley in a music store and was given an impromptu music lesson. The following year, as "Flip" Sloan, he recorded a single "All I Want Is Loving" for the short-lived Los Angeles label Aladdin Records. At the age of 16, he got a job as staff writer for music publisher Screen Gems and there formed a partnership with Steve Barri (b.1942). After attempting to record a hit single using various names, they were noticed by executive Lou Adler, manager of Jan & Dean, who used them as backing singers and musicians for the artists. With Sloan on lead guitar and Barri on percussion, they were credited on a number of their albums, with Jan Berry using Sloan's falsetto as lead vocal on the hit single "The Little Old Lady From Pasadena." Around the same time, Sloan and Barri also wrote the theme song for the popular *T.A.M.I Show*. In May 1964, they had their first chart success as writers with "Kick That Little Foot, Sally Ann" for Los Angeles singer "Round" Robin Lloyd, and continued scoring hits for surfing artists like Bruce & Terry and the Rip Chords. They even had their own surf-related singles and album as the Fantastic Baggys.

With their success, Adler hired them for his new publishing business Trousdale Music and the label Dunhill Records. Shortly after, Sloan wrote what would become his most celebrated song, "Eve of Destruction." Referencing the social issues of the time, including the Vietnam War, the Space Race, and the Civil Rights Movement, its controversial lyrics would see it banned by some radio stations. It was first offered to the Byrds who turned it down, and then the Turtles, who recorded their own version as a track on their debut album *It Ain't Me Babe*. Finally, folk-rock singer Barry Maguire, ex-member of the New Christy Minstrels, recorded a definitive version that had Sloan on acoustic guitar along with two members of the Wrecking Crew. Recorded in one take from words scrawled on crumpled paper, Maguire, not liking the song, appeared to rush it. Although his vocal was not intended for the final version, a rough mix was leaked to a local deejay and it began to get sufficient airplay for a more polished vocal not to be required. In 1971, the song would later be used as a rallying cry by supporters of the 26th Amendment, which changed the voting age from 21 to 18.

In March 1966, Adler requested the writing pair to work on a project for a Byrds/Turtles-type folk rock duo. Having already been asked to write songs to cash in on the growing movement, they chose "Where Were You When I Needed You." Originally intended for Herman's Hermits, it was recorded as the Grass Roots, with session musicians and Sloan on lead vocal. Demos sent to local radio stations gained interest, but the label wanted a real band that could tour under that name. Sloan and Barri found the Frisco band the Bedouins who met the criteria and they went on to tour and make tv appearances. Apart from the lead vocalist and the drummer, none of the others members appeared on recordings, which had Sloan and session musicians playing. After the failure of a subsequent album, the label decided to re-start and groom another group for the role. After one group declined, a third one was found with the 13th Floor from Los Angeles. As the new Grass Roots, they had their first top ten hit with a cover of "Lets Live For Today," and were given more input in the writing and playing.

After recording a solo album in 1968 called *Measure of Pleasure,* Sloan left the music business due to illness and a fallout with the label. He once remarked, "Songwriters don't cry tears, they cry diamonds."

Chart entries
Eve of Destruction – Barry Maguire (US 195 # 1; UK # 3)
The Sins of a Family – P F Sloan (US 1965 # 87)
Let Me Be – The Turtles (US 1965 # 29)
Child of Our Times – Barry Maguire (US 1965 # 72)

P F Sloan and Steve Barri
Kick That Little Foot, Sally Ann - Round Robin (US 1964 # 61)
Summer Means Fun - Bruce & Terry (US 1964 # 72)
One Piece Topless Bathing Suite *(with Don Altfeld)* The Rip Chords (US 1964 # 96)
Secret Agent Man - The Ventures (US 1966 # 54); Johnny Rivers (US 1966 # 3)
Where Were You When I Needed You - The Grass Roots (US 1966 # 28)
Only When You're Lonely - The Grass Roots (US 1966 # 96)
Things I Should Have Said - The Grass Roots (US 1967 # 23)
Wake Up, Wake Up - The Grass Roots (US 1967 # 68)

Carl Smith see Raynard Miner

James Marcus Smith (P J Proby) see also Steve Barri
Born Huntsville, Texas 1938.

Smith was the great-grandson of Western outlaw John Wesley Hardin, and as a young child sang harmonies with his mother with the radio on. His parents divorced when he was nine, and as part of the custody deal was sent to a military school, finally ending up at the Western Military Academy. Smith always wanted a career in movies, and at the age of 18 travelled to Hollywood with the aim of becoming an actor and recording artist. With agents giving him the stage name Jett Powers, he took singing and acting lessons and had small roles in a few movies, as well as cutting two singles for a couple of independent labels. In 1960, songwriter Sharon Sheeley had him change his stage name to P J Proby (after a former high school boyfriend) and got him a writing contract with Metric Music, the publishing branch of Liberty Records. After several unsuccessful recordings, he switched to writing songs and recording demos for top artists like Elvis Presley and Bobby Vee, with Johnny Burnette's "Clown Shoes" being the last UK chart hit credited to his real name in 1962.

Proby then went to London where he was introduced to tv producer Jack Good by his friends Sheeley and Jackie DeShannon. With Good, he recorded a number of chart hits, including "Hold Me," "Somewhere" and "Maria," the last two taken from the musical *West Side Story*. In January 1965, he was banned from theatres and tv shows after famously splitting his trousers at a show in Croydon, and as a result his popularity suffered. Proby then formed a partnership with songwriter Steve Barri (b. 1942) and over the next couple of years their songs brought chart success for artists like Herman's Hermits and the Turtles.

Chart entries
James Marcus Smith and Steve Barri
(Here They Come) From All Over the World - Jan & Dean (US 1965 # 56)
I Found a Girl - Jan & Dean (US 1965 # 31)
A Must To Avoid - Herman's Hermits (UK 1965 # 6; US # 8)
You Baby - The Turtles (US 1966 # 20)
Can I Get To Know You Better - The Turtles (US 1966 # 89)
Another Day, Another Heartache - The Fifth Dimension (US 1967 # 45)

Mike Smith see Dave Clark

Joe South
Born Joseph Alfred Souter, Atlanta Georgia 1940. Died 2012.
Nashville Songwriters Hall of Fame 1979.

As a young boy, South was given a guitar by his father and later built his own small radio station for playing his own songs. Modifying his name as a teenager, he had his first break in 1958 with the novelty song "The Purple People Eater Meets the Witch Doctor," a cover of the b-side to the Big Bopper's hit "Chantilly Lace." Reaching the top 50, it spurred South on to become a full-time songwriter. After a meeting with Bill Lowery, an Atlanta music publisher and radio personality, he was encouraged to begin a recording career in Atlanta with the National Recording Corporation. While there, he also worked as staff guitarist alongside other musicians that included Ray Stevens and Jerry Reed. The following year, two of his songs, "I Might Have Known" and "Gone Gone Gone, were recorded as album tracks by Gene Vincent. Returning to Nashville, South continued with session work, playing guitar on Dylan's album *Blonde on Blonde*, Aretha Franklin's hit "Chain of Fools," and Simon & Garfunkel's album *Sounds of Silence*. Also in the mid-Sixties, he wrote a number of hits for the Tams and Billy Joe Royal, before forming his own band, Joe South & the Believers, along with brother Tommy South and sister-in-law Barbara South. Among the songs he penned for the band were "I'll Come Back To You," "Great Day," "Don't It Make You Want To Go Home," and "Walk a Mile In My Shoes."

By 1969, South's writing style had radically changed in response to the worrying issues of the time, and it was clearly evident in his most famous song, "Games People Play." With the title taken from the 1964 bestselling book by Eric Byrne about social interactions, it was an international hit and went on to win two Grammys. Two years later, he would achieve his greatest chart success with Lynn Anderson's worldwide hit, "Rose Garden," which was also nominated for two Grammys.

Chart entries
Untie Me – The Tams (US 1962 # 60)
Silly Little Girl – The Tams (US 1964 # 87)
Down in the Boondocks – Billy Joe Royal (US 1965 # 9)
I Knew You When – Billy Joe Royal (US 1965 # 14)
I've Got To Be Somebody – Billy Joe Royal (US 1965 # 38)
Heart's Desire – Billy Joe Royal (US 1966 # 88)
Hush – Billy Joe Royal (US 1967 # 52); Deep Purple (UK 58; US # 4)
Games People Play – Joe South (US 1969 # 1; UK # 6)
The Greatest Love – Dorsey Burnette (US 1969 # 67)

Phil Spector
Born Harvey Philip Spector, Los Angeles 1939. Died 2021.
Rock and Roll Hall of Fame 1989.
Songwriters Hall of Fame 1997.

Born in the Bronx to Russian-Jewish parents, his father, deeply in debt, took his own life in 1949 and on his gravestone were inscribed the words, "To Know Him Was To Love Him." In 1953, his mother moved the family to Los Angeles where young Spector attended John Burroughs Junior High School before going on two years later to Fairfax High School. Already having learned to play guitar, Spector joined a loose-knit community of young aspirants that included future stars Sandy Nelson, Lou Adler, Bruce Johnston and Steve Douglas. Spector became a close friend of Marshall Leib and they formed a short-lived, unsuccessful band with pianist Michael Spencer. They then joined fellow Fairfax student Annette Kleinbard as a vocal trio. With money saved, they booked a recording session at Gold Star Studio along with a fourth member, bass singer Harvey Goldstein. They recorded one of Spector's songs, "Don't You Worry My Little Pet." Engineered by Stan Ross, it featured Spector's soon-to-be signature rapid-fire production with instrumental overdubs and even layered harmony vocals, albeit crudely done.

Ross was instrumental in tutoring Spector in record production. Taking the disc to town, it was picked up by Era Records, and after some thought, the four members came up with a name for their group, the Teddy Bears. A flip-side was also needed, and the label chose Spector's ballad "Wonderful Loveable You." With Goldstein about to be called up in the Army Reserve, he did not make the recording, and in fact was never invited to return to the group. Another of Spector's songs that drew attention was "To Know Him, Is To Love Him," inspired by the inscription on his father's headstone. With his heartfelt lyrics and Annette's delicately high vocal, it set the beautiful song apart from anything else that was in the charts at the time. Quickly done at the end of the session, it was taken up by Era's subsidiary label Dore in August 1958 as the b-side, but quickly switched when deejays preferred the new song. By December, it had topped the charts.

At the age of 19, Spector had just written, arranged, produced, played and sung the best-selling single in the country. Switching to the Imperial label, the Teddy Bears' subsequent releases, including an album, were unable to repeat the success, and with Kleinbard seriously injured in a car accident in 1960, Spector disbanded the group. While recording the Teddy Bears' album, Spector had also met former promotion man Lester Sill, who was a mentor for songwriting duo Leiber and Stoller. Along with his partner Lee Hazlewood, they agreed to support Spector's next project, the Spectors Three, consisting of Spector, Russ Titleman and female session singer Ricky Page. They had several singles on the Trey label, including the Spector-penned "I Really Do" and "Mr Robin."

In 1960, Sill had Spector apprenticed to Leiber & Stoller in New York, where he co-wrote "Spanish Harlem" with Leiber, a top ten hit for Ben E King, and as a sessionist played a guitar solo on the Drifters' "On Broadway." They also recommended Spector to produce, among others, "Pretty Little Angel Eyes" for Curtis Lee. In the meantime, Sill and Hazlewood had formed the new label Gregmark, and on Spector's return to Hollywood had him produce "I Love How You Love Me," a top five hit for the Paris Sisters (Albeth, Sherrell and Priscilla).

In 1961, Sill, having ended his partnership with Hazlewood, teamed up with Spector to establish the Philles label, the name being a hybrid of their first names (The following year, he would buy Sill's stock, becoming the country's youngest label owner at 22). While continuing to work freelance, he searched for new artists, and out of a possible three groups he wanted to produce, he chose the New York female vocal quartet, the Crystals. For their debut single he co-wrote "There's No Other (Like My Baby)" with Leroy Bates. With Barbara Alton's superb lead vocal, it peaked at number twenty on the charts, although Spector apparently neglected to pay them.

The following year, while temporarily working as an A&R producer for Liberty, Spector heard the song "He's A Rebel" written by Gene Pitney for the Shirelles, who turned it down because of its anti-establishment lyric. With it due to be released by Liberty with their singer Vicki Carr, Spector wanted it for the Crystals, but they were 3,000 miles away in New York. Wasting no time, he rushed to Gold Star studio, assembled a group of musicians, and had Darlene Wright of the Blossoms record it. Spector signed her to a contract with the new name Darlene Love, and it was recorded with Love on lead vocal, and the Blossoms (Fanita James and Gracia Nitzsche) as backing singers. When released on the Philles label, it was attributed to the Crystals and became a chart-topper. Carr had to wait three years before she had her first hit record with "It Must Be Him." Spector would have the Blossoms posing as the Crystals once more on the hit "He's Sure the Boy I Love."

Dolores "Dee Dee" Kenniebrew, one of the founding members of the Crystals, recalled later: " When we rehearsed it [He's a Rebel] we hadn't particularly liked it. Also, we'd already had two hit records in the States, plus and album, yet we still hadn't been paid. Phil Spector probably thought we were giving him too much hassle about money, so he got a studio group to record the song. Unfortunately, our first manager didn't get us a good contract and Spector was able to use the group's name."

Spector used royalties from the records to buy out his partners, and as the label's sole owner formed a new group, Bob B Soxx & the Blue Jeans, with Love, James and Bobby Sheen. Their first single was a cover of "Zip-a-Dee Doo-Dah," from the 1946 Disney movie *Song of the South*. During the recording, engineer Larry Levine overloaded the microphone on the guitar player causing distortion, and Spector told him to leave it like that. It was a method that other artists copied and later led to the invention of the fuzz box. Spector also co-wrote "Why Do Lovers Break Each Other's Heart," another chart hit for the group.

Around the same time, Spector needed another hit song for the Crystals, now with Dolores "LaLa" Brooks as lead vocalist. For two days he sat in his New York office with songwriters Jeff Barry and Ellie Greenwich and composed "Da Doo Ron Ron." Using the nonsense syllables as a dummy line until proper lyrics were written, Spector decided to keep it in the finished song and it became another huge success. Sonny Bono, a record producer who was at the recording, asked Spector if the song was "dumb enough" to be accessible to teenagers, and on playback Spector told him, "That's solid gold coming out of that speaker." And he was right, as it peaked at number three on the charts. The "Bill" mentioned in the opening lines was inspired by Bill Walsh, a friend of Spector who was present when the song was being written.

According to Love, she had recorded a lead vocal for the song, but Spector then changed his mind and brought in Brooks, who later recalled: "When I walked in the studio, all the musicians were there, and after they finished putting down the track, I sat there for hours. Me and Cher [a backing singer] went out to get something to eat. We come back, they're still putting down the track. All of a sudden, when the track is finished, Phil says, 'La La, go in the booth and put down the song now. I went in there, and cut down the song…"

In July 1963, Spector had successfully ended his partnership with Sill and had married Annette. He went back to New York looking for a follow-up song for the Crystals, and Barry and Greenwich gave him "Then He Kissed Me," for which Spector made some minor music contribution. Brooks was just 15 when she performed the song, and was the only member of the quartet present at the recording. To coax her vocal, Spector dimmed the studio lights and gave her specific instructions, "Think of someone kissing you…" The song reached number six on the Hot 100, and in 1967 was successfully covered by the Beach Boys as "Then I Kissed Her."

Almost simultaneously, Spector had auditioned the vocal trio the Ronettes, composed of sisters Veronica (Ronnie) and Estelle Bennett with their cousin Nedra Talley. As Ronnie & the Relatives they had had a string of unsuccessful singles on the Colpix label. Now looking to record elsewhere, Estelle had called Spector asking for an audition. Impressed by them doing an impromtu rendition of "Why Do Fools Fall in Love," he gave them a new song "Why Don't They Let Us Fall in Love," written with Barry & Greenwich, and had them record it at Gold Star. However, feeling they needed more time to refine their act, the release was withheld. Spector had not only been impressed by hearing 17-year-old Ronnie's vibrato voice, but was also developing a fixation for her too. Calling once again on Barry and Greenwich, they got together in his office and wrote "Be My Baby," which could have been interpreted as a declaration of his growing feelings for her (it worked anyway, as they would later marry).

Recorded at Gold Star, Spector had his right hand man Jack Nitzsche as arranger and his *de facto* house band, soon to be dubbed the "Wrecking Crew." The consistent layered use of several pianos, half a dozen guitars, bassists, drummers, percussionists, and sometimes strings and woodwinds in the mix, all played a part to create a tsunami of aural effects which was soon to be coined his "Wall of Sound." Hal Blaine later admitted that his iconic drum intro was done by accident after dropping a stick on the fourth beat. Like Brooks of the Crystals, Ronnie Bennett was the only member of the Ronettes to sing on the record, with Sonny Bono and Cher among the backing singers. Ronnie later explained that Spector had her rehearse the song for weeks, then spent another three days working on her vocal in the control room, even having her practice in the studio's ladies room where the acoustics helped her work out the "whoas" and the "oh-oh-ohs."

The single peaked at number two on the charts, and has since been cited as one of the greatest pop records ever made, at least as far as Beach Boy Brian Wilson and the Stones' Keith Richards were concerned. David Howard described it as "Spector's greatest achievement - two and a half sweaty minutes of sexual pop perfection."

By the fall of 1963, Spector was eager to do a follow-up single for the Ronettes. When they went on Dick Clark's *Caravan of Stars* nationwide tour, he kept Ronnie in California to record a new song, with Ronnie's cousin Elaine joining Estelle Bennett and Nedra Tally on the tour. The new song was "Baby, I Love You," written by Barry and Greenwich. For the recording at Gold Star in January 1964, Spector employed Bono, Cher and the Blossoms on backing vocals. It was yet another tour de force by the Wrecking Crew, especially Hal Blaine's powerhouse drumming on the intro, although it failed to repeat the chart success of "Be My Baby."

This was soon followed by the hits "(The Best Part of) Breaking Up," and "Do I Love You," both written for the Ronettes with Peter Andreoli and Vini Poncia of the pop group Trade Winds. A few weeks later, Spector had a chart-topper as co-writer with "Chapel of Love." It had been written a year before by Barry and Greenwich, who themselves had recently married, and was first recorded by Darlene Love. With Spector unhappy with her recorded version, it would remain unreleased for years. Meanwhile, a trio of young female singers called the Mel-Tones were looking for a record deal and passed an audition with songwriters Leiber and Stoller, who had set up their new Red Bird label in the Brill Building. They performed "Chapel of Love," and after rehearsing with Barry and Greenwich, it was decided to release it as a single on Red Bird with their new name the Dixie Cups. With Leiber and Stoller supplying additional lyrics, it was produced by all four songwriters and topped the charts for three weeks in May 1964. Spector had been brought in to help finish the song, but his contribution as writer remains unclear.

Just four months later came one of the last great songs by the Ronettes with "(Walking) In the Rain," which had Spector enlist New York husband-and-wife writers Barry Mann & Cynthia Weil. With its thunder and lightning sound effects, it won engineer Levine a Grammy nomination. Ronnie recorded her vocals in just one take, and late recalled: "{Mann, Weil and Spector] were writing it while we were in London. When I came back, I told them I loved the English rain and fog … When it came to the vocal, I went in the booth, closed my eyes and - boom! I said, 'Shall I do it again?' And they said, 'No, that was it.'"

However, the "British Invasion," beginning with the arrival of the Beatles, would signal the demise of the girl-group era, which Spector had had such a significant part in creating.

After seeing the Righteous Brothers perform on the same bill as the Ronettes, Spector was so impressed with their blue-eyed soul voices that he signed them up as his first white act after buying their contract from Moonglow Records. For their first recording, Spector had Mann & Weil write them a song. Taking hints from the Four Tops' current hit "Baby I Need Your Loving," they decided on the ballad "You've Lost That Lovin' Feelin," with Mann first writing the melody and the opening line, and both of them quickly writing the first two verses and the chorus. Spector's contribution was adding "gone, gone, gone, whoa, whoa, whoa," which was not to Weil's liking, but he did help lend a hand when they struggled with the bridge and ending. Bobby Hatfield also expressed disappointment to Spector for having to wait until the chorus before joining in with his tenor vocal. Spector famously replied that while he waited, he could "go directly to the bank!" The single became the label's second chart-topper.

With two of his songs already considered some of the best ever recorded, Spector was now set to give the world what many consider his masterpiece. After seeing the Ike &Tina Turner Review perform at a Sunset Strip nightclub, he invited them to appear on the *Big T.N.T Show,* a tv pop concert he was producing. Impressed by Tina's voice, he made a deal to get them released from their current contract and sign with Philles. Ike agreed, but only if recordings were credited to them both. Spector then had Barry & Greenwich help write a song for them.

At the then un-heard of cost of $22,000, Spector recorded "River Deep - Mountain High" at Gold Star, first taking two sessions with 21 musicians to lay down the track, and then bringing in Tina to do the vocals. A first attempt was deemed unsatisfactory, so after a week's rest she returned for a gruelling three-hour session until they had the perfect take. Although Ike had been invited to play guitar on the session, he never turned up (rumour has it that Spector paid him not to). The result was nothing short of a masterclass of production. The musicians present were Leon Russell (keyboards), Michel Rubini (piano), Jim Horn (sax), Barney Kessel (guitar), Glen Campbell (guitar), Earl Palmer (drums), Carole Kaye (bass) and Frank Capp (percussion). Although only a minor hit in the US, it was better received in Europe, peaking at number three in the UK charts in May 1966 (although only credited to Tina). Ike Turner later stated: "If Phil had released the record and put anybody else's name on it, it would have been a huge R&B hit. But because Tina Turner's name was on it, the white stations classified it as an R&B record and wouldn't play it. The white stations say it was too black, and the black stations say it was too white, so that record didn't have a home."

Spector's final chart release for the Ronettes was with the Barry & Greenwich "I Can Hear Music," which surprisingly just scraped into the Hot 100, although successfully revived by the Beach Boys two years later. In the summer of 1966, Spector brought in Jeff Barry and Bob Crewe to produce Ike & Tina Turner and the Ronettes. Still frustrated with the poor chart showing of what he deemed his best work and with a failed attempt to sell Philles to the A&M label, he lost his enthusiasm with the record industry and became somewhat of a recluse, only making a brief return in 1969 to work first with the Beatles and then with John Lennon and George Harrison on their solo projects.

Remaining largely inactive for the next three decades, Spector was later diagnosed with a bipolar disorder. Looking back on his career, Spector wrote: "I felt obliged to change music to art, the same way Galileo proved the Earth was round to the world and that the sun did not stand still." In 2009 he was convicted of the 2003 murder of Hollywood actress Lana Clarkson, and died in 2021 from complications caused by Covid-19.

Chart entries
To Know You Is To Love You – Peter and Gordon (UK 1965 # 5; US # 24); Bobby Vinton (US 1969
　# 34)

Phil Spector and Barry & Greenwich
Da Doo Ron Ron – The Crystals (US 1963 #3; UK # 5)
Not Too Young To Get Married – Bob B Soxx & the Blue Jeans (US 1963 # 63)
Wait 'Til My Bobby Gets Home – Darlene Love (US 1963 # 26)
Then He Kissed Me – The Crystals (US 1963 # 6; UK # 2); The Beach Boys (UK 1967 # 4
　(as Then I Kissed Her)
Be My Baby – The Ronettes (US 1963 # 2; UK # 4)
A Fine, Fine Boy – Darlene Love (US 1963 # 53)
Baby, I Love You – The Ronettes (US 1963 # 24; UK # 11); Andy Kim (US 1969 # 9)
Little Boy – The Crystals (US 1964 # 92)
I Wonder – The Crystals (UK 1964 # 36)
Chapel of Love – The Dixie Cups (US 1964 # 1; UK # 22)
All Grown Up – The Crystals (US 1964 # 98)
River Deep, Mountain High – Ike & Tina Turner (US 1966 # 88; UK # 3); Deep Purple
　(US 1969 # 53)

I Can Hear Music – The Ronettes (US 1966 # 100); The Beach Boys (US 1969 # 24; UK # 10)
I'll Never Need More Than This – Ike & Tina Turner (US 1969 # 114; UK #64)

Phil Spector and Ellie Greenwich & Tony Powers
Why Do Lovers Break Each Other's Heart? - Bob B Soxx & the Blue Jeans (US 1963 # 38)
(Today I Met) The Boy I'm Gonna Marry - Darlene Love (US 1963 # 39)

Phil Spector and Goffin & King
Just Once In My Life – Righteous Brothers (US 1965 # 9)
Is This What I Get For Loving You? - The Ronettes (US 1965 # 75)
Hung On You – The Righteous Brothers (US 1965 # 47)

Phil Spector and Mann & Weil
(Walking) In the Rain – The Ronettes (US 1964 # 23; UK # 3); The Walker Brothers (UK 1967 # 26); Jay & the Americans (US 1969 # 19)
You've Lost That Lovin' Feelin' – Righteous Brothers (US 1964 # 1; UK # 1); Cilla Black (UK 1965 # 2); Dionne Warwick (US 1969 # 16); Righteous Brothers (UK 1969 # 10)
Born To Be Together – The Ronettes (US 1965 # 52)

Phil Spector with others
First Taste Of Love *(with Doc Pomus)* Ben E King (UK 1960 # 27)
Spanish Harlem *(with Jerry Leiber)* Ben E King (US 1960 #10); Jimmy Justice (UK 1962 # 20); Sounds Incorporated (UK 1964 # 35) King Curtis (US 1965 # 89)
Be My Boy *(with Cory Sands)* The Paris Sisters (US 1961 # 56)
Young Boy Blues *(with Mort Schuman)* Ben E King (US 1961 # 66)
There's No Other (Like My Baby) *(with Leroy Bates)* The Crystals (US 1961 # 20)
Ecstasy *(with Doc Pomus)* Ben E King (US 1962 # 56)
Second-Hand Love *(with Hank Hunter)* Connie Francis (US 1962 # 7)
(The Best Part of) Breaking Up *(with Vince Poncia, Pete Andreoli)* The Ronettes (US 1964 # 39;
UK # 43); The Symbols (UK 1968 # 25)
Do I Love You? *(with Vince Poncia, Pete Andreoli)* The Ronettes (US 1964 # 34; UK 35)
Love Is All I Have To Give *(with Bobby Stevens)* Checkmates Ltd (US 1969 # 65)
Black Pearl *(with Tony Wine, Irwin Levine)* Sonny James (US 1969 # 13)

Philip Springer see Buddy Kaye

Tom Springfield
Born Dionysius Patrick O'Brien, London 1934. Died 2022.

As the elder brother of Mary O'Brien (future star Dusty Springfield), he attended the Royal Grammar School in High Wycombe, and later did his National Service at the Joint Services School for Linguistics, training conscripts in intelligence techniques. As a talented pianist, he sometimes played as part of a trio in the NAFFI. Later assigned to the Intelligence Corps, he teamed up with two musicians to form the vocal trio the Pedini Brothers, playing a mixture of ragtime, adapted Russian songs, and also Latin American, one of which was the self-penned "Magdelena." After leaving the military in 1954, he worked in banking for a time before pursuing a music career.

In 1960, after performing as one of the vocal group the Lana Sisters, Mary, along with Riss Long and Lynne Abrams, formed a folk duo called the Kensington Squares with Tim Field. She also invited her brother to join them as a new folk-pop vocal trio called the Springfields (Dion and his sister adopted the stage names Tom and "Dusty" Springfield, the latter being her childhood nickname given to her when playing football with boys in the street). With Tom's skill as a songwriter and Dusty's powerful vocal, they had their first hit with "Breakaway" in 1961. Their cover of "Silver Threads and Golden Needles" also became the first UK vocal group to make the US top twenty.

In late 1961, Field left the group to take care of his sick wife and was replaced by Mike Hurst. With him on board, they had their biggest success with Tom's much-covered "Island of Dreams," peaking at number five on the UK charts, followed by "Say I Won't Be There," which matched its chart position. With Dusty beginning to feel limited by their folk act and her brother's lead role within the trio, she decided to pursue a solo career, and the group announced they were disbanding while appearing on tv's *Sunday Night at the London Palladium* in October 1963.

While Dusty commenced what would be a spectacular solo career, Tom became songwriter and producer for the Australian folk-pop group the Seekers. Formed in Melbourne in 1962 with Athol Guy (double bass), Keith Potger (acoustic guitar) and Bruce Woodley (guitar), they were occasionally joined by jazz singer Judith Durham of the Escorts. With her wonderful soprano voice and connections with W&G Records, it led to her signing to the label as lead vocalist of the group. Their debut album *Introducing the Seekers* included their first single, "Kumbaya." During this period, Tom also wrote for other artists, including two songs with Clive Westlake - Frank Ifield's "Summer is Over" and sister Dusty's top ten hit "Losing You."

Toward the end of 1964, Tom (credited as Dion O'Brien) wrote and produced "I'll Never Find Another You" for the Seekers, their first UK chart entry and first chart-topper, thanks mainly to it being promoted by deejays on offshore Radio Caroline. In quick succession, it was followed by two more of his compositions. "A World of Our Own" was an international hit, covered three years later by singer Sonny James who had a country number one with it. "The Carnival Is Over" also topped the UK charts and was inspired by Tom's earlier exposure to Russian language, films and popular music. One of the songs that caught his attention had been an 1883 folksong called "Stenka Razin" about a Cossack leader. The original poem was set to the music of a popular Russian folk melody, and Tom adapted it into entirely new lyrics for "The Carnival is Over."

The Seekers' last chart entry was "Georgy Girl" in 1966. With lyrics written by UK singer/actor Jim Dale, it became the theme song to the movie of the same name, starring Lyn Redgrave and Alan Bates. It was also the group's highest charting single in the US, reaching number two, and was later nominated for an Oscar (although losing out to "Born Free"). Tom then joined songwriter Diane Lampert for "The Olive Tree," which was a solo single for Durham, although still part of the group. His final chart success came in June 1967, writing the ballad "Just Loving You" for British singer Anita Harris after seeing her perform on *Top of the Pops*.

Returning to Australia for a homecoming tour in March 1967, the Seekers played to 200,000 in Melbourne, at the time the largest ever audience for a concert in the Southern Hemisphere. During a New Zealand tour the following February, Durham announced she was leaving to pursue a solo career, and the Seekers officially disbanded shortly after a final televised performance by the BBC. Tom went on to write tv theme tunes and record two solo albums.

Chart entries
Breakaway – The Springfields (UK 1961 # 31)
Bambino – The Springfields *(trad.)* (UK 1961 # 16)
Island of Dreams – The Springfields (UK 1962 # 5)
Say I Won't Be There – The Springfields (UK 1963 # 5)
Hey Mama – Frankie Vaughan (UK 1963 # 21)
Come On Home – The Springfields (UK 1963 # 31)
Summer Is Over *(with Clive Westlake)* Frank Ifield (UK 1964 # 25)
Losing You *(with Clive Westlake)* Dusty Springfield (UK 1964 # 9; US # 91)
I'll Never Find Another You *(as Dion O'Brien)* The Seekers (UK 1965 # 1; US # 4);
   Sonny James (US 1967 # 97)
A World of Our Own – The Seekers (UK 1965 # 3; US # 19)
The Carnival Is Over – The Seekers (UK 1965 # 1)
Promises *(with Norman Newell)* Ken Dodd (UK 1966 # 6)
Walk With Me -The Seekers (UK 1966 # 10)
Georgy Girl *(with Jim Dale)* The Seekers (UK 1966 # 3; US # 2); The Baja Marimba
   Band (US 1967 # 98)
The Olive Tree *(with Diane Lampert)* Judith Durham (UK 1967 # 33)
Just Loving You – Anita Harris (UK 1967 # 6)
Adios Amor (Goodbye My Love) *(with Norman Newell)* José Feliciano (UK 1969 # 51)

Lewis Steinberg   see **Booker T Jones**

Geoff Stephens   see also **Tony Macaulay and John MacLeod, Les Reed.**
Born Geoffrey Stephens, London 1934. Died 2020.

After the war, Stephens' family moved to Westcliff-on-Sea, Essex and opened a guesthouse. While on the UK's east coast, he was able to listen to both the American Forces Network broadcast from Germany and Radio Luxembourg, and as a result was influenced by the American jazz and pop records they played. Although inspired by a high school teacher to become a writer, Stephens had no formal music training while growing up. As a consequence, he was unable to read music, and when he did become a songwriter it required others to transcribe the music he sang to them. After two years' national service in the Middle East, he moved to London with the goal of achieving his songwriting dream within three years.

With various jobs as school teacher, air traffic controller and silk screen printer, his music career got under way when he formed the Four Arts Society, writing songs and sketches for musical reviews and having BBC Radio accepting some of his satirical sketches for one of their programmes. In 1961, he had his first song "Problem Girl" accepted by music publisher Mills Music, whose Mike Leander had it recorded by the Chariots. As a result, Stephens worked for them briefly, and in March 1964, on the suggestion of publisher and producer Frank Poser, he teamed up with Les Reed. Neither of them had yet written a hit song, and after hearing part of a tune Reed had composed, Stephens thought that the words "tell me when" fitted perfectly. The common phrase, used when pouring a drink, was applied metaphorically in the song to a relationship as "tell me when you're ready to be mine." In January 1964, "Tell Me When" became a top ten UK hit for the Applejacks, with its lead singer Al Jackson, and (a rarity for the time) a female bass player called Megan Davies.

A few months later, Stephens wrote "The Crying Game." He recorded a demo with fellow writer John Carter and gave a copy to Decca producer Mike Smith, who then arranged for rock singer Dave Berry to record it. The song soon became a top five hit. According to Stephens, the line "I know all there is to know" was inspired by his father. Later in the year, Stephens and Peter Eden met Donovan Leitch in Southend and went on to produce his first hit single "Catch the Wind" as well as his debut album.

Two years later, Stephens gathered together studio musicians as the New Vaudeville Band to record his 1920's music-style "Winchester Cathedral." The demo, again performed by Carter, was the one used for the single release, and it not only topped the US charts in September 1966 but won a Grammy the following year for Best Contemporary Song. Around the same time, Stephens and Carter wrote the rather unorthodox "Semi-Detached Suburban Mr Jones" for Manfred Mann. The duo had drawn inspiration from a recent trend in which social issues were being highlighted in pop songs, while some interpreted it as being dismissive of middle class life. The song was also the first hit for the band's new lead singer Mike D'Abo, having replaced Paul Jones in July 1966.

The following year, Stephens and Reed had continued success with "There's a Kind of Hush" for Herman's Hermits. It had first appeared on the album by the New Vaudeville Band and was originally conceived as a neo-British music hall song, and when recorded by US teen band Gary & the Hornets as "Kind of Hush," it became a regional hit. The Hermits' 1967 version was a transatlantic top ten success. Over the next few years, Stephens wrote or co-wrote a number of hits which included "Sorry Suzanne" and "Lights of Cincinnati" (with Tony Macaulay), and "Sunshine Girl" and "Sentimental Friend" (with Carter).

In the Seventies, he joined Peter Callendar to write the million-selling single "Daddy Don't You Walk So Fast" for US singer Wayne Newton, before teaming up again with Macaulay to pen "You Won't Find Another Fool Like Me" for the New Seekers and "Silver Lady," a chart-topper for US singer/actor David Soul.

Chart entries
One Heart Between Two – Dave Berry (UK 1964 # 41)
The Crying Game – Dave Berry (UK 1965 # 6)
Winchester Cathedral – New Vaudeville Band (UK 1966 # 2; US # 1); Dana Rollin (US 1966 # 71)
Green Street Green – New Vaudeville Band (UK 1967 # 37)

Geoff Stephens and John Carter
Semi-Detached Suburban Mr James - Manfred Mann (UK 1966 # 2)
My World Fell Down - Sagittarius (US 1967 # 70 The Ivy League (US 1967 # 70)
Sunshine Girl - Hermans Hermits (UK 1968 # 8)
My Sentimental Friend - Herman's Hermits (UK 1969 # 2)

Geoff Stephens and Les Reed
Tell Me When - Applejacks (UK 1964 # 5)
There's A Kind Of Hush – Hermans Hermits (UK 1967 # 7; US # 4)
Claire – Paul & Barry Ryan (UK 1967 # 47)
Tears Won't Wash Away These Heartaches – Ken Dodd (UK 1969 # 22)

Geoff Stephens and Tony Macauley
Sorry Suzanne – The Hollies (UK 1969 # 3; US # 56)
Lights of Cincinnati – Scott Walker (UK 1969 # 13)
Smile A Little Smile For Me – The Flying Machine (US 1969 # 5)

Geoff Stephens with others
Peek-A-Boo *(with John Shakespeare)* New Vaudeville Band (UK 1967 # 7; US # 72)
Finchley Central *(with Alan Klein)* New Vaudeville Band (UK 1967 # 11)
Boy *(with Ken Howard & Alan Blaikley)* Lulu (UK 1968 # 15)

Cat Stevens
Born Steven Demetre Georgiou, London 1948.
Rock and Roll Hall of Fame 2014.
Songwriters Hall of Fame 2019.

The son of a Greek Cypriot restaurateur and a Swedish mother, they lived above the Moulin Rouge restaurant in London's Shaftesbury Avenue. With his parents divorcing while he was around eight years old, they continued to run the restaurant and live above it. Georgiou began his education at St Joseph Roman Catholic Primary School and developed an interest in playing the family's baby grand piano. As a teenager, his father bought him a guitar and he began writing songs. After a short stay in Sweden with his mother, he took a one-year course at Hammersmith School of Art, considering a career as a cartoonist, but songwriting became his primary goal and he began gigging under the name Steve Adams. Heavily influenced by the Beatles and the Kinks, as well as Dylan, Muddy Waters and Paul Simon, he also admired the work of musical composers like Ira Gershwin and Leonard Bernstein. Performing his songs in pubs and coffee houses, a failed attempt to form a band led to him preferring a solo career, and to change his name to Cat Stevens, partly down to a girlfriend saying he had cat-like eyes.

In 1966, 18-year-old Stevens was noticed by record producer and ex-Springfields guitarist Mike Hurst. Despite planning to leave to work in the US, Hurst was sufficiently excited by the young student's voice and songs to organise a recording session. They cut Stevens' self-penned "I Love My Dog" and Decca's Tony Hall was impressed enough to sign him as the first act on the new Deram label imprint, which was designed to showcase progressive young British talent. Aided by strong pirate radio airplay, "Love My Dog" peaked at number 28 on the charts in November. He later admitted he had essentially written the lyrics to the music of US jazz musician Yusef Lateef's "The Plum Blossom" from his 1961 *Eastern Sounds* album, for which he later paid him royalties and gave writing credit.

Following its success, Decca boss Sir Edward Lewis extended Stevens' contract with Hurst to release three singles within a year on Deram. "Matthew and Son" had been written before the deal with Deram had been signed, with the hook of the song originally intended for the song "Baby Take Me Back Home." The inspiration came from one of his girlfriends who complained about having to spend so much of her time working, and the song was a form of social commentary about "people being slaves to other people." Although Stephens probably had no real company in mind, he later claimed that the title was chosen simply because "the riff seemed to fit the words." It became a number two hit in January 1967 and appeared on his eponymous debut album.

Another track on the album was "Here Comes My Baby" which had been shelved as a single when "Love My Dog" took preference. Instead, it was recorded by the Tremeloes, and their slightly more upbeat version had minor changes to the lyrics and the final verse left out altogether. Nevertheless, it peaked at number four on the charts and became Stevens' first writing success for another artist. "I'm Gonna Get Me a Gun" followed, with its story of a young man obtaining a gun out of sheer frustration with his grinding, unrewarding job and the lack of respect from co-workers. As a result, it was perceived as a kind of fitting sequel to "Matthew and Son."

In 1965, Stevens had made a demo recording of "The First Cut Is the Deepest" while still having ambitions to become a songwriter. Written to promote his songs to other artists, he did not record it until early October 1967, neither did it appear on his second album. Instead, he had sold the song for £30 to US-born British soul singer P P Arnold (aka Patricia Ann Cole). The following year, she recorded it as a top twenty single, with it also appearing on her debut album *The First Lady of Immediate*. The following singles by Stevens failed to achieve the same kind of success, and his continuing popularity was partly achieved by the pirate Radio London playing his records before finally being closed down.

His 1967 album *New Masters* failed to chart in the UK, and two years later he contracted tuberculosis and almost died. Taking up meditation and reading about other religions, he began to question aspects of his own life and his spirituality. By doing so, he wrote dozens of songs, many of which would appear on later albums, including "Father and Son" on 1970's *Tea For the Tillerman*. This album, and several that followed, would be regarded as his finest work. He formally converted to Islam in 1977, taking the name Yusuf Islam the following year.

Chart entries
Love My Dog – Cat Stevens (UK 1966 # 28)
Matthew And Son – Cat Stevens (UK 1967 # 2)
Here Comes My Baby – The Tremeloes (UK 1967 # 4; US # 13)
Keep It Out Of Sight – Paul & Barry Ryan (US 1967 # 30)
I'm Gonna Get Me A Gun – Cat Stevens (UK 1967 # 6)

First Cut Is the Deepest – P P Arnold (US 1967 # 18)
A Bad Night – Cat Stevens (UK 1967 # 20)
Kitty – Cat Stevens (UK 1967 # 47)

William "Mickey" Stevenson
Born Detroit, Michigan 1937.
Songwriters Hall of Fame 2022.

Stevenson was raised by his mother, blues singer Kitty "Brown Gal" Stevenson, and stepfather Ted Moore. By the age of eight he was performing in a vocal trio with his younger brothers. Coached and produced by Stevenson's mother, they won first place in an Amateur Night at New York's Apollo Theater in 1950. Three years later, his musical ambitions were put on hold when his mother died. After attending Detroit's Northeastern High School, he joined the US Air Force in 1956 and became part of a special unit set up to entertain troops. While on furlough two years later, he saw a vocal group called the Four Aims (later to become the Four Tops), and it inspired him to quit the military and pursue a music career. He toured with bandleader Lionel Hampton as part of the Hamptones, and on his return to Detroit met Berry Gordy Jr, who spoke about setting up a new record label. In 1959, after working for a time as songwriter and producer for the gospel label HOB Records, Stevenson was hired by Gordy to head Motown's A&R department and also to establish the label's in-house studio band, soon to become the Funk Brothers. In 1961, he worked on the label's first chart-topper "Please Mr Postman" and the same year co-wrote with Gordy his first chart hit with Mary Wells' "I Don't Want to Take a Chance."

Stevenson went on to co-write many of Motown's hits. Among the most famous were "Dancing in the Street" (with Marvin Gaye & Ivy Jo Hunter), "It Takes Two" (with Sylvia Moy), "Stubborn Kind of Fellow" (with George Gordy) and "Needle in a Haystack" (with Norman Whitfield). He also toured the country with the Motown Review and created the Motown Orchestra to play and even conduct during the shows.

In 1968, Stevenson was replaced as A&R executive by Eddie Holland, and the following year he founded the label People Records, with which he recorded, among others, his wife Kim Weston and Hodges, James & Smith (The label would be dissolved several years later when James Brown's unrelated label of the same name was launched). The following year, he was appointed head of MGM's subsidiary label Venture Records to develop their share of the R&B and soul market, and in 1972 recorded his only solo album *Here I Am,* before shifting gear to follow his passion for producing stage musicals.

Describing his songwriting, he once revealed: "When I would write, I'd write a song and then I would turn around and read the lyrics. Forget the music - let's just see if it meant something as a lyric, like a poem or a short story."

Chart entries
Danger! Heartbreak Dead Ahead – The Marvelettes (US 1965 # 61)
Stranded in the Middle of Place – The Righteous Brothers (US 1967 # 72)

William Mickey Stevenson and Ivy Jo Hunter
Dancing in the Street *(with Marvin Gaye)* Martha & Vandellas (US 1964 # 2# UK # 28); The
    Mamas & the Papas (as Dancing In the Streets) (US 1966 # 73); Ramsey Lewis (US 1967
    # 84); Martha & the Vandellas (UK 1969 # 4)
Wild One - Martha & the Vandellas (US 1964 # 34)
Ask the Lonely - The Four Tops (US 1965 # 24)
I'll Keep Holding On - The Marvelettes (US 1965 # 34)
I'll Always Love You - The Spinners (US 1965 # 35)
My Baby Loves Me *(with Sylvia Moy)* Martha & the Vandellas (US 1966 # 22)
You've Been In Love Too Long *(with Clarence Paul)* Martha & the Vandellas
    (US 1965 # 36)

William Mickey Stevenson and Marvin Gaye
Beechwood 4-5789 *(with George Gordy)* The Marvelettes (US 1962 # 17)
Stubborn Kind Of Fellow *(with George Gordy)* Marvin Gaye (US 1962 # 46)
Hitch Hike *(with Clarence Paul)* Marvin Gaye (US 1963 # 30)
Price And Joy *(with Norman Whitfield)* Marvin Gaye (US 1963 # 10)

William Mickey Stevenson and Norman Whitfield
Price And Joy *(with Marvin Gaye)* Marvin Gaye (US 1963 # 10)
Needle in a Haystack - The Velvelettes (US 1964 # 45)

He Was Really Saying Something (*with Eddie Holland Jr*) The Velvelettes (US 1965 # 64)
It Should Have Been Me - Gladys Knight & Pips (US 1968 # 40)

William Mickey Stevenson and Clarence Paul
Once Upon A Time (*with Barney Ales*) Marvin Gaye & Mary Wells (US 1964 # 19; UK # 50)
What's the Matter With You Baby (*with Barney Ales*) Marvin Gaye & Mary Wells US 1964 # 17)
Hitch Hike (*with Marvin Gaye*) Marvin Gaye (US 1963 # 30)

William Mickey Stevenson and Sylvia Moy
Nothing's Too Good For My Baby (*with Henry Cosby*) Stevie Wonder (US 1966 # 20)
What Am I Going To Do Without Your Love - Martha & the Vandellas (US 1966 # 71)
It Takes Two - Marvin Gaye & Kim Weston (US 1967 # 14; UK # 4)

William Mickey Stevenson with others
I Don't Want To Take A Chance (*with Berry Gordy Jr*) Mary Wells (US 1961 # 33)
Jamie (*with Barrett Strong*) Eddie Holland Jr (US 1962 # 30)
Twistin' Postman (*with Robert Bateman & Brian Holland*) The Marvelettes (US 1962 # 34)
Playboy (*with Brian Holland, Robert Bateman, Gladys Horton*) The Marvelettes (US 1962 # 7)
What Good Am I Without You *(with Alfonso Higdon*) Marvin Gaye & Kim Weston (US 1964 # 61)
Devil With A Blue Dress On (*with Frederick "Shorty" Long*) Mitch Ryder & the Detroit Wheels (US 1966 # 4)
I Got What You Need (*with Dougg Brown*) Kim Weston (US 1967 # 99)

John Stewart
Born John Coburn Stewart, San Diego 1939. Died 2008.

The son of a Kentucky-born horse trainer, Stewart lived in the racetrack towns of Pomona and Pasadena. Going on to Mt. San Antonio Junior College in Walnut, he took part in their music and theatre activities. Inspired by the songs of Tex Ritter, he displayed an early talent for writing and playing ukelele, and composed his first song at the age of ten. While at Pomona Catholic High School, he formed the garage band Johnny Stewart & the Furies and toured southern California colleges and coffee bars. Just before his graduation in 1957, they recorded one single, "Rockin' Anna," which became a minor regional hit. Stewart then became a member of the Woodsmen. At the age of 19, he was encouraged by the manager of the Kingston Trio (for whom he had already written two songs) to form the folk-singing group the Cumberland Three with John Montrgomery and Gil Robbins (father of actor Tim Robbins).

In 1961, after releasing three Kingston Trio-style albums, Stewart was hired to join the Trio after founder Dave Guard had departed. With Stewart on board for the next six years, they took new directions and recorded a dozen albums, with Stewart writing many of their songs before finally disbanding in 1967. Stewart then toured as a solo artist and continued recording and writing songs for Capitol, while also beginning to sing with Buffy Ford, who had been part of the vocal group The Young Americans. When being pursued by Jefferson Airplane to become their lead singer, she joined Stewart instead, leaving them to sign Grace Slick.

One of the songs Stewart had written in 1966 was "Daydream Believer," which was originally intended to be part of a trilogy about suburban life. Stewart recalled that the idea had come to him after going to bed thinking what a wasted day it had been, having just daydreamed. The song was offered to We Five and Spanky & Our Gang, who both turned it down, but while at a party hosted by Hoyt Axton, producer Chip Douglas told him he was working with the Monkees and was looking for songs they could record. Accepting "Daydream Believer," RCA insisted that Stewart change one word of the lyric, and instead of "how funky I can be" it became "how happy I can be." It was recorded with all four Monkees present - Mike Nesmith on lead guitar, Peter Tork on piano, Mickey Dolenz on backing vocals, and Davy Jones on lead vocal. The single topped the US charts for four weeks in December 1967.

In 1968, Stewart released his debut album *Signals Through the Glass,* recorded with his future wife Buffy Ford. It included the ballad "July, You're a Woman," which Pat Boone had a minor hit with the following year. Stewart also wrote "Never Going Back," a track on his second album *California Bloodlines,* which was also a hit for the Lovin' Spoonful.

Chart entries
One More Town – The Kingston Trio (US 1962 # 97)
Daytime – Hedgehoppers Anonymous (UK 1966 # 57)
Daydream Believer – The Monkees (US 1967 # 1; UK # 5)
Never Going Back – The Lovin' Spoonful (US 1968 # 73)
July, You're A Woman – Pat Boone (US 1969 # 100)
Armstrong – John Stewart (US 1969 # 74)

Stephen Stills see also **Roger McGuinn, David Crosby**
Born Stephen Arthur Stills, Dallas, Texas 1919. Died 1996.
Songwriters Hall of Fame 2009.

Raised in a military family, Stills moved around the country. He later developed a love for blues and folk music, and also spent time in Latin American counties where he was also influenced by their music style. Developing partial hearing loss, he graduated from Lincoln High School in Costa Rica, but in the early Sixties dropped out of Louisiana State University to play in a number of bands including the Continentals (along with future Eagles' guitarist Don Felder). He also performed in Greenwich Village and ended up singing in a nine-member harmony group called the Au Go Go Singers, which included future Buffalo Springfield guitarist Richie Furay. Disbanding in 1965 after one album, Stills formed the rock-folk band the Company with some former members.

While on a tour of Canada, Stills met and befriended Canadian guitarist Neil Young (b.1945) of the Squires. When the Company broke up shortly after, he moved with Furay to California and failed an audition to become one of the Monkees (the part being given to Peter Tork, who Stills recommended). Stills and Furay then united with Young in Los Angeles to form Buffalo Springfield, along with ex-Standells drummer Dewey Martin and ex-Mynah Birds bass player Bruce Palmer. Their name came from a brand of steamroller which they saw parked on a Hollywood street during road repairs.

With a mix of county, folk, and psychedelic rock, and the hard-edged sound created by the twin lead guitars of Stills and Young, the band achieved critical success after signing with Atlantic in 1966. Their debut single "Nowadays Clancy Can't Even Sing" was a local hit, but in January 1967 they had their big break with the protest song "For What It's Worth." Written by Stills, it was inspired by the series of curfew riots in Los Angeles, with the name taken from a comment he made to a label executive, "I have a song here, for what it's worth." During his time with the band, Young wrote two of their chart hits, "Expected to Fly" and "On the Way Home," before going on to have a stellar solo career.

After Buffalo Springfield disbanded, Stills joined David Crosby and Graham Nash to form Crosby, Stills and Nash, and wrote many of their album tracks, including "Suite: Judy Blue Eyes" about his imminent breakup with girlfriend Judy Collins. In 1970, he also released his eponymous solo album, which included the single "Love the One You're With," which was later covered by the Isley Brothers.

Chart entries
For What It's Worth – Buffalo Springfield (US 1967 # 7); The Staple Singers (US 1967 # 66);
    King Curtis (US 1967 # 87)
Sit Down, I Think I Love You – The Mojo Men (US 1967 # 36)
Bluebird – Buffalo Springfield (US 1967 # 58)
Rock 'N Roll Woman *(with David Crosby)* Buffalo Springfield (US 1967 # 44)
Suite: Judy Blue Eyes – Crosby, Stills & Nash (US 1969 # 21)

Mike Stoller see **Leiber and Stoller**

Sly Stone
Born Sylvester Stewart, Denton, Texas 1943. Died 2025.
Rock and Roll Hall of Fame 1993 (with Sly & the Family Stone).
Grammy Lifetime Achievement Award 2017.

The second of five children, he moved with his family from Denton to Vallejo, California, where they were heavily involved in the Church of God in Christ. By the age of eight, he was already recording gospel music with siblings Freddie, Rose and Loretta as the Stewart Four, and a single "On the Battlefield b/w Walking in Jesus' Name," with him playing drums and guitar, was released in August 1956. With elder sister Loretta not pursuing a music career, she was replaced by the younger Vaetta. By the age of eleven, he had become proficient in a variety of instruments, including keyboards, and played in a number of school bands (primarily as a guitarist). One of these was the doo-wop group the Viscaynes, in which Sly and his friend Frank Arellano were the only non-white members, and together they worked the bars and clubs in Frisco's North Beach enclave.

During this period, Sly also recorded a few solo singles in Los Angeles under the name Danny Stewart, and with Freddie formed several other short-lived groups such as Joe Piazza & the Continentals and the Stewart Bros. After graduating high school, Sly studied music at the Vallejo campus of Solano Community College, and while in fifth grade a friend misspelled Sylvester as "Sly," and the nickname stuck. He also worked as a successful deejay for the R&B radio station KSOL-AM in San Mateo, guiding it into soul music and re-naming it K-SOUL. As a writer and staff producer for Autumn Records, he worked with other Bay-area bands such as the Beau Brummels and the Great Society. One of the singles he produced was Bobby Freeman's "C'mon and Swim" a top five hit in 1964, although his own opportunist single, "I Just Learned How to Swim" failed to chart. Sly was also a much-sought after sessionist and played keyboards for a number of performers including Dionne Warwick, Marvin Gaye, and the Righteous Brothers, as well as playing at one of the three Twist Party concerts held by Chubby Checker at San Francisco's Cow Palace in 1963.

In 1966, he was performing with his band Sly & the Stoners (which included Cynthia Robinson on trumpet) while brother Freddie was with a band called Freddie & the Stone Souls, along with Greg Errico and Jerry Martini. After recruiting bassist Larry Graham, they merged the two bands to form Sly & the Family Stone. (Rose Stone would not join the band until work began on "Dance to the Music.") For a multi-racial band to include women who were not only vocalists but musicians too, was a rarity at the time. They made their debut on the local Loadstone label with "I Ain't Got Nobody," but later signed with Epic to release their first album *A Whole New Thing*.

Their first success came with the single "Dance to the Music," credited to Sylvester Stewart, and a top ten hit in January 1968. Although following albums suffered from low sales, their fourth *Stand!* sold over three million copies and included "Everyday People," their first chart-topper at the end of the year. Unlike many of the funk/ psychedelic songs, this was mid-tempo with a more mainstream pop sound, with the band becoming one of the biggest names in music. They released two more top five singles, all composed by Sly, and their early morning performance at Woodstock in 1969 was cited as *the* legendary moment in the concert.

In the Seventies, Sly's music took a darker, more cynical tone amid the backdrop of racial tensions and the Vietnam War, and with his drug use and erratic behaviour signaling a waning power, it eventually put an end to the group. However, his legacy remains intact for being a pioneer of fusing soul, rock, gospel, and psychedelia, and by changing black music forever. *AllMusic* stated that with his politically-charged music, "James Brown may have invented funk, but Sly Stone perfected it."

As Sly would say it himself, "My only weapon is a pen, I'm a songwriter."

Chart entries
C'mon and Swim *(with Thomas Coman)* Bobby Freeman (US 1964 # 5)
S-W-I-M (*(with Thomas Coman)* Bobby Freeman (US 1964 # 56)
Dance To the Music - Sly and the Family Stone (US 1968 # 8; UK # 7)
Life – Sly and the Family Stone (US 1968 # 93)
Everyday People - Sly and the Family Stone (US 1968 # 1; UK # 36)
Stand! - Sly and the Family Stone (UK 1969 # 22)
I Want to Take You Higher - Sly and the Family Stone (US 1969 # 60)
Hot Fun in the Summertime - Sly and the Family Stone (US 1969 # 2)
Life and Death in G&A – Abaco Dream (US 1969 # 74)

Barrett Strong see also **Norman Whitfield**
Born Barrett Strong Jr, West Point, Mississippi 1941. Died 2023.
Songwriters Hall of Fame 2004.

The only boy of six children born on a farm to a minister, his family moved to Detroit in 1945. A self-taught musician, he learned to play a piano bought by his father without needing lessons. He began singing at Hutchins Intermediate School, where his classmates included Aretha Franklin and Lamont Dozier. He was also a cousin of Nolan Strong, lead singer of local doo-wop group the Diablos. With his sisters, he formed his own local gospel group the Strong Sisters, and by the age of 14 had started writing songs while studying at the Central High School. While still there, he emulated his hero Ray Charles with a band at the city's Dairy Workers Hall. Noticed performing there by singer Jackie Wilson, he was introduced to Motown's Berry Gordy Jr. Having already been turned down by Fortune Records, the Diablos' label, he became one of Gordy's earliest signings to his fledgling Tamla label in 1959.

Strong and Gordy collaborated on his first single, "Let's Rock/Do the Very Best You Can," which got some local airplay. However, it was the next single that became the label's first success. "Money (That's What I Want)," written by Gordy and his 16-year-old receptionist Janie Bradford, had Strong or Gordy playing piano, while the label's drummer Benny Benjamin was also present. With initial signs of it being a hit, Gordy transferred it to the Anna label, run by one of his sisters, which, unlike Tamla, had a deal for national distribution. Strong's name was added as co-writer before being removed as part of an on-going dispute, with Gordy claiming it had been a clerical error (although Strong maintained the basic idea for the hook phrase was his). In 1962, Strong teamed up with William "Mickey" Stevenson to write "Jamie," a top thirty hit for Eddie Holland, before spending time in New York and Chicago co-writing for non-Motown artists like the Dells and Mary Wells.

By 1967, Strong had returned to Detroit, where he began a long-standing partnership with songwriter Norman Whitfield. Together, they wrote two hit songs for Jimmy Ruffin, and also co-wrote "Take Me in Your Arms and Love Me," a moderate hit for Gladys Knight & the Pips. But one of his finest moments came working with Whitfield on "I Heard It Through the Grapevine." Strong already had the basics of a song while in Chicago, the idea having come to him while walking down Michigan Avenue where people often said the phrase. Whitfield added the single chorus line.

The first known recording was by the Miracles in August 1966, although Whitfield intended to have the Isley Brothers do it (a session may have been cancelled). The Miracles' version was not released as a single due to Gordy's veto at a quality control meeting and asking for a stronger version. In the meantime, Whitfield had Gladys Knight & the Pips record their own soulful version. Released as a single, it reached number two in the charts. Determined to have Gaye make it a hit, Whitfield had him record it over five sessions followed by a month of overdubbing his lead vocal with that of the Andantes' backing vocals. He then mixed in several Funk Brother rhythm tracks, and finally added a string section by the Detroit Symphony Orchestra. An argument also ensued when Whitfield wanted Gaye to perform the song in a higher key than his normal range. Nevertheless, the single topped the charts on both sides of the Atlantic.

Around the same time as this, Strong and Whitfield reached their creative peak with a run of hits for the Temptations. Beginning with "I Wish It Would Rain," written with Cornelius Grant and Roger Penzabene, it was followed with the top ten hits "Cloud Nine," "Runaway Child, Runaway Wild," and the chart-topping "I Can't Get Next To You," all recorded in the space of eight months. Devising the formula that became known as "psychedelic soul," their success would continue into the Seventies with "Ball of Confusion, "Just My Imagination," and the Grammy Award-winning "Papa Was a Rolling Stone."

Chart entries
Barrett Strong and Norman Whitfield
Gonna Gove Her All the Love I've Got - Jimmy Ruffin (US 1967 # 29; UK # 26)
I Heard It Through the Grapevine – Gladys Knight & the Pips (US 1967 # 2; UK # 47);
    King Curtis & the Kingpins (1968 # 83); Marvin Gaye (US 1968 # 1; UK # 1)
Please Return Your Love To Me *(with Barbara Neely)* The Temptations (US 1968 # 26)
Cloud Nine – Temptations (US 1968 # 6; UK 1969 # 15); Mongo Santamaria (US 1969 # 32)
Too Busy (Thinking About My Baby) *(with Janie Bradford)* Marvin Gaye (US 1969 # 4;
    UK # 5); The Billy Mitchell Group (US 1969 # 49)
Runaway Child, Running Wild – The Temptations (US 1969 # 6)
Don't Let the Jones Get You Down – The Temptations (US 1969 # 20)
I Can't Get Next To You – The Temptations (US 1969 # 1#; UK # 13)
That's the Way Love Is – Marvin Gaye (US 1969 # 7)
Friendship Train – Gladys Knight & the Pips (US 1969 # 17)
Don't Let Him Take Your Love From Me – Four Tops (US 1969 # 41)

Barrett Strong with others
Money (That's What I Want (*with Berry Gordy Jr, Janie Bradford*) Barrett Strong
    (US 1960 # 23); Bern Elliott & the Fenmen (UK 1963 # 14); The Kingsmen (US 1964 # 16);
    Jr Walker & the All-Stars (US 1966 # 52)
Jamie (*with William "Mickey" Stevenson*) Eddie Holland Jr (US 1962 # 30)
Stay In My Corner (*with Wade Flemons and Robert Eugene Miller*) The Dells
    (US 1965 # 10)
Take Me In Your Arms And Love Me *(with Cornelius Grant & Roger Penzabene)* Gladys
    Knight & the Pips (US 1967 # 98; UK # 13)

Chip Taylor
Born James Wesley Voight, Yonkers NY 1940.
Songwriters Hall of Fame 2016.

Along with his brothers (including future actor Jon Voight) he attended Archbishop Stepinac High School in White Plains before enrolling at the University of Hartford for a year. After a failed attempt at becoming a professional golfer like his father, he decided to pursue a music career. In 1958, performing as Wes Voight and the Town Three, he recorded a number of self-penned singles for King Records, including "I'm Ready To Go Steady," "I Want a Lover" and "Midnight Blues." Signing with Parlophone in 1960, he released "Movin' In" as Wes Voight, and two years later had his first release as Chip Taylor with "Here I Am" on the Warner Brothers label, which just missed out on the Hot 100. 1964 found him playing guitar in the New Jersey band Gigi Parker & the Lonelies, which also included Al Gorgoni, Hugh McCracken and Ted Daryll. Their single "Beatles Come Home," was written by Taylor and Darryll. He also scored his first chart hit as songwriter with "I Can't Wait Till I See My Baby," co-written with Norman Meade (aka Jerry Ragovoy) and recorded by soul vocalist Baby Washington. As a solo writer he gave Johnny Tillotson a top 50 hit with "Worry," and in 1966 teamed up with Gorgoni to form the duo Just Us, who released the album *I Can't Grow Peaches on a Cherry Tree* for the Kapp label, the title track of which peaked at number 34 on the Hot 100.

With a career now firmly focused on songwriting, his next success came with "I Can't Let Go," written with Gorgini. Originally recorded by blue-eyed soul singer Evie Sands on the Blue Cat label, it became a local hit in the New York area, but when recorded by the Hollies, it peaked at number two on the UK charts. Taylor had also been contacted by socialite Sybil Chrisopher who had formed the New York-based group the Wild Ones. Asked to write a song for them to release, Taylor took just minutes to write the chorus of "Wild Thing." After a successful demo, Gerry Granahan produced the Wild Ones' recording which had a lead vocal by Chuck Alden. It flopped when released in November 1965, but the following year the Troggs' manager Larry Page got to hear it and recommended that they record it as their next single. With Reg Presley's sexually-charged vocal, it spent two weeks at the top of the US charts.

Later that year, Taylor gave the Troggs another hit with the more-gentle ballad "Anyway That You Want Me." Although continuing to collaborate with writing friends like Gorgoni, Darryl and Billy Vera, Taylor produced one of his finest compositions "Angel of the Morning" in 1967. Inspired by listening to the Stones' "Ruby Tuesday" on his car radio while in New York, Taylor felt he needed to capture that kind of passion. Although turned down by Connie Francis for being too risqué, Taylor had Evie Sands record it, but with her label having financial trouble it was not promoted. The next recording was by UK singer Billie Davis for Lee Hazelwood's LHI label, but also made little impact. In 1968, US singer Merrilee Rush, lead singer of the Turnabouts, recorded the song at the American Sound Studio in Memphis with producers Chip Moman and Tommy Cogbill. Cogbill had kept a tape of the demo of the song for several months and had been looking for the right artist to record it. It peaked at number seven on the Hot 100. Two months later, British session singer P P Arnold, who had earlier provided backing vocals on Davis' version, had her own top 30 hit with the song.

In the Seventies, Taylor recorded solo albums before becoming addicted to professional gambling. Changing his direction, he went on to create a self-help program for himself and others and resumed his performing and recording career in 1993.

Chart entries
I Can't Wait Until I See My Baby *(with Wes Farrell)* Baby Washington ((US 1964 # 93)
Worry – Johnny Tillotson (US 1964 # 45)
Don't Make Me (Fall In Love With You) Babbity Blue (UK 1965 # 48)
Tommy *(with Ted Daryll)* Reparata & the Delrons (US 1965 # 92)
Welcome Home – Walter Jackson (US 1965 # 95)
On My Word – Cliff Richard (UK 1965 # 12)
Wild Thing – Troggs (UK 1966 # 2; US # 1); Senator Bobby (US 1967 # 20)
If You Were Mine, Mary – Eddie Arnold (UK 1966 # 49)
I Can Make It With You – Jackie De Shannon (US 1966 # 68); The Pozo-Seco Singers (US 1966 # 32)
Anyway That You Want Me – The Troggs (UK 1966 # 4); The Liverpool Five (US 1966 # 98); The American Breed (US 1968 # 88)
Angel of the Morning – Merrilee Rush & the Turnabouts (US 1968 # 7), P P Arnold (UK 1968 # 29); Evie Sands (US 1969 # 53)

Chip Taylor and Al Gorgoni
I Can't Let Go – The Hollies (UK 1966 # 1; US # 42)
Step Out of Your Mind - The American Breed (US 1967 # 24)
I'll Hold Out My Hand - The Clique (US 1969 # 45)

Chip Taylor and Billy Vera
Make Me Belong With You - Barbara Lewis (US 1966 # 28)
Storybook Children - Billy Vera & Judy Clay (US 1967 # 54)

Country Girl - City Man - Billy Vera & Judy Clay (US 1968 # 36)

R Dean Taylor
Born Richard Dean Taylor, Toronto, Canada 1939. Died 2022.

At the age of 12, Taylor made his first entry into the music world singing at various open-air Country & Western shows in the Toronto area, and by 1960 was performing as singer and pianist with several country bands.
In December that year, he recorded the self-penned "At the High School Dance" as R Dean Taylor & His Combo on the Audio Master label. It played across Canada and on CHUM radio, Toronto's leading station, with Taylor appearing on a CBC dance party tv show as well as touring for a time. In 1962, he went to New York and signed with the AMY-MALA label, cutting the singles "It's a Long Way to St Louis" and "I'll Remember." The following year, a friend in Detroit called Taylor about a new label called Motown with whom he could arrange an audition. While there, Taylor was fortunate enough to meet top producers Brian Holland and Lamont Dozier and, being impressed with his material, was signed to the subsidiary V.I.P label as songwriter and artist.

Taylor immediately began working with Holland writing lyrics for a number of the hits that followed. In March 1964, he recorded his scheduled first single, the satirical "My Ladybug (Stay Away From that Beatle)" but it was deemed too weak and never released. Another attempt came the following year with the subtle war protest song "Let's Go Somewhere," written with Holland, but that had only regional success.

In 1966, Taylor recorded "There's a Ghost in My House," written with Holland-Dozier-Holland, but later discovered there had been no promotion for it, the label having concentrated on more established acts. (In 1974 it would become a Northern Soul favourite when re-released on Motown UK). After co-writing hits for the Temptations and Four Tops, he produced and co-wrote "I Gotta See Jane" with Eddie Holland and Ronald Miller. Inspired after a rainy night's drive in Toronto, it also received little promotion in the US but charted in the UK.

After Holland-Dozier-Holland left Motown, Berry Gordy assembled a new songwriting/production team to write songs for Diana Ross & the Supremes. Dubbed "The Clan," the members were Taylor, Frank Wilson, Deke Richards, and Pam Sawyer, with Henry Cosby joining for production duties. Gordy checked them into a Detroit hotel and told them not to come out until they had written a hit song. They came up with "Love Child" which topped the charts in October 1968. Without Richards, the group later came up with the top ten hit "I'm Living in Shame," perceived to be a fitting sequel to "Love Child."

In 1970, Taylor resumed his recording career and became one of the first artists signed to Rare Earth, Motown's new subsidiary label dedicated to white artists. Written in late 1969, his song "Indiana Wants Me," with its desperate tale of a fugitive on the run from a murder charge, became a top ten hit in both the US and UK, largely due to the atmospheric sound effects of sirens, bullhorns and gunfire. In 1973, he established his own company Jane Records and built a recording studio in Los Angeles.

Chart entries
Just Look What You've Done *(with Frank Wilson)* Brenda Holloway (US 1967 # 69)
All I Need *(with Frank Wilson, Eddie Holland Jr)* The Temptations (US 1967 # 8; UK # 60)
I'll Turn To Stone *(with Brian Holland, Lamont Dozier, Eddie Holland Jr)* Four Tops
  (US 1967 # 76)
Gotta See Jane *(with Eddie Holland Jr, Ronald Miller)* R Dean Taylor (UK 1968 # 17)
I'm In a Different World *(with Brian Holland, Lamont Dozier)* Four Tops (US 1968 # 51;
  UK # 27)
Love Child *(with Henry Cosby, Frank Wilson, Pam Sawyer, Deke Richards)* Diana Ross
  & the Supremes (US 1968 # 1; UK # 15)
I'm Living in Shame *(with Henry Cosby, Frank Wilson, Pam Sawyer, Deke Richards)* Diana
  Ross & the Supremes (US 1969 # 10; UK # 14)

Dewey Terry see Don Harris and Dewey Terry

Mel Tillis
Born Lonnie Melvin Tillis, Tampa, Florida 1932. Died 2017.
Nashville Songwriters Hall of Fame 1976.
Country Music Hall of Fame 2007.

As a child, his parents moved to Pahokee, Florida, where a bout of malaria left him with a stutter (although not affecting his singing voice). Learning to play both guitar and drums, he went on to win a local talent show at the age of 16. He later joined the US Air Force after dropping out of the University of Florida, and while serving in Okinawa formed a band called the Westerners that performed in local nightclubs. Leaving the military in 1955, he returned to Florida and had various odd jobs before finding regular work on the railroad. He used his pass to visit Nashville, where he eventually met Wesley Rose of the publishing house Acuff-Rose Music. Encouraged to hone his songwriting skill, he moved to Tennessee and began writing full-time, often collaborating with Wayne Walker (1925-1979). His songs were recorded by a number of country artists, including Webb Pierce, Ray Price and Kitty Wells, as well as Brenda Lee. In the late Fifties, he signed for Columbia Records and in 1958 had a solo country hit with "The Violet and a Rose," followed by a duet with Bill Phillips on "Sawmill."

Continuing to have more success as a songwriter, he teamed up with Ramsey Kearney for Brenda Lee's top ten hit "Emotions," and in 1963 partnered Danny Dill to write "Detroit City" for country singer Bobby Bare (a later UK hit for Tom Jones). In 1967, he wrote "Ruby, Don't Take Your Love To Town," about a paralysed veteran looking on helplessly as his wife "paints up" to go out for the evening without him, believing she was meeting a lover. First recorded by Waylon Jennings and then Johnny Darrell, it was Kenny Rogers & the First Edition that scored top ten hits on both sides of the Atlantic in 1969.

Chart entries
Emotions (*with Ramsey Kearney*) Brenda Lee (US 1960 # 7; UK # 45)
So Wrong (*with Danny Dill, Carl Perkins*) Patsy Cline (US 1962 # 85)
Detroit City (*with Danny Dill*) Bobby Bare (US 1963 # 16) Tom Jones (UK 1967 # 8; US # 27)
Detroit City No. 2 (*with Danny Dill, Sheb Wooley*) Ben Colder (US 1963 # 90)
Ruby, Don't Take Your Love To Town – Kenny Rogers & the First Edition (US 1969 # 6;
   UK # 2)

Russ Titleman see Gerry Goffin

Allen Toussaint
Born Allen Richard Toussaint, New Orleans 1938. Died 2015.
Rock and Roll Hall of Fame 1998.
Songwriters Hall of Fame 2011.

The youngest of three children, Toussaint grew up in a shotgun house, with a father who worked on the railroad and played trumpet. Learning to play piano, he was given music lessons by an elderly neighbour, and in his teens played in a group called the Flamingos, which included guitarist Snooks Eaglin. Dropping out of school, he had his first break at the age of 17 when standing in for Huey "Piano" Smith at an Alabama performance by Earl King's band. After being introduced to Dave Bartholomew's band, he played with them at the Dew Drop Inn, a New Orleans nightclub. In 1957, he was a stand-in pianist on Fats Domino's recording of "I Want You to Know," and laying down parts that the star could not sing. That same year, he made his debut as producer with Lee Allen's "Walking With Mr Lee." After being spotted by A&R man Danny Kessler, he signed for RCA Records.   Essentially a bluesman, Toussaint had a poet's ear for lyrics and a smooth, honey-toned voice, although his debut recording in 1958 was an album of instrumentals. It included "Java," written by Toussaint with Alvin "Red" Tyler, Freddy Friday and Marilyn Schack, which in 1964 gave Al Hirt a number one hit on the Adult Contemporary chart.

In 1960, Toussaint was hired by Joe Banashak of Minit Records as an A&R man and producer, although also working freelance for other labels. The following year, he wrote, produced and played the piano solo on Ernie K-Doe's chart-topper "Mother-in-Law." That was quicky followed by co-writing Chris Kenner's hit "I Like It Like That," a later UK hit for the Dave Clark Five. For "Ruler of My Heart," he used the pseudonym Naomi Neville, his mother's name. First recorded by Irma Thomas on the Minit label in 1963, it was adapted by Otis Redding as "Pain in My Heart." Toussaint then filed a lawsuit against Redding and Stax Records, which was settled out of court, with Stax agreeing to credit Neville as songwriter.

Drafted into the US Army in 1963, Toussaint continued to record while on furlough, and on his discharge two years' later joined Marshall Sehorn to form the label Sansu Enterprises. Among artists on their roster were Lee Dorsey, Betty Harris and Chris Kenner. The core players of the rhythm section, used on many recordings and usually arranged by Toussaint, later became the Meters. Their increasing use of updated electric instrumentation and syncopation would pave the way for the development of the modern New Orleans funk sound. In 1966, he gave Lee Dorsey back-to-back chart hits with "Working in a Coalmine" and "Holy Cow."

In 1975, Toussaint's solo career peaked with the concept album *Southern Nights*. Although singles taken from it failed to chart, Glen Campbell scored a chart-topper with the title track two years later.

Chart entries
Mother-in-Law – Ernie K-Doe (US 1961 # 1; UK # 29)
I Like It Like That *(with Chris Kenner)* Chris Kenner (US 1961 # 2); The Dave Clark Five
   (US 1965 # 7)

I Cried My Last Tear – Ernie K-Doe (US 1961 # 69); The O'Jays (US 1965 # 94)
Lipstick Traces (On a Cigarette) Benny Spellman (US 1962 # 80); The O'Jays (US 1965 # 48)
Java *(with Alvin Tyler, Freddy Friday, Marilyn Schack)* Floyd Cramer (US 1962 # 49); Al Hurt (US 1964 # 4)
Pain in My Heart – Otis Redding (US 1963 # 61)
Whipped Cream – Herb Alpert & the Tijuana Brass (US 1965 # 68)
Ride Your Pony – Lee Dorsey (US 1965 # 28)
Get Out of My Life, Woman – Lee Dorsey (US 1966 # 44; UK # 22)
Confusion – Lee Dorsey (UK 1966 # 38)
All These Things – The Uniques (US 1966 # 97)
Working in a Coalmine – Lee Dorsey (US 1966 # 8; UK # 8)
Holy Cow – Lee Dorsey (US 1966 # 23; UK # 6)
Fortune Teller – The Hardtimes (US 1966 # 97)
My Old Car *(with Billy Backer)* Lee Dorsey (US 1967 # 97)
Nearer to You – Betty Harris (US 1967 # 85)
Go-Go Girl – Lee Dorsey (US 1967 # 62)
Everything I Do Gonna Be Funky (From Now On) – Lee Dorsey (US 1969 # 95)
It's Hard to Get Along – Joe Simon (1969 # 87)

Pete Townshend

Born Peter Dennis Blandford Townshend, London 1945.
Rock and Roll Hall of Fame 1990 (with The Who).
Grammy Lifetime Achievement Award 2001 (with The Who).

Chiswick-born Townshend came from a musical family, with his father a professional saxophonist in the RAF's dance band the Squadronaires, and a mother who sang with the Sidney Torch Orchestra. While still a toddler, his parents underwent a two-year separation before reuniting and moving to Acton. Although not showing an early interest in music (his early ambition pointed to journalism), it all changed in the mid-Fifties with repeated visits to the cinema to see the movie *Rock Around the Clock*, and eventually going to see Bill Haley & the Comets in concert. At the age of eleven, he enrolled at Acton Grammar School and was often bullied for having a large nose. That same year, a grandmother bought him a Spanish guitar, and he essentially taught himself to play, despite never being able to read music. With schoolfriends John Entwhistle (1944-2002), Phil Rhodes and Chris Sherwin, he formed what would be a short-lived group called the Confederates (also known as the Aristocrats and the Scorpions), whose trad-jazz music featured Townshend on banjo. Entwhistle was already an accomplished musician, having studied piano and French horn with the Middlesex Youth Orchestra.

In 1961, Townshend enrolled at Ealing Art College to study graphic design, where one of the students was future Stones' guitarist Ronnie Wood. At the same time, Entwhistle, who by now had become a civil servant, was invited by rhythm guitarist Roger Daltrey (b.1944) to join the skiffle/rock & roll band the Detours as bass player. Entwhistle suggested that Townshend join too. With Daltry later switching to lead singer, Townshend became the solo guitarist. With the help of Townshend's mother, they signed a management contract with local promoter Robert Druce and began to support established artists like Cliff Bennett and Johnny Kidd. In early 1964, after becoming aware of another group with the same name, a roommate of Townshend suggested they call themselves The Who. During one of their gigs in London, a drunken man, dressed in ginger, jumped on stage and sat at the drums during the interval. His wild style impressed the band enough to recruit him as their permanent drummer. His name was Keith Moon (1947-1978), who for several years had been playing semi-professionally with the Beachcombers.

That same year, they met freelance mod publicist Pete Meaden who dressed them in stylish clothes and courted a mod audience. Suggesting a change of name to the High Numbers (a mod term for style), he secured a deal with Fontana Records. Following a failed single "I'm the Face," with lyrics written by Meaden, the band dropped him, and their management was taken up by budding directors Kit Lambert and Chris Stamp (brother of actor Terence) who were looking for a band to appear in a film. At the same time, the band reverted back to being called The Who. In June 1964, while playing at the Railway Hotel in Harrow, Townshend's swinging-guitar style took chunks out of the low ceiling and damaged his instrument, but then he proceeded to destroy it altogether, something that would become a regular (and expensive) part of their live shows. After a demo by the band was rejected by EMI, expatriate US producer Shel Talmy showed an interest and secured them a contract with US Decca, with recordings sub-contracted through its UK subsidiary Brunswick.

With a reputation for having a hard-edged, raw-production sound due to his work with the Kinks, Talmy chose Townshend's "I Can't Explain" as their first single. Apparently, when asked how to summarise his feelings about listening to music by those that inspired him, most times his answer was "I can't explain." He also listened to the Kinks' "You Really Got Me" for inspiration, and would later admit that it was "straightforward Kinks copying." The single became a top ten hit, as did the follow-up, the innovative "Anyway, Anyhow, Anywhere," written with Daltrey, who helped with the final arrangement.

Their third single "My Generation" would become one of the benchmarks of British Sixties' pop with its call for youthful rebellion. Townshend claimed that it had been inspired by a report that the Queen Mother was allegedly offended by his 1935 Packard hearse and had it towed off a Belgravia street she often used. He also cited Mose Allison's "Young Man's Blues" about struggling to find a place in society. The single peaked at number two in the charts.

Over the next two years, Townshend continued to write successful singles. The inspiration for "Substitute" came from the Miracles' "The Tracks of My Tears" and his obsession with the line, "Although she may be cute/She's just a substitute," while the guitar riff on the verses was borrowed from the song "Where Is My Girl" by Robb Storme & the Whispers. Like "My Generation," the single "The Kids Are Alright" became another anthem, although release was delayed for six months. "I'm a Boy" had originally been intended to be part of a futuristic rock opera called *Quads*, where parents could choose the sex of their children. Although the idea was abandoned, the number two-charting single was retained.

According to Townshend, "Happy Jack" was linked to his childhood about a man who slept on a beach at the Isle of Man where his family holidayed. When kids made fun of him and buried him in the sand, the man would just smile in response. "Pictures of Lily" was inspired by a 1920s postcard his girlfriend had on her wall of Vaudeville star Lily Bayliss, on which someone had scribbled "Here's another picture of Lily - hope you haven't got this one." It led him to think that everyone had a "pin-up period."

During their impressive stage shows, Townshend had developed his "windmill" guitar stunt by swinging his right arm against the strings, and apparently inspired after watching Keith Richards warmup before a show. The Who's popularity in the US flourished in 1967, particularly after an appearance at the Monterey Pop Festival. "I Can See For Miles," first written and demoed in 1966, was considered by Townshend to be his best work up to that point. Around the time of Talmy's legal case against the band, Townshend had written the lyrics on the back of an affidavit, and was inspired by his jealousy of seeing his girlfriend with other men. Describing it as his "ace in the hole," he decided to save it for a time when they really needed a big hit. Released first in the US in September 1967, Townshend was hugely disappointed when it only reached the top ten on both sides of the Atlantic, and was now convinced the band would never have a chart-topping single.

In 1969, the band fully embraced the album market with the release of the extravagant rock opera *Tommy*, later the subject of a film. The set spawned one their most recognisable singles, "Pinball Wizard," celebrating the skills of a "deaf, dum and blind" pinball champion. Despite its critical success, Townshend referred to his lyrics as a "clumsy piece of writing." The album had mainly existed in his head while recording it, with other members of the band having no idea how the story would end until it was finished. Written to impress rock critic Nik Cohn, Townshend had brought him a rough mix of the album, but Cohn was not inspired. Almost as a gut reaction, Townshend realised Cohn was a pinball fanatic and sold him the idea of having Tommy a pinball savant. The ploy was successful, and Cohn gave the project a good review. In 1975, it was made into a successful movie starring Jack Nicholson, Tina Turner and Daltrey (playing Tommy), with Elton John's cover of "Pinball Wizard" scoring a top ten hit.

The Seventies saw the release of *Live at Leeds*, often cited as the best live album of all time, followed by the hugely successful single "Won't Get Fooled Again," originally intended for another rock opera that was later abandoned. In 1973, Townshend wrote and produced the album *Quadrophenia,* a cross-Atlantic success. Exploring the mods and rockers culture of the Sixties, it was made into a film by Ken Russell in 1979.

Townshend once remarked: "If you don't want anyone to know anything about you, don't write anything."

Chart entries
I Can't Explain – The Who (UK 1964 # 8; US # 93)
Anyway, Anyhow, Anywhere (*with Roger Daltrey*) The Who (UK 1965 # 10)
My Generation – The Who (UK 1965 # 2; US # 74)
Substitute – The Who (UK 1966 # 5)
A Legal Matter – The Who (UK 1966 # 32)
The Kids Are Alright – The Who (UK 1966 # 41)
I'm A Boy – The Who (UK 1966 # 2)
Happy Jack – The Who (UK 1966 # 3; US # 24)
Pictures Of Lily – The Who (UK 1967 # 4; US # 51)
I Can See For Miles – The Who (UK 1967 # 10; US # 9)
Call Me Lightning – The Who (US 1968 # 40)
Dogs – The Who (UK 1968 # 25)
Magic Bus – The Who (UK 1968 # 26; US # 25)
Pinball Wizard – The Who (UK 1969 # 4; US # 19)
I'm Free – The Who (US # 37)

Jackie Trent see **Tony Hatch and Jackie Trent**

Annette Tucker
Born Annette May Tucker, Los Angeles 1933.

As an aspiring songwriter, Tucker met fellow musician and writer Al Hazan by accident. While living next door to a singer/songwriter, a car accident resulted in Tucker quitting her job, giving her more time to observe her neighbour's creative process. One day, established songwriter Hazen happened to knock on her door by mistake and it led to them becoming a songwriting partnership. Together, they wrote her single "Stick Around," released in 1962 by Piper Records. The following year, determined to write rather than be a singer, she signed up with David Burgess's Four Star Music Publishers on Sunset Boulevard and was teamed up with another aspiring songwriter and lyricist Nancie Mantz. The first song they wrote together was "She's Something Else," recorded by Freddie Cannon in 1965. That same year, she co-wrote with Mantz and staff writer Jill Jones, the Knickerbockers' b-side "The Coming Generation." Working with husband-and-wife writing pair Linda and Keith Colley, she also scored a chart hit for the group with "High on Love."

Next came "I Had Too Much to Dream Last Night." After a series of rehearsals for a new band called the Electric Prunes, followed by one failed single, their label Reprise gave them one more chance. Convinced that they could not write their own songs, producer Dave Hassinger sought material from Tucker and Mantz. Tucker had already seen the band perform at a surprise party for her husband, and it was his cousin who had brought them to Hassinger's attention. Tucker came up with the title, and the song was originally conceived as an orchestral country ballad but ended up a psychedelic garage band song. Written in half an hour, the single was released in November 1966 and peaked at number eleven on the Hot 100. Tucker and Mantz went on to co-write many of the tracks on the band's first two albums, although their follow-up single, the top thirty "Get Me to the World On Time" was written with Jill Jones (according to Tucker, they had been told to write different types of songs for the band.) With reference to "Get Me to the Church on Time" from the musical *My Fair Lady*, the writers deliberately included what at the time were highly sexual lyrics.

After their departure from Four Star, the two writers joined Shapiro, Bernstein & Co before Mantz quit the business altogether following the tragic murder of her mother. Tucker then joined Kathy Wakefield to work for Jobete Music, where they wrote material for the Jackson 5.

In the Seventies, she taught songwriting at UCLA and at ASCAL workshops. Looking back on her career, she said: "That's the mystery of songwriting. You never know where the words or the melody come from, they just come."

Chart entries
One Track Mind *(with Linda Colley, Keith Colley)* The Knickerbockers (US 1966 # 46)
High On Love *(with Linda Colley, Keith Colley)* The Knickerbockers (US 1966 # 94)
I Had Too Much To Dream (Last Night) *(with Nancy Mantz)* The Electric Prunes (US 1966 # 11)
Get Me To the World On Time *(with Jill Jones)* The Electric Prunes (US 1967 # 40)
Green Light *(with Nancy Mantz)* The American Breed (US 1968 # 39)

Sylvia Tyson
Born Sylvia Fricker, Chatham, Ontario, Canada 1940.
Canadian Songwriters Hall of Fame 2019

With her father an appliance salesman and mother a church organist and choir leader, Fricker had already decided on pursuing a music career at an early age. Against her parents' advice, she moved to Toronto in 1959 to become an entertainer. While there, she met solo artist Ian Tyson, and they soon decided to perform together as the duo Ian & Sylvia, beginning professionally in 1961.

In 1961, Sylvia wrote her first and most famous song "You Were On My Mind," which was recorded by the duo the following year. According to Sylvia, it was written in a bathtub at a Greenwich Village hotel as "it was the only place… the cockroaches would not go." A more uptempo version was recorded in 1965 by the San Francisco-based folk-rock group We Five, while Barry Maguire recorded it for an album track. In early 1966, singer Crispian St Peters (aka Robin Peter Smith) scored a UK number two with the song, and also went on to top the Canadian charts with his follow-up "Pied Piper," written by Steve-Duboff and Artie Kornfeld. Sylvia and Ian were married in 1964 and together they recorded 13 albums before divorcing in 1975. Sylvia then had a solo career and in 1978 formed Salt Records.

Chart entries
You Were On My Mind – We Five (US 1965 # 3); Crispian St Peters (US # 36; UK # 2)

Paul Vance see Lee Pockriss and Paul Vance

Harry Vanda see George Young and Harry Vanda

Les Vandyke
Born John Worsley, Battersea, England 1931. Died 2021.

Born to a Greek Cypriot father and Welsh mother, the name Worsley was chosen by placing a pin at random on a map of England, although his father continued to call him Yannis Skordalides throughout his life. After leaving school, he worked as a draughtsman before completing two years' national service. With an ambition to become a singer, he changed his name to Johnny Worth. Performing in pubs and making one tv appearance, he came to the attention of the leader of the Oscar Rabin Band who signed him for the next five years, recording for various labels. He later joined the vocal quartet the Raindrops, which consisted of husband-and-wife Len Beadle & Jackie Lee and Vince Hill, and it was while appearing on tv's *Drumbeat* that he met composer John Barry and singer Adam Faith. With a long-held ambition to be a songwriter, he asked pianist Les Reed to arrange a demo of his song "What Do You Want?" Both Barry and record producer John Burgess liked it, and it was recorded by Faith. With Barry's arrangement, it shot to number one in November 1959. While still signed to Oriole Records, he decided to adopt another pseudonym, and by combining Reed's first name with his own telephone exchange, came up with Les Vandyke.

Vandyke would go on to write seven top ten hits for Faith, with the next single "Poor Me" giving the singer back-to-back chart-toppers. In 1961, he wrote "Well I Ask You," a number one for Eden Kane (who was also using a pseudonym (he was Richard Sarstedt, brother of Peter). This was followed a year later with "Forget Me Not," which peaked at number three. In 1963, Vandyke composed his only instrumental "Applejack" for ex-Shadows duo Jet Harris and Tony Meehan. Apparently, it did not feature Harris playing due to health issues, and his place was taken by Joe Moretti. With his own singing career at an end, Vandyke used alternating pseudonyms to write and compose music for a number of low-budget films including *What a Whopper, Some People, Johnny Cool,* and *Saturday Night and Sunday Morning.* In 1969, Vandyke and fellow songwriter David Myers left Southern Music to join the Trend record label, and together wrote "Baby, I Couldn't See" for the Foundations.

In 1971 he penned "Jack in the Box," the UK's Eurovision Song Contest entry. Performed in Dublin by Irish singer Clodagh Rodgers, it came 4th. Two years later, he wrote and produced "Gonna Make You An Offer You Can't Refuse," a hit for Jimmy Helms.

Chart entries
Poor Me – Adam Faith (UK 1960 # 1)
Johnny Rocko – Marty Wilde (UK 1960 # 30)
What Do You Want – Bobby Vee (US 1960 # 93)
Someone Else's Baby *(with Perry Ford)* Adam Faith (UK 1960 #2)
How About That! – Adam Faith (UK 1960 # 4)
Who Am I/This Is It – Adam Faith (UK 1961 # 5)
Well I Ask You – Eden Kane (UK 1961 # 1)
Pop Goes the Weasel *(trad; with George Hackney)* Anthony Newley (UK 1961 # 12)
Don't You Know It? – Adam Faith (UK 1961 # 12)
Get Lost – Eden Kane (UK 1961 # 10)
The Time Has Come – Adam Faith (UK 1961 # 4)
Forget Me Not – Eden Kane (UK 1962 # 3)
As You Like It – Adam Faith (UK 1962 # 5)
The River's Run Dry – Vince Hill (UK 1962 # 41)
Ain't That Funny – Jimmy Justice (UK 1962 # 8)
Some People – Carol Deene (UK 1962 # 25)
Don't That Beat All – Adam Faith (UK 1962 # 8)
Baby Take a Bow – Adam Faith (UK 1962 # 22)
Cupboard Love – John Leyton (UK 1963 # 22)
I'll Cut Your Tail Off *(as Johnny Worth)* John Leyton (UK 1963 # 36)
Blue Girl – The Bruisers (UK 1963 # 31)
Applejack – Jet Harris & Tony Meehan (UK 1963 # 4)
What Do Ya Say? – Chubby Checker (UK 1963 # 37)

Not Too Little Not Too Much – Chris Sandford (US 1963 # 17)

Billy Vera see Chip Taylor

Junior Walker
Born Autry DeWalt Mixon Jr, Blytheville, Arkansas 1931. Died 1995.

Called Junior by his stepfather, Walker began playing saxophone while still at high school. His career began in the mid-Fifties when he formed the jazz/R&B group the Jumping Jacks with three high school friends Willie Woods (guitar), Victor Thomas (organ) and Tony Washington (drums). His longtime friend Billy Nicks also formed a group called the Rhythm Rockers, with the two friends occasionally sitting in on each other's shows. Nicks obtained a permanent residency at a local tv station in South Bend. Indiana, and asked Walker and Woods to join him and keyboard player Fred Patton on a permanent basis. When Nicks was drafted into the army, Walker persuaded the band to move to Battle Creek, Michigan, and brought in Washington to play drums. Eventually Patton also left and Thomas stepped in. While playing in a club one night, a customer shouted out, "these guys are all stars." With that, they became Jr Walker and the All Stars.

In 1961, they were noticed performing by Johhny Bristol, who recommended them to ex-Moonglow Harvey Fuqua, who had his own labels in Detroit. Fuqua released several of the band's instrumental singles the following year, and when the labels were taken over by Motown's Berry Gordy, the All Stars began recording on their Soul imprint in 1964. Around this time, James Graves replaced Washington on drums. While playing a benefit show in Benton Harbor, Walker saw two teenagers performing a new dance they called the Shotgun, and in his motel room that night he penned a dance tune with that name. Recorded in Detroit, it became an immediate success, topping the R&B chart for four weeks, and peaking at number four on the Hot 100. A string of hits followed, all previously done by other Motown artists and all written by Holland-Dozier-Holland. In 1969, "What Does It Take (To Win Your Love)" peaked at number four on the Hot 100, despite Motown initially rejecting the song until sufficient radio airplay made them release it.

In 1979, Walker disbanded the All Stars to pursue a solo career with Norman Whitfield's label.

Chart entries
Shotgun – Jr Walker & the All-Stars (US 1965 # 4); Vanilla Fudge (US 1969 # 68)
Do the Boomerang *(with Henry Cosby, Willie Woods)* Jr Walker & the All Stars (US 1965 # 36)
Shake and Fingerpop – Jr Walker & the All-Stars (US 1965 # 29)
Cleo's Mood *(with Harvey Fuqua, Willie Woods)* – Jr Walker & the All-Stars (US 1966 # 50)
Shoot Your Shot *(with James Graves, Lawrence Horn)* Jr Walker & the All-Stars (US 1967 # 44)
Hip City *(with Janie Bradford)* Jr Walker & the All-Stars (US 1968 # 31)

William Weatherspoon and James Dean
Born William Henry Weatherspoon, Detroit, Michigan 1936. Died 2005.
Born James Anthony Dean, Detroit, Michigan 1943. Died 2006.

In 1956, Weatherspoon began singing with the Tornados, a local vocal group headed by ex-Moonlighters Charles Sutton. They recorded unsuccessfully for the Chess label and Robert West's Bumble Bee Records, where they released their "Geni in the Jug." Around 1960, the group disbanded and Weatherspoon joined the military for a time before working as a producer and songwriter for Detroit's Correc-Tone label. He contributed to the Pace Setters' 1963 recording of "The Monkey Whip." After the label folded, he began working for Motown where he was paired up with songwriter James Dean. Dean, a cousin of Motown's Holland brothers, had attended Hamtramck High School in Michigan and had served in the US Army before coming to Motown.

Tasked with writing for the label's relatively minor artists, they began with "What Becomes of the Brokenhearted," co-written with arranger Paul Riser. Although originally intended for the Spinners to record, Dean was persuaded by Jimmy Ruffin, older brother of the Temptations' lead singer David, to let him record it himself. He had left Motown to do his national service with the army and had just returned to record for Motown's subsidiary label. The song about unrequited love and its anguished lyrics about a man's heartbreak resonated with Ruffin. Produced by Weatherspoon and William "Mickey" Stevenson, it peaked at number seven on the Hot 100 in October 1966.

The writing pair then wrote and produced Ruffin's follow-up single "I've Passed This Way Before." After producing the Marvelettes' classic "When You're Young and In Love," written by Van McCoy, they gave Ruffin a moderate hit in March 1968 with "I'll Say Forever My Love," co-written with Stephen Bowden. Early the following year, Motown singer Marv Johnson's flagging career was given a boost with "I'll Pick a Rose For My Rose." Co-written with Johnson, the lyrics describe a man reflecting on lost love with the hope of rekindling it. Despite not making the US chart, it resonated more in the UK where it was a top ten hit. Later that year, Jimmy Ruffin released his album *Ruff'n Ready,* which contained four tracks written by Weatherspoon and Dean, including the already-released single "I'll Say Forever My Love." The song "Farewell is a Lonely Sound" had been written two years before with Jack Goga, and would now finally be released as a single as a last attempt by the label to get a hit song from the album, although it only charted in the UK. Another of their tracks, "It's Wonderful To Be Loved By You," would be released as a single in 1970, but again was only a hit in the UK.

When Holland-Dozier-Holland defected from Motown with lawsuits pending, Weatherspoon followed them and signed with their Invictus/Hot Wax/Music Merchant setup, going on to have moderate success with a number of minor artists. Dean joined Detroit producer Don Davis, and with former Motown writer John Glover scored a US chart-topper in 1976 with "You Don't Have To Be a Star (To Be in My Show)" by Marilyn McCoo and Billy Davis Jr.

Chart entries

What Becomes Of the Brokenhearted? *(with Paul Riser)* Jimmy Ruffin (US 1966 # 7; UK # 8)
I've Passed This Way Before - Jimmy Ruffin (US 1966 # 17; UK # 29; UK 1969 # 33)
It's So Hard Being a Loser *(with Stanley McMullen)* The Contours (US #1967 # 79; UK # 53)
I'll Say Forever My Love *(with Stephen Bowden)* Jimmy Ruffin (US 1968 # 77; UK # 52)
I'll Pick a Rose For My Rose *(with Marv Johnson)* Marv Johnson (UK 1969 # 10)
Farewell Is a Lonely Sound *(with Jack Coga)* Jimmy Ruffin (UK 1969 # 8)

Jimmy Webb
Born Jimmy Layne Webb, Elk City, Oklahoma 1946.
Songwriters Hall of Fame 1986.
Nashville Songwriters Hall of Fame 1990.

Raised in Laverne, Oklahoma, the son of a US Marine and Baptist minister, Webb had learned to play piano and organ by the age of 12, and, with father on guitar and mother on accordion, he sang in his father's churches, even later improvising and rearranging some of the hymns. Although at first restricted by his father to only listen to white gospel and country music on the radio, his musical direction would soon be influenced by the new music they played, especially singers like Elvis Presley and Glen Campbell. The first record he bought at the age of 14 was Campbell's "Turn Around, Look at Me." Four years later, he moved with his family to Colton, California, and studied music at San Bernadino Valley College. Following the death of his mother shortly after, his father returned to Oklahoma, giving his son $40 to continue his studies and pursue a career as a songwriter. Webb wrote many years later: "I like words. I like the way they clash around together and bang up against each other, especially in songs."

After working for a small music publisher in Hollywood, Webb gained a songwriting contract with Jobete Music, the publishing arm of Motown Records, and the first recorded song he wrote was "My Christmas Tree," which appeared on the Supremes' 1965 album *Merry Christmas*. The following year, he met singer and producer Johnny Rivers who signed him to a publishing deal with his Soul City Records. Webb gave him the song "By the Time I Get to Phoenix" to record for his album *Changes*. The inspiration for the song was Webb's breakup with his girlfriend Susan Horton, although they still remained friends after she re-married. He did not intend the lyrics to be geographically literal, but admitted: "It's a kind of fantasy about something I wish I would have done," calling it a "succinct tale" with an "O Henry-esque twist at the end."

That same year, Rivers turned to Webb to write songs for an album by a new soul-pop act he was producing called the Fifth Dimension. Webb contributed five tracks, including the album's title song, "Up, Up and Away," which became their debut single. A perfect example of sunshine pop, it scored a top ten hit and went on to win five Grammys, a record for a single song. Their follow-up album *The Magic Garden* featured eleven Webb songs, all inspired by his time with his girlfriend/wife. One of the songs, "The Worst That Could Happen" became a top three hit for the Brooklyn Bridge in December 1968. A few months after the album's release, ex-Wrecking Crew musician Glen Campbell charted with the definitive version of "By the Time I Get To Phoenix" and went on to win two Grammys.

Toward the end of 1967, Webb composed "MacArthur Park" after Bones Howe, producer of the group the Association, asked him to write a pop song with different movements and changing time signatures. Intended to be part of a cantata (vocal composition), it was later rejected due to its unorthodox lyrics and ambitious arrangement. It had been inspired by Webb's relationship and breakup with Horton, with the Los Angeles park being where they would occasionally meet for lunch and was symbolic of the end of their affair. According to Webb, everything in the song was real - the old men playing checkers and the cake left out in the rain were all things he had observed. On meeting Richard Harris at a fundraising event, the actor, who at the time had just started filming the musical *Camelot*, suggested that he would like to make a record for his pop music debut. After an invitation to meet up in London, out of several songs offered, Harris chose the last one, "MacArthur Park."

Recorded with the Wrecking Crew in Hollywood, the seven minutes, 21 seconds-song became a top ten hit on both sides of the Atlantic and went on to win a Grammy.

With the success of "By the Time I Get To Phoenix," Campbell later called Webb asking him to write another "place-based" song as a follow-up single. "Wichita Lineman" was inspired by driving through the high plains in Oklahoma and seeing a lineman perched on a telegraph pole and talking into a handset. Imagining him to be talking to his girlfriend, Webb set the song in Wichita, Kansas. Within hours, he delivered a demo of an unfinished version, with no bridge or third verse. Producer Al De Lory, whose uncle had been a lineman, had the Wrecking Crew musicians address what shortcomings there were to the music, and it became another top ten hit in November 1968.

The following year, Webb wrote two more chart hits for Campbell, the first another "place-based" song called "Galveston." The story about a soldier going into battle thinking about his lover back in his hometown, was seen by some as an anti-war protest. First released by Hawaiian singer Don Ho, Campbell's version became another top ten hit. This was soon followed by the top thirty "Where's the Playground Susie," which was a metaphor for the end of a relationship, using the playground as a symbol of their lost innocence and shared childhood.

As the decade came to an end, so too did Webb's run of chart hits. He made a number of solo albums with mixed reviews, wrote film scores and Broadway musicals, and had songs recorded by some of the biggest stars in the business. In the Eighties, he would win a Grammy for the song "Highwayman," recorded by supergroup the Highwaymen (Johnny Cash, Waylon Jennings, Willie Nelson and Kris Kristofferson).

Chart entries
Up, Up And Away – The 5th Dimension (US 1967 # 7); Johnny Mann Singers (UK 1967 # 6;
  US # 91); Hugh Masekela (US 1967 # 71)
By the Time I Get To Phoenix - Glen Campbell (US 1967 # 26; UK # 52); Marty Wilde
  (UK 1968 # 56); Georgie Fame (UK 1968 # 51)
Paper Cup – The 5th Dimension (US 1967 # 34)
Carpet Man - The 5th Dimension (US 1968 # 29)
McArthur Park – Richard Harris (US 1968 # 2; UK # 4)
Montage From How Sweet It Is (I Knew That You Knew) Love Generation (US 1968 # 86)
Do What You Gotta Do – Bobby Vee (US 1968 # 83); Nina Simone (UK 1968 # 2;
  US # 83)
The Yard Went On Forever – Richard Harris (US 1968 # 64)
Wichita Lineman – Glen Campbell (US 1968 # 3; UK # 7)
Worse That Could Happen – Brooklyn Bridge (US 1968 # 3)
Galveston – Glen Campbell (US 1969 # 4; UK # 14)
Didn't We – Richard Harris (US 1969 # 63)
Where's the Playground Susie? – Glen Campbell (US 1969 # 26)

Cynthia Weil see Barry Mann and Cynthia Weil

Ben Weisman
Born Benjamin Weisman, Providence RI 1921. Died 2007.

Raised in Brooklyn, his family had deep musical roots. At the age of five, under his father's supervision, he sang professionally at the neighbourhood temple during the High Holy holidays. In his teens, he was introduced to classical music, and for five years studied with concert pianist Grace Castagnetta. He then attended the Julliard School of Music. Drafted into the military at the start of the war, he became Special Services Music Director for the US Air Force. On his return, he began his musical career at New York's Brill Building, writing with Fred Wise and Kathleen Twomey, often with the collective pseudonym "Al Hill." After later signing an exclusive contract with music publishers Hill & Range, its co-owner Jean Aberbach requested him to write songs for Elvis Presley, beginning in 1956 with "First in Line," and later including the chart-topping "Rock-A-Hula Baby" (with Dolores Fuller). His friendship with Presley developed in the studio where Weisman was always invited to attend, especially as his demos were copied note-for-note and, without him there may have been problems. As a result he was nicknamed the "Mad Professor." Among his other successes were Bobby Vee's hit "The Night Has a Thousand Eyes," written with Dorothy Wayne and Marilynn Garrett, and Dusty Springfield's "All I See Is You," with Clive Westlake.

Chart entries
Ben Weisman and Fred Wise
Wooden Heart *(with Kay Twomey, Bert Kaempfert)* Elvis Presley (UK 1961 # 1); Joe Dowell

(US 1961 # 1)
Pocket Full of Rainbows - Deane Hawley (US 1961 # 93)
The Bridge of Love - Joe Dowell (US 1961 # 50)
Rock-A-Hula Baby *(with Dolores Fuller)* Elvis Presley (US 1961 # 23; UK # 1)
Follow That Dream - Elvis Presley (US 1962 # 15; UK # 34)
Let Me Go, Lover *(with Jenny Lou Carson, Kathleen Twomey)* Kathy Kirby (UK 1964 # 10)
I'll Touch a Star *(with Dolores Fuller)* Terry Stafford (US 1964 # 25)

Ben Weisman with others
The Night Has a Thousand Eyes *(with Dorothy Wayne, Marilynn Garrett)* Bobby Vee (US 1962 # 3; UK # 3)
Do the Clam *(with Dolores Fuller, Sid Wayne)* Elvis Presley (US 1965 # 21; UK # 19)
All I See Is You *(with Clive Westlake)* Dusty Springfield (UK 1966 # 9; US # 20)
Spinout *(with Dolores Fuller, Sid Wayne)* Elvis Presley (US 1966 # 40)

George David Weiss see also Bennie Benjamin
Born New York City 1921. Died 2010.
Songwriters Hall of Fame 1984.

Although originally planning a career as a lawyer or accountant, Weiss's first love took him to the Julliard School of Music, where he developed his skills in writing and arranging. Following his education, he became an arranger for some of the big bands of the day, including Stan Kenton and Vincent Lopez. For the next four decades, he was a prolific songwriter, with many songs written with Bennie Benjamin (1907-1989). He also composed film scores and Broadway musicals during the Forties and Fifties. In 1952, his writing partnership with Benjamim produced "Wheel of Fortune," a number one for Kay Starr, "Cross Over the Bridge" for Patti Page, and "How Important Can It Be?" for Joni James. In 1961, he arranged the melody and lyrics of "Wimoweh" into "The Lion Sleeps Tonight," a US number one for the Tokens. It had originally been written in 1939 as "Mbube" by South African musician Solomon Linda, and successfully recorded by the Weavers in 1951 as "Wimoweh." With around 150 artists having recorded the song, it earned an estimated $15 million in royalties, without Linda, long deceased, receiving any credit. With its inclusion in the movie and stage production of *The Lion King* a lawsuit followed between Linda's estate and Disney which was settled in 2006.

Also in 1961, Weiss co-wrote "Can't Help Falling in Love" with cousins Hugo Peretti and Luigi Creatore, its melody based on the popular French song "Plaisir d'amour," composed in 1784. It became a huge hit for Elvis Presley. Weiss continued partnerships with other writers throughout the Sixties, including Joe Sherman and George Dunning. In 1966, "Stay With Me," written with Jerry Ragovoy, was recorded at the last minute by soul singer Lorraine Ellison following a studio cancellation by Frank Sinatra, which Ragovoy was about to produce with a full orchestra. Calling in Ellison, the orchestra was retained and she delivered an impassioned vocal which took it into the charts. Weiss later teamed up with George Douglas (aka Bob Theile) for "What a Wonderful World." Theile found inspiration from the traumas of the post-Kennedy assassination, the Vietnam War and racial tensions, and along with Weiss chose Louis Armstrong to record it. It became a UK chart-topper in October 1967.

Chart entries
George David Weiss and Joe Sherman
That Sunday, That Summer - Nat King Cole (US 1963 # 12)
Toys in the Attic *(with George Duning)* Jack Jones (US 1963 # 92); Joe Sherman (US 1963 # 85)
Let Me Tell You, Babe - Nat King Cole (US 1966 # 90)
Let Me Cry On Your Shoulder - Ken Dodd (UK 1967 # 11)

George David Weiss and Bennie Benjamin
Wheel of Fortune - LaVerne Baker (US 1960 # 83)
I'll Never Be Free - Kay Starr (US 1961 # 94)
Oh! What It Seems To Be *(with Frankie Carlisle)* The Castells (US 1962 # 91)

George David Weiss with Hugo Peretti & Luigi Creatore
And Now - Della Reese (US 1960 # 6)
The Lion Sleeps Tonight *(with Solomon Linda, Paul Campbell, Albert Stanton)* The Tokens (US 1961 # 1; UK # 11); Karl Denver (as "Wimoweh" UK 1962 # 4)
Can't Help Falling In Love - Elvis Presley (US 1961 #2; UK # 1)

B'wa Nena - The Tokens (US 1962 # 55)
I'll Take You Home - The Corsairs (US 1962 # 68)
A Walkin' Miracle (*with Adam Levy*) The Essex (US 1963 # 12)
The Impossible Happened – Litte Peggy March (US 1963 # 57)

George David Weiss with others
Johnny Freedom *(with Jule Styne)* Johnny Horton (US 1960 # 69)
Stay With Me *(with Jerry Ragovoy)* Lorraine Ellison (US 1966 # 64); The Walker Brothers (as Stay With Me, Baby) (UK 1967 # 26)
What a Wonderful World *(with George Douglas)* Louis Armstrong (UK 1967 # 1)

Larry Weiss see Scott English and Larry Weiss

Bruce Welch see also Hank Marvin

Bryan Wells see Ron Miller

Clive Westlake
Born Gerald Clive Westlake, Wattsville, Wales 1932. Died 2000.

The son of a coal miner, Westlake studied at the Trinity College of Music in London, and was a music teacher at Robert Richardson Grammar School at Ryhope, near Sunderland, until 1959. Through the husband of singer Vera Lynn, he got into the music business by working as staff songwriter for the publishers Carlin Music. In 1964, he teamed up with Mort Schuman on "Here I Go Again," the first original single for the Hollies, the previous four having been covers. With ex-Springfields musician Tom Springfield, he wrote "Summer Is Over" a top thirty hit for Frank Ifield as well as "Losing You," a top ten hit for Tom's sister Dusty Springfield. With Ben Weisman, he gave her another top ten hit with "All I See Is You." After a break of two years, Westlake returned to writing songs for Springfield, with two self-penned songs, "I Close My Eyes and Count To Ten" (one of her biggest hits) and the moderate hit "I Will Come To You." His final success of the decade came with Tom Jones' "A Minute of Your Time," which peaked at number four in the charts in November 1968. With little further success, he eventually moved to Nashville in the Eighties.

Chart entries
Here I Go Again *(with Mort Schuman)* The Hollies (UK 1964 # 4)
What Am I To Yo? *(with Kenny Lynch, Mort Schuman)* Kenny Lynch (UK 1964 # 37)
Summer Is Over *(with Tom Springfield)* Frank Ifield (UK 1964 # 25)
Losing You *(with Tom Springfield)* Dusty Springfield (UK 1964 # 9; US # 91)
It's Gotta Last Forever *(with Kenny Lynch, Bill Giant)* Billy J Kramer & the Dakotas (US 1965 # 67)
All I See Is You *(with Ben Weisman)* Dusty Springfield (UK 1966 # 9; US # 20)
I Close My Eyes and Count to Ten) – Dusty Springfield (UK 1868 # 4)
I Will Come to You – Dusty Springfield (UK 1968 # 51)
A Minute of Your Time – Tom Jones (UK 1968 # 14; US # 48)

David White see John Madara and David White

Ronald White see also Smokey Robinson
Born Ronald Anthony White, Detroit, Michigan 1938. Died 1995.
Rock and Roll Hall of Fame 2012 (with the Miracles).

White was a childhood friend of fellow Miracles' co-founder Smokey Robinson and they had started singing together when White was 12. With Warren "Pete" Moore soon joining them, they formed a doo-wop group called the Five Chimes, along with Clarence Dawson and James Grice, all of who attended Detroit's Northern High School. With Dawson soon quitting and Grice leaving to get married, they were replaced by Emerson "Sonny" Rogers and his cousin Bobby and the quintet was re-named the Matadors.

In 1957 Sonny Rogers joined the US Army and was soon replaced by his sister Claudette Rogers, who had previously sung with The Matadorettes. After a two-year relationship, she would marry Robinson. Following a failed audition for Brunswick Records, they began working for Berry Gordy and signed with the Motown subsidiary Tamla as the Miracles. During the early years, White and Robinson performed a number of songs as Ron and Bill, while White also collaborated with him on a number of hits, including "My Girl Has Gone," "A Fork in the Road," as well as the Miracles' hit "Don't Look Back." Their most famous song was "My Girl," a chart-topper for the Temptations in December 1964. With White composing the music, Robinson claimed his lyrics were written with "all the women in the world in mind." The song was inducted into the Grammy Hall of Fame in 1998. It was White who also brought the relatively unknown Stevie Wonder to the label after hearing him play with his cousin.

In 1987, Robinson was inducted into the Rock and Roll Hall of Fame as a solo artist, although White and the other members of the Miracles were not included. In 2012 it was decided by a special committee representing the RRHOF to retroactively induct the group, including White and fellow members.

Chart entries
Everybody Gotta Pay Some Dues *(with Smokey Robinson)* The Miracles (US 1961 # 52)
You Beat Me to the Punch *(with Smokey Robinson)* Mary Wells (US 1962 # 9)
You Threw a Lucky Punch *((with Smokey Robinson, Don Covay)* Gene Chandler (US 1962 # 49)
Come On Do the Jerk (with *(with Smokey Robinson, Marvin Tarplin, Don Covay)* The Miracles (US 1964 # 50)
My Girl *(with Smokey Robinson)* The Temptations (US 1965 # 1; UK # 3); Otis Redding (UK 1965 # 11; 1968 # 36)
My Girl Has Gone *(with Smokey Robinson)* The Miracles (US 1965 # 14)
My Baby *(with Smokey Robinson, Pete Moore)* The Temptations (US 1965 # 13)
Don't Look Back *(with Smokey Robinson)* The Temptations (US 1965 # 83)
My Girl/Hey Girl *(with Smokey Robinson, Ronald White, Goffin & King)* Bobby Vee (US 1968 # 35)

Norman Whitfield see also Barrett Strong
Born Norman Jesse Whitfield, New York City 1940. Died 2008.
Songwriters Hall of Fame 2004.

Born and raised in Harlem, Whitfield spent most of his youth in local pool halls until, in his late teens, his family moved to Detroit where his father worked for his brother-in-law's chain of drug stores. After attending Northwestern High School, 19-year-old Whitfield began visiting Motown's Hitsville USA offices for a chance to find work. Noticed by founder Berry Gordy Jr, he was hired for their quality control department, deciding which records should be released. He also became part of the in-house songwriting staff and his first chart hit came in 1963 with "Pride and Joy," a top ten hit for Marvin Gaye, co-written with Gaye and William "Mickey" Stevenson. Along with Stevenson, he wrote "Needle in a Haystack" for the Velvelettes and later Martha & the Vandellas. More hits followed by collaborating with Eddie Holland, Barrett Strong and others.

In 1966, Whitfield took over Smokey Robinson's role as the main producer for the Temptations after his "Ain't Too Proud to Beg" performed better on the charts than Robinson's "Get Ready." He would go on to produce eight of their albums between 1969 and 1973. Among the famous songs he collaborated on as co-writer were "I Know I'm Losing You," "I Heard It Through the Grapevine," "Can't Get Next to You," and "Too Busy Thinking About My Baby."

"Cloud Nine" was the first Temptations hit recorded with their new lead singer Dennis Edwards, after David Ruffin was fired after missing a concert. He had also become difficult to work with after the label refused to bill the group as David Ruffin & the Temptations. The song also highlighted the group's new psychedelic funk sound akin to that of Sly & the Family Stone. It was also the first Motown song to use a wah-wah pedal when white guitarist Dennis Coffey brought it along and played it to Whitfield while arranging the song.

In the early Seventies, Whitfield teamed up with lyricist Barrett Strong to write a string of hits for the Temptations, including "Psychedelic Shack," "Ball of Confusion," "Just My Imagination," and "Papa Was A Rolling Stone." Despite that, friction between him and the band began to grow, with claims he was writing fewer love songs and moving toward social issues of the time, as well as putting more emphasis on their music instead of the vocals.

Chart entries
Norman Whitfield and Eddie Holland Jr
Price And Joy *(with Marvin Gaye & William "Mickey" Stevenson)* Marvin Gaye (US 1963 # 10)
Girl (Why You Wanna Make Me Blue) The Temptations (US 1964 # 26)

Needle In A Haystack *(with William "Mickey" Stevenson)* The Marvelettes (US 1964 # 45)
Too Many Fish In the Sea - The Marvelettes (US 1964 # 25)
He Was Really Saying Something *(with William "Mickey" Stevenson)* The Velvelettes (US 1964 # 45)
Ain't Too Proud To Beg - The Temptations (US 1966 # 13; UK # 21)
Beauty Is Only Skin Deep - The Temptations (US 1966 # 3; UK # 18)
I Know I'm Losing You *(with Cornelius Grant)* The Temptations (US 1966 # 8; UK #19)
Too Many Fish In the Sea / Three Litte Fishes *(with Saxie Dowell)* Mitch Ryder & the Detroit Wheels (US 1967 # 24)
Everybody Needs Love - Gladys Knight & the Pips (US 1967 # 39)
You're My Everything *(with Cornelius Grant & Roger Penzabene)* The Temptations (US 1967 # 6; UK # 26)
(Loneliness Made Me Realize) It's You That I Need - The Temptations (US 1967 # 14)
It Should Have Been Me *(with William "Mickey" Stevenson)* Gladys Knight & the Pips (US 1968 # 40)

Norman Whitfield and Barrett Strong
Gonna Gove Her All the Love I've Got - Jimmy Ruffin (US 1967 # 29; UK # 26)
I Heard It Through the Grapevine – Gladys Knight & the Pips (US 1967 # 2; UK # 47); King Curtis & the Kingpins (1968 # 83) ; Marvin Gaye (US 1968 # 1; UK # 1)
Please Return Your Love To Me *(with Barbara Neely)* The Temptations (US 1968 # 26)
Cloud Nine – Temptations (US 1968 # 6; UK 1969 # 15); Mongo Santamaria (US 1969 # 32)
Too Busy (Thinking About My Baby) *(with Janie Bradford)* Marvin Gaye (US 1969 # 4; UK # 5); The Billy Mitchell Group (US 1969 # 49)
Runaway Child, Running Wild – The Temptations (US 1969 # 6)
Don't Let the Jones Get You Down – The Temptations (US 1969 # 20)
I Can't Get Next To You – The Temptations (US 1969 # 1#; UK # 13)
That's the Way Love Is – Marvin Gaye (US 1969 # 7)
Friendship Train – Gladys Knight & the Pips (US 1969 # 17)
Don't Let Him Take Your Love From Me – Four Tops (US 1969 # 41)

Norman Whitfield and Roger Penzabene
Don't You Miss Me A Little Bit – Jimmy Ruffin (US 1967 # 68)
I Wish It Would Rain – The Temptations (US 1968 # 4; UK # 45); Gladys Knight & the Pips (US 1968 # 41)
The End Of the Road - Gladys Knight & the Pips (US 1968 # 15)
I Could Never Love Another (After Loving You) – The Temptations (US 1968 # 13; UK # 47)

Ronnie Wilkins see John Hurley and Ronnie Wilkins

Brian Wilson and Mike Love see also Jan Berry, Roger Christian
Born Brian Douglas Wilson, Inglewood, California 1942. Died 2025.
Born Michael Edward Love, Baldwin Hills, Los Angeles 1941.
Rock and Roll Hall of Fame 1989 (with the Beach Boys).
Songwriters Hall of Fame 2000 (Wilson).
Grammy Lifetime Achievement Award 2001 (with the Beach Boys).
Songwriters Hall of Fame 2025 (Love).

The first of three brothers born to Murry and Audree Wilson, Brian showed an aptitude for learning melodies by ear at a remarkably young age. Along with brothers Dennis (1944-1983) and Carl (1946-1998), they were often treated harshly by their disciplinarian father, a part-time songwriter. Learning to play accordion, he sang solo in a church choir and was said to have perfect pitch. At the age of 12, his family bought an upright piano and Brian taught himself to play his favourite songs. With an uncle later teaching him to play boogie-woogie and Carl introducing him to R&B music, Brian began teaching his brothers harmony parts after listening to vocal arrangements by the Four Freshmen. In his senior year at Hawthorne High School, he submitted an essay that stated his ambition to "make a name" for himself in music.

One of Brian's closest friends was his cousin Mike Love, whose mother was the sister of Murry Wilson. The two families lived close to each other and often socialised, with singalong sessions that developed their vocal styles - Brian's falsetto, Mike's bass, and Carl's middle-register. On his 16th birthday, his parents bought Brian a two-track tape recorder, opening up a whole new sonic world and laying the groundwork for him becoming a record producer. With his own music room set up in the house, he enlisted both parents and Carl for four-part harmonising. Dennis was always reluctant to join in, finding more pleasure in outdoor pursuits like surfing. In his senior year at high school, Brian was asked to form a combo to play at a student rally. When one of two school friends dropped out, Brian enticed brother Carl, who had recently taken to playing guitar, to join them as the short-lived Carl & the Passions.

On graduation, Brian elected to go to El Camino College, taking courses in psychology and music appreciation. While there, he befriended fellow football player Alan Jardine (b.1942) who had his own combo the Tikis, and they began performing together. Eventually, Brian, Mike and Al formed the short-lived Kenny & the Kadets which played at local parties, while Carl and his young neighbourhood friend David Marks (b.1948) jammed with their guitars. Mike inherited an interest in music from his mother, and, like Brian, became interested in both R&B and street-corner harmony groups. It was a time when kids all over the city were embracing rock and roll and the dream of it making them rich. All Brian wanted was a subject to sing about, and that's where Dennis came in...

One of the first ideas to form a proper group came from Mike in early 1961. After discussing the idea with Dennis on a visit to Malibu Beach, they put the idea to Brian. Around the same time, Jardine was also talking to Brian with the same idea. He and his combo had already tried out an unsuccessful recording at Hite and Dorinda Morgan's new recording studio (Hite being a friend of Murry's), and on a second attempt had taken along Brian to assist, although it was finally abandoned. Alan later asked Brian to bring along Mike and his brothers to help them record "The Wreck of the John B," but, still unimpressed, the Morgans asked them to come back with something original. At that point, it was Dennis who said, "No one had ever written a song about surfing," (although that was not the case). With that, Brian and Mike grabbed pens and started scribbling down lyrics, while Jardine played a rough melody on his guitar (the Morgans were probably not even aware of the latest craze).

On Labor Day weekend, Brian's parents went on vacation, leaving the boys money to buy food. Instead, they rented musical equipment and for the next five days rehearsed a song they simply called "Surfin'" with Brian on keyboards, Carl on guitar, Alan on upright bass, and Dennis on drums. While rehearsing, they came up with the name the Pendletones, after the woollen shirts surf groups were sporting. There were the anticipated arguments once the Wilsons returned home, but Murry soon realised they were on to something and gave them his support. In early November, they recorded "Surfin'" and a couple of songs the Morgan family had written, and then signed a songwriting contract with the Morgans' publishing company Guild Music. Hite Morgan took a tape of the recordings to the A&R man at the local label Candix Records, suggesting the name of the group be the Surfers. Realising there was already a group by that name, it was left to the label's accountant to suggest the name, Beach Boys (although the members were unaware of it until the record was released). On November 27th 1961, "Surfin'" was released and had sufficient airplay to see it peak at number 75 on the Hot 100. All that was left to do was for Murry to convince Capitol, one the world's biggest record labels, to sign them on a lucrative contract.

Murry Wilson took out a loan to pay for more studio time for the boys, but when Candix fell into bankruptcy he looked for a better deal. In the meantime, Brian was writing more songs with Mike as well as with his friend, 22-year-old bank teller and aspiring songwriter Gary Usher (1938-1990) and they recorded them at Western Recorders with sound engineer Chuck Britz. By this time, Jardine had left the group citing creative differences, and his place taken by 13-year-old David Marks. In May 1962, Murry's perseverance paid off when the group signed an interim recording contract with Capitol. The first single released was Brian and Mike's "Surfin' Safari" which became a top 20 hit, and the subsequent album *Surfin' Safari,* consisted mainly of original songs written by Brian and Mike, although the emotive ballad "The Lonely Sea," was written with Usher. The second album *Surfin' USA* quickly followed, with the title track being Brian's re-working of Chuck Berry's "Sweet Little Sixteen." According to Brian, the inspiration came from the surfing brother of his girlfriend who gave him a list of all the best surfing spots, many of which Brian namechecked in the song. It peaked at number three on the Hot 100, and a few years later, Berry's name was credited as co-writer.

In early 1963, Brian had attended a party held by Jan Berry and Dean Torrence, who recorded as Jan & Dean. When Brian played "Surfin' USA" to them, they suggested they could release it themselves as a single, but were refused. Instead, Brian offered them an unfinished song he had been working on but had since lost interest. With Berry and Torrence adding additional lyrics, they recorded "Surf City" and took it to the top of the US charts, to the lifelong chagrin of Murry Wilson, who felt his son had simply given away a hit single for the group.

The third album *Surfer Girl,* released in September 1963, was mainly a collection of surfing songs, with members of the famous Wrecking Crew utilised for the first time. The recordings also saw the return of Jardine (although Marks would remain for a few more months). Three of the tracks, surprisingly not released as singles, saw a marked development in Brian's production techniques. "Catch a Wave," with Mike's sister Maureen emulating the sound of rolling waves with a harp glissando, was *the* classic surfing song, while "Little Deuce Coupe," written with radio personality friend Roger Christian (1934-1991), was one of their signature car songs. However, the standout track was Brian and Usher's introspective "In My

Room," which came about from Brian once telling his friend that the sanctuary of his room (the music room) was his whole world. Usher's success with Brian would be short-lived due to Murry and their mutual dislike for each other.

The next album, the car-inspired *Little Deuce Coupe,* recycled some of the car songs from previous albums, with five new ones co-written with Christian, but it also included the anthemic "Be True To Your School," the single version of which had the girl group the Honeys emulating cheerleaders that the Wilsons recalled from their high school days. The following year's *Shut Down Volume 2* included two of Brian and Mike's finest songs. According to Mike, "Fun, Fun, Fun," with its tale of a teenage girl deceiving her father to go hot-rodding with his Ford Thunderbird, was modelled after Chuck Berry's "Nadine," while the opening guitar riff was based on his "Johnny B Goode." Also noticeable were touches of Phil Spector's work. The extraordinarily beautiful "The Warmth of the Sun" about the pain and heartbreak of a failed romance was partly inspired by the death of JFK just two months before. "Don't Worry Baby," arguably one of the group's greatest songs, was written by Brian with lyrics by Christian, and inspired by Brian's disciple-like admiration for Phil Spector's work, especially the song "Be My Baby." Initially intended for the Ronettes, it had been rejected by Spector, leaving Brian to bring in the Wrecking Crew and make what many consider his masterpiece. The car-related lyrics related to Brian's girlfriend Marilyn often unburdening his troubles with a simple "Don't worry, baby."

Their sixth album *All Summer Long,* released in July 1964, consisted of more complex and innovative arrangements and refined vocals, spawning one of their most memorable songs, Brian and Mike's "I Get Around." Partly inspired by brother Dennis's lifestyle, it relates to their newfound fame and the desire to find new places to go. In the wake of the British Invasion, it became their first chart-topper, signalling for the first time a growing rivalry with the Beatles. In a move away from car songs, Brain and Mike's "Little Honda" paid tribute to the Honda 50 motorcycle, popular at the time, and shorty after was recorded by the Usher-produced group the Hondells, who took it into the US top ten. The fine ballad "Girls on the Beach," although not release as a single, became the theme to the 1965 film of the same name. 1964's *Christmas Album* and the resulting hit single "Little Saint Nick" was in direct response to Spector's classic seasonal album of 1963.

Four months later, came the ground-breaking album *The Beach Boys Today!,* which followed Brian's nervous breakdown and a departure from touring. Displaying a marked difference to previous work with its thematic approach and intimate subject matter, it led to the group being considered as album artists rather than a singles act and is now rightly considered as one of the greatest albums of all time. Three of the singles were taken from side one, with a fourth "Help Me, Ronda" being re-recorded as "Help Me, Rhonda" and giving them their second chart-topper. But it was side two of the album that had musicologists taking special notice, with all but one track being beautiful crafted ballads, including a cover of the Students' "I'm So Young." With tracks like "Kiss Me Baby" and "She Knows Me Too Well," Brian was making a cohesive artistic statement that he would explore fully with *Pet Sounds*. Next came *Summer Days (and Summer Nights!)* with its lead-off track and single "California Girls" being one of Brian and Mike's finest moments. Their appreciation for homegrown women was partly inspired by the group's first tour of Europe and apparently conceived by Brian while on an acid trip and thinking about Western movies. With its dazzling orchestral intro, it became one of their best-selling singles up to that time. It was also the first recording that featured new member Bruce Johnston (b.1942), formerly of the duo Bruce & Terry, who was now replacing Brian on tour. "You're So Good To Me," another surprising non-candidate for a hit single, was written by Brian and Mike in just twenty minutes. The following *Party!* album consisted mainly of cover-songs, including several by the Beatles, but the one that made the most impression was their version of Fred Fassert's "Barbara Ann," Recorded by the Regents in 1961, it had Brian and Dean Torrence sharing lead vocals against a backdrop of party chatter, and it went on to peak at number two on the US charts.

In January 1965, 22-year-old Brian announced his withdrawal from the group following the recent nervous breakdown while on a flight. His aim was to concentrate on songwriting and production. Galvanised by the current work of the Beatles, he would produce "the greatest rock album ever made," with more complex arrangements and vocal parts than on any of his previous work. Viewing it as a solo album, he would make full use of the Wrecking Crew with songs that could not be easily replicated live. According to most sources, Brian met his future lyricist at United Recorders. 26-year-old Tony Asher was a copywriter working on advertising jingles, and after exchanging ideas, a collaboration was proposed. Within days of working at Brian's home, they had written their first song, "You Still Believe In Me," and over the next two to three weeks Brian had developed melodies and chord progressions to match the lyrics. Another of their early completed songs was "Caroline, No," inspired by one of Asher's past girlfriends. Initially conceived as "Carol, I Know," Brian misheard it as "Caroline, No," which they agreed sounded more poignant. Recorded without the other group members (they were on tour), it included Brian's two barking dogs for the non-musical tag at the end, and was released as a solo single in March 1966.

That same month, their "Sloop John B" was released. Recorded the previous December, the cover of the Kingston Trio's 1958 hit "The John B Sails," had been suggested to Brian by Jardine, a keen folk music fan. With Capitol needing another hit single by the group, it peaked at number three in the charts and became a worldwide hit. "Wouldn't It Be Nice," for which Mike would later be given co-writing credit (along with many others), was released as a double a-side with "God Ony Knows," which Brian had originally considered as a solo single for brother Carl. Arguably one of the finest pop records ever recorded, this was, like the album itself, another Brian masterpiece. Despite Carl's heaven-sent vocal, the sonic tapestry of the bridge, and the final coda with Brian and Bruce, it was a not big hit in the US. Compared to their previous albums, *Pet Sounds* was only a moderate commercial success in the US (largely due to Capitol releasing a greatest hits album just two months later), but went on to receive huge critical acclaim and is now still regarded by many as the greatest pop album of all time.

While doing the groundwork for *Pet Sounds*, Brian had also been working with Asher on an R&B song initially called "Good, Good Vibrations," which had been inspired by Brian's mother telling him how dogs could pick up invisible vibrations and bark at certain people. With Asher's original lyrics being (luckily) discarded, Brian felt he needed more time to work on the song, and as a result it was left off the album.

Brian now set his mind on exploring new directions for his next project and was in need of a new lyricist who could share his imagination. In July 1966, he reconnected with Van Dyke Parks (b.1943) who he had first met the previous December, and between them they developed *Smile*, a revolutionary album that Brian touted as his "teenage symphony to God." From the very first attempts at "Good Vibrations" through to May 1967, it consumed over 80 hours of recording sessions and 50 hours of tape, before finally being abandoned as the most famous unreleased album in music history. However, remnants of it would be re-recorded on future albums.

The most famous, of course, was "Good Vibrations," released on *Smiley Smile* in September 1967. Although Brian did not want the song included, he was out-voted by the group, who saw its hit potential. With revised lyrics by Mike, it not only became a transatlantic chart topper, but one of the legendary pop singles of all time. The other famous *Smile*-era song that was resurrected for the album was the complex "Heroes and Villains." Inspired partly on the Western ballads of Marty Robbins, Van Dyke's lyrics were based on the early history of the US, with references to the Spanish and Native-American Indians. Brian put together a composite of what parts remained in just three days at his home studio, and although not happy with the finished version, it was included on the album and released as another charting single, but with the production credit going to all group members for the first time.

The next album, the soulful *Wild Honey*, and the two singles lifted from it, the title track and "Darlin," both had Carl as lead vocalist. At one time, Brian had even contemplated giving away "Darlin'" to the band Three Dog Night. The title track of the next album *Friends* was Brian's attempt to bring back waltz-time music back into pop. This was soon followed by the album *20/20*, so-called for being the group's 20th album. It consisted mainly of outtakes from earlier work, but was more noticeable for Brian's growing absence from the recordings.

Conflicts with Brian had begun to surface more regularly, with Mike wanting the group to continue with their immaculately produced pop music and feeling that since the days of *Smile* Brian was getting too "far out." His growing dependence on drugs and his reclusive nature added fuel to the argument. One last shining moment was Brian and Mike's "Do It Again," which preceded the album's release by months, and was their attempt to revisit their surfing sound, not seen since 1964's *All Summer Long*. Inspired and written by Mike after a day spent at the beach, its sweep of nostalgia proved more popular in the non-surfing UK where it scored their second chart-topper. Another highlight of the album was Carl's slick version of the Ronettes' "I Can Hear Music," the first song by the group that had no involvement from Brian. On a darker side, the track "Never Learn Not to Love," was a revised version of "Cease To Exist," written by the infamous Charles Manson, who for a short time had befriended Dennis Wilson.

In April 1969, the group issued Capitol a lawsuit for unpaid royalties and mismanagement, thus severing their seven-year relationship. Before launching their own Brother Records, they still owed Capitol one last single, so Brian called in his father Murry for help. Almost at the drop of a hat, they came up with "Break Away," a rock-solid, life-affirming song that became the group's last hit of the decade.

Over the years to come, there would still be shining moments for the group, with albums like *Sunflower* and *Surf's Up*, the latter's title track being another *Smile* remnant, but now credited as one of Brian's finest works. Although losing his younger brothers far too early, Brian went on to record a number of solo albums and even reconstructed and recorded what he imagined *Smile* would have been, and the critics loved it.

On his advice to other songwriters, Brian wrote: "I would recommend that they follow through if they have an idea. Follow through with it. Don't quit halfway through like a baby. Go through the whole shebang and carry it through instead of quitting halfway."

Chart entries
Surfin' (US 1961 # 75)
Surfin' Safari (US 1962 # 14)
Ten Little Indians (US 1962 # 49)
Surfin' USA *(with Chuck Berry)* (US 1963 # 3; UK # 34)
Surfer Girl (US 1963 # 7)
Be True To Your School (US 1963 # 6)
Little Saint Nick (US 1963 #25; UK # 43)
Fun, Fun, Fun (US 1964 # 5)
I Get Around (US 1964 # 1; UK # 7)
When I Grow Up (To Be A Man) (US 1964 # 9; UK # 27)

Dance, Dance, Dance (US 1964 # 8; UK # 24)
Do You Wanna Dance? (US 1965 # 12)
Help Me, Rhonda (US 1965 # 1; UK # 27)
California Girls (US 1965 # 3; UK # 26)
The Little Girl I Once Knew (US 1965 # 20)
Wouldn't It Be Nice (US 1966 # 8)
Good Vibrations (US 1966 # 1; UK # 1)
Wild Honey (US 1967 # 31; UK # 29)
Darlin' (US 1968 # 19; UK # 11)
Do It Again (US 1968 # 20; UK # 1)

Brian Wilson
Custom Machine – Bruce & Terry (US 1964 # 85)
My Buddy Seat – The Hondells (US 1964 # 87)
Sloop John B *(Trad. Arranged by Brian)* (US 1966 # 3; UK # 2)
Brian Wilson and Mike Love
Little Honda – The Hondells (US 1964 # 9)

Brian Wilson with Jan Berry and Roger Christian
Surf City - Jan & Dean (US 1963 # 1)
Drag City - Jan & Dean (US 1963 # 10)
Dead Man's Curve *(with Artie Koenfeld)* Jan & Dean (US 1964 # 8)
Ride the Wild Surf - Jan & Dean (US 1964 # 16)
Sidewalk Surfin' - Jan & Dean (US 1964 # 25)

Brian Wilson with others
Caroline, No *(with Tony Asher)* Brian Wilson (US 1966 # 32)
God Only Knows *(with Tony Asher)* The Beach Boys (US 1966 # 39; UK # 2)
Heroes and Villains *(with Van Dyke Parks)* The Beach Boys (US 1967 # 12; UK # 8)
Friends *(with Carl Wilson, Dennis Wilson and Al Jardine)* The Beach Boys (US 1968 # 47; UK # 25)
Break Away *(with Reggie Dunbar aka Murry Wilson)* The Beach Boys (US 1969 # 63; UK # 6)
In My Room *(with Gary Usher)* Sagittarius (US 1969 # 86)

Frank Wilson
Born Frank Edward Wilson, Houston, Texas 1940. Died 2012.

As a youngster, he was taught to play piano by his mother, a domestic servant, and also sang in his uncle's vocal group the Gibbs Five. After attending Southern University in Baton Rouge for a year, he took part in a civil rights protest and subsequently lost his scholarship. With an ambition to become a performer and songwriter, he moved to Los Angeles while still in his teens and joined the gospel group the Angelaires. Singer Brenda Holloway heard him perform and persuaded him to move into secular music, and he went on to make a number of recordings for local labels, using the pseudonyms Sonny Daye, Chester St Anthony and Eddie Wilson. Thanks to Holloway, Wilson was invited to join Motown, whose Los Angeles offices had been set up by producers Marc Gordon and Hal Davis.

His first writing credit came with Patrice Holloway's "Stevie," the label's very first West Coast release. Asked by Berry Gordy to relocate to Detroit, one of his first records there was to have been his "Do I Love You (Indeed I Do)." Although many demos were pressed in 1965, it was never officially released, partly due to Wilson deciding to focus on producing rather than a recording career, and for Gordy not keen on his vocals and allegedly preferring his producers not to have successful recording careers. Only several copies of the demo survived, and due to its scarcity it became highly collectible, especially around the UK's Northern Soul clubs, until officially released there by Motown in 1979. It remains one of the most rarest and most valuable records in pop history. Wilson teamed up with producers Davis and Gordon to write a number of chart hits, and also wrote two hits for Brenda Holloway, including "You Made Me So Very Happy" with Gordy, Brenda and her younger sister Patrice. His biggest success came with the Supremes' 1968 chart-topper "Love Child," written with Motown staff writers Hank Cosby, Pam Sawyer, Deke Richards and R Dean Taylor.

In the Seventies, his work with the Supremes continued with "Up the Ladder To the Roof" (with Vincent DiMirco) and "Stoned Love" (with Kenny Thomas). Moving back to L.A, he co-wrote "Keep on Truckin'" and "Boogie Down" for ex-Temptations' Eddie Kendricks.

Chart entries
Castles in the Sand *(with Hal Davis, Marc Gordon, Mary O'Brien)* Little Stevie Wonder (US 1964 # 62)
I'm So Thankful *(with Marc Gordon)* The Ikettes (US 1965 # 74)
Whole Lot of Shakin' in My Heart (Since I Met You) The Miracles (US 1966 # 46)
Somebody (Somewhere) Needs You *(with Marc Gordon)* Darrell Banks (US 1966 # 55)
Just Look What You've Done *(with R Dean Taylor)* Brenda Holloway (US 1967 # 69)
All I Need *(with Eddie Holland Jr, R Dean Taylor)* The Temptations (US 1967 # 8; UK # 60)
You've Made Me So Very Happy *(with Brenda Holloway, Patrice Holloway, Berry Gordy)* Brenda Holloway (US 1967 # 39); Blood, Sweat & Tears (US 1969 # 2; UK # 35)
Chained – Marvin Gaye (US 1968 # 32)
Love Child *(with Henry Cosby, Pam Sawyer, Deke Richards, R Dean Taylor)* Diana Ross & the Supremes (US 1968 # 1; UK # 16)

Steve Winwood see also **Dave Mason**
Born Stephen Lawrence Winwood, Birmingham, England 1948.
Rock and Roll Hall of Fame 2004 (with Traffic).

Handsworth-born Winwood's father was not only a foundryman but a semi-pro musician who mainly played clarinet and saxophone, and it was no wonder that as a child he was playing piano, drums and guitar, and having a love for both swing and jazz music. With a gifted voice, he also sang in a church choir in nearby Perry Barr. After going to school, he had music classes at the Birmingham & Midland Institute where one of his friends was future Fleetwood Mac member Christine Perfect. At the age of eight, although underage, he was performing in clubs and bars with the Ron Atkinson Band, along with his father (on tenor sax) and elder brother Mervyn "Muff" Winwood (on bass guitar), and while still at school in his teens became part of the city's blues rock scene, playing a Hammond organ while backing famous US blues artists while on UK tours.

In August 1963, while the Winwood brothers were performing as the Muff Woody Jazz Band at the Golden Eagle pub in Birmingham, they were noticed by Spencer Davis (1939-2020), a former Birmingham University student and ex-member of the London skiffle group the Saints. Davis recruited them, along with drummer Pete York, to form the Rhythm & Blues Quartet. In June 1964, they were seen performing by Chris Blackwell, who was so impressed with their playing and Steve's distinctive high tenor voice, that he immediately signed them to his fledgling independent label, Island Records. It was Muff who came up with the name the Spencer Davis Group, as he seemed to be the only member enjoying doing interviews, thus letting the others members off the hook.

In late 1965, the band had their first UK chart-topper with "Keep on Running," written by reggae musician Jackie Edwards, a house songwriter for the label, who also gave them a second number one with "Somebody Help Me." Due to lack of promotion by the Atco label, neither charted in the US. However, their UK success now meant Winwood could afford to buy his own Hammond organ. Inspired by the Beatles and Stones to write original material, Winwood had already co-written "When I Come Home" with Edwards, but it was shelved in favour of "Somebody Help Me," until they appeared performing it in the 1966 comedy film *The Ghost Goes Gear*, after which Blackwell agreed to release at as a single.

Later that year, while under pressure from Blackwell for another hit, Davis and the Winwoods wrote and rehearsed "Gimme Some Lovin'" in just twenty minutes, and on its release it just missed out on the top spot. The following year, Winwood and their producer Jimmy Miller came up with the organ-driven "I'm a Man," a top ten transatlantic hit, but also the last single before the Winwood brothers quit the group in April 1967, with Stevie joining Traffic and Muff working as an A&E man for the label.

Winwood had first met future Traffic members Jim Capaldi, Dave Mason and Chris Wood when they jammed together at the Elbow Room in Birmingham. All Midlanders, guitarist Mason had been a roadie for the Spencer Davis Group, sax and flute player Wood had played with the bands Locomotive and Sounds of Blue, and drummer Capaldi had played with the Hellions, as well as with Winwood in Deep Feeling. Winwood had already talked with Capaldi about forming a group and writing together.

It was Capaldi who came up with the name Traffic while the four of them were waiting to cross the street in Dorchester, and they rented a cottage in Berkshire to write and rehearse their songs. Moving into psychedelic rock, the first song they came up with was "Paper Sun," inspired by Capaldi from a newspaper headline he read while sharing a boarding house with Winwood. With an upright piano in the living room, they sat down and wrote the song which later became a top five hit. Their best known song, "Hole in My Shoe," was written and performed by Mason, and featured a spoken-word midsection by

Blackwell's stepdaughter Francine Heimann fantasying about a ride on the back of a giant albatross. Although becoming their biggest hit, it was disliked by the other members as not representing their musical or lyrical style. All four members wrote the next hit single "Here We Go Round the Mulberry Bush" which was featured in the 1968 romantic teen movie of the same name starring Barry Evans and Judy Geeson.

In late 1967, they released their debut album *Mr Fantasy*. Despite containing none of the previous singles, it was well received by critics. With Mason departing the band, they continued as a trio, and Winwood and Capaldi wrote the ballad "No Face, No Name, No Number," the band's final single. While they were on hiatus, Winwood began jamming with his friend, ex-Cream guitarist Eric Clapton, and in early 1969 they got together with ex-Cream drummer Ginger Baker and ex-Family bassist Rick Grech to form the short-lived "supergroup" Blind Faith. Their eponymous album had no singles but did include Clapton's classic "Presence of the Lord." After completing a US tour with the band, Clapton lost interest and began working with Delaney & Bonnie.

In late 1969, Winwood and Grech joined Ginger Baker's Airforce for a time, with Winwood then pursuing a successful solo career. Looking back on a lifetime of music, he once stated: "I think a lot of people came into rock n' roll to try and change the world. I came into rock n' roll to make music."

Chart entries
When I Come Home *(with Jackie Edwards)* The Spencer Davis Group (UK 1966 # 12)
Gimme Some Lovin' *(with Spencer Davis, Muff Winwood)* The Spencer Davis Group (UK 1966 #2; US # 7)
I'm a Man *(with Jimmy Miller)* The Spencer Davis Group (UK 1967 # 9; UK # 10)
Paper Sun *(with Jim Capaldi)* Traffic (UK 1967 # 5; US # 94)
Here We Go Round the Mulberry Bush *(with Jim Capaldi, Chris Wood)* Traffic (UK 1967 # 8)
No Face No Name No Number *(with Jim Capaldi)* Traffic (UK 1968 # 40)

Mark Wirtz
Born Mark Philip Wirtz, Strasbourg, Germany 1943. Died 2020.

After being raised in Cologne during the war, he moved with his family to England in 1962. He began his music career studying at London's Fairfield College of Arts and Science and later studied drama at the Royal Academy of Dramatic Art where he was part of the college rock band, the Beatcrackers. In 1963, they were signed by EMI producer Norman Newell as Mark Rogers & the Marksmen and recorded one single, "Bubble Pop." Two years later, Wirtz had started his first independent production company and worked on recordings by veteran singer Marlene Dietrich, as well as releasing solo instrumentals under various pseudonyms. In 1966, he wrote and produced the instrumental single "A Touch of Velvet - A Sting of Brass" by the Mood-Mosaic, with vocals supplied by the Ladybirds, and it was soon taken up as a theme tune by pirate radio stations.

The following year, he accepted an offer by Norrie Paramor of EMI to become an in-house producer, working alongside the Beatles and Pink Floyd, often with engineer Geoff Emerick. In May 1967, he produced the single "My White Bicycle" for the short-lived psychedelic rock band Tomorrow, which featured singer Keith West (aka Keith Hopkins), and also worked with Kippington Lodge (a band that included members Brinsley Schwartz and Nick Lowe), producing and arranging the single, "Shy Boy."

While working on the project *Mood Mosaic,* Wirtz began developing the idea for a rock opera, inspired by a dream he had about an aged door-to-door grocer called Jack in a turn-of-the-century village. Mocked by children, he dies unexpectedly, and as the town folk react with anger over the inconvenience it now created, the children are heartbroken with remorse. The idea was to cut a single, and if it was a hit, people would want an entire opera.

Although EMI were skeptical, using the pseudonym Philwit, Wirtz went on to write the aptly-named "Excerpt From a Teenage Opera," and gave it to West to record, along with backing vocals from the Corona Academy childrens choir. Although the single peaked at number two (sadly denied the top spot by "The Last Waltz"), EMI refused to give the go-ahead for an album until there was a successful second single. Meanwhile, Wirtz continued developing stories about individual village characters, and a second single materialised called "Sam," about a man and his steam engine. Although still a modest hit, it coincided with the sudden demise of pirate radio and changes to the label's marketing approach, and as a result Wirtz eventually lost interest in the project.

In more recent years, snippets of the opera already produced emerged on a new album, showing glimpses of what it could have been - pop music's very first rock opera. In 1969, Wirtz left EMI to return to independent production.

Chart entries
Excerpt From a Teenage Opera *(with Keith Hopkins)* Keith West (UK 1967 # 2)
Sam *(with Keith Hopkins)* Keith West (UK 1967 # 38)

Fred Wise see Ben Weisman

Jimmy Wisner see also William Jackson
Born James Joseph Wisner, Philadelphia Pa 1931. Died 2018.

As a youngster, he received classical training and in the late Fifties attended Temple University studying psychology. In 1959, he formed the Jimmy Wisner Trio with drummer Chick Kinney and Ace Tesone on bass. Together, they backed different artists who toured through Philadelphia (including Mel Tormé and Dakota Staton). Their first album *Blues For Harvey* was released on Felsted Records in 1961. Laer that year, came the single "Asia Minor." Co-written with Roger Mozian and played on a honky-tonk upright piano, it merged Grieg's classical Piano Concerto in A Minor with a rock n' roll beat. Fearing that it would tarnish his reputation as a well-respected jazz musician, Wisner used the pseudonym Kokomo. After it was rejected by nearly a dozen labels, he set up his own label Future Records to release it, along with distributor Harry Chipetz and engineer Amel Corset. When finally picked up by Felsted, it peaked at number eight on the US charts, and also charted in the UK despite a radio ban by the BBC. Three more singles as Kokomo were released on Felsted, including "Like Teen," but chart success eluded them.

Wisner then launched a successful career as songwriter, producer and tv and film composer. In 1963, he wrote "Somewhere" with his then-wife Norma Mendoza, a top twenty hit for the Tymes, and he soon formed a longer-standing writing relationship with William Jackson, with hits such as ""Don't Throw Your Love Away," a UK number one for the Searchers in 1964, and "What in the World's Come Over You," a top thirty chart hit for the Rockin' Berries the following year. As producer and arranger, Jimmy "the Wiz" worked with various artists, including Bobby Rydell, Freddy Cannon, Neil Sedaka, Len Barry, and Spanky & Our Gang, and for a couple of years at the end of decade headed Columbia's A&R department.

Chart entries
A Perfect Love *(with Bob Marcucci, Peter De Angelis)* Frankie Avalon (US 1960 # 47)
Asia Minor *(with Roger Mozian, Edward Grieg)* Kokomo (aka Jimmy Wisner) (US 1961 # 8;
   UK # 35)
Somewhere *(with Norma Mendoza)* The Tymes (US 1963 # 19)

Jimmy Wisner and William Jackson
Willyam, Willyam - Dee Dee Sharp (US 1964 # 97)
Don't Throw Your Love Away - The Searchers (UK 1964 # 1; US # 16)
The Magic of Our Summer Love - The Tymes (US 1964 # 99)
Here She Comes *(with Roy Straigis)* The Tymes (US 1964 # 92)
What in the World's Come Over You - The Rockin' Berries (UK 1965 # 23)

Bobby Womack
Born Robert Dwayne Womack, Cleveland, Ohio 1944. Died 2014.
Rock and Roll Hall of Fame 2009.

The third of five children growing up in the Cleveland slums, his mother once told him that he could "sing his way out of the ghetto." All five children were told not to touch their father's guitar while he worked at a steel mill, but of course they all did, and it was only then that they became aware of eight-year old Bobby's talent. As a result, all five brothers were bought guitars, and with Bobby being left-handed, he played it upside-down before realising it could be restrung. By the mid-Fifties, siblings Bobby, Friendly Jr, Curtis, Harry and Cecil, were touring the Mid-west gospel circuit as the Womack Brothers, along with their father on guitar and their mother on organ. With Curtis usually the lead singer, Bobby was sometimes allowed to sing with him, their voices in contrast, with young Bobby's gruff baritone and his elder brother's smooth tenor. In 1955, they released the single "Bible Tells Me So/Buffalo Bill" on the Pennant label. While touring, the Womacks met up with Sam Cooke, leader of the Soul Stirrers, who became their mentor. With his help, they were booked to go on national tours with the Staple Singers.

When Bobby dropped out of high school in 1960, Cooke hired him as guitarist in his backing band, and the following year signed the Womack brothers to his new label SAR Records. After releasing several gospel singles, Cooke suggested they change their name to the Valentinos, relocate to Los Angeles, and make the transition from gospel to a more soul and pop sound. As a result, their first single "Lookin' For a Love" was a pop version of the gospel song "Couldn't Hear Nobody

Pray" that had been recorded earlier. Produced and arranged by Cooke, it became an R&B hit. Quickly followed with "I'll Make It Alright," another chart entry, it prompted a support spot on a James Brown tour.

In 1964, the Valentinos had their last release with "It's All Over Now," written by Bobby with sister-in-law Shirley Womack, the wife of elder brother Friendly Jr. It entered the charts in June that year, just as the Rolling Stones had commenced their first US tour. After hearing the song on radio, the Stones recorded their version nine days later at Chess Records in Chicago. With the Valentinos' version just scraping into the Hot 100, the Stones' version became a top thirty US hit and a UK chart-topper just a month later. Although at the time Bobby had told Cooke he didn't want the Stones' to record it, once the first royalty cheque came in, he said that they could have any of his songs they wanted.

Following the murder of Cooke in December 1964, the Valentinos broke up and the label folded. Bobby married Cooke's widow, Barbara, and attempted a solo career, but the backlash created by the marriage brought a hostile reception by radio stations. Instead, he began a busy period of session work, contributing to recordings by artists that included King Curtis and Wilson Pickett, and also toured and recorded with Ray Charles. Around 1965, he relocated to Memphis and worked at Chip Moman's American Studios, playing on recordings by Joe Tex, the Box Tops, and Aretha Franklin. His songwriting output was noticed by Wilson Pickett, who went on to record 17 of his songs, including "I'm in Love" and "I'm a Midnight Mover" (co-written with Pickett). In September 1968, following brief stints at Chess and Atlantic, Womack signed with Minit Records and recorded his debut album *Fly Me to the Moon,* the title track of which gave him his first solo success.

In the early Seventies, Womack divorced Barbara, recorded a number of successful albums, and continued to collaborate with other artists. Reflecting on his career, he said: "People think you have to go through a lot of changes to become a soul singer. You just have to go through life."

Chart entries
It's All Over Now *(with Shirley Womack)* The Rolling Stones (UK 1964 # 1; US # 26) The
 Valentinos (US 1964 # 94)
Baby, Help Me – Percy Sledge (US 1967 # 87)
I'm In Love *(with King Curtis)* Wilson Pickett (US 1968 # 45)
Jealous Love (US 1968 # 50)
I'm a Midnight Mover (*with Wilson Pickett*) Wilson Pickett (US 1968 # 24; UK # 38)
I Found A True Lov*e (with Reggie Young)* Wilson Pickett (US 1968 # 42)
How I Miss You Baby (*with Darryl Carter)* Bobby Womack (US 1969 # 93)

Stevie Wonder
Born Stevland Hardaway Morris, Saginaw, Michigan 1950.
Songwriters Hall of Fame 1983.
Rock and Roll Hall of Fame 1989.
Grammy Lifetime Achievement Award 1996.

Born six weeks premature, it led to a disease that aborted eye growth and left him blind, and when his parents divorced when he was three, his mother moved with her children to Detroit. Stevie attended Whitestone Baptist Church, and by the age of eight had become the choir's soloist. He had already learned to play piano, drums and harmonica and had started writing songs. In the meantime, his parents had reunited and had two more children. With a friend John Glover, Stevie formed a singing partnership called Stevie & John and performed on street corners and at parties. Glover's cousin Gerald White was the brother of the Miracles' Ronnie White. When he heard Stevie sing his own composition "Lonely Boy," White took Stevie and his mother for an audition at Motown. Apparently, on first hearing Stevie play, it dazzled Motown boss Berry Gordy Jr who reportedly exclaimed, "Boy! That kid is a wonder!" The name stuck, but it was apparently producer Clarence Paul who came up with the name Little Stevie Wonder. His legal name was also changed to Morris, reportedly an old family name. Due to his age, Gordy drew up a rolling five-year contract in which royalties would be held in trust until the boy was 21. With his mother paid expenses, Stevie would receive $2.50 a week and have private tuition while on tour.

With Wonder now attending Fitzgerald Elementary School, he was also put in the care of producer Paul, and for the next year they worked together on two albums, *Tribute to Uncle Ray* (mainly a cover of Charles' songs) and the instrumental *The Jazz Soul of Little Stevie,* which had two compositions co-written with Wonder. In August 1962, he released his first single, "I Call It Pretty Music, But the Old People Call It the Blues," written by Gordy. Peaking just outside the Hot 100, two unsuccessful singles followed, and, on their release, the two albums also stalled. Meanwhile, Wonder had enrolled at the Michigan School for the Blind in Lansing. In October 1962, he embarked on the two-month Motortown Revue tour with Marvin Gaye, the Supremes, the Miracles and Mary Wells. Stevie's 20-minute performance at Chicago's Regal Theater was recorded for the album *Recorded Live: The 12 Year Old Genius,* and released in May 1963*,* along with the single "Fingertips" written by Clarence Paul and Henry Cosby, which topped both the US R&B and Hot 100 charts. At the age of 13, he became the youngest ever artist to achieve that feat.

The next few singles were unsuccessful, and with Wonder's voice now changing as he was getting older, some of the label's executives considered dropping him, but producer and songwriter Sylvia Moy persuaded Berry to give him another chance. In fact, producer Paul was beginning to find it easier to work with Wonder's now-mature tenor voice.

Agreeing to drop the "Little" from his name, Moy and Cosby set about writing a new song for him, based on an instrumental riff that Wonder had devised. The resulting song was the dance-orientated "Uptight (Everything's Alright)," with Moy's lyrics depicting a poor man's gratitude for a rich girl seeing beyond his poverty. Not having the lyrics in braille for the recording, Moy sang one line ahead of him, so Wonder just had to repeat it as he heard it. This began a run of US top forty hits that remained unbroken for over six years (apart from seasonal Christmas releases).

Like most Motown artists, Wonder went on to record material chosen for him by the label's executives, often collaborating with staff writers. The 1966 single "A Place in the Sun" was the first of three singles that would feature songwriter Ron Miller (1932-2007), the others being "For Once In My Life" and "Yesterme, Yesteryou, Yesterday," while "I Was Made To Love Her" gave his mother Lula May Hardaway co-writing credit and also had Wonder add-libbing the last line, "You know Stevie ain't gonna leave her."

Wonder continued into the Seventies co-writing hits for other artists, including the number one "Tears of a Clown" for Smokey Robinson & the Miracles, "It's a Shame" for the Spinners, and "Until You Come Back To Me" for Aretha Franklin. But it was his solo career that took the music world by storm with a string of ground-breaking albums, beginning with 1972's *Talking Book*, followed by *Innervisions*, *Fulfullingness' First Finale*, and *Songs in the Key of Life*, as well as having five chart-topping US singles.

Looking back on his stellar career, he wrote: "Music, at its essence, is what gives us memories. And the longer a song has existed in our lives, the more memories we have of it."

Chart entries
Uptight (Everything's Alright) Stevie Wonder (US 1965 # 3; UK # 14); The Crusaders (US 1966 # 95); Nancy Wilson (US 1966 # 84); Ramsey Lewis (US 1966 # 49)
Just A Little Misunderstanding (*with Clarence Paul, Morris Broadnax*) The Contours (US 1966 # 85; UK # 31)
Loving You Is Sweeter Than Ever (*with Ivy Jo Hunter*) The Four Tops (US 1966 # 12)
Hey Love (*with Clarence Paul, Morris Broadnax*) Stevie Wonder (US 1966 # 90)
I Was Made To Love Her (*with Lula Mae Hardaway, Henry Cosby, Sylvia Moy*) Stevie Wonder (US 1967 # 2# UK # 5); King Curtis & the Kingpins (US 1967 # 76)
Little Ole' Man (Uptight Everything's Alright) (*with Sylvia Moy, Henry Cosby*) Bill Cosby (US 1967 # 4)
I'm Wondering (*with Syvia Moy, Henry Cosby*) Stevie Wonder (US 1967 # 12# UK # 23)
Shoo-Be-Doo-Be-Doo-Da-Day (*with Sylvia Moy, Henry Cosby*) Stevie Wonder (US 1968 # 9; UK # 46)
You Met Your Match (*with Lula Mae Hardaway, Don Hunter*) Stevie Wonder (US 1968 # 35)
I Don't Know Why (*with Paul Riser, Don Hunter, Lula Mae Hardaway*) Stevie Wonder (US 1969 # 39; UK # 14)
My Cherie Amour (*with Sylvia Moy, Hank Cosby*) Stevie Wonder (US 1969 # 4; UK #4)

Chris Wood see Dave Mason

Roy Wood
Born Birmingham, England 1946.
Rock and Roll Hall of Fame 2017 (with ELO).

Attending Moseley School of Art during the early Sixties, the first (and only) instrument Wood was trained on was drums, and at the age of six he was allowed to play with a big band at his sister's wedding. Six years later, he went to see the Shadows play at Birmingham Town Hall and was influenced by Hank Marvin's guitar sound. As a result, he obtained a guitar and taught himself to play, and at the age of 14 formed a group called the Falcons. In 1963, he turned professional with local band Gerry Levene & the Avengers, before moving to play with Mike Sheridan & the Nightriders (later becoming the Idle Race). Around this time, he had also begun to write songs, and in 1964 was expelled from art school.

In December 1965, Wood got together with Trevor Burton, lead guitarist of local band Danny King & the Mayfair Set, and Chris "Ace" Kefford, bass guitarist of the Vikings, to form a group from among the city's best musicians, similar to how the Who had been formed. The three of them held jamming sessions at Birmingham's Cedar Club and invited the Vikings' guitarist/singer Carl Wayne and drummer Beverley "Bev" Bevan to join their new group. Wayne (1943-2004) had previously formed the G-Men in the late Fifties before joining the Vikings as lead singer, while Bevan's music career had started with Denny Laine & the Diplomats. The two musicians agreed to join the new group, now called the Move.

In January 1966, the band made their debut appearance at the Belfry Hotel in Stourbridge, followed by further bookings in the areas, with a repertoire of Motown covers and west coast hits, and with Wayne handling most of the lead vocals. Masterminded by Secunda, they secured a weekly residency at London's Marquee Club and their on-stage stunts' initiated by their manager, drew much attention, despite getting them banned from some venues. In December, they were signed by independent record producer Denny Cordell to Deram Records. Up to now, Wood had composed only two songs, but in January 1967, he wrote "Night of Fear," the main riff and base line taken from Tchaikovsky's *1812 Overture*. The lyrics about moving shadows in the hall and pictures on the bedroom wall had hints of psychedelia and alluded to the narrator having drug-induced hallucinations. Nevertheless, it saw it peak at number two on the UK charts.

The following single, Wood's "I Can Hear the Grass Grow" was based on a book of fairy tales which he had written while at art college, with the title coming from a letter a photographer had received from someone unknown that read: "I listen to pop music on the radio because where I live it's so bloody quiet that I can hear the grass grow." Once again, hints of drug use were dispelled, with Wood claiming it was about mental illness. Now recording on the Regal Zonophone label, their most famous single was "Flowers in the Rain," which was another based on Wood's book of fairy tales. It also gained long-lasting fame by being the first record played by deejay Tony Blackburn on BBC's new Radio One on September 30th 1967. According to Blackburn, it was a mad panic whether the records had been sorted into the proper order, and as the programme went on air, he had just picked the first record he could lay his hands on. As part of the publicity campaign for the single, Secunda and the group issued a risqué postcard that had representations of British Prime Minster Harold Wilson in bed with his secretary Marcia Williams. Taken to court, Wilson won an injunction preventing the use of the material, and all royalties for the song were sent to charities of Wilson's choice.

With Kefford also now departed to pursue a solo career, "Blackberry Way" became the band's first chart-topper in 1968, but with its bleak counterpoint to their previous songs, Wayne refused to sing lead vocal, giving Wood the honour. In March 1969, Jeff Lynne of the Idle Race and Rick Price of Sight and Sound were both invited to join the band, but only Price agreed, soon replacing the departing Burton. "Curly" was the last single to feature Wayne and the first for Price, and was issued as a single, despite Wood and Bevan's disapproval.

Following Wayne's departure in January 1970, Jeff Lynne finally joined the group in 1970 for the single "Brontosaurus." His arrival would encourage them both to eventually follow their individual ambitions, resulting in the grand offshoots, Lynne's Electric Light Orchestra and Wood's Wizzard.

Wood later revealed: "I've always been a bit of a Jekyll and Hyde. I always feel that you should keep singles as commercial as possible so that the people can walk down the road and whistle a song. But on the other hand on albums I think you can afford to show people what you can do."

Chart entries
Night Of Fear – The Move (UK 1967 # 2)
I Can Hear the Grass Grow – The Move (UK 1967 # 5)
Flowers In the Rain – The Move (UK 1967 # 2)
Wild Tiger Woman – The Move (UK 1968 # 53)
Fire Brigade – The Move (UK 1968 # 3)
Blackberry Way – The Move (UK 1969 # 1)
Hello Susie – Amen Corner (UK 1969 # 4)
Curly – The Move (UK 1969 # 12)

George Young and Harry Vanda
Born George Redburn Young, Glasgow, Scotland 1947. Died 2017.
Born Johannes Hendrikus Jacob van den Berg, Voorburg, Netherlands 1946.

Following the UK's "big freeze" of 1962-63, 15 members of the Young family took the offer of assisted travel to go and start a new life in Australia. For the first six years, the family lived at the Villawood Migrant Hostel in the suburbs of Sydney. Young attended Chester Hill High School across from the migrant hostel until expelled in 1964 for having long hair. Later that year, he formed a beat group called the Starlighters. All five members were migrants at the hostel. Lead singer Stevie Wright, former member of Chris Langson & the Langdells, came from Leeds, and ex-Mojos drummer Gordon "Snowy" Fleet from Bootle, while bassist Dick Diamonde and lead guitarist Harry Vanda were both from Holland. The name of the band was changed to the Easybeats after the arrival of Fleet, who coined it after the BBC radio pop show of the same name.

The Easybeats' first performance was as a residency at Sydney's Beatle Village club, where they first met producer Ted Albert, who managed to get them a record deal with Parlophone's Australian label. In March 1965, they made their radio debut at the 2UW Theatre, followed by their tv debut on the show *Sing Sing Sing.* That same year, they released their first single "For My Woman," written by Young and Wright, but found success with the four-track EP *She's So Fine*. Recorded in Melbourne, it peaked at number three on the country's chart. Further hits followed and they quickly gained a teen following.

In June 1966, they signed with United Artists with entrepreneur Mike Vaughan as manager, and moved to the UK to work with producer Shel Talmy. Their debut UK single "Come and See Her," written by Young and Wright, was taken from the album *It's 2 Easy*. The following year, the two of them wrote what would become their best-remembered song, "Friday on My Mind." A worldwide hit when released in October 1966, it described the drudgery and tedium of the working week, although any working-class anthem connotations were dismissed by Young, who saw it more as their view of the world.

In 1967, the band toured Australia and the US, losing member Fleet along the way, and at the end of the year they formed their own recording company, Staeb Productions. The following year, the Young and Vanda ballad "Hello, How Are You?" became their final UK chart success. Different from anything that came before, the first version, more of a psychedelic pop song, was produced by Bill Shepherd but was quickly rejected. Turning to arranger Alan Tew, they cut the single version with orchestration. Despite a hit, Young felt they should have stuck to the formula of power pop songs.

When the Easybeats disbanded in 1969, Young and Vanda formed a production and songwriting partnership providing songs for other artists and themselves to record. In 1973, they returned to Sydney and worked for Ted Albert's Albert Productions as in-house producers.

Chart entries
Friday on My Mind – The Easybeats (US 1966 # 16; UK # 6)
Hello, How Are You – The Easybeats (UK 1968 # 20)
Bring a Little Lovin' – Los Bravos (US 1968 # 51)
St Louis – The Easybeats (US 1969 # 100)

Kenny Young see Artie Resnick and Kenny Young

Neil Young see Stephen Stills

SOURCES

Books
Colin Larkin, *The Virgin Encyclopedia of Sixties Music* 1997
Joel Whitburn, *Top 40 Hits* Billboard 1992
Joel Whitburn *Across the Charts - The 1960s* Record Research Inc. 2008
Joel Whitburn *Top Pop Singles 1955-2006* Billboard 2008
Daffyd Rees, Barry Lazell & Roger Osborne, *40 Years of the NME Charts* 1992
Jim Cogan & William Clark, *Temples of Sound - Inside the Great Recording Studios* 2003
Samuel Niman, *The Ultimate UK Official Charts 1960-2024* 2025
Martin C Strong, *The Great Rock Discography* 2004

Lou Adler Craig Werner, *A Change is Gonna Come: Music, Race and the Soul of America* 2000.
Arthur Alexander Mark Lewisham, *The Beatles: All These Years* 2013; Jason Ankeny *AllMusic* Mar 18 2007
Ian Anderson Scott Allen Nollen, *Jethro Tull: A History of the Band 1868-2001* 2001, *Kerrang!* 1984
Paul Anka Paul Anka & David Dalton, *My Way: An Autobiography* 2025
Burt Bacharach and Hal David Burt Bacharach, *Anyone Who Had a Heart: My Life and Music* 2014; William Farina, *The German Cabaret Legacy in American Popular Music* 2013; Warwick interview, *People*; David Interview, *DISCoveries* 1997.
Randy Bachman and Burton Cummings Cummings interview, *Toronto Star* 2014
Clint Ballard Jr Songfacts.com
Syd Barrett Barry Miles, *Pink Floyd: The Early Years* 2011
Jeff Barry and Ellie Greenwich Mary Weiss interview, *Telegraph magazine* April 14 2007
Jan Berry Mark A Moore, *The Rock n Roll Life of Jan Berry* 2021
Don Black Vincent Dowd *BBC News* July 20 2020; James Inverne & Don Black, *Wrestling with Elephants: The Biography of Don Black* 2010
Otis Blackwell Brian Gilmore *Don't Be Cruel: Otis Blackwell's Triumph*, American Songwriter 2013
Sonny Bono *Pop Chronicles* 1967
Leslie Bricusse Bricusse, *Pure Imagination: The Life and Good Times of a Songwriter* 2015
Gary Brooker and Keith Reid *Uncut* interview April 4 2008; Claes Johansen, *Procol Harum: Beyond the Pale* 2001
James Brown R J Smith, *The One: The Life and Music of James Brown* 2012
Eric Burdon Jeff Kent, *The Last Poet: The Story of Eric Burdon* 1989
Felix Cavaliere and Eddie Brigati Marc Myers, "The Day They Grooved to "Groovin'" *Wall Street Journal* April 2013
Clarke, Hicks and Nash Graham Nash, *Wild Tales: A Rock & Roll Life* 2013; Mike Ragogna, *Sex, Freedom, and Marianne Faithfull's Voice in the Afterlight of the 1960s* 2011; Nash interview *Mojo* 2021; Malcolm Searles *A Biography of the Hollies* 2021
Sam Cooke Cliff White & Daniel Wolff, *You Send Me: The Life and Times of Sam Cooke* 2011
David Crosby Peter Doggett, *Crosby, Stills, Nash & Young: The Definitive Biography* 2020
Mac David *The Tennessean* Sept 29 2020
Ray Davies Johnny Rogan, *Ray Davies: A Complicated Life* 2016
Desmond Dekker *The Independent* Oct 2 2016
Jackie DeShannon Dave Marsh, *The Heart of Rock and Soul* 1989; *Uncut* April 2021
Neil Diamond Laura Jackson, *Neil Diamond: The Biography* 2005
Donovan www.songfacts.com; *Mojo* June 2011; *Wall Street Journal* April 9 2017
Bob Dylan Philippe Margotin & Jean-Michel Guesdo *Bob Dylan - All the Songs* 2022
John Fogerty Craig Werner, *Up Around the Bend* 1998; John Fogerty, *Fortunate Son: My Life, My Music* 2016
Jerry Fuller www.songfacts.com
Mort Garson *Shindig!* Oct 2020
Gibb Brothers *The Mail on Sunday* Nov 1 2009; David Meyer, *The Bee Gees - The Biography* 2013
Gerry Goffin and Carole King Henry Spencer, *Carole King - A Beautiful Journey* 2024

Berry Gordy Jr Berry Gordy, *To Be Loved: The Music, the Magic, the Memories of Motown: An Autobiography* 1994
Graham Gouldman *The Guardian* Jan 24 2025
Peter Green *New Musical Express* April 26 1969; Martin Celmins, *Peter Green: Founder of Fleetwood Mac* 2025.
Tim Hardin Robert Hilburn, *Los Angeles Times* Mar 18 1994
George Harrison Robert Rodriguez, *Revolver: How the Beatles Reimagined Rock n Roll* 2012
Tony Hatch and Jackie Trent *Mojo* January 2013; Hatch interview, *classicbands.com;*
Isaac Hayes and David Porter Rob Bowman, *Soulsville USA: The Story of Stax Records* 1997
Justin Haward *Daily Express Saturday Magazine* May 3 2008; Marc Cushman, *Long Distance Voyagers - The Story of the Moody Blues Vol 1* 2018
Jimi Hendrix Keith Shadwick *Jimi Hendrix: Musician* 2003
Holland-Dozier-Holland Howard Priestley, *Love Factory: The History of Holland Dozier Holland* 2021
Mick Jagger & Keith Richards Keith Richards interview *Life* 2010; Mick Jagger Remembers *Rolling Stone* Aug 2020; *According to the Rolling Stones* 2003; Robert Palmer, What Makes the Rolling Stones the Greatest Rock & Roll Band in the World, *Rolling Stone* Dec 1981
Jerry Leiber and Mike Stoller Bassam Habal *Behind the Hits: An Interview with Mike Stoller of the Legendary Songwriting Duo The Music Soup;* Richard Crouse, *Who Wrote the Book of Love* 2012
John Lennon and Paul McCartney Steve Turner, *The Complete Beatles Songs* 2018
Jerry Lordan www.songfacts.com; Royston Ellis, *Cliff Richard & the Shadows - A Rock N Roll Memoir* 2014
Henry Mancini Henry Mancini & Gene Lees, *Did They Mention the Music?* 1989
Barry Mann and Cynthis Weil *Uncut* 2016
Steve Marriott and Ronnie Lane Sean Egan, *Long Agos and Worlds Apart: The Definitive Small Faces Biography* 2024
Gerry Marsden Gerry Marsden, *I'll Never Walk Alone - An Autobiography* 2021
Bill Martin and Phil Coulter Sandie Shaw, *The World at My Feet* 1991
Barry Mason and Les Reed *The Mail on Sunday* Feb 6 2011
Roger McGuinn Interview, www.songfacts.com; James K Billy, *From Folk Roots to Rock Legend - The Life and Music of the Byrds Visionary Leader* 2025.
John Medora and David White *New York Times* Feb 16 2015; *Cashbox* Dec 21 1963.
Reynard Miner "Jackie Wilson on Columbia Records" May 22 2009; Dave Marsh, *The Heart of Rock and Soul* 1989
Sylvia Moy *Mojo* Feb 2009
John Phillips www.songfacts.com; Matthew Greenwald, *Go Where You Wanna Go - The Oral History of the Mamas and the Papas* 2002
Wilson Pickett Tony Fletcher, *In the Midnight Hour: The Life and Soul of Wilson Pickett* 2016
Gene Pitney David McGrath, *Gene Pitney: The Singer, the Songs, the Songwriters* 2021
Doc Pomus and Mort Schuman Alex Halberstadt & Peter Guralnick, *Lonely Avenue: The Unlikely Life and Times of Doc Pomus* 2007
Otis Redding Scott Freeman, *Otis: The Otis Redding Story* 2001
Smokey Robinson Charlie Parson, *Smokey Robinson: A Journey Through Soul, Songwriting, and Enduring Influence* 2025; Peter Benjaminson, *Mary Wells: the tumultuous life of Motown's first superstar* 2012
Tommy Roe Interview, *Forgotten Hits* March 18 2016
Bobby Russell Tony Hicks interview, *The Guardian* Feb 24 2006
Jimmy Ryan Ciccone interview, *Goldmine*; Jimmy Ryan, *The Superstar Chronicles* 2021
John Sebastian Walter Everett, *The Foundations of Rock* 2009
Neil Sedaka Neil Sedaka, *Stepping Out* 1976
Pete Seeger Alec Wilkinson, *The Protest Singer: An Intimate Portrait of Pete Seeger* 2009
Gloria Shayne The Story Behind the Song, www.franciscanmedia.org
Grace Slick Michael Gallucci Top 10 Jefferson Airplane Songs *Ultimate Classic Rock* Jan 2016; Grace Slick, *Somebody to Love?: A Rock-and-Roll Memoir* 1999.
Phil Spector David Howard *Sonic Alchemy: Visionary Music Producers and Their Maverick Recordings* 2004; Mick Brown, *Tearing Down the Wall of Sound: The Rise and Fall of Phil Spector* 2012; Kenniebrew interview, *Daily Express Saturday Magazine* Aug 25 2007

Stephen Stills Peter Doggett, *Crosby, Stills, Nash & Young: The Definitive Biography* 2020
Sly Stone Jason Ankeny *AllMusic* Mar 2022; Aaron Owens, *Memoirs of a Funk Pioneer* 2023
Pete Townshend Peter Townshend, *Who I Am* 2012
Jimmy Webb Terry Gross, *Jimmy Webb: From Phoenix to Just Across the River* NPR Feb 2004
Brian Wilson and Mike Love Michael F Taylor, *The Beach Boys - Pet Tracks* 2023
Steve Winwood *Pop Chronicles* 1970; John Van der Kiste, *While You See a Chance - The Stevie Winwood Story* 2018
Stevie Wonder Mick Hutchinson, *Have Eyes to Wonder: Stevie's Early Years 1950-1971* 2025
Roy Wood John Van der Kiste, *Roy Wood: The Move, Wizzard and Beyond* 2014

www.ingramcontent.com/pod-product-compliance
Lightning Source LLC
Chambersburg PA
CBHW081350230426
43667CB00017B/2775